Indian Summer

INDIAN SUMMER

*The Secret History of the
End of an Empire*

ALEX VON TUNZELMANN

SIMON &
SCHUSTER

London · New York · Sydney · Toronto

A CBS COMPANY

First published in Great Britain in 2007
by Simon & Schuster UK Ltd
A CBS COMPANY

1 3 5 7 9 10 8 6 4 2

Simon & Schuster UK Ltd
Africa House
64–78 Kingsway
London WC2B 6AH

www.simonsays.co.uk

Simon & Schuster Australia
Sydney

A CIP catalogue for this book is
available from the British Library.

ISBN-10: 0-7432-8588-3
ISBN-13: 978-0-7432-8588-9

Typeset in Sabon by M Rules
Printed and bound in Great Britain by
CPI Bath

To Nick and Carol,
with love and thanks

CONTENTS

PART III: THE BEGINNING

PART IV: AFTERWARDS

ACKNOWLEDGEMENTS

In Britain, I would like to thank Her Majesty The Queen for allowing me access to the Royal Archives at Windsor, and the staff there, especially Pamela Clark; the staff at the Mountbatten Papers at Southampton University, especially Karen Robson and Chris Woolgar; the National Archives at Kew; the department of Asian & African Studies at the British Library, London; the Newspaper Library at Colindale; the Churchill Archives Centre at Churchill College, Cambridge; the Centre of South Asian Studies at Cambridge; the Modern Papers Department at the Bodleian Library, Oxford, especially Colin Harris and Helen Langley; the School of Oriental and African Studies, London; and the London Library. In India, I would like to thank all the staff at the National Archives, and at the Nehru Memorial Museum & Library, both in New Delhi.

During the course of writing this book, I made repeated approaches to the Mountbatten and Nehru-Gandhi families, in the hope that I would be allowed to use the private archive of letters that passed between Jawaharlal Nehru and Edwina Mountbatten. Though their responses were courteous, neither family was keen to cooperate. Only a handful of carefully selected historians has ever been allowed to look at any part of this correspondence, a pity in view of the light it would undoubtedly shed on some of the twentieth century's most fascinating personalities and politics. Lord Mountbatten himself is said to have wanted the correspondence published. At the time of writing, the letters remain closed.

Many people were generous in giving me their advice and thoughts. I would particularly like to thank M.J. Akbar, William Dalrymple, Saul David, Nicky Goldberg, Anna and James Hatt, Lawrence James, Julia Jordan, Edward Luce, Eleanor Newbigin, Dora Napolitano, Alexander van Praag, Nicole Taylor, Eugénie von Tunzelmann and Siraj Ulmulk. Special thanks must go to Nayantara Sahgal, for sharing with me her lucid and perceptive memories of the period and the people in this book and allowing me to see her wonderful collection of photographs and private letters. I would also like to thank Jeremy Paxman for giving me invaluable opportunities to hone my research skills, and for encouraging me to write my own book. Two friends in particular have offered indispensable help: Maddie Rowe, whose expert comments have been as witty as they have been perceptive; and Adi Bloom, whose exceptional reader's eye and infectious enthusiasm for all things subcontinental have been inspiring.

The events of 1947–48 are still highly controversial, and some of those who spoke to me have asked not to be named. They may be assured of my gratitude nonetheless. Any errors in this book are entirely my responsibility.

For the production of this book, I would like to thank my editors, Andrew Gordon, George Hodgman and Chris Bucci; also Jennifer Barth, Kari Brownlie, Martin Bryant, Eva Diaz, Joanne Edgecombe, Lisa Fyfe, Sue Gard, Vicki Haire, Meryl Levavi, Vanessa Mobley, Emily Montjoy, Lindsay Ross, Kenn Russell, Rory Scarfe, John Sterling, and everyone at Simon & Schuster in London, Henry Holt in New York and McClelland & Stewart in Toronto. I am extremely grateful to Natasha Fairweather and to all at A.P. Watt, especially Philippa Donovan, Rob Kraitt, Naomi Leon and Linda Shaughnessy.

Finally, I would like to thank my parents for too many things to list here, but expressly for their unfailing support, wit, generosity, guidance and love throughout this project. It is a privilege to be able to dedicate this book to them.

INDIAN SUMMER

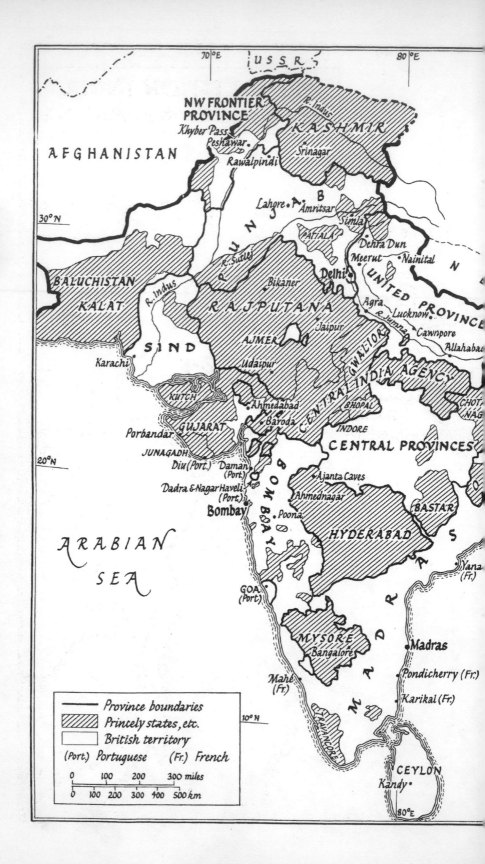

USSR

NW FRONTIER
PROVINCE

Khyber Pass
Peshawar •
• Rawalpindi

R. Indus

KASHMIR

Srinagar •

AFGHANISTAN

30°N

Lahore • P U N J A B
• Amritsar
Simla •
PATIALA
Dehra Dun •
Meerut • • Nainital

R. Sutlej

BALUCHISTAN
KALAT

• Bikaner

Delhi •

Agra •
• Lucknow

UNITED PROVINCE

R. Indus

R A J P U T A N A

S I N D

• Karachi

AJMER •

Jaipur •

R. Jumna

• Cawnpore

• Allahabad

Udaipur •

KUTCH

GWALIOR

CENTRAL INDIA AGENCY

CHOT.
NAG.

20°N

GUJARAT

• Ahmedabad
• Baroda

Porbandar •

JUNAGADH

BHOPAL

INDORE

CENTRAL PROVINCES

Diu (Port.)
Daman
(Port.)
Dadra & Nagar Haveli
(Port.)

Bombay

• Ajanta Caves

B O M B A Y

Ahmednagar •

BASTAR

ARABIAN

• Poona

HYDERABAD

SEA

GOA
(Port.)

Yana
(Fr.)

M A D R A S

MYSORE
Bangalore •

• Madras

Mahé
(Fr.)

• Pondicherry (Fr.)

• Karikal (Fr.)

TRAVANCORE

—— Province boundaries

///// Princely states, etc.

☐ British territory

(Port.) Portuguese   (Fr.) French

CEYLON
Kandy •

0   100   200   300 miles

0 100 200 300 400 500 km

80°E

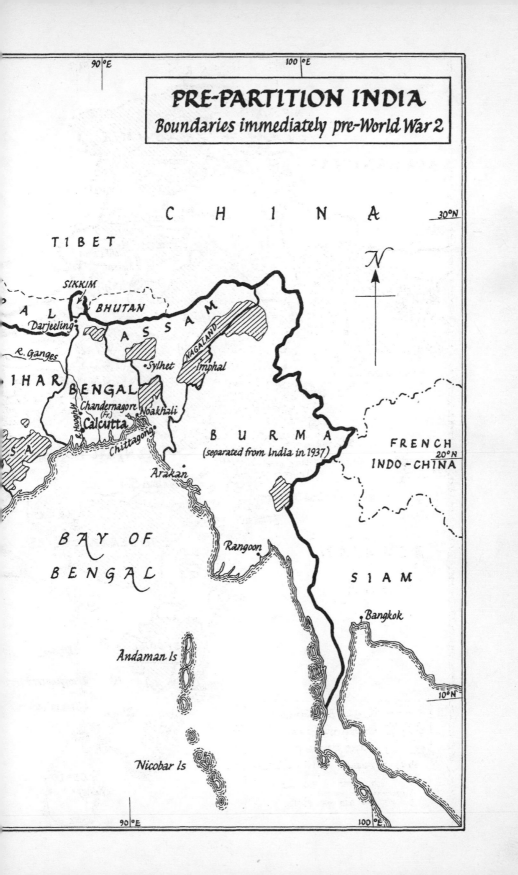

PRE-PARTITION INDIA
Boundaries immediately pre-World War 2

CHINA

TIBET

30°N

SIKKIM

NEPAL

BHUTAN

Darjeeling

ASSAM

NAGALAND

R. Ganges

Sylhet

Imphal

BIHAR

BENGAL

Chandernagore (Fr.)

Noakhali

Calcutta

R. Hooghly

Chittagong

ORISSA

Arakan

BURMA

(separated from India in 1937)

FRENCH
INDO-CHINA

20°N

BAY OF
BENGAL

Rangoon

SIAM

Bangkok

Andaman Is

Nicobar Is

10°N

90°E

100°E

The subcontinent after partition

India and Pakistan became independent within the Commonwealth in Aug. 1947. India became a republic in 1950.

90°E

100°E

CHINA

30°N

TIBET

BHUTAN

°Darjeeling

ASSAM

NAGALAND

•Imphal

R. Ganges

EAST PAKISTAN

Sylhet

IHAR

Dhaka•

TRIPURA

WEST

Chandernagore•
(Fr.)

BENGAL

(BANGLADESH (1971)

Calcutta

Chittagong•

SA

BURMA

(Independent republic 1948)

20°N

BAY OF
BENGAL

Rangoon

SIAM
(THAILAND)

Bangkok

Andaman Is

10°N

Nicobar Is

90°E

100°E

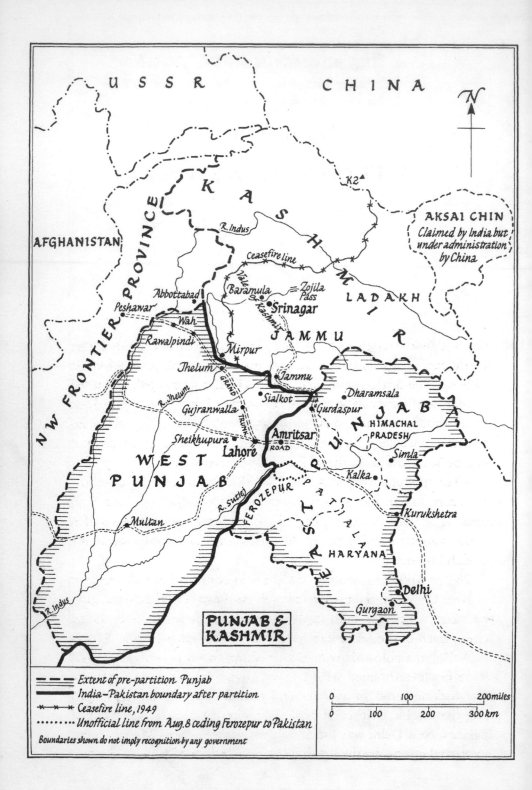

USSR

CHINA

AFGHANISTAN

K A S H M I R

K2

AKSAI CHIN
Claimed by India but
under administration
by China

R. Indus

Ceasefire line

Vale of Kashmir

Baramula

Zojila Pass

Srinagar

LADAKH

N W   F R O N T I E R   P R O V I N C E

Abbottabad

Peshawar

Wah

Rawalpindi

Mirpur

JAMMU

Jhelum

R. Jhelum

Jammu

GRAND TRUNK ROAD

Sialkot

Gurdaspur

Dharamsala

Gujranwalla

Sheikhupura

Amritsar

Lahore

P U N J A B

HIMACHAL
PRADESH

W E S T

P U N J A B

Simla

Kalka

R. Sutlej

FEROZEPUR

P A T I A L A

Kurukshetra

Multan

HARYANA

R. Indus

Delhi

Gurgaon

PUNJAB &
KASHMIR

– – – Extent of pre-partition Punjab
——— India–Pakistan boundary after partition
✕ ✕ ✕ Ceasefire line, 1949
· · · · · · Unofficial line from Aug. 8 ceding Ferozepur to Pakistan
Boundaries shown do not imply recognition by any government

0   100   200 miles
0   100   200   300 km

A Tryst with Destiny

On a warm summer night in 1947, the largest empire the world has ever seen did something no empire had done before. It gave up. The British Empire did not decline, it simply fell; and it fell proudly and majestically on to its own sword. It was not forced out by revolution, nor defeated by a greater rival in battle. Its leaders did not tire or weaken. Its culture was strong and vibrant. Recently it had been victorious in the century's definitive war.

When midnight struck in Delhi on the night of 14 August 1947, a new, free Indian nation was born. In London, the time was 8.30 p.m.[1] The world's capital could enjoy another hour or two of a warm summer evening before the sun literally and finally set on the British Empire.

The constituent assembly of India was convened at that moment in New Delhi, a monument to the self-confidence of the British government, which had built its new capital on the site of seven fallen cities. Each of the seven had been built to last for ever. And so was New Delhi, a colossal arrangement of sandstone neoclassicism and wide boulevards lined with banyan trees. Seen from the sky, the interlocking series of avenues and roundabouts formed a pattern like the marble trellises of geometric stars that ventilated Mughal palaces. New Delhi was India, but constructed – and, they thought, improved upon – by the British. The French Prime Minister Georges

Clemenceau had laughed when he saw the new city half-built in 1920, and observed: '*Ça sera la plus magnifique de toutes ces ruines.*'[2]

Inside the chamber of the constituent assembly on the night of 14 August 1947, 2000 princes and politicians from across the 1.25 million square miles that remained of India sat together on parliamentary benches. Yet amid all the power and finery, two persons were conspicuous by their absence. One was Mohammad Ali Jinnah, the leader of the Muslim League, who was in one of those parts of the Empire that had just become Pakistan. His absence signified the partition of the subcontinent, the split which had ripped two wings off the body of India and called them West and East Pakistan (later Pakistan and Bangladesh), creating Muslim homelands separate from the predominantly Hindu mass of the territory. The other truant was Mohandas Karamchand Gandhi, who was sound asleep in a smashed-up mansion in a riot-torn suburb of Calcutta.

Gandhi's absence was a worrying omen. The seventy-seven-year-old Mahatma, or 'great soul', was the most famous and the most popular Indian since Buddha. Regarded as little short of a saint among Christians as well as Hindus, he had been a staunch defender of the British Empire until the 1920s. Since then, he had campaigned for Indian self-rule. Many times it had been almost within his grasp: in 1922, 1931, 1942, 1946. Each time he had let it go. Now, finally, India was free, but that had nothing to do with Gandhi – and Gandhi would have nothing to do with it.

In the chamber the dignitaries fell silent as the foremost among them, Jawaharlal Nehru, stepped up to make one of the most famous speeches in history. At fifty-seven years old, Nehru had grown into his role as India's leading statesman. His last prison term had finished exactly twenty-six months before. The fair skin and fine bone structure of an aristocratic Kashmiri Brahmin was rendered approachable by a ready smile and warm laugh. Dark, sleepy, soulful eyes belied a quick wit and quicker temper. In him were all the virtues of the ancient nation, filtered through the best aspects of the British Empire: confidence, sophistication, and charisma. 'Long years ago,' he began, 'we made a tryst with destiny. And now the time comes when we shall redeem our pledge; not wholly or in full measure, but substantially. At the stroke of the midnight hour, while the world sleeps, India will awake to life and freedom.' The clock struck and, in that instant, he became the new country's first Prime Minister. The reverential mood in the hall was broken abruptly by an unexpected honk from the back. The dignitaries jerked their heads round to the source of the sound, and a look of relief passed over their faces as they saw a devout Hindu member of the assembly blowing into a conch shell – an invocation of the gods. Mildred Talbot, a journalist who was present, noticed that the interruption had not daunted the new Prime Minister. 'When I happened to spot Nehru just as he was turning away, he was trying to hide a smile by covering his mouth with his hand.'[3]

It was the culmination of a lifetime's struggle; and yet, as Nehru later confided to his sister, his mind had not been on the splendid words. A few hours before, he had received a telephone call from Lahore in what was about to become West Pakistan. It was his mother's home town, and a place where he had spent much of his childhood.[4] Now it was being torn apart. Gangs of Muslims and Sikhs had clashed in the streets. The main gurdwara – the Sikh temple – was ablaze. One hundred thousand people were trapped inside the city walls without water or medical assistance. Violence was a much-predicted consequence of the handover, but preparations for dealing with it had been catastrophically inadequate. The only help available in Lahore was from 200 Gurkhas, stationed nearby, under the command of an inexperienced British captain who was only twenty years old. They had little chance of stopping the carnage. The horror of that night in Lahore set the tone for weeks of bloodshed and destruction. Perhaps the Hindu astrologers had been right when they had declared 14 August to be an inauspicious date. Or perhaps the Viceroy's curious decision to rush independence through ten months ahead of the British government's schedule was to blame.

Emerging into the streets of Delhi, Nehru was greeted by the ringing of temple bells, the bangs and squeals of fireworks and the happy shouting of crowds. Guns were fired, in celebration rather than in anger; an effigy of British imperialism was burned, in both.[5] Soon afterwards, Nehru arrived at the Viceroy's House, a gated citadel at the end of Kingsway, New Delhi's two-mile processional avenue. He and Rajendra Prasad, the leader of the constituent assembly, were to see the last of the viceroys, Earl Mountbatten of Burma.[6]

Mountbatten was young for a viceroy at forty-seven, but no less assured for it. Tall, broad-shouldered and handsome, he had a brilliant Hollywood smile, easy wit and immediate charm; it might never have been guessed that he had been born a prince, were it not for his ability to switch to a regal demeanour. The new earl and his countess, Edwina, had kept an appropriate distance from the festivities. While freedom was declared, the couple had spent the night at home, pottering around their palace, and helping the servants tidy away anything marked with an imperial emblem. They had taken a brief break to watch the latest Bob Hope movie, *My Favorite Brunette*. It was a pastiche of the fashionable noir genre: the story of a wayward but irresistible baroness, played by the sultry Dorothy Lamour, whose feminine wiles drag a number of men into a dangerous conspiracy. No more than a handful of those in the Viceroy's House that evening could have realized what a very apposite choice of film it was.

While Nehru had been declaring his nation's independence and worrying about the emerging crisis in Lahore, Mountbatten had been sitting in his study alone, thinking to himself – as he later recollected – that 'For still a few minutes I am the most powerful man on earth.'[7] At 11.58 p.m., he settled on a last act of showmanship, creating the Australian wife of the Nawab of Palanpur a highness, in defiance of Indian caste customs and British policy. It was an act epitomising Mountbatten's character. King-making was his favourite sport. Two minutes later, and the power had vanished.

Nehru and Prasad were greeted by the Viceroy's wife, Edwina Mountbatten, still on lively form despite the lateness of the hour. Vivacious, chic and slim, at forty-five Edwina was still in her prime. Her position as one of the world's richest women had never made her happy. But, over the course of the previous few years, she had finally found a role for herself, leading health and welfare campaigns for the Red Cross and the St John Ambulance Brigade. The heiress to millions had never been happier than when she was working in the hot, rough and filthy refugee camps that had been set up across the riot-scarred Punjab. In India, Edwina had blossomed, both in the revelation of her own work and in her close friendships with the Indian leaders, particularly Gandhi and Nehru. It was the second of these friendships that was already the subject of gossip in Delhi society.

The warmth shared by India's new Prime Minister and Lady Mountbatten was obvious. It was equally obvious that Lord Mountbatten minded not at all. In contrast to the erupting turmoil across the subcontinent, the scene between imperial lord and victorious revolutionary that night was one of astonishing civility. For half a century Nehru had devoted his life to this single goal of throwing off the yoke of the British Empire. Now it was done, and his first action as Prime Minister was to pay a call to the power he had just displaced – and to offer it a job. 'When one thinks of the sad years that have led up to recent events,' noted Lady Mountbatten, 'I suppose this was the most surprising development of all.'[8]

Nehru and Prasad were invited into Mountbatten's study, followed by an unruly gaggle of reporters. Photographers scrambled on to the furniture, standing on French-polished tables to get the best angles, firing off a blitz of flashbulbs which shattered noisily over the journalists who squeezed to the front. The exhausted Prasad began to stammer an invitation for Lord Mountbatten to become Governor General of the new Indian nation, but lost his words. Nehru stepped in to complete them, and Mountbatten graciously accepted. He then poured out glasses of port for those present. 'To India,' he proclaimed, holding his glass aloft. Nehru replied: 'To King George VI.' Few missed the significance of the moment. Some years before, Nehru had refused to attend a banquet in Ceylon on the grounds that toasts would be proposed to the King and the government.[9]

But while in Delhi the gentlemen toasted nations and kings, their new world was turning into a battlefield. As Viceroy, Lord Mountbatten had wielded unprecedented power over the fates of two nations and 400 million people. He had transferred power in a way that, within the next couple of days, would trigger a state of civil war in both nations, followed by a war between the two of them. Millions of people would be displaced; millions would be wounded; hundreds of thousands, perhaps millions more, would die. During the next few days, riots would spread across the divided states of the Punjab and Bengal, and a holocaust would begin.

The following night, the Mountbattens held a grand reception for Nehru at their palace. In the gorgeous expanse of the Mughal Gardens, water flowed from fountains around terraces of pink stone from Jaipur; squirrels scampered up the trunks of bougainvillea trees; the heavy scent of roses hung around sunken beds. The party was a dazzling swansong for British India. Everyone had expected that such a day would be glorious in India's history; but, thanks to Mountbatten, it had somehow been made glorious in Britain's as well. Thanks to his impressive gift for public relations, the end of Empire was presented as the purpose of Empire – India was as a well-nurtured and fattened chick, raised to fly from the imperial nest while Britain, the indulgent parent, looked on with pride. And so the British were able to celebrate their loss alongside the Indians who celebrated their victory. Comforting fictions were established that happy night: that the British left India with dignity, having seen the error of their ways through Gandhi's soft but compelling persuasion; that the Indian independence campaign won its prize by non-violence and civil disobedience; that the departure of the British was completed with enough goodwill to pave the way for genuine friendship between India and the west, and separately between Pakistan and the west; that the end of the British Empire in India was a triumph for freedom.[10]

The world was redefined that night, but not in the way that most of those present thought. On either side of Old Europe, two new powers were rising to world superiority – and both took a close interest in the new dominions of India and Pakistan. In the east, Stalin's Russia was in the process of supporting communist movements across Europe and Asia, bolstering the influence of Moscow and extending its borders. In the west, the President of the United States of America had announced the Truman Doctrine just five months before. He had stated his intent to promote democracy across the world, and resist the tide of communism flowing forth from Russia. The Americans had become particularly concerned about its flow into India, and Russian agents were already suspected of funding Indian communist parties in Bengal. That very night,

Nehru's sister and close confidante, Vijaya Lakshmi Pandit, was in Moscow, preparing to present her credentials to Stalin as free India's first ambassador. Though its envoys were on good terms with Nehru, the United States government was alarmed by these developments, and moved fast to create a new alliance with Pakistan. During the nineteenth century, Britain and Russia had played the 'Great Game' for control of Central Asia, focusing on Afghanistan and the territory that would become West Pakistan. In 1947, the United States was gearing up to play a new Great Game against Russia – and the slow but significant rise of a fundamentalist Islamic movement would ensure that Afghanistan and Pakistan would remain at the centre of international politics well into the next century.

As darkness fell on 15 August 1947, Delhi's Mughal Gardens glowed with thousands of tiny lights set among the jacaranda trees, and with hundreds of distinguished guests. Among the long avenues of gold mohur and flame-of-the-forest, princes chatted cordially to freedom fighters, and Hindu radicals to British soldiers. There was a sense of hope and magic, as two of the twentieth century's greatest men fulfilled their ultimate ambitions. Nehru became leader of a free India, and Mountbatten played the role of a king – with Edwina as his queen. Few of the guests watching this display would have suspected that the celebration was about to be blown apart.

PART I

EMPIRE

CHAPTER I

IN THEIR GRATITUDE
OUR BEST REWARD

IN THE BEGINNING, THERE WERE TWO NATIONS. ONE WAS A vast, mighty and magnificent empire, brilliantly organized and culturally unified, which dominated a massive swathe of the earth. The other was an undeveloped, semi-feudal realm, riven by religious factionalism and barely able to feed its illiterate, diseased and stinking masses. The first nation was India. The second was England.

The year was 1577, and the Mughal emperors were in the process of uniting India. The domain spread 1200 miles along the tropic of Cancer, from the eerie white salt flats of the Rann of Kutch on the shores of the Arabian Sea, to the verdant delta of the holy River Ganges in Bengal; and from the snowy crags of Kabul to the lush teak forests of the Vindhyan foothills. The 100 million people who lived under its aegis were cosmopolitan and affluent. In 1577, the average Indian peasant enjoyed a relatively higher income and lower taxation than his descendants ever would again. In the bazaars were sold gold from Jaipur, rubies from Burma, fine shawls from Kashmir, spices from the islands, opium from Bengal, and dancing-girls from Africa. Though governed by Muslims under a legal system based loosely on sharia law, its millions of non-Muslim subjects – Hindus, Sikhs and Buddhists – were allowed freedom of conscience and custom.[1]

This empire was ruled by the world's most powerful man, Akbar

the Great. Akbar was one of the most successful military commanders of all time, a liberal philosopher of distinction, and a generous
patron of the arts. He lived in unmatched opulence at Fatehpur
Sikri, in rooms done out in marble, sandalwood and mother-of-
pearl, cooled by the gentle fanning of peacock feathers. His hobbies
were discussing metaphysics, collecting emeralds, hunting with chee-
tahs and inventing religions; he had as his plaything the Koh-i-Noor
diamond, a gigantic, glittering rock weighing over 186 carats, then
almost twice its present size.[2] His family came from Mongolia, and
his court showed a strongly Persian influence. But Indians were
accustomed to foreign rule. Since the death of the indigenous
Emperor Asoka in 232 BC, large parts of the subcontinent had been
conquered by Turks, Afghans, Persians and Tocharians, as well as by
Mongols. During a long and dramatic life, Akbar himself conquered
and ruled over an area the size of Europe.

In England, meanwhile, most of the population of around 2.5
million lived in a state of misery and impoverishment. Politically
and religiously, the country had spent much of the sixteenth century
at war with itself. Around 90 per cent of the population lived rurally
and worked on the land, going hungry during the frequent food
shortages. They were prevented from moving in to industry by the
protectionist racket of guild entry fees. Begging was common, and
the nation's 10,000 vagabonds the terror of the land. The low standard of living endured by much of the population – two-fifths of
which lived at subsistence levels – and squalid conditions in towns
ensured that epidemics of disease were common. The Black Death
still broke out periodically, as did pneumonia, smallpox, influenza
and something unpleasant called 'the sweat'. Life expectancy stood
at just thirty-eight years – less than modern Sudan, Afghanistan or
the Congo, and about the same as Sierra Leone.[3] The vast majority
of the English people was illiterate and superstitious: the discontent
of communities often boiled over into rioting and witch-hunts.

But by the 1570s, from the filthy soil of England, the first green
shoots of a pleasant land were sprouting forth. The economy began
to recover from years of inflation and political instability. Efforts
were made by the Queen, Elizabeth I, towards religious tolerance,
and by her government towards forcing communities to take some

responsibility for the poor. After years of cultural backwardness, London society began to aspire to refinement. 'They be desirous of new-fangles,' complained the Elizabethan writer Philip Stubbs; 'praising things past, condemning things present, and coveting things to come; ambitious, proud, light-hearted, unstable, ready to be carried away by every blast of wind.'[4] In 1577, a blast of wind drove the English to a world beyond the borders of Europe. At the request of the Queen, the pirate and explorer Francis Drake set sail from Plymouth to bother the Spanish fleet in the Pacific, and thence to circumnavigate the globe.

Drake was not the only man at the court of Elizabeth whose mind was improbably turning to world domination. In 1577, the philosopher, kabbalist and magus John Dee conjured up the first image of a 'Brytish Impire'. At the time, Dee's suggestion would have seemed fanciful, though very few Englishmen could have known enough about geopolitics to say so. Next to Akbar, Elizabeth was indeed a weak and feeble woman, with her dubious breeding, her squabbling and faction-ridden court, her cluttered and rickety palaces, and her grubby, unsophisticated, cold, dismal little kingdom. Nonetheless, the greater monarch generously agreed to humour her shabby emissaries at his fabulous court. They were overwhelmed: both Agra and Fatehpur Sikri were far larger than London, and many times more wondrous. Ralph Fitch, a merchant, described gilded and silk-draped carriages pulled by miniature oxen, and roads lined with markets selling victuals and gemstones. 'The King hath in Agra and Fatepore, as they do credibly report, a thousand Elephants, thirty thousand Horses, fourteen hundred tame Deer, eight hundred Concubines; such a store of Ounces, Tigers, Buffles, Cocks and Hawks that it is very strange to see', he wrote home.[5] Fitch's eventual return with stories of riches undreamt of by the wondering English came at an apt moment in history. The mighty Spanish Armada had been defeated, and England was starting to feel confident and expansive. Fitch was swiftly made a governor of Elizabeth's Levant Company. It was the beginning of four centuries of intimacy and exchange, a love–hate relationship between India and Britain which would change the histories of both countries – and that of the whole world – beyond what even the magus Dee could have predicted.

Twenty-three years later, in 1600, Elizabeth granted a charter to 'The Governor and Company of Merchants of London trading into the East Indies' for fifteen years. That expiry date was cancelled by her heir, James I, giving the East India Company exclusive trading rights in perpetuity. The only caveat: if it failed to turn a profit for three consecutive years, it voided all its rights. Thus a beast was created whose only object was money. It would pursue this object with unprecedented success.

Over the following sixty years, the East India Company men's adventures in diplomacy brought them close to the Mughal emperors, and allowed them to gain precedence over their Dutch and Portuguese rivals. Despite their obvious superficial differences, the Indians and the British were to find that they shared many of the same values and tastes. Both societies functioned through rigid class structures, gloried in their strongly disciplined military cultures, and nurtured a bluff, unemotional secularism among their upper classes. Both prized swaggering but ultimately gallant men, and spirited but ultimately demure women. Both enjoyed a sturdy sense of their own long histories and continual ascendancy. Complicated codes of etiquette were vital to their interaction; hunting on horseback and team sports dominated their social lives. As time went on, they would even discover a shared taste for punctilious and obstructive bureaucracy.

The British relationship with India would be of a different quality from those it had with its other colonies. India was always the 'Jewel in the Crown': and the British found that they often respected, understood and liked the Indian people, in a way that they did not on the whole respect, understand or like the Chinese, the Aborigines, or the various tribes of Africa. The sympathy was so convincing that intermarriage between Britons and Indians became quite commonplace in the early years of the East India Company. Many Britons emigrated permanently to India, where they set up home, started families and raised dynasties.[6]

But the history of empire did not remain so cosy for long. After the English republic fell and the monarchy was restored, King Charles II would turn the East India Company into a monster. With five acts, he gave it an amazing array of rights without responsibilities. By the

1670s, the Company could mint its own coin, maintain its own army, wage war, make peace, acquire new territories and impose its own civil and criminal law – and all without any accountability, save to its shareholders. This was pure capitalism, unleashed for the first time in history. Combined with the gradual fragmentation of Mughal control, which had begun after Akbar's death in 1605, it would prove to be almost unstoppable.

This private empire of money, unburdened by conscience, rampaged across Asia unfettered until the 1850s. Guided only by market forces, it was both incredibly successful and incredibly brutal. Adam Smith, the high priest of free trade and originator of the 'invisible hand' theory of markets, was appalled by the result of a completely unregulated corporation. 'The difference between the genius of the British constitution which protects and governs North America, and that of the mercantile company which oppresses and domineers in the East Indies, cannot perhaps be better illustrated than by the different state of those countries,' he wrote in his 1776 classic, *The Wealth of Nations*.[7] The British government was beginning to agree; and over the following decades regulation began to creep in, act by act. Eventually, in 1834, the parliament in London decided that an empire based on trade was in poor taste, and drew up a new charter. The East India Company was still to govern, but no more to trade. Presenting the scheme to parliament, Thomas Babington Macaulay freely admitted that licensing out British sovereignty to a private company was inappropriate. 'It is the strangest of all governments,' he said, 'but it is designed for the strangest of all empires.'[8] But the British Crown could not bring its beast to heel. That would take a revolt by the Indians themselves.

In the century after Robert Clive's famous victory at Plassey in 1757, the East India Company had embarked upon a run of military enterprises. Its armies fought the Burmese twice, annexing Burma in 1852; the Afghans once; and the Sikhs twice, taking the entirety of the Punjab by 1849. They took Gwalior in 1844, and conquered Sind in 1843, Nagpur in 1853, and Oudh in 1856. By then, almost 70 per cent of the subcontinent could be called British territory.[9] There had been some efforts at improving the lot of the people of India, too, though not all of them were welcomed. Efforts were made to set up British schools in which Indians might be educated. Suttee, the burning of live Hindu widows on the funeral pyres of their dead husbands, was banned in 1829. The Company also attempted to stamp out thuggee, a brutal lifestyle adopted by bands of professional thieves. The thugs were given to strangulation of their victims and devoted to Kali, the goddess of death. They were held responsible for many thousands of murders in the early nineteenth century.[10] But this policy-making and interference, these wars and laws, finally drew the attention of the Indian people to the fact that they had been subjugated. Companies, it was thought, did not conquer, and therefore no threat had been detected. The Mughals had been lulled by the promise of ever greater riches, and had invited the East India Company across their own threshold. Once inside, it had been able to suck the wealth and riches out of India, and impose its own regime – all by the grace of the Indian rulers.[11] 'The English have not taken India', wrote Mohandas Gandhi succinctly in 1908; 'we have given it to them.'[12]

There would be one great attempt to take it back by force, and that was the Indian Mutiny of 1857.[13] Famously, the spark for the Mutiny was the Company's adoption of the Enfield rifle on behalf of its sepoys, the Indian soldiers serving in its army. The cartridges for this particular model were supplied in greased paper, which had to be bitten through before they were used. Rumours spread among the sepoys that the grease contained tallow derived from cow or pig fat, thereby offending both Hindus, who revered the cow, and Muslims, who were forbidden to eat the pig. It has never been proven whether the grease was actually objectionable, or whether the protests were opportunistically started by Indian agitators to damage the East India Company.[14]

Whatever the truth, the Company made a public point of replacing its grease with a version made from ghee and beeswax: but this action came too late. The rumours had served their purpose. The scandal was the final insult in a catalogue of British wrongs against the Indians. The conquest of states, the commandeering of private lands, the propping-up of corrupt local landlords who used torture to extract revenues, the arbitrary imprisonments without trial, the evangelism of Christianity, and the attacks on Indian cultural traditions – for not everyone had welcomed the outlawing of suttee – had pushed Company dominance too far.[15]

After several small-scale rebellions, the Mutiny exploded with full force at the town of Meerut, just north-east of Delhi. On 24 April 1857, eighty-five troopers of the 3rd Light Cavalry had refused to use their cartridges. A court-martial composed of fifteen Indian officers found against the troopers on 8 May and sentenced them each to five to ten years' hard labour. The following day, two regiments at Meerut turned on their officers, sprung the eighty-five imprisoned sepoys from jail, and pillaged the town. The English were shot, beaten to death, hacked at with swords, burned alive. Among the victims was a seven-year-old girl, her skull sliced in two by a single stroke from a blade; and pregnant twenty-three-year-old Charlotte Chambers, the foetus ripped out of her womb and dumped contemptuously on her breast.[16]

By the morning of 11 May, the mutinous troops had marched south to Delhi and joined with a garrison there. The rebels took the Red Fort, home of the heir to the Mughal Empire, Bahadur Shah II. Bahadur Shah was a gentle and unimposing Muslim of eighty-one years of age. He occupied his hours with poetry and courtly etiquette, was said to believe rather eccentrically that he could transform himself into a gnat, and had no jurisdiction beyond the walls of the Red Fort. He had been propped up and pensioned by the Company, which found him useful in sustaining the illusion of Indian self-government.[17] The rebels seized on this reluctant and bewildered old man, and persuaded him that he ought to demand his long-lost power back.

The restoration of the Emperor, precarious though it was, suggested that there was a credible alternative to British private rule. As the news spread, uprisings surged across north and central India, agitating one-third of the subcontinent by mid-June. But India was a country of deep divisions, in which disparate factions had only been united by their opposition to foreign rule. Where the British were ejected, these factions were left to face the enormity of their differences. Meanwhile, the British retained the support of the Sikhs of the Punjab, the Pathans of the North-West Frontier, the Gurkhas of Nepal, and the armies of Bombay and Madras. Neither Calcutta nor Simla, the two seats of the Company's administration, was attacked.[18] Almost all the princes stayed loyal to the British. The problem which had dogged the subcontinent since the death of Asoka, and would continue to dog it until 1947, was becoming clear. Karl Marx had recently been struck by the problem of India's deep internal divisions. It was, he wrote, 'A country not only divided between Mohammedan and Hindu, but between tribe and tribe, between caste and caste; a society whose framework was based on a sort of equilibrium, resulting from a general repulsion and constitutional exclusiveness between all its members. Such a country and such a society, were they not the predestined prey of conquest?'[19]

Within weeks, the British government sent its troops to the Company's aid. The British comeback would prove to be as brutal as it was predictable. Whole villages were burnt, men lynched and shot, and women raped. The streets of Delhi were stormed and lay filled with the bloated and stinking corpses of sepoys, provoking an outbreak of cholera which killed many of the remaining inhabitants. Holy idols were smashed as the plunderers searched for hidden jewels. Muslim rebel leaders were sewn into pigskins, and force-fed pork; Hindus were doused with cows' blood. Other instigators were strapped to the muzzles of cannon, and blown to pieces.[20] Bahadur Shah II ran away, and hid in the tomb of Akbar's father, Humayun – a mausoleum to the south of Delhi that stood as a monument to prouder Mughal days. The British found him, carried him off, and confined him to a house in Delhi; there he was kept to be gawped at by any European who cared to inspect him.[21] One family had a particularly lucky escape. Police Constable Gangadhar Nehru was fleeing Delhi across the Jumna River with his wife, Indrani, and their four children. The family was from Kashmir, with the typically pale skins and hazel eyes of that region's people – so pale that some British soldiers mistook one of the daughters for an English girl, and accused Gangadhar of kidnapping her. Only his son's proficiency in English, and the testimony of a passerby, saved the family.[22] Four years later, Indrani would give birth to another son, Motilal Nehru, who would in his turn father the first prime minister of independent India.

And so, in 1858, the relationship between Britain and India moved into its most intense phase: the raj.[23] On 2 August, the Government of India Act transferred all the East India Company's rights to the British Crown – which made it clear that the status quo would remain. Across great expanses of India, the maharajas, rajas and nawabs would be left in charge, with only a British Resident present in their capitals to keep an eye on things. The East India Company had long reasoned that ruling would be far easier through existing structures than through new creations. The landowners and princes propped up by the British enjoyed almost unlimited power, and consequently felt no need to challenge the British raj. In 1858, Queen Victoria proclaimed: 'We hold ourselves bound to the natives of our Indian territories by the same obligation of duties which bind us to all our other subjects. In their prosperity will be our strength; in their contentment our security; and in their gratitude our best reward.'[24]

In response to this spirit of cooperation, India became the favourite investment opportunity of European financiers. Industry boomed, with the production and processing of tea, coffee, cotton, jute and indigo. New roads and railways criss-crossed the plains, and wove in and out of the hills. The first steamships began to arrive at Bombay. After the Suez Canal opened in 1869, it was possible to get from Europe to India in just three weeks – half the time it had taken aboard the old sailing boats. Young Britons would often serve a tour of duty in India, either on military or civil service. It was easy for these fellows to get used to the luxuries to which a white skin and the low cost of living entitled them. Attitudes hardened, rather than liberalized, as the Empire went on: Indians were commonly referred to as 'natives' in the eighteenth century, 'coolies' by the end of the nineteenth, and 'niggers' by the beginning of the twentieth. Eventually, the Britons would return to sleepy cottages in the Home Counties, bringing back rugs, jewels and a taste for curried food, along with a dreamy nostalgia for their days as lords of a tropical paradise. The enthusiasm caught on at the highest level. Queen Victoria herself, the first and last Empress Regnant of India, was deeply interested in Indian culture and even learnt to speak Hindustani. She was tutored by her most trusted attendant, Abdul Karim, to whom she developed an attachment that verged on the romantic. Though she never made it to India herself, she sent her son, the future Edward VII, to meet the princes and shoot tigers in 1875. He was accompanied by a young aide-de-camp, Prince Louis of Battenberg.[25]

By the late nineteenth century, the cream of Indian society began to enjoy its British connections. Fashionable Indians went to Oxford or Cambridge for their education, and London for their tailoring: they read voraciously the classics of English literature, and often spoke English as their first language. New generations were growing up with notions of equality, democracy, citizenship, blind justice and fair play, only to discover that none of these rights actually applied to them. Indians were all but prevented from joining the administration of their own country by the deliberately obstructive entry procedure for the Indian Civil Service. Certain clubs, public places and even streets were designated 'Europeans only'.

The Indian upper classes found it hard to reconcile their proud Anglophiliac upbringings with the reality of their exclusion. At Eton, Harrow and Winchester, they identified themselves with the gilded youth of a glorious empire. Only in adulthood did they discover that their race relegated them to the second rank. 'The fact that the British Government should have imposed this arrangement upon us was not surprising; but what does seem surprising is that we, or most of us, accepted it as the natural and inevitable ordering of our lives and destiny', wrote one of those Harrow-educated sons of India, many years later. 'Greater than any victory of arms or diplomacy was this psychological triumph of the British in India.'[26]

Those words would be written by Gangadhar Nehru's grandson, Jawaharlal Nehru. But in 1877, Britain was still ascending towards the peak of its global influence. Exactly 300 years after a sorcerer had suggested the idea to another Queen of England, Victoria assumed the imperial throne *in absentia* during a splendid durbar in Delhi, her crown resting on a gilded cushion. As the massed ranks of the Indian Army cheered their new Empress, one of the most terrible famines of all history was underway in the south. Five million would waste and die, while the Viceroy and his government clucked about maintaining 'strict regard for the severest economy' and refused to undertake any further 'disastrous expenditure'.[27] The mechanisms of Empire had primed India for revolution. The only surprise would be just how long it would take.

CHAPTER 2

MOHAN AND JAWAHAR

ON 2 OCTOBER 1869, A SON WAS BORN INTO A MIDDLE-CLASS
family in Gujarat, a collection of princely states under British authority on the western coast of India. Mohandas Karamchand Gandhi
had an ordinary childhood, culminating, as ordinary childhoods
often do, in a teenage rebellion. This revealed a boy whose desire to
experiment was usually halted by an immobilizing timidity in the
actual act of defiance. He tried smoking, and stole gold from his
family to finance it; but this upset him morally, and so he stopped.
Though from a strictly vegetarian family, he tried eating meat; but
this upset him physically, and then morally as well, and then he
dreamt of a live goat trapped in his stomach, bleating, so he stopped
that too. Once he was egged on to visit a prostitute, but stood in the
brothel having a crisis of confidence until the woman shouted at him
to go away. On another occasion, he and a cousin ventured into the
jungle to kill themselves by overdosing on datura, the narcotic seeds
of the thorn apple – but, once they found the plant, they lost their
nerve.[1]

This boy's family was reasonably well off and of a middling but
respectable caste. Hindu society had been divided for over 1700
years into four main castes, reflecting second-century social groups:
Brahmins (priests), Kshatriyas (warriors), Vaishyas (merchants),
and Sudras (farmers). Within each of these were hundreds of

minute subdivisions, and below them a mass of outcastes, or 'untouchables' – those unfortunates who, condemned by the bad karma of previous incarnations, were destined to spend their lives sweeping, begging, scrubbing latrines and cleaning up corpses. The Gandhi family were Vaishyas, and within that were of the Bania subdivision. Banias were notorious for being hard-bargaining sales-men, a trait which young Mohan evidently inherited, and would one day apply to spiritual and political ends with unprecedented effect.

Mohan's rebellion was perhaps more unusual because the sup-posed cure for youthful misbehaviour had already been administered. Karamchand and Putliba Gandhi had already married their thirteen-year-old son to a girl from a staunchly religious family. The girl who had been chosen, Kasturbai Makanji (known accord-ing to local tradition as Kasturba later in life, when she became matriarch of the household) was also just thirteen.[2]

During daylight hours, etiquette decreed that Mohan and Kasturbai should ignore each other completely. Even an affectionate word between husband and wife was considered taboo. As darkness fell, they were left to their own devices – though neither had much idea what those should be. Mohan went to the bazaar to buy pam-phlets, hoping to learn about his conjugal rights and duties. He was taken with the concept of fidelity, and decided it should be his task to extract this from little Kasturbai. He told her that she could no longer leave the house without his consent.

But, despite her youth, Kasturbai had already mastered the most effective technique available to women who live in extremely restric-tive societies: that of passive resistance. She was a devout Hindu from a very traditional background, and would not openly disobey her husband. Instead, she found a loophole.

Mohan's mother asked Kasturbai to accompany her to the temple every day. Because this request was made in the daytime, when the young spouses were not supposed to communicate, Kasturbai was unable to ask Mohan's permission. To disobey the command of the matriarch, on the other hand, would have been a terrible sin. So Kasturbai went with Putliba to the temple, and returned to have her first fight with her husband, which she won by the sheer power of logic. Mohan was forced to remove the restrictions he had placed on Kasturbai.[3]

This small incident would hardly be worthy of note, except for the fact that it formed the basis for Gandhi's entire political method. In later years, when he found that he was at a disadvantage being an Indian in a white world, he would remember and develop the tactic of a woman in a man's world. All Gandhi's most famous tactics – passive resistance, civil disobedience, logical argument, non-violence in the face of violence, emotional blackmail – had came from Kasturbai's influence. He freely admitted this: 'I learned the lesson of non-violence from my wife.'[4]

Though his father had been Prime Minister of the princely state of Porbandar, young Mohan had not yet found any reason to involve himself in politics. Porbandar was over 800 miles from Bombay, where, in 1885, a Scotsman called Allan Octavian Hume founded the Indian National Congress. Congress enjoyed no legal status, but acted as a forum and a mouthpiece for Indian (as well as progressive British Indian) opinion. It was far from being a revolutionary organization; its foundation was approved by the Viceroy.[5] Its modest claims included a greater share of government for educated Indians, along with citizenship and equal rights with other members of the British Empire.

In Gujarat, Mohan and Kasturbai went through adolescence, and Kasturbai became pregnant for the first time. But their lives were to be disrupted by the illness of Mohan's father, Karamchand, who was consigned to his bed with a fistula in 1885. The son took on the duty of nurse. 'Every night whilst my hands were busy massaging my father's legs, my mind was hovering about the bedroom,' he admitted. It was an ill-fated juxtaposition. One night, Mohan's uncle offered to massage Karamchand. Eagerly accepting, Mohan went to Kasturbai. Though it was considered a sin against God to have sex with a pregnant woman, Mohan did so; and, just five or six minutes afterwards, received the most horrible shock of his young life. A servant knocked at the door to tell him his father had died.

Mohan rushed to Karamchand's room, overwhelmed with grief and, more importantly, with guilt. 'I saw that, if animal passion had not blinded me, I should have been spared the torture of separation from my father during his last moments', he later wrote. In the boy's distraught mind, his lust had killed his father. Pleasure was immediately conflated with destruction. In the development of his philosophy and his life, Mohan began to look for salvation in self-denial and discomfort. His father's death was 'a blot I have never been able to efface or forget', he confessed at the age of fifty-six.

As if to confirm Mohan's sense that he had brought a curse upon himself, Kasturbai gave birth to a weak and ailing infant. 'I may mention that the poor mite that was born to my wife scarcely breathed for more than three or four days,' wrote Gandhi. 'Let all those who are married be warned by my example.'[6]

In June 1888, the couple had a healthy baby, Harilal. Three months after his son was born, Mohandas Gandhi set sail for London.

Going to London was a brave move for the nineteen-year-old Mohandas. He faced opposition from his mother, who made him swear a solemn vow in front of a Jain monk to abstain from what she correctly imagined were the corrupting influences of London life: eating meat, drinking and whoring. He faced even more daunting opposition from the Bania community. When the elders in Bombay heard that Mohandas was planning to cross the Arabian Sea, they met to discuss the matter – and concluded that, because none of them had ever been to Britain, it must be 'polluting' to do so. If Mohandas went, he would be rejected by his caste, and would forever rank among the outcaste sweepers and scavengers.[7] Mohandas ignored these dire pronouncements, and got on the next boat. He would not see his wife and child again for three years.

In 1888, London was one of the greatest and richest cities on earth. Mohandas was not impressed, finding it expensive and strange, with bland food and incomprehensible customs. 'At night the tears would stream down my cheeks, and home memories of all sorts made sleep out of the question', he wrote.[8] He had an interest in medicine but, mindful of his family's opposition to the dissection of dead bodies, instead enrolled at the Inner Temple to study law.[9] In London, Mohandas dressed in a very different garb from the one in which he would eventually find fame. He was seen in Piccadilly wearing a pin-striped morning suit, stiff Gladstonian collar, silk topper and spats over his patent shoes, as well as what a fellow Indian student remembered as being 'a rather flashy tie'.[10] But this fashionable rig represented a meticulous nature, not profligacy. Adrift in the decadent luxury of London, Mohandas tended towards ever more stringent economies. He lodged in one room in Baron's Court. He walked everywhere. He stopped ordering spices from India, and subsisted on a diet of porridge, cocoa and plain boiled spinach. He became popular: with one bottle of wine between each four students at Inner Temple dinners, everyone wanted to sit beside the teetotaller from Gujarat.[11]

One day he stumbled across one of Victorian London's few meat-free restaurants, the Centre in Farringdon Road, and joined the Vegetarian Society of England.[12] Thanks to his new friends in the Society, he started reading Christian writers, such as Leo Tolstoy and John Ruskin, who would rank among his strongest influences. They also induced him to read the Bhagavad Gita for the first time.[13] From this point he began to develop his personal philosophy. It was rooted in Hindu scripture, but incorporated many of the anti-materialistic and abstinent values of early Christianity and Jainism. He considered it to be applicable to all faiths. Central to his message was a motto: 'God is truth'.[14]

Mohandas returned to India in 1891. He went through a purification ceremony to re-enter his caste, and began to practise law in Bombay. The results were lacklustre. When, in 1893, a businessman offered him a job in South Africa for three years, he decided it was best to take this opportunity, and left his family again.

The trip to South Africa was to change the course of his life. For the first time, Gandhi would experience the full force of colonial racism. Only a week after his arrival, he was physically thrown from a train at Maritzburg. Having bought a first-class ticket, he had presumed it was his right to sit in the first-class compartment. The conductor thought otherwise, and had him ejected by a policeman. He proceeded by stagecoach, and was beaten up by the coach-leader because he had asked to sit inside the coach, rather than on a dirty piece of sackcloth on the footboard. On his eventual arrival in Johannesburg, the Grand National Hotel refused to let the well-dressed Indian barrister have a room.[15]

Mohandas Gandhi had arrived in what was, for an Indian, one of the most hostile territories on earth. The 150,000 Indians in South Africa were described in the statute books as 'semi-barbarous Asiatics, or persons belonging to the uncivilised races of Asia', and were subject to an array of punitive restrictions designed to make their lives as difficult and unprofitable as possible.[16] Gandhi launched a campaign that demanded equal rights for Indians in South Africa as citizens of the British Empire. On 22 May 1894, he inaugurated the Natal Indian Congress – modelled on the Indian National Congress, of which he had read but never yet attended. The suspicion of the authorities was immediately aroused. Two years later, when he brought his wife and children to South Africa, it was made obvious that the Gandhis were not welcome. The port supervisors refused to let their ship dock for twenty-three days. When they disembarked, Gandhi was attacked by a mob of white men, who threw stones, bricks and eggs at him, before setting on him with punches and kicks. He was saved by the wife of the police superintendent, who bravely interposed herself, armed only with a parasol. Later that day, a lynch mob surrounded the house where the Gandhi family was hiding.

For once in his life, Gandhi was persuaded not to confront his enemies, on the grounds that this would put his family and friends in even more danger. Instead he disguised himself as a policeman, with a tin pan wrapped under his turban for defence, and thus attired made it to the local police station.[17] He had been so badly beaten after getting off the ship that it was two days before he could make a statement, but he refused to bring charges against his attackers.[18] This disinclination to see punishment enacted distinguished Gandhi from other political agitators. Here was something new – and it would attract murmurs of surprise, and even admiration, in the international press.

During 1897, with Kasturba pregnant again, Mohandas invited several young law clerks to live with the family. He started to implement rules inspired by the vision of society offered by Ruskin and Tolstoy, aimed at egalitarian, cooperative living, and a pure devotion to God through asceticism. One of the founding principles was that everyone was supposed to empty and clean their own chamber pots – a task which Hindus normally delegated to the Untouchables. Kasturba was appalled, not least because of the rule that she and Mohandas had to clean any that had been forgotten. One day, when a Christian Indian of Untouchable parentage accidentally left his pot unemptied, she found it. She refused to move it, to which Mohandas replied that he would clean it himself. For a Hindu wife to allow her husband to defile himself is considered an even greater degradation than to pollute her own body. Weeping with anger and humiliation, Kasturba lugged the pot down the stairs outside the house. Little did she realize that Mohandas was watching. He lost his temper, shouting that not only must she carry around buckets of excrement, but that she should do so cheerfully. She threatened to walk out, at which point Mohandas grabbed her roughly by the arm. He dragged her to the gate and tried to shove her through it. She sobbed that she had nowhere to go. At this, he relented, and let her back.[19]

The incident illustrated Gandhi's growing belief that personal life was an integral part of politics. He insisted on leading by example, no matter what the consequences were for himself, his family, his friends or his followers. In 1899, he demonstrated this again on a grander scale when the Boer War broke out. In spite of his personal sympathy with the Dutch settlers, Gandhi's reaction was that the Indians must support the British. If they demanded British rights, he reasoned, they must shoulder British responsibilities. He set up the Indian Ambulance Corps and actively recruited his countrymen in the name of the Queen-Empress. The Indians served without pay, and would march up to twenty-five miles every day, bearing the British Empire's wounded on stretchers back to their camps. Gandhi's courage, hard work and patriotism paid off. He was awarded the War Medal, and the Indian Ambulance Corps was mentioned in dispatches.[20]

The Ambulance Corps was an early example of Gandhi's flair for the grand gesture. The defining motif of self-sacrifice was important. After the birth of his fourth surviving son, Devadas, in 1900, he attempted to become a *brahmachari* – a celibate. This decision was strengthened by the family's move from their villa to the first of his formal ashrams (semi-monastic community retreats) in 1904.

Gandhi believed that the community would grow more intimate overall if its members had no special favourites, either through sexual intimacy or family ties.[21] There was also the aspect of sin. In his young teens, Mohandas had learnt in the most devastating way to associate sex with moral and physical ruin. In adult life, he began to consider any form of physical pleasure – food, comfort and intoxication, as well as sex – to be degrading, and any form of physical torment – fasting, scrubbing latrines, wearing prickly homespun cloth, being beaten up by the police – to be righteous.

In 1907, Gandhi coined the term *satyagraha*, a Sanskrit word, meaning literally 'truth-force'. The intent was to imply a powerful but non-violent energy.[22] During October 1908, while he was in prison for civil disobedience, his commitment was to be tested. Kasturba fell seriously ill. It was possible for Gandhi to have himself released at any time: all he had to do was plead guilty, pay the modest fine, and walk out from the prison gates. But Gandhi was not prepared to admit guilt. Friends, family, life and death meant less to him than truth, faith and politics. 'I am not in a position to come and nurse you', he wrote to Kasturba; 'if it is destined that you shall die, I think it is preferable that you should go before me . . . Even if you die, for me you will be eternally alive.' He assured her that he had 'no intentions' of remarrying after her death, and told her that her demise would be 'another great sacrifice for the cause of Satyagraha'.[23] Kasturba survived.

When Gandhi returned to India in 1915, he still did not appear to be the sort of man who shook empires. He seemed to be exactly the opposite. In the King's birthday honours of 3 June 1915, Mohandas Gandhi of Ahmedabad was awarded the Kaiser-i-Hind (Emperor of India) medal for services to the British Empire.[24] It was Sir Rabindranath Tagore, the Bengali poet and Nobel Laureate, who bestowed upon Gandhi the title by which he would become known. Tagore dubbed him 'Mahatma', meaning 'great soul'. But the great soul would require a great lieutenant to link him to the temporal world. In one of history's more surprising pairings, the lieutenant would be an upper-class Brahmin lawyer, the sophisticated product of Harrow and Cambridge, who spoke Indian languages only haltingly, and did not believe in God at all. And yet, despite their differences, the combined strength of Mohandas Gandhi and Jawaharlal Nehru would one day command the attention of the world.

While Gandhi was experimenting with truths, another Indian youth was preparing to go to England for his education. This boy was a far more promising student than Gandhi had been at the same age. He was also more sophisticated, more confident, more charming, much wealthier and conspicuously better looking. It was little surprise that young Jawaharlal Nehru was the apple of his father's eye – and that father happened to be one of India's top lawyers and an emerging figure in the Indian National Congress, Motilal Nehru.

Motilal Nehru was a colossus, of broad shoulder and imposing countenance. It was often remarked that, in profile, he resembled a Roman emperor. He dominated any gathering, both physically and intellectually. He was incisive, bullish, witty, warm, and occasionally fiery. He impressed everybody. Even the British attempted to change their own race rules so that they could invite him to join their clubs.[25] He presided over a cheerfully integrated, Westernized and lavish household in the grandest mansion in Allahabad, Anand Bhavan. Under Motilal's roof, no distinction was drawn between Hindus, Muslims, mixed-race Anglo-Indians, Untouchables and Europeans.[26]

As the beloved only child of a very privileged family, young Jawahar (as he was known) was haughty, refined and more than a little spoiled. Lacking brothers or sisters, and schooled at home without classmates, he soon learned to direct his thoughts and questions inwards. He developed a capacity for merciless self-judgement which, ultimately, would set him apart from other statesmen.

Jawahar only made it to the age of five or six before feeling the full power of his father's fearsome temper. Motilal had two smart fountain pens in his study; his son took one without asking. A massive search ensued, during which the terrified Jawahar kept silent. The pen was eventually discovered in his possession, and Motilal administered a ferocious beating to the tiny boy. Even forty years later, when he was a veteran of several beatings at the hands of armed policemen, Jawahar's memory of this first encounter with violence remained raw. 'Almost blind with pain and mortification at my disgrace I rushed to Mother,' he wrote, 'and for several days various creams and ointments were applied to my aching and quivering little body.'[27] But he did not hate his father for the pain he had suffered, nor even for the injustice of such a punishment. The explosive Nehru temper was hereditary, and the boy, though naturally of a gentle and even quiet disposition, soon learned to imitate his father's outbursts. Later in life, he would become notorious for thumping those who irritated him.[28]

The counterpoint to this awestruck relationship with his father was the simple, comforting love Jawahar had from his mother, Swarup Rani. She cuddled him after Motilal's thrashings, and offered him the beguiling images of Hinduism while Motilal doggedly maintained his secularism. For a while, Jawahar felt himself pulling towards the softer, more spiritual side of the Nehru household. He experimented with religion and, under the influence of his tutor, Ferdinand T. Brooks, even signed up to one. Theosophy had been invented in 1875 in England, and relied on fusing parts of Hinduism and Buddhism with the late nineteenth-century European fashions for mysticism, esoteric rituals, and attempted communion with the spirit world. Annie Besant, one of the religion's most notable devotees and later a leading advocate for Indian independence, inducted Jawahar herself. He was thirteen years old.[29] Not long afterwards Mr Brooks left, and young Jawahar's creed departed shortly after.

Initially Jawahar had scorned his father's strict rationalism as unimaginative. But ultimately, as with the temper, he could not help but emulate it. Faced with the indulgent comforts of his mother's love, and the hard-headed challenge of his father's, Jawahar preferred the challenge. Though he adored her, part of him began to look down on his mother. Her love for him, he wrote, was 'excessive and indiscriminating'. If Jawahar was to become a man, it was clear which path he had to follow; and religion, he concluded superciliously, 'seemed to be a woman's affair'.[30]

In 1900, his first sister was born and named Sarup, which she hated. On marriage, she would rename herself Vijaya Lakshmi, but was always known as Nan. A second sister, Krishna, known as Betty, would follow seven years later. Jawahar doted on Nan, but the gap of eleven years between them prevented her from becoming a confidante until later in life.[31] The lonely boy continued to live a large part of his life inside his head, as a recurring dream he began to have at around this time illustrates. 'I dreamt of astral bodies and imagined myself flying vast distances', he wrote. 'This dream of flying high up in the air (without any appliance) has indeed been a frequent one throughout my life; and sometimes it has been vivid and realistic and the countryside seemed to lie underneath me in a vast panorama.' The Russo-Japanese War was in progress, and news of Asian victories over Europeans sparked Jawahar's imagination. At night he dreamt of flying over Indian domains; during the day, he pictured himself as a noble knight, sword in hand, freeing beautiful Asia from her wicked European overlords.[32]

In 1905, when Jawahar was fifteen, he went with his parents and Nan on a journey to the heart of the overlords' territory. They reached Britain in May, and deposited Jawahar at Harrow School in north London. Following in the footsteps of Winston Churchill seventeen years before, he joined the Head Master's House, an imposing red-brick building on the High Street. Life at Harrow was designed to confuse outsiders, with its esoteric traditions, colour-coded bow ties, and private language of beaks, bluers, shepherds and philathletes. Initially this made him homesick, but Jawahar soon learned to conform to the school's eccentricities. 'I had deliberately not resisted them so as to be in harmony with the place,' he later acknowledged. But, within this complicit young denizen of the British establishment, there were already hints of a more controversial future. When he received a volume on Garibaldi as a school prize, Jawahar found himself identifying strongly with the revolutionary soldier, atheist and republican, who had made possible the unification of Italy less than half a century before.[33]

After two years Jawahar became bored with Harrow, though in adult life he remembered it with nostalgia. Many years later, when he had become a revolutionary soldier, atheist and republican, he would dig out a dusty volume of Harrow school songs from the library at Anand Bhavan. There, over six thousand miles from the Head Master's House, he sat with his nieces Lekha, Tara and Rita, singing rousing choruses of 'Jerry, You Duffer and Dunce' and 'When Grandpapa's Grandpapa was in the Lower Lower First'.[34] Grandpapa's grandpapa had been a landowner in Delhi, and appeared regularly at the Mughal court.[35] But the mature Jawahar would be able to enjoy his European refinements without compromising his Indian identity.

At seventeen, Jawahar persuaded Motilal to let him go up to Trinity College, Cambridge, where he read natural sciences. A lover of nature, he specialized in chemistry, botany and geology. In his spare time, he went riding, learned ballroom dancing, coxed a college rowing boat in the Lent races, and pursued a satisfying social life.[36] Jawahar later wrote with a happy sentimentalism of winter evenings spent by the fire, talking about culture, politics, sex and morality until the embers died out, and the sharp cold of a draughty old sandstone college forced him and his friends to bed.[37] The conversations about sex struck him in particular. 'Most of us were strongly attracted by sex and I doubt if any of us attached any idea of sin to it,' he wrote. 'Certainly I did not; there was no religious inhibition.' And, a few lines later, he added: 'I enjoyed life and I refused to see why I should consider it a thing of sin.'[38] His defensiveness on the matter is intriguing, but there are no further clues to follow. Certainly he was not yet the intoxicating draw for women that he would be in his later years.

At around this time, his father's thoughts were also turning to matters of Jawahar's heart. The choice of possible brides was not one to be taken lightly, and Motilal asked for his son's opinion in 1909, causing Jawahar to reply, caustically, 'I am not violently looking forward to the prospect of being married to anybody.'[39] While resisting the idea of marriage in general, Jawahar did note that his enthusiasm would be far greater if the bride could be found from outside the Kashmiri Brahmin community. But this was not to be. Motilal answered legalistically, pointing out that intermarriage between castes was invalid under Hindu law and, because the British had never legislated to overrule that point, a free choice was simply not possible.[40]

Many letters passed between father and son on this theme, and it became increasingly obvious that Jawahar's secular upbringing and British veneer were going to make traditional Hindu matchmaking an awkward business. 'You express a hope that my marriage should be romantic', he wrote to his father. 'I should like it to be so but I fail to see how it is going to come about. There is not an atom of romance in the way you are searching [out] girls for me and keeping them waiting till my arrival. The very idea is extremely unromantic. And you can hardly expect me to fall in love with a photograph.'[41] But Motilal was not to be put off, and eventually found Kamala Kaul, a girl from Delhi. Pretty though she was, Jawahar found something to object to in the ten-year age gap between them. 'I could not possibly marry her before she was eighteen or nineteen, and that is six or seven years hence', he wrote. 'I would not mind waiting as I am not in a matrimonial state of mind at present.'[42]

After Cambridge he went to the Inner Temple in London to follow his father into the legal profession. His studies did not grip him; social and political life did, and two years went by as Jawahar 'hovered about London', becoming interested in Fabianism, socialism, votes for women and Irish independence. This left-wing awakening was done in the company of some old public-school friends, and expensively. Motilal had always been a generous father. At Cambridge, Jawahar had £400 a year, which was almost half a professorial salary.[43] He had proven to be good at spending it, and had often run short of cash. 'I was merely trying to ape to some extent the prosperous but somewhat empty-headed Englishman who is called a "man about town",' he later confessed. 'This soft and pointless existence, needless to say, did not improve me in any way.'[44] Regular requests for another £100 here and there arrived back in Allahabad; sometimes, there was just a cable with the single word 'Money'.[45] This occasioned at least one Motilal fury being delivered in written form; but the debts were always paid. And Jawahar's easy life in London was not without its uses. In 1911, Motilal commissioned his son to purchase for him a full suit of court dress – buckled knee breeches over silk stockings, a tail coat with gold embroidery, a bicorne hat and a ceremonial sword. Despite his criticism of the British regime, Motilal was both loyal and important enough to have been one of the very few Indian commoners commanded to attend the Delhi durbar of King-Emperor George V.[46]

*

In the autumn of 1912, a young English gentleman, Jawaharlal Nehru, returned to India, the land of his birth. He had been away for seven years, punctuated by two trips home. He had received a world-class education of the grandest type, read plenty of fashionable books, developed a raffish interest in radical politics, and spent a large amount of his father's money. Nehru's verdict on himself at age twenty-two was characteristically sharp: 'I was a bit of a prig with little to commend me.'[47]

In India Jawahar duly began to take on legal cases, and was soon delighting his father with a substantial income. He was interested in politics, but had a crippling fear of speaking in public – especially if he had to do it in Hindustani, rather than English.[48] The rest of his time was divided between the bar library and the club, and featured an endless rotation of the same old men discussing the same legal topics in the same stuffy, colonial lounges. It was a life of stupefying tedium, and Jawahar quickly fell into despair. A quote from the pacifist Goldsworthy Lowes Dickinson struck him hard: 'And *why* can't the races meet? Simply because the Indians *bore* the English.' Jawahar added, darkly, 'It is possible that most Englishmen feel that way and it is not surprising.'[49]

This glum lad was hardly cheered by the arrival of what was supposed to be the happiest day of his life on 8 February 1916. The wedding of Jawaharlal Nehru and Kamala Kaul was one of the leading social events of the year, described later by their friend Asaf Ali, with very little overstatement, as the 'royal wedding'.[50] It had been arranged for the first day of spring. A special train, swagged opulently with ribbons and bunting and garlanded with flowers, brought the groom and three hundred guests up from Allahabad to Delhi. A town of tents and marquees was set up outside the walled city, beneath a sign with the words 'Nehru Wedding Camp' spelt out in flowers. There were bedroom tents, living-room tents and dining tents, each hung and carpeted with oriental rugs and furnished with Motilal's usual lavishness. The encampment had a full staff and its own orchestra.

Astrologers chose the hour just after midnight as the most favourable for the ceremony. The groom rode to the Kaul family mansion in Old Delhi on a white horse, followed by a procession of guests. Jawahar wore a brocade sherwani and silk turban; Kamala a traditional pink sari. Because Hindu priests usually took the bride's jewellery as part of their fee, it was customary for her ornaments to be made of flowers – but the Nehrus were wealthy enough that chains of gold as well as blossom could hang around Kamala's slender neck. She was, according to the groom's second sister, Betty, 'one of the most beautiful women I knew or ever have known'.[51] Under a canopy, the couple exchanged vows as the priests chanted and poured ghee into the fire, and plumes of black smoke billowed up into the night sky.

The next day brought more celebrations of an even more sumptuous style back at the Nehru Wedding Camp. Kamala wore a stunning cream-coloured sari, embroidered with real pearls, which had taken a group of craftsmen working on the verandahs of Anand Bhavan several months to bead.[52] Motilal had designed the jewellery in which he bedecked her, so much of it that she seemed to be 'ablaze' with diamonds, pearls, emeralds and rubies.[53] A further ten days of rejoicing was declared for the guests, all at Motilal's expense.

The only person not enchanted by the festivities was the groom, who looked grumpy in every photograph. In chapter six of his autobiography, Nehru announced curtly that 'My marriage took place in 1916 in the city of Delhi.'[54] The strange turn of phrase admitted him no agency: not 'I married', but 'My marriage took place'; he did not name the bride. Immediately, he moved the subject on to a trip to Kashmir and Ladakh that summer, a sort of honeymoon *en famille*. Motilal hired a fleet of houseboats on the picturesque Dal Lake at Srinagar. But a lazy married life did not hold Jawahar's attention, and he persuaded his family to trek up into the mountains. Motilal brought his luxuries with him: the party rode up on horseback, with the frail Swarup Rani carried in a sedan chair, and took a dozen servants to wait on them in their palatial, wooden-floored tents.

Even this expedition did not satisfy Jawahar's urge to escape. Leaving Kamala with his parents, he set off on a perilous climbing adventure to the Zojila Pass with a cousin, during which he was, to his great excitement, nearly killed when he slipped down a crevasse.[55] The newlyweds were not especially happy in their marriage, which was later described by their niece Nayantara Sahgal as 'a grievous mistake for two profoundly different people'.[56] Jawahar, rhapsodizing at elegiac length on the beauty of the Kashmiri land-scape, was clearly not so taken with the charms of his wife; and she, now living with his parents in a strange half-Westernized house-hold, began to show signs of distress. Soon after their Kashmiri holiday, Jawahar was called back to Allahabad on business. Kamala stayed in Kashmir, where she did little but eat cherries and develop headaches.

The birth of a daughter, Indira, the following year did little to rec-oncile Jawahar to family life, for he had at last found a purpose outside it. Mohandas Gandhi had kept a low profile since returning to India the previous year, but had caused a scandal and, nearly, a riot when he spoke freely at the opening of Benares Hindu University in February 1916. In front of an audience of British and Indian emi-nences, and a large number of students who had been angered by the arrest of some of them that day, he launched into one of the most incendiary speeches he would ever make. 'I compare with the richly bedecked noblemen the millions of the poor,' he said, indicating the former on the platform behind him. 'And I feel like saying to these noblemen: "There is no solution for India unless you strip your-selves of this jewellery and hold it in trust for your countrymen in India". . . . Our salvation can only come through the farmer. Neither the lawyers, not the doctors, nor the rich landlords are going to secure it.'[57] He went on to discuss violent acts of revolution – in the context of dismissing them, but the audience missed the subtlety, and heard only the Mahatma talking of the throwing of bombs and the assassination of viceroys. Several princes walked out, including the chairman, the Maharaja of Darbhanga. The students were thrilled. The speech brought Gandhi to the attention of the nation, and to that of Jawaharlal Nehru.[58]

Few political figures have been so widely misunderstood as Gandhi, in his own time or today. He emerged at a time when monarchies were falling, and communism loomed; he was contem-porary with Lenin. To many listeners, aware of the march of events in Russia, Gandhi's speech sounded like a rallying cry to Indian socialism, with its talk of the casting off of jewels, and the power of the workers. This was, indeed, the reason that young radicals like

Jawahar were so attracted to him. But a closer examination of Gandhi's words reveals something different, and much more profoundly religious. He had confronted the moral behaviour of society, not its structure. Gandhi called for the princes to stop wearing their finery and instead 'hold it in trust' for their subjects. This is not the same thing at all as telling the masses to rise up and seize it. Gandhi was not challenging the princes' right to hold wealth, nor even their right to reign. He was asking for a change of heart.

Gandhi's condemnation of princely luxury was part of a much broader preoccupation with returning India to what he supposed had been a prehistoric 'golden age' of godliness, simplicity and humility.[59] He had begun to reject Western ideals of progress and technology, and insisted that India's future lay in a return to simple village life, not industrialization. As a symbol of this, he adopted hand-spinning on a wooden wheel, and used only *khadi* – hand-spun – textiles. He developed a distaste for synthesized drugs and surgery, which he associated with Western medicine, describing them as 'black magic'.[60] Doctors, he believed, 'violate our religious instinct' by prioritizing the body over the mind, and curing diseases which people had deserved by their conduct. Lawyers, meanwhile, had propped up British rule by espousing British law, and were as 'leeches' on the people, their profession 'just as degrading as prostitution'.[61] This position had fuelled continual conflict in his own family life. Unsurprisingly, he was far from supportive of his sons' ambitions to pursue careers in medicine or law. 'I know too that you have sometimes felt that your education was being neglected', Mohandas wrote to his third son, Manilal. But, he contended, 'Education does not mean a knowledge of letters but it means character building. It means a knowledge of duty.'[62] His eldest son, Harilal, fared worse. After Mohandas denied him a legal scholarship to London, he ran away from home, married a woman without his father's consent, was disinherited, and ended up unemployed, destitute and bitter. When Manilal tried to lend Harilal money, Mohandas was so furious that he banished Manilal from his presence for a year. Manilal ended up sleeping rough on a beach.[63]

It is not easy being a saint, and it is perhaps even less so to live with one. 'All of us brothers have been treated as a ringmaster would treat his trained animals', Harilal wrote to his father in the course of a twelve-page letter deploring Mohandas's treatment of his wife and sons.[64] And yet, to a wider audience beyond his immediate family, Gandhi's charisma, determination and fearlessness were inspiring.

At the end of the First World War, India found itself subject to a new onslaught of oppression. The subcontinent had been heavily taxed, repeatedly hit for loans, and had given 1.5 million of its men into the service of a distant military effort. Indian harvests had been requisitioned to fill European bellies, with the effect that the bounteous land that produced them suffered shortages. Four out of every five British soldiers engaged in defending the vulnerable North-West Frontier against Afghans and tribal warfare had been called away to fight for the Allies. As a result, militant pan-Islamic fundamentalists were able to gain a strong foothold in the Punjab, as well as in Bengal. Across the rest of India, Hindu nationalism seized the opportunity to capitalize on public discontent.

In March 1915, the Defence of India Act had given the courts extraordinary powers to detain suspects without trial, and to imprison, deport or execute political agitators in the Punjab and Bengal. By this stage, even the moderates of the Indian National Congress began to object. In 1917 Edwin Montagu, the Secretary of State for India, made a vague pronouncement about the object of British policy being towards the 'gradual development of self-governing institutions'.[65] The reality did not match the rhetoric.

It is within the context of this tightening of the imperial shackles that the swift and dazzling rise of Gandhi can be understood. The Indians were a people belittled, starved and fearful. 'And then Gandhi came', wrote Jawaharlal Nehru.

> He was like a powerful current of fresh air that made us stretch ourselves and take deep breaths; like a beam of light that pierced the darkness and removed the scales from our eyes; like a whirlwind that upset many things, but most of all the working of people's minds. He did not descend from the top; he seemed to emerge from the millions of India, speaking their language and incessantly drawing attention to them and their appalling condition.[66]

Gandhi's satyagraha was an alternative to fear, an option more radical and, crucially, more Indian than that proposed by the moderate Congress. His effect on audiences was breathtaking. Jawahar's sister Nan heard him speak in Allahabad. 'I found myself struggling to pull off some gold bangles I had on my wrist so that I could put them into the bag when it came. Afterwards I couldn't think why I'd been so moved. But he had this quality of magic about him.'[67] His triumphal entry into Congress brought in its wake great crowds of new supporters: not just Brahmin lawyers, but peasants, farmers and labourers. He ordered the Brahmin lawyers to the villages, to recruit yet more of the common people: the effect was double-sided, for many among them had never truly seen the poverty of their own countrymen. His arrival changed everything, putting the upper classes in touch with the lowest and raising the lowest to a new status of nobility. For the first time since the Mutiny, India had a widely popular political movement that rejected the way of life imposed upon it from the distant chambers of London.

CHAPTER 3

CIVIS BRITANNICUS SUM

ON 28 JUNE 1914, AN AUSTRIAN ARCHDUKE AND HIS WIFE
were shot in Sarajevo by a nineteen-year-old terrorist. Assassinations
were not unusual at the time – victims in recent years had included
the Presidents of Mexico, France and the United States, the
Empresses of Korea and Austria, a Persian Shah, and the Kings of
Italy, Greece and Serbia. Portugal had two kings assassinated on the
same day in 1908.[1] But the murder of Archduke Franz Ferdinand
would swiftly assume its legendary status as the trigger for the Great
War. Swift to feel its tremors was the fourteen-year-old great-grandson of Queen Victoria, His Serene Highness Prince Louis of
Battenberg.

Prince Louis was born on 24 June 1900, at which point forty-
eight people would have had to die, abdicate, or marry Catholics in
order for him to become King of Great Britain and Ireland, and
Emperor of India. He was always known within the family as
'Dickie'. Dickie's father, another Prince Louis of Battenberg, was
the First Sea Lord of the Royal Navy; his mother was Princess
Victoria of Hesse, the sister of the Tsarina of Russia. This made him
cousin to almost every king, prince and grand duke in the monkey-
puzzle family tree of European royalty.

The Battenbergs were not especially wealthy, and their prove-
nance placed them firmly in royalty's second class.[2] (The line had

been created by Prince Alexander of Hesse, who fell in love with and married a countess considered too lowly, and was summarily demoted by his disgusted family. They had never been keen on him anyway: Prince Alexander was widely supposed to have been the illegitimate son of his mother's chamberlain, Baron Augustus Senarclens von Grancy.[3]) Still, even a tangential relationship to royalty proper was a smart thing to have in the early twentieth century, and the younger Prince Louis enjoyed a fairy-tale childhood touring Europe's palaces, and playing with his Russian cousins, Olga, Tatiana, Marie, Anastasia and Alexei. He was particularly fond of Marie, who was a year his senior, and wondered if he ought to marry her one day.[4] The question would never arise; the First World War would spark a further cull of royalty and neither the House of Battenberg, nor Grand Duchess Marie, would survive.

Four months to the day after Franz Ferdinand's death, the elder Prince Louis of Battenberg was removed from his position as First Sea Lord. Prince Louis had been British since 1868, and had served in the Royal Navy since he was fourteen years old. But by October 1914 Britain was at war with Germany, and there were far too many Germans visible in high places. For King George V, of the house of Saxe-Coburg Gotha, the public tide of anti-German feeling was alarming. He was largely German; his wife, the former Princess May of Teck, was wholly German; his recently deceased father, King Edward VII, had even spoken English with a strong German accent. It was uncomfortably obvious where all this might lead, and a high-profile sacrifice was required to satisfy the public. Prince Louis was at the top of the list.

And so the King and his First Lord of the Admiralty, Winston Churchill, agreed to throw one of their most senior military experts on to the pyre at the beginning of the war, because his name was foreign. The Prime Minister, H.H. Asquith, wrote cheerfully to his confidante Venetia Stanley that 'our poor blue-eyed German will have to go'.[5] There was another reason, too, though it was not discussed openly: both Churchill and Asquith had lost confidence in Prince Louis's abilities. No one was honest enough to say this; Prince Louis was, therefore, asked to resign, and was told to say publicly that he was doing so out of a patriotic desire not to embarrass the government with his Germanness.[6] Churchill avowed to Prince Louis that, 'No incident in my public life has caused me so much sorrow,' though privately he had been pushing to install his old friend Lord Fisher in the job for some time.[7] Prince Louis maintained great dignity in the face of this shameful treatment, aside from briefly bursting into tears on the shoulder of George V.[8] He tendered his resignation as requested, and faded away into a private life of unemployment. For his teenaged son Dickie, a naval cadet at Osborne, the sense of injustice was devastating. Many years later, he would still describe it as 'the worst body-blow I ever suffered'. He was seen standing to attention on his own beside the flagpole at Osborne, weeping.[9] 'It doesn't really matter,' he told a friend, when he had calmed down. 'Of course I shall take his place.'[10]

But the humiliation of the Battenbergs was not complete. On 17 July 1917, a mass rebranding of royalty was ordered by George V. The King led by example this time, dropping Saxe-Coburg Gotha (which was, in any case, a title – nobody knew what his surname was, though they suspected without enthusiasm that it might be Wettin or Wipper), and adopting the British-sounding Windsor. Much against their will, the rest of the in-laws were de-Germanized. Prince Alexander of Battenberg became the Marquess of Carisbrooke; Prince Alexander of Teck became the Earl of Athlone; Adolphus, Duke of Teck, became the Marquess of Cambridge. The unfortunate Princesses of Schleswig-Holstein were demoted, in the King's words, to 'Helena Victoria and Marie Louise of *Nothing*'.[11] And the unemployed Prince Louis of Battenberg would be Louis Mountbatten, Marquess of Milford Haven.

The former Prince Louis detested both his inelegant title and the reasoning behind it. 'I am absolutely English,' he told George V. 'I have been educated in England and have been in England all my life. If you wish me to become now Sir Louis Battenberg I will do so.'[12] It was a noble offer, dimmed only slightly by Prince Louis's presumption of a knighthood – he dismissed the idea of being Mr Louis Battenberg as 'impossible' – and the Teutonic cast of his sentences.[13] The compromise was rejected. Henceforth, Prince Louis would be a marquess, and Battenberg a cake.

But the family's losses in the Great War were far more devastating than the misplacement of a little social prestige. Exactly one year to the day after the Battenbergs became Mountbattens, a massacre took place that would decimate their family and shock the world beyond. On 2 March 1917, Prince Louis's brother-in-law Tsar Nicholas II of Russia had been forced to abdicate. A little over a year later, the ex-Tsar and his family were moved to the mining town of Ekaterinburg. There they were incarcerated in a mansion which the Bolsheviks had renamed, with their usual knack for the ominous, the 'House of Special Purpose'. That purpose was to become apparent within just two months. Early on the morning of 17 July 1918, the former imperial family was ordered into the basement, along with a doctor, a serving-girl, a cook and a valet. The family and staff were shot, and the survivors, Marie and Anastasia, repeatedly bayoneted as they screamed and struggled. The Tsarina had made them sew jewellery into their bodices for safe keeping, and the gemstones deflected both bullets and blades. The bodies were dragged outside, one of the grand duchesses still wailing and another choking on blood. The squad was reduced to bludgeoning the girls with the butts of rifles. The bodies were loaded on to a cart and dumped in an abandoned mineshaft in the Koptyaki Forest. Shortly afterwards they were retrieved, set on fire, doused in sulphuric acid and buried at the roadside.[14]

These events haunted the young Lord Louis Mountbatten, as Dickie had been renamed now that he was the son of a peer, rather than the son of a prince. The teenaged Dickie took to keeping a portrait of his first sweetheart, Grand Duchess Marie, beside his bed. Once in love, Dickie rarely fell out of it, and the portrait of Marie would hang in his bedroom for the rest of his life.[15]

Young Dickie's challenge for the war years was to make his mark in the same Royal Navy from which his father had been so rudely ejected. Dickie was, from childhood, adventurous: quick and deft of thought; intrepid, but usually slapdash with it. A school report from the spring term of 1915 noted that 'He is very diligent and interested in his work. At present he is rather inaccurate but I think that his steadiness should soon overcome this failing.'[16]

Three distinguishing features of his personality were beginning to emerge. The first was a strong streak of romanticism. Aged fourteen, he broke his ankle while tobogganing and was confined to bed. He placed an advertisement in a local newspaper, billing himself accurately, though misleadingly: 'A young naval officer, injured and in hospital, desires correspondence.' He received 150 replies, many from women proposing marriage. Always too coy to act the rake, Dickie passed the letters on to the crew of his brother's ship, the *New Zealand*, without answering a single one of them himself.[17]

The second feature was a great gift for storytelling, unspoilt by any preoccupation with the truth. The above tale of capturing 150 swooning, girlish hearts, for instance, was often told by Mountbatten himself in later life. And yet a search through the local Dartmouth newspapers from the winter of 1915–16 turns up no such advert, and the giving-away of the letters means that there is no evidence in the Mountbatten archive, either. The tale may be true, or it may be 'rather inaccurate', but it makes a nice story. As such it is similar to many of Mountbatten's favourite anecdotes.

The third, and perhaps the strongest, of Mountbatten's distinguishing features was a passion for formality. He adored ceremony, and developed an infatuation with orders and rank. He would amass an extraordinary collection of decorations: the octagonal collar of the Royal Victorian Order with its eight gold roses; the Maltese cross of the Order of St John, with two lions and two unicorns rampant between its points; the heron- and ostrich-plumed hat and the jewelled strap of the Most Noble Order of the Garter. Most delightful of all was surely the star and sash of the Most Exalted Order of the White Elephant. This distinguished Thai order was founded in 1861 by King Mongkut Rama IV, perhaps better known to Westerners in fictionalized form as the hero of Rodgers and Hammerstein's musical *The King and I*. But the Order of the White Elephant is no fiction, and at his country house, Broadlands, Dickie's still hangs proudly on its pink sash.[18]

Springing from a long line of royal sticklers, fussers and pedants, Mountbatten had been bred for pageantry. It was a good thing, for he seemed not to have been bred for the navy. A fellow officer later admitted that Mountbatten 'knew nothing about the sea at all; he went into the Navy because it was in his family rather than in his blood.'[19] One of his instructors reported that Mountbatten was slower than the average cadet, and that he would only ever keep up by hard work. Fortunately, Mountbatten had an insatiable appetite for hard work, and a burning ambition which would both literally and figuratively keep his head above water. At the age of eighteen, he had been made second-in-command of his first ship, a patrol vessel called HMS *P31*. His greatest achievement was to have it moored at Westminster and visited by King George V and Princess Mary – an event which set the tone for his career, in which the stage-managing of publicity coups would be paramount.[20]

In 1919, Dickie was released from the Navy to go to Cambridge, where he matriculated at Christ's College. Entrance to the two most hallowed of English universities in those days had little to do with academic merit, and a lot to do with connections and money. The intensely anti-intellectual Prince of Wales, Prince Edward ('David'), had already been through Magdalen College, Oxford, where he found it necessary to keep his private tutor with him at all times. His younger brother Prince Albert ('Bertie'), who had been placed sixty-eighth out of sixty-eight in his final examinations at Osborne, was at Trinity College, Cambridge. Another brother, Prince Henry, was so profoundly dim of wit that even the royals themselves looked down on him (David was said to have remarked that the only reason 'poor Harry' recognized the National Anthem was because everybody stood up). He was about to start alongside his brother at Trinity. Unfortunately the royal family viewed education with the same suspicion with which a villageful of medieval peasants viewed witchcraft. The King refused to let Bertie and Harry live among their college peers. Instead he put them up at Southacre, a large house which was a good distance out of town, and consequently the shy Bertie made no friends at all, while Harry spent most of his university career setting up mousetraps in the conservatory. The young princes were fortunate in having one person who could provide a link to the distant social whirl of undergraduate life – their cousin, Dickie Mountbatten.

Being at Cambridge at the same time as the princes was a stroke of luck for Dickie. The Empire, though at its largest ever extent, had been troubled by the war. There was an opportunity at the heart of the royal family for someone with an instinctive feel for public relations, someone who could stand as a great British hero, steady the national identity, and move the throne forwards into a new democratic age. It was widely assumed that this would be the enormously popular golden boy, David, who would one day reign as Edward VIII. But, as royal families have long learned, it is no bad thing to have a spare besides an heir. By moving into the close cabal that surrounded the royal family, Dickie was moving closer towards fulfilling his own ambition: to restore his family to the very top of British public life.

Even before the war, the British Empire had been modifying its relationship with its colonies. Four of its great territories – Australia, New Zealand, South Africa and Canada – now held 'dominion status', allowing them a measure of self-government. It was incongruous that India remained a mere colony. The incongruity was enhanced by the fact that India had provided wartime supplies of food and soldiers, the latter widely recruited by Mohandas Gandhi, who still professed that those who wished for rights must act like they deserved them. But the British government in India appeared to be moving towards greater control. In February 1919, it introduced the Rowlatt Bills, two pieces of anti-terrorist legislation which were intended to reinforce the totalitarian powers that had been granted to the judiciary in wartime. Gandhi saw these bills as an open challenge. On 18 March 1919, the Imperial Legislative Council forced the Rowlatt Act into law, despite the opposition of every Indian member. Three weeks later, on 6 April, Gandhi called a *hartal* – a day of prayer and fasting that effectively functioned as a general strike. It was the first major nationwide and interfaith protest against the British government since the Mutiny. Some protesters became so incensed that the non-violent character of the hartal was forgotten, and riots broke out. The British grew frantic, and far-fetched rumours spread among the troops. British soldiers heard that Gandhi himself had sponsored circulars inciting Indian patriots to murder European men and ravish European women.[21] Gandhi had done nothing of the sort. On the contrary, he condemned his followers' heated behaviour.[22]

But the most significant incident, which would change the whole course of British imperial history, was to take place in Amritsar, north of Delhi. On 10 April 1919, two Indian leaders who had been organizing the hartals were arrested. In consequence, there was a massive riot. Forty thousand people ran amok in the city, pillaging and burning buildings, and killing five white men as well as seriously injuring two women. The next morning, Brigadier General Reginald Dyer arrived from Jullundur to take command of the scorched city.

Dyer had served in the eastern Empire for over thirty years. He was known for his short fuse, but maintained an excellent rapport with the Indian soldiers under his command.[23] On assuming command in Amritsar, he issued a proclamation warning that gatherings would be fired on. 'Respectable persons,' it warned, 'should stay indoors.'[24] By the morning of 13 April, the proclamation was being disobeyed, though not for nefarious purposes. That day happened to be a Sikh festival, Baisakhi Day, which was also celebrated by Hindus as the first day of harvest. Dyer sent his troops on to the streets to repeat the proclamation in Urdu and Punjabi, and added a curfew to the ordinances. Owing to the intense heat, and the small number of soldiers available, few citizens had any chance of hearing the proclamation. Many of them ran to hide at the first sight of British troops.[25]

At four o'clock that afternoon, Dyer received reports that a meeting was taking place in Jallianwala Bagh. The Bagh was an area of enclosed scrubland with only three narrow exits – one of which had been closed up. As usual on a Sunday afternoon, it was full of people. Hundreds used the Bagh as a social meeting place every day, and the crowd was swelled to thousands by out-of-town families who had come in for the festival. In one corner was the political meeting that had so outraged Dyer. A wooden platform had been set up near a well, and various poets and activists were speaking to the crowd.

Just before 5.15 p.m., Dyer arrived with 100 Gurkha, Sikh, Pathan and Baluchi riflemen, and 40 more Gurkhas armed with knives.[26] He stopped outside one of the two open exits, and sent a man in to estimate the size of the crowd – 5000, the report came back. Later estimates suggested it must have been between three and ten times that figure. The troops marched in and set up their rifles. Dyer's instructions were specific: aim straight and low, fire at the fullest part of the crowd, and pick off any stragglers who try to escape. No warning was given before the troops opened fire.

The gathering, though technically illegal, had been peaceful until Dyer showed up. At his order, 1650 bullets were fired into the throng of men, women and children. Soldiers deliberately blocked the exits, trapping people in the killing ground. In desperation, they clawed their way up the walls, scrambled over their injured friends, and leapt down the open well, which filled with 120 bodies drowning and suffocating in water thick with blood. The slaughter went on until the ammunition was spent. Official estimates put the death toll at 379, with at least 1200 more injured. Popular estimates went much higher. Many of the victims were too scared to seek medical assistance from the British hospitals, and the curfew prevented families from searching for their dead.[27]

Dyer showed no remorse in the aftermath of his massacre. Instead, he had high-caste Indians whom he suspected of political agitation rounded up and publicly flogged. Any Indian who dared approach the street where a Christian missionary had been dragged off her bicycle was forced to crawl face-down in the dirt.

Dyer's action had been vicious, decisive and unforgettable, and would polarize political opinion across the Empire. Strict military censorship slowed the spread of news, but so shocking a tale could not stay secret for long. By 30 May, it had reached Bengal. The national poet, Rabindranath Tagore, immediately resigned his knighthood. 'The time has come when the badges of honour make our shame glaring in the incongruous context of humiliation,' he explained to the Viceroy.[28] Motilal Nehru wrote that, 'My blood is boiling', causing his daughter Betty to add that, 'If his blood was in that condition, my brother [Jawahar]'s was like superheated steam.'[29] Amritsar was the most influential single incident in the radicalization of Congress, and in the radicalization of the Nehrus.[30]

More surprising, perhaps, was the great upsurge in popular backing for Dyer. 'I thought I would be doing a jolly lot of good,' said the man himself, and there was no shortage of people who agreed with him.[31] The House of Lords passed a motion in his support. The *Morning Post* newspaper started a drive to raise funds for his retirement; £26,000 was collected, from members of the public and celebrities, including Rudyard Kipling, and the Duke of Somerset. When Sir Edwin Montagu rose in Parliament to condemn Dyer for terrorism and racial humiliation of the Indians, he was shouted down by Conservative members crying, 'It saved a mutiny,' accusing him of Bolshevism, and screaming anti-Semitic insults. The session nearly turned into a physical fight.[32] Even among Indians there was support for Dyer. The Sikh leaders in Amritsar made him an honorary Sikh, staging a special ceremony in their holiest site, the Golden Temple.[33]

But perhaps the most surprising response of all came from Mohandas Gandhi, the leader of the formerly peaceful campaign which had ended in such carnage. On 18 April, newspapers printed a letter from Gandhi expressing regret for the civil disobedience campaign. 'I am sorry, when I embarked on a mass movement, I underrated the forces of evil', he wrote, 'and I must now pause and consider how best to meet the situation.'[34] Discussing the victims of Dyer's massacre, he declared that they 'were definitely not heroic martyrs', and criticized them for having 'taken to their heels' rather than face death calmly.[35] He continued to profess that he believed the British would see justice done.[36] Gandhi had fought for the British Empire for the entirety of his adult life. He believed in it; what he wanted for the Indian people was that they be recognized and treated as full subjects, and that they act in a way to deserve such an honour.

The plea against arbitrary justice in the Roman Empire, as famously invoked by St Paul at Philippi, was 'Civis Romanus sum' – I am a Roman citizen. Many years later, the Indian writer Nirad Chaudhuri converted this to 'Civis Britannicus sum' – I am a British citizen. Chaudhuri was widely seen in post-imperial India as being an apologist for British rule, but in fact he was making a point no different from Gandhi's in 1919. It was an appeal for inclusion within the British imperial family; a sentiment young Dickie Battenberg, estranged by his German name, would have felt as he saluted the Union Jack at Osborne with tears of humiliation rolling down his cheeks.[37]

The Hunter Commission was set up on 14 October 1919 to inquire into the massacre and other disorders in Bombay, Delhi and the Punjab. It took five months to conclude that Dyer had been in the wrong. Congress ran its own inquiry into events, with young Jawaharlal Nehru sent to inspect the Bagh and take evidence. Later that year, Jawahar got on the night train to Delhi at Amritsar. It was full, and he crept into the only upper berth that was not occupied by a sleeping body. Only the next morning did he realize that he was travelling in a carriage full of loud, blustering officers of the Indian Army. The loudest and most blustering among them was Brigadier General Dyer himself, bragging of his exploits at Amritsar. 'He pointed out how he had the whole town at his mercy and he had felt like reducing the rebellious city to a heap of ashes, but he took pity on it and refrained,' Jawahar remembered. 'I was greatly shocked to hear his conversation and to observe his callous manner. He descended at Delhi station in pyjamas with bright pink stripes, and a dressing-gown.'[38]

Dyer was asked to resign from the army. He escaped prosecution and lived out his remaining years quietly in Bristol. Gandhi was eventually moved from his patriotic position with great difficulty, having given the British administration every opportunity to prove itself responsive. Had the British at this point allowed moderate concessions, the following years might have been a great deal easier for them as well as for their king's Indian subjects. Unfortunately, they did nothing. Fourteen months after Tagore had resigned his knighthood, Gandhi belatedly returned to the Viceroy his Kaiser-i-Hind medal. He declared his first national satyagraha campaign, and he and Congress declared themselves in favour of *swaraj* – meaning self-rule, defined as 'political and spiritual' independence.[39]

In London, it was felt that the reputation of the Empire had taken a serious knock. King George V had sensibly issued a pardon for all those involved in the Punjab rioting just before Congress opened its session of December 1919. The Congress president, Motilal Nehru, joined Gandhi in sending grateful thanks to the King 'for his act of mercy'.[40] In reality, the act had been pragmatic. The Empire's image needed a boost, and the energies of its subjects needed to be refocused on patriotic pride. The government hit upon a simple solution. The King's son David, Prince of Wales, was young, handsome and popular. Though he spent all of his free time in nightclubs dancing with other men's wives and moaning about his royal burden, the press obediently presented him as a clean-cut young soldier hero and the most eligible bachelor in Europe. He was the ideal 'face' of the British Empire – and so he would be sent to tour his future domain. This would serve a triple purpose. First, David could act as an ambassador for British rule. Second, he could learn about the many lands and peoples that would one day be subject to him. And, third, it would get him away from his debauched Mayfair set – not least his unsuitable girlfriend Freda Dudley-Ward, who was married to someone else.

David's cousin Dickie Mountbatten was not really a member of that set, being slightly too young and too gauche to join in. But his carefully nurtured friendships with David's less glamorous brothers Bertie and Harry had brought him to the inner circle of royal life. One night, David was talking about his trips abroad at a Buckingham Palace dinner, and suggested to the rapt Dickie that he should come along as his aide-de-camp.

The process of inspecting his future Empire, and letting it inspect him, was to prove tiresome to the Prince of Wales. David was lonely on HMS *Renown*. The only people he considered to be friends were Dickie and an equerry called Piers Legh. 'Dickie is keen & cheery about everything, though of course he is such a baby!!' the prince wrote to Mrs Dudley-Ward on the day after he sailed from Portsmouth, 17 March 1920. 'But he's a vewy clever boy & goes out of his way to be nice & kind & sympathetic & attentive to me as I think he guesses a little how I'm feeling. I'm so glad I've got him with me & I think we are going to be great friends.'[41]

The cousins did indeed become great friends, and quickly. Dickie was the only person the prince saw during his long cruises around the world to whom he could relate on equal terms and, conspicuously, the only person aboard ship who could call the prince 'David', rather than 'Sir'. The two men shared the same sense of humour, so common among royalty, centred around practical jokes. And they were both lovesick: David for Mrs Dudley-Ward, and Dickie, apparently, for a new girl each week. 'Dickie has been sitting in my cabin for 1/2 hr while I undressed & has told me all his "love affairs" as he calls them!!' the prince wrote to Mrs Dudley-Ward. 'He makes me laugh, sweetie, particularly when he mentions the word love!!'[42]

Dickie had been pining for an Englishwoman, Audrey James, to whom he was tentatively engaged following a dogged pursuit – but she would chuck him on his return, and absence did not appear to be making his heart grow fonder, either. On tour, he flirted with all the cheerful abandon of one let off the leash, and delighted in dancing and playing Ludo with 'a lot of pretty girls'.[43]

The tour's first destination was Barbados ('I haven't landed yet sweetheart but it looks a proper bum island this Barbados,' David confided to Mrs Dudley-Ward)[44], and it was there that the standard for the trip was set. David spent the days moping about in between ponderous ceremonials and formal parties, while Dickie plied him with horseplay and dancing partners in an attempt to lighten things up. The two men soon found themselves riding together, drinking together, going to parties together, learning to surf together, sleeping on deck with their beds pushed together, and even, one hot afternoon in Fiji, bathing together. 'Plenty of room for two!!' David exclaimed as he and Dickie threw themselves into a tiled pool at Government House and ordered reviving cocktails.[45] (Back in Britain, the King was not impressed. 'You and Dick in a swimming pool together is hardly dignified, though comfortable in a hot climate, you might as well be photographed naked, no doubt it would please the public,' he wrote acidly.)[46] Most of all, they joked together. They tied up officers and dunked them in a bath. They attempted to train David's pet wallaby, Digger, to perform tricks. They flooded bathrooms. They raided gentlemen's cloakrooms, and dressed up in silly outfits: 'Dickie & I found some of our host's clothes & opera hats & tennis boots in his room (he was away) & we dolled ourselves up & made everybody laugh too which was so amazing! But as you can guess my beloved my mild hilarity was merely due to some very good brown sherry His Ex gave us for dinner though I wasn't in any way toxi-boo.'[47]

The rest of the crew began to find this pair ever more insufferable, even when they were not toxi-boo, and their resentment tended to focus on Dickie. Even the otherwise loyal Piers Legh started to refer to the prince's cousin as 'Dirty Dick' and 'the Hun' in letters home.[48] By 18 April, the situation had reached crisis point. A deputation from the staff went to the Admiral with a lengthy list of Dirty Dick's many transgressions. The Admiral duly gave him a talking-to, though, as his crimes amounted to little more than having an annoying personality, it is hard to imagine what he might have done about them. David was distraught, and attributed the crew's complaints to jealousy. He began to worry about what the crew would say about his new best friend once they were back. 'I don't want my "little brother" Dickie badly spoken of at home!!' he declared. 'I'm so fond of that boy & he means so much to me when I'm away from TOI, far more than Bertie ever has or ever will.'[49]

By the time the tour arrived back in Portsmouth on 11 October 1920, Dickie Mountbatten's social climb was complete. He was now, without doubt, the closest friend of the Prince of Wales and future king – closer even than the prince's own brother. David and Dickie's next and most important challenge was already set up. They were to be sent to conquer India.

CHAPTER 4

DREAMING OF THE EAST

ON 29 JUNE 1920, THE PRINCE OF WALES WROTE TO HIS LOVER Freda Dudley-Ward about his planned trip to India the following year. 'I'm intent on Dickie coming again!!' he wrote. 'I just couldn't do without that boy on the next trip & the Admiral likes him & wants him too & it won't harm his naval career, in fact he'll benefit by it!!'[1] When he looked back over his royal career thirty years later, David's enthusiasm for cousin Dickie was not so obvious; though the influence of his ghost-writer was. 'It was my impression at the time that his interest in the manifold problems of India was confined to that part of the country bounded by the white boards of polo fields,' he mused, with the haughtiness that only the pot can muster for the kettle. 'However, not so many years were to elapse before he was to be established in the Viceroy's House at New Delhi, engaged in the process of liquidating the immeasurable Imperial trust he and I, each in our own way, had endeavoured to defend in our youth.'[2]

The peak of the British Empire's extent and influence is often said to have been in the early 1920s, and thoughts of it ending at that time were widely considered to be absurd. The *New York Times* had stated boldly on 10 July 1921 that 'British imperialism would be compelled to evacuate Great Britain itself before it would willingly evacuate India',[3] sentiments with which the future King-Emperor and his retinue would doubtless have agreed. Perhaps they did not realize how close the imperial trust was to being liquidated – without their consent.

On 26 October 1921, Dickie and David left Portsmouth on the battlecruiser HMS *Renown*. On 12 November, they came ashore at Aden on the south coast of Arabia, the westernmost British colony ruled from Delhi. The pair of them drove past large gatherings of black spectators hemmed in by the occasional white man in a pith helmet. Union Jacks fluttered in the sky, and a huge banner was unfurled. It addressed the Prince of Wales with a loyal exhortation: 'Tell Daddy we are all happy under British rule'. And it was from this acceptably loyal outpost of his future empire that David embarked finally for the Jewel itself.

For months, the pages of English-language newspapers in India had filled up with advertisements selling printed portraits of the prince for two rupees, and advising ladies to purchase abundant wardrobes of new gowns for the myriad social events during his stay. But the greater part of the excitement was generated by fear: a very real fear that Gandhi's call for 'civil revolution' might explode into a revolution of the more usual, uncivil type.[4] If anything were to happen to the Prince of Wales while he was in India, the consequences would be unthinkable. As the *Renown* drew closer to Bombay across the Arabian Sea, the British administrators, and the media, seemed to hold their breath.

The prince set foot in his future imperial domain at 10.20 in the morning of 17 November 1921 at Bombay. A royal barge ferried him from the *Renown* across the silver waves to the half-finished, roseate arches of the Gateway of India. He emerged from his barge, a slight, golden-haired figure in a neat white naval uniform, amid clouds of spent gunpowder from the massive salute afforded him by the fleet of British warships anchored just offshore. Preceded by three chaprasis clad in scarlet, the prince progressed to a garlanded pavilion on the quay. There he inspected the guards of honour, and sat on a gilded throne to read out King George V's message to the Indian Empire. That done, he was put into a state carriage, and drawn by four horses to Government House for a formal luncheon.[5] The *Times of India* estimated that 200,000 people lined the route between Apollo Bunder and Sandhurst Road.

The prince's itinerary had been planned according to long-established royal tradition. He was to progress around India attending interminable parties, opening buildings, killing as much wildlife as possible and only interacting with the common people by waving at them from a parade. The sentiments of the royal party were made plain in the booklet of Hindustani phrases produced by Dickie and Sir Geoffrey de Montmorency, and circulated on board HMS *Renown*. It comprised a list of basic numbers and verbs, plus a few everyday expressions. These included:

Ghoosul teeyar kurro – Make ready the bath
Yeh boot sarf kurro – Make clean these boots
Peg do – Give me a whisky and soda
Ghora lao – Bring round the horse
Yeh miler hai; leyjao – This is dirty; take it away
Tum Kootch Angrezi bolte hai? – Do you speak any English?
Mai neigh sumujhta – I don't understand

The words for 'please' and 'thank you' are nowhere to be found.[6]

So far, it seemed, so good. But a smooth disembarkation could not allay fears that the prince's four-month tour would end in disaster – and the probable culprit was obvious. Gandhi, according to the prince, 'was regarded as a sinister if somewhat ludicrous figure' in government circles. This was perhaps an understatement. The year before, Winston Churchill had astonished a dinner party by suggesting that he have Gandhi bound hand and foot at the gates of Delhi, and let the Viceroy sit on the back of a giant elephant and trample the Mahatma into the dirt.[7] Most of the government kept their opinions rather less forthright, and the prevailing mood appears to have been trepidation rather than vengeance. 'Would he try to spoil my show?' asked the prince.[8] In fact, Gandhi was just as concerned by the possibility of mob violence as were the British. He called for a hartal to mark the prince's arrival in Bombay, but specifically and repeatedly stated that it should be peaceful and dignified.[9]

But Gandhi's hold over the masses was feebler than his reputation suggested. As the prince sat down for his luncheon and the crowds that had greeted him dispersed, celebration turned swiftly to anger.

The effect was immediate and terrifying, as the city which had looked so serene only an hour before erupted in violence. 'From Government House, one could hear the sounds of distant rioting and occasional shots,' the prince noted.[10] For once, Hindus and Muslims were united, as both ganged up on Parsi and Indian Christian communities. Shops were looted. Tram cars were pelted with stones. The police station at New Nagpada was set upon, and three Indian constables were brutally murdered by a howling mob.[11] Meanwhile, the royal tour attempted to continue as normal, and the shaken prince was taken to watch some polo at the Willingdon Club. He then returned to Government House for a reception in a very stuffy room, at which he had to shake hands with three thousand people while attempting not to perspire too noticeably. (One guest at the reception was so struck by the frequency with which the prince mopped his reddened brow that he wrote a letter to the *Times of India* complaining about it.)[12]

Gandhi appealed for an end to the carnage. 'The Swaraj that I have witnessed during the last two days has stunk in my nostrils,' he wrote. 'I invite every Hindu and Mussalman to retire to his home and ask God for forgiveness and to befriend the injured communities from the bottom of their hearts.'[13] The Mahatma's words did little to calm the situation. By the time that the prince returned to Bombay the following week, several parts of the city had been devastated. A mob had set fire to a barrel of alcohol at the Null Bazaar and burnt the whole building down, causing damage estimated at 100,000 rupees. Errant Gandhians had smashed up liquor shops, and one such establishment had been raided by a marauding band of Pathans. A group of Parsis had attacked a motorcar and forced the Hindu occupants to remove their Gandhi caps. The Hindus fled, leaving the Parsis to tear the car to pieces. Amid reports of attacks on anyone wearing Western dress, seven Europeans were admitted to the General Hospital with injuries over the weekend, and one was killed. The official estimated death toll stood at 36, with between 150 and 200 more lying injured in hospital.[14]

With both Gandhi and the British authorities railing against the masses, the prince was packed off on his train, heading north towards the deserts of Rajputana. In Bombay, the people had looked poor, the city dirty and crowded, and the atmosphere bleak. In Baroda, the opposite of each of these was true. The prince was greeted with six garlanded elephants, bearing jewelled silver how-dahs; a line of silver carriages, drawn by caparisoned oxen with gilded horns; and rows upon rows of plumed horses ridden by Baroda's state guard. He was driven through vast crowds of people, said to comprise the entire population of the state, to the Nazar Bagh palace. The prince walked on a carpet of cloth-of-gold all the way from his carriage up a magnificent flight of stairs to a hall with a silver sofa, where he and the Gaekwar of Baroda held court for the local dignitaries.[15]

The Indian states would have many more chances to impress the disoriented Prince of Wales as he travelled on through Udaipur to the extraordinary blue-painted town of Jodhpur. It was there, on 30 November 1921, that the prince got to stick his first pig on a dawn hunt, and then his second soon afterwards. The ladies of the party, spectating from towers built at the edge of the open ground, were disappointed that he stuck both of his pigs out of sight in the jungle. They had to be content with listening to a 'piercing and long-drawn squeal' from deep in the undergrowth, the cry of a beast skewered by a princely spear.[16]

David enjoyed pig-sticking so much that he and Dickie went again the next day. This time, Dickie's luck was in. 'It was one of the best mornings I have ever spent anywhere,' he wrote effusively in his diary.[17] Unwary researchers in the Mountbatten archive may still shake out an envelope bearing the emblem of the Maharaja of Jodhpur, and be confronted by a decaying, matted lump of hair and skin. It is proudly labelled: 'Tip of tail of Boar speared by me at Jodhpur 1st Dec 1921 – D'.[18]

If the elephants at Baroda had impressed the prince, the welcome at Bikaner would astound him. For two miles before the palace of Lalgarh, the road was lined with thousands of steeds of the Ganga Rissala Bikaner Camel Corps, bearing the sumptuously robed and jewelled nobility of the state. The prince spent an arduous day inspecting Boy Scouts and, that night, he and Dickie saw an elabo-rate programme of entertainment at the Junagarh Fort. The inner court was lit with thousands of coloured fairy lights, which were dramatically extinguished as fourteen exquisite nautch girls appeared, bearing lit candelabra on their heads. Dickie burnt himself while inspecting a piece of glowing charcoal that a performer had held in his mouth during a fire-dance. Another performer danced barefoot upon swords, spear-points, saws, and a heap of delicate shells which he left perfectly unbroken.[19]

It would have been easy for the Prince of Wales to forget about the nightmare he had glimpsed briefly in Bombay – that is, until he got to the United Provinces. The provinces, in the north-east of India between Delhi and the Himalayas, were one of India's most politically sophisticated regions. This was the home territory of the Nehru family, and would be the scene of the best-organized protests against the prince's visit. The royal party first arrived in Lucknow on 9 December. It was a destination with particular resonance, having withstood two lengthy sieges by rebel sepoys during the Mutiny. The prince gamely joined in a polo match, and was allowed to win; the Raja of Jahangirabad presented him with the cup.[20] But, beyond the white boards of that particular polo field, support for the tour was proving hard to drum up. The royal party blamed Gandhi personally for a range of dirty tricks which they believed had been employed to keep the crowds away. It was said that Congressmen had told the people that they would be shot by police if they went too near the prince's procession; further, that the prince had been so horrified by India's poverty that he had poisoned the customary free food, in order to effect a mass cull of the poor.[21] Such rumours may have been spread, but not by Gandhi. He went in for far more straightforward persuasion. Meanwhile, David was tickled to see trucks driving around Lucknow painted with the slogan 'Come and see the Prince and have a free ride'. It was, he admitted, 'a form of enticement that never had to be employed when my father travelled about India'.[22]

That night, David was encouraged to dance away his woes at Government House. 'I am afraid that I prefer native states to British India,' Dickie complained,[23] but the evidence suggests that he had a good time – his card for the evening reveals that he danced with so many new girls that he could not remember all their names. There was a foxtrot with 'Red Ostrich Feather', a one-step with 'Pink Gray

Stockings', and two more foxtrots with 'Miss Slim Ankles'.[24] Despite appearances, though, the girl-crazy days of 1920 were behind him. Miss Slim Ankles was destined for disappointment, for he had been writing to the Hon. Edwina Ashley all tour.

Edwina Ashley was a year younger than Dickie Mountbatten. Her maternal grandfather was Sir Ernest Cassel, an enormously successful banker and close friend of King Edward VII – who had stood as her godfather and after whom she had been named.[25] Sir Ernest bequeathed to his first granddaughter the greatest portion of his estate. This included properties in Mayfair, Bournemouth, Newmarket and Switzerland; a considerable collection of art treasures and valuable furnishings; and a trust fund worth something close to £3 million (equivalent to over £100 million today). From her father's side, Edwina would ultimately inherit even more money, along with the estates of Broadlands in Hampshire, and Classiebawn in Sligo. It was from that side that she also inherited a colourful family tree, ranging from Prime Ministers Melbourne and Palmerston to the Algonquin princess Pocahontas.

Despite all this gilding, Edwina had endured an austere and lonely childhood. Her mother had died in 1911, after which her father, Lord Mount Temple, had taken a new wife – described later by Dickie as 'a wicked woman, a real bitch'.[26] Because Edwina and her sister could not get on with their stepmother, they were doomed to a youth of freezing showers and endless lacrosse at a hearty girls' boarding school in Eastbourne. Edwina was bullied on account of her grandfather being rich, German and Jewish, and later described school as 'sheer hell'.[27] She was afterwards subjected to an internment at a domestic science college in Suffolk, where wealthy young ladies had to wear mob-caps and long green overalls while learning to cook, clean and sew. These privileged girls would never be expected to use their accomplishments in a vocational context: they were being taught how to supervise their future staff, and instilled with a suitably soul-destroying sense of 'traditional' femininity.[28] Edwina kept writing to Sir Ernest about how unhappy she was. Finally, after six months of button-sewing, table-laying and learning to comport herself, she was rescued by him and packed off to travel round France and Italy. Edwina was to have a grand tour, seeing for herself the art, culture and society of Europe, under the watchful eye of Jane Cranston, a chaperone who was under strict instructions not to let Edwina attend evening parties or befriend bachelors. But Miss Cranston would soon find that her pretty young charge had already had enough propriety to last her a lifetime. Edwina's photograph albums from the trip juxtapose a few improving classical ruins with a lot of brooding young men in well-tailored breeches.[29]

Dickie and Edwina had met in October 1920, at a dance given by Mrs Cornelius Vanderbilt at Claridge's Hotel in London.[30] They met again at Cowes during the Regatta Week of 1921, when the keener-eyed society doyennes noticed the pair dancing together every night. Mrs Vanderbilt was among those doyennes, and invited them both on a ten-day cruise around Belgium and France on the Vanderbilt yacht. Edwina had several suitors, but Dickie was trying so hard to get her attention she could hardly fail to notice. One evening they slipped away from their maids to dance at a seaside cafe called the Omar Khayyam. On their last night, Dickie seized an opportunity offered by Edwina's seasickness, convincing her that the way to conquer it was to sleep on deck in a lifeboat in which, so it happened, he too would be spending the night.[31]

After they returned home, Dickie invited Edwina to meet his parents. Shortly afterwards, the new couple went on another holiday in Scotland, with various friends including Dickie's princely cousins, David and Bertie. Dickie had been on the verge of proposing to Edwina when he received a severe shock. A telegram arrived with the unexpected news that his father had died following a heart attack. Dickie hastened back to his family. Days later, Edwina returned to London to comfort him. She had meant to go straight to Brook House to tell her grandfather and guardian, Sir Ernest Cassel, about her new boyfriend. On getting off the train, she discovered that she was a few hours too late. Cassel, too, had just died of a heart attack, as unexpectedly as had the Marquess of Milford Haven.[32]

Under such circumstances, the blossoming romance deepened. When Dickie sailed for India with David, Edwina had been photographed standing on the quay between Dickie's sister Louise and David's brother Bertie, a soulful expression on her face.[33] Later, Dickie had pressed Edwina to join him. 'I need you so badly', he wrote to her. 'You just don't know what a difference your coming out to India is going to make.'[34] Unable yet to access her grandfather's estate, Edwina borrowed £100 from her great-aunt for a second-class berth, and studied the passenger lists until she found the name of a vague acquaintance she could ask to act as her chaperone. A long, hot journey followed, through the Mediterranean and the Red Sea: 'I just lay on my bunk with the ceiling fan slowly turning, and dreamed of the East,' she remembered.

As Edwina sailed towards Bombay, her beau moved on with the Prince of Wales to the troublesome city of Allahabad. For those on the tour, any remaining dreams of eastern promise were to be rudely interrupted. Here, the peaceful protest was to reach its zenith – despite the local magistrate's efforts to keep the ringleaders caged by arresting Motilal Nehru and his thirty-two-year-old son, Jawahar.

Since the days of being 'a bit of a prig', Jawahar had undergone a political epiphany. A group of peasants had come to Allahabad to beg the leaders of the freedom movement to take up their case against cruel and oppressive landlords. Jawahar agreed to visit their village and discuss their concerns. This three-day trip had transformed him from a shy and cosseted lawyer – who, by his own admission, was 'totally ignorant' of the conditions in which the great majority of Indians worked and lived – into a revolutionary. 'Looking at them and their misery and overflowing gratitude, I was filled with shame and sorrow,' he wrote; 'shame at my own easygoing and comfortable life and our petty politics of the city which ignored this vast multitude of semi-naked sons and daughters of India, sorrow at the degradation and overwhelming poverty.'[35]

By the time of the Prince of Wales's tour, Jawahar had been confirmed as a rising star of the freedom movement, and one more radical than his august father. Motilal had been opposed to satyagraha in the first instance, and argued that the sending of a few individuals to prison would make little difference. In particular, he was unhappy with the thought of Jawahar ending up there. A doting father does not send his only beloved son to Harrow and Cambridge in the expectation that he will end up in a jailhouse. Yet Jawahar was determined to pursue satyagraha. Though even Gandhi advised him to do nothing that would upset Motilal, he could not be dissuaded.

Father and son argued for several days. Jawahar pointedly began to eat bread and milk in the evenings from a steel bowl, amid the rest of the family's crystal and Dresden china. Before one dinner he was fiddling with a piece of twine from a parcel, and commented: 'I wonder what it feels like to have a noose round one's neck?' Swarup Rani nearly fainted; Motilal walked out and slammed the door. 'Has this family no sense of humour left?' asked Jawahar, crossly.[36] That night, Motilal secretly tried sleeping on the floor, wanting to understand the hardship his son would suffer in prison.[37]

On the evening of 6 December 1921, the Prince of Wales was in his train en route for Bharatpur. That same night, Jawahar was up late in the Congress office in Allahabad, when a clerk burst in with the news that they were surrounded by police and that the building was being searched. Jawahar maintained his cool – 'it was my first experience of the kind, but the desire to show off was strong,' he later admitted. He refused to flinch while the police went around tipping out files and arresting his colleagues. Eventually, provoked by the news that raids were taking place elsewhere in the city, he returned home to check on his family – only to find the police there too. Both Jawahar and Motilal were arrested.[38] Between December 1921 and January 1922, the British authorities arrested an almost unbelievable total of 30,000 people in connection with the hartals.[39] It was hard for them not to arrest even more. Jawahar's sister Betty remembered that everyone was so keen to support Gandhi's cause that 'people who were *not* arrested would pile into prison vans, which arrived at the jails with more prisoners than the jailers expected or could handle. The officials were at their wits' ends; what could you do with people like that?'[40]

The arrest of the Nehrus stirred up Congress supporters across the United Provinces and beyond.[41] Stories seeped through the tight ring of press censorship suggesting 600 arrests in Bombay, and rioting in Calcutta.[42] When the Prince of Wales descended from his train at Allahabad on the 12 December, it was to an eerie hush. Allahabad had been a typical Indian city the day before, filled with noisy, colourful bazaars, bustling rickshaws, children playing and fighting, the fragrant smoke of burning incense, the bubbling of milk boiling for sweets, and the crackling of samosas being fried on roadside stalls. Now the streets were deserted, the houses shuttered. The city was a ghost town, with silent troops lining the empty streets, saluting the lonely state carriage that bore the uncelebrated prince. From a population of 150,000, only a couple of thousand spectators had turned out – and those that had were conspicuously white of skin.[43] 'It was a spooky experience,' David later confessed. 'I attempted to maintain a rigid and majestic pose in the carriage in order to show that I had risen above the insult. But curiosity got the better of me; and, peering up the empty side streets, I was gratified to see peeking furtively round the corners of the blocks the heads of many Indians.'[44]

Though some locals were unable to resist stealing a glance at their future King-Emperor, there was no doubt that the people of Allahabad had administered a ringing slap to the princely face. Even the stalwart *Times of India* was forced to admit that, 'There is no use blinking the fact that the non-co-operators have scored their first success.'[45] A few days later, the contrast between unpopular raj and popular nationalism was made stark, when large numbers of Allahabad citizens turned out to support the Nehrus as they went on trial. Jawahar's wife and mother were among the chosen few spectators who watched him go up before the magistrate. Four-year-old Indira sat on Motilal's knee throughout the proceedings.[46] Jawahar was accused of distributing notices asking people to observe a hartal, and responded by stating that he neither recognized the British government of India, nor regarded the court as legitimate. He described the proceedings as a farce, and refused to answer any further questions.[47] The magistrate gave him six months in jail and a fine of 500 rupees, which he refused to pay. Motilal was given the same sentence, and both were carted off to Lucknow Prison.

Now that the Nehru family was enjoying George V's 'hospitality', it was ironic to reflect that, only shortly before, the district magistrate of Allahabad demanded that Motilal Nehru invite King George's son to stay with him. Because Anand Bhavan was the grandest house in Allahabad, the government intended to requisition it for the prince's use. Motilal had refused to comply.[48] The Nehrus remained in prison until 3 March 1922, when the authorities belatedly discovered that there had been no law against distributing notices asking people to observe a hartal, and that therefore they had never actually committed a crime.[49]

For Christmas, the royal party had moved on to the old capital of Calcutta. The authorities had prepared for hartals and riots – as well as going to great lengths to drum up cheering crowds. Offices of Congressmen and Muslim agitators were raided; 200 sword-sticks were found in one dissenter's house; 10,000 arrests were made in the ten days leading up to the prince's arrival.[50] The prince arrived to an unprecedented level of policing, with armoured cars patrolling the side streets and a cordon around the entire city. The city's shops were shut, its taxis nowhere to be seen, and the roads lined thinly, with hardly any Indians visible. Even the generous British newspapers could only run to estimating 5000 spectators present, with 10,000 police guarding them. The protest passed off with only one or two minor riots in the suburbs.[51]

The Prince of Wales ate Christmas dinner at Government House, alongside numerous state governors, their wives, their hopeful unmarried daughters, and a few approved Indians, including Captain Raja Sir Hari Singh, son of the Maharaja of Kashmir. A fairy-lit Boxing Day ball was held in honour of the royal guest. It was a dazzling event, and markedly multicoloured. Hindu, Sikh, Muslim and Anglo-Indian guests mingled with British officials. Lady Ronaldshay wore a gown of heavy yellow crêpe de Chine; the Maharani of Burdwan wore a gown of gold tissue embossed with roses, with an overlaid sari of gold lace; Mrs Shelley Banerjee wore charmeuse trimmed with lace and jet; and Mrs Sunanda Sen wore purple brocade accented with golden sprigs of maidenhair fern. Dickie danced the foxtrot with Miss Scott, and the Calcutta One-Step with Miss Gamble.[52]

After Christmas, David opened the Victoria Memorial Hall, a magnificent museum in Calcutta. He quoted his great-grandmother Queen Victoria's proclamation of 1858 about the Indians: 'In their prosperity will be our strength; in their contentment our security; and in their gratitude our best reward.' With impressive optimism, he added: 'It is fitting that this memorial to the Great Queen-Empress should be opened at a time when her dreams for the Indian Empire have come true.'[53] Perhaps, among the fashionable and integrated elites of Calcutta, it was possible to believe that they had.

On 13 January, the prince arrived at the wealthy city of Madras. A complete hartal had been planned, but did not come off in the manner Gandhi would have intended. As Dickie wrote, 'As in Bombay, so here, on finding that their Non-Violence system produced no results they resorted to Violence.'[54] It ended up as a riot, with troops and policemen stoned, cars and buildings vandalized. British troops were forced to use armoured cars and bayonets just a stone's throw from where the prince was staying at Government House. In the heart of the European quarter, the mob came across a pavilion decorated with flags and palms, under the protection of a solitary policeman. They knocked him over and destroyed the decorations, trampling the torn remnants of the Union Jack into the mud. They smashed up and attempted to burn down the Wellington cinema and a car showroom next door. A British journalist was horrified to discover a dead body with its head beaten in, lying in the road outside the cinema.[55] Dickie reported another casualty: a Government House taxi deliberately ran over a man aiming a brick through the windscreen, 'leaving him a somewhat shapeless mass in the road'.[56]

By the next day, order had been restored and the prince was cheered at the races.[57] Swiftly, the tour got back on track. On 15 January, Dickie went to visit the Theosophical Society in Madras, which was presided over by the eccentric Baroness de Kuster, a friend of his sister. The baroness attempted to explain reincarnation and astral projection to a sceptical Dickie, and imparted to him that Annie Besant had recently identified the future Emperor of India, David, as the reincarnation of a former Emperor of India, Akbar the Great. 'David was not over-pleased at the idea of having been a "black man", so I did not inform him that his soul had previously been shared by a group of horses,' Dickie noted.[58]

The royal tour ground on, zigzagging up through the belly of India and stopping in Bangalore, Mysore, Hyderabad, and Indore. By 4 February, it had reached Bhopal, where Dickie and David were the guests of the only woman ruler in Asia, the Nawab Sultan Jahan Begum. The Begum was an ardent Muslim, and usually ruled from behind a purdah screen. The rare sight of her tiny figure, swathed in a blue burka, next to the white-uniformed Prince of Wales, gave the tour's photographers some of their best opportunities.[59] But it was an image more connected to the past than to the future. Gandhi's non-cooperation movement had reached a crescendo. Protests against the prince had been extensive, and had come from all quarters of Indian society – crossing boundaries of wealth, caste and religion. Elsewhere in the Empire, colonies were being offered self-government. The provisional government of the Irish Free State had just met for the first time, under the leadership of freedom fighter Michael Collins. Collins had, controversially, accepted a form of dominion status within the British Empire, providing a model for what might shortly be offered to India. The Irish Free State was not to prove a resounding success, but its inception revealed an empire shifting gear from conquest to retreat.

Gandhi could have had every expectation of a swift victory. Best of all, the British were just about to do the worst thing possible from their point of view and arrest him. Gandhi's imprisonment would be met with an international outcry; his trial would make headlines all over the world; inevitably, he would have to be released, and subsequently listened to. This would put the British in exactly the same position as they had recently occupied in Ireland, where they had had to overlook Michael Collins's terrorist activities and negotiate with him. Gandhi would be offered a deal, just as Collins had been offered a deal. All he had to do was stand firm.[60]

It came as some surprise, then, that Gandhi did not stand firm. Instead, he called off the non-cooperation movement, cancelled all further agitation against the British and backed down, declaring that his followers had sinned against God; that to continue the campaign would be to obey Satan; and that India was not ready for self-government. His reason was a single incident of mob violence that occurred in the small town of Chauri Chaura in the United Provinces, the day after the Prince of Wales had been photographed with the Begum of Bhopal.

Gandhi was nowhere near Chauri Chaura at the time of the incident: he was 800 miles away in Bardoli. But the facts that were reported to him three days later overwhelmed him with a sense of personal responsibility. A peaceful demonstration had been taking place in the town. The Indian constables policing it had attacked some demonstrators. The demonstrators had turned on the constables; this had upped the stakes, and the constables shot into the crowd. When their bullets ran out, they ran to the police station for shelter. The demonstrators surrounded the station, set fire to it, and burned the constables alive. Twenty-two policemen were killed.[61]

The event differed neither in character nor greatly in scale from the previous riots in Bombay or Madras. Yet something about Chauri Chaura particularly upset Gandhi. 'Let the opponent glory in our humiliation or so called defeat,' he wrote. 'It is better to be charged with cowardice and weakness than to be guilty of denial of our oath and to sin against God.'[62] He went on a five-day fast to purify himself, and withdrew from all further satyagraha activities, with the exception of the boycott on British goods. He declared an intention to concentrate henceforth on 'constructive' activities: absolute non-violence; the setting-up of Congress organizations in every village; a spinning-wheel in every home; the rejection of ornamentation; Hindu–Muslim unity; 'purification' of the Hindus by abstention from drink and drugs; and 'killing the snake of untouchability'.[63] Put simply, these were unachievable aims. The British themselves could not have drawn up a more prohibitive list of conditions against their own departure.

Gandhi's sudden withdrawal sent the British into a panic. Sir George Lloyd, the Governor of Bombay, was ready to take him into custody. Back in London, Edwin Montagu, the Secretary of State for India, was preparing to announce the Mahatma's arrest in the House of Commons. But it was obviously absurd to arrest an agitator immediately after he had stopped agitating. The Viceroy, Lord Reading, summoned his emergency council, but it could not reach a decision. In the end, he himself made the call. Soon after midnight, his secretary telegraphed a coded message to London, informing Montagu that the arrest was off.[64]

Lloyd was so furious he threatened to resign, and later declared, with a touch of hyperbole, that 'Gandhi's was the most colossal experiment in world history, and it came within an inch of succeeding.'[65] But his shock, confusion and anger could not compare to that felt by Gandhi's own followers. 'The drastic reversal of practically the whole of the aggressive programme may be politically unsound and unwise,' Gandhi told them with lucid self-awareness, 'but there is no doubt that it is religiously sound.'[66] Jawaharlal Nehru, still languishing in a British jail for his own part in the satyagraha campaign, was devastated. Fifteen years later, the sense of disappointment was still tangible when he argued that 'the non-violent method was not, and could not be, a religion or an unchallengeable creed or dogma. It could only be a policy and a method promising certain results, and by those results it would have to be finally judged. Individuals might make of it a religion or incontrovertible creed. But no political organization, so long as it remained political, could do so.'[67]

The split between Nehru and Gandhi was deeply damaging for Congress. Nehru, who declared that religion 'filled me with horror' and was 'the enemy of clear thought', had never signed up to fight a holy war; Gandhi, who believed that 'no man can live without religion' and that 'those who say that religion has nothing to do with politics do not know what religion means', could never have envisaged anything else.[68] Exhilarated though he had been by Gandhi's whirlwind arrival on the political scene, Nehru quickly realized that the Mahatma's argument provided the British with the permanent means to defeat him.

The rest of the tour passed in relative calm, with the only story being the gossip about Dickie Mountbatten and Edwina Ashley. Edwina had finally reached the east she had dreamed of, and swiftly discarded her chaperone. She arrived in the riot-torn city of Bombay to realize that she could only afford a third-class train ticket to Delhi. It would have meant sitting, eating and sleeping on bare boards for two days, clumped together with poor Indians and their livestock. Edwina was happy to do so, but the clerk flatly refused to sell the elegant young Englishwoman a third-class ticket.[69] This functioned as a useful opportunity for the handsome former prince Dickie to come gallantly to a fair maiden's rescue – he sent to her aid an Indian Army colonel, who put her on the mail train.[70] Her beau met her at the station on 12 February, and they fell happily into each other's arms. Two days later, there was a St Valentine's Day dance at the Viceregal Lodge. Mountbatten wrote in his diary: 'I danced 1 and 2 with Edwina; she had 3 and 4 with David, and the 5th dance we sat out in her sitting-room, when I asked her if she would marry me, and she said she would.'[71] Edwina chose an old Indian ring from Schwaiger's art gallery.[72] Three days later, Dickie was off with David to Patiala. The Vicereine, Lady Reading, dispatched a dismissive letter to Edwina's father. 'I am afraid she has definitely made up her mind about him,' she wrote of the happy couple. 'I hoped she would have cared for someone older, with more of a career before him.'[73] Dickie did not believe that his youth was a problem. 'I have never really sown any wild oats,' he confessed to his mother, 'and as I never intend to, I haven't got to get over that stage which some men have to.'[74]

On 17 March the Prince of Wales boarded the *Renown* at Karachi, and sailed for Ceylon and Japan. The breath that had been held since his arrival in Bombay exactly four months before could finally be let out. 'Regret not unmingled with relief may be said to sum up the feelings of most loyal subjects of the British Crown, on the occasion of the departure of the Prince of Wales from our shores to-day,' commented the *Statesman*. 'Probably the feeling of relief is predominant.' It concluded that 'the reception accorded to His Royal Highness has been such as to make every true friend of this country hang his head in shame.'[75] A sense of shame and depression would be felt on both sides. The prince's tour had revealed the acute unpopularity of the British in India. Gandhi's campaign against it had revealed the weakness of the alternative.

CHAPTER 5

PRIVATE LIVES

ON 18 JULY 1922, LORD LOUIS MOUNTBATTEN MARRIED THE
Hon. Edwina Ashley at St Margaret's Church, Westminster. It was
the wedding of the year.[1] Policemen linked arms to hold back the
crowd of 8000 people, which had not been deterred by the drizzly
London weather.[2]

The guests included most of the royal family, led by Queen Mary,
imposing in plumes, feathers, and fat strands of pearls; and her
seventy-seven-year-old mother-in-law, Queen Alexandra, stylish in a
jewelled turban and a long coat edged with black fur. The groom
arrived, looking impossibly tall, slim and handsome next to his
diminutive best man, David, the Prince of Wales. The bride debuted in
a gown of silver tissue. Among her bridesmaids were the four sisters of
Prince Philip of Greece, wearing gigantic lace bonnets.[3] (Just weeks
afterwards, a coup in Greece would nearly be the end of them. They
would be saved by the timely intervention of the British Foreign Office,
with the future husband of the British Queen cradled in an old orange
crate. Mountbatten, in later years, would do little to discourage the
story that it was he who had organized the rescue – but this was pure
fantasy.)[4] The newlyweds emerged to great cheers from the crowd, and
went on to host a reception for 1400 guests at Brook House, before
driving off towards Edwina's country house in the Rolls-Royce Silver
Ghost that the bride had bought the groom for a wedding present.

Despite her position as the heiress to an immense fortune, Edwina had been brought up with austerity. She had always travelled third class (apart from when an Indian railway clerk had prevented her from doing so) and existed on a modest allowance. The first time she was allowed to have lunch with a man unchaperoned was when Dickie took her to Claridge's after they became engaged; the first time she used make-up was when she wore a pale pink lipstick on her wedding day.[5] After she married, the economies ended. During the five indulgent months of their honeymoon, Dickie and Edwina went to stay with Dickie's uncle, the Grand Duke of Hesse, and toured Europe in the Silver Ghost. The jewellery Edwina received as wedding gifts attracted so much attention that Dickie took to sleeping with a gun under his pillow. When a thief broke into their bedroom, in Angoulême, he made enough of a kerfuffle while scrabbling around in the bedsheets for it to scare off the would-be felon.[6] From Europe, the newlyweds sailed to New York, and crossed the United States, ending up in Hollywood. They stayed at Pickfair, the Beverly Hills mansion owned by movie stars Mary Pickford and Douglas Fairbanks. The Fairbankses were away, so Charlie Chaplin graciously stepped in to act as their host. Chaplin offered them a unique wedding present: the chance to star in one of his short films. The plot was inspired by the couple's true life adventures, for Edwina plays the victim of a gang of jewel thieves. She is saved by Chaplin in trademark guise as the little tramp, and by a prettily made up Dickie.

Edwina's vast wealth and Dickie's social connections allowed the Mountbattens to live the most fashionable of lives. Edwina indulged Dickie's fantasies of naval glory by giving him a special suite at their London home, Brook House in Mayfair, modelled on a ship's cabin. The walls and ceilings were enamelled in white, and fake pipes and cables artfully arranged. Portholes were carved out of a wall, and electric fans blew through them to lull Dickie with a gentle sea breeze. He slept in a bunk, complete with brass rail to prevent him from falling out, should a typhoon strike Park Lane. There was a life-size mannequin of an admiral, dressed in a selection of relics of Prince Louis of Battenberg, including his hat, uniform and decorations; an imposing sight indeed in a newlywed's bedroom. Edwina's suite, meanwhile, was filled with lace, silk and swansdown.[7] Dickie was allowed in only sporadically. 'Slept with Edwina!!' he would write triumphantly in his diary after one of these rare intimacies.[8]

From the outside, the Mountbattens looked like the most golden couple in London. But it took only two years of marriage for Edwina to tire of having plighted her troth exclusively to Dickie. Dickie was deeply attached to the Navy, and spent more of his time fussing over it than over her.[9] When he did fuss over her, he fussed too much. Dickie had come from a happy, intimate home, and wanted to recreate a family in which everything was a team effort. Edwina had grown up in a household in which privacy and independence had been the norm, sometimes to the point of dysfunction. Dickie's marital behaviour was exactly the opposite of what Edwina wanted: starving her of attention for months at a time, then smothering her with domesticity.

The couple had two daughters together, Patricia in 1924 and Pamela in 1929. Often they had the young Prince Philip of Greece to stay after he began his education at Cheam prep school in 1930.[10] Behind this illusion of wedded bliss, Edwina embarked on a long and ostentatious series of affairs. These started very early on, even if one discounts the claim Charlie Chaplin once dropped into conversation about Edwina having made a pass at him during her honeymoon.[11] Dickie's posting to the Dardanelles aboard HMS *Revenge* in 1923 left his young wife alone to the gaudy pleasures of London's night life, and she – still quite recently emancipated from her maiden existence – made the most of them. 'Went to see David at St James's Palace,' Dickie wrote warily in his diary on 3 December 1925. 'He had a queer story about Edwina.'[12]

There would be many more queer stories to come. In October 1926, the *San Francisco Chronicle* ran a lurid story entitled 'A Royal "Spanking" for Gay Lady Mountbatten'. Though not quite as scandalous as it sounds to modern ears, the article was damaging enough. It contained a list of her misdeeds, which were said to have included an inappropriate Charleston with Fred Astaire, and a florid description of the rebuke she had allegedly received from Queen Mary.[13] By then, Dickie knew all too well that his wife was doing more than the Charleston with some of her 'ginks', as her admirers became known. He was devastated. His younger daughter, Pamela, later said that he had nurtured a romantic dream about 'a wife that was purer than pure', whom he could put on a pedestal and would support his career indefatigably: 'And then, of course, he finds that she's not like that at all.'[14] He wrote Edwina a piteous letter:

> I wish I knew how to flirt with other women, and especially with my wife. I wish I'd sown more wild oats in my youth, and could excite more than I fear I do. I wish I wasn't in the Navy and had to drag you out to Malta. I wish I had an equal share of the money so that I could give you far handsomer presents than I can really at present honestly manage. In other words, I'd like to feel that I was really worthy of your love.[15]

'I feel I've been such a beast,' was Edwina's typical reply. 'You were so wonderful about everything and I do realise how hard it all was for you, altho' I know you think I don't. I feel terribly about it all.'[16] But the terrible feeling never prevented her from doing it again. Edwina did not bother to be secretive about her affairs, and hints of her liaisons were scattered through newspaper headlines, gossip columns and the memoirs of nightclub hostesses.[17] In 1928, the Mountbattens called in the newspaper magnate Lord Beaverbrook to help quash an American divorce case in which Edwina would have been cited as co-respondent.[18]

Despite the Mountbattens' marital dramas, the marriage did not break up. There had been a decisive row, with Edwina sitting in her bath, sobbing, and telling Dickie that she wanted to be free. Dickie agreed to leave the next morning, and retired to bed. His cool reaction worked: it was Edwina who came to his room to make up. They agreed to stay together, though with, effectively, an open relationship.[19] Dickie had realized, with a commendable grasp of reality that would elude him in his working life, that he could not have his wife to himself. Edwina would be allowed her boyfriends: and Dickie, somewhat perfunctorily, would take a girlfriend. He met Yola Letellier, the wife of a French newspaper owner, at a polo game. According to Dickie's younger daughter, Pamela, 'He didn't fall head over heels, but he found her very attractive, to flirt with, to dance with, and to enjoy life with.'[20] Though it may have been adultery in a technical sense, Dickie's relationship with Yola would demonstrate his instinctive urge for fidelity. They would stay together, in one form or another, for decades.

Edwina was furious about Dickie's consolation affair. 'It was all right for her to have her own boyfriend, but she wasn't so keen on my father having his girlfriend,' remembered Patricia. 'She suffered from this dreadful jealousy all her life and even when she didn't want him herself she still hated the thought of him with anyone else.'[21] Edwina swiftly and unhelpfully befriended her husband's girlfriend, going to great lengths to create trouble. On one occasion, Dickie arrived in Paris for a weekend with Yola to find a note saying that Edwina had taken her to Austria.[22] When he complained, Edwina let rip in the most unreasonable tones. 'I have never in any way tried to pinch her from you', she wrote angrily. 'I don't want our friendship spoiled . . . by this ridiculous attitude you have been taking up: jealousy, hurt feelings, and all over nothing.'[23] But the person in the marriage who suffered most frequently from jealousy was Edwina. She was jealous of Yola, extracting a promise from Dickie not to marry her if he were widowed; she was jealous of the Navy; she was even jealous of her own daughters. Even when Patricia was a grown woman, she had to conspire to meet her father in secret to avoid incurring her mother's wrath.[24]

In contrast to her intense jealousy towards women, Edwina never showed any sign of the least resentment towards the men in her husband's life. There was quite a number of them; and there have been persistent rumours that he was homosexual. Several of his closest friends were gay, including Noël Coward, Tom Driberg, and a left-wing ex-Guards officer called Peter Murphy who virtually cohabited with the Mountbattens for many years. Coward had met the Mountbattens after their trip to America with the Prince of Wales in 1924. He had always had a 'hero-worship for the Royal Navy', and the friendship blossomed despite the fact that the two men were quite different.[25] 'Temperamentally we were diametrically opposed,' Coward admitted; 'practically all our interests and pleasures and ambitions were so divergent that it was difficult to imagine how, over such a long period of time, we could have found one another such good company.'[26] And yet they did. By the 1930s, they were close enough that Coward went on holiday with the Mountbattens in Gozo: 'I spent one of the gayest months I have ever spent with him and Edwina in Malta', he later wrote; it should probably be assumed he meant 'jolliest'.[27] Coward passed his time lounging around at the Mountbattens' house, the Casa Medina, stripped to the waist, and tanning himself to a dark teak finish.[28] On his return to England, he wrote a thank-you letter to Dickie, addressing him as 'Dear dainty Darling', and went on:

> I could *not* have enjoyed my holiday more . . . Please be careful of your Zippers Dickie dear and don't let me hear of any ugly happenings at Flotilla dances.
>   Love and kisses
>   Signal Bosun Coward
> (I *know* Bosun ought to be spelt 'Boatswain' but I *don't* care!)[29]

The fact that Mountbatten was not threatened by gay men does not automatically imply that he himself was gay; it could be taken to signify the opposite. His reaction on being told that one of his servants was gay was characteristically unflustered. 'Of course,' he replied. 'All the best valets are.'[30] The conclusion drawn by most of those who knew him was that, while he enjoyed flirtation with everyone, Dickie was not terribly interested in actually having sex with anyone.

As their marriage floundered, the Mountbattens' separate pursuits grew ever more important. While Edwina partied, Dickie invented things. He became obsessed with time-saving devices. He equipped himself with elasticated shoes, had his braces stitched permanently to his trousers, and wore a buttonless waistcoat that could be pulled on over his head like a jumper. His valet even reported that Dickie invented a 'Simplex' shirt with built-in Y-fronts, 'that he could slide into like a stretch suit'. Edwina had started to find her husband tiresome and unattractive.[31] But her extramarital social life was not making her happy, either. She was by no means the only person to notice that London in the 1920s was a whirl of overcrowded parties that felt empty. It was a theme of the time, most memorably captured in Evelyn Waugh's *Vile Bodies*, but also occupying any number of less celebrated literary works such as *Jig-Saw*, the first novel by Edwina's friend Barbara Cartland. Noël Coward's party farce *Hands Across the Sea* was a straight parody of the Mountbattens; apologetically, he sent them six tickets for the premiere in recognition of the fact.[32] Edwina's life was a constant rotation of luncheon-parties, garden-parties, cocktail-parties, dinner-parties and weekend house-parties. When she was not at parties, she was planning parties, or buying new dresses for parties, or carrying on illicitly with the men she had met at parties, or recovering from the hangovers she had incurred by going to too many parties. The Mountbattens often received three or four invitations for the same evening. 'To those who knew her best it seemed she was just burning up energy because she did not know what else to do with it,' commented one semi-authorized biographer.[33] As she approached thirty, she began to plot an escape. She planned to travel the world, and her first choice of destination – Moscow – betrayed the stirring of a new political interest in her mind.

Mohandas Gandhi had suffered greatly from his retreat after Chauri Chaura. In his absence, control of Congress had passed to Motilal Nehru and C.R. Das. At the end of 1922, they had formed a group called the Swarajya Party within Congress, aiming at a swift transition to dominion status. This was well supported in India, but the British Home Member of the Indian government, Sir Malcolm Hailey, put a stop to it. The 'responsible government' stated as the aim of British policy since 1919, he said, did not imply a fully responsible government, nor one that had dominion status. 'It may be,' he said during the debate, 'that full dominion self-government is the logical outcome of responsible government, nay, it may be the inevitable and historical development of responsible government, but it is a further and final step.'[34] Indian hopes were dashed again.

Motilal Nehru followed Jawahar's lead, and gave up everything for Gandhi: his legal career, his fine clothes, his Western dining room, his stable of horses and his wine cellar. Only one trapping of his former life remained. 'I have done all these things for you, Bapu,' his daughter Betty remembered him saying to Gandhi, 'but I am an old man and accustomed to my ways. Whether you like it or not, I am going to have my two pegs [whiskies] before dinner.'[35]

Meanwhile, the relationship between Gandhi and the younger Nehru was intense, fraught and semi-paternal. The two men had wildly different political and philosophical ideas, but a peculiarly potent sympathy with each other, both emotional and practical. Gandhi needed a link to the temporal world; Nehru needed a guru. It suited Gandhi well to groom this young radical, for he had found no serious political heir among his four sons. In fact, by the middle 1920s, his relationships with them had become extremely difficult. When eighteen-year-old Manilal was caught in an embrace with a young, married Indian woman, Mohandas coerced her into shaving her head, and extracted from Manilal a vow of lifelong chastity.[36] In 1926, still languishing under his vow, Manilal fell in love with a Muslim woman called Fatima. Mohandas was outraged. 'Your desire is against your religion', he wrote to Manilal. 'It would be like putting two swords in one scabbard ... Your marriage will be a great jolt to Hindu–Muslim relations.'[37]

Manilal did not marry Fatima, though he was finally released from his vow at the age of thirty-five, and married a Hindu woman. It was then the turn of Mohandas's third son, Devadas, who fell in love with Lakshmi, the daughter of Chakravarty Rajagopalachari, one of the leading lights of Congress and a member of the Brahmin caste. The fathers would only agree to the inter-caste marriage if Devadas and Lakshmi waited for five years to see if their feelings changed. Happily, they did not. The couple married in 1933.[38]

Despite the many failures of his *brahmacharya* policy, Gandhi persisted in enforcing it at his ashrams, and broke up several marriages by persuading the women to renounce sex.[39] It was a field in which he and Nehru could never be reconciled. Nehru wrote that Gandhi's sex ban 'can only lead to frustration, inhibition, neurosis, and all manner of physical and nervous ills'.[40] As for Gandhi's decree that birth control was a particular sin, for it allowed a person 'to indulge his animal passions and escape the consequences of his acts', Nehru considered it to be outrageous. 'Personally I find this attitude unnatural and shocking, and if he is right, then I am a criminal on the verge of imbecility and nervous prostration.'[41]

Nehru was aware that the gulf between Gandhi and himself was deep. Much of his autobiography chronicled their differences. And yet the two continued to be the closest of friends. 'People who do not know Gandhiji personally and have only read his writings are apt to think that he is a priestly type, extremely puritanical, long-faced, Calvinistic, and a kill-joy,' Nehru wrote. 'He is the very opposite . . . His smile is delightful, his laughter infectious, and he radiates light-heartedness. There is something childlike about him which is full of charm.'[42]

Whatever his moral eccentricities and political failures, Gandhi's charm and charisma ensured that he remained popular both within Congress and in the nation at large. The millions of admirers he attracted from among the general public greeted him not as a politician, but as a spiritual guru. They cannot be accused of mis-construction. Nehru went around the United Provinces with Gandhi during 1929, and was struck by the masses of ordinary people who turned up – amounting to tens of thousands every few miles. Gandhi's tour was a basic affair. He brought no means of amplifica-tion and, consequently, these heaving throngs had little chance of making out what he was saying. 'Probably they did not expect to hear anything,' Nehru observed; 'they were satisfied if they saw the Mahatma.'[43] He was right, and it went further than that. An American correspondent watched in awe as people surged forward towards Gandhi at the end of one of these meetings, desperate to touch the hem of his garment.[44] Sanskrit has a useful word which Nehru used to describe Gandhi's appearances: *darshan*, meaning the act of seeing or being seen by a divinity.

Among those who found Gandhi inspirational was Kamala Nehru. 'Close contact with Gandhiji opened up a new world to her,' remembered her daughter, Indira.[45] Kamala, like many Hindu girls, had been taught that the highest accomplishment at which a woman could aim was the emulation of Sita – the legendary wife of Rama, whose obedience and chastity were rewarded with rejection and slander, and whose achievement was to bring up twin sons alone, deliver them unto the husband who had rejected her, and then roll over and be swallowed up by the earth.[46] But Kamala had married Jawaharlal Nehru, who thought little of meek obedience and still less of pretty ignorance. She had been only seventeen when they married, and barely educated – but she became a brave, spirited and politically active woman. Visits to Europe with her husband strengthened both her notions of racial identity and her feminist tendencies. She wrote from London: 'When I think of the plight of my sisters my heart bleeds for they are indifferent to the question of their own rights. Day by day I am getting more and more determined that on my return home I shall take my sisters along with me, I shall urge them to place their trust in God and fight for their own freedom, educate their daughters so that they are not in trouble like us and join the struggle for independence so that we do not have to spend our lives in shame.'[47] Yet, despite her increasing interest in politics, she and her husband were barely happier together than they had been on their disjointed honeymoon. Jawahar was struck to see paintings for sale at bazaars, depicting Kamala and him with the caption 'Adarsha jori' – 'The ideal couple'.[48]

Kamala was never in good health after the birth of the couple's daughter, Indira, in 1917. In 1924, she and Jawahar had a premature baby boy, who soon perished. The experience further ruined her constitution, and she developed tuberculosis. Jawahar was obliged to take her to Europe for long periods so that she might recuperate in Alpine sanatoria. Even outside India, Jawahar took no rest from Congress activities, travelling tirelessly around the European capitals, followed, somewhat to his pride, by the British secret service, which he described as 'the best in the world'.[49]

Lonely and bored, Kamala struck up a correspondence with Syed Mahmud, a Muslim friend of Nehru's from his Cambridge days. She encouraged him to correct her Urdu, and debated with him her new-found interest in women's rights.[50] She urged him to educate his daughters and to remove the women of his family from the strictures of purdah. 'I want you men to be put in purdah for some years, and then I should ask you what it is like.'[51]

She was able to confide to Mahmud her innermost feelings, which at that time could be dark and unhappy. 'I am of no use to the world and am making it heavier every day by doing nothing: only eating and sleeping,' she confessed. 'I cannot earn my living and am a burden to everybody. I wish that my end will come soon. Your brother [Jawahar] cannot do his work owing to me. There is no other way to free him of his burden.'[52] Mahmud later described her as 'an angel of the house', 'goodness personified', and confessed that she was 'like a sister to me'.[53] But, for all that her friends could see Kamala's virtues, her own husband remained distant, and only intermittently affectionate.

In the summer of 1927, Motilal arrived at Kamala's Swiss sanatorium, and with his entrance the austerity of Jawahar's household vanished. Kamala, Betty, Indira and Jawahar went all around Europe with him first-class, staying in luxury hotels and driving in limousines. In Berlin, Jawahar and Motilal received an invitation from the Soviet government to go to Moscow for the tenth anniversary celebrations of the Russian Revolution. Jawahar was thrilled by Moscow, and by his perceptions of comradely idealism, though he was horrified by the brutality of the Stalinist regime. Motilal felt the horror, but not the thrill. The suite in the Grand Hotel was filled with gold and velvet furniture covered up with coarse cloth: its tsarist opulence did not fit with communist tastes. It was freezing, and Betty was alarmed to discover that there was no hot water to bathe in – 'though Father succeeded by making a tremendous fuss'.[54]

When Jawahar finally returned to India, he was driven by a new confidence. His fellow Congressmen began to joke that 'vodka has gone to his head'.[55] 'In a hundred fiery speeches all over India he preached the doctrine of complete independence', wrote Betty. 'So radical was he that even Gandhiji protested that he was moving too fast, and Father was terribly worried.'[56] Motilal's concern was that his son on the left, and Subhas Chandra Bose on the right, would split Congress. Towards the late 1920s, the independence movement had lost much of its vitality. Nehru had been in Europe; Gandhi's focus had been on his two personal campaigns, *swadeshi* – self-sufficiency, or the campaign to buy Indian-made goods – and khadi, or hand-spinning of cloth. It came as something of a surprise to all sides when, in March 1927, the British government announced that it was appointing a commission to look into India's future.[57]

The Simon Commission, led by Sir John Simon and including a junior Labour MP called Clement Attlee, arrived in India in February 1928, to investigate possible changes to the Indian constitution.

Indian politicians were outraged: every single man on the Commission was British, and they had had enough of Britons imposing constitutions upon them. Immediately, Congress and the Muslim League came together to organize protests. 'Once again, by lack of elementary tact, the British did for us what we could not seem to do ourselves,' wrote Betty, wryly, 'they unified India.'[58] The protests would give Jawaharlal Nehru his first experience of violence at the hands of the state.

Sixteen people with a flag had been defined as constituting an illegal procession, and so Nehru led a group of exactly that description through the back streets of Lucknow. They had not gone more than a couple of hundred yards when mounted policemen rode them down and let fly with their lathis, bamboo sticks with metal tips. As he saw his fellow demonstrators being thrashed, Jawahar's instinct was to hide – but he forced himself instead to face the aggression. A policeman approached him on horseback, and Jawahar simply asked him to go ahead, before turning his head away. From high atop his horse the policeman struck two blows on Jawahar's body. Jawahar did not fall, and was saved from further injury by the intervention of local officials.[59]

The next day, when the Simon Commission actually arrived, a few thousand assembled for a protest on the maidan. They were charged by mounted policemen, who galloped their horses right up to the crowd, trampling innocent bystanders as they went. Once again, the policemen hit out with batons and lathis. Nehru had to fight down the urge to strike back.[60]

Nehru and his compatriots emerged from their beating with their flesh thoroughly mortified. He himself had received a serious injury to his arm, which would trouble him for the rest of his life, though he was too proud to admit it in his autobiography. 'Injuries severe but not serious', he telegraphed to friends in London. 'Hope survive the British Empire.'[61]

It looked like he might, for the British general election of May 1929 returned a minority Labour government: weak, but determined to move on Indian policy. Lord Irwin was summoned back to London in June; he returned to Delhi in October, and made a proclamation:

In view of the doubts which have been expressed both in Great Britain and India regarding the interpretation to be placed on the intentions of the British Government in enacting the Statute of 1919, I am authorised on behalf of His Majesty's Government to state clearly that in their judgment it is implicit in the declaration of 1917 that the natural issue of India's constitutional progress as there contemplated is the attainment of Dominion Status.[62]

It had taken twelve years to clear up that misunderstanding; an incredible amount of time during which many opportunities had been lost. It would take a further eighteen years before India actually achieved dominion status. A great many more opportunities, a very large amount of money, and hundreds of thousands of human lives would be sacrificed along the way.

CHAPTER 6

WE WANT NO CAESARS

IN INDIA, THE BRITISH GOVERNMENT HAD LONG ENFORCED A monopoly on salt. It was illegal to go to the beach and collect it, and more illegal still to sell it on. When salt was sold legitimately, a tax went directly to the British government, providing a total of three per cent of its revenue from India.[1] This gave Gandhi the cue for the most iconic of all his campaigns, the one which sealed his international fame: the Salt March.

In 1930, Gandhi announced that he would organize his first civil disobedience campaign against the British for eight years. To Nehru's great satisfaction, he also declared – perhaps as a sign of lessons learned from the debacle after Chauri Chaura – that Congress should not desist if the protest turned violent.[2]

Gandhi's choice of the salt tax as a target for his protest was inspired, though it was met with a bemusement verging on disdain when he first presented it to Congress.[3] British taxes had never been a major target of the nationalist campaign, perhaps because they were so low: in peacetime, the raj never took more than 7 per cent of India's income.[4] But the salt tax hit the poor disproportionately hard. It had particular resonance because salt was a product of nature, freely given up by the sea. Gandhi planned to go and collect it. As an ascetic, he himself had not eaten salt for six years – but was prepared to start again for a good cause.[5] This was a brilliantly simple protest, which could involve men, women and children of all ages, castes and creeds. With the ageing Gandhi in humble garb, walking with a staff and leading his people to freedom, its symbolism was exquisitely pitched for a Western audience as well as for the Indian masses.[6] In March 1930, Patricia Kendall was among the many American journalists who interviewed this strange and mystical Indian, who was fast becoming a celebrity in world politics. 'It is always delightful to talk to Americans,' Gandhi greeted her. 'Unfortunately I have little time just now, as I am preparing to march to the sea and break the salt laws of this satanic Government.'[7] On 12 March, he strode out of the Sabarmarti ashram, followed by seventy-eight men. 'Let nobody assume that after I am arrested there will be no one left to guide you,' he announced. 'It is not I, but Pandit Jawaharlal who will be your guide. He has the capacity to lead.'[8]

Gandhi and his fellow satyagrahis marched 241 miles to the shores of the Arabian Sea, attracting many more marchers as they went. A crowd of thousands, waited upon by the international media, arrived at the coastal village of Dandi on 5 April. They prayed all night and, the next morning, Gandhi led them down to the ocean, and picked up a handful of salt from the shore. The marchers immediately crowded into the sea and filled all manner of kettles and pans, boiling them over fires to evaporate the water, leaving behind in each a few muddy crystals of contraband.

The effect across India was sensational. Along 5000 miles of coastline, many thousands of Indians went to the shore and simply picked up or boiled down their own salt. The British administration in Delhi, aware that it was being made to look foolish, started making the situation worse by arresting people. These included Nehru and Gandhi, the latter's detention provoking a demonstration by 100,000 people in Bombay. And 25,000 others followed their leaders into British prisons. The American journalist Webb Miller made his way with some difficulty past the British authorities to watch a satyagraha protest at the salt pans north of Bombay. His eyewitness report shocked the world. Around 2500 satyagrahis clad in white khadi, led by Gandhi's son Manilal and the poet Sarojini Naidu, marched towards the salt deposits. Indian police guards,

commanded by a handful of British officers, ran forward to meet the
first column of marchers and struck at them brutally with their steel-
tipped lathis. 'Not one of the marchers even raised an arm to fend off
the blows', Miller wrote.[9] The air filled with the grisly thud of steel
against undefended skull. The first line fell in pools of their own
blood, many struck unconscious. The rest marched on until they,
too, were beaten down. Then a second column formed, and the
same thing happened again. Hundreds of bodies piled up, bones
broken, flesh slashed open, white clothes spattered and soaked with
crimson. But not a single satyagrahi fought back. Frustrated, the
police began harassing the casualties, beating them brutally, kicking
them in their stomachs and groins, and throwing their bruised bodies
into ditches. That afternoon, Miller counted 320 injured and 2 dead
in the shed that served as a field hospital.

Later that year, the British Prime Minister, Ramsay MacDonald,
convened a Round Table Conference to address India's future. He
had invited representatives of 'every community' to London:
maharajas, Hindus, Muslims, Sikhs, Buddhists, Anglo-Indians,
Untouchables, trades unions, the Burmese, and women – who could
not really be said to constitute a community, but certainly had plenty
of grievances. Congress had been invited, but did not participate. To
Nehru's disgust, the most visible Indian figure was the passionate but
divisive Aga Khan, the super-rich hereditary leader of Shia Ismaili
Muslims.[10]

The first session of the Round Table Conference opened in
London on 12 November 1930, to an interminable chorus of parti-
san speeches by the dozens of representatives. As the journalist
Malcolm Muggeridge acidly put it, the invitation of so many delegates ensured that 'everything under the sun [was] represented
except the 25,000 in gaol and the 300,000,000 cultivating their
small patches of overworked soil.'[11] MacDonald's optimism soon
wilted: 'Hindu-Moslem not coming together,' he wrote despondently
in his diary on 18 December. 'They have no mutual confidence &
Hindu too nimble for Mosl: brethren.'[12] The only agreement which
could be made by the end was to plan for an All-India Federation.

In January 1931, Gandhi, Nehru and other leaders were released
by the Viceroy, Lord Irwin, probably the most sympathetic Viceroy

India had yet seen. He invited Gandhi to the Viceroy's House, and did not even object when the old man brought his own illegal salt to consume pointedly in front of him. In London, Churchill launched into an outraged condemnation of the spectacle of 'a seditious Middle Temple lawyer, now posing as a fakir of a type well-known in the East, striding half-naked up the steps of the Vice-regal palace', but Irwin ignored him.[13] He was later asked whether Gandhi had been very tiresome, to which he replied sharply: 'Some people found Our Lord very tiresome.'[14]

From 15 February to 5 March, Irwin and Gandhi prepared a pact. Congress would discontinue its campaign of civil disobedience, lift the boycott on British goods, and send a delegate to the second Round Table Conference. In return, political prisoners would be freed, the swadeshi campaign would be approved, and those Indians who lived near the sea would be allowed to make salt unhindered. India as a whole saw its Bapu ('Father') being welcomed into the Viceroy's House, and was jubilant. But Nehru wept when news reached him of the pact, which he saw as a betrayal of Congress principles. The pact reserved British control over defence, foreign policy, finance and the position of minorities. It did not challenge the extortionate tax rates on peasants; salt could be made, but not sold; and there would be no investigation into allegations of police brutality.[15]

The sympathetic Lord Irwin was replaced, in a most untimely move, by the far more hostile Lord Willingdon. Under much pressure from Willingdon, who wanted him out of the way, Gandhi eventually agreed to go to the Round Table Conference as Congress's sole delegate – to the further dismay of Nehru.[16]

Gandhi arrived in Folkestone on 12 September aboard SS *Rajputana*, which was mischievously reported to be carrying a ton of holy Ganges mud for some idolatrous purpose.[17] It had already become obvious that Gandhi's celebrity would overshadow any political interest in the conference. London was also playing host to a Hollywood celebrity at that time, in the form of Charlie Chaplin, and someone with a keener sense of publicity than judgement hit upon the idea of introducing the two.[18]

They met at a house just off the East India Dock Road, surrounded by a formidable battalion of the world's media and crowds of curious East End folk. Chaplin arrived first, and went straight to the upstairs front room, where he waited and tried to think of things to say to the Mahatma. A cheer from the crowd heralded Gandhi's arrival. He followed Chaplin upstairs, and the two men waved to their public from a first-floor window. They made an odd couple, each so exceptionally famous in so different a context that their simultaneous appearance on one sofa was almost a cosmological event. 'Now came that uneasy, terrifying moment,' Chaplin remembered, 'when I should say something astutely intelligent upon a subject I knew little about.'[19] Bravely, he ventured to declare himself sympathetic to India's freedom struggle, and asked Gandhi about his opposition to machinery. Gandhi gave his usual answer, about the real meaning of independence being the shedding of unnecessary things, while the photographers snapped away, flashbulbs popping.[20] Perhaps the experience did not leave Chaplin entirely untouched. Five years later, he released *Modern Times* – a film in which he starred as a factory worker struggling against the oppressions of the machine age.

Invited to Buckingham Palace, Gandhi turned up in his loin-cloth, delighting the world's media all over again. In India, Lord Willingdon was tickled to imagine the scene. 'I wonder what Your Majesty thought of the curious little man,' he wrote, 'and whether you could realise, from the few words that you spoke to him, what a terribly difficult little person he is.'[21] It was the King rather than Gandhi who chose to be difficult. He made a point of saying that Britain would have no truck with Indian terrorism, and that he was going to see that a stop was put to it. 'Gandhi spluttered some excuse,' remembered the King's secretary, 'but H.M. said he held him responsible.'[22] As Gandhi was about to leave, the King was heard to collar him again: 'Remember, Mr Gandhi, I won't have any attacks on my Empire.' Gandhi replied, with deft courtesy: 'I must not be drawn into political argument in Your Majesty's Palace after receiving Your Majesty's hospitality.'[23] David, the Prince of Wales, had been chatting with some Indian princes, when he noticed Gandhi shaking hands with his father. One of the other princes murmured to David, 'This will cost you India.'[24]

At the conference itself, nothing much was achieved. For two months, discussions circled pointlessly, with snipes about precedence and protocol both reflecting and exacerbating a lack of trust all round. Thousands of miles away, Nehru asserted that the scales were loaded against Congress. He was right: but this situation had not been helped by Congress sending Gandhi as its sole delegate.[25] For all his fame, the Mahatma was one man, and therefore appeared to be in a minority. B.R. Ambedkar for the Untouchables, Tara Singh for the Sikhs, and the Aga Khan and Mohammad Ali Jinnah for the Muslims, all demanded separate concessions for their communities – and were more than able to shout Gandhi down. The whole performance was looking increasingly like a flop. On 8 November, Congress wired Gandhi to summon him home; he ignored the wire, and stayed on, to no advantage whatever.

Gandhi eventually departed from Victoria Station on 5 December, to choruses of 'For he's a jolly good fellow' and the Indian nationalist anthem, 'Vande mataram' ('Hail motherland'). When Gandhi eventually arrived back at Bombay, it was to a chorus of boos and the waving of black flags by 2000 Untouchable protesters, who viewed his insistence that they should not be given a separate electorate from caste-Hindus as an act of repression.[26]

The Round Table Conference had been a failure for everyone involved. A third session at the end of 1932, ungraced by celebrity, troubled neither the press nor the populace.

By the early 1930s, even the British Prime Minister supported the idea of Indian self-rule. And yet independence would take until 1947. To a considerable extent the delay may be attributed to the actions of three men: Winston Churchill, Mohammad Ali Jinnah, and Mohandas Gandhi.[27]

One of the great faults of the British attitude to India was simply that it was pigheaded. It preferred the illusion of imperial might to the admission of imperial failure; it put prestige before common sense. And the most pig-headed of all British politicians when it came to India was Winston Churchill who, following the defeat of his party, had returned to the back-benches as an opposition MP. 'I hate Indians,' he declared. 'They are a beastly people with a beastly religion.'[28] Churchill was fond of quoting his father, the former

Chancellor of the Exchequer Lord Randolph Churchill. 'Our rule in India is as it were a sheet of oil spread out over and keeping free from storms a vast and profound ocean of humanity,' the elder Churchill had said.[29] As a metaphor, it was apt, though for different reasons than he intended. An oil slick does not protect the sea from storms, but stifles all life beneath it. Winston Churchill made it his business to incapacitate any attempt to move the Indian nation towards self-government. Clement Attlee remembered of the Simon Commission recommendations that 'it took a very long time to get through and a great deal of harm was done during the debates by Winston and his die-hards. Halifax [formerly Lord Irwin], who was Viceroy, believed that there was a good chance that we might have got it accepted and had an all-Indian Government but for Churchill and his die-hards. That is one of the things one has to chalk down against the old boy.'[30]

But within Indian division, Churchill saw an opportunity. An argument continually repeated saw the large Muslim and Untouchable minorities as being under serious threat in Hindu-majority India. The British, in their role as paternalistic rulers, had a moral duty to protect them. If the British left, it would be a dereliction of that duty; therefore the British could not leave India. The existence of the Muslim League served to strengthen this argument. Meanwhile, it suited the Muslim League to have friends in the British establishment.

Despite the cultural and religious differences in India in 1931, there was not yet a mainstream demand for partition. Muslims, Sikhs and Untouchables may have requested separate electorates, to safeguard their representation among the caste-Hindu majority; but they did not demand separate nations. The call for Pakistan would only come to prominence as a result of the alienation of India's ablest Muslim politician, Mohammad Ali Jinnah, who had walked out of the second Round Table Conference in disgust and, at that point, appeared to be politically finished. The opposite was true. Jinnah would soon emerge as one of the most successful politicians of the twentieth century: creating his own country, leading it, and almost single-handedly reviving Islam as a modern political force.

Jinnah was a successful barrister, born in Karachi and called to the bar at Lincoln's Inn. Tall and slender, he hardly ate, and smoked fifty Craven A cigarettes a day.[31] He was often described as looking cadaverous, but this description does no justice to his dynamism. With his smooth coiffure and glittering stare he looked more like a cobra than a corpse. Margaret Bourke-White described at length 'the Oxford-educated Jinnah' with his 'razor-sharp mind and hypnotic, smoldering eyes'.[32] Jinnah had not, in fact, been educated at Oxford: he had attended a madrassa in Karachi and a local mission school. But it was easy to believe that this urbane gentleman, described by the *New York Times* as 'undoubtedly one of the best dressed men in the British Empire', his public speaking rich with quotations from Shakespeare, was part of the British elite.[33]

Jinnah had begun his political career in Congress. He made himself a figurehead for Hindu–Muslim unity, and was acclaimed as such by Hindu Congress luminaries. He had joined the Muslim League in 1913, confident that he could act as a bridge between the political parties. But it was the emergence of Gandhi as the spiritual leader of Congress in 1920 that began to elbow Jinnah out. 'I will have nothing to do with this pseudo-religious approach to politics,' Jinnah had said, rejecting the call for satyagraha. 'I part company with the Congress and Gandhi. I do not believe in working up mob hysteria. Politics is a gentleman's game.'[34] But politics is rarely gentlemanly, and as if to prove it there was a profound and deadly clash of personality between Jinnah and the other English gentleman of Congress, Jawaharlal Nehru. Like his compatriot and friend, the poet Muhammad Iqbal, Jinnah disdained 'the atheistic socialism of Jawaharlal'. 'We do not want any flag excepting the League flag of the Crescent and Star,' he would declare. 'Islam is our guide and the complete code of our life.'[35]

Despite his position as one of the key figures in the rise of twentieth-century Islam, Jinnah was no fundamentalist. His Islam was liberal, moderate and tolerant. It was said that he could recite none of the Koran, rarely went to a mosque, and spoke little Urdu. Much has been made of his reluctance to don Muslim outfits, his fondness for whisky, and his rumoured willingness to eat ham sandwiches.[36] In fact, he never pretended to be anything other than a progressive Muslim, influenced by the intellectual and economic aspects of

European culture as well as by the teachings of Mohammed.[37] The game he played was carefully considered: here was a Muslim who understood the British sufficiently to parley on equal terms, but asserted his Islamic identity strongly enough that he could never be seen to grovel. His refusal of a knighthood was significant; so, too, was his demurral in the face of Muslim attempts to call him 'Maulana' Jinnah, denoting a religious teacher.[38] Some historians go so far as to describe him as a 'bad' Muslim, revealing more about their own ideas of what a Muslim should be than about Jinnah's faith. In any case, the Muslim League suffered from no shortage of good Muslims. What it had lacked was a good politician. And Jinnah was without question one of the most brilliant politicians of his day.

Jinnah had married Rattanbai 'Ruttie' Petit, the daughter of a prominent Parsi banker, when he was forty-two and she just eighteen. Rebellious and beautiful, Ruttie had been a close friend of Jawaharlal Nehru's sister, Nan Pandit; she was closer still, indeed almost passionately so, to Padmaja Naidu, who would later become Jawahar's lover.[39] The deeply personal and incestuous nature of Indian politics is plain from these relationships.

Jinnah's marriage was not an easy one. After the birth of their daughter, Dina, he and Ruttie separated. Ruttie died on her thirtieth birthday in 1929, following a long affliction with a digestive disorder.[40] Jinnah was devastated at her death, and moved to London with Dina. He took a large house in Hampstead, was chauffeured around in a Bentley, played billiards, lunched at Simpson's and went to the theatre. He considered standing for parliament in the Labour interest, but was rejected by a Yorkshire constituency, allegedly with the verdict that it would not be represented by 'a toff like that'.[41] His sister Fatima gave up a career as a dentist to become, in effect, his hostess, though that title belies her full significance. Fatima Jinnah was a woman of intelligence and drive, and was influential in her brother's move towards Islamic nationalism.

Jinnah had returned to politics to fight the Muslim League's corner at the Round Table Conference, which pitted him directly against Gandhi. 'I had the distinct feeling that unity was hopeless, that Gandhi did not want it,' he told a journalist in the 1940s.[42]

After the conference, he returned to private life – until a friend reported to him a comment made by his arch-rival, Jawaharlal Nehru. In conversation at a private dinner party, Jawahar had remarked that Jinnah was 'finished'. Jinnah was so furious that he packed up and headed back to India immediately, with the stated intent to 'show Nehru'.[43] He returned ready to fire up the Muslim League, which he would transform from a scattered band of eccentrics into the second most powerful political party in India.

But probably the most surprising obstacle to Indian independence was the man who was widely supposed to be leading the campaign for it – Mohandas Gandhi. Gandhi's need for spotless moral perfection hamstrung his party's progress. His principal object was to make the Indian people worthy of freedom in the eyes of God. The object of actually achieving freedom from the British was secondary. Gandhi's most influential work, *Hind Swaraj*, published in 1908, set out very clearly his point of view: that European civilization was corrupt, atheist and destructive, but that merely driving the British out of India would not serve to make India free. To be free, Indians needed to relinquish violence, material possessions, machinery, railways, lawyers, doctors, formal education, the English language, discord between Hindu and Muslim, alcohol, and sex. It is for this reason that his campaigns so often faltered. Gandhi stood for virtue in a form purer than politics usually allows. Whenever he had to make a choice between virtue and politics, he always chose virtue. He strove for universal piety, continence and humility, regardless of the consequences. Even if a person were faced with death, or a group with obliteration, he would sanction no compromise of moral integrity. It is impossible to assess how the Indian nationalist struggle might have proceeded without Gandhi, but there are ample grounds for thinking that a more earthly campaign led by a united Congress, perhaps under the joint leadership of Motilal Nehru and Mohammad Ali Jinnah, could have brought dominion status to India in the 1920s.[44] Gandhi's spiritual style of leadership was a source of inspiration to millions but, politically speaking, it was erratic. Within Congress, too, it created divisions. Congress was not a church, and Gandhi's mystical judgements were often difficult even for his closest followers to accept.

A year after his appearance at the Round Table Conference, Gandhi started a new campaign on caste. There were already tensions about his direction among his colleagues, and this religiously and politically fraught issue would exacerbate them. Gandhi's own attitude to caste, which he had long accepted as the 'natural' order of society, was complex.[45] His renaming of the Untouchables as 'Harijans' (children of God) was, for him, a way of showing respect for their role. This brought up one of the most fundamental divisions between Nehru and Gandhi. Nehru saw social and economic hardship as a cause of suffering, and therefore wanted to end it; Gandhi saw hardship as noble and righteous, and therefore wanted to spread the blessings of poverty and humility to all people.

In September 1932, Gandhi announced that he was going to embark on a 'Fast Unto Death' until the British government withdrew its plan to give separate electorates to the Untouchables under the new Indian constitution. The British were surprised. They had presumed he would be in favour of a measure intended to improve the representation of outcaste Hindus in government. But Gandhi was adamant. Separate electorates would put a permanent bar between the Untouchables and other Hindus. It was not division he wanted, but respect for the Untouchables within Hinduism.

Nehru was horrified that Gandhi had chosen 'a side-issue for his final sacrifice'.[46] It was not that he considered caste unimportant. The Nehru family had been demonstrably opposed to Untouchability for longer than Gandhi – Motilal Nehru had appalled his more devout friends by employing an Untouchable to work as his valet and, even more shockingly, another as his cook.[47] But Jawahar worried that Gandhi was losing focus on the larger issue of independence. It also upset him that Gandhi would opt for a 'religious and sentimental approach to a political question'.[48]

Meanwhile, the remarkable B. R. Ambedkar, who had already clashed with Gandhi at the Round Table Conference, moved in for an open attack on the Mahatma. Ambedkar had been born an Untouchable but, thanks to his brilliance and hard work, instead of cleaning up feculence he had studied law in London and earned a doctorate from Columbia University in New York. Ambedkar was outraged that Gandhi was fasting against the granting of separate electorates to Untouchables, while apparently not objecting to the same concession being given to Muslims or Sikhs.[49] He found the Mahatma's glorification of humble village life and lowly self-sacrifice patronizing, and swiftly realized that Congress had good reason to fear his people, who numbered millions of potential voters, being removed from its fold.[50] In late September, Ambedkar went to Poona, where Gandhi was languishing in Yeravda Jail, being fussed over by nine doctors.[51] After almost a week of hot debate, both men compromised to sign the Poona Pact. The pact gave Untouchables a guaranteed number of seats, but not a wholly separate electorate. In return, wells, schools, roads, temples and institutions which had previously been closed to Untouchables would be opened to them.

Ambedkar claimed victory. 'There was nothing noble in the fast', he wrote. 'It was a foul and filthy act. The fast was not for the benefit of the Untouchables. It was against them and was the worst form of coercion against a helpless people to give up the constitutional safeguards of which they had become possessed ... It was a vile and wicked act.'[52] Gandhi's supporters claimed victory, too, but a serious blow had been struck against the Mahatma's image. The 'Father of the Nation' had been brought into direct conflict with that nation's most downtrodden people. Among many Untouchable groups, his reputation would never recover.[53]

There was a sad epilogue to the story. On 15 January 1934, a colossal earthquake hit Bihar, a rural province on the Gangetic plain beneath the Himalayas of Nepal. The devastated area stretched from Allahabad to Darjeeling, and from Kathmandu to Patna. The death toll was estimated at 20,000.[54] Gandhi visited Bihar in March, and spoke to the bereaved, destitute and homeless people. The earthquake, he told them, 'is a chastisement for your sins'. And the particular sin that he had in mind was the enforcement of Untouchability.[55]

Even Gandhi's closest supporters were horrified. The victims of the earthquake had included poor as well as rich; Untouchables, Muslims and Buddhists as well as caste-Hindus. But Gandhi was explicitly blaming the victims, appropriating a terrible disaster to promote his own religious ideas. Nehru, who had been helping the relief effort in Bihar, read Gandhi's remarks 'with a great shock'.[56]

But the most effective refutation came from Rabindranath Tagore, long one of the Mahatma's greatest advocates. Tagore argued caustically that this supposedly 'divine' justice, if such it was, constituted the least just form of punishment imaginable.[57]

With even his closest adherents condemning him in public, Gandhi's political star was plummeting. In September 1934, he resigned from the Indian National Congress. He singled out some of his younger followers, and bestowed upon their bowed heads his public blessing. Through these men – including Vallabhbhai Patel, who had organized a successful satyagraha against the land tax in Bardoli, and the Brahmin lawyer Chakravarty Rajagopalachari – he would continue to influence the political sphere from the background. But principal among his followers was always Jawaharlal Nehru. The two men came to depend on each other personally as well as politically. Jawahar's father, Motilal Nehru, had died in 1931, leaving a vacancy in his life. Gandhi still had four sons; but in 1936, there was a very public scandal involving his eldest. Harilal declared that he had converted to Islam, began calling himself Abdullah Gandhi, and attacked his father in print. He continued to be seen drunk in public, which scarcely suggested fervent adherence to the teachings of the Koran.[58] At around this time, Gandhi suffered from the first of a series of nervous breakdowns. He left Kasturba and his followers, and moved into a one-room hut in central India, far from railways or post offices, and among a population mostly consisting of Untouchables.[59] As after Chauri Chaura, he withdrew from the political scene, and focused on spiritual leadership. His hope for the future now was Jawaharlal Nehru.

During much of the drama surrounding Gandhi's caste campaign and conflict with Ambedkar, Jawahar had been serving lengthy prison sentences for deliberately flouting confinement orders and speaking out against the government. In August 1934, he was briefly released on parole. He saw Kamala who was, by then, critically ill with tuberculosis. He returned to prison desperately afraid. 'Bad news and the waiting for news made the days intolerably long and the nights were sometimes worse,' he wrote.[60] In October, he was offered a grim choice by the authorities. If he gave his word that he would stay away from politics for the duration of his sentence, he would be freed to tend to his dying wife.

Jawahar was torn between his anxiety for Kamala and his loyalty to the freedom movement. He was taken again to visit her. She was running a fever and seemed barely conscious. As he was leaving, she called him over, and whispered in his ear: 'What is this about your giving an assurance to Government? Do not give it!'[61] Back he went to prison, full of admiration. But their new closeness was not to last long. A few months later, at the beginning of 1935, Jawahar was allowed to visit Kamala for another couple of days – but found that she had grown distant. 'Somehow things went wrong', he wrote in his diary. 'I felt there was a psychological change. She seemed reserved.' He brought her poems and pieces of writing, but she showed no interest. Instead, she told him that she had decided to devote the rest of her life to religious contemplation, and no longer wanted a sexual relationship. 'Apparently I was not to come in the way of God.'[62]

In May, with Jawahar still in prison, Kamala went to a clinic in Germany. It proved difficult to book a berth to Europe. King George V's silver jubilee was coming up and, ironically, India's most prominent dissident family would be squeezed into a ship crammed with hundreds of loyal British subjects going to celebrate the endurance of their Empire.[63] On 4 September, Jawahar was released suddenly from prison on compassionate grounds, and went immediately to his wife.

It was a long journey, and Jawahar could not help but be worried, despite his semi-estrangement from Kamala. 'I feel rather lost here', he wrote to his sister, Nan, on his arrival in Nazi Germany. 'I was shocked to see Kamala. She had changed greatly for the worse.'[64] He was surprised to find German children offering him the Hitler salute: 'Occasionally as I pass a small group of children their arms shoot out suddenly and without warning and they snap out – Heil Hitler! It is all done very smartly.'[65] He made a point of seeking out and using one of the few remaining Jewish shops.[66] Every day, he went to the sanatorium to see Kamala. She smiled, her eyes shining, but was too weak for conversation.[67]

Kamala died early in the morning of 28 February 1936. She was cremated and her ashes given to Jawahar, so that he might take them to Allahabad and cast them into the sacred confluence of the Ganges and the Jumna. As he flew back over the deserts of Arabia with the sad little urn by his side he thought, 'She is no more, Kamala is no more, my mind kept on repeating.' When his plane reached Baghdad, Jawahar sent a cable to the London publishers of his just-finished autobiography. He wanted to dedicate the book: 'To Kamala who is no more.'[68]

After Kamala's death, Jawahar's relationship with his only child, eighteen-year-old Indira, became more important. With her father in prison and her mother ill, Indira had been an introverted girl. Jawahar's cosmopolitan sisters had viewed the uneducated Kamala as something of a bumpkin. They could be just as dismissive of Kamala's daughter. Aged about thirteen, Indira overheard her aunt, Nan, describe her as 'ugly and stupid'.[69] Like her parents before her, Indira reacted to her miserable home life by throwing her energies into politics. Betty returned home one day to find the house full of children dressed in homespun kurta suits. Indira had started her own organization, the Monkey Brigade, to promote nationalist activity among children.[70]

Kamala's beauty and spirit had ensured that, outside her marriage, she had had no shortage of admirers. Most significant among these was a Parsi called Feroze Gandhy. In 1930, Feroze had been an eighteen-year-old student, watching the beautiful, fragile Kamala, twelve years his senior, lead a demonstration at Allahabad. She had fainted, and he had rushed to her aid. He had helped her back to Anand Bhavan, and the very next day dropped out of college to volunteer for Congress work. Over the following weeks and months he had been frequently observed following her on her tours, carrying her lunchbox. Feroze had even taken up the task of cleaning out the tuberculous woman's spittoon – something from which the servants at Anand Bhavan recoiled.[71]

To much raising of eyebrows from those who had observed his devotion to Kamala, Feroze first proposed to Indira three years later. She refused, and he kept proposing until 1937, when she finally accepted on the steps of Sacré-Coeur in Paris. Jawahar was among the disapprovers, and asked her to return from Europe to Allahabad to think it over. She refused to speak to him until he let her return to Feroze.[72] After a five-year wait for her to finish her education at Oxford, and many more fights with her father, she would marry Feroze in a Hindu ceremony. During the late 1930s, Feroze had begun to spell his surname 'Gandhi' – a small change which would be of inestimable value to his wife's future career.[73]

On 29 May 1932, the *People* newspaper in London printed a vague allusion to an affair between an upper-class society hostess and a black man.[74] The lady was supposedly identifiable as Edwina Mountbatten, and the allegation of an interracial indiscretion horrified Buckingham Palace so much that she was forced to bring a libel proceeding.[75] Her supposed lover, also unnamed, was presumed to be the distinguished American actor and civil rights activist Paul Robeson. Similar rumours swirled around her relationship with Leslie Hutchinson, a nightclub singer to whom she gave a cigarette case engraved with an affectionate message and her own name.[76]

The case opened in July, with Edwina's barrister declaring that, 'It is not too much to say that it is the most monstrous and most atrocious libel of which I have ever heard.'[77] Unusually, she was permitted to give evidence herself: and denied that she had ever so much as met Robeson. The defence replied with an unmitigated apology. Edwina won substantial damages, which she refused to claim. Whether or not there was actually any truth in the story is another of the many romantic mysteries in her life. It was said that Robeson was deeply hurt by Edwina's denial of ever having met him.[78]

Fed up with England, Edwina had a new impetus to travel. She went to the South Seas, where she joined a trading schooner and looked after the ship's pigs. She took an epic journey to Persia with Dickie's sister-in-law Nada, Marchioness of Milford Haven, with whom it was rumoured she was having an affair. The two drove themselves from the Black Sea across the Levant to the Persian Gulf, and on through Tehran to Persepolis, with nothing but basic camping equipment and a couple of formal outfits in case they met anyone distinguished. They did, of course, stopping to dine in Baghdad with King Feisal.[79] In Paris, she went to see a fortune-teller who said she saw her sitting on a throne and ruling with her husband; she laughed the prediction off.[80]

'Edwina's travels were a great mystery to me, and to a good many other men who knew her intimately,' one of her closest male friends later told a biographer. 'It was as if she wanted to get away from men for a while.'[81] Not all men: further travels were undertaken with a boyfriend, the handsome Harold Phillips, known as 'Bunny'. Dickie knew of the relationship, and enabled it. 'The fact that I encourage the Rabbit', he wrote to Edwina, 'is not that I don't care but that I love you so very much that I want you to be happy and I like him better than all your friends and have no doubt that he is *au fond* nicer than me.'[82] She occasionally returned home from these travels, bringing some sort of exotic baby animal – Sabi the lion cub, Rastas the honey bear, Bozo the bushbaby – which would be kept as a pet until it became too partial to eating shoes, or grew so large it frightened the guests, at which point it would be deposited at the Whale Island Zoo in Portsmouth. Among this menagerie was a chameleon, which could change its colour at a moment's notice. Edwina named it Gandhi.

Edwina's scandals were nothing compared with the story that was just about to break. On 20 January 1936, after a reign of twenty-five-and-a-half years, King George V died. Mountbatten's old friend David, Prince of Wales, now became King Edward VIII of Great Britain and Ireland, Emperor of India. David had never been keen on the idea of being King. He thought of leaving it all behind to wed a divorcée as early as 1920, when he repeatedly wrote to Freda Dudley-Ward from his imperial tours about the possibility of their marrying, wondering casually: 'who knows how much longer this monarchy stunt is going to last'.[83] But by the mid-1930s Mrs Dudley-Ward had been forgotten, and he had fallen in love to the point of obsession with Wallis Warfield Simpson.

That summer, the Mountbattens attended a house-party at Balmoral, Queen Victoria's beloved castle in Scotland. Their host, the King, was accompanied as usual by the wife of Mr Ernest Simpson. Photographs show David and Dickie playing 'arrow golf', of which the precise rules are obscure: they appear to involve breaking things. Others show Edwina and Wallis giggling together, arm in arm, the resemblance between the two unmissable. The liaison between the King and Mrs Simpson was hardly discreet. Esmond Harmsworth, chairman of Associated Newspapers and of the Newspaper Proprietors' Association, was also among the guests.[84] Despite this, and in fact because of it, there would be no mention of the King's mistress in the British press until he was actually forced off the throne.

All over the world, everyone was talking about the King and Mrs Simpson – everyone, that is, apart from the King's own subjects, most of whom were still completely in the dark. For an Englishman abroad, it could be rather embarrassing. Noël Coward, who was in Washington, took the audacious step of writing to Dickie to ask him to sort it out. 'It is impossible to pick up any paper here without feeling sick', he wrote. 'I am only writing to you on a sort of hunch that . . . you might conceivably be able to bring a little personal influence to bear.'[85]

The Mountbattens refrained from intervening directly until 1 December, when Dickie wrote David an impassioned and supportive letter.[86] It made no difference. Ten days later, for the first time in history, a King voluntarily abdicated the British throne. On the evening of 9 December, Edward VIII called his brothers – the Dukes of York, Kent and Gloucester – and his cousin Lord Louis Mountbatten to Fort Belvedere, his country house. Mountbatten's valet remembered his master emerging: 'His face was ashen and his lips taut . . . we returned to London without conversation.'[87]

After twenty-four hours of hectic squabbling over money, poor, stuttering Bertie, Duke of York, prepared to take the throne as King George VI, with the air of one condemned. 'I feel,' he said, 'like the proverbial sheep being led to the slaughter, which is not a comfortable feeling.'[88] It was said that he collapsed and sobbed for an hour in Marlborough House while David wound up his reign, with their mother Queen Mary attempting to calm him down.

While the BBC prepared to introduce him on the radio as Mr Edward Windsor, a title was hastily invented and bestowed upon the ex-King Edward VIII. 'I have found it impossible to carry the heavy burden of responsibility and to discharge my duties as King as I would wish to do,' declared the new Duke of Windsor, 'without the help and support of the woman I love.'

Millions of people across the Empire listened to that broadcast. Even in faraway Allahabad, Jawaharlal Nehru, his sister Nan and her husband Ranjit Pandit were 'glued to the radio' at Anand Bhavan. The ex-King's words 'moved me very much', admitted Nan.[89] With those words, Britain was plunged into a tumult of confusion, anger, sorrow and speculation – though very little republican feeling. One exception to the loyalist mood was made by Edwina Mountbatten, who shocked society by turning up to a party immediately after the event in a 'startlingly gay' dress of aquamarine with a wrap of bright blue ostrich feathers. Most women were wearing mourning outfits of black.[90]

After David's abdication and exile, Dickie had to pursue an unchivalrous damage-limitation strategy, distancing himself as much as possible from the disgraced ex-King. On 11 December – the very day of the abdication – he had written a charming and personal letter to 'My dear Bertie'. 'Heartbroken as I am at David's departure and all the terrible trouble he has brought on us all', he wrote, 'I feel I must tell you how deeply I feel for Elizabeth and you having to shoulder his responsibilities in such trying circumstances.'[91] Dickie would later gain some notoriety for turning his ship hard a'port at top speed – but, on this occasion, it worked. On the first day of the new year, Bertie, reigning as King George VI, re-appointed Mountbatten as his personal naval aide-de-camp, and handed him another gong, the Knight Grand Cross of the Royal Victorian Order. A lesson had been learned: that control is better exerted from above than from below. Henceforth Mountbatten would switch to fostering royal protégés rather than attempting to ingratiate himself with royal patrons.

On 1 April 1937 the Government of India Act came into force, bringing the vote to almost 35 million people. When the election results came in, Congress, under the presidency of Nehru, had won a great victory. The news was nowhere near as good for the Muslim League, which failed to win any outright victories. In the Punjab, for instance, the Unionist Party commanded the largest portion of the Muslim vote. 'I shall never come to the Punjab again,' declared Jinnah; 'it is such a hopeless place.'[92]

Jinnah had not expected to win overall, but he had pinned his hopes on achieving a strong enough share of the vote that Congress would have to offer the Muslim League seats in its cabinets. But so decisive were its majorities that Congress had no need to do so. The British Indian civil servant Penderel Moon called Congress's rejection of the League at this point 'a fatal error – the prime cause of the creation of Pakistan'.[93]

Congress decided that, while it continued to mistrust Britain's intentions, it would for once act pragmatically. Elected Congressmen were permitted to take their offices, and lined up to take their oaths of loyalty to the King-Emperor. Nehru's sister, Nan Pandit, was invited to join the cabinet in the United Provinces – becoming only the second female cabinet minister in the British Empire.[94] She remembered mumbling the oath with the greatest disinclination. Afterwards, she looked so shaken that the Governor, Sir Harry Haig, asked her if she was feeling all right.

'Thank you, I'm well,' she replied. 'It's just that the King is stuck in my throat.'

'Well, you must wash him down, then,' said a smiling Sir Harry, passing her a drink.[95]

But, behind the celebrating, Muslim parties all over India were taken aback at Congress's rejection of League participation – which, they feared, was a sign of the Hindu arrogance that Jinnah had long been warning them about. Quickly they began to align themselves with him. India's Muslims were in no way homogeneous, ranging from mystical Sufis to puritanical Deobandis, and previously only a small minority would have argued for separate Muslim representation.[96] But now the very moderate Punjabi Unionist Party joined the League; the Muslim premiers of Bengal and Assam both gave their support, too. More important than the politicians, perhaps, was the support of local religious leaders: the League began to attract the support of large numbers of pirs, maulvis and maulanas. Jinnah was suddenly transformed from an electoral failure into the champion of free Islam against Hindu dominance.

A new idea of Muslim liberation began to gather pace. In 1930, a group of Indian Muslim students at Cambridge University, led by Choudhry Rahmat Ali, had brought out a pamphlet called

'Now or Never'. Ali and his colleagues set forth a demand for what they called Pakistan – comprising the provinces and the initial letters of Punjab, Afghania (the North West Frontier Province), Kashmir and Sind, and a 'tan' from Baluchistan. In Urdu, Pakistan meant 'land of the pure'.[97] This elegant name would soon catch on, not long after Jinnah was presented with the idea by a students' group in the late 1930s.

In August 1938 Jinnah met Lord Brabourne, the acting Viceroy, and offered him a deal. If the British recognized the League as the sole mouthpiece for Muslims, the League would support the British. Jinnah said publicly that he was prepared to be 'the ally of even the devil' if Muslim interests required it. 'It is not because we are in love with imperialism,' he told the League's annual session, 'but in politics one has to play one's game as on a chessboard.'[98] At the time, Brabourne saw no great advantage for the British in Jinnah's friendship. When war broke out the following year, that would change.

Meanwhile Congress itself was being split again. Jawaharlal Nehru had been President since 1935, and had spent most of 1936 travelling around India and meeting the people he hoped to represent. He was received with a series of darshans almost Gandhian in their fervour. Songs were composed in his honour; fantastic stories were told of his valour and bravery. A woman in Madras created a line of toiletries called the 'Nehru Specialities', and sent samples to him. His vanity was slightly offended by the 'most disagreeable picture of mine' branded on all the bottles, but otherwise he found them amusing and distributed the samples of Nehru Brilliantine, Nehru Pomade, and Nehru Lime Juice & Glycerine among his friends.[99] Pamphleteers and orators called him 'Bharat Bhushan' ('Jewel of India') and 'Tyagamurti' ('O, Embodiment of Sacrifice') – nicknames which were gleefully picked up by his family. 'When Bhai [Brother] came down to breakfast we bowed deeply and asked how the Jewel of India had slept, or if the Embodiment of Sacrifice would like some bacon and eggs,' remembered Betty.[100] The reaction of the chosen one to all this acclaim was characteristically self-deprecating. 'It went to my head, intoxicated me a little, and gave me confidence and strength. I became (I imagine so, for it is a difficult task to look at oneself from outside) just a little bit autocratic in my ways, just a shade dictatorial.'[101]

By the time that the question of his potential re-election came up in 1937, there were serious rumblings about where exactly Nehru was leading Congress. The most persuasive of these was an extraordinary piece published in the *Modern Review* at the time, entitled 'The Rashtrapati' (President). It described Nehru as a godlike figure, moving through multitudes as their serene and natural leader; then turned to criticism of how this adoration had spoiled the man. 'What lies behind that mask of his, what desires, what will to power, what insatiate longings?' it asked.

> Men like Jawaharlal, with all their capacity for great and good work, are unsafe in democracy. He calls himself a democrat and a socialist, and no doubt he does so in all earnestness, but every psychologist knows that the mind is ultimately a slave to the heart and logic can always be made to fit in with the desires and irrepressible urges of a person. A little twist and Jawahar might turn a dictator sweeping aside the paraphernalia of a slow-moving democracy ... His conceit is already formidable. It must be checked. We want no Caesars.[102]

This powerful vilification was published under the pseudonym 'Chanakya', after an ancient political philosopher, and caused great outrage among Nehru's loyal followers. What they did not realize was that 'Chanakya' was actually Jawaharlal Nehru himself. To ensure secrecy, he had submitted the piece via Padmaja Naidu, who had become his lover and confidante after Kamala's death. In Nehru's writing, there is no piece more telling of his personality than 'The Rashtrapati'. Introspection, honesty, wit and mischief: few other politicians in history could have written such a lucid essay in self-deconstruction.

But the opposition to Nehru in Congress consisted of more than himself. While he was touring India, the party had been reshaped by the ascendancy of the extreme right-wing Subhas Chandra Bose, and the return of the increasingly erratic Gandhi. Gandhi disliked Bose, but, with Nehru again in Europe, had accepted him as the President of Congress for 1938. Bose soon made an unambiguous statement that he meant to impose a deadline for the British to leave

India – after which, if they were still there, he would abandon the principles of non-violence. A horrified Gandhi tried to persuade Nehru to return, oust Bose and take over, but Nehru refused to interfere. Bose stood firm, and won a shock victory against Gandhi's candidate, the little-known provincial politician Pattabhi Sitaramayya.

Bose was carried away with his own remarkable triumph over the Mahatma. He started calling himself Netaji – 'dear leader' – in a deliberate imitation of Adolf Hitler's title, 'Führer'. In February 1939, twelve members of the Congress Working Committee resigned and Bose was left politically adrift. He was effectively beaten into resignation by May. With his brother Sarat he retreated to Bengal, where they formed their own party, the Forward Bloc. Though banned from leaving the country by the British authorities, he escaped Calcutta in January 1941 disguised as a Pathan. Via a daring dash through Afghanistan and Moscow, he found his way to Germany under an Italian passport in the name of Orlando Mazzotta.[103] And Germany, in 1941, was where the attention of the whole world was focused.

CHAPTER 7

POWER WITHOUT RESPONSIBILITY

ON 1 SEPTEMBER 1939, HITLER'S ARMIES INVADED POLAND. Three days later, the Viceroy, by then Lord Linlithgow, summoned Gandhi and Jinnah. The Indian leaders demonstrated how seriously they took this faraway war by bickering over whether they should go in Gandhi's or Jinnah's car to the meeting, a scrap which Jinnah, for what it was worth, won.[1] The Viceroy did not take their contribution seriously, either. He informed them that India had already declared war on Germany – without their approval.[2]

Gandhi's position on non-violence was absolute. Aggression could never be returned. He did not believe that women should resist rape, but preferred that they should 'defeat' their assailants by remaining passive and silent.[3] Correspondingly, he did not believe that the victims of war should resist attackers by physical force, but rather ought to offer satyagraha – that is, non-compliance with the invaders. 'If there ever could be a justifiable war in the name of and for humanity, war against Germany to prevent the wanton persecution of a whole race would be completely justified,' he wrote. 'But I do not believe in any war.' He advised the British to give up the fight against Hitler and Mussolini: 'Let them take possession of your beautiful island ... allow yourself, man, woman and child, to be slaughtered, but you will refuse to owe allegiance to them.'[4] Furthermore, in one of his most controversial arguments, Gandhi advised the Jews in Germany to offer passive resistance to the Nazi regime – and to give up their own lives as sacrifices.[5] He told the Jews to pray for Adolf Hitler. 'If even one Jew acted thus,' he wrote, 'he would salve his self respect and leave an example which, if it became infectious, would save the whole of Jewry and leave a rich heritage to mankind besides.'[6]

Gandhi compounded this error of judgement by offering praise to Hitler. 'I do not consider Herr Hitler to be as bad as he is depicted', he wrote in May 1940. 'He is showing an ability that is amazing and he seems to be gaining his victories without much bloodshed'.[7] Apparently, he saw some parallel between his own efforts to return India to the Indians, and Hitler's invasion of French territory to reclaim that lost to Germany under the terms of the Treaty of Versailles at the end of the First World War. He regretted that Hitler had employed war rather than non-violence to achieve his aims, but nonetheless averred that the Germans of the future 'will honour Herr Hitler as a genius, a brave man, a matchless organizer and much more.'[8]

Louis Fischer brought up this subject with Gandhi in 1946. By that time, the concentration camps had been discovered, and the true, awful extent of the Holocaust revealed. It might have been expected that the benefit of hindsight would have tempered the old man's views. It had not. 'Hitler killed five million Jews,' Gandhi told Fischer. 'It is the greatest crime of our time. But the Jews should have offered themselves to the butcher's knife. They should have thrown themselves into the sea from cliffs . . . As it is they succumbed anyway in their millions.'[9]

Gandhi's ambivalence towards the Nazis was matched by his feelings about the Japanese. Roosevelt's personal envoy to India, Louis Johnson, was dismayed. 'Gandhi appeared to him to favour Japan,' a British diplomat reported to London, 'under the impression that if the English were out of the way, India could make an agreement with Japan.'[10] Gandhi may have favoured Japan; certainly Bose did; but there was one man at the centre of Congress politics who consistently opposed the Axis powers. Nehru's steadfast opposition to fascism marked him out from his comrades. He was advised by them to tone it down, for in the event of a Japanese conquest of India he would undoubtedly suffer for his forthrightness: his response was to speak out louder. 'Hitler and Japan must go to hell,' he declared. 'I shall fight them to the end and this is my policy. I shall also fight Mr Subhas Bose and his party along with Japan if he comes to India.'[11]

On 14 September Congress issued a demand for total independence, which was ignored. A month later, Linlithgow announced that it was 'unthinkable' to proceed without consulting the Muslims, and reiterated the offer of dominion status for India somewhere in the unspecified future.[12] Some said that the Viceroy had deliberately insulted Congress in order to force its ministers to resign from the government.[13] If so, it worked. On 10 November, they all left office. Jinnah declared a 'Deliverance Day' from the 'tyranny, oppression, and injustice' of Congress, provoking an outburst from Nehru – which mattered very little, for he had resigned. Gandhi mourned the loss of Hindu–Muslim cooperation, without which he saw 'no real freedom for India'.[14]

If the Viceroy was out to sabotage Congress, he would have pleased the new Prime Minister, Winston Churchill, who took office on 10 May 1940. Churchill's reactionary stance on India was so extreme that it depressed even committed imperialists like his India Secretary, Leo Amery. Had Nehru been privy to Churchill's cabinet orations, all his worst fears about the British policy of divide and rule would have been confirmed. Churchill described Hindu–Muslim antagonism as 'a bulwark of British rule in India', and noted that, were it to be resolved, their concord would result in 'the united communities joining in showing us the door'.[15]

Divide and rule had worked exceptionally well. Both sides now hated each other even more than they hated the British. But perhaps it had worked too well: the last thing the British wanted on their hands was a civil war. Shortly before Churchill came to office, the Muslim League had, for the first time, voted in favour of a separate state of Pakistan. Jinnah was acclaimed as the 'Quaid-e-Azam', or 'great leader', for his championing of this policy. It was said that he had told a few close associates that the demand for Pakistan was a 'tactical move', rather than a serious aim.[16] Either way, it served to stir up trouble. Tara Singh, a Sikh radical, immediately declared that 'If the Muslim League wants to establish Pakistan they will have to pass through an ocean of Sikh blood.'[17]

Nehru, meanwhile, was in prison again at Dehra Dun at the foot of the Himalayas. He spent his time planting an English country garden of sweet peas and nasturtiums, and over the course of nine months spun 112,500 yards of yarn – some of which Indira would wear as her wedding sari, in place of the usual silk.[18] He had nightmares about being cornered by an oppressive force. In his dreams, he tried to cry out, but could not; in reality, the sleeping Jawahar howled, terrifying his fellow inmates.[19] Congress's campaign for a free India was going nowhere.

Dickie Mountbatten's war was going better than Jawaharlal Nehru's, although only on the surface. 'Thank God I'm not a German', he had written in 1937 to his cousin Prince Louis of Hesse, who was.[20] He was put in charge of a destroyer, HMS *Kelly*. It was, according to his valet, 'a moment he treasured almost as much as the birth of his two daughters' – but in the case of the ship there ensued a catalogue of misadventures.[21] Returning from a botched expedition to rescue another British ship, Mountbatten was thrashing the *Kelly* through a turbulent North Sea at twice the usual speed when he ordered a swift change of direction. The *Kelly* rolled fifty degrees, losing all the boats, davits and rails on the starboard side, as well as an unfortunate stoker.[22] A few weeks later, the *Kelly* was in the Tyne estuary, when Mountbatten – obeying orders – sailed it into the middle of a minefield. It was a British one, but no less explosive for that; Mountbatten promptly smacked into a mine, and his ship went into port for one of its regular repair-jobs.[23] During a blizzard on 9 March 1940, a fearful grating was heard aboard as something tore through the *Kelly*'s bows. Mountbatten, perhaps with some self-knowledge, had primed his radio operators to send the immediate signal 'Have been hit by mine or torpedo. Am uncertain which' in such an eventuality. HMS *Gurkha* sent back the laconic 'That was not mine but me' – the *Kelly* had, in fact, struck another British ship.[24] Exactly two months later, Mountbatten found himself off the coast of Holland, after getting distracted in pursuit of a U-boat. It was not long before the Germans found him there, too, owing to his overzealous use of signalling lights. He stopped when he saw the wake of a torpedo streaking through the water towards his ship.

'That's going to kill an awful lot of chaps,' he remembered thinking; twenty-seven, in fact, though the ship was prevented from sinking.[25] During the six months it took to repair the *Kelly* after this incident, Mountbatten was put in charge of HMS *Javelin*, which had its bow and stern blown off and forty-six of its crew killed when he sped past a German flotilla too noisily, attracting torpedo fire; and then compounded the error by swinging round to port, presenting the largest possible target.[26]

The *Kelly* was constantly in and out of the dockyards. Soon after one of these patch-ups, a young naval officer called Terry Healey watched Mountbatten ram the newly restored *Kelly* straight into the bows of another British ship. Terry's brother, Denis, would end up being Mountbatten's senior at the Ministry of Defence two decades later, where he would often recall the story. 'He had to have his own bows repaired all over again,' Denis Healey remembered; 'but his birth saved him from the court martial any other officer would have faced.'[27]

It was not only Mountbatten's birth that was on his side, but a tremendous amount of luck. In 1941, the *Kelly* – along with HMS *Kashmir* – was sent to attack Crete, where the Germans had acquired a British airfield. The ships did so in the early hours of 23 May, allowing British troops to retake the airfield, but attracting a swarm of twenty-four Junkers dive-bombers. 'Christ, look at that lot,' Mountbatten was heard to remark.[28] It took just two minutes for the bombers to sink the *Kashmir*, and only a couple more for the *Kelly* to follow it. Mountbatten, who had vowed never to abandon ship, remained on the bridge. The ship abandoned him – plunging Mountbatten violently into the brine. He dragged himself under the bridge screen by using his tin hat as a weight.

'I started swallowing water,' he remembered later. 'I knew I'd be finished if I couldn't stop this so I put my left hand over my mouth and nose and held them shut. Then I thought my lungs would burst. Finally I began to see daylight and suddenly shot out of the water like a cork released.'[29] Mountbatten and his fellow survivors swam around in the churning waters, slicked with fuel oil and strafed with machine-gun fire from the bombers above, dragging their injured comrades aboard rafts. The captain led three cheers for the *Kelly* as its hull finally sank beneath the surface. HMS *Kipling*, another British ship from Mountbatten's flotilla, appeared at this opportune moment. One hundred and thirty-six souls had been lost, but 128 survived. The next day, an oil-soaked Mountbatten came ashore in Egypt, to be greeted by his nephew Philip with the characteristically distasteful exclamation: 'You look like a nigger minstrel!'[30]

Back at home in London, Mountbatten's celebrity friends were on tenterhooks – or, at least, one of them was. 'Very worried on reading in paper that HMS *Kelly* sunk off Crete', wrote Noël Coward in his diary. 'Feared Dickie Mountbatten lost. Rang up Ministry of Information. Found that he had been saved. Very relieved.'[31] A little over five weeks later, Coward went to a screening of *Down Argentine Way* with Dickie and Edwina. Afterwards, they dined at the Mountbattens' house in Chester Street, and Coward was treated to the full story of the *Kelly*'s sinking. If Dickie was anything, he was a world-class yarn-spinner – and Coward was smitten. 'Absolutely heart-breaking and so magnificent,' he gushed. 'He [Dickie] told the whole saga without frills and with a sincerity that was very moving. He is a pretty wonderful man, I think.'[32] Less than three weeks later, he told Dickie of his idea to make a film based on the sinking of the *Kelly*. Mountbatten was delighted, and immediately promised the support of the Admiralty.[33] And that was how the British government ended up financing a very odd movie indeed – one of the few propaganda films in history to show the heroes suffering a disastrous routing by a stronger and more competent enemy.

Coward and Mountbatten got together at Broadlands to work on the script, and both men were in their element: Coward pretending to be a naval officer, and Mountbatten pretending to be a showman. 'I am purposely making it as little like you as possible', wrote Coward to Mountbatten. 'My Captain (D) is quite ordinary with an income of about £800 a year, a small country house in Plymouth, a reasonably nice looking wife (Mrs. not Lady), two children and a cocker spaniel.'[34] The cocker spaniel was neither here nor there, for 'Captain Edward Kinross' was to be given Mountbatten's character intact and his speeches verbatim, and would even wear Mountbatten's own cap at the correct jaunty angle.[35]

The Ministry of Information soon decided that a film about a British ship being sunk would be bad publicity. It withdrew its support. Coward rang up Mountbatten; Mountbatten took the script directly to the King and Queen; something unknown occurred; the Ministry's support was mysteriously reinstated.[36] All the opposition that came up during filming was dealt with according to a similar protocol. Making his debut as a sailor was actor Richard Attenborough. 'He was a showman,' Attenborough later said of Mountbatten. 'He had a wonderful sense of the theatrical drama, and of course he was incredibly good looking, and in his naval uniform, I mean, he was everybody's idea of a major movie star.'[37] But Mountbatten was not the movie star: that was the shorter and stouter Coward, and consequently *In Which We Serve* is one of the few films in which an actor playing a real-life character is less good-looking than the genuine article. Even so, Coward did his best to act up to his subject's reputation. His Kinross, like Mountbatten, ingratiates himself with his men by demonstrating a crystal-clear memory for their names and achievements. Celia Johnson, as his wife, shared with Lady Louis a witty and opinionated character as well as a striking physical resemblance. A lengthy and emotional speech about competing with a ship for her husband's affections would have been familiar to the real Edwina. Meanwhile, the real Dickie ensured that real sailors on leave played all the extras.[38]

In Which We Serve was premiered on 17 September 1942, to rapturous reviews. Coward won an honorary Academy Award for 'outstanding achievement in production' at the 1943 Oscars; the film was nominated for Best Picture the following year, but lost to *Casablanca*. On 27 October 1942, Coward received a letter from Dickie 'embodying a suggestion from his cousin'.[39] The cousin was King George VI, and the suggestion a knighthood. The profoundly royalist Coward admitted himself 'flung into a frenzy'. He would accept, of course, he replied to Dickie: 'I only wish secretly that it could be a little different from the usual award on account of that particular accolade having fallen rather into disrepute lately through being so very indiscriminately bestowed.'[40] As it turned out, knighthoods were not so very indiscriminately bestowed, for

Coward's was blocked (by Churchill, he thought) before it could be made official.[41]

Dickie's wartime adventures left Edwina alone in London and, for the first time, able to find a role that fulfilled her ambition. Her father, the Conservative minister Lord Mount Temple, had been one of those Britons who found the disciplined machismo of Nazi Germany all too seductive by the middle 1930s, when he had with lamentable timing founded the Anglo-German Fellowship. Edwina, whose love for her Jewish maternal grandfather had far outshone the distant relationship she had with Mount Temple, did not find Hitler's politics appealing. She paid for many of her German Jewish relatives to escape to London, and installed them in suites at the Ritz.[42] The satisfaction that came from making a practical difference changed her life. She volunteered for the St John Ambulance Brigade in October 1940, and spent many nights visiting air-raid shelters, particularly in Stepney and around the East End. A St John lieutenant remembered that on Edwina's night tours of shelters 'her hat was at just the right angle, and there was never a hair out of place. She'd go down into those filthy shelters, so dainty and clean herself, with a smile for everybody; and you should have seen their faces light up.'[43] But Edwina did more than just waft around impressing Cockneys with her personal grooming. She inspected shelters thoroughly, noting anything from a missing light bulb to a total absence of lavatories, and then lobbied officials and government ministers tirelessly over every detail. Her technique for improving standards was a combination of feminine wiles and outright bullying: she would flutter her eyelashes one minute as shamelessly as she might pull rank the next. But she could not be ignored. She also began to talk in increasingly anti-colonialist and even anti-capitalist tones.[44] Edwina's upper-crust friends generally dismissed these views as affectations. The Conservative MP Chips Channon had a drink with the Mountbattens and the King of Greece at the Dorchester on 25 February 1942, and noted that 'Edwina M – is now a complete Socialist, which for anybody in the position of a millionairess, a semi-royalty, and a famous fashionable figure, is too ridiculous.' Ridiculous or not, it was evidently doing her, and her marriage, no

harm. 'She looked a dream of beauty and seemed fond of Dickie.'[45]
They were getting on better than ever, perhaps because they rarely
saw each other more than once or twice a week. Richard Hough, to
whom Mountbatten spoke openly about his marriage, wrote: 'They
certainly never went to bed together; that had ceased years ago.
When they did meet it would be on some formal occasion or, like a
divorced couple, at weddings or funerals.'[46]

In October 1941, the Prime Minister, Winston Churchill, had
recalled Mountbatten from a tour of the United States, where he had
been attempting to charm the Americans into the war. Churchill
was nostalgic for the fast-receding days of Britain's supremacy, and
its embodiment in famous men. He would speak in reverential tones
of his 'great ancestor', by whom he meant the Duke of Marlborough
who had trounced Louis XIV's armies at Blenheim, Ramillies and
Oudenaarde. In Mountbatten, he saw resurrected many of
Marlborough's virtues: fearlessness, patriotism, chiselled features,
aristocratic breeding, an easy rapport with women. Over the next
year, it would become clear that Marlborough, Churchill and
Mountbatten shared another trait: their love of the grand gesture,
untempered by concern for human lives.

Churchill wished to install Mountbatten in a new position as
Adviser on Combined Operations. Mountbatten demurred, saying
that he would prefer to remain in the Navy. 'Have you no sense of
glory?' Churchill replied. 'I offer you a chance to take part in the
highest direction of the war and all you want is to go back to sea.
What could you hope to achieve except to be sunk in a bigger and
more expensive ship?'[47] Mountbatten gave in and, on 4 March 1942,
was promoted to Chief of Combined Operations.

It had been a giddy ascendancy. Before transferring to Combined
Operations, Mountbatten been a mere Captain in the Navy, commanding a small fleet of destroyers. Churchill's promotion gave him
the acting ranks of Vice-Admiral of the Navy, Lieutenant-General of
the Army and Air Marshal of the Royal Air Force. The Chiefs of
Staff, men of far greater strategic experience than their new peer,
regarded him as a dangerously callow upstart – and supposed he had
only been promoted as Churchill's pet.[48]

The plan was for Combined Operations to annoy Hitler as much as possible along his north-western front, mainly to distract the German Army from the then more critical front in the east. Mountbatten's appointment was largely political, a sop to the Americans and the Russians.[49] General Dwight D. Eisenhower turned up in London in May 1942 and specifically requested that Mountbatten be made commander of a putative invasion of France. 'In America I have heard of a man ... his name is Admiral Mountbatten,' he told the Chiefs of Staff. 'I have heard that Admiral Mountbatten is vigorous, intelligent and courageous, and if the operation is to be staged originally with British forces predominating, I assume he could do the job.' Sir Alan Brooke eventually broke the frosty silence that followed by pointing out, 'General, possibly you have not met Admiral Mountbatten. This is he, sitting directly across the table from you.'[50] Eisenhower gamely supported Mountbatten's candidacy even after he had met him. It was not such a bad appointment. A big, obvious flourish was needed, rather than military success – and, when one needed a big, obvious flourish, the man to call for was Mountbatten.

The raid on the French port of Dieppe, which was planned from April 1942, was an experiment. It had become a truism in Allied Command that any invasion of northern France via the English Channel would have to begin by securing two or three major ports, ideally without wrecking them. Dieppe, a smallish port on the Normandy coast, was to serve as a test case.

The location being settled, there followed two months of faffing, squabbling, buck-passing and indecision, the curses of Combined Operations. Too many high-ranking individuals had a say in the planning, but the attention from most of them was intermittent. Insofar as there was a commander at all, it was the unproven Mountbatten. He first planned to land forces on either side of Dieppe and attack in a pincer movement. General Bernard 'Monty' Montgomery told him flatly that this plan was amateur, and he ought to go for a frontal assault as well. Mountbatten caved under the weight of the senior man's scorn. Next he planned that the raid be preceded by air strikes, a provision to which Churchill agreed on 1 June. But Mountbatten missed the next crucial meeting a few days later by being in Washington, and in his absence the idea was dropped. This pattern continued. Plans for big-gun support by a battleship or a pair of cruisers were dropped in favour of an ineffectual flotilla of little destroyers. Plans to use a small force of about 500 experienced Marines and commandos were dropped in favour of a massive force of 5000 newly imported Canadian troops, who had never been trained for an amphibious operation, on the grounds that their government was keen to get them into the field.[51]

The first rehearsal took place at Bridport on 13 June, and was a shambles, with men being seasick, tanks being lost and troops landing in the wrong place.[52] The second, on 23 June, was more coherent, though not much. The operation was scheduled for the next clear day. Almost as if the heavens themselves were warning the raid off, there followed three weeks of the filthiest weather the Channel could throw up. The Chiefs of Staff began to realize – correctly, as it later transpired – that the Germans must have worked out what they were up to by this point, not least because every one of the 10,000 Allied troops selected to take part had been told.[53] On 8 July Montgomery recommended that the whole thing be called off. The idea might never have been seen again, had not Mountbatten brightly suggested that they relaunch the operation six weeks later, still aiming at Dieppe – setting up the ultimate elaborate double-bluff.

This madcap plan was met with disbelief by the Chiefs of Staff. Mountbatten was apparently able to win over these august strategists with the argument that – in his words – 'the very last thing they'd ever imagine is that we would be so stupid as to lay on the same operation again.'[54] His charm was, as Jawaharlal Nehru would later remark, dangerous.

At 5 a.m. on 19 August 1942, a group of commandos landed on either side of Dieppe, while a frontal assault by Canadian troops came straight at the beach. The commandos to the west achieved their objective; those to the east, partially so. The bombardment of the front failed, and all parts of the operation ran hopelessly late. The main body of troops approached the beach an hour and a half after the Germans had realized they were being attacked. Captain Denis Whitaker, of the Royal Hamilton Light Infantry, remembered the moment when they realized that the bombardment had had no

impact on the town's defences. Where they had been expecting devastation and rubble, unbroken window panes shone in the morning
sun. The situation was worse than they knew. The fifty-three tanks
that had been supposed to cover them had not arrived, and every
German post was fully manned and ready.

The men who mounted the beach walked into a killing field.
German machine guns picked off scores of Allied troops before they
even landed. Those that did staggered but a few steps before being hit
by tracer fire and mortar bombs. Heaps of bodies piled up as the men
fell, those behind wading through seawater scarlet with the freshly
spilled blood of their fellows. All around them, bullets whacked into
arms, legs and stomachs with dizzying efficiency. The beach offered
no cover: infantrymen attempted to jam themselves into the shallow
pools left by the sea behind jagged rocks, to little avail. Around half
of the tanks eventually arrived; several promptly threw their treads on
the sharp stones of the beach. Those men who attempted to get out
and repair them were cut down in a hail of fire.

Back in the destroyers, the situation was uncertain. Lieutenant Dan
Doheny was sent ashore for a recce. He arrived amid the carnage and
jumped for cover behind a tank to see his friend Lieutenant John
Counsell. 'It's an awful F.U.,' Counsell said. 'They were waiting for us.
They knew we were coming.' As he said this he pitched forward into
Doheny, a bullet in his back. Stretcher-bearers swiftly ran out of bandages and morphine. The first landing craft that tried to get to the beach
to evacuate survivors was swarmed. So many of the troops piling on to
it were shot in their attempt to get up the ramp that the doors would
not close; it sank, captain and crew killed. At 9.40 a.m., the withdrawal signal was sent through, and attempts to get the remaining
men on the beach back to the flotilla began. They took what shelter
they could as bomber squadrons from the RAF, RCAF and the
Luftwaffe filled the air. Planes dropped from the sky: 106 were downed
(against only 48 of the Luftwaffe), and 60 pilots killed. At twenty minutes past noon, the ships turned back for Britain in tattered disarray.[55]

All the brave efforts of the men on the beach had been in vain.
Without air support, without proper cover from tanks, without the
timely arrival of the pincer-movement commandos, and without the
advantage of surprise, they had been doomed. Not one man got as

far as the centre of the town. More than 2000 were left behind to be taken prisoner, and watched their own fleet turn tail. Meanwhile, the tide came in, drowning many of the gasping soldiers who still lay wounded on the beach. A few managed to pull themselves out of its reach, and bled to death on higher ground. Their wretched deaths brought the total killed to over 1000 men. The Canadian troops suffered a horrifying rate of 65 per cent casualties.[56] Hundreds of bodies, riddled with German bullets, were washed out to sea by the gentle swell of the waves.

Mountbatten, Churchill and Eisenhower attempted to put the best possible gloss on this catastrophe. But it is Mountbatten who has borne most of the opprobrium. His apologists shift the blame on to Montgomery's admittedly poor advice, or speculate that the outcome would have been the same whoever was in charge. But such a defence is in the worst taste. Mountbatten was an inexperienced and over-confident commander, with a known propensity for taking risks. And, even if some of the planning decisions cannot be pinned on him, he was unquestionably responsible for the fiasco of the intelligence operation. After he had arrived at Combined Operations he had filled its offices with his cronies, who swiftly became known as the 'Dickie Birds'. Harold Wernher, brother-in-law of Dickie's brother George, had been put in charge of supply chain management; Peter Murphy, Dickie's sometime live-in chum, headed up a nebulous office considering political ramifications of military affairs; and Bobby, the Marquis de Casa Maury, an occasional racing driver who managed the Curzon Cinema in Mayfair, had been made Head of Intelligence. Some of the Dickie Birds got on all right with their tasks; others did not.[57] Bobby Casa Maury was one of the latter sort. He got everything wrong in his assessment of Dieppe. He had reported that Dieppe's defences were puny; they turned out to be comprehensive. He had said that the defending force was one battalion of the 110th division of the German Army, headquartered in Arques-la-Bataille, four miles south of Dieppe; this was impressively wrong on three counts, for the real defence was a regiment (comprising three battalions), headquartered at Envermeu, six miles from Arques, and it was of the 302nd division. The 110th had been at the Russian front since the war began.[58] This information was not difficult to find. The description of Dieppe's defences that appeared in the *New York Times* on 20 August 1942, taken from old newswire reports, was significantly more accurate than the one prepared by Casa Maury for the operation itself.[59]

Mountbatten must also take the blame for the loss of the crucial element of surprise in the operation. It was he who had suggested the double-bluff: and, despite his official biographer's insistence that the Germans knew nothing about the plan to attack Dieppe specifically, it was well-known in the German Army that the Allies might be planning a Channel raid of some sort. The German commanding officer in Dieppe had actually received a report that the combination of dawn and high tide on 19 August might be chosen for such a raid.[60] Even had the Germans not been on high alert, the plan for the operation contained a crucial weakness, to which Mountbatten's attention had been drawn. Troops landing on the beach needed to surprise the Germans, which would be impossible if the two flanking pincer raids had already landed at local villages half an hour before, and bombardment from the British destroyers on the town had commenced five minutes before.[61]

Mountbatten himself repeatedly attempted to dodge the blame, and even to propagate the feeble and insulting fiction that the sacrifice of over 1000 young men was a great boon to the commanders rather than a result of their incompetent planning. Useful lessons were showcased at Dieppe, but many of them could equally have been learned from books, or indeed – for Mountbatten was not partial to books, unless they were about genealogy or polo – by asking Churchill about what had happened at Gallipoli.[62] Furthermore, all of the mistakes made had been suggested at the planning stage before Dieppe, or were apparent from the rehearsals. Mountbatten was happy to accept the attractive titles and smart uniforms of high office, but reluctant to take the responsibility along with the power.

On 15 February 1942 the Allies – and Britain in particular – had received a devastating shock when the supposedly 'unconquerable' Singapore was taken by the Japanese. Singapore's huge guns pointed out to sea, and were mounted in concrete; the Japanese simply went around the back and attacked from the land. The parallel with Lawrence of Arabia's capture of Aqaba in 1917, one of the most famous escapades in British military history, is so strong that it seems extraordinary that a British command would not have anticipated such an approach. Yet it did not. Without firing a single shot, Colonel Hunt surrendered with 60,000 troops of the Indian Army.[63]

This brought Japan right up to India's doorstep, threatening British interests on a new and potentially devastating front. 'If the Japanese adopt a bold policy,' the Joint Planners warned Churchill, 'we are in real danger of losing our Indian Empire – with incalculable consequences to the future conduct of the war.'[64] The old man reacted instantly when stung in his Indian Empire. Until then, the British had not bothered to improve upon their offer of dominion status with a date or a constitution. But whether or not they planned on keeping India, they could not lose it to the Japanese; and its defence could be facilitated by some form of cooperation from Indian politicians. Meanwhile, Churchill was under attack domestically and internationally for his reactionary stance on Indian freedom. The Labour leader, Attlee, told Churchill his views were 'not widely shared', and that imperialist braggadocio was 'fatally short-sighted and suicidal'.[65] Roosevelt leant on him harder still.[66]

Besieged on all sides, even Churchill had to accept that only some sort of settlement would satisfy the Americans and result in a useful war effort from the Indians. Just three weeks after the Japanese took Singapore, he sent Labour MP Sir Stafford Cripps to Delhi. In India, the march to independence had been milling about pointlessly for so long that its leaders were completely taken aback.

Cripps arrived in India on 22 March 1942. Gandhi met him, and soon deduced that the Mission intended to offer a straightforward bargain. Britain was prepared to offer India dominion status after the war, in exchange for the main parties giving their full support to the Allies while it lasted. Protesting that he was unwilling to participate in violence, Gandhi withdrew to his ashram. Nehru took over negotiations, for he was prepared to fight Japan if it would result in an agreement. But Cripps's eventual offer soured his ambivalence into dissatisfaction. Heavy concessions to the princely states, and a voting system weighted by caste and creed, would deprive Congress of overall control. Furthermore, dissenting provinces would be permitted to leave the Indian Union.

Gandhi may not have been negotiating, but he kept an eye on Nehru's actions. He feared that the policy was a deliberate attempt once again to divide and rule, which would ultimately lead to the 'Balkanization' of India; consequently, he put pressure on Congress to reject it; consequently, they did.[67] The Muslim League rejected it too, for it did not specifically designate a Pakistan – but the offer was a vindication for Jinnah's strategy. The right of Muslim provinces to stay out of a Congress-dominated India had been acknowledged. In the course of just twelve years, Pakistan had gone from decorative acronym to a feasible prospect for millions of Muslims.[68]

The failure of the Cripps mission was disappointing in India. But it was just as devastating in Whitehall. A rash deal had been made in 1940, whereby Britain assumed a heavy burden of financial responsibility for the defence of India. The Chancellor began to predict Indian sterling balances – the amount effectively owed by Britain to India – rising as high as £400 million, even £450 million, by April 1943; and no ceiling was in sight.[69] By the end of 1944, the balances were so large that economist John Maynard Keynes thought that it might be necessary to take another large loan, or a gift, from the United States to cover them.[70] Few were under any illusions about what the conditions might include. Lord Beaverbrook expressed the opinion of many in Whitehall when he said that, 'It would be better to pay India a considerable tribute rather than permit the United States to intrude into the affairs of that country.'[71] The United States had taken little interest in India until the rise of Gandhi had made it interesting. But, owing to the Americans' own long memory of colonial rule, as well as the nation's principles of liberty and democracy, there was a general feeling against empires – and against the British Empire in particular.

Churchill's trenchant refusal to give up on the Empire was leaving him increasingly isolated. By 1942, even the Viceroy was thinking in terms of an exit strategy. 'We are not going to remain in India,' Linlithgow told the American journalist Louis Fischer. 'Of course, Congress does not believe this. But we will not stay here. We are preparing for our departure.'[72]

CHAPTER 8

A NEW THEATRE

IN JUNE 1942, LOUIS FISCHER SPENT A WEEK AT GANDHI'S ashram, and observed the preparations for a new campaign under the slogan 'Quit India'. The slogan was not only catchy, but accurate: the British administration was to be harried, disobeyed and besieged until it simply upped and left, war or no war, economy or no economy, responsibility or no responsibility. The Quit India resolution, passed by Congress on 8 August 1942, announced that Congress would 'no longer [be] justified in holding the nation back from endeavouring to assert its will' against the British administration, and sanctioned 'a mass struggle on non-violent lines under the inevitable leadership of Gandhiji'.[1] The struggle would only begin at Gandhi's word; but this was a call for treason as far as the British were concerned. The first arrests were made in the early hours of the morning of 9 August.

Over the following days, India exploded in violent uprisings, described by the Viceroy, Lord Linlithgow, as the 'most serious since that of 1857'.[2] There were Quit India hartals across the country, which turned into riots. The police and the army fought back, often brutally, leaving an official civilian death toll of 1028; bazaar gossip put the total at 25,000.[3] Effectively, Congress had given the raj an excuse to imprison hundreds of its leaders, including Gandhi himself and Nehru – who, according to his sister, was almost thankful for it, so uncomfortable had he felt opposing the war effort.[4] The resolution could never have succeeded. Britain could not evacuate India in the middle of the Second World War, with Japan looming on its eastern front. But the empty space created in politics by the Congress leaders being in prison gave the Muslim League its chance to rush in.

According to Jinnah, it was not in the interests of the Muslims for the British to abandon them in a potentially hostile swamp of Hinduism.[5] The logical position of the League was actually to keep the British in India – at least for as long as it took to convince them of the case for Pakistan, and perhaps indefinitely. The effect of Gandhi's Quit India misstep, and the League's hugely successful campaign during the 1940s, can be seen from the election statistics. In the general election of 1945–6, the Muslim League would win about 75 per cent of all Muslim votes. In every previous election, its share of the Muslim vote had hovered around 4.6 per cent.[6] During the war years, Gandhi and Congress handed Jinnah a sixteenfold increase in his support. Quit India damaged the chances of a united India at least as much as any single act of the British administration ever had.

Linlithgow wrote to Churchill, admitting that he was concealing the severity and the extent of the violence from the world. But the Americans found out, and sent their own mediators to Delhi. The Americans' 'zeal in teaching us our business is in inverse ratio to their understanding of even the most elementary of problems', Linlithgow complained to the Secretary of State for India, Leopold Amery. It would be bad if the Americans came, he averred; it would be worse still if they tried to talk to Gandhi or Nehru. He pleaded with Amery 'to arrest at least for a time this flow of well meaning sentimentalists'.[7] But the flow of Americans continued, and Indians delighted to see them spoiling official occasions for the British by wearing the wrong clothes, disregarding procedure and cheerfully ignoring distinctions of rank.[8]

But the imprisoned leaders of Congress were impotent. After five months in prison, Gandhi's frustration grew to the point where he threatened to fast.[9] The British had been expecting this very move. 'He is old, and you know you can't feed the old man,' Linlithgow had told Louis Fischer. 'He is like a dog and can empty his stomach at will . . . I cannot permit the old man to interfere with the war effort.'[10]

Gandhi scheduled his fast to begin on 9 February, and continue for twenty-one days. 'This fast can be ended sooner by government giving the needed relief', he wrote to Linlithgow.[11] The Viceroy replied that he held Congress leaders responsible for the terrorism that had followed Quit India, and that he could not give into terrorism. On the point of the fast, he was softer. 'I would welcome a decision on your part to think better of it,' he wrote, 'not only because of my own natural reluctance to see you wilfully risk your life, but because I regard the use of a fast for political purposes as a form of political blackmail (*himsa*) for which there can be no moral justification, and understood from your own previous writings that this was also your view.'[12]

This argument provoked an angry letter from the Mahatma, by return of post. 'Posterity will judge between you as the representative of an all-powerful government and me as a humble man who has tried to service his country and humanity through it', he wrote.[13] But the government's opinions on how to deal with Gandhi and his fasts had hardened. 'My own views have always been clear', wrote Linlithgow. 'They are that Gandhi should be allowed to fast to death.'[14] No negotiation would be entered into: 'Important thing is to avoid parleying with him or giving him an excuse for that hair-splitting correspondence at which he is so expert.'[15]

Gandhi's fast began at the Aga Khan's palace in Poona, in which he was imprisoned, with the world's media clustered expectantly around. Three days later, the Hindus in the Viceroy's council had still not resigned in sympathy with the Mahatma, for fear that Jinnah would make the most of it if they did. 'Fast is falling rather flat,' reported Linlithgow with satisfaction.[16] Churchill, meanwhile, found the whole business irritating. 'I have heard that Gandhi usually has glucose in his water when doing his various fasting antics', he wrote to Linlithgow. 'Would it be possible to verify this?'[17] 'This may be the case,' replied Linlithgow, 'but those who have been in attendance on him doubt it, and present surgeon general Bombay (a European) says that on a previous fast G was particularly careful to guard against possibility of glucose being used.'[18]

From that day on, Gandhi began a marked deterioration. As he weakened, the Americans became increasingly upset at the distress of

Gandhi's followers and the stubborn inflexibility of the British. Roosevelt – 'probably under the influence of Madame Chiang-Kai-Shek and Mrs. Roosevelt', the British thought[19] – asked his envoy to persuade the Viceroy to release Gandhi. Linlithgow refused to see the envoy, and told him that intervention by the United States government would be 'disastrous'.[20]

On the night of 21 February, Gandhi suffered a seizure. General Smuts, who had dealt extensively with Gandhi in South Africa many years before, sent Churchill a personal message. 'Gandhi's death should be avoided by all means if possible,' he advised, 'and it is worth considering whether forcible feeding by injections or otherwise should not be applied to him, as in previous cases in English practice.'[21] 'I do not think Gandhi has the slightest intention of dying,' replied Churchill, 'and I imagine he has been eating better meals than I have for the past week.'[22] This was something of an overstatement – even outside his fasts, Gandhi was not known to open a bottle of hock at breakfast. But the apt timing of Gandhi's heart failure to coincide with a conference of Congress leaders in Delhi, and his recovery immediately afterwards, appeared to confirm British suspicions. 'It now seems almost certain that the old rascal will emerge all the better from his so-called fast', Churchill wrote to Linlithgow, advising that 'the weapon of ridicule, so far as is compatible with the dignity of the Government of India, should certainly be employed.'[23] To this, the Viceroy replied at length. 'I have long know Gandhi as the worlds [sic] most successful humbug', he wrote. 'I am suggesting slyly to certain American correspondents here that it has not been so much a matter of having their heartstrings plucked as of their legs being pulled.'[24] Churchill was satisfied. 'What fools we should have been to flinch before all this bluff and sob-stuff.'[25]

A further tragedy awaited Gandhi that year. In December 1943, while he was still in prison, his wife Kasturba fell ill with bronchitis. The disease was soon compounded by pneumonia. Her doctors advised that Gandhi stay away from Kasturba, or at least keep his face a distance from hers. 'But no one dared say even that to him,' remembered his devotee Sushila Nayyar, herself a qualified doctor. 'Gandhiji did not believe in germ theory. So the best course I felt was to say nothing.'[26]

As Kasturba neared death, Mohandas took over her care. Two days before she died, she pleaded for castor oil; he would not give it. 'A patient should never try to be his or her own doctor,' he told her. 'I would like you to give up using medicine now.'[27] The last battles of the Gandhi family took place over Kasturba's deathbed. Devadas had penicillin flown in from Calcutta to treat his mother. Gandhi was opposed from the outset and, when he heard that the penicillin was to be given by injection, forbade it. Devadas and his father had a fight, with Gandhi pleading, 'Why do you not trust God?'[28] Kasturba had no penicillin. Instead, her husband filled the room with his followers, who sang devotional songs.

On 21 February, the black sheep of the family, Harilal, turned up. He had been invited to the prison by the government, not by his family – though Mohandas had recently caught Kasturba praying to an icon of Krishna for her eldest son to visit. When Harilal arrived he was drunk. Gandhi's entourage ushered him out of his mother's presence, while she sobbed and beat her forehead with her hands.[29]

The next day, Kasturba died, after a long, slow and painful illness, her suffering unrelieved except by prayer. That night, Sushila Nayyar visited Gandhi as he lay in his bed. 'How God has tested my faith!' he exclaimed. 'If I had allowed you to give her penicillin, it could not have saved her. But it would have meant bankruptcy of faith on my part . . . And she passed away in my lap! Could it be better? I am happy beyond measure.'[30] Only Mohandas's closest disciples were permitted to glimpse his real feelings. After the cremation his sons gathered their mother's ashes to throw into holy rivers. Gandhi's disciple Miraben, formerly Madeleine Slade, the daughter of a British admiral, walked back to the prison with the Mahatma. On that walk, she saw him cry for the first time.[31]

Back in England, Dickie Mountbatten, amazingly, had kept his job. Churchill was not especially perturbed by the horror of Dieppe. He had proved his point, which was that to invade across the Channel at this point was impossible. Instead of being sacked, Mountbatten was given a new set of toys to play with. 'Winston adored funny operations,' remembered an intelligence liaison officer.[32] Mountbatten planned a raid on the Channel Islands, leading General Brooke to complain that he 'was again putting up wild proposals disconnected with his direct duties.'[33] He planned to sneak troops into the north of Norway, whence they would descend on Axis forces like valkyries in little armoured snow-carts. He puzzled over the anchorage of the Mulberry harbour, demonstrating models to Churchill in his bathtub aboard the *Queen Mary*.[34] At one stage, he championed an enormous, rolled-up spiral of roadway, called the Swiss Roll, which would be released by rocket propulsion. Unfortunately, when he invited a group of admirals and generals to watch him demonstrate it, the Swiss Roll went off-course and rolled most of them into the sea.[35]

Geoffrey Pyke, one of a group of scientists Mountbatten nurtured at Combined Operations, was his co-conspirator in the greatest of all his flights of fancy. Habakkuk was to be an aircraft carrier, fashioned out of a colossal, moulded iceberg. It could be frozen in Canada or Russia, and then dragged to the North Sea to fight Hitler. Pyke invented a special extra-strong ice, which he named Pykecrete, made from paper pulp and seawater. A prototype Habakkuk, sixty feet long, thirty feet wide and twenty feet deep – about the size of twelve double-decker buses – was set up on Canada's Patricia Lake, so that Mountbatten could sell the idea to the Joint Chiefs of Staff in Quebec. With typical theatrics, Dickie produced two blocks of ice – one standard, one Pykecrete – pulled out a revolver, and shot each one. The standard ice exploded; the Pykecrete survived, and so impressively that the bullet glanced off it and stung the American Chief of Naval Operations in the leg before lodging in the wall. The Americans vetoed the project.

In August 1943, Mountbatten had confessed to Churchill: 'I have a congenital weakness for feeling certain I can do anything.'[36] Churchill seemed to believe he could do anything, too, for he proposed Mountbatten for the new role of Supreme Allied Commander, South East Asia. Roosevelt agreed: he had met Dickie during the latter's propaganda tour of the United States in the autumn of 1941, and liked him.[37] In the military, it appeared that Churchill and Roosevelt were more or less the only two men who did. 'Dickie Mountbatten is, of course, quite unfit to be a Supreme Commander,' said Montgomery. 'He is a delightful person, has a quick and alert brain and has many good ideas. But his knowledge of how to make war is really NIL.'[38] 'Seldom has a Supreme Commander been more deficient of the main attributes of a Supreme Commander than Dickie Mountbatten,' agreed Brooke.[39] But it was Admiral Cunningham, the new First Sea Lord, who summed up the reaction most succinctly. 'I think most people in the Service have just laughed.'[40]

Mountbatten left for Delhi, brimming with delight at his appointment. 'It is the first time in history that a Naval officer has been given supreme command over land and air forces,' he wrote to Edwina. 'It will mean another stripe.'[41] But the person to whom Dickie most wanted to show his stripe was nowhere in evidence. His wife was now Superintendent-in-Chief of the St John Ambulance Nursing Division, and had no interest in going out to Asia to act as the Supremo's hostess. 'I really don't know how I will be able to do this job without you', wrote Dickie plaintively to her. 'Wouldn't it be romantic to live together in the place we got engaged in, and in a job which is really more important in the war than our host's was . . .'[42] But Edwina stayed put in London.

Mountbatten's role at South East Asia Command (SEAC) was ill-defined, and he was regarded with suspicion by much of the existing hierarchy. His own superiors had conflicting interests: the British Chiefs of Staff intended for SEAC to recapture Burma, Malaya, Singapore and the rest of the former European colonies; the Americans only really cared about helping China and were wary of imperialist tendencies among their European allies.[43] In the absence of strong direction, Mountbatten decided that morale needed the boosting power of a new logo. He dedicated many hours to sketching a Japanese rising sun impaled on a sword before someone informed him that the branding of Allied uniforms with such an emblem would, in the event of capture by the Japanese, guarantee the immediate execution of the soldiers in them. His final design of a phoenix was less controversial, though no more lauded: the troops nicknamed it the 'pig's arse'. Still, that probably cheered them up, which was the point. To boost morale further, Mountbatten attempted to persuade his cousin, King George VI, to visit. The King was receptive to the idea, but Churchill blocked the trip. Anglo-American relations were now very prickly over India, and a triumphant tour by the King-Emperor would have been provoca-tive.[44] Mountbatten, meanwhile, was reduced to visiting hospitals, and making careful notes on any lack of staff or equipment. 'I really can't bear to see someone's stomach being cut open and all their guts pulled out,' he noted, 'but it is difficult to refuse what is evidently regarded as a great privilege.'[45] It escaped no one's attention whose example had inspired this initiative, though there was a general con-sensus that she was better at it, and some even thought she might have been better at the rest of the Supreme Allied Commander's job, too. 'There wouldn't have been 7,000 of us in Command HQ if Edwina had been "Supremo",' said one of Dickie's staff at the time. 'There would have been 700, and we'd have been in Singapore six months before Hiroshima instead of after.'[46]

By the middle of 1944 Mountbatten had moved his headquarters from Delhi to the beautiful Botanic Gardens at Kandy in Ceylon, which was 2000 miles from the front line.[47] This distance was prob-ably no bad thing. Mountbatten was, it must be admitted, a hopeless strategist. It was left to commanders of proven competence – notably William Slim and the 14th Army – to win the battles. Mountbatten spent a lot of time sitting in Kandy devising complex and man-power-heavy operations against the Japanese, which were cancelled by the Chiefs of Staff whenever he finished putting them together.[48]

Meanwhile, outside India, something alarming was happening. Subhas Chandra Bose had fallen in with the Nazis. The political vacuum created by Quit India had not only benefited the Muslim League; it had allowed the Indian National Army (INA), Bose's mili-tia, to get a foothold. In Germany, Bose met Hitler, Mussolini and high officials from the Japanese governments, and, to the disgust of Nazi eugenicists, involved himself with a German woman.[49] He was indulged with the creation of an Indian Legion in the German Army, though the reputation it soon carved out for itself as brutal and ill-disciplined did him no credit.[50]

In the summer of 1943, Bose emerged from the foam off the coast of Singapore, a fascist Aphrodite spewed up from the deep, with a Japanese submarine serving as his scallop shell. The Germans had put him in a U-boat at Hamburg three months previously, and he had swapped ships off the coast of Madagascar. He was taken to Tokyo, and given command of the formerly British Indian soldiers that had been captured in Singapore. More than half of them had refused to fight for the Japanese, and were put in camps where thousands perished. But Bose managed to persuade 10,000 more among the survivors to join the turncoats, and was able to add 20,000 recruits from Malaya.[51] In October 1943 he declared a provisional government of Free India, and made himself Head of State, Prime Minister, Minister of War, and Minister of Foreign Affairs. He set up his government's headquarters in the Andaman Islands, a tropical archipelago in the Bay of Bengal, and declared war on the United States and Britain. In January 1944 he moved his base to Rangoon in Japanese-occupied Burma, and marched on India with 7000 of his men.

While Bose geared up for an attack on Assam, the Allied commanders did their best to keep Mountbatten out of their way. 'Dickie has been interfering in your battle again,' General Browning told General Christison, who had been commanding the defence at Arakan. 'I've told him he must not and he is going to come and apologize to you. Don't be nice to him, he's so keen he'll only do it again!'[52] In the hope of finding someone who would be nice to him, Mountbatten went to visit his deputy, the American General Joseph Stilwell, on the Chinese front. Stilwell, known as 'Vinegar Joe' for his acid tongue, was not a fan of the British – 'the bastardly hypocrites do their best to cut our throats on all occasions. The pig fuckers' – but had been unusually affable towards Mountbatten. Close contact soon caused him to revert to his natural state. 'The Glamour Boy is just that,' he decided. 'Enormous staff, endless walla-walla, but damned little fighting.'[53]

Returning from his visit to Stilwell's front on 7 March 1944, Mountbatten finally received his war injury. He drove his jeep over a bamboo stump and it flicked up into his face, hitting him in the left eye. Even the threat of blindness could not diminish his enthusiasm for action. Five days later, he was ignoring doctors, tearing off bandages and heading back to bother the real commanders.[54] The battle of Imphal was beginning, with the large British garrison besieged by a smaller but effective force of Japanese. The Japanese were reinforced by the INA, which reached Imphal by May. The British garrison held them off until the monsoon rains came, literally dampening the efforts of Bose's men. The siege collapsed into retreat by 22 June, and the ragged remains of the INA, depleted by desertion and suicide, surrendered in Rangoon in May 1945.

Bose himself escaped from Saigon on the last Japanese plane out of that city, but would not live out the year. In August 1945 he died when his plane crashed in Formosa. Conspiracy theories abounded that Bose had survived, and was raising a new army in China, Tibet or the USSR; these were believed in high enough circles that even Gandhi professed them for a while, though he later recanted.[55] The story of Bose's survival continues to have its adherents. In 1978, the elderly Lord Mountbatten would receive a letter of the most baroque character from the Indian High Commissioner to London. He accused Mountbatten of helping Nehru to cover up Bose's escape to the Soviet Union, 'perhaps because the British did not want to pick up a quarrel with their erstwhile ally and Nehru did not want to have a rival.'[56]

Whatever happened to Bose, the INA was finished as a political or military force. Despite his disgust at Bose's totalitarian leanings, Nehru was moved by the passion of his soldiers. The trial of INA officers at the Red Fort in December 1945 would persuade him to swallow his long-held principle that, because he did not recognize the British regime, he could not participate in its legal system. He donned the wig and gown of a British barrister for the last time in his life to defend them.

Mountbatten's greatest asset, besides his own charm, was his wife. Back in Europe, Edwina had been asked by General Eisenhower to work for the Red Cross in field hospitals. Edwina's hospital visiting technique, later to garner so much approval in India, was developed in Europe during 1944. She always carried make-up, a comb, a clothes brush and a shoe-shine pad so she looked her best, always inspected hygiene and organizational facilities with a keen eye for nursing procedure, and always spoke to every single patient in the hospital.

Later that year, her husband invited her to lead the recovery effort in South East Asia. On 9 January 1945, she arrived in Karachi and immediately embarked on a tour of the local hospitals. She met up with her husband shortly afterwards in Delhi. *Woman* magazine wrote a gushing profile of her a few years later, in which it was claimed that she said in Delhi: 'Keep one of my afternoons free. Dickie and I want to go and hold hands in the bungalow where he proposed to me.'[57] The source for the comment was a friend of hers, who wrote to Edwina to apologize. She was unbothered: 'the sentence in question sounded deliciously romantic to the readers of "Woman", and I believe they lap it up!!'[58] Delicious though it may have been, the story was not completely unfeasible. On this occasion, Dickie and Edwina enjoyed an affectionate reunion, which Dickie was confident enough to describe as 'our new-found relationship'.[59]

When Dickie had left for SEAC, Edwina's affair with Bunny Phillips had been so serious that he had toyed with the idea of divorce – not on grounds of personal affront, but because he did not want to stand in their way. Instead he found Bunny a job in SEAC, and the marriage held. The arrangement was unusual but, according to the Mountbattens' daughter Pamela, it worked: 'Because my mother was happy with Bunny, it made her much easier in the home as well.'[60] Their affair had lasted nearly a decade when, in the summer of 1944, Bunny uneasily announced that he was going to marry another woman. Edwina was devastated. Dickie wrote his wife an extraordinarily charitable letter of sympathy.

> I must tell you again how deeply and sincerely I feel for you at this moment when, however unselfish you may be about A. [Bunny]'s engagement, the fact that it is bound to alter the relationship – though I feel convinced not the friendship – which has existed between you, is bound to upset you emotionally and make you feel unhappy.
>
> You have however still got the love and genuine affection of two chaps – A. and me – and the support of all your many friends . . .
>
> A. always knew that I had accepted the fact that after the war you were at liberty to get married and I could not let either of you get the impression that anything I had ever done had stood in the way.[61]

Edwina was moved. 'As well as helping so tremendously at what must be a difficult time in my life,' she wrote, 'it has made me realise more than ever before how deeply devoted I am to you and what very real and true affection as well as immense admiration I have for you.'[62] When she came out to the east, she sparkled with new enthusiasm – and transferred much of it to her adoring husband before she left again in April. Getting Edwina's attention was never easy, but, whenever Dickie managed it, he glowed in the light of her approval. The two would sit at breakfast and compare their total numbers of British hands shaken, or hospital patients comforted.[63]

Mountbatten was in London when news of the Japanese surrender came through. He returned to Singapore for the surrender ceremony with the left-wing journalist and MP Tom Driberg. On their way, they visited Burma, where Driberg was able to witness both Mountbattens in action. In Rangoon, they attended a dinner party with the resistance leader, Aung San – to whom Mountbatten was supposed to present a ceremonial dagger as a token of the Allies' gratitude. Mountbatten had already noted of Aung San and his Burma National Army that 'I am completely on their side', a view which had taken some of the shine off him as far as Churchill was concerned. 'I hope Mountbatten is not going to meddle in Burmese politics,' he had noted severely, as the campaign for an independent Burma gathered pace.[64] The imperial loyalists who organized the evening were obviously more Churchill than Mountbatten, and had churlishly seated Aung San at a lower table at the far end of the room, omitting his name from the list of toasts. Mountbatten flatly refused to speak unless Aung San was invited to do so, too. The hosts gave in, and, according to Driberg, 'Aung San's was the speech of the evening.'[65]

As the Mountbattens and Driberg drove on towards Singapore, they stopped at the prisoner-of-war camps that still housed many British soldiers. At each camp, the performance was the same. Dickie and Edwina would leap on to a truck, and he would order the men to break ranks and cluster around. He would speak for approximately ten minutes, combining general world news with an update on how long it might be until the former POWs could be taken home. Edwina on her own was every bit as impressive, if not more so. She had organized a council to bring together the Red Cross and other welfare organizations, and visited even those camps in the most perilous parts of the interior. 'Conditions indescribable', she wrote in her diary, but her spirits remained high.[66] One officer remembered Edwina visiting his POW camp in a remote part of Thailand. She sprung, unexpectedly, from a convoy of army jeeps, and was swarmed by a crowd of curious POWs. 'I know I am the first white woman you have seen for years,' she joked, 'but remember I have got a husband knocking about here somewhere.' She visited the field hospital, taking the name and address of each invalid. Many of their mothers later received personal letters from Edwina, saying that she had seen their sons and found them well. Before she left, Edwina passed on the news that 20,000 Japanese soldiers at the nearby headquarters had accepted the surrender. 'She left the camp to roars from the men,' remembered the officer admiringly.[67]

'To me she was the famous playgirl of the twenties and thirties, and some people said she's only coming out here to pursue an affair,' remembered Lieutenant Colonel Paul Crook. But, when he watched her tour Singapore camps, making lists of needs and sourcing them the next day from SEAC, Crook was won over. He was impressed with her fearlessness in visiting dangerous areas, which were off limits to much of the military – let alone to military wives. 'The bravery of it all was quite remarkable,' he added.[68] One American general put it more baldly: 'She is so smart she scares me.'[69]

Though he was fond of Dickie, Driberg was not blind to the man's faults. In Penang, it was discovered that the batman had packed Mountbatten's set of full-sized decorations rather than the miniatures that are correctly worn with evening dress. Dickie threw a tantrum. After several frantic telephone calls between aides-de-camp, the miniatures were found back at South East Asia Command. Luckily, 'There was just time before the dinner for an RAF aircraft to fly them from Kandy to Penang.'[70]

On 12 September, Mountbatten accepted the Japanese surrender in Singapore. Afterwards, Driberg and Edwina went on to Saigon. A couple of weeks before, the last Emperor of Indochina had abdicated in favour of nationalist leader Ho Chi Minh, and the Democratic Republic of Vietnam had been declared. Very early in the morning of 23 September, French forces, supported by British

Gurkhas, stormed buildings occupied by the Viet Minh, whom they suspected of planning an insurrection. This strike did not begin the First Indochina War, but those on the spot could tell that a build-up was underway. Driberg had contacts which he believed could get him in with Ho, and offered his services as a mediator. Mountbatten relayed this to London, and the Foreign Office sent back its authorization – but, before it arrived, Driberg had to leave.[71] The situation in Indochina was part of a far greater picture. From the ashes of a worldwide war, a new world was rising.

Among the highest ranks of the British Empire, few were ready for the shift into a post-colonial era. One man, however, was. 'It is horrifying', Mountbatten had written in his diary shortly before the end of the war in the east, 'to think that the American and Indian press evidently still regard us as merely Imperial monsters, little better than Fascists or Nazis.'[72] When Attlee vacillated and Churchill blustered over setting a date for Burmese self-government, it was Mountbatten who tried to persuade them to set a firm timetable for the handover.[73] It was Mountbatten, too, who had opened negotiations with Aung San; it was Mountbatten who had wanted to negotiate with Ho Chi Minh; it was Mountbatten who had persuaded the Dutch to negotiate with Sukarno in Indonesia. In all of these matters, he was led by his wife. Referring to Indonesia, he admitted: 'Nobody gave me an idea of the strength of the nationalist movements. Edwina was the first person to give me an inkling of what was going on.'[74] From then on, said Driberg, 'she showed an instant strong sympathy with any Asian nationalist who was being oppressed by some American-backed right-wing regime.'[75]

It cannot be pretended that Mountbatten was a brilliant sailor, nor even that he was a competent one. It cannot be pretended that he was a brilliant commander-in-chief. And it is certainly true that he could be hasty, negligent, and easily distracted by trivialities. Nonetheless, he was the man of the coming age. Perhaps uniquely among the high ranks of the British armed forces, he was liberal, personally charming, and apparently favoured Asian nationalism over Western imperialism. He may have been a bit of a joke in Whitehall. But, only fifteen months after the end of the war, Dickie Mountbatten would be called upon to act as the saviour of his country.

CHAPTER 9

NOW OR NEVER

WITH THE WAR WON, WINSTON CHURCHILL CALLED A GENERAL election. The race pitted Churchill, victorious and iconic, against the flat and efficient Clement Attlee. Despite his friendship with Churchill, Dickie Mountbatten shared the political colours of his wife. During the campaign, he answered the door at Broadlands to a Tory canvasser. 'I don't have a vote because I'm a peer,' he told her. 'If I did, I'd vote Labour. You can try going round the back. I think my butler's a Conservative.'[1]

To the surprise of almost everyone, and most of all Churchill, there was a Labour landslide, and Attlee became Prime Minister. In his speech opening the new parliament, Attlee had the King announce that his government planned 'the early realization of full self-government in India'.[2] The contention that India should be given back to the Indians did not sit well with Churchill and the opposition, but they had little room for manoeuvre. The war had ended, and Britain was broke. The gap in the balance of payments at the end of the war had widened to £2.1 billion (then $8 billion), roughly the cost of administering the Empire for two years. Keynes had told Attlee frankly that he was facing a 'financial Dunkirk', and the only option was to seek aid of around $5 billion from the United States.[3] The funds available to repair wartime devastation would hardly benefit Britain: they were diverted to the nations which had hosted land battles, such as France, Holland and Belgium.[4] The Treasury was all but empty, and the debts of Empire lay in the middle of it like an open drain. An economic aspiration had started the British Empire. An economic reality would end it.

There was a practical urgency to the desire to dump the Empire, which had shown up most clearly during the Bengal Famine of 1943. During the war, the British had shipped grain and railway stocks out of India, weakening its domestic food supply network. At the beginning of 1943, Churchill ordered a cut of 60 per cent in sailings to the subcontinent, saying that the Indian people and the Allied forces there 'must live on their stocks'.[5] But Bengal had been lashed by a massive cyclone in October 1942, and in the wake of that by three tidal waves.[6] The rice harvest had been relatively poor during 1942 and 1943, prompting panic-buying in the market, stockpiling by producers, and a massive increase in the price of foodgrains that coincided unhappily with a fall in real-term agricultural wages.[7]

Around six million people were affected by the subsequent famine, and between one and two million of them died.[8] Hospitals filled up with wretched and emaciated peasants, suffering from dysentery, anaemia, cholera and smallpox; patients came in sweating from malarial fevers, and breaking out in the hard papules of scabies.[9] Almost all of the dead were poor people in rural areas, excepting those few in the cities who contracted disease from the wandering sufferers. In the cool bungalows and elegant mansions of Calcutta, rich Europeans and Indians alike supped on plenty. Supplies were available, just at a price that the poor could not afford. Shameful fortunes were reaped from misery and hunger.[10]

The famine was the direct result of the failure of the Bengal government and, indeed, the government of India as a whole, to regulate the market – thus allowing the price of rice to rise out of the reach of rural agricultural workers. When the governments realized their mistake, they compounded it by handing the market over to 'unrestricted free trade' in March 1943.[11] The blame for the famine cannot entirely be laid upon the British, for the government of Bengal was run by elected Indians;[12] but the gross inhumanity shown by that government was matched in London. During the crisis, the army veteran Lord Wavell took over as Viceroy. He repeatedly telegrammed Churchill, telling him that millions of people were dying in India and that extra food was needed. In reply, 'Winston sent me a peevish telegram to ask why Gandhi hadn't died yet!'[13] Churchill refused to release the government's readily available food stocks, on the grounds that British people might need them at some point. Despite enormous pressure from Wavell in Delhi and the India Secretary, Leo Amery, in London, Churchill and the Bengal government persisted in a policy whose effect was a sort of genocide by capitalism. The government of India, in a panic, lied and pretended that the food stocks were on the way.[14] The damning official report concluded that the famine had been avoidable, and its management had been a catastrophe.

By 1946, the subcontinent was a mess, with British civil and military officers increasingly desperate to leave, and a growing hostility to their presence among Indians. In January British RAF servicemen mutinied in India and the Middle East, demanding to be sent home. Soon after, there were a couple of small anti-British rebellions in the Royal Indian Navy, but these were swiftly crushed and the officers court-martialled. Graffiti began to appear on Navy property in Bombay: 'Quit India', 'Revolt Now', 'Kill the British White Bastards'. In February, the crews of HMIS *Talwar*, *Sutlej* and *Jumna* refused to work or eat. HMIS *Narbada* turned its guns on the Bombay Yacht Club. The Congress flag was raised, and a riot broke out in the town. In Karachi, the crew of HMIS *Hindustan* shouted 'Jai Hind' – the old INA slogan, 'Victory to India' – and opened fire on the town, but were quickly arrested. The next day, the Army fired on the mutineers at Bombay and crushed them swiftly too.[15]

The reaction to these mutinies had shown that the British could still put down dissent if they wished. That would not be the case for much longer. The granting of leave to civil and military officers after the war would mean that many parts of India had to be run by a skeleton staff. More importantly still, as one civil servant pointed out, to reassert British power physically after the war would have been politically impossible: 'neither British opinion nor world opinion would have tolerated it.'[16]

Now that they were gearing up to leave, though, the British authorities decided to turn some of the politicians they had previously imprisoned to good use, and it was in this spirit that Wavell suggested Nehru go to Malaya at the beginning of 1946. Malaya had seen strikes and unrest among its Indian population, on account of the treatment accorded to the INA prisoners. Nehru had been released from prison only nine months before. Now he was to be the emissary of cohesion and calm, but apparently not everyone had been informed. The Malayan administration planned to line the streets with armed soldiers. The Supreme Allied Commander of South East Asia, Dickie Mountbatten, put a stop to that. He insisted that Nehru be received as a distinguished statesman, and that, rather than policing the streets to warn people off, lorries be sent to bring Indians in from the suburbs especially to see him.[17]

The visit was an extraordinary and unexpected success. Nehru arrived at Government House in Singapore on 18 March 1946, accompanied by his sister Betty's husband, Raja Hutheesing, and it was there that he met Mountbatten for the first time. He was given tea, and driven by Dickie to meet Edwina and other welfare workers at the YMCA Rest Room for Indian Servicemen on Waterloo Street.[18] There he was greeted by the public with the sort of reception more usually reserved for the likes of Bing Crosby or Rita Hayworth. The YMCA building was surrounded by cheering and shouting Indians, in crowds so dense that Mountbatten and Nehru had trouble getting in. As the two men disappeared inside, dozens of Nehru's fans surged forward and began to clamber through the windows after them.[19]

In the St John Ambulance canteen, which Edwina had set up in a Nissen hut, the crowd surged forward and knocked Raja Hutheesing over. Edwina was knocked down too, and fell flat on the floor under the stampeding crowd. 'Your wife; your wife; we must go to her,' shouted Nehru to Mountbatten. The two men linked arms and barged forward to find her, but she had already scrambled out of the crush. Nehru and Mountbatten helped her up and carried her to safety.[20] As first meetings go, theirs could hardly have established a greater informality.

Afterwards, Edwina was the first to emerge from the YMCA, which she did to a roar of approval from the crowd. The roar intensified as Dickie appeared, and the two of them, laughing, pushed through to their car. They turned to watch with amusement how Jawahar would fare. There was a pause before he appeared; when he did, the crowd reached an almost frightening peak of frenzied adulation. The fans still in the building rushed forward and Jawahar, along with a small clutch of officials, was shoved roughly down the steps.

That night, Nehru and Hutheesing dined informally at Government House with the Mountbattens. At Mountbatten's request, Nehru agreed to forgo the planned jamboree around the laying of a wreath on the INA memorial the next day.[21] His conciliatory attitude was demonstrated again later that morning, when he held a meeting in the Jalan Besar stadium. A flag was hoisted to the singing of anthems and the shouting of slogans. Soon this deteriorated into the INA's trademark cry: 'Blood! Blood! Blood!' But, instead of feeding the crowd's frenzy, Nehru took the microphone to rebuke them. He told them that the time for violence had passed, and that the peaceful, constitutional route was now the clearest path to Indian freedom. (Never a complete Gandhian, he added that he would not hesitate to call on them should the need for violence arise.) As the Director of Intelligence for SEAC commented, 'His tone throughout was conciliatory and calming, and undoubtedly caused a measure of disappointment.'[22]

Nehru's trip, and Mountbatten's reception, had set a new tone of civility in Anglo-Indian relations. Alan Campbell-Johnson, Mountbatten's omnipresent press attaché, remembered that 'the two men made a deep personal impression on each other.'[23] Nehru had felt warm enough to send Mountbatten a copy of his new book, *The Discovery of India*, inscribed 'in memory of a pleasant evening and with all good wishes'.[24] On 25 March he went on to Penang, but media attention had moved back to Delhi – where the Cabinet Mission was arriving to negotiate the end of the British Empire.

The arrival of the Cabinet Mission was greeted by *Time* magazine with a front cover showing a scowling Jinnah with the caption, 'His Muslim tiger wants to eat the Hindu cow'. *Time*'s pro-Congress line reflected a widespread opinion in the United States that India should remain as one nation. As Roosevelt had told the British chargé d'affaires in New York a few years before, any partition of India 'sounded terrible' in the United States, echoing as it did their own civil war.[25]

It is obvious from the records of the Cabinet Mission that, by this point, the British were desperate for a settlement. The Mission's plan proposed a federal India, with a ten-year constitutional review which would have allowed Muslim provinces to leave the Indian Union if they wished. To the astonishment of everyone, including his own supporters, Jinnah accepted the plan – effectively giving up his campaign for an immediate Pakistan. It has been suggested that he was bluffing, because he knew Nehru would reject the plan. If so, it would have been an extraordinary risk to take.[26] It is more plausible that Jinnah actually meant to accept it. His intention, since the very beginning of his career, had been to prevent minority Muslim interests from being submerged under a Hindu-majority government. The Cabinet Mission's plan did indeed provide for that, and paved the way for Pakistan in a decade. It may simply have been good enough.[27]

Almost everyone on the Mission regarded Gandhi as the biggest culprit in holding up negotiations. Sir Francis Fearon Turnbull, a civil servant, was impressed with Gandhi's clever drafting and legal mind, but not in the least with his attitude. 'The nasty old man has grasped that he can get what he asks for', he wrote, '& so goes on asking for more & more.'[28] Wavell, the Viceroy, agreed. 'Gandhi was the wrecker', he wrote to the King.[29] Even Lord Pethick-Lawrence, the new Secretary of State for India noted for his mild manners and cruelly nicknamed 'Pathetic-Lawrence' on account of them, became exasperated by the Mahatma. He 'let fly in a way I have never heard him before', wrote Turnbull. 'Said he was coming to believe Gandhi did not care whether 2 or 3 million people died & would rather that they should than that he should compromise.'[30]

In the middle of June, Wavell got fed up with negotiating. 'O! dear, my poor Archie does wish himself back among soldiers', wrote his wife, Queenie, to her friend Edwina Mountbatten. 'It is very difficult and trying when all your life you have dealt with men who mean what they say and know what they want, to talk and talk and talk with those who almost invariably say what they don't mean.'[31] Wavell announced his intention to form an interim government of six Congress Hindus (including one Untouchable), five Muslim Leaguers, a Sikh, a Parsi and an Indian Christian. Jinnah had already accepted the plan, and it was rumoured that Nehru and Vallabhbhai Patel were ready to acquiesce. But Gandhi lent heavily on Congress to reject it, on the grounds that there was no Congress Muslim in the government. Gandhi meant well: he hoped to demonstrate to Muslims that Congress was their party too. In retrospect, though, most commentators have agreed that his derailment of the plan was a point of no return. The Muslim League's mistrust of Gandhi reached a fever pitch: from then on, the partition of India was inevitable.[32] It fell to Nehru, on 10 August, to inform Wavell that he was prepared to form a government.

As soon as Nehru accepted the premiership, Jinnah dropped his support for the plan. The council of the Muslim League declared a Direct Action Day for 16 August. 'We will have,' Jinnah announced, 'either a divided India or a destroyed India.'[33] It looked like he might get both. On the morning of 16 August, Calcutta erupted into a frenzy of violence. Groups of Muslims, Hindus and the small community of Sikhs attacked each other in the streets. Others formed murder squads to venture into different quarters of the town, killing, beating and raping anyone they could find. Their sadism knew no bounds. Nirad Chaudhuri, a Calcutta resident, described a man tied to the connector box of the tramlines with a small hole drilled in his skull so he might bleed to death as slowly as possible. He also heard of a boy of about fourteen years old, who was stripped of his Hindu clothing so that the mob might ascertain that he was circumcised – proving he was a Muslim. The boy was flung into a pond and held under with bamboo poles, 'with a Bengali engineer educated in England noting the time he took to die on his Rolex wristwatch, and wondering how tough the life of a Muslim bastard was.'[34]

For the next week, gangs terrorized the city. The riots spread through Bengal and Assam, and triggered copycat killings in the Punjab and the North-West Frontier Province. By the time the bloodshed finally subsided, deaths and serious injuries in Calcutta alone were estimated at 15,000 or 20,000, and the streets were piled with corpses to the height of two storeys in some areas.[35] The bloated carcasses of holy Hindu cows lay stinking and fly-covered beside the bodies of their owners. The American photojournalist Margaret Bourke-White arrived to see 'a scene that looked like Buchenwald';

no light comparison, for she had herself seen that, too.[36] Nehru went to Calcutta with his younger sister, Betty, to spearhead the government's effort to open first-aid camps and canteens. 'Many of these people who came to us seemed utterly bewildered,' Betty remembered; 'even those who had taken part in the killings seemed not to know why. Often they said to Bhai [Brother], "We don't know. It's you politicians who have done this, because we have lived in peace for years".'[37] Those politicians were still not prepared to compromise. When Nehru officially became Vice President of the Viceroy's interim government on 2 September 1946, Jinnah instructed all Muslims to display black flags and declared a day of mourning.[38]

Catapulted into a position of responsibility over a dramatically deteriorating nation, Nehru needed more than ever the steadying hand of his guru. But the Mahatma Gandhi was in no mood to lead Congress. 'I have no power,' he told journalist Louis Fischer. 'I have not changed Congress. I have a catalogue of grievances against it.' Nor had he much more patience for compromise with the Muslims. Fischer interviewed Gandhi in the summer of 1946, and found him at his most intemperate. 'Jinnah is an evil genius,' Gandhi told him. 'He believes he is a prophet.' He alleged that Jinnah had 'cast a spell over the Moslem, who is a simple-minded man'. He concluded that he thought the Muslim League would ultimately join the interim government. 'But the Sikhs have refused. They are stiff-necked like the Jews.'[39]

Many of Gandhi's acolytes were untroubled by these incendiary comments. But serious dissent was caused among even the most loyal of them by his 'brahmacharya experiments' during 1946 and 1947. The aged Mahatma had been 'testing' his vow of celibacy by sleeping at night in bed with a naked or partially clothed woman. The object of the experiments was to transcend physical arousal. One night, when the police turned up to arrest him, they found him in bed with a girl of eighteen. The British authorities decided that discretion was the better part of valour, and hushed up the police report.[40]

Nirmal Kumar Bose, a distinguished anthropologist who had volunteered his services to Gandhi as a secretary, wrote a detailed memoir of the experiments. According to him, several women were

involved, and many among them became personally possessive of
Gandhi, some to the point of emotional crisis. Gandhi's grandniece,
Abha, who started sleeping next to the Mahatma when she was just
sixteen and he seventy-four, spoke of the experience in later life. 'I
don't remember whether he had any clothes on or not,' she told an
interviewer. 'I don't like to think about it.' Sushila Nayyar said that
Gandhi had told another of his young relatives, Manu, that they
both needed to be naked to offer the purest of sacrifices, because 'We
both may be killed by the Muslims at any time.'[41] There was a dis-
quieting incident with Nayyar herself, when cries and two loud slaps
on flesh were heard from Gandhi's hut. The ashramites who ran to
their aid found Gandhi and Nayyar both in tears, though neither
would explain why. Bose later asked Gandhi whether he had struck
Nayyar. Gandhi denied it, and insisted that his behaviour was above
board.[42] But even if the Mahatma's intentions were pure, the objec-
tors argued, it was disrespectful to treat women as instruments. He
responded with more denials. Bose remembered that, 'If anybody
questioned Gandhiji's purity in respect of sex, he could fly into an
anger.'[43] Along with several others, Bose felt he had no option but to
resign from Gandhi's service. The Mahatma was unmoved. 'If I can
master this,' he is supposed to have said of his experiments, 'I can
still beat Jinnah.'[44] But at seventy-seven, Gandhi had been sapped of
political power. His importance to the independence process was by
then talismanic.

Whitehall was awash with intrigue. In the House of Commons,
Churchill had replied to the Cabinet Mission plan by arguing that,
'We cannot enforce by British arms a British-made Constitution
upon India against the wishes of any of the main elements in Indian
life.'[45] By the main elements, he meant eighty million Muslims, sixty
million Untouchables, and the princely states that comprised a third
of the land and a quarter of the population: all of which feared for
their fate under a caste-Hindu majority rule.

'To my mind, the most important point is that we should do all
we can to persuade and encourage the principal elements in India to
remain attached to the British Empire,' the lawyer Walter Monckton
had written to Churchill two days after the Cabinet Mission Plan

was announced. 'I see little prospect of inducing Congress to take such a line . . . The Muslim League, on the other hand, are naturally ready – though they will not be anxious to express their readiness publicly – to see the British connection retained.'[46]

Churchill read Beverley Nichols's controversial *Verdict on India*, a profoundly conservative book which argued that the British could not quit without creating a separate homeland for the Muslims. Afterwards, he declared to his wife that he was depressed by the scorn with which the raj was viewed in India and America; that 'out of my shadows has come a renewed resolve to go fighting on as long as possible and to make sure the Flag is not let down while I am at the wheel', he wrote. 'I agree with the book and also with its con-clusion – Pakistan.'[47] Churchill's vocal support of Pakistan would be instrumental in creating the world's first modern Islamic state, and in sabotaging any last hopes of Indian unity.

Exactly how far the alliance between Churchill and Jinnah went is hard to tell from the few remaining records. It has been rumoured that they had formed a secret pact several years before. Churchill, then Prime Minister, was said to have pledged to grant Jinnah Pakistan in return for Muslim League support of the Allied war effort. It is true that Jinnah repeatedly offered deals of this kind to the Viceroy, but there is scant evidence that he corresponded directly with Churchill on the matter.[48] Of course, any such letters would have been very unlikely to survive: for not only would they show Jinnah conspiring to keep the British in India, but they might have opened Churchill to charges of treason.[49]

Extensive letters between Churchill and Jinnah from 1946 survive in both men's papers.[50] They do not reveal a particularly close friend-ship, but do show Churchill's keen interest in the Muslim League. He wrote to Jinnah that any Muslim state ought to remain in the Commonwealth. 'Having got out of the British Commonwealth of Nations,' he wrote, 'India will be thrown into great confusion, and will have no means of defence against infiltration or invasion from the North.'[51] This statement was unqualified. Perhaps Churchill was pointing out the vulnerability of the north Pakistan border against the Afghans and the Russians; perhaps he was implying that a future Pakistan – to the north of India – might be able to invade India.

Either way, the implication that Pakistan needed British help was there.

In December the British government flew Nehru, Jinnah and Wavell to London to talk to Pethick-Lawrence, Cripps and Attlee.[52] On 5 December, the unfortunate King George VI found himself sitting between Nehru and Jinnah at a Buckingham Palace luncheon. The atmosphere was so poisonous that he summoned Attlee three days later to discuss it. 'The two main political parties in India had no real will to reach agreement among themselves', he wrote; 'the situation might so develop as to result in Civil War in India, & there seemed to be little realization among Indian leaders of the risk that ordered govt. might collapse.' He concluded: 'The Indian leaders have got to learn that the responsibility is theirs & that they must learn how to govern.'[53] Nehru lasted through only three days of squabbling before flying home, seething at the intransigence he perceived in London. On 9 December he convened a constituent assembly, in which the Muslim League refused to participate.

In Britain, Jinnah fared better. At Buckingham Palace, he found that the King was in favour of Pakistan; on talking to the Queen afterwards, he found her even more in favour; and finally he spoke to Queen Mary, who was '100% Pakistan!' He later told this anecdote to the Viceroy's principal secretary, Sir Eric Miéville. 'I replied that I was sorry Their Majesties had acted in such an unconstitutional way as to express their opinions on political matters connected with their Indian Empire,' wrote Miéville, 'at which he laughed quite a lot.'[54] Jinnah spent a Saturday at Churchill's country house, Chartwell, on 7 December; the meeting was evidently a success, for he afterwards invited Churchill to a luncheon party at Claridge's on 12 December.[55] By this point, their relationship had warmed up. On 11 December 1946, Churchill wrote secretly to 'My dear Mr Jinnah':

> I should greatly like to accept your kind invitation to luncheon on December 12. I feel, however, that it would perhaps be wiser for us not to be associated publicly at this juncture.
>
>   I greatly valued our talk the other day, and I now enclose the address to which any telegrams you may wish to send me can be sent without attracting attention in India. I will always sign myself

'Gilliatt'. Perhaps you will let me know to what address I should
telegraph to you and how you will sign yourself:'[56]

Jinnah was to write to Churchill in the guise of Miss Elizabeth
Gilliatt of 6 Westminster Gardens. (Images of Mr Toad dressed as a
washerwoman must be dismissed – Miss Gilliatt was Churchill's secretary, not an alter ego.) After this letter, the trail goes cold. Hardly
any further correspondence between Churchill and Jinnah is to be
found among either man's papers, beyond a few brief notes enclosing press cuttings or speeches. It seems likely that there would have
been additional letters of substance after one so cordial as the above.
If so, they were probably destroyed. Little may be told from this
fragment, though the cloak-and-dagger approach implies that the
two men were up to something interesting. Churchill's behaviour
over the next year would be extremely favourable to Pakistan and to
Jinnah personally. There can be no doubt that his public championing of the Muslim League's cause in the House of Commons
throughout 1946 and 1947, and of Pakistan's thereafter, was crucial
both to the creation of Pakistan and to the British government's support for its interests over the years to come. If Jinnah is regarded as
the father of Pakistan, Churchill must qualify as its uncle; and, therefore, as a pivotal figure in the resurgence of political Islam.

Across the Atlantic, the United States was also refining its interest in
Indian politics. American foreign policy had two main goals. One
was the ending of colonialism. The other was that communism must
be prevented from spreading. Great empires should retreat, setting up
model democracies in their stead – which, it was thought, would
naturally tend towards peace, secularism and liberal economics. In
the case of India, though, the United States feared that the exit of one
ruling foreign power would create a vacuum into which another
would be sucked. There were two main contenders on India's borders – Mao's China and Stalin's Russia – and the acting Prime
Minister, Jawaharlal Nehru, was openly friendly with both. It did not
take a great deal of imagination to construct a 'domino scenario'
whereby these two communist nations begat communist India, and
Washington did not intend to let events slide in that direction.[57]

Jawaharlal Nehru may have occasioned some suspicion on grounds of his friendships, but his family had used the war to carry out a brilliant public relations campaign in the United States, significantly increasing that nation's interest in Indian independence. Nehru's nieces Lekha and Tara Pandit, daughters of his sister Nan, had been sent to Wellesley College during the war. They became popular with nationalist and civil rights organizations, and were introduced to a miscellaneous collection of celebrities, including Danny Kaye, Joan Crawford, and Helen Keller. The girls stayed with their Uncle Jawahar's old friend, and Edwina Mountbatten's alleged lover, Paul Robeson.[58] Swiftly, it was made clear that official American opinion was keen to associate itself with the cause of Indian independence. A pair of speckled orchids, tied with gold ribbons, was sent to the girls, accompanied by a note saying, 'Let me know if there is anything I can do for you. I cannot do enough for Nehru's nieces.'[59] They had come from Louis Johnson, President Roosevelt's personal envoy to India. Johnson had cabled to Roosevelt that Nehru had been 'magnificent in his cooperation with me. The President would like him and on most things they agree . . . He is our hope here.'[60]

The Nehru girls' mother, Nan Pandit, visited them in December 1944. She also took the opportunity to represent India at the Pacific Relations Conference. Nan lunched with Eleanor Roosevelt in New York, and President Harry S. Truman at the White House. She toured the country speaking in favour of Indian independence, in public and on the radio. Her success was immediate. 'I didn't listen much to what you were saying, but your voice is like moonbeams and honey and I love you and am on India's side!' said one breathless male caller.[61] The presence of this sophisticated Indian woman in their midst only enhanced what the American government already thought. On 29 January 1945, Acting Secretary of State Joseph Grew told the media that the United States 'would be happy to contribute in any appropriate manner to a satisfactory settlement. We have close ties of friendship, both with the British and with the people of India.'[62]

American opinion had added weight, for the British government had no choice but to borrow money from its prosperous ally. The

loans Britain took from the United States to finance the Second
World War and subsequent reconstruction were so vast that the final
payment would not be made until 31 December 2006. Meanwhile,
Britain had quietly stopped paying the loans – approaching
£1 billion at 1947 rates – that the USA had lent it for the First World
War. Being so far in the Americans' pocket was an invidious situation. Britain was beginning to find out what it was like to be the
humbled dependency of a much more powerful state.

Attlee did not like American interference in the India question any
more than had Churchill. 'I do not like the idea of a statement by the
USA on India,' he said. 'It looks like a pat on the back to us from a
rich uncle who sees us turning over a new leaf.' He noted, furthermore, that any intervention from America 'would irritate the
Moslems'.[63] American diplomats leant heavily on Jinnah and Nehru
to accept the Cabinet Mission's plan and get on with their own independence. But the Indian leaders would not be squeezed out of their
entrenchments.[64]

By the end of 1946 the Viceroy, Wavell, had lost the confidence of
both sides of the Indian nationalist movement. Gandhi began to
canvass for his removal in September.[65] By the end of November,
Nehru, too, was publicly accusing him of favouring Jinnah.[66] Jinnah
wrote an impassioned letter to Attlee and a similar one to Churchill,
accusing Wavell of being under the thumb of Congress.[67] Attlee realized, with his usual brisk unsentimentality, that he was going to
have to fire Wavell. 'A great man in many ways, you know, but a
curious silent bird, and I don't think silent people get on very well
with Indians, who are very loquacious.'[68] The search began for one
who would not mind talking to the Indians. Attlee considered the
problem for some time before settling on his candidate, Dickie
Mountbatten – who had proven experience with 'all kinds of
people', and who was 'blessed with a very unusual wife'.[69] Attlee was
under no illusions about the anomaly of a semi-royal acting as a figurehead for democracy and freedom. Privately, he confided to friends
that Dickie was 'rather a Ruritanian figure, don't you think?'[70]

The description was apt, for since he had returned from South
East Asia Mountbatten had engaged himself almost full time in a
project worthy of the Order of the Red Rose. In one of the most

daring bloodless coups ever attempted, he would install the House of Mountbatten on the British throne – the same throne which, only thirty years before, had ordered his father's ruin. Mountbatten's involvement in the marriage between his nephew, Philippos Schleswig-Holstein-Sonderburg-Glücksburg, and the King's daughter, Princess Elizabeth, can hardly be overstated. He introduced the couple, engineered meetings between them, and went to great lengths in grooming Philip to become a consort.

Philip's credentials for marrying the world's most eligible woman were tenuous. His father was a playboy who had disappeared into the champagne-bars of the Côte d'Azur; his mother, abandoned, had gone mad and become a nun; his sisters had all married Nazis; he himself was only a naval lieutenant, and a penniless one at that. He had been a prince of Greece before a coup ousted his family, but the revolution had left him poor and nameless. He met Princess Elizabeth for the first time on 22 July 1939, when the royal family visited the Royal Naval College at Dartmouth under the proud supervision of Dickie Mountbatten. Philip was eighteen years old; Elizabeth was thirteen, and playing with a clockwork train. Their eyes met over lemonade and ginger biscuits, and Philip was among the cadets invited to lunch on the royal yacht. There he impressed the princesses by being able to jump high and eat an abnormal quantity of shrimp, though not simultaneously. When the time came for the yacht to sail, the cadets followed in rowboats and motorboats for a while; Elizabeth watched the tall, blond, strikingly handsome Philip row his little boat further than anyone else.[71]

Less than eighteen months after the smitten Princess Elizabeth had watched her handsome quasi-prince rowing after the royal yacht, the Conservative MP Chips Channon spent a few days in Athens. He met Philip at a cocktail party and, during the course of extensive gossiping, established that, 'He is to be our Prince Consort, and that is why he is serving in our Navy.'[72] At this stage the prospect seemed improbable. The Greek royals were impoverished, shabby and foreign. It was Dickie who organized a campaign to fashion young Philip into an eligible naval hero. The most important factor in this transformation would be to secure for him British nationality. For some reason, no one – not even the genealogically preoccupied Mountbatten – remembered the 1705 Act of Naturalization of the Most Excellent Princess Sophia, Electress and Duchess Dowager of Hanover, and the Issue of Her Body. As a descendant of Sophia, Philip had been British since birth. Unaware of this, Mountbatten embarked upon a frenetic two-and-a-half-year campaign. On 23 August 1944, he flew from South East Asia Command to Cairo, near Philip's station at Alexandria, to 'sound out' Philip and the King of Greece about whether the former could assume British nationality. He told the British High Commissioner, incredibly, that the British King had ordered his secret mission, on the grounds that Philip could 'be an additional asset to the British Royal Family and a great help to them in carrying out their royal functions'.[73] In fact, the King had already warned Mountbatten off: 'I have been thinking the matter over since our talk and I have come to the conclusion that we are going too fast', he had written to him two weeks before.[74] Soundings were taken; they were, apparently, satisfactory; Mountbatten was on the plane back to Karachi that same afternoon.

In October 1945, the matter of Philip's naturalization came before the cabinet. Attlee postponed any further discussion owing to the undesirability of aligning the British government with the Greek royalist cause. But by then the teenaged Princess Elizabeth was playing 'People Will Say We're in Love' from the musical *Oklahoma!* non-stop on her gramophone; and Philip had been seen helping her with a fur wrap at the wedding of Mountbatten's daughter Patricia. Mountbatten moved quickly, making personal appointments with the King, the Prime Minister, and the Foreign Secretary, while expending considerable effort in enlightening his media contacts about Philip's gallantry.[75] 'Please, I beg of you, not too much advice in an affair of the heart', Philip wrote to his uncle, 'or I shall be forced to do the wooing by proxy.'[76]

Mountbatten was summoned to meet the Prime Minister, Clement Attlee, for quite another reason on 18 December 1946. According to Attlee, Dickie was taken aback at the offer of the viceroyalty of India – 'Bit of a shock for him, you know' – and initially was reluctant to accept owing to the probable hitch in his naval career.[77] But the consent of the Lords of the Admiralty for Mountbatten's removal was obtained with noteworthy ease.[78] Even the King was keen: 'Rather unexpectedly he warmly approved of the idea right away,' remembered Attlee. 'Not everyone would let a member of the royal family go and take a risky job, hit or miss, in India as he did.'[79] It is hard not to feel sympathy for a King who had recently endured several years of intense lobbying for his daughter's hand in marriage, and may well have had enough of Cousin Dickie for the time being.

Aside from his naval career, there was another factor in Mountbatten's reluctance to accept the viceroyalty: Edwina. Bunny Phillips's marriage had been hard on her; a giddy romance with the conductor Malcolm Sargent had irritated her husband and daughters; she suffered from arteriosclerosis, and would soon have to undergo a partial hysterectomy. Dickie worried constantly about how hard she worked, her fragile health, and her depression. Since the war ended, they had been presented with all sorts of baubles, including the Freedom of the City of London, the Sword of Honour, and Dickie a viscountcy – 'though he expected an earldom', according to one of their friends.[80] 'Dickie got reduced in rank down to rear-admiral and Edwina wasn't saving people all day and night as she had been. I think, secretly, they were feeling a little low.'[81]

Despite his need for a new focus, there is plenty of evidence which indicates that Mountbatten's disinclination to take up the viceroyalty was genuine.[82] Letter after letter to Attlee shows Dickie setting up new and imaginative obstacles in his own path. First he said he would only do the job 'at the open invitation of the Indian parties',[83] which was obviously impossible to obtain as it would have involved them agreeing. Next, he demanded a complete change of policy as regarded viceregal protocol, so that he and Edwina could visit Indians at will and unencumbered by staff.[84] This he was unexpectedly granted. Finally, he hit upon the sticking point. On 7 January 1947, he asked Attlee to set an 'exact date for the termination of the British Raj'.[85]

The British government, in consultation with Wavell, had long been working to an end-date of 31 March 1948. British troops were already being moved out of India; and, after that time, Wavell considered that their numbers would have dipped below the minimum required to maintain order.[86] Attlee remembered in his memoirs: 'I decided that the only thing to do was to set a time-limit and say: "Whatever happens, our rule is ending on that date." It was, of course, a somewhat dangerous venture.'[87]

Even the most cursory glance at the letters between Attlee and Mountbatten reveals this memory to be false. It was Mountbatten who pushed to set a firm date – Attlee resisted. 'My dear Dickie,' he wrote on 9 January. 'As at present advised we think it is inadvisable to be too precise as to an actual day, but I will bear the point in mind.'[88] Alarmed, Mountbatten replied: 'I notice with some concern that it is now considered inadvisable to name a precise and definite day.'[89]

'I do not think that you need worry', Attlee wrote back. 'We shall get a clear statement of timing, but an exact day of the month so long ahead would not be very wise. There is no intention whatever of having any escape clause or of leaving any doubt that within a definite time the handover will take place.'[90]

But Mountbatten would not back down, and refused to be satisfied with Attlee's suggestion that they agree on 'the middle of 1948'.[91] Still Attlee resisted. The reason for his intransigence was that he was under intense pressure from the British administrators in India not to set a date. A report by Sir Frederick Burrows, Governor of Bengal, advised him that the announcement of a date would precipitate civil war, 'massacres on shocking scale (with Gandhi one of the first victims) and famine'.[92] Attlee received similar notices from the governors of the Punjab and the United Provinces. Wavell sent his personal opinion too, in the strongest terms: 'I am sure that announcement about the withdrawal in 1948 should not repeat not be made until after my successor has taken office and has had at least a week or two to study situation. I do not think that it is fair on him to have to take over situation which may already have developed unfavourably, nor on me to have to carry out in my last few weeks of office a line of action which I consider miss-timed [sic] and ill-judged.'[93]

Attlee communicated all this to Mountbatten, but the Viceroy-Designate refused to be intimidated. On this point, the cabinet stood by him. The two arguments that had swayed them in the past still convinced them now. First, that a firm deadline would force the

Indian parties to cooperate; second, that without one 'we should be suspected, as earlier Governments have been, of making communal differences an excuse for continuing British rule in India'.[94] Attlee cabled all this to the royal train, then making its way around South Africa. Once he had received the King's nod, he announced the new plan, the new viceroyalty and a date: 1 June 1948, flexible to within one month.[95] Mountbatten's instructions from Attlee, while vague in their wording, were clear enough in their implication. It was the 'definite objective' of His Majesty's Government to negotiate a plan for the transfer of power, with India or the divided bits of India remaining in the British Commonwealth if possible. Mountbatten was to stop short of compulsion. If his negotiations had reached no conclusion by 1 October 1947, Attlee had mandated him to get Britain out in nine months at most, regardless of whether the Indians were ready or not.[96]

Mountbatten's appointment was widely greeted with a cheer. Congratulatory letters poured into Broadlands, from friends, colleagues, journalists, ambassadors, members of the public, the Hampshire Cricket Club, the Central Chancery of the Order of Knighthood, David Joel Ltd (Manufacturers of Joinery and Furniture), and the entire company of the London Ballet.[97] Most were positive, though one of the bluntest exceptions came from Admiral Sir Reginald Plunkett-Ernle-Erle-Drax. 'Some people, I gather, expect that, when we move out, Indian unrest will develop to a state bordering on civil war', he wrote. 'Then Muslim & Hindu in India, like Jews & Arab in Palestine, will continue to quarrel until one of the contending parties invites the Russians to come in & help them. After that, the date of World War no. 3 is anybody's guess. However, I am v. ignorant of these problems & I trust that the pessimists are wrong. Every good wish to you in your difficult task.'[98]

'Thank you very much for your very kind letter of congratulation,' replied Mountbatten. 'I appreciate all the kind things you say.'[99]

With immense dignity, Wavell refrained from criticizing his successor, though privately he was furious at the abrupt manner of his dismissal. He busied himself by filling the incinerators in the Viceroy's House with stacks of documents that might have caused embarrassment to the British – either by revealing their attitudes to Indian political figures, or by detailing British mismanagement of India.[100] The choice of Mountbatten did attract some public criticism. Conservative MP Brendan Bracken deplored Mountbatten's closeness to Nehru, and described the former as 'a miserable creature, power-mad, publicity-mad'.[101] Bracken was not the only one to notice the Mountbatten–Nehru connection, and to draw the conclusion that there must be something fishy about it.[102] The Associated Press of America reported that Mountbatten's appointment had been made to appease Nehru. Nehru denied this in a terse statement, pointing out that he had met Mountbatten on just two previous occasions: in Singapore in 1946, and once afterwards as Mountbatten was passing through Delhi, when they discussed nothing more exciting than the transport of paddy.[103]

Bracken and the AP had seized the wrong end of the stick. Nehru was suspicious about Mountbatten's appointment, and mistrustful of the man himself. Attlee's announcement, Nehru wrote to his London-based friend Krishna Menon, 'has shaken people up here and forced them to think furiously'.[104] He went on: 'The two men that Mountbatten is bringing with him, Miéville and General Ismay, are not the type which inspires confidence regarding Mountbatten's outlook.' He asked Menon to try to see Mountbatten and get an impression of him. 'Much will depend on what kind of a directive Mountbatten is bringing with him, and how he intends to function here. He can obviously make things easier or more difficult.'[105]

Poor, accident-prone Dickie, long known in the Admiralty as the 'Master of Disaster'[106], had been given more power over 400 million subjects of the British King-Emperor than any preceding Viceroy.[107] The task of reconciling the Indian politicians, re-establishing public order and finding a formula for an independent India was awesome, and quite beyond Mountbatten's experience. India would have been within its rights to panic but, from the British government's point of view, Dickie's appointment had been a clever move. He was a gung-ho sort, and could be relied upon to remove himself, and his nation, by any means necessary. And, by this stage, the British government did not care much what means were necessary. The end was its only concern.

On the evening of 18 March 1947, Dickie and Edwina held a farewell reception at the Royal Automobile Club in Pall Mall. It was a double celebration for them. That very morning, Mountbatten had secured a great victory, signalled by an announcement of the superfluous naturalization of Lieutenant Philip Mountbatten, RN, in the *London Gazette*.[108] He had planned to call his nephew 'HRH Prince Philip'. Philip preferred to start again as a commoner, but it is hard to imagine that Dickie had nothing to do with his choice of surname. 'Most people think that Dickie's my father anyway,' Philip later acknowledged.[109] With Philip's engagement to the heiress presumptive soon to be announced, the House of Mountbatten was now right at the front of the line for the British throne.

At the reception that night, the Mountbattens stood for two hours to meet their 700 guests, including a smattering of royals, the Prime Minister, various India-related politicians, the Archbishop of Canterbury, and copious servicemen. Also in attendance, as usual, was Noël Coward. Dickie and Edwina's cocktail party put him in a pensive mood. 'I wonder if they will come back alive', he wrote in his diary that evening. 'I think that if it is possible to make a go of it in the circumstances they will, but I have some forebodings.'[110] He was not the only one. As Mountbatten climbed aboard his aeroplane at Northolt the next day, he said to his aide-de-camp: 'I don't want to go. They don't want me out there. We'll probably come home with bullets in our backs.'[111]

A sense of foreboding was justified. The next fifteen months were to be the most dangerous, the most triumphant, the most terrifying, the most passionate, and the most controversial of the Mountbattens' lives.

PART II

THE END

CHAPTER 10

OPERATION MADHOUSE

A RELATIVELY SMALL GATHERING AWAITED THE DESCENT OF A plane to Palam Airfield, south-west of New Delhi, in the early afternoon of 22 March 1947. In it were representatives of the Muslim League and Congress, whose appearances a well-informed bystander would have had no trouble decoding. Liaquat Ali Khan, General Secretary of the Muslim League, wore a European suit with an astrakhan Jinnah cap. Jawaharlal Nehru, effective leader of Congress, wore a Gandhi cap and Indian sherwani suit. The 14th Punjab Regiment, the Royal Air Force and the Royal Indian Air Force had mounted guards of honour for the occasion. A collection of photographers waited in the heat, polishing the dust from their lenses.

The York transporter plane made its lazy approach to the runway. The wheels came down, the back end sank to meet the tarmac, the nose levelled, and the aircraft juddered to a halt. As the four engines whirred down into silence, the door opened and a group of people emerged into the Delhi haze. Foremost among these was Viscount Mountbatten of Burma, the new Viceroy-Designate, forty-six years old, handsome and gleaming in his full dress uniform, with rows of medals stretching from breastbone to armpit. (He had originally been advised to turn up in plain clothes. Disappointed, he referred the matter to the Labour MP Woodrow Wyatt, who reassured him that the government would send a band and a delegation, and that he could therefore appear in full fig.[1]) Following the Viceroy-Designate was Viscountess Mountbatten, in a chocolate brown suit.

In her husband's words, Lady Mountbatten was 'looking absolutely terrific, absolutely knock-down charm, marvellous figure'.[2] She had recovered physically from her illness that spring, but had no desire to be in India – describing the posting as a 'horror job'.[3] There had been a hint of sullenness on the flight, when Edwina had shocked her staff by stuffing the diamond tiara her husband had specially designed and bought for her into an old shoebox and chucking it carelessly into an overhead rack.[4] But her knock-down charm was back on as she lingered on the red carpet, chatting to Liaquat and Nehru.

The Mountbattens drove to the Viceroy's House, where they were greeted by the Royal Scots Fusiliers and Lord and Lady Wavell. A lone British officer in the crowd attempted a cheer, which petered out in the gloomy silence. 'Is *nobody* happy here?' he asked, but those nearby pretended not to have heard.[5]

Lords Mountbatten and Wavell withdrew to the latter's study for a manly word, while Edwina retired to her new apartments. She had brought a Sealyham terrier, Mizzen, with her, and asked for something to feed it. Half an hour later, two servants turned up, bearing roast chicken on a silver salver. Edwina froze at the sight. Seizing the plate over Mizzen's barking head, she ran into the bathroom, locked herself in and ate the lot.[6] This incident has usually been omitted by biographers, perhaps because to modern eyes a story about an extremely thin woman who locks herself in a bathroom to eat looks uncomfortably like evidence of an eating disorder. It originally appeared in a Mountbatten-sanctioned version of events, interpreted as a response to rationing back in Britain. But Dickie and Edwina had just flown to India in considerable luxury, breaking their journey at the British High Commands in Malta and Suez, and it is unlikely they were starved on the way. Under the circumstances, it is hard not to see the incident as a demonstration of Edwina's unhappiness.

Meanwhile, her husband was being briefed by his predecessor on the situation he was about to inherit. Mountbatten's memory of his meeting with Wavell, recounted much later in life to his pet historians

Dominique Lapierre and Larry Collins, has the spin of an old sea-yarn to it. According to Dickie, Wavell escorted him into the study, shut the heavy teak doors behind them, and opened with: 'I am sorry indeed that you've been sent out here in my place.'

'Well, that's being candid,' Mountbatten shot back. 'Why? Don't you think I'm up to it?'

'No,' Wavell is supposed to have replied, 'indeed, I'm very fond of you, but you've been given an impossible task. I've tried everything I know to solve this problem and I can see no light.' He gloomily opened his safe, and removed from it the diamond badge of the Grand Master of the Order of the Star of India, along with a plain manila file entitled 'Operation Madhouse'. 'Alas,' the departing Viceroy lamented, handing over the badge and file, 'I can see no other way out.'[7]

The words Mountbatten attributes to Wavell do not recall that officer's usual brusque tone.[8] Nor does the supposed affection of Wavell for his successor ring true. And no manila file called 'Operation Madhouse' has found its way into the British or Indian National Archives, though Wavell does refer to a similar plan called the 'Breakdown Plan' in his diary.[9] 'Wavell was frankly pretty defeatist by then,' Attlee recalled. 'He produced a plan worked out by his ICS advisers for the evacuation of India with everybody moving from where they were by stages right up through the Ganges valley till eventually, apparently, they would be collected at Karachi and Bombay and sail away. Well, I thought that was what Winston would certainly quite properly describe as an ignoble and sordid scuttle and I wouldn't look at it.'[10] This description is unfair, for the plan was less about panic than pragmatism. Wavell believed that the great achievement of the raj was the unification of India. He also knew that the partition of the same would be incendiary. It was, he thought, in Britain's best interests to stand well back before lighting the touch-paper. He wanted to hand over power gradually to demo-cratic provinces and Indian princedoms, in localized groups, while retaining British jurisdiction at the centre. When all the bits and pieces were under Indian control, the British could bow out dis-creetly – leaving the Indians to deal with the civil war that would almost certainly be left behind.

The Breakdown Plan was far from perfect, and made no attempt to save the Indian people from disaster. But the point was that the disaster would not be occurring on Britain's watch. Moreover, it was what Congress had been demanding for years: that Britain simply quit India. Yet it had not been thought acceptable in Whitehall – partly because the resulting civil war would reflect badly on Britain, but also because it would not work quickly enough. According to the Indian government's political adviser, Sir Conrad Corfield, the American government was now leaning on London 'to confer on India the advantages of undiluted democracy as soon as possible'.[11] The Americans were ever more concerned about the outward creep of communism from Russia and China, and cannot have been reassured by the fact that, a week before Mountbatten's viceroyalty began, British intelligence services reported the first clear case of direct financial aid passing from the Soviets to the Communist Party in India.[12] That same week, the British Foreign Secretary, Ernest Bevin, had been in Moscow: Stalin told him that Russia would not interfere in Indian independence, but noted that it was a time of grave dangers. This did not placate the British. 'It would clearly be imprudent to take Stalin's profession of non-interference at its face value, particularly having regard to certain recent signs to the contrary', wrote the India Secretary, Lord Pethick-Lawrence, to Mountbatten.[13] Suddenly, the focus of President Truman's campaign against communism shifted from Greece and Turkey – which had been worrying the United States for some weeks – abruptly eastwards.

The morning after the Mountbattens' arrival, the Wavells departed with dignity and cordial handshakes, their plane taking off promptly at ten. Most of Delhi's white population was dismayed to see them go. Wavell's directness and unemotional approach had made him popular; the manner of his sacking had predisposed many to dislike his successor. Mountbatten's press attaché, Alan Campbell-Johnson, had already discovered that the consensus in Delhi was against his master.[14] The Europeans felt that he knew nothing about India and was little more than a playboy. The fact that Mountbatten spent his first day arranging press and photography for his grand swearing-in did little to contradict their view.

On the bright Monday morning of 24 March, the dignitaries of British India congregated at the Viceroy's House, under the massive gold dome and ornate chandeliers of the Durbar Hall. English gentlemen in tailcoats and pith helmets strode up the steps alongside turbaned Sikhs; Indian ladies in silk saris chatted to Congressmen in homespun kurtas; princes glittered in their ancient jewels. The crowd hushed as a fanfare of trumpets heralded Dickie and Edwina's appearance through the back doors: he a handsome prince in shining regalia with a sword clasped by his side, she a beautiful princess in a flowing gown of ivory brocade, with that carelessly treated diamond tiara flashing brilliant sparkles of light back at the photographers.

The Mountbattens marched sedately and in perfect synchrony up the aisle, an ethereal and slender pair of white-clad and gold-strewn presences, shimmering in the crowded hall. They came to a halt in front of two enormous thrones under a towering scarlet-draped canopy, and turned towards each other, then around to face their audience and a salvo of exploding flashbulbs.[15] Surrounded as he was by all these new and exciting outfits, the Viceroy puffed up with delight. 'What a ceremony!' Mountbatten remembered later in life. 'I put on everything. My white full dress uniform. Orders, decorations, medals, the whole lot ... Obviously, I wore the Garter. Then I wore the Star of India, I was the Grand Master of the Order, I wore the Star of the Indian Empire, and then I wore the Victorian Order and that made the four; that's all you're allowed to wear. And I wore the aiguillettes as personal ADC to the King Emperor.'[16]

It is easy to laugh at Mountbatten's obsession with decorating himself, and with his fussing over protocol. But these trivialities were prerequisites for the job. A large portion of the Viceroy's responsibilities had to do with awarding honours, remembering faces, seating people appropriately at parties, writing correct letters and invitations, remembering how to address the divorced wife of the second son of an earl after she had remarried a sea captain, and so on. In all of these matters, Mountbatten's skills were peerless. But the key to perfect protocol is knowing when to break it, and Mountbatten had reserved a surprise for his audience. 'This is not a normal viceroyalty on which I am embarking,' he admitted, in a forthright address which newspapers back in London reported with some shock. 'Every one of us must do what he can to avoid any word or action which might lead to further bitterness or add to the toll of innocent victims,' he said. 'I am under no illusion about the difficulty of my task. I shall need the greatest good will of the greatest possible number and I am asking India today for that good will.'[17] This was the sound of the British Empire owning up to its limitations, and the old guard of the raj might have been outraged. Fortunately, the acoustics in the hall were so bad that few could hear. Nevertheless, both Nehru and Liaquat were observed to be paying very close attention and, during the last sentence, even the poised Lady Mountbatten could be seen to turn her head slightly to look at her husband.[18] Mountbatten had established his style with immediate effect. The new regime was to be frank, inclusive and open-minded. It was now full steam ahead to the transfer of power, and the old guard could come on board or stay on shore as they pleased.

During the week that followed, Mountbatten's vision of sophisticated imperial elegance rapidly deteriorated. His wife was miserable; the parade of Indian leaders through his study conjured up a portent of insoluble quarrels; and, above all, the full horror of India's communal violence would set in. Tension in the Punjab had been tightening for years, owing to the visible economic difference between wealthy caste-Hindus and Sikhs, and relatively impoverished, labouring Muslims. That March, it had finally snapped. The worst riots in a century had left thousands dead, mostly Sikhs massacred by Muslims in Rawalpindi and Multan.[19] On the very day after Mountbatten arrived, rioting broke out in Delhi itself. Chandni Chowk is the main street of Old Delhi, running from the Lahore Gate to the Red Fort. Its wide avenue was lined with stalls selling the requisites of Delhi life: fine woven dupattas, sweet lassi, festive tinsel. Amid the labyrinth of alleyways and bazaars running off the Chowk are diverse shrines, including one of the Sikhs' most important temples, the Sisganj Gurdwara, and India's largest mosque, the Jama Masjid. The district was a tinderbox for trouble, loaded that day by a Muslim meeting at the mosque in support of Pakistan, and ignited, according to eyewitnesses, by the 'recklessly provocative behaviour' of Sikh protesters. The Sikhs arrived at the busy marketplace in two lorries and assorted jeeps, and 'careered about', brandishing swords. (The Chief Commissioner of Delhi noted rather flippantly that this had the effect of 'accidentally injuring some Muslims'.[20]) At least two people were killed and six seriously injured.[21] It was not much of a welcome party for the new Viceroy.

Perhaps with the safety of the Mountbattens in mind, the district magistrate imposed draconian edicts. For seven days, a curfew would run from 6 p.m. until 7 a.m. For a fortnight, no group of more than five individuals would be permitted to assemble for any purpose. For a week, all newspapers, commentary, photographs and even cartoons would be subject to official censorship. These measures did not make much difference. On 25 March, the Chief Commissioner, apparently long past the point of taking his reports seriously, wrote that 'the night passed peacefully except for a certain amount of shouting', and noted that there had been seven stabbing and brickbatting incidents on the previous day, in which eleven people had been injured. A police picket had opened fire when it was set upon by a mob armed with stones, a number of arrests had been made and 'some bad characters have also been rounded up'. He concluded that, 'All is quiet today up to the time of writing (10.30 A.M.),' which was not much of a boast. Indeed, another hand added below that, 'After lunch some stabbings and a clash by the Jumna [sic] Masjid.'[22]

If the local situation seemed bad, the national was far worse. On the Wednesday after Dickie and Edwina's arrival, riots broke out in Calcutta, killing 8 and injuring 111. In Patna, the police went on strike and occupied the arms depot at Gaya; the Prime Minister of Bihar blamed communists. By Thursday, casualties in Calcutta had risen to fourteen, and fires ripped through the east of the city. The police were rapidly losing control. First they attempted to subdue the mob with tear gas; when that did not work, they resorted to bullets, and fired eighteen rounds into the crowd.

By Friday, the Punjab was incongruously quiet – but only, said *The Times*, because 'all the members of one community or the other either [had been] slaughtered or [had] fled'.[23] In Amritsar, 160 lay dead in the streets after rioting. Fourteen policemen were injured at riots in Mardan, in the North-West Frontier Province. Back in Calcutta, a further eight were killed and thirty-two injured when bombs were thrown. The police gave up, and called in the Army.

The next Sunday, 30 March, was the god-king Rama's birthday, a day of celebrations for Hindus. In Calcutta, it was celebrated with even greater rioting, which spread across the Hooghly River to the industrial city of Howrah. The death toll rose again, amid stabbings, bombings and the throwing of acid: 46 dead, 400 injured. In Bombay, a deceptive peace was broken in the evening when three separate riots broke out. Bombs were thrown, and temples set ablaze. Muslims and Hindus pitched battles in the city, fighting with clubs, knives, iron bars and whatever weapons they could improvise. The police were attacked, and responded with gunfire. Hundreds were injured, and dozens killed: the bodies lay uncounted in the streets. A car was ambushed and its four passengers imprisoned inside by the mob while they set it alight. The passengers burned alive, screaming for mercy. The next day, all that remained was four human skeletons within the burnt-out metal skeleton of their car.

While all this was going on, Mountbatten had to meet the Indian leaders. For that first week, the two least compromising and highest-profile among them declined his invitation – though he had been so anxious to meet these two in particular that he had written to each of them before his viceroyalty had begun.[24] Mohammad Ali Jinnah, representing the Muslim League, remained in Bombay, making inflammatory speeches. Mohandas Gandhi, representing Mohandas Gandhi, was living among the outcastes in distant Bihar, and refused to take advantage of the viceregal aircraft. Among those Mountbatten did meet, the impression was already less than encouraging. Many of the princes seemed determined to press for the independence of their states, rather than transferring their allegiance to an independent India – a plan which would fragment the subcontinent into dozens, perhaps hundreds, of private kingdoms. The Maharaja of Bikaner blamed the Nawab of Bhopal for dividing the princes along communal lines. The Nawab of Bhopal said the Maharaja of Bikaner was nothing more than a patsy of Congress. Both begged Mountbatten not to let the British leave India at all.[25] This opinion was not confined to the princes. John Matthai, the

Minister for Transport, told him that, 'But for Congress, there was no body in India which would not move Heaven and Earth to keep the British.'[26] Other politicians presented further unexpected difficulties. Liaquat Ali Khan subtly suggested that Mountbatten must have made his controversial swearing-in address at the behest of Congress. Mountbatten vehemently denied it, but Liaquat said that three highly placed sources had told him it was so.[27] Vallabhbhai Patel of Congress, ominously nicknamed 'the Iron Man', was a forceful Hindu-nationalist lawyer, clever and cool. He was impervious to Mountbatten's famous charm, describing the new Viceroy as 'a toy for Jawaharlalji to play with – while we arrange the revolution'.[28]

Only one man seemed to offer a glimmer of hope. 'Pandit Nehru struck me as most sincere,' Dickie wrote after their first meeting on 24 March, and praised his 'fairness of mind'. But even this interview promised greater problems yet to come. Nehru spoke at length about Jinnah, but was too astute to impugn his nemesis openly. Instead, he managed with great subtlety to sow in Mountbatten's mind the seeds of ill favour, perhaps realizing – either consciously or unconsciously – that criticism always bites harder when it comes dressed up as praise. Thus Jinnah, he said, was 'one of the most extraordinary men in history', and a 'financially successful though mediocre lawyer', who avoided taking any action that might split his party, such as holding debates or answering questions. The assessment had the taint of sour grapes to it, but Mountbatten did not seem to notice.[29] Three days later, Jinnah made a speech in Bombay that confirmed Nehru's picture of him as a thorn in everyone's side. He alleged that the British had deliberately conspired against the Muslims: trying to force them into staying in India rather than creating their own state of Pakistan, in order to produce greater bloodshed and destruction after the raj's departure.[30] He was in a better position than anyone else in India to know that the opposite was true, for the person who had been attempting to conspire with the British to create Pakistan for more than seven years was Jinnah himself.

While the Viceroy struggled to generate a rapport with the Indians, his Vicereine was doing far better. Edwina began by entertaining the wives of her husband's guests but, within a couple of days of arriving, she established her own political network. In the first few days, she sought out and befriended Gandhi's right-hand woman, Amrit Kaur, who was to become one of her greatest friends and the new government's Minister for Health; Vallabhbhai Patel's influential daughter, Maniben; Liaquat's wife, the Begum Ra'ana Liaquat Ali Khan, who like Edwina herself was deeply involved in health and welfare work; the Untouchable leader, B.R. Ambedkar; the radical feminist Kamaladevi Chattopadhyaya; and the poet and politician Sarojini Naidu, who coincidentally had been a childhood friend of her mother's.[31] Very few of the women or, indeed, the men she met had ever been allowed into the Viceroy's House before.

Women were prominent in Indian politics, a trend which Edwina Mountbatten, along with many Indian women, attributed to Gandhism. Non-violence, passive resistance and boycotts were all tactics which could be practised by women without breaking social conventions; and Nehru had insisted as early as 1937 that the Congress manifesto pledge to remove all social, economic and political discrimination against women. As a result, there were more powerful women in India's Congress than there were in Britain's Labour Party or in America's Democratic Party at the time. The Muslim League, too, had Fatima Jinnah and the Begum Liaquat, unofficial but significant and visible figures, at the highest level. As Edwina would later tell an audience in London, 'We shall have to wake up in this country when we see how the women of India have achieved emancipation to such a remarkable degree in spite of the backwardness of the country, the illiteracy of the people, the low standard of life, and all kinds of disadvantages from the point of view of religious feeling and other obstacles.'[32]

For years Edwina had been looking for a role in which she could actually do something and, to her surprise, it would be in India that she found it. One of her most important friendships was quickly established with the sharp and personable Congress politician Vijaya Lakshmi 'Nan' Pandit. 'Edwina plunged headlong into informality,' remembered Nan. 'Politics were forgotten and women discussed women's problems.'[33] But it was with Nan's brother, Jawaharlal Nehru, that she formed the most important connection of all.

Jawahar and Edwina became close almost immediately on her arrival. Shahid Hamid, the private secretary to Field Marshal Sir Claude Auchinleck, alleged that Edwina's relationship with Jawahar was 'sufficiently close to have raised many eyebrows' by 31 March 1947 – and claimed to have heard the gossip from Nehru's confidant, Krishna Menon.[34] At first glance this seems implausible, not least because Hamid's memoirs have been widely disputed. By 31 March, the Mountbattens had been in India for only a week. Yet even so quickly it is possible to be attracted to a person, to feel a sympathy with them and even to develop the beginnings of a romantic attachment. They were together remarkably often during that first week, and the informality of their friendship was obvious. He addressed a meeting of the Red Cross; she accompanied him, and photographs show her looking up at him, enraptured. At the reception for delegates of the Asian Relations Conference on 28 March, the pair drew their armchairs together for an involved conversation. In one photograph, Nehru is being interrupted, and looks startled. Lady Mountbatten, elegant in a long floral-print dress, has her attention focused entirely on the Congress leader. That same evening, at the Mountbattens' first garden party, there was a shortage of chairs during a dance recital. The yogic Jawahar forsook his, and instead sat cross-legged on the floor at Edwina's feet. After the party, Edwina accompanied Jawahar back to his house on York Road for a nightcap – with her daughter, but without her husband.[35]

In March 1957, Edwina would write to Jawahar that it was the anniversary of 'Ten years ... monumental in their history and so powerful in the effects on our personal lives.' Simultaneously, he wrote to her that March 1957 marked 'Ten years!'[36] Even if their close friendship had not yet developed a romantic aspect, it is obvious that it had been firmly established.

To Lord Mountbatten, this first week of Indian reality had come as a nasty shock. While Edwina began to find her footing, Dickie rapidly lost his. When he wrote the first of his personal reports to London on 31 March, India – with its impossible politicians, its religious combustions, its villages laid to waste by bloodthirsty mobs, its corpses in burnt-out cars, its tangled, ghastly web of tensions, histories and grievances, and the enormous weight of expectation to fix all of this laid heavily upon his shoulders – had already reduced the beaming new Viceroy of 24 March to jelly. Aghast, he wrote to Attlee:

> The scene here is one of unrelieved gloom ... At this early stage I can see little ground on which to build any agreed solution for the future of India. The Cabinet is fiercely divided on communal lines; each party has its own solution and does not at present show any sign of being prepared to consider another.
>
> In addition, the whole country is in a most unsettled state ... The only conclusion that I have been able to come to is that unless I act quickly I may well find the real beginnings of a civil war on my hands.[37]

If anything, Mountbatten was understating the case. The real beginnings of civil war were already on his hands, and he was in no position to deal with them. Britain had only 11,400 soldiers in India (a number which would fall to 4000 over the course of the twelve months from April 1947), and the country had been in a state of unrest for at least a year.[38] Only one man had ever seemed capable of holding back this swelling tide – and he was the elderly Gujarati who would meet the new Viceroy for the first time that afternoon.

Mohandas Gandhi arrived at five o'clock, a tiny, flyweight figure leaning on Maniben Patel for support. He posed for photographs in the afternoon sun with the Mountbattens, and formed an instant bond with Edwina. As they went back into the house, Gandhi rested his hand on the Vicereine's shoulder – a gesture of fellowship, acceptance and trust which he habitually reserved for his ashramites. Most of the photographers were already packing up their equipment, but one shutter in the garden clicked. The next morning, the image it captured was on front pages across the world.

Whether Gandhi formed so immediate a connection with Lord Mountbatten is uncertain. Back inside the Viceroy's House, Edwina made an excuse to leave, so that her husband and the Mahatma could get down to business. They did not. Gandhi first assured Mountbatten that he would come back for two hours every day that week; then started to tell his life story. 'I felt there was no hurry and deemed it advisable to let him talk along any lines that entered his head,' noted Mountbatten cautiously. Two hours later, having spoken at great length of his legal training in England, his life in South Africa, and his travels in India, and not at all about a settlement for independence, the Mahatma got up and left. The Viceroy was slightly bemused, but determined to remain upbeat. 'We parted at 7.15, both of us, I am sure, feeling that we had progressed along the path of friendship.'[39]

The next day Gandhi returned, bringing an ascetic meal of curds to take under a tree in the garden while the Viceroy pointlessly offered him tea and scones. The Mahatma launched upon an unsuspecting Mountbatten his plan to quell the bubbling discontent between Hindu and Muslim. It was an extraordinary suggestion. Jinnah was to be made Prime Minister, and could form a cabinet entirely composed of Muslims if he wished. Congress would agree to cooperate freely and sincerely. This would, Gandhi believed, satisfy the Muslims that the new India was not to be a 'Hindustan', and that their rights and freedoms would be represented.

That day was April Fool's Day, but Gandhi's scheme was not a joke. He intended that Jinnah should be offered a chance to form an exclusively Islamic cabinet, despite the fact that the Muslim population of India was only around 25 per cent, with the majority Congress Party meekly serving beneath them, and apparently did not foresee any potential upset in the already inflamed Hindu and Sikh communities as a consequence of this. Nor did he acknowledge that an artificially constructed and undemocratic minority government would represent a continuation of what India had most loathed about the British raj: it would mean the rule of a very vast number of people by the unelected elite of a culture radically different from their own. Such a government would have had no real chance of success, and must quickly have fallen or been toppled after the British had left. At that point, it could only have been replaced by a predominantly Hindu administration. Moreover, in case Jinnah were wise enough to refuse the leadership, Gandhi proposed a codicil. If Jinnah would not form a cabinet, the same offer was to be made to Congress, with the Muslim League acting as obedient handmaidens to a purely Congress rule. Either way, it was virtually guaranteed to result in disaster for India's 100 million Muslims, the sidelining of the Muslim League, and the ultimate domination of Congress. The scheme was so risky, and the probable result so obvious, that many Muslims thought Gandhi was conspiring to discredit Jinnah and ensure the long-term goal of a Hindu nationalist state.[40]

Gandhi had put forward the same idea several times in the past, and it had been dismissed by previous viceroys as impossible.[41] By 1947, even Gandhi's colleagues in Congress were beginning to suspect that he had gone 'a bit senile'.[42] Mountbatten described himself as 'staggered' by Gandhi's suggestion, but was not yet sure enough of his balance to dismiss the plan outright.[43] Nehru was more realistic, and told him it would not work. A note of frustration had become discernible lately in Nehru's tone when he spoke of the Mahatma. He described the old man as 'going round with ointment trying to heal one sore spot after another on the body of India, instead of diagnosing the cause of this eruption of sores and participating in the treatment of the body as a whole'.[44] A couple of weeks later, Gandhi was forced to drop the plan on the grounds that Congress was not prepared to accept it. The rejection prompted his withdrawal from formal involvement in negotiations for the transfer of power, though he would continue to contribute from the sidelines.[45]

Mountbatten's initial meetings with Gandhi had been bad. His meetings with Jinnah would be worse. The Viceroy decided that he would open with the same gambit that Gandhi had used on him: to leave politics aside in the first instance, and instead chat about himself. And so he launched cheerfully into the story of his Indian tour with the Prince of Wales in the twenties, his engagement to Edwina in Delhi, his exploits as Supremo and so forth, to the bewilderment of his guest. 'He could not see why we should not talk business at once,' Mountbatten remembered, 'but finally resigned himself to listen to my Indian reminiscences.'[46] Fortunately, Mountbatten was interrupted by the arrival of some press photographers. With Lady Mountbatten joining them, Mountbatten and Jinnah went into the gardens to have their pictures taken. 'A rose between two thorns,' quipped Jinnah – slightly too late, for Edwina had just moved around from between them to Jinnah's left-hand side, casting her in the role of a thorn, and him in the role of the rose. Some historians have hinted that Jinnah's faux pas may not have been entirely unintentional.[47] Mountbatten assumed it was, and roared with laughter. Either way, the joke thawed the atmosphere. After they returned to the study, Mountbatten reported that Jinnah relaxed considerably and even started talking about his own background and life in London. 'In fact we ended on a surprisingly friendly note. He had come in haughty and frigid but the joke at the photograph had suddenly unfrozen him and I felt we had begun to make friends and would be able to do business together.'[48]

It is safe to say that Mountbatten and Jinnah never ended up making friends. Much has been made of the former calling the latter various unpleasant names in his notes – including 'psychopathic case', 'bastard' and 'evil genius'.[49] The remarks presented in context appear less offensive, for Mountbatten was in the habit of writing very lively notes. It is easy enough to find him calling Nehru 'a demagogue' and 'reprehensible', Patel 'hysterical', and Gandhi 'an inveterate and dangerous Trotskyist'.[50] At first, both Mountbattens tried hard with the Jinnahs. When Jinnah returned the evening after their first meeting to dine at the Viceroy's House with his sister Fatima, they stayed until well after midnight, and according to Mountbatten 'the ice was really broken'.[51] He was adamant that Jinnah should be brought into the government to work alongside Nehru. When he suggested this to Jinnah, it did not go down well. 'If I had invited the Pope to take part in the Black Mass,' Mountbatten reported to London, 'he could not have been more horrified.'[52]

'Dickie and I have of course found the Jinnahs the most difficult,' Edwina admitted to Isobel Cripps. They were personally charming, she said, and remarkably intelligent: 'I cannot help but liking [sic] them both very much indeed.' But she and Dickie despaired of getting them to compromise. 'Yet one sympathises so much with their fears and apprehensions and wants to do everything one can to give the necessary safeguards and as fair a deal as is humanly possible.'[53] Edwina had Fatima to tea that week, and struck up a conversation about how encouraging it had been to see Muslim and Hindu students integrating happily at Lady Irwin College. 'Don't be misled by the apparent contentment of the Muslim girls there,' Fatima told her, bleakly; 'we haven't been able to start our propaganda in that college yet.'[54]

It is impossible to dismiss the notion that Fatima Jinnah's coolness to Edwina Mountbatten may have been informed by the latter's close and obvious friendships with Gandhi and Nehru. Previous vicereines had not gone visiting Gandhi's hut in the sweeper colony; they had certainly not gone alone to dine with the handsome widower Nehru. Edwina did both, and regularly. Fatima Jinnah was a perceptive woman, well-connected in political circles, and can hardly have been unaware of Edwina's friendship with her brother's rival. Whether or not she believed the more scandalous gossip, it is only logical that the connection with Jawahar would have raised suspicions that Edwina had a leaning towards Congress. Any further suspicion that Mountbatten might be influenced by his wife would have been well founded. Dickie's interest in Asian politics had, by his own admission, followed Edwina's.

As April began, the situation in the country at large was getting worse, and little was being done about it. On 6 April, it was reported that riots had left 350 dead and 4000 homeless in the town of Gurgaon, around 20 miles from Delhi on the road to Jaipur; from Noakhali came reports of people being roasted alive.[55] Gandhi went on a twenty-four-hour fast 'to vindicate swaraj through Hindu–Muslim unity, hand spinning, and the like.'[56] It did not achieve much, but it was more than the Viceroy could do. Just four days later, on 11 April, five major cities – Calcutta, Delhi, Amritsar, Agra and Peshawar – were placed under curfew following riots. In Calcutta, a food shortage was beginning to hit. The market and most of the shops were closed. Great heaps of rubbish had been piling up in the streets for a fortnight, for the Untouchable sweepers were too scared to perform their normal function.[57] The simultaneous collapse of public hygiene and public nutrition had predictable consequences in the form of a cholera epidemic. Three hundred and fifty people had been admitted to hospital already, the numbers increasing exponentially.

On 15 April, something hopeful happened at last, when Gandhi and Jinnah issued a joint proclamation against violence. It was not a sign of any softening in their personal relationship. The two men had not seen each other for two and a half years, and did not even meet to discuss their joint declaration. Mountbatten had asked Jinnah to appeal for a truce in the communal disturbances in conjunction with Congress.[58] Jinnah had agreed, but only on the grounds that the 'unknown nobody' of a Congress President, J.B. Kripalani, should not be invited to sign.[59] Gandhi agreed to sign it in Kripalani's place, telling Mountbatten that it was a great political step and that he was pleased to have given him the idea in the first place. 'Although I have absolutely no recollection of Mr Gandhi making any such suggestion,' Mountbatten noted, 'I felt it would be politic not to point this out. For although I believed it to have been my own idea I am only too delighted that he should take the credit.' He was not, however, convinced by Gandhi's motives. At the same meeting, Gandhi asked Mountbatten to hand over full control of unpartitioned India to the interim government. Mountbatten answered that he could not, for it would mean handing over the reins to Congress and ignoring the Muslim League, which would precipitate civil war. Gandhi replied with a smile that, by signing the declaration, Jinnah had forsworn violence in perpetuity: he could not start a civil war now, even if he wanted to. Mountbatten was deeply shocked. It seemed to him that Gandhi was proposing to take advantage of Jinnah's good intentions to crush Muslim dissent. 'I find it hard to believe that I correctly understood Mr Gandhi', he wrote.[60]

Whatever its motives, the joint declaration was a significant diplomatic achievement. But it proved only that Jinnah had as little control over Muslim India as Gandhi had over the Hindus. Communal violence continued across the entire subcontinent, increasing in Delhi, Calcutta, Bombay, Peshawar and Cawnpore. Within days of the proclamation, newspapers were reporting that the North-West Frontier Province had descended into chaos, with widespread arson attacks and brutal violence against the Hindu minority. The situation became so awful that Mountbatten was obliged to take action. He did so, as usual, by calling a meeting in Delhi. Mountbatten, Nehru and Sir Olaf Caroe, Governor of the North-West Frontier Province, congregated at the Viceroy's House on 18 April. Khan Abdul Jabbar Khan, Prime Minister of the North-West Frontier Province, was summoned away from his erupting province and flown by RAF special aircraft from Peshawar to join in. It was agreed that all non-violent political prisoners in NWFP jails would be released, which seemed like a step forward; but most of the 5000 prisoners refused to leave their prisons.[61]

The North-West Frontier was far from the only problem on the Viceroy's plate. Mountbatten went straight from that meeting into another with the Sikh leaders Tara, Kartar and Baldev Singh, who demanded partition of the Punjab, and hinted that they aimed at an independent state or province of their own. Khalistan, or 'Sikhistan' as it was nicknamed, was to include Simla and perhaps even Lahore.[62] 'Any hopes that I still entertained of being able to avoid the partition of the Punjab if Pakistan is forced on us were shattered at this meeting,' Mountbatten reported to London; 'all three Sikhs made it quite clear that they would fight to the last man if put under Muslim domination.'[63]

On 24 April, Mountbatten had another meeting with Patel. It was to prove one of his trickiest. 'Since you have come out here,' Patel accused him, 'things have got much worse. There is a civil war on and you are doing nothing to stop it. You won't govern yourself and you won't let the Central Government govern. You cannot escape responsibility for this bloodshed.'[64] Patel demanded that he turn over full authority to the government to allow it to fight what he considered to be the insurgents: Muslim League armies in the Punjab, the North-West Frontier and Assam.

'Like you and Stafford, both Dickie and I like Vallabhai [sic] Patel very much indeed', wrote Edwina to Isobel Cripps, 'although we quite realise the dominant attitude he adopts and his rather dictatorial manner. He and Dickie, however, are getting on very well indeed and when he behaves like a bit of a gangster, Dickie, as you well [sic] imagine, does not lag behind!'[65] Patel had described one of Mountbatten's actions in a written minute as 'pointless and inappropriate', sparking a massive argument between the two men. Mountbatten demanded that he tear the minute up and withdraw it; Patel refused, and Mountbatten said he would proceed directly to Nehru, resign the viceroyalty, and fly home immediately unless Patel left the government instead. 'He questioned whether I would throw up the viceroyalty after only a month in the job,' he remembered. 'I replied that he evidently did not know me. I could be tougher than him and unless he withdrew his minute then and there I would send for his Prime Minister and announce my resignation to him.' To Mountbatten's immense satisfaction, Patel gave in.[66]

By the end of April, Mountbatten's situation seemed bleak. His relationships with Gandhi, Jinnah and Patel were all in troublesome states; the princes presented a range of awkward grievances that he had not yet even begun to address; the Sikhs were threatening civil war; and violence continued to flare up across the country. A malaise began to spread among the Viceroy's staff. Alan Campbell-Johnson confided his misgivings to the Chief of Staff, Lord Ismay. Ismay was a good deal older than Campbell-Johnson, and had spent much more time in sticky diplomatic corners. He shrugged off Campbell-Johnson's concerns, saying, 'I like working for lucky men.'[67] Campbell-Johnson cheered up immediately. Mountbatten was nothing if not lucky.

That luck came to his aid almost immediately. On 28 April, Dickie and Edwina flew to Peshawar, an ancient Pathan town near the border with Afghanistan in the North-West Frontier Province. Like many frontiers, the north-west was a wild and tribal place. Muslim Leaguers wore green; Congress-aligned unionists (also mostly Muslim) wore red. Friction between the two was common, and often violent. This was the territory of the Pir of Manki Sharif, a fearsome Islamic fundamentalist nicknamed the 'Manki Mullah'. Still only in his mid-twenties, the Manki Mullah excited the interest of the press with his burning eyes and flowing black beard, preached an extreme interpretation of sharia law, and commanded a following of some 200,000 devotees.[68] Only a month before, on 28 March, the Manki Mullah had been captured in the Muslim League office in Peshawar. Since then he had languished in prison, to the enormous benefit of his reputation; and his Greenshirts, enraged, had been rioting. The Redshirts had rioted back, and the city had been placed under stringent curfews while the police struggled to cope.

Fearing the worst, Caroe and Jabbar Khan had persuaded the Redshirts not to demonstrate during Mountbatten's visit, and had effectively cordoned off the centre of Peshawar. As a result, on the morning of the Viceroy's arrival, at least 50,000 Greenshirts assembled on the outskirts of the town at Cunningham Park, shouting political slogans and stamping their feet.[69]

The scene was too great a temptation for Mountbatten's brazen self-confidence. He insisted on driving right to the centre of Cunningham Park, where he seized Edwina's hand and climbed gamely to the top of an embankment. The sight of an enormous sea of coloured turbans and green flags gave the Mountbattens temporary pause. For the first time, they were facing a hostile crowd. It was a very large one, and potentially deadly – Caroe later estimated that there would have been between 20,000 and 40,000 rifles in the crowd, many of which were being jabbed threateningly into the air.[70]

Edwina quickly came to her senses, and simply smiled and waved. Dickie did likewise and, to the great surprise of everyone except himself, did not get shot. Instead, the crowd gave him a ten-minute ovation, and some even chorused a previously unimaginable phrase: 'Viceroy *zindabad*!' ('Long live the Viceroy!').[71] In all probability, the warmth of the reception had little to do with Dickie's charm, and much more to do with the fact that he had chosen that day to wear a military uniform of the same Islamic green hue as the flags, banners and shirts of the Muslim League that fluttered in the breeze for miles across the park.[72] His decision may have been sartorial rather than political, but the effect was not lessened. Sometimes, Lord Mountbatten's love of dressing up paid off.

A BARREL OF GUNPOWDER

WHEN THE MOUNTBATTENS WENT ON FROM THEIR JOYFUL reception at Peshawar up to the tribal territories, it was possible to believe that their attempts to woo the Muslims of India were going well. The day after Peshawar, they flew to the Khyber Pass, that famous corridor between the dangerous peaks of the Hindu Kush through which Alexander, Timur and Babur had marched on India, now guarded by Muslim Afridi tribesmen who were generally reckoned to be among the ablest fighting forces in the world. Seated on fine carpets in the dappled shade of tamarisk trees, the elders greeted Mountbatten in Pashtun and invited him to join their *loya jirga*, or tribal council. They told him that, when the British left, they wanted control of the Khyber Pass. He replied that it would be up to the tribes to negotiate with the new authorities, which seemed to satisfy them, though they did mention that they might prefer to negotiate with Afghanistan than with a Congress-run India.

The elders proceeded to hold forth against Nehru. Mountbatten avoided responding and instead told a nice story about his days in the Navy and a brave ship called HMS *Afridi* that had fought valiantly in the North Sea. This went down well, and the Afridis presented him with a rifle. Edwina got a pair of slippers. According to *The Times*, 'The Jirga dispersed in high good humour.'[1]

Back in Delhi, things did not seem so agreeable after Mountbatten returned to begin what his political adviser, Sir Conrad Corfield, referred to as his 'Dutch auction' of British India.[2] Mountbatten asked Sir Frederick Burrows, Governor of Bengal, whether he still felt that he was sitting on a barrel of gunpowder. 'Good Lord no,' replied Burrows, 'we got off that a long time ago and are now sitting on a complete magazine which is going to blow up at any time.'[3] As if to prove the point, Jinnah made a statement on 30 April demanding that Pakistan consist of all the Muslim-majority provinces: Sind, the Punjab, the North-West Frontier Province and Baluchistan in the west, and Bengal and Assam in the east. Such a Pakistan would certainly have included Calcutta, for though that city's population was mainly Hindu it was crucial to the economy of the surrounding Muslim-majority lands of east Bengal. It could have included the historically Muslim cultural and business centres of Delhi, Lucknow, Aligarh, Agra and Cawnpore.[4] Anything less, particularly any sub-partition of Bengal or the Punjab, would result in a 'truncated or mutilated, moth-eaten Pakistan', Jinnah told the press.[5] Visitors to Jinnah's elegant Delhi villa had their attention drawn to a silver map of India he had put up on his mantelpiece, with his claims for Pakistan picked out in vivid green.[6] But Bengal and the Punjab were hotly disputed. Each had large areas of non-Muslim-majority populations, and, owing to centuries of intermingling, more areas yet where there was no clear majority at all.

The obvious answer was to divide the provinces up. But partitioning Bengal and the Punjab was not an option that readily appealed to anyone. Bengal had been split in two, most contentiously, by the Viceroy Lord Curzon back in 1905, and that had gone so badly that the King had revoked it at the Delhi Durbar in 1911. When Mountbatten raised the possibility of partitioning the provinces with Jinnah, the latter blanched, and argued that those provinces had strong internal identities: that Hindus identified themselves more strongly as Bengalis or Punjabis than as Hindus or Congress supporters, and that the integrity of their provinces ought be preserved above all. But Mountbatten pointed out that such arguments would also apply to India as a whole, and if they were accepted there could be no Pakistan. 'I am afraid I drove the old gentleman quite mad,' reported Mountbatten jovially, 'because whichever way his argument went I always pursued it to a stage beyond which he did not wish it to go.'[7]

While her husband returned to Delhi, Lady Mountbatten extended her tour for two days. At the suggestion of Vallabhbhai Patel, she had decided to travel around the hostile region on her own.[8] On 30 April she was in Rawalpindi, and from there she visited the Wah Relief Camp for victims of recent rioting. Photographs in the press showed her crouching down to talk face to face with refugee women, establishing an informality that was a departure from the style of previous vicereines.[9] Even to Edwina, who had served in London during the war, the scene at Wah was shocking – 'like the Blitz at its worst', she wrote.[10] The wards were filled with dust and bereft of drinking water. Very few of the beds had sheets. Visitors and children were allowed in and out of the infectious diseases wards freely: as a result, measles had spread everywhere, including the maternity ward, and both dysentery and pneumonia were rife. Most upsetting of all, though, were the injuries which had been inflicted by human hands. People had been carried in from the villages with horrific burns. 'They seem to be very fond of tying whole families together, pouring oil on them and then lighting them as a single torch,' Lord Mountbatten remarked.[11] Among the survivors were young children whose hands had been hacked off.[12]

From Wah, Edwina flew to the towns of Dera Ismael Khan and Tank, where she spent five hours walking in the burning heat among heaps of rubble left by communal riots. She asked people directly what they needed, and when the answer came – clothing – she took the matter to local officials, and was able to promise that some would be provided within a few days. The next day, she flew to Amritsar to visit more areas devastated by rioting. In the afternoon, Jawahar's cousin, Rameshwari Nehru, showed her around similar locations in Lahore.[13] On 2 May she was supposed to fly to Multan for more of the same, but a dust storm prevented the aircraft from landing. With the greatest difficulty, her aides persuaded her that she would have to return to Delhi.[14] She had nonetheless visited nine hospitals, seven refugee centres, and four riot areas. She had been seen to speak to Hindu, Sikh and Muslim victims alike.

This first tour made a great impact on Edwina herself as well as on the Indian public – and on Jawaharlal Nehru who, as a result of her efforts, began to view her with an 'undying admiration', according to his friend Marie Seton.[15] After it, she made a serious effort to involve herself in improving the public health situation. She corresponded with high officials who, by etiquette if not by inclination, were unable to ignore her, and forwarded notes to Dickie with advice for the setting up of health clinics in refugee camps. It was obvious from the tone of her letters that she was not content to observe events, but meant to direct them. She questioned the government's policy on refugees, and recommended a range of practical interventions. She suggested setting up a full-time clinic in each refugee centre. Within two weeks, it was done.[16]

Having been prevented from visiting Multan on the first trip, Edwina returned a fortnight later. She visited a camp of 2000 refugees in the middle of the city, and met separate delegations of Hindu and Muslim women to assure them that her husband was doing everything he could to help them. Whether he was or not, Lady Mountbatten's attention was fully engaged. During the visit, she noticed that the civil hospital needed lamps for its operating theatre. On her return to Delhi, she wrote to the brigadier in charge of the medical directorate in New Delhi and, after a struggle, obtained one.[17]

The deprivation Edwina saw on her tours, and its contrast with her cosseted life in Delhi, shamed her deeply. Previous vicereines had done their share of opening hospitals and presenting cups to schoolchildren; but any small discomfort could be assuaged by the many and fabulous luxuries of the Viceroy's House. 'Lady Mountbatten remarked to me that she always suspected, and now knew, just how easy it is to get engulfed in this labyrinthine palace and live self-contained and cut off from the outside world,' Alan Campbell-Johnson had recorded after only two days in India.[18] Yet Edwina was unwilling to abandon her charity at the forbidding iron gates. Delhi was on strict food rationing by the spring of 1947, but those in official circles had rarely felt the gnaw of hunger until she arrived.[19] So strict were her prescriptions that many of the officials who dwelt in the house attempted to secure luncheon and dinner invitations elsewhere every day.

Edwina also insisted on rewording the court circular so that she and the Viceroy 'received' every guest; formerly, they had 'received' top dignitaries, 'seen' middling ones, and 'interviewed' the minor sort. People were no longer 'honoured' with the viceregal invitation or presence, but simply 'invited', their parties 'attended'. 'In the changed circumstances in India when dealing so largely with Indians this means a very great deal,' Edwina wrote to Lady Reading, 'and I have been amazed at the number of very favourable comments which have been made on this decision. After all, it is surely example and behaviour which keeps up the prestige of the Crown and one's country – not mere words.'[20] Under Edwina's new rules, at least half of the guests at any of their frequent entertainments were Indian. 'It makes me absolutely sick to see this house full of dirty Indians,' remarked one English lady to another within earshot of the Mountbattens' daughter, Pamela. The Viceroy was so horrified that he asked the provincial governors to send anyone expressing such sentiments back to Britain.[21]

May began, and with it came the first crippling outbreak of the inevitable 'Delhi belly', which felled both Mountbatten and Ismay. It did nothing for the Viceroy's mood. As he admitted to Edwina, it had become depressingly apparent to him that there was no chance of transferring power to a united India.[22] 'The more I look at the problem in India the more I realise that all this partition business is sheer madness and is going to reduce the economic efficiency of the whole country immeasurably,' he reported to London. 'No-one would ever induce me to agree to it were it not for this fantastic communal madness that has seized everybody and leaves no other course open.' He was beginning to suspect that both sides were deliberately avoiding a settlement. 'The most we can hope to do, as I have said before, is to put the responsibility for any of these mad decisions fairly and squarely on the Indian shoulders in the eyes of the world, for one day they will bitterly regret the decision they are about to make.'[23]

On 2 May, he sent his draft plan back to London for the government's consideration. Two days later, the *Hindustan Times*, a newspaper edited by Gandhi's son Devadas and owned by his patron, G.D. Birla, launched the first Congress attack on

Mountbatten. 'For the first time since Mountbatten assumed the Viceroyalty the feeling that he may not be playing fair has come among the Congressmen and Sikh leaders', it read.[24] Gandhi told Mountbatten that, since signing the joint declaration, Jinnah would no longer be able to resort to violence and would have to accept whatever plan was put before him. Mountbatten had had time to come up with a response to this familiar ruse. 'I told him Jinnah signed in good faith when he thought I was going to give a fair decision and that I did not for one moment suppose the Muslims would not immediately go to war if I attempted to betray them in this manner,' he remembered.[25] But Gandhi was not persuaded. 'The communal feuds you see here are, in my opinion, partly due to the presence of the British,' he told a Reuters correspondent. 'If the British were not here, we would still go through the fire no doubt, but that fire would purify us.'[26]

'He knows quite well that the things he may suggest are difficult,' explained one of Gandhi's followers, Agatha Harrison, to Edwina. 'My long and close touch with this man convinces me that *only sustained contact will yield any result* . . . I have seen Mr Gandhi used spasmodically, and then – because people find him baffling – they give up and feel what he suggests for action is impossible.'[27] The Viceroy was beginning to feel very much baffled, and increasingly disposed to give up. It was left to Edwina to charm the Mahatma, which she did; and he charmed her back. His 'dear sister', as he called her, would claim for the rest of her life that Gandhi was the most wonderful man she had ever met. From this point on, cordial relations between the Viceroy's House and Gandhi were almost exclusively maintained by Edwina, who regularly visited Gandhi's hut in the insalubrious Bhangi Colony, home to many of Delhi's Untouchables. Dickie never went.

Mountbatten deliberately allowed a meeting with Gandhi to run late on 2 May, for he had an eye on his next interviewee: Mohammad Ali Jinnah. He was convinced that progress might be made if these two estranged leaders could be induced to speak. 'I managed to be a bit unpunctual,' he remembered, 'and their interviews overlapped.'

The seating in the Viceroy's study consisted of large, imposing

leather armchairs, too heavy to move. Gandhi and Jinnah each settled into one as far away from the other man as possible. They
proceeded to speak in hushed mutters, with Mountbatten trotting
back and forth as an interlocutor. If either had hoped to avoid speaking directly to his rival, he would not escape so easily. Mountbatten
took advantage of the quiet to put it to them that they should
meet again at Jinnah's house. There was no excuse not to agree, and
so they did.[28] That evening, Gandhi came close to endorsing
Mountbatten publicly at his prayer meeting. 'We have no right to
question the Viceroy's honesty until he betrays our trust,' Gandhi
concluded. It was 'until', rather than 'unless', but still close enough
to encouragement to yield press enthusiasm the next day.[29] The
public gap between Mahatma and Mountbatten had been closed.
Edwina's friendship with Gandhi would ensure that it stayed closed
forever after.

As they had agreed, Gandhi and Jinnah met on 6 May. The meeting went on for three hours, and achieved nothing much. It was
established, again, that the two disagreed over partition, and agreed
that violence should cease. It would soon be established again, too,
that neither man's call for such a cessation would be heard.

That same day, the Mountbattens made the long journey up to the
hill station of Simla, 7200 feet up in the Himalayan foothills. The
British had adopted Simla in 1832, when the Governor General
started coming every summer for its fresh Alpine climate, days away
from the heat, humidity and filth of Calcutta. It became the official
summer capital of India. Here, among thick forests of deodar trees,
meadows blossoming with wild flowers and spectacular views to
the snow-capped high Himalayas, the British built a fantastical
vision of home. Soon the crags were dotted with precariously situated Scottish baronial castles and half-timbered Tudor cottages. 'It
looks like a place of which a child might dream after seeing a pan-
tomime', wrote the Viceroy, Lord Dufferin, in 1885. 'That the capital
of the Indian empire should thus be hanging on by its eyelids to the
side of a hill is too absurd.' He was smitten.[30]

The British continued to come to Simla, sometimes for eight
months of each year, with the European ladies and gentlemen carried

up in the local jhampan sedan chairs. They were followed by hundreds of coolies, who had been press-ganged from their surrounding farms into the service of Her Majesty's Government, lugging dispatch-boxes, carefully packed crockery, musical instruments, trunks full of theatrical costumes for amateur dramatics at the Gaiety Theatre, crates of tea and dried provisions, faithful spaniels in travelling-boxes, rolled-up rugs, aspidistras, card tables, favourite armchairs, baskets of linen, and tons upon tons of files; all the paraphernalia of the raj literally borne on the shoulders of one long caravan of miserable, sweating Indian peasants. Eventually, in 1891, a narrow-gauge railway was opened, weaving in and out of 103 tunnels up from the plains at Kalka – a journey which still took at least six hours. The British never questioned whether all this was worth it. Gandhi may have criticized the administration's annual repair to Simla for being 'government working from the 500th floor', but that was exactly the point.[31]

Mountbatten had originally planned to invite Gandhi, Jinnah, Nehru, Liaquat, Patel and the Nawab of Bhopal to Simla for an informal weekend.[32] After it became apparent that the Sikhs were a pressing concern, and the Mahatma started to get on Mountbatten's nerves, the list changed to exclude Gandhi and include Baldev Singh.[33] It was eventually decided that Simla had 'unfortunate associations' – Lord Wavell's attempt to stage a conference there had ended in disappointment.[34] But the plan did not expire. When Krishna Menon suggested that Dickie take Nehru away for a couple of days to Kashmir, Mountbatten approved of the idea, though not the location. He thought, rightly, that such a trip would cause problems with the Maharaja of Kashmir, who had welcomed Nehru the year before by arresting him as soon as he set foot in the state. To Menon's disappointment, he settled on Simla again.[35]

Nehru had endured a viceroy's hospitality in Simla before. Two years previously, shortly after being released from a long imprisonment, he had stayed at a government-owned house called Armsdell. 'Red-liveried *chaprasis* are in evidence, and both the soap and the notepaper are embossed "Viceregal Lodge"!' he had written to his daughter, Indira. 'I find it quite impossible to use this Viceregal notepaper, though I have succumbed to the soap. Rather odd this atmosphere for me. I do not feel too happy about it.'[36] The contrast two years later was profound. Jawahar joined Dickie and Edwina for a cosy house-party in the morose splendour of the Viceroy's Lodge, perched atop the high peak at the far end of Simla's razorback ridge. 'House hideous', wrote Edwina with characteristic brevity. 'Bogus English Baronial, Hollywood's idea of Viceregal Lodge.'[37]

Initially, Nehru was tense. He did not enjoy bogus baronial, nor the sight of jhampan coolies, finding the idea of a poor man carrying a rich one distasteful. Yet soon he relaxed when the Mountbattens took him for tea at the Viceroy's Retreat. This charming, secluded cottage, hidden among dense forests near the village of Mashobra, was about half an hour's drive from Simla along precipitous roads. It was set among some of the most captivating scenery in the whole of India. Lush gorges plunged dramatically down thousands of feet to glittering sapphire tributaries of the mighty Sutlej River, and colossal mountains rose up thousands of feet behind them. Wild cacti and delicate orchids sprouted forth from the roots of conifers; families of monkeys swung through the pines and picked keenly at strawberry bushes; above the treetops, eagles circled.

Jawahar walked with Dickie and Edwina around the orchard terraces and up mountain paths, which wound up the hill from which Lord Kitchener's former mansion, Wildflower Hall, could be glimpsed atop the next peak.[38] Though once a flamboyant youth, Nehru had become a man of simpler tastes. Yet there were two pleasures he could never resist: the vitality of mountain scenery, and the company of an interesting woman. At Mashobra, he had both. Soon he was happily teaching Dickie and Edwina to walk backwards up slopes to rest their muscles; the Mountbattens, too, 'fell in love with the place,' noted Campbell-Johnson, 'and are quite determined to come back again.'[39]

There was plenty of hard work to be done, but the atmosphere remained convivial. Nehru had brought his daughter, Indira, and the Mountbattens one of theirs, Pamela. Pamela opened a door and found the acting Prime Minister standing on his head, a daily yoga ritual. She was taken aback when he cheerfully carried on a conversation from that position.[40] Even the steady stream of depressing telegrams from 500 floors below could not dampen the mood. News of an Indian Mutiny Day in Bengal, and threats of an accompanying 'holocaust', came to nothing. For once, that province was quiet, even after Gandhi used a prayer meeting in Calcutta to blame Muslims for its partition.[41] There were riots in Amritsar and Hyderabad, but these places were far away, and seemed like another world entirely. Nehru was at his most cooperative, expressing the hope that Mountbatten might stay on after the transfer of power as Governor General of both India and Pakistan. When it came to the drawing of the new borders, he agreed with Mountbatten that the British ought to take no responsibility. 'The less H.M.G. did in this direction the better for all concerned,' Nehru was reported as saying. He was equally amenable to another pressing aspect of Mountbatten's personal concerns. 'Pandit Nehru stressed that the psychological effect of power being transferred earlier than 1948 would be an invaluable factor in the long-term view of Indo-British relationship.'[42]

After two days, Mountbatten received the exciting news he had been awaiting. Back in London, the cabinet had authorized his plan for the transfer of power. Only six weeks into his viceroyalty, it seemed that he had already solved the insoluble problem. Immediately he issued a statement saying that he was ready to present the Indian leaders with the plan, and invited Nehru, Jinnah, Patel, Liaquat and Baldev Singh to attend a meeting at the Viceroy's House in Delhi on 17 May at 10.30 a.m.[43]

So well had things been going with Jawahar that, on a whim, Dickie broke protocol and ignored the advice of his staff to show his new chum a copy of the secret plan in the study after dinner that very night. But when Jawahar read through the top secret papers his disposition turned from affable to shocked, and from shocked to furious. At two o'clock the next morning he stormed into Krishna Menon's bedroom. The draft proposals, he wrote to Dickie that night, 'produced a devastating effect upon me.' They presented, he said, 'a picture of fragmentation and conflict and disorder, and, unhappily also, of a worsening of relations between India and Britain.'[44]

The plan from which Nehru recoiled was known as 'Plan Balkan', a name hardly more inspiring than 'Operation Madhouse', and indeed approximately synonymous.[45] Having for centuries enforced rule by unelected men from London, the British government had recently developed an unprecedented enthusiasm for the will of the people – preferably, for the will of as many people as possible. There would be an India, there would be a Pakistan, and each province could choose which one to join. But the principle of self-determination would be extended further yet. Should Bengal or the Punjab be divided in their wishes, each state could be split; or it could choose to become an independent nation. Should the troublesome North-West Frontier Province wish to become independent, it could do so too. As for the 565 princely states, each of those could also determine its own future in or out of the two dominions, 'presumably as feudatories or allies of Britain', Nehru commented sharply.[46] What Nehru had foreseen was the prospect of Balkanization, but on the colossal scale of the subcontinent: the proliferation of dozens, perhaps even hundreds, of small and potentially antagonistic nation-states. Too small to survive alone, these would inevitably end up serving the interests of peripheral giants: not just Britain, but the United States, Russia, China, and Afghanistan. It would stir up civil conflict, undermine the central authority, and split the army, police and services.[47]

Jawahar was 'white with rage', Dickie remembered. 'You know, he used to get these tantrums, having been in prison. He took a long while to control himself.'[48] Dickie was upset, but quickly realized that the situation might have been worse yet. Had his plan been rejected publicly a week later by Nehru, he told his staff, 'Dickie Mountbatten would have been finished and could have packed his bag. We would have looked complete fools with the Government at home, having led them up the garden to believe that Nehru would accept the Plan.'[49] He immediately cancelled the announcement he had been due to make that morning, and delayed the meeting with the leaders from 17 May to 2 June – prompting the press to report incorrectly that this was either because of the British parliamentary recess, or because Gandhi had rejected Pakistan. High up in the Himalayan foothills, Mountbatten, Nehru, the Reforms Commissioner V.P. Menon, and the Governor of the Punjab, Evan Jenkins, attempted to smooth the plan into an acceptable shape.

Suddenly, even the helpful psychological effect of an early transfer of power had dissipated: 'The Viceroy said that Pandit Nehru had also stressed to him that the present proposed timetable was too much of a rush.'[50] In just three hours, Menon and Nehru drew up a new plan, with the consent but not the direct involvement of Mountbatten. Telephone calls were made to Congress potentates, and it was confirmed that the revised plan would be accepted.[51] Neither the Muslim League, the princes, nor any other body in India would be given the chance to review the plan before its announcement.[52]

On 14 May, Mountbatten descended from Simla in his open-top Buick, describing himself as 'feeling fighting fit'. As for his relations with Nehru, they had apparently been improved, rather than damaged, by the trouble in the hills. 'We have made real friends with him and whatever else happens I feel this friendship is sincere and will last.'[53]

Mountbatten's optimism was not shared by leaders back in London, who felt they had indeed been 'led up the garden' and were seriously considering having the Viceroy supplanted. Patience with faraway India was at a low ebb, for the domestic situation was in turmoil. On 8 May, the Chancellor had announced that Britain would freeze further payments on all its war debts until the creditors agreed to reductions. The exchequer was more than £3 billion in the red, thanks to the war: it owed Egypt £450 million, Ireland £250 million, Australia and New Zealand £200 million each, and further enormous sums to Argentina, Norway and Brazil. But the largest creditor of all, with £1250 million owed, was India.

Attlee drafted, but did not send, a stern telegram to Mountbatten on 13 May. He pointed out that the cabinet had been under the impression that Nehru would definitely accept Mountbatten's plan, and that consequently they had made no substantial alterations to it. Any mistakes in it were Mountbatten's, not theirs.[54] The following day, Attlee's private secretary wrote him a note about 'the plan . . . for a Minister to go out to India to settle matters there with full powers and the minimum of reference home'. The secretary strongly recommended that Attlee himself went to Delhi: 'This gesture would, I feel, fire the imagination of the world.'[55] But Attlee recoiled from such a prospect, and no other minister could be found: they were all too ill, too busy or too inexperienced. In the end, Mountbatten was summoned back to London to explain himself.

It was a reprimand, and Mountbatten took it very badly. Without hesitation, he threatened to resign. Edwina, together with V.P. Menon, calmed him down.[56] It was Edwina, too, Menon's daughter remembered, who extracted a concession from Nehru to offset the revisions to the plan. She persuaded him that India should accept an initial phase of dominion status.[57] This was no mean feat. Dominion status had been seen as an unacceptable halfway house by Congress since its declaration of 'purna swaraj' (complete self-rule) in 1930, and by Nehru, who had been behind that declaration, for longer still. It is a clear demonstration of Edwina's extraordinary intimacy with Jawaharlal Nehru and her influence over policy. Menon's daughter was not the only one to express such a view. 'I have often wondered how Jawaharlal was won over by Lord Mountbatten', wrote Nehru's close friend Abul Kalam Azad, the highest-ranking Muslim in Congress. 'Jawaharlal is a man of principle, but he is also impulsive and amenable to personal influence . . . perhaps even greater was the influence of Lady Mountbatten.'[58] Where several viceroys and Sir Stafford Cripps had failed, Edwina Mountbatten succeeded – saving her husband's political career as well as the entire process of the transfer of power.

It was announced that Mountbatten would be returning to London for an unscheduled visit, the press apparently swallowing the cover story that the government had decided it must have 'final discussions' with him 'in view of the importance of these arrangements'.[59] On 18 May, the Mountbattens and V.P. Menon left for London by air. They emerged drawn and unsmiling at Northolt Airfield the following afternoon. 'He has met the Indian leaders and heard their views, but fires still rage in Lahore, and disorders are at their height in the Punjab!' exclaimed the Pathé News announcer, as if pitching a new adventure comic. 'Only twelve months now remain in which to complete the transfer of power to the Indians!'[60]

Mountbatten met with the opposition, in the forms of Churchill, Anthony Eden, John Anderson and Lord Salisbury, and reassured them off the record that it might be worth their while to take up

Nehru's concession. If they were prepared to offer India a very early transfer of power, they could expect it to accept dominion status rather than full independence.[61] The next day, Churchill wrote to Attlee that 'if those terms are made good, so that there is an effective acceptance of dominion status for the several parts of a divided India, the Conservative Party will agree to facilitate the passage of this session of the legislation necessary to confer dominion status upon such several parts of India.'[62] There was no ambiguity in his words. It was the phase of dominion status, as secured by Edwina, that persuaded him to support the bill.

Mountbatten himself was deeply passionate about the idea of the Commonwealth, and retaining the Indian territories within it was a preoccupation of his and the opposition's, not the government's. 'It is the definite objective of His Majesty's Government to obtain a unitary Government for British India and the Indian States, if possible within the British Commonwealth', Attlee had written in his commission to Mountbatten back in February.[63] That last clause had been added at the specific request of Dickie himself.[64] Mountbatten supported it out of a sense that international brotherhood was a splendid thing for world peace and understanding. The opposition's reason was not dissimilar, though with a heavier emphasis on its advantages for Britain. As Leopold Amery wrote to Churchill shortly afterwards, 'we can only hope that, somehow or other, the Britannic orbit will remain a reality in this parlous world even if, to assume the worst, Indian politicians are unwise enough to wish to break the formal link.'[65] On the government side, the new India Secretary Lord Listowel, who had replaced Pethick-Lawrence just weeks before, was in strong accord with the Conservative view.

Mountbatten saw Churchill again on 22 May, finding him still in his bed – a sight well-known to the old man's colleagues. Churchill habitually organized breakfast meetings over a cigar and a weak whisky and soda, often attended by his malodorous poodle, Rufus, and his budgerigar, Toby, the latter perching on a square sponge atop the Churchillian pate.[66] On this occasion, Mountbatten remembered that Churchill was 'extremely pleasant' to him. 'Winston Churchill said he wished to congratulate the Government on their perspicacity in appointing someone of my intelligence,' he told historians Larry Collins and Dominique Lapierre in the 1970s. 'I do want that quoted.' In a letter written to Attlee immediately after the meeting in question Churchill implied that, in fact, his feelings about Mountbatten were rather more ambivalent, and that he would like his Conservative colleagues to be allowed to question him further in secret.[67] It is no easy feat to maintain one's focus while being scolded by a man with a budgerigar on his head, and perhaps Mountbatten's confusion is attributable to such a distraction. Certainly Mountbatten seemed 'very anxious' about the old man's attitude when he spoke to Amery later that week. 'Dominion status has done something to ease the position with Winston, but he still fears some explosion', Amery noted.[68] All accounts agree that Churchill gave Mountbatten a message to deliver to Jinnah. 'This is a matter of life and death for Pakistan, if you do not accept this offer with both hands,' the Conservative leader advised the Muslim. Mountbatten emphasized to his staff that Churchill's opinion was the only one in the world likely to sway Jinnah.[69]

The signs of cooperation from the Muslim League were mixed. Jinnah used Mountbatten's absence to voice a demand for a 1000-mile corridor through the Indian Union to connect East and West Pakistan – something which the British had already dismissed, and Nehru immediately denounced as 'completely unrealistic'.[70] On the other hand, the Jinnah made an uncharacteristically generous announcement about the Viceroy. 'Lord Mountbatten's efforts will secure full justice to the 100 millions of Mussalmans,' he wrote. 'I am not in the habit of flattering anyone, but I must say that throughout our discussions and examination of the various points, I was impressed by the high sense of integrity, fairplay and impartiality on his part and, therefore, I feel that Lord Mountbatten will succeed in his great mission.'[71]

Beyond the main parties, signs continued that the communal interests were gearing up to welcome Mountbatten back. A Hindu fundamentalist party, the All-India Dharma Sangh, issued a summons to its followers. Hindu holy men began to pour into New Delhi, opposing partition, cow slaughter, and the ban on Untouchability which the constituent assembly had passed on 29 April. At the same time, fundamentalist Muslims poured in from the

United Provinces and the Punjab. Bands of Khaksars, a militant group known as the 'Servants of the Dust', were seen to be gathering in the city and wearing fascist-style uniforms; large numbers were arrested, and had their weapons confiscated, but still more came.[72]

The Mountbattens left Northolt airfield on the morning of 29 May. Two days later they were in Delhi, Dickie clutching the new version of his plan, as approved by the British cabinet; Edwina bearing placatory gifts for Fatima Jinnah.[73] The plan had been sold to the British government. Now, it had to be sold to the Indians.

CHAPTER 12

LIGHTNING SPEED IS
MUCH TOO SLOW

THE PLAN HAD BEEN APPROVED; THE ACTS DRAFTED;
Mountbatten returned to Delhi, chastened but still hopeful. 'We are
just starting our fateful week with the temperature already over 112°
and the whole scene very explosive but we hope for the best', wrote
Edwina on 2 June.[1] 'I find myself all alone,' said Gandhi. 'Even the
Sardar [Patel] and Jawaharlal think my reading of the situation is
wrong and peace is sure to return if partition is agreed upon . . . the
future of independence gained at this price is going to be dark.'[2]

That morning, the future leaders of India and Pakistan were summoned to the Viceroy's study for a two-hour briefing on the new
plan. Sitting around the table with him were Nehru, Vallabhbhai
Patel and J.B. Kripalani for Congress, Jinnah, Liaquat and Abdur
Rab Nishtar for the League, and Baldev Singh for the Sikhs. 'I got
the feeling that the less the leaders talked, the less the chance of friction and perhaps the ultimate breakdown of the meeting,' noted
Mountbatten, and consequently filibustered for as long as possible.
His ploy was to declare upfront that he was not asking for the leaders' agreement to the plan – for he knew that it met no one's
demands. If they accepted that the plan was a solution in the interests of the country, that would be enough. He asked the leaders to let
him have their responses by midnight. Jinnah told Mountbatten he
would return at eleven o'clock after consulting his committee and,

sending the others off to read their copies of the plan, Mountbatten held him back 'to impress on him that there could not be any question of a "No" from the League.' After he left the room, Alan Campbell-Johnson picked up a scrap of paper that the Quaid-e-Azam had left behind him, covered in scribbles from the meeting. The words 'Governor General' were written in inverted commas and underlined in the middle of the page; around it was a collection of symbols. 'I am no psychologist,' admitted Campbell-Johnson, 'but I think I can detect the symbols of power and glory here.' In contemplating his success, Jinnah had drawn a collection of phallic shapes, all pointing proudly upwards.[3]

One troublesome icon having been dealt with, another showed up. Gandhi had spent the previous week railing against the new plan, and trying to revert to the Cabinet Mission plan of 1946 – which he had been instrumental in refusing. The Congress Working Committee was thoroughly annoyed with him, and Mountbatten too had had his fill of the Mahatma. 'He may be a saint but he seems also to be a disciple of Trotsky', the Viceroy wrote to London. 'Judge then of my astonished delight on finding him enter the room with his finger to his lips to indicate that it was his day of silence!' Mountbatten spent forty-five minutes explaining why the Cabinet Mission plan could not be enforced if any party was opposed to it, with Gandhi scribbling replies on the backs of old envelopes.[4]

At midnight, Jinnah returned to the Viceroy's House, ready to hurl another spanner into Mountbatten's fragile works. As the constitutional leader of the Muslim League, he said, it was not in his power to accept the plan tomorrow. However, he would do his best to ensure the council of the League would accept it, and would bring it up at their next meeting – in a week's time.

This was exactly the sort of manoeuvre guaranteed to make Congress back out, and Mountbatten knew it. He told Jinnah that he had only secured Congress acceptance on the basis that the Muslim League would accept simultaneously, but Jinnah would not budge. 'If that is your attitude,' Mountbatten told him, 'then the leaders of the Congress Party and the Sikhs will refuse final acceptance at the meeting in the morning; chaos will follow, and you will lose your Pakistan, probably for good.'

Jinnah shrugged. 'What must be, must be.'

'Mr Jinnah!' exclaimed Mountbatten. 'I do not intend to let you wreck all the work that has gone into this settlement. Since you will not accept for the Moslem League, I will speak for them myself.' He told Jinnah that, in the meeting, he would announce that he was satisfied with Jinnah's assurances, a hair-splitting legalistic move that would hopefully fool Congress into thinking Jinnah had accepted: 'and if your Council fails to ratify the agreement, you can place the blame on me.' When he mentioned Jinnah's assurances, he would look at Jinnah – and Jinnah should nod his head in agreement.

Mountbatten looked at Jinnah then. Silently, the Quaid-e-Azam nodded his head.[5]

The next morning, the leaders of all parties arrived back at the Viceroy's House, tired and acquiescent. Mountbatten was prepared to listen to their many reservations in private, but decided that none should be allowed to speak at the meeting in case they upset each other. And so, for the first time in history, no party raised an objection against a plan for independence. Immediately after they had not objected, Mountbatten theatrically raised and then thumped on to the table a plan for the transfer of power. In the first paragraph, this revealed the unexpected fact that power was to be transferred by 15 August 1947 – ten months in advance of the June 1948 deadline, and just ten weeks from the 3 June meeting itself.[6] The room's silence changed its quality from one of studied etiquette to one of shock. The Viceroy dismissed the bewildered leaders into the searing brightness of a Delhi day, and could reflect on his personal moment of glory. Both parties had been forced to compromise – Congress accepting partition, Jinnah more or less accepting what would probably be a moth-eaten Pakistan – but he, Mountbatten, had finally been able to set a date.[7]

Mountbatten left the leaders as little thinking time as possible between their acceptance of the plan and their distinctly untriumphant addresses to the nation on All-India Radio that afternoon. 'It is with no joy in my heart that I commend these proposals, though I have no doubt in my mind that this is the right course,' said Nehru, sadly. Jinnah, too, noted that 'We cannot say or feel that we are satisfied,' and finished on the slogan 'Pakistan zindabad' ('Long live Pakistan'), apparently misheard by some listeners as a exultant crow of 'Pakistan's in the bag!'[8] Mountbatten declared again that he would have preferred to preserve the unity of India. 'But there can be no question of coercing any large areas in which one community has a majority, to live against their will under a Government in which another community has a majority. And the only alternative to coercion is partition.'[9]

In London, the terms of the plan were announced in the House of Commons at half past three that afternoon. Leo Amery had promised Mountbatten he would write a letter to *The Times* 'to steady Conservative opinion here, in case Winston proved fractious', but even Winston was in a placatory mood.[10] 'I am sure that Dickie has done marvellously,' noted Harold Nicolson, who was present. 'But it is curious that we should regard as a hero the man who liquidates the Empire which other heroes such as Clive, Warren Hastings and Napier won for us. Very odd indeed.'[11] So it may have seemed, but Mountbatten was serving his country with as much loyalty, courage and determination as had those other heroes. Mountbatten turned a stagnating mess into perhaps the most successful retreat from empire in history – from the point of view of the imperialist nation, at least. If his conduct has provoked censure as well as acclaim, then perhaps that is the price any hero must pay; Clive, Hastings and Napier have.

The following day, 4 June, Mountbatten gave a bravura performance of the charisma that had allowed him to pull off this feat. At the press conference he had called to announce the plan, he was warm, witty and spectacular, disclosing the startling closeness of independence in answer to a question like a stage magician pulling a rabbit from a hat. Mountbatten had chosen 15 August 'out of the blue', he admitted – it was the second anniversary of VJ Day, but nothing more significant than that.[12]

Just before the Mountbattens had left England in March, Edwina had answered a relative's concerns briskly. 'Don't worry,' she had said. 'This is going to be a marvellous experience – and Dickie says we'll be back as soon as we can – and that means not long.'[13] By the end of May, Mountbatten had browbeaten the government into making it even less long than it might have been. Attlee had given

Mountbatten an exit-date of 1 June 1948. This was a tight schedule in any case, bearing in mind the complexity of Indian politics and the possible repercussions of the process. And yet, undaunted by the task before him, the last Viceroy took the bizarre and unilateral decision to speed independence up.

'When I got out to India I realized . . . that, although we in London had visualized the programme of transfer for June, 1948, to be moving at lightning speed, in India it was regarded as being much too slow,' Mountbatten would tell a meeting of the East India Association in London the following year. 'Everybody there was agreed on this point: the leaders, leading British officials, my staff advisers.'[14] This was manifestly untrue. After seeing the plan at Simla, even Nehru had told him he was going too fast.[15] Another Congress politician told him that the timetable would only have been workable if the British had announced a five-year date for their departure two or three years previously.[16] For the Muslim League, Liaquat stated that he did not believe under any circumstances, united or divided, India could stand on its own legs by June 1948.[17] Several of the princes had begged the British to stay. As for the British officials and Mountbatten's staff advisers, the archives show them to have been explicitly opposed to haste.[18] V.P. Menon had advised Mountbatten that 'The psychological effect of power having been transferred earlier than 1948 will be an invaluable factor in the long-term view of Indo-British relationship.'[19] But Menon made it clear that this would hold true only if there was a complete transfer of power to the whole of India of dominion status, followed by 'not less than four or five years' during which the parts of the country would draw up their constitutions. He envisaged a joint defence policy and a joint Governor General of India and Pakistan in this eventuality, which is very different from what actually happened. In fact, the only person who seemed to agree unreservedly with Mountbatten that power had to be handed over so far ahead of time was his public relations adviser, Alan Campbell-Johnson.

'A terrific sense of urgency had been pressed upon him by everybody to whom he had spoken', Campbell-Johnson wrote.[20] But the records do not show anyone else pressing Mountbatten to hurry up: not the British government, not his advisers, not the Sikhs, not the

Muslim League, not Gandhi, and not even the majority of Congress. Nehru and Patel may have hinted that they were keen to get on with governing, but neither expressed any demand that Mountbatten set a date in August that same year. The rush was Mountbatten's, and his alone.

A few months before the Mountbattens went to India, their marriage was in one of its healthier phases. Photographs of the time show them smiling, affectionate and relaxed, and their letters reveal a matching picture. A few weeks afterwards, they reached a nadir, and by the beginning of June were constantly fighting. It is hard to believe that this turbulence did not have an effect on Mountbatten professionally – especially as he had to work closely with Nehru and Gandhi, two men whose company his wife plainly preferred to his own. Edwina had not wanted to be in India in the first place, and in the first few weeks put pressure on her husband to ensure that they would be on their way back to Britain as soon as possible.[21] Dickie had always striven to impress her with his achievements at work. Perhaps, if he could carry out the transfer of power swiftly and efficiently enough, he might still save his marriage.[22]

Within days of the announcement that there would be two successor administrations in India, talk had turned to which of them would be Britain's favourite.[23] The smart money was on Pakistan. Muslim organizations in general, and particularly the League, had spent many years cultivating links with Britain. Pakistan was likely to be the weaker of the two states, and would be seeking out foreign alliances more hungrily than would India. Moreover, its western part was geographically advantageous. West Pakistan would border Persia, Afghanistan and China, three nations of strategic interest to Britain and the United States. It was close enough to Russia to be even more interesting on that count.

Gandhi raised the question of favouritism with Mountbatten in early June, requesting that the British announce there would be no differentiation between the two dominions. The Viceroy took the matter up with the India Office in London, but received a cagey reply. 'We all felt strongly that we should be extremely guarded in dealing with this request of Gandhi's', wrote Lord Listowel; 'we feel

that we should be very careful not to say that we shall not in any circumstances have closer relations with Pakistan than with India.'[24]

'I have done my job,' said Jinnah on 9 June, with some justification.[25] He went on to address the last meeting of the Muslim League
in the Imperial Hotel that day. The Imperial was Delhi's grandest
hotel, a short distance south of Connaught Circus on the avenue of
Queensway. A perfectly spaced colonnade of royal palms screened its
smooth, green lawns and pristine art deco frontage from the noise,
smells and wandering livestock outside. That Monday, as usual, the
better-heeled of Delhi's visitors were taking tea on the terrace. The
gentle murmur of conversation, and the clink of china and silver,
were the only sounds emanating from a serene company of dignitaries, American journalists and grand European ladies. Upstairs, in
the ballroom, Jinnah took to the stage in front of 425 delegates to
present them with Mountbatten's plan.

Suddenly, a mob of fifty Khaksars – the fundamentalist sect that
had been massing in Delhi for a month – burst through the palm
colonnade on to the lawn, waving sharpened spades and shouting,
'Get Jinnah!' The hotel guests scattered; cups of Darjeeling tea
smashed on the marble tiles, and chairs and tables overturned as the
Khaksars stormed through the lounge and up the staircases. There
they were met by Muslim League national guards, and a battle
ensued. Jinnah would have been entitled to panic: the only serious
assassination attempt ever made against him had been by a Khaksar
who had broken into his house and stabbed him, four years previously. Instead he remained perfectly calm, and continued with his
meeting while clashes, screams and thuds echoed up the stairs. He
was addressed in the Persian style as 'Shahenshah-e-Pakistan' –
Emperor of Pakistan. 'I am a soldier of Pakistan, not its Emperor,' he
swiftly replied. The Mountbatten plan was accepted by 300 votes to
10. Soon the police arrived to subdue the combatants with tear gas,
and Jinnah escaped without a scratch. The Imperial was not so fortunate. That evening, red-eyed guests still blinking away the tear gas
sat down for dinner at its Shahnaz restaurant on broken furniture. A
party from the Viceroy's House arrived, and was taken to the
Mughal Suite on the first floor. Edwina Mountbatten was one of
those who picked their way through the wreckage to enjoy a banquet

of *homard à l'armoricaine* and *selle d'agneau farci de la paté*, with a chilled glass of Chablis Premier Cru 1936.[26]

On 18 June, the Mountbattens flew to the beautiful lakeside city of Srinagar, for a visit to the largest of India's princely states, Kashmir. Nehru had already warned Mountbatten that the Muslim-majority Kashmir might prove to be a problem. Mountbatten knew the Hindu Maharaja, Sir Hari Singh, having first met him in Calcutta at Christmas dinner in 1921, for which Sir Hari had been specially selected as one of the British government's best behaved princely allies. Their acquaintance had been sufficiently cordial that Dickie and Edwina had holidayed with him at Srinagar as late as 1946.[27]

It was known that the Maharaja wanted Kashmir independent, a scheme unpalatable to Nehru, Gandhi and the British. The Mountbattens' visit to Kashmir was not a raging success. At the opening banquet, Dickie accidentally set off a bell that had been installed under the table, which alerted the band to play 'God Save the King'. The band dutifully struck up, at which guests dropped their chicken curry and scrambled to their feet. Mountbatten and the Maharaja's son cracked up with laughter; but the Maharaja himself was thunderous with rage. The following day, the Maharaja dispatched the Viceroy on a long, lonely fishing trip.[28] When he was allowed to return, Mountbatten found Sir Hari reluctant to be in his company. The two only spoke during drives together. On one of these, Mountbatten assured the Maharaja that he would be allowed a free choice of which dominion to join after 15 August, emphasizing the importance of ascertaining the will of the Kashmiri people, but making it clear that any moves to independence would be foolish and dangerous.[29]

Mountbatten had asked Nehru to brief him on Kashmir just before he left for Srinagar, and received an essay in return arguing that, despite its overwhelming Muslim population of 92 per cent in Kashmir proper (excluding Jammu) and 77 per cent overall, 'The normal and obvious course appears to be for Kashmir to join the Constituent Assembly of India.' Furthermore, 'It is absurd to think that Pakistan would create trouble if this happens.'[30] Nehru himself was a Kashmiri by descent, and his detachment would repeatedly fail him when dealing with his ancestral state. Nonetheless, there was another reason for his desperation to secure Kashmir. If the North-West Frontier Province went to Pakistan, India would lose the Hindu Kush mountains – its natural defence against attack from the north. Mountbatten was insisting that a plebiscite be held in the NWFP, to the despair of Nehru and Gandhi. If both the NWFP and Kashmir went to Pakistan, there would be nothing but farmland between India and the Soviets, the Afghans, the Pakistanis, and the Chinese.[31] The danger from the north was real and immediate, especially after 2 July, when Afghanistan revived its old claim to territory on the North-West Frontier, comprising most of the land between the Indus and the border. Fears abounded that the Afghans were being encouraged by the Russians, though some in India wondered whether their action was more to do with pan-Islamic ambitions. Nehru received a package of papers from an anonymous correspondent. 'After Jinnah's Pakistan has liquidated all Hindus inside its boundaries the big JEHAD of the twentieth Century will begin,' it said. The correspondent went on to allege that Muslims in India had been directed to act as fifth columns among the Hindus, and 'In the name of religion Mohammedan women are being ordered to entice Hindu men.'[32] Nonsense though this was, the number of similar protests indicates that communal feeling was becoming ever more perilous.

One month later, the North-West Frontier plebiscite would register a decisive vote to join Pakistan, with 289,244 for Pakistan against only 2874 for India. Mountbatten declared himself most satisfied with having 'insisted on the referendum in spite of the strongest possible opposition' from Congress.[33] Neither he, nor his staff, nor anyone in London, seems to have realized that the die had been cast for conflict in Kashmir.

The Mountbattens returned from Kashmir on 23 June. That day, the Punjab voted in favour of its own partition; Bengal had already done so. Sir Cyril Radcliffe, a London barrister, was flown in to take up the onerous and vulnerable job of drawing the lines of partition. He had been nominated by the British government with the approval of Jinnah.[34] The Muslim League's victory over the principle of basing statehood on identity inspired all sorts of new demands. The 3.5 million Pathans in the north-west were raising a call for a separate state of Pathanistan, and the 'Frontier Gandhi', Abdul Ghaffar Khan, added his voice to that call on 2 July.[35] The original Gandhi also supported Pathanistan, though Jinnah condemned it as 'disastrous'.[36] The following day, Tamil separatists in the south cabled Attlee from Madras to note that they also wanted a separate Dravidanadu for Muslims and Dravidian people.[37] Shortly afterwards, it was reported that the Naga tribes in Assam were keen to establish a Nagastan; their leaders turned up in Delhi, threatening to fight 'to the last drop of their blood' to win independence.[38] The Sikhs were split over whether or not to accept partition, and some among them still hoped for a separate Khalistan. A Sikh protest day against the partition of the Punjab was declared. Many went to their gurdwaras wearing black armbands, and rumblings began to be heard from agitators. 'With clear vision, determination, and vigour that is characteristic of our virile race, we shall extricate ourselves out of this whirlpool of annihilation that is facing us', read one pamphlet. 'Our phoenix-like rise shall signal the fall of our enemies.'[39]

This rapidly expanding chaos made the British keener still to escape from India. In late June, riots in Lahore and Amritsar had left hundreds of houses burnt down. People running from their blazing homes were shot in the street for breaking the curfew order. Nehru was horrified, and asked Mountbatten to declare martial law. 'If you will forgive a personal touch, I should like to tell you that my mother came from Lahore and part of my childhood was spent there', he wrote to Mountbatten. 'The fate of Lahore, therefore, affects me perhaps more intimately than it might many other people who are not connected with that city.'[40] It affected Jinnah, too. 'I don't care whether you shoot Muslims or not,' he told Mountbatten, 'it has got to be stopped.'[41] The Sikh minister Baldev Singh advised him to 'shoot everyone on sight'. But the British government had made it clear that they would send no more troops or resources. Britain's debit balance for imports and exports was running at over £50 million. The Chancellor, Hugh Dalton, had just announced that imports of tobacco, newsprint, petrol and some foods were to be scaled back drastically. There was nothing to spare for India. All Mountbatten could propose was the setting up of a multi-faith security committee, which would sit in Delhi and resolve that things would be better if everyone stopped killing each other.

On 4 July 1947 – the 171st anniversary of another independence day in another of Britain's colonies – the Indian Independence Bill was introduced into the House of Commons. Not only in India had its passage been perilous. Three days earlier, Churchill had written to Attlee in tones of profound outrage, demanding that the name of the bill be changed to 'The India Bill, 1947' or 'The India Self-Government Bill'. India was becoming a dominion, he argued, not an independent state: if the word 'independence' remained, he would not be able to vote for it.[42] Had the bill's name been changed at this stage, Congress could not have accepted it. On the other hand, the prospect of forcing the bill through parliament without Conservative Party support raised the unthinkable possibility of it being defeated. Either eventuality would keep Britain in India and sabotage all the progress that had been made.

Under the circumstances, Attlee did the best thing he could possibly have done. He did not reply to Churchill's letter until the morning of 4 July itself, and then pointed out that it was too late to change anything. Churchill, who was recuperating after a hernia operation and had less of a fight in him than usual, gruffly accepted this, noting that his protest would remain on record.[43]

A founding principle of Mountbatten's plan was the reappointment of himself as joint Governor General of both new dominions for a short period after 15 August. Nehru had acquiesced; Jinnah had hedged, and recommended separate Governors General with a Supreme Arbitrator – in which post he was happy to have Mountbatten – to oversee such matters as the division of financial assets and arms stocks.[44] Foolishly, Mountbatten had assumed that Jinnah would eventually come round to the idea of a single Governor General. As might have been guessed from his doodle on 2 June, Jinnah wanted to become Governor General himself.[45]

During the last week of June, Jinnah announced that he would be unable to accept any position apart from Governor General of Pakistan in six weeks' time. 'What I thought would happen funnily enough', wrote Edwina to Patricia, 'and which neither Daddy nor any of his staff EVER contemplated has occurred'.[46] Mountbatten tried to convince Jinnah that he would have more power as Prime

Minister of Pakistan – an argument which a lawyer as assiduous as
Jinnah would immediately have seen to be false. 'In my position it is
I who will give the advice and others who will act on it,' replied the
Quaid-e-Azam, who had clearly read the terms of the Indian
Independence Bill very closely. 'Do you realise what this will cost
you?' asked Mountbatten. 'It may cost me several crores [tens of
millions] of rupees in assets,' Jinnah replied. 'It may well cost you
the whole of your assets and the future of Pakistan,' snarled
Mountbatten, and stormed out of the room.[47]

Attlee told the cabinet that Jinnah's demand 'was no more than an
indication of his own egotism'.[48] Vain though Jinnah may have been,
it would be unfair to attribute his action solely to a lust for fancy
titles. He had turned down a British knighthood and sternly rebuked
those who attempted to dub him Emperor of Pakistan.

A more convincing reason for Jinnah's refusal of Mountbatten's
candidacy was personal. Delhi was no place to keep a secret, and the
gossips soon ensured that Jinnah found out about Mountbatten
showing Nehru the then-secret plan at Simla on 10 May. He also
found out that Nehru had been allowed to rewrite it.[49] It was obvious that the Viceroy liked Nehru, and even close friends of
Mountbatten would later admit that his corresponding dislike of
Jinnah had become obvious by this point.[50] Mountbatten had
repeatedly proclaimed his preference for a united India, creating
fears in the Muslim League that a joint Governor Generalship might
favour the reabsorption of Pakistan, in line with Congress hopes.[51]

But there was more to it than that. Yahya Bakhtiar, a Baluchistani
politician who was a close associate of Jinnah's, argued that a joint
Governor Generalship under Mountbatten would have meant
Pakistan 'getting destroyed at inception'. By July, Jinnah had very
strong reasons to suspect that Mountbatten was wrapped around
Nehru's finger. 'Nehru in those days was having a roaring love affair
with Lady Mountbatten,' added Bakhtiar, 'said to be with the tacit
approval of Mountbatten.'[52]

There is an intriguing tale told by S.S. Pirzada, later Foreign
Minister of Pakistan, that Jinnah had been handed a small collection
of letters that had been written by Edwina and Jawahar. 'Dickie will
be out tonight – come after 10.00 o'clock,' said one of Edwina's.

Another revealed that: 'You forgot your handkerchief and before Dickie could spot it I covered it up.' A third said: 'I have fond memories of Simla – riding and your touch.'

Pirzada claimed that Jinnah discussed what to do about these letters with Fatima and his colleagues. In the end, Jinnah concluded that 'Caesar's wife should be above suspicion', and had the letters returned.[53] If this incident really did occur in late June 1947, it provides a credible reason for Jinnah's sudden switch from agreeing that Mountbatten could be a Supreme Arbitrator to refusing him any role whatsoever in Pakistan. Perhaps Edwina and Jawahar were just good friends at this point and the rumours of a roaring love affair jumped the gun; such details may be something that only the two of them will ever know. But exactly how roaring the love affair may have been by this point is of little consequence. They were known to be close, and they were known to have political influence with each other. The Pakistani government could not be expected to tolerate a situation in which its Governor General's wife was to any substantial degree intimate with the Prime Minister of India. Jinnah could not have accepted Mountbatten's candidacy.[54]

On the evening of 2 July, Jinnah came to see Mountbatten, and told him flatly that the Muslim League would not negotiate further. Mountbatten sat with the Quaid-e-Azam for over four hours attempting to persuade, cajole and even bully him into changing his mind. The Viceroy dangled the carrot of British favour, and raised the stick of economic disadvantage: but Jinnah was completely immovable.[55]

As soon as Jinnah's position was known, the India Office drew up a top-secret memorandum. There was a specific danger in the provisional constitution: the powers granted to the Governor General of each dominion were 'exceedingly wide', allowing him a free hand in controlling most institutions of state, including the judiciary; not requiring him to act on the advice of his constituent assembly; and prescribing no limit to his tenure of office. 'This position is innocuous and convenient if the Governor-General is a disinterested and transitory Englishman such as Lord Mountbatten,' noted the India Office, whose staff perhaps did not know him awfully well. 'Quite different considerations plainly arise if the holder of the office is an

ambitious Indian.' The memorandum predicted serious disturbances
after the transfer of power, and recommended that full plans for the
evacuation of all British troops and civilians be made without hesitation.[56]

Mountbatten was personally hurt by Jinnah's decision, and his
sense of crisis was so acute that he flew Lord Ismay back to London
to present the situation to the cabinet. Ismay reported that
Mountbatten feared that, 'If he accepted the Congress invitation
after being largely responsible for partition, he might be subsequently criticised for siding with Congress and for failing in
impartiality during his period of office as Viceroy.' This was an
accurate prediction. But both Attlee and Lord Listowel felt strongly
that Dickie should be persuaded to stay on. Listowel argued that
Mountbatten could influence India to stay in the Commonwealth
and to negotiate defence arrangements that would be beneficial to
Britain. Moreover, he admitted, 'The partition of assets between the
two Dominions would in any event work out unfavourably for
Pakistan; Lord Mountbatten would be in a better position than
anyone else to exercise a moderating influence on Congress policy in
this matter.'[57] Though the cabinet conceded that Mountbatten's personal reputation might suffer, it resolved to ask him to carry on as
Indian Governor General – in the interests, principally, of his own
country.

Ismay next went to discuss the matter with Churchill, who was
happy to accept Jinnah's candidacy for Governor General of
Pakistan. He was also concerned that India retain a strong British
influence in the form of Mountbatten. He emphasized that
Mountbatten would be particularly useful in three key roles: 'He can
strive to mitigate quarrels between Hindu and Moslem, safeguard the
position of the Princes, when that is involved, and preserve such ties
of sentiment as are possible between the Government of Hindustan
and that of the other Dominions (or Commonwealths) of the
Crown.'[58] All of these roles would have been just as relevant in
Pakistan as in India, but Churchill already had good reason to be
confident of Pakistan's obedience: he trusted Jinnah to run it in a way
that would serve British interests. Meanwhile Jinnah, who saw as
clearly as anyone else the advantage of having one overseeing body to

regulate the partition awards, arms and resources distribution and so on, lobbied Churchill and Attlee to set up a council from among the British government to act as such. The intention was clear. He still wanted a Supreme Arbitrator, but not Mountbatten. His suggestion was ignored.[59]

On 9 July, under pressure from the cabinet, the opposition, and the King, Mountbatten agreed, with great reluctance, to stay on.[60] 'Everyone seems to think the decision has been a right one', wrote Edwina to Lady Reading, 'although I myself am still worried at its implications, not personal of course, but as to whether it was really the right decision for the people of this country.'[61] The achievement of separate Governors General was, however, a great victory for Jinnah, and no one could be in any doubt at his satisfaction. He held press conferences in fanless rooms, amid hordes of sweating journalists, at which he wore an immaculate white silk suit and smoked cigars while informing them cheerfully about his modern, democratic and inclusive vision for Pakistan.[62]

For all Jinnah's publicity, it was Mountbatten's name that shone out from the headlines. That day, the world's media had been able at last to confirm what they had keenly suspected for months, if not years. Lieutenant Philip Mountbatten, RN, was engaged to marry Princess Elizabeth of Great Britain, the woman who would be Queen. The Mountbatten connection was not lost on the press: the *Times of India* printed a warm editorial noting the Viceroy's contributions to Philip's upbringing. Dickie himself was elated: 'I am sure she couldn't have picked a better man', he wrote to Attlee.[63] Edwina wrote to Lady Reading that Philip was 'extremely cultured, well-read, of a progressive mind . . . In fact he will I think be a breath of fresh air into the Royal circle'.[64]

Thoughts of thrones and crowns and ermine were soon to consume them all. Mountbatten had persuaded India's political leaders to accept his plan. For his next trick, he would have to persuade each of the 565 princely rulers to join one of the two new dominions. The clock was ticking. Less than a month remained before the British would finally leave India.

CHAPTER 13

A FULL BASKET OF APPLES

ON 18 JULY, THE KING SIGNED THE INDIA INDEPENDENCE ACT in London, and the Mountbattens celebrated their silver wedding anniversary in Delhi, twenty-five years after having become engaged in that city.[1] They received numerous congratulatory gifts and messages from a cross-section of society – everything from an intricate solid silver model of a palace from the Maharaja of Bikaner, to grubby notes from schoolchildren – but the most memorable of all was the very first to arrive. At an early hour of that morning, a message arrived from Gandhi. Pointedly, it was written to Edwina, addressing her as 'Dear Sister'. Edwina was deeply touched. 'I hope that your joint career here will blossom into citizenship of the world', the Mahatma wrote.[2] But, though the Mountbattens' careers were blossoming, they were not doing so jointly. Dickie would come up to Edwina's room every night to kiss her goodnight before returning to work. Every night, there was a row.[3]

Other friends were beginning to worry about Edwina. 'As for yourself, my dear I wish you would gain a little weight', wrote one. 'I do hope you're finding time to relax.'[4] She was not. For one thing, there was her anniversary party to manage: guests included Nehru, Jinnah, all of the cabinet and most prominent Congress and Muslim League figures, which must have made for a vexing seating plan. Jinnah turned up half an hour late, uncharacteristically. Auchinleck's secretary, Shahid Hamid, remembered meeting Jinnah in a corridor, and remarking on his apparent insouciance. 'My boy,' Jinnah replied, 'do you think I would come to this damn man's party on time? I purposely came late to show him I despise him.'[5] The relationship between the Mountbattens and Jinnah was now in a parlous state. At the dinner, Edwina described Jinnah as being 'in an unbearable mood and quite hopeless . . . God help Pakistan.'[6]

In addition to hosting this dinner, Edwina embarked upon two major healthcare initiatives that week. On 17 July, she made a public appeal for nurses and midwives through the Countess of Dufferin Fund. Three days later, she launched a campaign to recruit 14,200 health visitors in the fight against tuberculosis.[7] She took a special interest in a Nursing Council Bill, a piece of legislation that had been drifting around unpassed since 1943. It had been proposed to set standards for public health, and Edwina was desperate to get it passed before partition. She embarked upon a campaign of intense lobbying among her political contacts, but at the very last moment it looked as though the bill might fail. It might have been expected that the Vicereine would speak to the Viceroy over such a matter. Instead, Edwina went to talk to Jawahar. Within two days, the bill had been approved.[8]

Behind the scenes, her political activities were explicitly left-leaning. 'I wish I could completely share people's views about Ernie Bevin as to his sincerity and vision, but I just can't', she wrote to a friend. 'I feel myself that his hatred of the Communists and his fear of them blinds him in making decisions that very largely affect foreign as well as home policy.' Jawahar introduced her to a wider spectrum of political figures. At his house she met Indonesian exiles escaping the latest 'ghastly Dutch aggression', and heard their 'shattering' stories.[9] International news was at its most dramatic that week. On 19 July, Mountbatten's and Nehru's friend Aung San was sitting in a meeting of his executive council when gunmen burst in and shot him dead, along with six colleagues.[10] Meanwhile, Liaquat was reporting to Mountbatten that relations between the future officials of Pakistan and India had become so tense that they could no longer work together. The secretaries of Pakistani departments had been turfed out of their offices and sent to work among the clerks; there was no space to do so, and so the grounds of the government offices were now full of pitiable little groups of Pakistani officials, reduced to setting up desks under trees. 'I was one of the strongest opponents of rushing partition through by the 15th August,' Liaquat told Mountbatten, 'but I now wish to God you could get partition through by the 1st August.'[11]

Against this background of upheaval, Mountbatten felt that he had to refocus attention on the matter in hand, and on 20 July issued each of his staff with a tear-off calendar. The day of the month was at the top and, underneath it in bold, the words: 'X days left to prepare for the Transfer of Power'.[12] Yet it was he himself who could not be detached from trivialities. In the middle of July 1947, while negotiations about defence, finance, partition, the possible independence of several princely states and the future of 400 million people raged around him, the Viceroy spent hours fussing about flags. 'In previous reports I have expressed the hope that I would be able to persuade the new Dominions to have the Union Jack in the upper canton of their flags as do other members of the Commonwealth', he cabled to London. 'This design has not been accepted by either part.'[13] The Muslim League felt that it would be distasteful to juxtapose the Christian crosses of the Union Jack with the crescent of Islam; Congress agreed that the retention of the British emblem would upset hardliners; the British government did not really give a hoot what they did. Having lost that battle, Mountbatten turned his attention to the woefully minor issue of Governor General flags – the ensigns that would be flown on top of residences and car bonnets. A week later, he nearly came to blows with Jinnah when the Quaid-e-Azam rejected his designs. 'He was only saved from being struck by the arrival of the other members of the Partition Council at this moment,' Mountbatten reported to London. 'However, I sent Ismay round to beat him up as soon as possible, and Jinnah claimed that I must have misunderstood him.'[14]

There was one more enormous obstacle to be overcome before partition, and that was the question of what would happen to India's princely states. Each of the 565 princely states in India had a separate agreement with the government, ensuring the paramountcy of the British Crown over its affairs. It had taken centuries to bring the states under paramountcy, and many still operated through arcane systems of government and society. It was the boast of the Empire's supporters that the reassuring eminence of the Indian Civil Service, staffed almost entirely with public-school-educated British men, kept things on track. Some thought this the pinnacle of British achievement, allowing the states their freedom of cultural diversity while tempering the worst excesses of absolute rule. The idea was to leave rulers as independent as possible; in case of trouble, for the British to offer the ruler in question 'private counsel'; and, should that not fix the trouble, to intervene. In the event of gross totalitarianism or outright rebellion, the British raj would remove the individual prince who had proved to be a bad egg, install a more responsible scion of his family, and leave the dynasty intact.[15]

Unfortunately, this appealing portrait of a smooth, tolerant and accountable system was a fiction. In reality, the British presence in India was relatively small and unable to keep watch over so many princes. The notion that the 'British race' had a monopoly on freedom and democracy was unsupportable with regard to the lengthy traditions of public debate, heterogeneous government and freedom of conscience that had existed for centuries in the Indias of Asoka and Akbar.[16] If anything, the presence of the British damaged these traditions, and actually safeguarded the princes from any new incursion of democracy. The British Army was always on hand to give succour to each imperilled tyrant, and stamp out any attempts by the people to express their discontent. As one staunch imperialist boasted, the princes had been 'mostly rescued from imminent destruction by British protection'.[17] And so imperialists were able to perfect a classic piece of doublethink: railing against what they called 'Oriental despotism' on one hand, while propping it up with the other.

Even the illiberal Lord Curzon had been appalled by the standard of princely behaviour during his viceroyalty, half a century before. He had written to Queen Victoria that 'for all these failures we are responsible. We have allowed the chiefs when young to fall into bad hands. We have condoned their extravagances, we have worked at their vices.'[18] Though he conceded that some of the princes were 'capable and patriotic men', many more were 'frivolous and sometimes vicious spendthrifts and idlers'. In the latter category, he counted such men as the Maharaja Rana of Dholpur, 'an inebriate and a sot'; the Raja of Chumba, who had 'crippled himself by intemperance'; the Maharaja of Patiala, 'little better than a jockey'; the Raja of Kapurthala, who was 'only happy when philandering in Paris'. 'As Your Majesty knows,' he added, 'the Maharaja Holkar is half mad and is addicted to horrible vices.' This last was a particularly pointed comment – Victoria liked Holkar, because he had once sent her a telegram on her birthday. It was unfortunate, for 'half mad' underestimated his insanity by around 50 per cent. He would stand at a high window overlooking his subjects and issue random edicts as they popped into his head, once ordering the abduction of every man wearing a black coat. Once, he harnessed the bankers of Indore to a state coach and whipped them soundly as he drove them around the city.[19]

During his tour of India in 1921, the young Dickie Mountbatten had admired the princely states, but was shocked by their inequality. In Udaipur, he wondered at the habit of feeding pigs when people were starving, an injustice that prompted him to note, 'There are times when I do sympathize with the Bolsheviks.'[20] Princely excesses were common in states where the vast majority of people were destitute. The Jam Sahib of Nawanagar had 157 cars and a wife with 1700 saris.[21] The Nawab of Junagadh spent £21,000 on a wedding for two of his dogs.[22] The Maharaja of Patiala moved into London's Savoy Hotel, occupying all thirty-five suites on the fifth floor, and ordered that 3000 fresh roses be brought to decorate his rooms every day.[23] Visitors to the miserly Nizam of Hyderabad would have seen that he used what looked like a crumpled ball of old newspaper as a paperweight – little suspecting that wrapped in it was the 185 carat Jacob Diamond, twice the size of the Koh-i-Noor.[24] The Gaekwar of Baroda's second wife, Sita Devi, earned herself the nickname of 'India's Wallis Simpson' when she plundered the state treasury to finance her jewellery habit. Sita Devi made away to Switzerland with untold riches, including the incomparable Baroda pearl carpet. This remarkable object measured six feet by seven and a half feet, and was made up of 1.4 million pearls, 2520 rose-cut diamonds, and hundreds of emeralds and rubies, embroidered on to deerskin and silk in delicate arabesques.[25]

The journalist Webb Miller was treated to a glimpse of a typical princely attitude at the Cecil Hotel in Simla in 1930. His Highness Ali Nawaz Khan, the Mir of Khairpur, was dining that night. The Mir was striking to behold: so grotesquely fat that he could not get his face closer than two feet to the table. 'His paunch was bespattered with soup spilled on its way from the plate to his distant mouth,' remembered Miller.[26] This glutton, who commanded a private army as well as forty lucky wives back in his state, had ordered his desperately poor subjects to oppose Gandhi, the independence movement and even any move to dominion status. 'The interests of the Indian native rulers are identical with those of the British government,' the Mir's minister told Miller silkily. 'They believe if the present status is altered it will injure their interests.'[27] The Mir was by no means unique. Four decades after Curzon's letter to Victoria, the then Viceroy, Lord Wavell, wrote a remarkably similar one to his monarch, George VI. According to him, the Nizam of Hyderabad was 'an eccentric miser with a bad record of misrule', the Maharaja of Kashmir 'little better', the Maharaja of Gwalior 'a nice lad and means well, but cares more for his horses and racing than anything else', the Khan of Kalat 'stupid', the Maharaja of Travancore 'a non-entity', and the Maharaja of Indore 'a poor creature, physically and morally'.[28]

These are some of the grosser examples of princely behaviour, and should not be taken as a slander against every individual prince. Some among them were men and women of great intelligence, ability and compassion. A Gaekwar of Baroda introduced the first free, compulsory education in India in 1894. A Maharaja of Travancore introduced progressive land reforms in the early 1880s. One turn-of-the-century Maharaja of Cochin was greatly admired for his modernizing legal reforms – though he became so frustrated at the complacency of his British patrons that he abdicated in 1914.[29] But the existence of a few commendable examples does not vindicate the system. The reason that the Indian princely states were uniquely badly ruled was the very fact of British protection. Aside from their consciences, the princes had no incentive to govern well. Foreign invaders would be dealt with, domestic challenges neutered, and the ravening mob readily suppressed, all by the might of the British Indian Army.

Mountbatten set up a States Department in July, convinced by then of the need to absorb the states into India or Pakistan rather than surrender them to the capricious rule of their princes.[30] India's offer to the states was straightforward. Control over defence, foreign affairs, and communications would go to the government of India. Their domestic affairs, including their privy purses, were to be their own concern. Nehru had told Mountbatten that 'I will encourage rebellion in all States that go against us,' which had caused the Viceroy to question his friend's sanity.[31] 'On the subject of the States,' Mountbatten reported to London, 'Nehru and Gandhi are pathological.' He was relieved that the unsentimental Vallabhbhai Patel had been made head of the department rather than the more emotional Nehru.[32] For Patel's part, he realized immediately that Mountbatten, with his own semi-royal status and personal friendships with many of the princes, was uniquely suited to help India achieve its aim of leaving no state behind.

Britain's intentions towards the states had been deliberately left unclear by Attlee. Mountbatten was supposed to 'aid and assist the States in coming to fair and just arrangements with the leaders of British India as to their future relationships'. But there was also the command that 'You will do your best to persuade the rulers of any Indian States in which political progress has been slow to progress rapidly towards some form of more democratic government.'[33] Mountbatten interpreted this to mean that he should exert pressure upon each prince to go with the majority of his people in deciding whether to join India or Pakistan. He agreed to help Patel, and pledged to deliver 'a full basket of apples' before 15 August. To London, he confided that he would take a great risk and side entirely with Congress, on the basis that his help would constitute a strong bargaining point. 'I am positive that if I can bring in a basket-full of States before the 15th August, Congress will pay whatever price I insist on for the basket', he wrote. 'I need hardly say that unless we can pull this off, India will be in a bit of a mess after the 15th August.'[34]

With no Pakistani representative to match Mountbatten and Patel in the states department, the states would turn into a major point of conflict between Indian and Pakistani interests. But Jinnah did not clamour for the inclusion of a Muslim Leaguer. It was not that he took no interest; he did, and actively. But he was not especially concerned about whether states acceded to Pakistan or remained independent. His strategy was simply to stop them acceding to India. If enough states could be persuaded to stay out, Nehru and Patel would inherit a moth-eaten India to go with his moth-eaten Pakistan. And so the stage was set for one of the bitterest, most scandalous and most secretive battles of the transfer of power, in which Mountbatten and Patel would try every possible tactic to scare the princes into India, and Jinnah would do everything he could think of to scare them out of it.

On 9 July, representatives of the states met in New Delhi to ascertain their starting positions. The great majority inclined to join India. But four of the most important states – Hyderabad, Kashmir, Bhopal and Travancore – wanted to become independent nations. Each of these states had its own unique set of difficulties. The Nizam of Hyderabad was the richest man in the world; he was a Muslim, and his people were mostly Hindus. His state was enormous, and both France and the United States were rumoured to be ready to recognize it.[35] The Maharaja of Kashmir was a Hindu; his people were mostly Muslims. His state was even bigger than Hyderabad, but more limited by its lack of trade routes and industrial potential. The Nawab of Bhopal was an able and ambitious Muslim prince, and one of Jinnah's advisers: unfortunately for him, his state had a Hindu majority, and was stuck right in the middle of India, over 500 miles from the likely border with Pakistan. Uranium deposits had recently been discovered in Travancore, lending the situation there a greater international interest.

Mountbatten and Patel both adopted a pincer attack. On one hand, they described the princes as their 'personal friends' and offered them ambassadorships, honorifics and privileges; on the other, they threatened them with disaster. 'I hope the Indian States will bear in mind that the alternative to cooperation in the general interest is anarchy and chaos,' growled Patel.[36] Mountbatten, meanwhile, used his royal connections to exert pressure on the princes to accede to India. Two of the agents acting for the princes felt so aggrieved by Mountbatten's tactics that they compared him, rather

excitably, to Hitler.[37] The Nawab of Bhopal attempted to get the
states to band together, so that they might hold out for independence: such a coalition might have formed an area the size of
Pakistan. Not only Lord Mountbatten, but also Lady Mountbatten,
crushed the plan, according to the Maharawal of Dungarpur: 'It
was an end brought about by one man and his wife.'[38]

Though Mountbatten's heavy-handed strategy is certainly open to
criticism, his aim was to bring the states' people into a democratic
India. British historians who have scolded Mountbatten for that aim
have argued that the princes were strong supporters of Britain during
the war, and that they had rights under the British paramountcy
system which were discarded.[39] Such arguments ignore the political
and immediate realities of the situation. Many of the princes were
regarded as tyrants by the All-India States Peoples' Conference (president, 1935–46: Jawaharlal Nehru), an organization set up to
represent the interests of the princes' 100 million subjects – who
counted as 'British protected persons'.[40] By supporting the princes
against the people and against the new dominions of India and
Pakistan, Britain would have undermined the entire process of transferring power to democratic institutions.

No significant figure in London was prepared to stand up for the
princes. The request of some states for independence and dominion
status had been described by Pethick-Lawrence as 'rather fanciful' on
18 April: they had never been formal British territory, and the British
could hardly go around enrolling them into the Empire at this point,
even if they begged to be conquered.[41] By the middle of July, when
some in Whitehall were beginning to question Mountbatten's
devices, Attlee allowed a telegram to be sent to him questioning
whether he was riding too rough. Mountbatten's response was to the
point: 'I am trying my very best to create an integrated India which,
while securing stability, will ensure friendship with Great Britain. If
I am allowed to play my own hand without interference I have no
doubt I will succeed.'[42] The India Office backed down completely
and allowed him his hand back. Nor was the opposition prepared to
stick its neck out. The Nizam cabled Churchill in June asking him to
demonstrate his sympathy and support for the Indian princely order,
a cause which he had championed in the past. Churchill replied with

what can only be described as a snub, merely thanking him for his kind message.[43]

Mountbatten spent July hustling recalcitrant princes into the Indian fold. The Maharaja of Indore was most displeased when Mountbatten sent a crack team of fellow princes to cajole him. Faced with the intimidating sight of the Gaekwar of Baroda, four Maharajas, and his best friend, the Raja of Sandur, he absconded from his palace and had to be retrieved. When he returned, he 'unceremoniously kicked out five of the Rulers literally into the passage, keeping only the Gaekwar'. The Gaekwar's persuasive skills failed to turn him around. 'It may not be a bad thing to have a thoroughly unsatisfactory State like Indore remaining outside the Dominion, as an example of what happens to States that try and stand on their own,' Mountbatten reported. 'If he does not change his mind and come in I prophesy that the people of Indore will kick their Ruler off the Gaddi [throne] before the end of September.'[44]

The Hindu Maharaja of Jodhpur, who had just turned twenty-four and had only succeeded to the throne in June, provided a dramatic moment. Jinnah had been courting him, with plans that Patel feared would create 'a dagger into the very heart of India', a spur of Pakistan that would run down through Jodhpur into Bhopal. Mountbatten explained to the Maharaja that he was legally entitled to join Pakistan, but reminded him of his Hindu majority. 'Your Highness is free to stay out, if you like,' Patel added. 'But if there is trouble in your State as a result of your decision, you will not get the slightest support from the Government of India.'[45] The Maharaja was shaken by this clear threat. He turned up at the Viceroy's House, and was fobbed off with V.P. Menon while Mountbatten dealt with a Hyderabad delegation in Edwina's study next door. Apparently, Menon was not to the Maharaja's satisfaction. He pulled out a pistol concealed behind the nib of a very large fountain pen and screamed that he would 'shoot him down like a dog if he betrayed the starving people of Jodhpur'. Menon talked him down, and the Maharaja eventually put the gun away – later making a present of it to Mountbatten, who 'gave him hell' for the incident.[46]

There was further trouble with Travancore. It was incorrectly rumoured that the state had already reached a private agreement with Britain over the fate of its uranium deposits, prompting Nehru to threaten that he would send the Indian Air Force to bomb it.[47] Meanwhile, the Maharaja of Travancore refused to throw his lot in with India on the grounds that Nehru had established diplomatic relations with the Soviet Union.[48] When Mountbatten cornered him, the Maharaja professed to see himself as only the Dewan, or Prime Minister, of Travancore. The real Maharaja, he explained, was the god Padmanabha, an aspect of Vishnu.[49] The Maharaja's actual Dewan, Sir C.P. Ramaswami Aiyar, turned up at the Viceroy's House with a set of files to present to Mountbatten. 'The first of these contained a number of rather amusing cartoons, to which he took the greatest exception,' Mountbatten reported, 'and in particular one published that morning showing him being spanked by me at this very meeting!' Another file 'contained cuttings to prove that Gandhi was a dangerous sex maniac who could not keep his hands off young girls.[50] It took Mountbatten two hours to calm Aiyar down. Aiyar returned to Travancore, and shortly afterwards was viciously attacked with a swordstick and almost killed by a rogue agent of the local communist party. The States Peoples' Conference put pressure on the Maharaja, who admitted defeat and telegraphed his instrument of accession to Mountbatten immediately. 'The adherence of Travancore after all C.P.'s declarations of independence has had a profound effect on all the other States and is sure to shake the Nizam,' Mountbatten noted with satisfaction.[51]

But it did not. The Nizam of Hyderabad, along with the Maharaja of Kashmir, was to prove Mountbatten's biggest stumbling-block. The Nizam employed Sir Walter Monckton, a London lawyer with exceptionally strong connections in the British establishment, to fight his corner. Monckton advised the Nizam that, as an independence ruler, he could increase his army and start munitions factories as well as appointing his own ministers. 'I shall do all I can to see that the new Viceroy understands the vital part which Indian India must continue to play,' Monckton wrote.[52]

On 3 June, after Mountbatten had announced the plan for the transfer of power, Monckton lunched with both Mountbattens and discussed the fate of Hyderabad. The very next day, he took his concerns to Jinnah. 'Mr. Jinnah said that Hyderabad could still give a lead to other States by declaring for independence,' Monckton noted. 'This would very likely hold Mysore independent and would be a source of strength to Travancore.' Jinnah even suggested that the independent states could form a bloc to defend themselves against India.[53]

By late July, Jinnah was writing to the Nizam in his most honeyed tones. 'I shall always remain a friend of Your Exalted Highness and the Mussalmans of Hyderabad,' he declared, professing his willingness to help the delegation Hyderabad was sending to him. 'But please do not take any final decision; and I hope, as you say in your letter[,] you will do so with my "concurrence and knowledge".'[54] Meanwhile, Mountbatten had managed to convince himself that Monckton was on his side. 'Monckton and I have now agreed together on a co-ordinated plan of campaign to bring the Nizam in, and I have offered to fly down if Monckton feels that he requires my help to pull it off', he wrote to London. 'As a last resort I shall offer to make his second son "His Highness"'.[55] Both the Nizam and Monckton had set their sights rather higher than that, as Monckton's note to Jinnah of the same week makes clear. Monckton wrote that the Nizam would definitely prefer to have a closer relationship with Pakistan than with India, but that his geographical position made this difficult. He requested that Jinnah explain what steps he could take 'to assist and rescue Hyderabad' in the event of political or economic pressure by India. Specifically, he asked whether Pakistan could guarantee that food, weaponry and troops be supplied. He wondered whether Pakistan would come to Hyderabad's aid in the event of an internal revolt fomented by India, or whether Pakistan might help Hyderabad gain an outlet to the sea.[56]

Monckton's note is stark evidence that Hyderabad was seriously considering a defensive war against democratic India. It may also have been considering a war of conquest – for Hyderabad was at least 100 miles from its closest port, and there could be no way to create an outlet to the sea without annexing Indian territory. The threat loomed large, until Jinnah pushed his luck too far. 'Jinnah in effect said that the State must earn its own independence by standing on its own feet and making all sacrifices', Monckton wrote on 6 August, 'even, if necessary, including the abdication of the Nizam.'[57]

The Nizam had no intention of abdicating, and was forced to look again to Mountbatten and Patel. He sent Monckton back to Delhi to pull out all the stops. Monckton saw Ismay and Mountbatten on the afternoon of 10 August, and railed furiously against the Congress position. He deplored Patel's intimidation tactics, which hinted that Hyderabad might face a blockade from India, and threatened to write to Churchill if the pressure was not let up.[58]

On 25 July, Mountbatten – in full uniform, and gilded all over with decorations and orders – clinked his way up the red carpet to the Chamber of Princes at the Council House in Delhi. Beside him strode the senatorial figure of Vallabhbhai Patel. After the photographers had been chased from the chamber, Mountbatten stood to address a glittering throng of nobility. With his trademark combination of form and familiarity, Mountbatten informed these august presences that they ought to accede either to India or to Pakistan. He reminded them that the key factors in their choice should be the feelings and welfare of their subjects, and the geography of their states; he assured them that they would suffer no financial loss or erosion of sovereignty. As Patel looked on sagely, he warned them they were being made an offer that was not likely to be repeated. After 15 August, he would no longer be the Crown representative – and they would have to negotiate with the Indian or Pakistani governments directly. He added a detached observation that any armaments they might think of stockpiling would soon be obsolete.

So dazzling was Mountbatten's performance that, even though he had just threatened the princes quite brazenly with conquest and subjugation by a future Indian government, the tone of the meeting quickly warmed up into a sort of friendly banter. The high point came when the Dewan of Kutch, representing the ailing Maharao of Kutch who had gone to Britain for medical treatment, questioned Mountbatten. The Dewan protested that he did not know his Maharao's mind, and could not raise him from his sickbed with a telegram. Mountbatten picked up a glass paperweight that happened to be on his rostrum. 'I will look into my crystal,' he said, 'and give you an answer.' A full ten seconds of astonished silence ensued as Mountbatten peered into the paperweight. Finally, with faultless comic timing, the Viceroy intoned: 'His Highness asks you to sign the Instrument of Accession.'[59] Many of the princes laughed, and few even thought to complain as chits were passed round warning them that the Viceroy was very busy and that they would not be allowed to speak.[60] No commoner could have pulled off such a daring act of lese-majesty; but many of the princes knew Dickie as a friend and a near-equal.

That night, Jinnah attended a small dinner-party at the Viceroy's House. There was an awkward scene, during which Jinnah implied that Mountbatten was abusing the states by forcing them to accede too quickly, and pointed out that the British government did not share this urgency. Afterwards, Jinnah claimed that Edwina Mountbatten agreed with him. The specific subject of Kashmir came up. Jinnah noted that an accession either to India or to Pakistan would spark revolts, though he stated that he would apply no pressure.[61] Apparently, this did not resolve the tensions. At the end of the dinner, Jinnah deliberately broke protocol by rising to leave the dining room at the same time as the Mountbattens.[62]

Two big flies remained in the Kashmiri ointment: the Maharaja, still evading any form of straight discussion, and Jawaharlal Nehru. Nehru again tried to visit Kashmir at the end of July, describing it as his 'first priority'.[63] He had to be stopped by Mountbatten, Patel and Gandhi, on the grounds that this would be taken as political lobbying. According to Mountbatten, when Patel attempted to talk him out of it, 'Nehru had broken down and wept, explaining that Kashmir meant more to him at the moment than anything else.'[64] Gandhi went instead, took goat's milk and fruit under a chinar tree with the Maharaja and his family, and told them to obey the wishes of their people. He was afterwards accused of lobbying for India in Nehru's place.[65]

On 28 July, Mountbatten held a reception at which he, Patel and V.P. Menon joined forces to bully the princes. The Maharajas stood around nervously to watch this daunting triumvirate work on each of their fellows in turn. 'Who's H.E. [His Excellency] getting to work on now?' one asked. 'There's no need for him to work on me. I'm signing to-morrow!'[66] Mountbatten would not be able to provide Patel with a completely full basket of apples, but it is striking that he managed to secure as many as he did. After independence, Patel would maintain his focus on the states, corralling them into groups, extracting from them their vestigial rights and responsibilities, and assimilating them into the body of democratic India.

Most of the princes, reduced to the status of adequately remunerated mascots, would disappear quietly into estate management or gin palaces, as they pleased. But an impressive number of exceptions ran for office in the new democratic India. Among Indian princely families who were guaranteed privileges at the time of their accession, more than one-third have produced electoral candidates for public office.[67] Whatever may be said about Mountbatten's tactics or the machinations of Patel, their achievement remains remarkable. Between them, and in less than a year, it may be argued that these two men achieved a larger India, more closely integrated, than had 90 years of the British raj, 180 years of the Mughal Empire, or 130 years of Asoka and the Maurya rulers.

CHAPTER 14

A RAINBOW IN THE SKY

'NATIVE RACES WITHIN THE EMPIRE ARE SHOWING AN EVER more lively appreciation of their status', reported the British *Imperial Review* in August 1947. 'The whole outlook has changed, and the native has been educated to echo the shibboleths of democracy.' Self-congratulation reverberated in the *Review*'s tone, as it surveyed the indigenous movements in New Zealand, Canada and South Africa: 'the Maori and the Red Indian, under fostering and enlightened care, have shown a surprising and gratifying ability to survive . . . A mere advisory body does not satisfy the Bantu. He wants more executive power, something nearer equality.'[1] Past and present were being revised at a speed to match Mountbatten's haste in India. Had not the British Empire always been a kindly, generous, and even selfless father figure, gently shepherding flocks of dumb savages towards freedom and democracy? Old volumes of Lord Macaulay's essays were retrieved from the attic and dusted off, and his assertion that the day India achieved self-rule would be 'the proudest day in British history' presented as incontrovertible evidence that, indeed, that had always been absolutely true.[2] There seemed to be no real difference in atti-tude between Macaulay and Mountbatten. It followed, then, that what went between must have been progress.[3]

The new spirit of post-colonial liberation seemed to be every-where. News from Indonesia provided the sense of superiority: the

Dutch had embarked upon a new wave of atrocities against the indigenous rebels. News from Palestine added to the motivation: British military lorries were blown up by Jewish terrorists, and two young sergeants hanged from a tree near Natanya at the end of July. When the staff at the Viceroy's House sat down to watch their Sunday film, Bernard Shaw's *Caesar and Cleopatra*, in the first week of August, they were treated to the bizarre but apposite spectacle of white actors with cut-glass English accents dressed up in fake tan, black wigs, linen and beads, refusing to submit to the Roman Empire with cries of 'Leave us to settle our own affairs!', 'Yes, go back to your own country!', 'Egypt belongs to us, not to you!', and 'Egypt for the Egyptians!'

In India itself, security remained perilous. On 27 July huge crowds of Sikhs, estimated at over 10,000, attempted to enter the All-Punjab Sikh Conference in Lahore, and were fired upon twice by police. Dalip Singh, presiding, observed that 'The British scheme for the partition of the country provides for an Empire for the Muslims in India.'[4] Responding to the signals of future trouble, Mountbatten took a personal role in organizing a Punjab Boundary Force, under the command of Major-General T.W. Rees, whom he described as 'a marvellous little man'.[5] General Rees was supported by two high-ranking advisers, one Muslim, one Sikh; he had 50,000 mixed troops at his command, including a high proportion of British officers. 'It is probably the largest military force ever collected in any one area of a country for the maintenance of law and order in peace-time,' noted Alan Campbell-Johnson.[6] On the same day, Attlee announced drastic cuts in foreign spending.

The British government was feeling the cold sweat of a financial crisis that threatened to overwhelm it. The next day, Sir Stafford Cripps met the American Under-Secretary of State in Paris, and tried to persuade him to relax the terms of its $3.75 billion loan, of which Britain had only $1 billion left. By this point, the government in London was having secret plans drawn up in case the United States did not let it off the hook. These included a below subsistence ration of 1700 calories per person per day, and the conscripting of school-children into agricultural work.[7] Five days later Churchill, recovered from his illness, delivered a rousing speech at his birthplace,

Blenheim Palace. He told an audience of 60,000 Conservatives that the only hope of national recovery was to have an election and throw out the Labour government.

With these troubles brewing, the Mountbattens' relationship suffered further. 'The last two days have been pretty good Hell', Ismay wrote to his wife on 5 August. 'Both Dickie and Edwina are dead tired, nervy as they can be, and right across each other. So that in addition to my other troubles, I have been doing peace-maker and general sedative . . . It's very wearing for them, and for me.'[8] While Edwina was concerned with world events and the plight of the growing number of victims of violence in the Punjab, Dickie seemed to be incapable of seeing beyond protocol. That day, he bothered Jawahar with a list of dates upon which the Union Jack might continue to be flown in India after independence. It is hard to imagine an issue of less pressing import that could have consumed the Viceroy's time just ten days before the transfer of power. That evening, Edwina went alone to see Jawahar.[9]

Despite his preoccupation with trivialities, even Mountbatten could not ignore the fierce controversies thrown up by the two partitions of Bengal and the Punjab. For centuries, both regions had been melting-pots of cultures, a jumbled variety of Muslims and Hindus living side by side, with Sikhs, Buddhists, Animists and Christians fitted in too. In times of peace, it had not mattered much to which of these religions a Punjabi or a Bengali adhered. As Jinnah himself had admitted, most people within the regions tended to consider their local identity before their religious affiliation. But the importance of religious identity had been growing in the twentieth century, notably in India and more slowly in the world beyond it.

The reason for this effect can in part be traced to the British policy of 'divide and rule'. Undoubtedly, the raj did plenty to encourage identity politics. The British found it easier to understand their vast domain if they broke it down into manageable chunks, and by the 1930s they had become anxious to ensure that each chunk was given a full and fair hearing. But picking a few random unelected lobbyists, based on what the British thought was a cross-section of Indian varieties, was not a reliable way to represent 400 million people. India's population could not be divided into neat boxes labelled by religion and cross-referenced with social position. India was an amorphous mass of different cultures, lifestyles, traditions and beliefs. After so many centuries of integration and exchange, these were not distinct, but rippled into each other, creating a web of cultural hybrids and compromises. A Sunni Muslim from the Punjab might have more in common with a Sikh than he did with a Shia Muslim from Bengal; a Shia might regard a Sufi Muslim as a heretic; a Sufi might get on better with a Brahmin Hindu than with a Wahhabi Muslim; a Brahmin might feel more at ease with a European than he would with another Hindu who was an outcaste. When the British started to define 'communities' based on religious identity and attach political representation to them, many Indians stopped accepting the diversity of their own thoughts and began to ask themselves in which of the boxes they belonged. At the same time, Indian politicians began to focus on religion as a central part of their policies – defining themselves by what they were, and even more by what they were not.[10]

This phenomenon is shown at its clearest with Jinnah, who began his career as the leading light of Hindu–Muslim unity, and ended it by forcing the creation of a separate Islamic-majority state. But the arc of Jinnah's career merely amplifies that of Indian politics as a whole. Congress was a largely secular and inclusive organization during Motilal Nehru's prime in the first twenty years of the twentieth century. Though it was the opposite of his intention, the emergence of Gandhi gave confidence to religious chauvinists. While Gandhi himself welcomed those of all faiths, the very fact that he brought spiritual sensibilities to the centre of politics stirred up extreme and divisive passions. Fundamentalist Hindus were rare presences on the political scene before Gandhi. In the wake of Gandhi, though, Hindu nationalists were able to move into the central ground of politics; while organizations like the Hindu Mahasabha and the Rashtriya Swayamsevak Sangh (RSS), dedicated to the formation of a Hindu nation, swelled their ranks from the fringes. This was no slow, invisible political trend: it was happening visibly during the spring and summer of 1947, when holy sadhus clad in saffron robes marched around the streets of Delhi, bellowing forth political slogans.[11] Rajendra Prasad, who was to become the

President of the new Constituent Assembly, wrote to Nehru on 7 August telling him that since July he had received 164,000 letters and postcards demanding that cow slaughter be made illegal – a common concern of devout Hindus, but one which is often used and taken as an anti-Muslim strategy. It was the Muslims in India, and the Untouchables, who ran the lucrative leather and beef industries, mostly for export.[12] The threat of a ban on cow slaughter naturally drove Muslims and Untouchables into the arms of more radical political organizations, which they felt would stick up for them. Whether the British caused division by carving up politics on the basis of religion, or whether they were simply responding to a trend in Indian society for Hindu nationalism and the beginnings of an Islamic resurgence, is an endlessly debatable question.

In an atmosphere of such tension, almost every part of the partition lines could be disputed by someone. But the three greatest controversies to haunt India's and Pakistan's future were those of two Punjabi districts, Gurdaspur and Ferozepur; and one Bengali district, Chittagong.

The Punjab is a great sweep of plain, laced with rivers, stretching from the Himalayas in the north to the Thar Desert in the west. It is one of the most fertile agricultural regions in the world, frequently described as the 'bread-basket' of India. According to a religious breakdown of the population, the western wing along the Indus had to go to Pakistan; the eastern wing between the Sutlej and Jumna Rivers had to go to India. The central sections were in dispute, mainly because they were rich, populous districts, and strategically important. Religiously speaking, the populations in those central tracts were far too integrated and too complex for a straight partition of their land. The economic case was labyrinthine. There would be conflicting interests over the divisions of holy shrines, railways, defensive frontiers, and water supplies.

A Punjab Boundary Commission had been set up to report to Sir Cyril Radcliffe, with four judges – two Muslims, a Hindu and a Sikh. These judges were given no mandate to negotiate with political leaders or other interested parties, which might have been supposed to be their most crucial function. Instead, they simply heard the cases presented, and then predictably divided in two when it came to the judgement – the Muslims sticking together, and the Sikh siding with the Hindu. Radcliffe was left to consider these inconclusive verdicts, and consequently had no choice but to make the decision of where to draw the dividing line entirely according to his own opinions. Suffering terribly from the heat, he was left alone with a secretary in a bungalow in the grounds of the Viceroy's House, amid daunting piles of maps, submissions and reports. He was not supposed to speak to any of the Indian leaders about his work, including the Viceroy; perhaps blessedly, he enjoyed a complete ignorance of Indian politics, and had never previously been east of Gibraltar.[13] He later admitted that it would have taken two years to draw up a just partition.[14] The Governor of the Punjab, Evan Jenkins, told Mountbatten it would have taken twice that to partition it peacefully.[15] Radcliffe had forty days.

In 1556, aged fourteen, Akbar had been crowned emperor at Gurdaspur.[16] In 1947, its significance was that it provided the only useful land-link between India and Kashmir. Further east along the Indo-Kashmiri border, the Himalayas rose so high as to prohibit a readily navigable route. Mountbatten has been accused of interfering with the decision on Gurdaspur, and certainly its fate had worried Nehru.[17] Most of it did eventually go to India, but there is good reason to think it would have done so anyway. As early as February 1946, when Lord Wavell had drawn up an estimate for what might constitute Pakistan, he had insisted that Gurdaspur must be kept with Amritsar. If it were not, Amritsar would be encircled to the east, west and north by Pakistan, rendering the Sikh position untenable. This would have proved a decisive factor in the apportioning of Gurdaspur regardless of the road link to Kashmir.[18] On that basis, Mountbatten's innocence of the charge of interfering with Gurdaspur is credible, though not proven beyond doubt.

The case of Ferozepur entails a lot more doubt, and a lot less innocence. Ferozepur was a narrowly Muslim-majority district running along the south bank of the Sutlej River, with a population of over half a million people. It included a major arsenal as well as the headwaters that irrigated the princely state of Bikaner. A salient within it, sticking out forty miles into Sikh lands and effectively encircling Amritsar to the south, had been assigned to Pakistan.[19]

This can be seen from a provisional map sent from Mountbatten's private secretary, George Abell, to Evan Jenkins on 8 August. The map showed the approximate border, which was to be finalized the next day. 'There will not be any great changes from this boundary', Abell wrote.[20] But the Ferozepur salient was of evident concern to Bikaner, which had already agreed to go to India. Kanwar Sain, the Chief Engineer of Bikaner, said that he and his Prime Minister visited Mountbatten on 11 August. They told him that, if the Ferozepur headwaters went to Pakistan, so too would their state.[21]

Mountbatten did not respond to this threat, though Sain remembered that his face changed colour; but apparently he took it seriously. Late that night, Radcliffe received a visitation in the suave form of V.P. Menon, who invited him to lunch with Mountbatten and Lord Ismay the next day. Christopher Beaumont, secretary to the Boundary Commission, was unusually excluded from the invitation. Beaumont later testified that Radcliffe returned from that lunch 'agitated', would not disclose what was said, and immediately redrew the line of partition to award Ferozepur to India. Both Beaumont and one of Mountbatten's secretaries thought that the Viceroy was under pressure from Nehru as well as from Bikaner to make Radcliffe change the line. Evan Jenkins received a telegram bearing the two words: 'eliminate salient'.[22]

Throughout the rest of his life, Mountbatten kept up the position that he had never interfered with Radcliffe. This was a lie, as he himself allowed in at least one private letter. Mountbatten wrote to Ismay in April 1948, with the instruction that he should burn the letter. It survived, and provides a potentially less dishonest Mountbatten side of the story. Radcliffe, he says, came to him with the Ferozepur problem, and Mountbatten hinted that it would be fine to 'make any adjustments necessary' – with the caveat that, owing to the difficulty presented by the Sikh population in the Punjab, he would prefer any concession to Pakistan to be made in Bengal.[23]

Mountbatten's account to Ismay still does not tie up entirely with Beaumont's testimony, which attributes the raising of the subject very clearly to Mountbatten rather than to Radcliffe. There is no reason to assume he was telling the whole truth to Ismay. But, even if he was, the other side of the bargain presented to Radcliffe was not fulfilled: there was no matching concession to Pakistan in Bengal. Mountbatten's official biographer has suggested that the award of the Chittagong Hill Tracts in Bengal to Pakistan compensated for Ferozepur.[24] But the award of Chittagong was supposed to make up for Pakistan's loss of a far greater prize: Calcutta.

Back in March, when Mountbatten's principal secretary had expressed the opinion that 'Pakistan would definitely be unworkable without Calcutta', Mountbatten had proposed that Chittagong might do as a port instead.[25] But Chittagong was far smaller than Calcutta, nowhere near as developed, and much less convenient for overland transport. Muslim-majority East Bengal was mainly agricultural, with a strong jute farming industry. But all the actual manufacturing and heavy industry was based in Hindu-majority West Bengal. The Governor, Sir Frederick Burrows, had predicted that an independent East Bengal without Calcutta would become a 'rural slum'. It was felt among Muslims that partition of Bengal was a way of sabotaging East Pakistan. Mountbatten agreed. During the meeting, he made it clear several times that the whole point of the current policy was to allow Pakistan 'to fail on its demerits'. If the plan presented to Jinnah was awful enough, the British thought, he could be made to reconsider the whole idea of Pakistan.[26] They were wrong; Jinnah would surprise them by accepting Pakistan anyway.

On 26 April, Mountbatten asked Jinnah how he would feel if Bengal, as a whole, became independent rather than joining Pakistan. Jinnah replied unhesitatingly: 'I should be delighted. What is the use of Bengal without Calcutta; they had much better remain united and independent; I am sure that they would remain on friendly terms with us.'[27] Congress, on the other hand, was under no circumstance prepared to countenance a fully independent Bengal, and the Muslim League in East Bengal was under no circumstance prepared to join India. What was created, then, in East Bengal, soon to be East Pakistan and afterwards Bangladesh, was a nation deliberately designed to be incapable of supporting itself. At least one half of Pakistan was set up to fail.

Even the poor sop of Chittagong for Calcutta threw Congress

into a frenzy. This was predicated on the grounds that the Chittagong Hills had a non-Muslim majority: most of the inhabitants were Buddhist or Animist. On 13 August, two days before the transfer of power, Patel wrote to Mountbatten deploring the probable award of the Chittagong tracts to Pakistan as 'manifestly unjust'.[28] The letter insinuated that not only might the people of Bengal resist the award of Chittagong to Pakistan by force, but that they would be justified in doing so; and that the Indian government would have to support them, both morally and militarily.

Mountbatten was furious with Patel: 'The one man I had regarded as a real statesman with both feet firmly on the ground, and a man of honour whose word was his bond, had turned out to be as hysterical as the rest.'[29] The plain fact was that, even with Chittagong taken into account, India had done much better out of the partition of Bengal than had Pakistan. East Pakistan was also to be deprived on its north side of the high ground claimed by the Muslim League, which would have included the hill station of Darjeeling. There were sound arguments of geography, trade and communications for including most of the north districts between East Bengal and the borders of Bhutan and Nepal in Pakistan. These had been clear during the earlier partition of Bengal in 1905, when they had been included in the east. But for the partition of 1947 such concerns as geography, trade and communications had to be subordinated beneath religious identity, and the religious identity of the northern part of East Bengal was, in the main, non-Muslim. It went to India, creating a tight corridor across the Himalayas between West Bengal and Assam, around the back of East Pakistan.

There was some debate among Mountbatten's staff over when Radcliffe's award should be published. Some suggested the earliest possible point, because it would be useful to the police and army. Others thought that, since it was bound to cause trouble, it was best left until 14 August. Mountbatten himself, after initially asking Radcliffe to publish the award on 10 August, ultimately suggested something even more radical than leaving it till the last minute – which was to make the announcement after independence.[30] This was technically impossible, for states could not exist without borders.[31] But Mountbatten argued that independence day itself should not be marred by the inevitable trouble that would follow the award's publication.[32]

Mountbatten saw Radcliffe on 9 August and asked him to postpone the award.[33] Radcliffe refused point blank. He had finished the partitions of Bengal and the Punjab, and had almost finished partitioning Sylhet in Assam; any delay would be politically motivated. After a great deal of viceregal persuasion, he finally conceded that all three awards could be delivered simultaneously on 13 August. Handily, this would coincide with Mountbatten getting on a plane to Karachi. He would not be back in Delhi until the evening of 14 August, and the printing presses would be closed for the national Independence Day celebrations on 15 August. The awards arrived, and were put in a safe, where they would stay, apparently unperused, until 16 August.

Mountbatten's personal report to London of 16 August deliberately misrepresented these dealings. 'It was on Tuesday, 12th August, that I was finally informed by Radcliffe that his awards would be ready by noon the following day, just too late for me to see before leaving for Karachi,' he averred on the official record. Another line in the same report got closer to the truth: 'It had been obvious all along that, the later we postponed publication, the less would the inevitable odium react upon the British.'[34]

To Mountbatten's expressed relief, his two most troublesome foes – Gandhi and Jinnah – were soon to be out of his life. On 9 August, Gandhi arrived in Calcutta. He moved into the mansion of a Muslim widow in the suburb of Belliaghatta with H.S. Suhrawardy, the Muslim League Prime Minister of Bengal, in an attempt to restore communal harmony. On the night of 13 August, a crowd of a thousand Hindu youths threw stones at the house, smashed windows and shouted at Gandhi to move to Park Circus, a Muslim area where Hindu houses lay vacant and ruined.[35] 'Gandhi has announced his decision to spend the rest of his life in Pakistan looking after the minorities,' Mountbatten reported to London. 'This will infuriate Jinnah, but will be a great relief to Congress for, as I have said before, his influence is largely negative or even destructive.'[36] Verdicts outside the Viceroy's House were similarly bleak. 'Mr

Gandhi today is a very disappointed man indeed,' noted the *Times of India*. 'He has lived to see his followers transgress his dearest doctrines; his countrymen have indulged in a bloody and inhuman fratricidal war; non-violence, khadi and many another of his principles have been swept away by the swift current of politics. Disillusioned and disappointed, he is today perhaps the only steadfast exponent of what is understood as Gandhism.'[37]

Jinnah's parting was more cheerful. On 7 August, he had left Delhi for Karachi, flying in the Viceroy's silver Dakota with Fatima. He arrived at Mauripur airport, and descended wearing a sherwani and an astrakhan cap. Cheering crowds broke through the police cordon to greet him, and pursued him all the way to his new residence, Government House.[38] Four days later, he was formally elected President of the constituent assembly, and delivered an extraordinary speech – so extraordinary, in fact, that it begs the question of what his intentions had ever been in proposing the idea of Pakistan. Some historians have put forward the notion that he may have intended it all along as a bargaining chip; and that, when Mountbatten advanced the date of the transfer of power and made it clear that the British were leaving, the rug was pulled from under his feet.[39]

Jinnah's speech on 11 August made it very clear that he intended Pakistan to be a secular state. 'You may belong to any religion or caste or creed – that has nothing to do with the business of the State,' he declared, guaranteeing equality in Pakistan for all faiths and communities. He went further still: 'In course of time all these angularities of the majority and minority communities, the Hindu community and the Muslim community – because even as regards Muslims you have Pathans, Punjabis, Shias, Sunnis and so on, and among Hindus you have Brahmins, Vashnavas, Khatris, also Bengalees, Madrasis and so on – will vanish,' he said. 'Indeed, if you ask me, this has been the biggest hindrance in the way of India to attain freedom and independence, and but for this we would have been free peoples long, long ago.'[40] These were peculiar words from the man who had long hindered independence precisely by reinforcing the division between Hindu and Muslim, and add weight to the theory that Jinnah may have been less serious about Pakistan as a Muslim homeland than as a playing piece. Perhaps, all along, he had pursued not an Islamic state, but rather a non-Hindu-majority state. There was no time to worry about it. On 13 August, an exhausted Radcliffe delivered his award; the last few princely states were still squabbling over better deals; Gandhi, in Calcutta, tried desperately to hold Hindus and Muslims together; and Nehru, in Delhi, began to read reports of new outbreaks of disorder in the Punjab with growing concern. One hundred and fifty people, mostly Sikhs, had been murdered there in the previous twenty-four hours.[41]

That afternoon, the Mountbattens flew to Karachi for the first of their independence days. In the evening, the Jinnahs threw a party at Government House. There was a state banquet, at which Fatima Jinnah and the Begum Liaquat Ali Khan teased Mountbatten about the midnight plans for Delhi's independence ceremonies, and remarked how shocking it was that a government should be in thrall to the pronouncements of astrologers. 'I refrained from retorting that the whole Karachi programme had had to change because Jinnah had forgotten that it was Ramazan,' Mountbatten wrote sniffily, 'and had had to change the lunch party he had himself suggested to a dinner party.'[42]

On the verandah, the band played an eclectic selection of tunes – from 'Finlandia' to 'A Whistler and His Dog' – while the guests sipped soft drinks and ate ice cream and cakes. Jinnah, though elegant as ever, was showing the strain of the previous few weeks. The journalist Mildred Talbot, who was present, reported that his 'appearance so shocked me that little else registered on my mind during the evening. I hadn't thought it possible but he was even more slender and a worse colour than when we had seen him in Delhi last November. He looked like a walking, talking corpse. The nightmare I had that night was directly attributable to that vivid impression.'[43] Despite his appearance, Jinnah was at his warmest that night. He and Mountbatten had their friendliest ever conversation, with Jinnah thanking Mountbatten for the creation of Pakistan and for staying on in India, and imploring him to defend Pakistan's interests, too.[44]

The next morning, the Mountbattens and the Jinnahs drove to Assembly Hall in a superannuated Rolls Royce that had been borrowed from a prince. Jinnah wore a silk sherwani, while both

Mountbattens were in their trademark dazzling white. 'Mountbatten was looking very dashing,' remembered one British soldier who was on duty during the parade, 'with an all-over, almost *Chorus Girl* tan.'[45] All four waved and smiled as they drove through Karachi to the piping of the Royal Highlanders. Mountbatten doffed his cap as they passed the bronze statue of Mohandas Gandhi that stood between the secretariat and the chief court, a gift from Karachi's Hindu merchants, who had threatened civil war within twenty-four hours if it were removed. Earlier that day, someone had put an Muslim fez on it: this had tactfully disappeared by the time the parade passed. When Mountbatten uncovered, Jinnah, too, raised his hand in an acknowledgement of his great rival.[46]

At the assembly hall, the four descended from their car, which was by then so overheated that it burst into flames.[47] Inside the hall, Mountbatten noticed that there was only one special chair set up. He was still busy thinking that Jinnah ought to have a special chair, too, when Jinnah sat himself down on the throne and indicated that Mountbatten should take one of the humbler seats.[48] Both men gave gracious speeches, complimenting each other on a carefully chosen list of virtues. Edwina pressed Fatima Jinnah's hand with affection as Jinnah gave his magisterial address.[49] 'History seems sometimes to move with the infinite slowness of a glacier and sometimes to rush forward in a torrent,' said Mountbatten when it was his turn to speak. 'Just now, in this part of the world our united efforts have melted the ice and moved some impediments in the stream, and we are carried onwards in the full flood. There is no time to look back. There is time only to look forward.'[50] Jinnah read out the goodwill messages Pakistan had so far received. The very first was from one of the parties with the greatest interest in Pakistan's future, President Harry S. Truman of the United States of America. It was followed by similar good wishes from Egypt, France, Syria and Nepal.[51] The band played 'God Save the King' before the meeting broke up. Mildred Talbot cast some doubt on the supposed new spirit of camaraderie between Mountbatten and Jinnah. 'If it were in truth a "parting between friends" as they both declared,' she wrote, 'it was the coldest friendship I have ever seen.'[52]

After the ceremony, the Mountbattens and the Jinnahs emerged into the sunlight for a state parade. The atmosphere was reported as being one of 'curious apathy' – whether this represented a general antipathy towards Pakistan, or just the fact that most of Karachi's population was Hindu, was not certain.[53] Mountbatten had been warned the day before by the Criminal Investigation Department of a plot to throw bombs at Jinnah during the procession. He had tried to persuade Jinnah to cancel it, 'but he was in his strongest "no" mood'.[54] Instead, Jinnah advised Mountbatten not to join him in the open car; but the Viceroy would not baulk before Jinnah, and, in any case, he thought his presence might guard against any attempt by Hindus or Sikhs. 'I knew that no one in that crowd would want to risk shooting *me*!'[55] The parade went on. 'I won't pretend I wasn't scared,' Mountbatten later admitted. 'I was, and did my best not to show it, but the new Governor-General of Pakistan did not seem in the least bit frightened. I was deeply impressed by his calm courage and high sense of duty.' The car trundled along, Mountbatten unable to relax until the view of Government House drew close and they arrived back through the gates. 'Never had my feelings been warmer to the man with whom I shared this traumatic experience', he wrote.

Jinnah flashed Mountbatten a grin, leaned forward to touch him on the knee and said, 'Thank God I've brought you back alive.' Mountbatten's tension got the better of his etiquette. 'You brought me back alive?' he exclaimed. 'It's I who brought you back alive.'[56] But the important thing, as he soon afterwards admitted, was that they had both come back alive – and that there was a new cordiality in the air between the Governors General of India and Pakistan. Before the Mountbattens climbed on to their aeroplane at midday, Fatima Jinnah bid them farewell. To Edwina's surprise, she kissed her goodbye affectionately on both cheeks.[57] But the cheerful mood sobered as the Viceroy's plane flew over the Punjab boundaries on its way back to Delhi, the large fires of villages aflame clearly visible from the air.[58] In the villages of the Punjab, the beginnings of the partition disaster were already underway.

'My warmest thanks to you on this day which sees the successful achievement of a task of an unexampled difficulty', Attlee cabled to

Nehru family portrait, circa 1899. Left to right: Swarup Rani, Motilal, Jawaharlal.

'A beam of light that pierced the darkness': Mohandas Gandhi and his wife Kasturba.

A reluctant Jawahar marries
Kamala Kaul, 1916.

'I think we are going to be great
friends': David (front), the future
King Edward VIII, on his imperial
tour with Dickie Mountbatten.

Hollywood honeymoon: Dickie and Edwina Mountbatten (2nd and 3rd right) on set with Charlie Chaplin (centre) and Cecil B. DeMille (3rd left).

Gandhi (left background, bare-chested) arrives with his Salt Marchers at Dandi, 6 April 1931, to collect salt in defiance of British law.

Ramsay MacDonald, standing, presides over the 2nd Round Table Conference, London, 1931. This attempt to move towards Indian self-rule failed, owing in part to the massive number of delegates. Gandhi is sitting centre, fourth right from MacDonald.

Balmoral, summer 1936: King Edward VIII (in cloak) is joined by friends, including (left) Dickie Mountbatten, and (right) Wallis Simpson and Edwina Mountbatten. A few months later, the King would abdicate to marry Mrs Simpson.

Grand strategy conferences

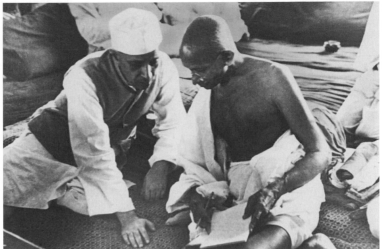

Jawaharlal Nehru and Mohandas Gandhi agreeing the 'Quit India' plan in defiance of the British raj, 1942.

World War II Allies, 1943. Seated centre left, Winston Churchill; centre right, Franklin D. Roosevelt; standing, centre, Dickie Mountbatten. Sir Hastings Ismay is to the left of Mountbatten. Seated to the left of Churchill is Admiral Ernest King, who Mountbatten accidentally shot in the leg.

Captured in a rare moment of mutual good humour: Jawaharlal Nehru and Mohammad Ali Jinnah, 1946.

24 March 1947: Dickie Mountbatten is sworn in as Viceroy of India. Edwina is to the right of Dickie. Standing to the left of the picture can be seen Jawaharlal Nehru, in black sherwani and white cap; to the left of Nehru is Vallabhbhai Patel, in white khadi. Liaquat Ali Khan is standing to the right of Edwina, in a light suit and a black cap.

28 March 1947: At the Viceroy's first garden party, Edwina sits on a sofa with Nan Pandit and Pamela Mountbatten. Jawahar sits at Edwina's feet.

Front page news, 31 March 1947: Gandhi, at his first meeting with the Mountbattens, leans on Edwina for support.

It was no secret that the Mountbattens got on less well with the Muslim League leaders. Left to right: Liaquat Ali Khan, Jinnah, Dickie, Fatima Jinnah, Edwina.

'Like the Blitz at its worst': Edwina inspecting riot damage in the Punjab, April 1947.

3 June 1947: for the first time in history, no party raises an objection to the plan for independence. Clockwise around the table from centre: Dickie, Jinnah, Liaquat, Abdur Rab Nishtar, Baldev Singh, K. R. Kripalani, Vallabhbhai Patel, Jawahar.

Independence days

Pakistan's Independence Day, 14 August 1947. 'I won't pretend I wasn't scared': driving through Karachi, Dickie and Jinnah maintain brave faces despite an assassination threat.

India's Independence Day, 15 August 1947: a rainbow appears in the sky as the new flag is raised. Dickie salutes; to the right, Edwina and Jawahar in conversation.

15 August 1947, Delhi: crowds greet the Mountbattens.

Calcutta, August 1947:
Gandhi (with grand-niece
Manu) plugs his ears against
the screams of rioters.

'A great and unique love': brought together by their work with the victims of India's partition, Jawahar and Edwina can be seen holding hands during a visit to a refugee camp in this rare photograph.

October 1947: crowds gather in riot-torn Delhi to hear Gandhi and Nehru call for peace.

'We have so long been the "Aunt Sally" of politics in India that our reappearance in that role is hardly surprising': the Mountbattens in Gwalior during the Kashmir crisis, December 1947.

'His sister slipped up before each photograph and tried gently to uncurl his desperately clenched hands': the dying Jinnah photographed by Margaret Bourke-White, 1948.

Henri Cartier-Bresson/Magnum Photos

'A thousand years later that light will still be seen in this country': Jawahar climbs the gatepost of Birla House to tell the crowds of Gandhi's murder, 30 January 1948.

Nehru Memorial Museum & Library

'Only the eyes revealed stark anguish': Jawahar (centre) at Gandhi's funeral, 31 January 1948. Edwina sits behind him.

Mashobra, May 1948: Dickie and Pamela Mountbatten in their car, just outside the Governor-General's Retreat. Edwina and Jawahar are in the back.

'They really dote on each other in the nicest way': Edwina and Jawahar walking together in the forests around Mashobra.

'Hundreds of thousands will be sorrowful at the news that you have gone': Edwina and a downcast Jawahar at the Mountbattens' farewell dinner.

More goodbyes: Dickie bids farewell to Rajagopalachari while, in the background, Jawahar kisses Edwina's hand.

'It was not a bang but with a kiss you left us': Edwina hugs India's new Governor-General, Chakravarty Rajagopalachari, as the Mountbattens leave for London, 21 June 1948.

Keeping in touch:
Edwina and Jawahar
in London, 1955.

'He had sat between
Mrs Kennedy and her
sister and with the
light of love in his
eyes': Indian state
visit to Washington,
1961. Left to right:
Jacqueline Kennedy,
Jawahar, Indira
Gandhi, John F.
Kennedy.

'Theirs had been a harmony
of difference, cemented by
their mutual admiration for
the Mahatma, on the one
hand, and the very human
Edwina, on the other':
Dickie is the first British
visitor to Jawahar's lying in
state, 1964. With Dickie is
Jawahar's sister, Nan
Pandit.

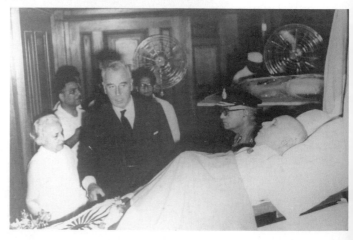

Mountbatten that night – adding a special thanks to Edwina. Mountbatten replied delightedly that it was 'the most encouraging telegram I have ever received'.[59] He communicated Attlee's thanks to Edwina in a heartfelt letter, perhaps intending to rebuild the relationship after the storms of the previous weeks: 'surely no husband in history has had the proud privilege of transmitting a telegram of appreciation from the Prime Minister to his wife', he wrote. 'I'm proud to be that exception.' He concluded with an appreciation of his own: 'Thank you, my pet, with all my heart.'[60]

In Delhi, the bunting was going up, and a joyful atmosphere prevailed. On every street, workmen climbed scaffolding to repaint walls and hang banners, wiring thousands of orange, white and green lightbulbs around trees and fences, swagging them across the roads. In the great shopping arcades of Connaught Circus, the national flag hung in every window. Drapers filled their windows with bales of silk in the national colours; restaurants offered special independence menus; cinemas proclaimed free shows of Indian movies for students and children. Gentlemen's outfitters sold out of sherwanis: according to the *Times of India*, 'An Indian dressed in a western suit is already beginning to feel self-conscious.'

In the cramped, ancient alleys of Old Delhi, steam billowed forth from vats of boiling milk, filling the air with the delicate scents of rosewater and cardamom as the city's confectioners toiled to meet endless orders for sweets. The heavy rationing of sugar was not permitted to spoil the fun: 'the blackmarketeer is having the time of his life, combining patriotism with business.'[61] Nehru gave a splendid speech to a huge crowd, undiminished by the sheeting monsoon rain. 'I felt happy at coming into close personal contact with great crowds again', he wrote to his sister, Nan, who had left for her ambassadorial posting in Moscow a few days before. 'I still seem to appeal to them.'[62] He was thrilled to see the flags unfurling all over the capital, stamping a new Indian identity on the British city. 'You do think they're really going, don't you,' a respected political analyst asked an American journalist; 'this is not just a subterfuge so they can come back when their crisis at home is over?'[63] But they were going. As the chimes sounded and the unexpected blast from a conch shell startled the delegates in the chamber of the

Constituent Assembly, a nation that had struggled for so many years, and sacrificed so much, was freed at last from the shackles of Empire.

Yes, Britain was finally free.

By the following morning the world had turned once, and changed for ever. India and Pakistan were dominions. Britain had surrendered the keystone of its Empire. And yet at 8.30 sharp the Mountbattens were once again sitting on gold and scarlet thrones in New Delhi's majestic Durbar Hall. Lord Mountbatten, resplendent in a uniform, was saluted by trumpet fanfares from the upper gallery. Meanwhile, according to Mildred Talbot: 'Probably every woman present marveled at the cool appearance of Lady Mountbatten who, in the midst of Delhi's indescribable summer heat, was stunning in gold lamé, arm-length gloves, and the appropriate jewelry including a gold tiara.'[64]

This almost monarchical ceremony installed Mountbatten in his new democratic role as Governor General of India. For, though there had been a revolution, the Empire had not been overthrown. The British had got away with their dignity intact, and their majesty undimmed. The Mountbattens drove to the Council House for an inaugural meeting, at which Lord Mountbatten read out a message to India from his cousin, King George VI. 'Freedom-loving people everywhere will wish to share in your celebrations,' the King had written, 'for with this transfer of power by consent comes the fulfilment of a great democratic ideal to which the British and Indian peoples alike are firmly dedicated.'[65] An overdue retreat had been turned into a great British victory.

No cynicism blighted the mass celebrations that day. While the dignitaries of the Constituent Assembly delivered their speeches in the Council Chamber, the Indian tricolour was raised above the building for the first time. For a few minutes, there was silence along the grand avenue of Kingsway, as the hundreds of thousands assembled (some on roofs, or hanging out of trees) took in the long-wished-for sight. But a gradual rumbling soon swelled into a cheer, which was renewed as Nehru came out on to the balcony. When the Mountbattens emerged, another shout of approval went up. Before he and his wife got into their state coach, Lord

Mountbatten, knowing exactly how to serve the moment, turned and saluted both his friend Nehru and the Indian flag.

After lunch and a quick change, the Mountbattens were driven in a parade down the whole length of Kingsway to India Gate, through streets so packed with crowds that they were unable to get out of their coach. In the blistering heat of that afternoon, Princes' Park was crammed with hundreds of thousands of free Indians. The park was a monument to royalty, with a colossal statue of King George V in a pagoda at the centre, and the palaces of five of India's most magnificent princes arranged in a circle around it: the Nizam of Hyderabad, the Gaekwar of Baroda, and the Maharajas of Patiala, Bikaner and Jaipur. On Independence Day, it brimmed with ordinary people. Where 30,000 had been expected, at least ten times that number turned up: some estimates said as many as a million. An instant democracy blossomed, as peasant crowds stormed the grandstand which had been reserved for dignitaries, and cheerfully occupied it six to a chair.[66] The crush was such that people could not lift a foot for fear they would never get it back to the ground. The Mountbattens' daughter Pamela remembered that 'it was raining babies! Because lots of women had brought their babies with them and they were being crushed. So they threw them up in the air in despair of having these babies crushed, and you just sort of caught a baby as it came down.'[67] Nehru's daughter, Indira Gandhi, saw one woman decide that her baby was probably safer with Lady Mountbatten, and pass it over. Edwina held the infant tightly in her arms.[68]

Pamela was with Vallabhbhai Patel's daughter, Maniben. Maniben was a tiny, fragile-looking woman, and Pamela began to fear seriously for her life as the crowd squeezed tighter. They were rescued by Nehru, who created a distraction by lifting off a nearby Indian's topee and bashing another on the head with it. He climbed up on to a man's shoulders, and surfed forwards over the shoulders of the crowd towards them. 'Panditji came galloping over people, wearing sandals,' Pamela remembered. Nehru pulled them towards the flag platform, which would provide something to stand against.

'Where do I put my feet?' asked Pamela. 'I cannot walk on people.'

'Of course you can walk on people,' he replied. 'Nobody will mind.' Pamela indicated her high-heeled shoes, at which he added, 'Well, take those shoes off then nobody will mind.'

'And we walked over human bodies the whole way,' remembered Pamela, 'and the extraordinary thing about that day was that nobody did mind.'[69]

Taken aback, Mountbatten and Nehru decided to abandon the carefully planned programme of ceremonial. Instead, the Governor General simply shouted from his carriage that the new Indian flag should be hoisted up, as he pulled fainting children out of the crowd and into safety. The new Indian tricolour unfurled to a chorus of joyous uproar. (The British flag was not hauled down first. Mountbatten had seen to it that all Union Jacks had been removed the night before.)[70] As a salute was fired, a rainbow broke across the sky – a detail that one would dismiss as fanciful, were it not for the fact that so many observers insisted they had seen it.[71] Mountbatten pointed up at this well-timed natural phenomenon, and the crowd went wild again. 'I had never noticed how closely a rainbow could resemble the new Dominion flag of saffron, white and green,' he mused in his report to the British government the next day.[72]

The rest of the day was taken up with parties, speeches and almost impossible progressions through the undiminishing throngs in the streets. The Mountbattens' coach was besieged as it returned to the Viceroy's House (renamed Government House for the new era). As the coach trawled through the crowds, it picked up several stowaways. Four Indian ladies and their children crammed inside next to the Mountbattens, along with the Polish wife of a British officer. An Indian press photographer clung to the back. Nehru himself, unable to get to his car, sat cross-legged on the hood. The photographer was particularly struck by the people's reaction to the Mountbattens, as they shouted out, 'Pandit Mountbatten ki jai!' ('Hail Mountbatten!') The next day, he was moved to tell Mountbatten's press attaché: 'At last, after two hundred years, Britain has conquered India.'[73]

PART III

THE BEGINNING

CHAPTER 15

PARADISE ON EARTH

WHAT HAD BEEN ONE WAS NOT NOW TWO, BUT LEGION. INDIA and Pakistan were dominions within the British Commonwealth of Nations. Hyderabad, Kashmir, Bhopal, Indore, Kalat and Junagadh were of uncertain status, having refused to accede to either dominion, though Bhopal and Indore would soon accede to India, and Kalat ultimately to Pakistan. Owing to Jinnah's laid-back policy, none of the ten princely states which were expected to go to Pakistan had acceded; British paramountcy was gone, and theoretically any of these could be recognized as independent nations. Even so, by the morning of 15 August, India was by population the second largest country in the world. On its eastern and western edges, the two chunks of Pakistan comprised the sixth largest country in the world. East and West Pakistan were separated by at least 725 miles of Indian territory, or a twenty-day journey by steamship around the edge. There was a good deal of bad feeling between India and Pakistan, and no borders – at least, none known to any but Sir Cyril Radcliffe and his secretary, for still the maps lay locked up on Mountbatten's orders in a safe in Government House. In London, a Ministry of Works carpenter in a white apron and a Homburg hat briskly unscrewed the plaque to the left of the door on King Charles Street that read 'India Office', and replaced it with a new one: 'Commonwealth Relations Office'.[1]

On the morning of 16 August, Jawaharlal Nehru closed the celebrations, and hoisted the Indian tricolour over the Red Fort in Old Delhi, the splendid palace of Shah Jahan, grandson of Akbar. Half a million people crowded into the wide street around the fort, whose red sandstone towers had been the setting for generations of potentates. The great Mughals had shown their majesty from its ramparts at daybreak every morning. The last Mughal, Bahadur Shah II, had briefly ruled the Indian mutineers from its pillared halls. King George V, in plumes and medals, had ridden forth from it for his coronation as Emperor of India in 1911. Now it was the turn of a man who hoped to represent democratic India. Over the archway leading into the audience hall of the fort, its ornate white marble walls inlaid with jewels cut and polished to represent delicately blossoming flowers, a famous Persian inscription reads: 'If there is a paradise on earth, it is this'. The crowd agreed, cheering Nehru wholeheartedly; and Edwina Mountbatten, standing at the Prime Minister's side, wore an expression of unreserved joy. She had come fresh from another fight with Dickie, this time over his acceptance of a new earldom. Dickie wrote to his daughter Patricia that Edwina was 'in despair' at being promoted from Viscountess to Countess, 'for she disapproves *so much* of all these nonsensical titles.'[2]

'That the double change-over occurred amid widespread rejoicings and peaceful demonstrations happily confounds the Jeremiahs who foresaw trouble', read the *Times of India*'s confident editorial.[3] It spoke too soon. Nehru's speech from the Red Fort was the last happy moment of the transfer of power. That afternoon, Mountbatten handed Radcliffe's finished award to the leaders in Delhi, and cabled it to their counterparts in Karachi. 'Nobody in India will love me for my award about the Punjab and Bengal', Radcliffe had written bluntly to his stepson three days earlier, 'and there will be roughly 80 million people with a grievance who will begin looking for me. I do not want them to find me.'[4] He had the good sense to get on a plane to London on 17 August, and afterwards burnt all his papers relating to the partition.[5]

It was inevitable that none of the parties would be happy, which was why Mountbatten had secured on 22 July an agreement from both governments-to-be that they would accept the award, whatever it was. They did so without pleasure. In Pakistan, the Communications Minister, Abdur Rab Nishtar, described the award as 'the parting kick of the British',[6] while Liaquat was livid at the loss of Gurdaspur. In India, the reaction was no less grim. 'Bhai [brother] and the other Congress leaders read it with deepening misery', wrote Nehru's sister, Betty Hutheesing.[7] Patel could not contain his rage at the award of the Chittagong Hill Tracts to Pakistan. But it was the Sikh minister Baldev Singh's wordless dejection that augured the worst for the trouble to come.[8] The Sikh population that he represented, scattered between West Pakistan and India, received the news hardest of all. The inclusion of the western Punjab and Lahore in Pakistan provoked an immediate response. A wave of violence, familiar in its intent but renewed in its vigour, spilled forth across the Punjab.

When Mountbatten had still been thrashing out the details of his plan, Gandhi had told him that there were two alternatives. Either British rule would be continued, or else there would be a bloodbath. 'What should I do, then?' Mountbatten had asked. Gandhi's reply was typical. 'You must face the bloodbath and accept it.'[9]

The bloodbath would have to be faced with an immediacy and on a scale that shocked all the governments involved. Within hours of independence, the Punjab, which had been disturbed for several days, suffered a total collapse of public order. Penderel Moon was in Lahore in 15 August and found it mainly deserted or on fire. While he was discussing the situation in broad daylight with another British official, a gang of Muslims broke into a Hindu house across the street and plundered it. The official told him that the Muslim police had been siding with the mob, to the extent of offering armed cover from the roofs while Muslim rioters ransacked Sikh gurdwaras.[10] On the afternoon of 16 August Sir Claude Auchinleck, now Supreme Commander of the Indian and Pakistani armies, reported to Mountbatten that the new dominion of India was already in a state of civil war.

Less than a month before, the future governments of India and Pakistan had issued a joint declaration insisting that 'in no circumstances will violence be tolerated'. There can be no doubt that the governments were genuine in their intention to preserve order, just as there can be no doubt that they had neither the imagination nor the capacity to do so. It had been believed, fancifully but firmly, that the local police and General Rees's Boundary Force would be able to take care of any spots of bother.[11] But the extent and vigour of communal tensions had been catastrophically underestimated.

On 17 August, Nehru dropped everything and flew to the Punjab to meet Liaquat. Side by side, the two men appealed for peace through public appearances and broadcasts. Meanwhile, Lord and Lady Mountbatten flew to Bombay to see off the first contingent of British troops, and to celebrate all over again. By the shores of the Arabian Sea, on Bombay's Ballard Pier, Mountbatten asked the 5000 men to break ranks and cluster around, just as he had so often in Burma during the war. He made a jovial speech, and had a message of good wishes from Nehru read out.

Dickie and Edwina proceeded to a tea party at the Taj Mahal Hotel, and afterwards drove to Government House. The drive, just five miles around Back Bay, took almost an hour owing to the number of people lining the route – the Bombay police estimated 750,000.[12] The Indian tricolour was waved all day by Lady Mountbatten and the crowds alike; they also waved the Union Jack. Just eighteen months before, remembered the journalist Phillips Talbot, the naval mutineers in Bombay had roused great crowds with cries of 'Death to Englishmen!' and 'Britishers: Go Back!' Now the cry was 'Jai England!' and 'England zindabad!'[13] 'A senior British official was misty-eyed when he told me about it later,' Talbot noted.[14] Police cordons were broken as crowds swarmed the car. Dickie was overjoyed, and shouted 'Jai Hind!' all the way along Marine Drive. People climbed on to the footboard of his carriage to touch the hems of his gleaming naval whites, and he was 'literally caressed for hundreds of yards by rapt admirers', according to the *Times of India*.[15]

Dickie returned to Delhi, while Edwina stayed in Bombay to visit her usual round of worthy institutions. It was the cheerful photographs of her kneeling on the floor to play with the happy, healthy children at the United Mills Welfare Centre that made it into the official album of the trip; but the grimmer scenes at the Matunga labour camp and the filthy slum area made a greater impact on her personally. Edwina trudged for hours around the grim hovels in which many thousands of the city's poor lived, and was quoted in the newspapers describing the conditions as 'appalling'.[16] But the press baulked at reporting the full force of her comments, which decried the slums as a 'constant reproach to the citizens of the great and wealthy city of Bombay', and called on those citizens to wipe out this shame. The reception she received from the locals was one of rapturous approval.[17]

Edwina arrived back in Delhi on 19 August. In the four days since partition, the Punjab had been reduced to open anarchy. Seventy thousand Muslims from India had already arrived in Lahore. The Pakistani government opened camps for 40,000, but the rest were obliged to fend for themselves. Meanwhile, Hindus and Sikhs fled the city. In April 1947, the Hindu and Sikh population of Lahore had been estimated at 300,000. It was now, just four months later, barely 10,000.[18] In Amritsar, on the Indian side of the border, a large group of Muslim women was stripped naked, paraded through the streets and raped by a Sikh mob. Some Sikhs were able to rescue a few of the women and hide them in the Golden Temple until the army could arrive. The rest of the women were burnt alive.[19] Murders were running at several hundred a day, and a bonfire had been made of Muslim houses. The police on both sides either stood by or, in many cases, joined in. The phrase 'a thousand times more horrible than anything I saw during the war' became a cliché among British and Indian officers. One officer was confronted with the sight of four babies that had been roasted to death over a fire.[20]

A strong desire for revenge following the massacres of Sikhs by Muslims in March meant that the Sikh campaign was being organized with striking efficiency, recruiting and mobilizing ex-servicemen and arming them from private stockpiles. Groups of anywhere between 20 and 5000 men (and sometimes women and children) would meet in gurdwaras and organize themselves into jathas, or fighting mobs, to raze Muslim villages. They were well armed with machine guns, rifles and shotguns, as well as grenades, spears, axes and kirpans, the ceremonial blade carried by all Sikhs.[21] Usually, their Muslim adversaries only had staves. The pattern of attack was well established. When Muslim villagers saw a jatha coming, they would climb on to their roofs and beat gongs to alert neighbouring villages. The Sikhs would send in a first wave to shoot them off the roofs, a second wave to lob grenades over the walls, and a third wave to cut survivors to pieces with kirpans and spears. A fourth wave of older men would then go in and set light to the village, while outriders would ride around, swinging their kirpans to fell any escapees.

Retaliation against these atrocities was swift and furious. On 23 August a train full of Sikh refugees was attacked by Muslims at Ferozepur, leaving 25 dead and 100 wounded. In Quetta, riots kicked off between Muslim League supporters and Pathans. After three boys were paraded through the streets, bearing injuries sustained from riots in West Punjab, both sides turned on the local Hindus.[22] One week after partition, Delhi was a temporary home to 130,000 Muslim refugees on their way to Pakistan, a quarter of whom had arrived in the preceding fortnight. Five thousand were crowded into a squalid refugee camp in front of the Jama Masjid; sixteen other camps were set up to host the rest.[23] Inside these enclaves, according to Lord Ismay, 'conditions defied description': there was no water, no food, no sanitation and no security.[24]

Mountbatten has been widely held responsible for the scale of the partition disaster, and for the failure to deal with it once it started. For his management of the situation, according to his fiercest critic, Andrew Roberts, 'Mountbatten deserved to be court-martialled on his return to London.'[25] This is a serious accusation, and worth examining in some detail. The criticism has been aimed from three angles. First, Mountbatten is accused of ignoring the specific problem of the Sikhs, who were particularly disgruntled by their lot under his plan, and capable of organizing their disgruntlement into military action. Second, he is accused of failing to use British troops to stop the trouble once it started. Third, he is accused of having rushed through the whole transfer of power so fast that preparations made for the effects of partition were either inadequate or absent.

On the matter of the Sikhs, Mountbatten had long been alerted. During his very first week in India, he had asked V.P. Menon for an assessment of the Sikh situation.[26] He had had extensive contact with the moderate Sikh Minister of Defence, Baldev Singh; he had also spoken to the more militant Akali Dal leaders, Tara Singh and Kartar Singh. He had heard their demand for an independent Khalistan.

Khalistan was impossible, as Kartar Singh himself admitted.[27] The Sikhs had a great deal of land and people scattered throughout the Punjab, but they were a majority in no part of it – and neither Hindus nor, more emphatically, Muslims would have consented to live in a Sikh state. Inevitably, once the partition of the Punjab had been decided upon, the Sikhs would have to be split. The only alternative would have been to leave the Punjab intact and give it in its entirety to India or Pakistan. Pakistan was the stronger contender, for the Punjab had over 16 million Muslims against fewer than 8 million Hindus and 4 million Sikhs, and a strong Muslim League presence in its government.[28] But without any firm word on their security or freedom of conscience the Sikhs were reluctant to enter into an Islamic nation.[29] Several Punjabi Sikh groups threatened civil war if they were forced into Pakistan.

Mountbatten had been warned that the Sikhs would object to their deal before partition. Liaquat repeatedly asked him to imprison Sikh leaders and to ban the kirpan.[30] Mountbatten did not, and this has often been used to hold him responsible for Sikh involvement in the massacres.[31] But he had only refrained from acting, on the advice of senior neutral experts. On 5 August, Mountbatten had a secret meeting with Patel, Jinnah and Liaquat, which directly implicated the Sikh leaders in a number of plots – including that to assassinate Jinnah in Karachi on 14 August. Jinnah and Liaquat again demanded the arrest of Tara Singh and his associates, but Patel warned that this would make the situation worse. Mountbatten did not take Patel's word for it, but wrote to Evan Jenkins, Governor of the Punjab, and his two successors, Sir Chandulal Trivedi and Sir Francis Mudie, to ask them for their opinion. All three were firm and unanimous in their accord with Patel.[32]

Had Mountbatten imprisoned the likes of Tara Singh and Kartar Singh for crimes they had not yet committed, and had he banned the kirpan, he would have faced a tremendous backlash from the Sikhs before the transfer of power. This was exactly opposite to Britain's interests, and therefore he could not do it. Even if he had imprisoned the leaders, it is unlikely that the Sikhs would have been pacified. From the character of the fighting during August and September 1947, it was obvious that they had created an organized militia. Had Tara Singh and Kartar Singh been removed, more heads would have sprung up to replace them. As Nehru wrote afterwards, 'It is just childish nonsense or deliberate malice for anyone to contend that [the] arrest of Tara Singh or a few others could have made any difference to a vast explosive situation.' Nehru also noted another point, too often ignored, that 'The charges are based on premises that the Sikhs were originators of and guilty party in all that happened,' premises which he described as 'completely wrong'.[33] Mountbatten did exactly as he was advised by his governors and staff: he duly reported the Sikh problem to London – which did not volunteer any extra reinforcements – and set up the Punjab Boundary Force with it in mind.[34] Without hindsight, it is hard to see that he could have done more.

Mountbatten has also been charged with not deploying more British soldiers to maintain order, and to guarantee safe conduct for refugees between the two dominions.[35] To a great extent, this would have been the responsibility of the Ministry of War, the Ministry of Air, and the Admiralty, rather than Mountbatten, but it is true that he did not bother those ministries for reinforcements.[36] Had British troops been used, he argued, 'They would doubtless have incurred the odium of both sides.'[37] As it was, the Punjab Boundary Force was widely seen as being an arm of British imperialism.

After 15 August, Mountbatten was the servant of the Union of India; and his Prime Minister, Jawaharlal Nehru, had made unequivocal his opinion: 'I would rather have every village in India go up in flames than keep a single British soldier in India a moment longer than necessary.'[38] Mountbatten's staff agreed with Nehru. When the Governor General showed an inclination to send a British brigade to police Delhi, Auchinleck argued that British troops could only be used to protect British lives.[39] British services were overstretched, and commanders had been pointing out for at least a year that the release of soldiers from India was a high priority: India was no longer relevant to British defence.[40] Field Marshal Montgomery had visited Delhi in June, and met Nehru, to whom he expressed his desire to withdraw all British troops as fast as possible. 'He asked me if there was any chance of our changing our minds later and asking some British troops to be left in India,' noted Nehru. 'If this happened it would upset his programme. I told him that there was not the least chance of this happening and we wanted British troops in India to be taken away completely.'[41] The situation was unambiguous: the British government, the British services and the Indian government all insisted that British troops should be removed from India at the earliest possible opportunity. It is fanciful to imagine that Mountbatten could have acted in direct contradiction of the wishes of all three of these bodies.

Finally, there is the question of whether Mountbatten's extraordinary rush to transfer power caused the disaster. Undoubtedly, Mountbatten went much faster than anyone asked him to. But the arguments against Mountbatten's speed all rely on a mistaken assumption: that, if the Viceroy had stuck to Attlee's timetable, he would have had the time and resources to subdue the Punjab. He had neither. Attlee had made it clear that Britain was going to leave India regardless of its situation in June 1948. Once this had been stated, even a dramatic show of force against rioters could only have postponed the violence until then. There is no reason to think that the slow-boiling of communal tempers under martial law for an extra nine months would have reconciled everybody to live happily ever after. There is every reason to think that the result would have been just as bad, if not worse.[42] Chakravarty Rajagopalachari, who would the following year take over from Mountbatten as Governor General of India, was one of many who expressed this view. 'If the Viceroy had not transferred power when he did', he wrote, 'there could well have been no power to transfer.'[43]

For Britain to impose martial law would have put the governments in Delhi and in London in a dubious situation. In the first place, there was no appetite in Britain for further British casualties in foreign wars. Only seven British officers were killed in India between partition and the end of January 1948; had the British Army taken full responsibility, it is logical to suppose that there would have been many more.[44] In the second place, had Mountbatten cracked down hard on the Punjab before 15 August, he would have caused untold

trouble both inside India and with Britain's international allies, especially the United States. Assertions of British dominance were neither
desirable nor practical. They risked antagonizing the Indian people
and politicians further, and spreading serious discontent from the
Punjab to other parts of India – an effect that was already visible
from sympathy riots in the North-West Frontier Province. Neither
Britain nor India needed in the middle of 1947 to risk any more
Brigadier General Dyers carrying out any more Amritsar massacres.

But most important of all was the issue of resources. The British
government was in the middle of its worst financial crisis since the
Great Depression. There was very little popular understanding of
what was going on in the Punjab, and even less interest. The British
had recently emerged from six years of war. Hundreds of thousands
had been killed, and millions expended. Their normal industries had
been battered, their towns destroyed, their families broken up and
stuck back together. Still they languished under the strictures of
rationing, which were getting tighter, not looser. To these ordinary
people, the Empire was a superfluous accoutrement. Edie
Rutherford, a forty-three-year-old housewife from Sheffield, had a
typically indifferent reaction to the mass of press coverage about the
effective end of her nation's Empire and the independence of 400
million of her fellow subjects. 'I swear most folk couldn't care less',
she wrote in her diary on 16 August 1947, 'and I resent the inference
that we have had them enslaved up to now. Most folk are simply
glad to be shot of them, to put it vulgarly yet truthfully.'[45] Churchill's
warnings about indignant Britons awakening sharply to defend their
Empire came to nothing. Even he himself had relented. 'I do not
think we shall lose very much by leaving India at the present time,
and that feeling is undoubtedly widespread here,' he had mused in an
unsent letter to Jinnah.[46]

Mountbatten's early withdrawal might not have allowed sufficient time for the Indian and Pakistani governments or armies to get
their acts together, but it did a service to Britain – whose interests,
after all, he had been employed to serve. It has been argued that the
British government should have felt a responsibility for the millions
of Punjabis who were, after all, British subjects until August 1947. In
moral terms, probably it should have. But in practical terms it felt a

lot more responsibility for the millions of British subjects who lived in Britain itself, to whom it would still be accountable after 15 August. Faced with a choice between abandoning a nation a very long way away, and antagonizing the nation on its doorstep, the government chose the former. The decision may not have been a happy one, but no government in that position could have behaved differently.

On all three counts for which Roberts would have had Mountbatten court-martialled – the mishandling of the Sikhs, the lack of British Army support, and the speed of the transfer of power – there is a strong case in his defence. As Viceroy, Mountbatten was charged with serving the interests of Britain. He did this rigorously. Naturally, his focus on British interests meant that both India and Pakistan were ill-served by his viceroyalty – but that was inevitable. Moreover, for all his later boasts that Attlee had granted him 'plenipotentiary powers', Mountbatten's hands were tied by what London would give him.[47] He could not magic soldiers out of thin air.

From Mountbatten's point of view, the greatest mistake was staying on as Governor General of independent India. At the stroke of midnight on the morning of 15 August 1947, he had been transformed from a servant of British interests to a servant of Indian interests. The best interests of Britain had been served by a swift exit, a slapdash partition, the creation of Pakistan, and the repatriation of British armed forces. The best interests of India might well have been served by exactly the opposite. After 15 August, Mountbatten was in the unenviable position of having to deal with a combusting and hamstrung India that had been left that way by his own successful management of his previous job. He had been deeply reluctant to accept the governor-generalship, but had had little choice under pressure from his king, government and opposition. From his point of view, though, his reputation would have endured far better had he been on his plane heading for London alongside Sir Cyril Radcliffe.

Ten days after the transfer of power, the scale and awfulness of what was underway had still not been realized in Delhi. 'We are only *just* alive', wrote Edwina to her friend Kay Norton, 'but the last gruelling five months have been well worth while after all the incredible happenings and demonstrations of the last 10 days.' She expressed the hope that the refugee situation would soon be resolved.[48] In the days after writing those words, both she and Jawaharlal Nehru visited the Punjab, and the grim truth began to sink in.

In 1946, Nehru had made three predictions to journalist Jacques Marcuse. 'One, India will never be a Dominion. Two, there will never be a Pakistan. Three, when the British go, there will be no more communal trouble in India.' Marcuse was back in Delhi just after partition to interview him again, but could not bring himself to remind Nehru of their previous conversation. In the end, Nehru brought it up himself. 'You remember, Marcuse, what I told you? No Dominion, No Pakistan, No . . .'

Both men were silent for a moment, until Nehru added wistfully, 'Wasn't I wrong?'[49]

On 24 August, he set out at six o'clock in the morning in an aeroplane for the Punjabi town of Jullundur, and spent hours travelling by car and jeep across the dusty plains. He emerged to walk through deserted ruins which had been lively, noisy and welcoming villages. Now there was no sound, no life; just corpses, cinders, and dried-up splashes of bloodstain in the dust. He saw a caravan of 100,000 refugees, moving despondently away to a new land unknown. He talked to as many as he could. 'I cannot imagine another day when he could have felt more strongly that all his hopes, his dreams, his faith in human nature were crashing down in pieces,' remembered his secretary, H.V.R. Iengar. Finally, he made it to bed at two o'clock the next morning, before getting up at half-past five to fly to Lahore. The passengers on the plane slumped back in their seats, exhausted and miserable; except for Nehru, who was engrossed in reading a slim volume. Iengar asked him what it was. He explained that it was a Sanskrit play: *Mrcchakatika*, or *The Little Clay Cart*.[50] It is the witty and scandalous story of a hero, Charudatta, 'the tree of plenty to the poor', 'a treasure of manly virtues, intelligent, liberal, and upright', who has given up his hereditary riches to the people. Charudatta falls in love with a spirited, bold and compassionate woman, Vasantasena. But Vasantasena is claimed by another man – the frivolous, hasty and foolish brother-in-law of the King. 'There is no changing nature,' a character remarks; 'nothing can keep an ox out of a field of corn, nor stop a man who covets another's wife.' In the end, Charudatta not only wins the love of Vasantasena, but through 'noble daring wrested an empire from its ancient lords'.[51] Much in this ancient tale must have resonated.

Two days after Nehru had set out, Edwina flew to Jullundur with her close friend and India's first female cabinet minister, Amrit Kaur. She had gone after consulting Maniben Patel, who had told her that it would be helpful to have a reliable eyewitness report on the situation, in addition to the raising of morale her trip might effect.[52] The local authorities were in such disarray that no welcome party had turned up to meet Edwina and Amrit, apart from a lost baby buffalo that had wandered on to the tarmac. Eventually, they managed to commandeer a jeep, and toured seven refugee camps and hospitals in Jullundur and Amritsar that first day, distributing medical supplies and food when they could, and making notes of what was needed after they ran out. As Edwina came to the end of her tour, she was told of an attack on a lorryload of refugees who had come in from Sialkot. Without hesitation, she returned to the Victoria Memorial Hospital to visit the survivors. Afterwards, she went to see the Sikh leader, Tara Singh, in person. According to Alan Campbell-Johnson, he was 'at last beginning to tremble at the wrath he has readily invoked'.[53] The next morning she was off to Lahore in Pakistan, visiting a Muslim refugee camp and a school before breakfast. She continued through Rawalpindi, Sialkot and Gujranwalla before returning to Delhi.

The trip established Edwina's position at the prow of the government's relief efforts, making her one among many visible women in senior positions in the Indian administration. Independent India had been constituted along remarkably progressive lines. From the outset, Indian women would earn equal pay for equal work – a right not conferred upon British women until the 1970s. 'A lot of people will dispute the advisability of such a thing in this country, and it remains to be seen what will happen here,' Lady Mountbatten told a meeting of the East India Association in London the following year; 'but I am convinced that India was perfectly right to decide that there should not be any discrimination between men and women, that every field of service should be open to those women who were qualified to serve. Men and women must be equal before the law and if that is so they must then receive equal pay for equal work.'[54]

But behind this image of feminist progress lay a long, dark shadow of female despair. At Calcutta in 1946, and subsequently, the vengeance of the rioters had been wreaked deliberately on women. As the great migrations and great slaughters following partition got underway, so too did a sustained and brutal campaign of sexual persecution. The use of rape as a weapon of war was conscious and emphatic. On every side, proud tales were told of the degradation of enemy women. Thousands of women were abducted, forcibly married to their assailants, and bundled away to the other side of the border. Many never saw their families again. Thousands more were simply used and then thrown back into their villages. There were accounts of women who had been held down while their breasts and arms were cut, tattooed or branded with their rapists' names and the dates of their attacks.[55]

As if such ordeals were not horrific enough, the media and public officials publicly glorified a distinctly feminine martyrdom. It was constantly suggested that the high point of female heroism was to commit suicide rather than face the 'dishonour' of rape, as if the shame and guilt for the crime would fall on the victim rather than on the perpetrator. The desperate actions of such women were admired as an example of feminine virtue rather than deplored as an example of female subjection. India might have had the most visible female politicians of any nation, but the notion that a woman's chastity was worth more than her life abounded, even among the political class. Jawahar's cousin, Rameshwari Nehru, visited Thoa Khalsa, where ninety Sikh women had committed collective suicide by jumping into a well rather than face a Muslim attack. 'It was eighteen days after the incident that we arrived at this sacred spot', she wrote. 'The bodies of those beautiful women had become swollen and floated up to the surface of the water. Their colourful clothes and long, black hair could be seen clearly. Two or three women still had [the bodies of] infants clinging to their breasts.' She was with a large group of observers come to gawp at this gruesome spectacle. 'We thought of it as our great good fortune that we had been able to visit this site and worship these *satis*'.[56]

The violence in the Punjab was getting worse, rather than better. On the night of 25 August, the small town of Sheikhupura, near Lahore – with a population of 10,000 Muslims, and 10,000 Hindus and Sikhs – exploded into a massive pitched battle, for no reason anyone could ascertain. It had previously been known as one of the quietest spots in the West Punjab. Twenty-four hours later, several thousand people, mostly Sikh and Hindu, had been murdered in a frenzy of stabbing, shooting, beating and burning, and parts of the town were ablaze. No effort had been made to quell the violence. The Muslim police actually aided it. A journalist who visited Sheikhupura the next day found a civil hospital in a disgusting state, with flies teeming thickly over the blood-soaked rags that substituted for bandages, and the stench of death in the muggy monsoon air. Most Sikhs were too scared to go to hospital, and were sheltering in their gurdwara without even basic facilities. 'Here there were more appalling sights', he wrote; 'men and women whose hands had been cut off and whose forearms were black putrescent fly-covered stumps, and children, even babies, who had been cut and slashed. Perhaps the most heart-rending spectacle of all was the young mothers who had lost their children.'[57] Visiting days later, Nehru described himself as 'sick with horror'; still the stink of blood and burnt human flesh was inescapable.[58] His car was stopped by Muslims, shouting at him to stop the war. 'Are you not ashamed of yourselves?' Nehru shouted back. 'Have you no conscience left? What do these houses and these dead bodies show? Who is conducting this war?'[59]

Nehru wrote to Mountbatten in deep depression. 'I suppose I am not directly responsible for what is taking place in the Punjab', he wrote. 'I do not quite know who is responsible. But in any event I cannot and do not wish to shed my responsibility for my people. If I cannot discharge the responsibility effectively, then I begin to doubt whether I have any business to be where I am.'[60] Only the courageous spirit of Edwina Mountbatten could lift him from this gloom. Indira Gandhi remembered one evening in her father's house when a telephone call came through from Patel. A train had just arrived in

Delhi from the Punjab, filled with dead bodies. Edwina turned up at Jawahar's door, and changed her high heels for sensible shoes. 'I am just going to the station,' she announced. 'And of course there was no security, no arrangements,' said Indira. 'She just went.'[61]

The violence kept spreading. By 26 August, the great industrial city of Ludhiana was aflame. At the end of August, Lahore was described as a 'city of the dead' by the *Times of India*. Its mall was deserted, its shops shuttered, its roads empty except for military vehicles. No Hindus or Sikhs were visible outside the refugee camps. Those refugees brought stories of thousands shot by police and the army in the nearby towns; 16,000 languished in the camps, with hardly any food; 8,000 or 9,000 were supposed to be in one camp at Jullundur, and most of them had had just one meal in the five days up to 24 August.[62] At some of the camps, food was not free; unsurprisingly, few among the refugees had brought supplies of cash. Local banks closed down under threat of looting, and it was not long before even the wealthy went hungry. Driving to the town of Hasilpur, Penderel Moon noticed great heaps of what he thought was manure piled up along the roadside. When he got closer, the horrible truth became clear, and he exclaimed, 'They're corpses!' Three hundred and fifty Hindu and Sikh men, women and children were piled up in heaps, arms and legs sticking out at odd angles, bodies hideously contorted. They were the victims of a Pathan mob that had passed through that morning. In the town he found a weeping group of women and children desperately fanning the flies away from two or three blood-drenched survivors. 'It was hard to endure,' Moon remembered. 'We could do nothing to help.'[63] It was announced that every available plane of the British long-haul carrier BOAC would be sent to India and Pakistan to evacuate Europeans. Paradoxically, the Europeans were those in the least danger.[64]

On 29 August, in the middle of the Punjabi holocaust, the Punjab Boundary Force was actually disbanded at the order of a Joint Defence Council meeting in Lahore. Mountbatten, Auchinleck and General Rees were profoundly opposed to this action, but their hands were forced by the other members, including Nehru, Baldev, Liaquat and Jinnah, and by public opinion. Indian and Pakistani representatives alike argued that the force needed to be reformed under the command of each national government. Each government wanted direct military control over its new borders; rumours circulated in the press that the force was hoarding the best officers. On the ground, the force was accused of having communal sympathies. Rees admitted that the internal atmosphere of the force had become impossible to maintain by the end of August, though he noted that there were many examples of courage and lack of prejudice among the troops. One Sikh major, guarding a train full of Muslim refugees, took three bullets and six spear wounds while fearlessly fighting off a mob of his co-religionists.[65] There were much more credible allegations of partiality against the police, but the visibility of the force made it a focus for resentment. Edwina had returned from the Punjab the day before, and repeated to Dickie that such allegations were now widespread. Reluctantly, he gave in. The one effort he had been able to make towards protecting the Punjabis had fallen flat.[66]

On the last day of August, Calcutta, too, finally succumbed to the communal fury, and there was a furious demonstration against Gandhi's mission. A mob broke into the Belliaghatta mansion in which he was staying, bearing a wounded Hindu who they alleged had been stabbed by a Muslim, and demanded he call for revenge. He refused to do any such thing: without a tremor he stood to face them, quietly, with arms folded. Someone threw a brick. Another hit at him with a lathi, and narrowly missed him. The eighteen days of peace in Calcutta between the Mahatma's arrival and the end of August had been the longest and most notable interlude of calm in that city for a year, and were a direct result of Gandhi's awe-inspiring presence in the popular imagination. But the peace could not hold, and the dozens rioting that night had to be dispersed by police armed with tear gas.[67]

That same evening, the film at Government House in Delhi was *Men of Two Worlds*, a thoughtful drama about colonialism in Africa. A young musician from Tanganyika is sent to London, and returns fifteen years later as a health worker. He finds himself caught in a bitter conflict with his village's witch doctor. His Western sophistications offend his tribe's traditions – and the British workers in the village cannot agree about whether or not their civilization is worth emulating, either. It is not known who was choosing the films at

Government House, but he or she must have been a perceptive critic. One of the biggest questions facing the war-ravaged subcontinent was whether Nehru's Western ideals, or Gandhi's traditional medicine, would heal India. As it turned out, neither would work fast enough. Within a week of the film's screening, the situation right in the heart of India's capital was to get much, much worse.

CHAPTER 16

THE BATTLE FOR DELHI

'ONE MILLION DEAD': THIS IS THE MOST CONVENIENT NUMBER to have come out of the wildly varying estimates of how many people may have been killed following partition. Mountbatten preferred the lowest available estimate, which was 200,000, and has been widely condemned for it: the denial of holocausts is always a sticky business, and yet more so when one may be implicated personally.[1] Indian estimates have ranged as high as 2 million. Many historians have settled for a figure of somewhere between half a million and 1 million. The figure of 1 million dead has now been repeated so often that it is accepted as historical fact. 'What is the basis for this acceptance?' asked the historian Gyanendra Pandey. 'That it appears like something of a median?'[2] Unfortunately so, for the truth is that no one knows how many people were killed, nor how many were raped, mutilated or traumatized. The numbers anyone chooses say more about their political inclination than about the facts. Fewer than 400,000 suggests an apologia for British rule; 400,000 to 1 million moderation; 1 million or more usually indicates that the person intends to blame the deaths on a specific party, the most usual culprits being one or more of Mountbatten, Patel, Jinnah or the Sikhs.

Beyond the dead, there were more numbers, too, plucked from the extrapolations and imaginations of regional officials, army, police and historians. Refugees on the move by the beginning of September: 500,000, or perhaps 1 million. Women abducted and raped: 75,000, or perhaps 125,000. Total who would migrate from one dominion to the other between 1947 and 1948: 10 million, or perhaps 12 million, or perhaps 15 million. The Indian National Archives contain sheaves of charts scribbled by British and Indian officials, recording 87 killed in Bengal here, 43 injured in Madras there. 'The figures make no pretence to accuracy,' admitted the Home Department. The Punjab government reported that its casualty estimates were 'increasing daily as investigation uncovers further tragedies'; the North-West Frontier Province government referred to 'stray murders', which were not counted.[3] Usually it was impossible to count the number of victims amid the 'confused heap of rubble & corpses' that was left behind after riots.[4] Sir Francis Mudie, Governor of the West Punjab, remembered that he had to 'ignore any report of a riot unless it alleged that there were at least a thousand dead. If there were, I asked for a further report, but I cannot remember any case in which I was able to do anything.'[5]

In Stalin's famous words, one death is a tragedy; one million deaths is a statistic. In this case, it is not even a particularly good statistic. The very incomprehensibility of what a million horrible and violent deaths might mean, and the impossibility of producing an appropriate response, is perhaps the reason that the events following partition have yielded such a great and moving body of fictional literature and such an inadequate and flimsy factual history. What does it matter to the readers of history today whether there were 200,000 deaths, or 1 million, or 2 million? On that scale, is it possible to feel proportional revulsion, to be five times more upset at 1 million deaths than at 200,000? Few can grasp the awfulness of how it might feel to have their fathers barricaded in their houses and burnt alive, their mothers beaten and thrown off speeding trains, their daughters torn away, raped and branded, their sons held down in full view, screaming and pleading, while a mob armed with rough knives hacked off their hands and feet. All these things happened, and many more like them; not just once, but perhaps a million times. It is not possible to feel sufficient emotion to appreciate this monstrous savagery and suffering. That is the true horror of the events in the Punjab in 1947: one of the vilest episodes in the whole of history, a devastating illustration of the worst excesses to which human beings can succumb. The death toll is just a number.

Amid these dark tales came one remarkable sign of hope. In Bengal, Gandhi had been faced with the collapse of his hard-won peace. Once again, packs of armed goondas (gangsters) ruled the streets of Calcutta. The years had not been kind to Gandhi. The Salt March had been the apogee of his power and influence; the 1930s a struggle, bitter and increasingly opposed, culminating in a private breakdown; the early 1940s a calamity, with the ill-judged Quit India campaign and mass departure of Muslims from Congress; the later 1940s a wilderness, with his presence treated as an irritation. And yet, despite intense personal disaffection and marginalization by his colleagues, the Mahatma would rally for a final, spectacular swansong. With Calcutta detonating around him, he decided to fast.

Used against the British raj during the war, Gandhi's fasts had become useless as a political weapon. The British government had decided to let Gandhi die, concluding that the short-term consequences of Gandhi's death might be easier to manage than the long-term consequences of Gandhi's life. But as a moral weapon the fasts had power, and now a moral weapon was required. Against the goondas of Calcutta, Gandhi's fast would prove astonishingly successful.

On 2 September, the Mahatma renounced all food and sustenance except sips of water, and reclined on a cot in a public room at the house in Belliaghatta. The effect was unprecedented. Over the course of little more than a day, the city calmed, and the processions to his house changed their temper from angry mob to penitent pilgrimage. From all parties and all faiths, leaders came to beg with him to give up his fast and save his life. He replied that it was not a question of saving his life. The fast was 'intended to stir the conscience and remove mental sluggishness'; if the people's consciences were stirred, there might be the side-effect that he would live. The hours passed, with burly goondas turning up to weep contritely by the Mahatma's bedside. Finally, on the evening of 4 September, when all the city leaders had signed a pledge that there would be no further trouble in Calcutta, Gandhi broke his fast with a drink of fruit juice.[6] 'In the Punjab we have 55,000 soldiers and large-scale rioting on our hands', an awestruck Mountbatten wrote to him. 'In Bengal our forces consist of one man, and there is no rioting.'[7] To the wonder of all observers, Gandhi's achievement would endure beyond his presence in the city. Aside from a few isolated incidents – no more than in normal times of peace – Calcutta remained orderly for months.

Recovering quickly, the seventy-seven-year-old Mahatma left Calcutta and headed for the place where the need for his moral power was greatest: the Punjab. On the way, he planned to break his journey briefly at Delhi. But, by the time he got there, the capital itself would become the new focus of communal fury.

At the end of August the Mountbattens had gone back up to Simla. The day after they arrived, they had held a farewell party for an aide-de-camp who was returning to England. His train was hijacked, and all 100 Muslims on board murdered – except his own bearer, who hid under a seat. The day after that, the Mountbattens heard that their treasurer and his wife had been killed in another train massacre.[8] In Delhi, panic began. From the city centre, smoke could be seen unfurling from nearby villages and the town of Gurgaon. Three hundred Muslims fled to Palam airfield, where they had to be protected by Indian Army troops.[9]

Appalled, Edwina told Dickie she was going back to the capital.[10] On 4 September, he was summoned back, too. The Mountbattens arrived the following day, along with Lord Ismay, recalled from his holiday in Kashmir.[11] By that time, Delhi was in turmoil. Blood-chilling reports landed hourly on the desks of government officials. A bomb exploded in the Fatehpuri Masjid, a seventeenth-century mosque at the western end of Chandni Chowk. The police arrived to find a mob throwing bricks at it while troops fired on them. Two Hindus were shot dead.[12] In Karol Bagh, between New and Old Delhi, children of all faiths were sitting their matriculation examinations in a local high school, when goondas stormed in and demanded that the Muslim boys be separated from the rest. The boys were taken into another room and slaughtered like animals.[13]

Mountbatten set up an emergency committee, which met for the first time that afternoon. Patel was full of rage, while Nehru sat at the table with an expression of all-consuming sorrow on his face.[14] 'If we go down in Delhi,' Mountbatten told them firmly, 'we are finished.'[15]

He immediately set up a large and splendid map room in Government House, fitted out with lots of charts, graphs and telephones. His staff stayed up for two nights getting all the little flags into the correct places to represent the Punjab boundary. So exhausted was the lieutenant colonel in charge of this effort that he fainted while showing the committee around the room on 8 September.[16] Mountbatten devoted much of his own time to concerns such as whether visitors ought to come through a special entrance and be given a special pass.[17]

At the suggestion of Nehru, Edwina Mountbatten was put in charge of the emergency committee's refugee group. While Dickie was still fiddling with his map room, Edwina established and chaired the United Council for Relief and Welfare. It was a swift, effective and hands-on attempt to deal with the reality of the situation. Edwina coordinated fifteen separate relief organizations, two government ministries and one Mahatma into a single targeted team with clear instructions and purpose.[18] She began touring the worst areas of trouble, mobilizing volunteers and personally directing the Red Cross effort to improve water, sanitation and medical supplies. Through the United Council, she suggested initiatives ranging from the establishment of a sister organization in Pakistan, all the way down to the setting up of Girl Guide knitting circles to provide pullovers for refugees.[19] A sure sign of her effectiveness was that the Governor General's aides-de-camp began to try to avoid being on her staff. Anyone required to serve with Edwina would have to help with a variety of gruesome tasks in unpleasant locations. She stopped her car when she saw injured or dead people, got out, dodged bullets, and retrieved their bodies to take them to hospitals or morgues. She also ordered her husband's personal bodyguards to forget about him and patrol the hospitals, following a number of unspeakable attacks on helpless patients as they lay in the wards.[20] In Edwina's wake, the main Emergency Committee also got into its swing, cancelling all holidays – including Sundays – to keep the economy going, punishing errant officials, and arranging a volunteer police force.

The battle to bring Delhi back under control was prolonged and vicious. On 6 September, a bomb was thrown into New Delhi's packed railway station, aimed at fleeing Muslims. The police arrived

and fired into a massed Hindu crowd. By this point, 450 were reckoned to have been killed in the previous forty-eight hours of rioting
alone. But the worst was still to come. The following day, outbursts
of violence erupted all across Delhi, so simultaneously and so brutally that many thought it must have been planned. Looters
descended on Connaught Circus, the huge central plaza of New
Delhi, built by the proud British as concentric circles of graceful
neoclassical arcades. This forum was filled with a baying mob,
which began to smash up Muslim-owned shops. The army arrived,
and attempted unsuccessfully to disperse the crowd with bullets and
tear-gas. Nehru himself arrived a little later armed with a stick,
plunged into the crowd and chased looters away from outside the
Odeon Cinema. The orgy of destruction was not confined to goondas. Nirad Chaudhuri, who was present, described middle-class
couples strolling away from the scene, loaded down with stolen
handbags, cosmetics and bottles of scent. He also saw tongas, the
light horse-drawn taxis mainly driven by Muslims, left burning by
the sides of the road. Their drivers had been dragged from them and
murdered. When he returned to his house, he looked back on a view
of the city colonnaded with pillars of smoke from arson attacks, and
soundtracked by the screams of fire engines and bursts of gunfire.
That evening, 6000 Muslims fled from their homes in the middle-
class Lodi Colony to the Pak Transfer Office in Connaught Place.[21]

The rest of 7 September was punctuated by repeated blasts of fire
from Sten guns.[22] Serious rioting was simultaneously underway in
the princely state of Mysore in the south. In Bangalore shops were
looted, apparently by police as well as civilians, and Congressmen
arrested for lawbreaking.[23] In Karachi that day, Jinnah was holding
a garden party for the Emir of Kuwait, which was gatecrashed by
500 government workers demanding the rescue of their families
from Delhi. Karachi itself had seen a slew of train attacks, bombings
and assaults.[24]

By this point, thousands of Muslims had clustered in any part of
Delhi that offered sanctuary: the Jama Masjid; the Purana Qila (Old
Fort); Muslim graveyards and Mughal ruins; the Pakistani High
Commission; the houses and gardens of well-known Muslims,
including Nehru's two Muslim cabinet ministers, Abul Kalam Azad

and Rafi Ahmed Kidwai; and even Humayun's Tomb, the same gorgeous marble mausoleum that had briefly sheltered the fleeing Mughal Emperor Bahadur Shah II ninety years before. Outside the camps, things kept getting worse. On 8 September at Sabzimandi, north of Old Delhi, a confrontation between troops and rioters lasted for twelve hours, leaving the roads 'littered with bodies', and the town 'burnt to ashes', according to the British High Commissioner.[25] Paharganj, just north of Connaught Circus, was reported to be 'like a battle-field', its streets filled with dead animals, its buildings ablaze, and the constant pattering of machine-gun fire in the air.[26] All flights from Bombay and other cities into Delhi were cancelled. Reports suggested that 600,000 were involved in rioting in the city, and Muslim estimates put their death toll at 10,000. The telephone, telegraph and post systems shut down, as did all public transport.[27] A shoot-to-kill order was issued to Delhi police and armed forces. Patel called the Sikh leaders to a meeting, and threatened to set up 'concentration camps' and put all Sikhs in them unless the leaders appealed for an end to the violence. They duly did.[28] All weapons were banned except, to Jinnah's fury, Sikh kirpans, which had to be sheathed.[29] In conjunction with Pakistan's Prime Minister, Liaquat Ali Khan, Nehru organized an airdrop of more than 100,000 leaflets over the Punjab, saying that lawbreakers would be hunted down without mercy or hesitation. By the end of the day, the number of Muslims in the Pak Transfer Office in Connaught Place had doubled to 12,000.

The following day, the riot spread to Bara Hindu Rao, on the north side of Old Delhi. Insurgents had equipped themselves with hand grenades and firearms, and the police and troops had great difficulty in regaining order. More than 5000 residents had to be evacuated the following morning.[30] The Pakistani High Commissioner, who had no means of communicating with his government and had long run out of food, absconded to the airfield with the intention of escaping to Karachi. Mountbatten heard in time, and sent a member of his staff to go and pull the man off the plane. The Governor General was acutely aware that the arrival of a hysterical diplomat 'would have sent Mr. Jinnah through the roof'.[31] Such was the confusion that the Pakistani government received the impression that its High Commissioner had been murdered, and a diplomatic incident was only narrowly avoided.[32] The High Commissioner was persuaded to delay his departure for two days and allow Lord Ismay to accompany him but, once they got to Pakistan, Ismay was unable to force the terrified man to return to Delhi.[33]

Filled with aggrieved Sikhs, Hindus and Muslims, the capital had become a crucible for the rages that had boiled up across the Punjab. Large-scale riots were no longer a daily, but an hourly threat. In terror, the citizens of Delhi began to mark themselves out with visible signs that they were not Muslim. Hindus shaved their hair to leave a traditional 'shikha' tuft on the crown, and left shirts unbuttoned to show the white sacred thread worn across the chest. Indian Christians began to sew large red crosses on to their shirts. All the shops in central Delhi displayed placards saying 'Hindu Shop', regardless of their ownership. These public displays of religious identity only made the conflict more tribal.[34]

'We are dealing with a situation which is analogous to war,' announced Nehru on All-India Radio, 'and we are going to deal with it on a war basis in every sense of the word.'[35] But his tough stance isolated him from many in Congress, who conspicuously refrained from condemning Hindu atrocities in fear that they would lose the support of the Hindu majority. Nehru reminded the party's president, Rajendra Prasad, that under Gandhi's leadership Congress had always condemned even minor acts of violence. Now its politicians refused to criticize murder, rape and communal hatred. 'I have no stomach for this leadership', Nehru wrote in disgust. 'Unless we keep to some standards, freedom has little meaning'.[36] All hopes were now pinned on the small, khadi-draped figure who arrived in the capital by train that day.

Gandhi arrived back to great acclaim and expectations. 'Delhi will now be saved,' Muslims told each other. 'Muslims will now be saved.'[37] It was not just Muslims that would be saved, but Nehru, too. Gandhi returned from his triumph in Calcutta with his reputation at a new high, and immediately made his support public for Nehru's unpopular policies of protecting Muslims, maintaining full religious tolerance, and avoiding war with Pakistan. His arrival had come at a time of desperate need. For those who had survived the riots so far, conditions in Delhi were grim. Communal feeling was so ingrained that, despite Nehru's efforts, Indian government aid had only found its way to Hindu and Sikh refugees. Muslim refugees had been left to the Pakistani High Commission and non-governmental peace committees. Gandhi insisted that the government take responsibility for all faiths.[38] Finding that the Untouchable settlement at the Bhangi Colony was now a refugee camp, Gandhi roomed in the grand New Delhi mansion of his sponsor, G.D. Birla. He visited dangerous sites, though with difficulty. When he visited Hindu camps, so uncontrollable was the 'rush for *darshan*', according to the *Times of India*, that he did not get a chance to speak.[39] One of the first people to visit him was Edwina Mountbatten. Through her efforts for the refugees she formed a working bond with Gandhi that was even closer than her friendship with him in the months before partition.

In response to the crises of September, Nehru flourished. One of his oldest friends, Sri Prakasa, remembered sitting in sickened silence at the thought of the crisis when Nehru came and sat by his side. 'There are only two things left for us now, Prakasa,' Nehru said with affection. 'To go under or overcome our difficulties. And we are not going under.'[40] He devoted himself to his constant work with courage and diligence. 'Almost alone in the turmoil of communalism,' noted Alan Campbell-Johnson, 'he speaks with the voice of reason and charity.'[41] He set up a city of tents in his garden and filled that and his house with refugees, including two Muslim children he had personally rescued from a roof in Old Delhi while a riot raged below.[42] Every day, he walked in the streets and listened to people tell him their sorrows. 'I know, I know, mere bhai [my brother], it is my sorrow too,' he replied.[43] The old Nehru temper flared up frequently. Jawahar was being driven in his official car when he noticed a Hindu passerby with a cart full of loot from a Muslim neighbourhood. Immediately, he leapt out and told the thief to take it back. 'They have their Pakistan, we will have our Hindustan,' replied the man, at which Jawahar flew into a rage, grabbed him by the throat and shook him. 'If I must die it is an honour to do so at your hands, Panditji,' gasped the man. Jawahar dropped him in disgust and returned to his car.[44]

During that first September fortnight, Jawahar's friendship with Dickie Mountbatten strengthened. 'He has come suddenly to see me alone on more than one occasion – simply and solely for company in his misery; to unburden his soul; and to obtain what comfort I have to give', Dickie wrote to the King.[45] But Jawahar's relationship with Edwina Mountbatten became more important still. While Dickie chaired committees, both Jawahar and Edwina fearlessly went out into the streets of Delhi to deal with the rioters. Edwina was with her friend, the Health Minister Amrit Kaur, when they heard that Jawahar had gone out alone. They found him attempting to stop a crowd of armed men. 'Brought him back!' Edwina wrote.[46] Another evening, Jawahar heard of an attack planned on the Jamia Millia Islamia, a Muslim college outside Delhi. The college was in the middle of riot-torn countryside. At night, the students, fearing for their lives, turned off their lamps and stood guard. They could hear splashes as Muslims from nearby villages were chased into the Jumna River, pursued by mobs intent on drowning them. Without waiting to organize a bodyguard for himself, Jawahar got into a taxi and drove alone through the treacherous countryside straight there – only to find Edwina already on the site, without guards, trying to pacify the would-be raiders.[47] 'Did we get our freedom so that you could kill each other?' Jawahar shouted at the mob. 'He was,' noted one observer, 'a man who had no fear.'[48]

Again and again, events brought the two together. Richard Symonds, a friend of Edwina's who was working alongside her in Delhi and the Punjab, noted the value of her friendship with Jawahar for the relief effort. 'If we had problems where the Prime Minister's attention was needed,' he remembered, 'she'd got it.'[49] At eleven o'clock one evening, Jawahar's sister Betty was in her brother's house at York Road, when a telephone call came through from Edwina. Jawahar was not in, so she took the call – noting with interest that the Governor General's wife had telephoned her brother personally, rather than having an aide-de-camp ring up. 'Haven't you heard that there is fighting between a Hindu and a Muslim camp?' Edwina asked. 'The rumor [sic] is that a Muslim from his camp shot a Hindu woman in their camp. So now the Hindus are up in arms throwing stones at the Muslims who are unable to protect themselves; and there aren't enough guards. So I am going down there and I called to see if your brother would like to come with me, but of course . . .'

Without hesitation, Betty offered to come in Jawahar's place. Edwina at first demurred. 'I can't have you hurt or dead on my hands,' she said; but eventually she agreed that Betty might be helpful. Shortly afterwards, she arrived in a jeep, escorted by another in front and one behind, with discreetly armed guards. Together, the women drove out of the city to the Muslim camp in question. It was surrounded by an enormous and agitated crowd of Hindus and Sikhs, who were attempting to set it on fire. The few guards present could do little and had been backed against the wall. The man whose wife had been shot was leading the arsonists, screaming, 'Nehru is protecting the Muslims and this is what they do!'

Edwina climbed out of the jeep, pushed past her guards and positioned herself between the mob and the camp gate. She turned to face the crowd, bricks and stones whizzing over her head, 'as calmly as though she were at a garden party in the Moghul Gardens', remembered Betty. Edwina started to address the mob, but her command of Hindustani was not adequate. Betty took over, jumping on top of the jeep and shouting for the crowd to stand down. She told them that her brother was away, but would be back the next day and would be sure to find the murderer.

Some of the protesters calmed down at her words, but the widowed man still attempted to incite them further. 'All right,' Edwina said to Betty. 'Now tell them that if they continue this way we will order the guards to shoot down the agitators, it doesn't matter which side they are on.'

Betty realized immediately that calling the mob's bluff was a risky strategy. Even with their guards, she and Edwina were massively outnumbered by the rioters. If it came to a fight, they would probably be torn to pieces. But, lacking other options, she shouted out the message. To her great relief, it worked. The shouting stopped, and the crowd dispersed.

When the panic had subsided, Edwina and Betty went into the camp to talk to the terrified Muslims, who pleaded their innocence and said they had no guns. Betty was inclined to believe them. Most were half-naked, and none had many possessions. An hour later, they headed back to York Road, to find Jawahar just returned. Edwina told him the story. 'Poor Bhai was so tired and distressed that he flew into one of his fine rages, angry at both sides,' Betty recalled. He started an investigation the very next morning. It found that the dead woman had long been ill with tuberculosis. Worn out by caring for her, her husband had shot her himself – and blamed it on a Muslim. Unlike most of those involved in the partition war, who escaped prosecution, he was later convicted of murder.[50]

At the beginning of September 1947, Edwina noted in her diary her surprise at how deeply fond of Jawahar she had become.[51] The feeling was obviously mutual. In at least one photograph of the two of them visiting a refugee camp, Jawahar's hand can be seen clasped protectively around Edwina's. Jawahar's niece, Nayantara Pandit, came to live with him in October, and observed the relationship first hand. 'It was a very deep emotional attachment, there's no doubt about that,' she remembered. 'I think it had all the poignance of the lateness of the hour . . . that terrible cut-off-ness from the world, and anxieties about India, where are we going, all the rest of it. And then to find this – and for her, apparently, also a great and unique love.'[52]

Dickie would subtly facilitate Edwina's relationship with Jawahar, just as he had with her other lovers; more so, in fact, for he liked Jawahar. But stoicism comes at a cost, and there is a glimpse of it in a letter Dickie wrote to Noël Coward in October. The film at Government House had been Coward's masterpiece *Brief Encounter*, released two years previously and recommended to Dickie by Noël at the time.[53] In it, a woman married to a kind but undemonstrative man falls in love with a passionate doctor. She goes through a spectrum of feelings, from exhilaration to despair; her husband simply keeps doing the crossword. Dickie, too, was firmly entrenched in the role of the accepting husband, though he preferred genealogy to crosswords. The congruence between the film and his own situation can only have been enhanced by the fact that Coward had based scripts on the Mountbattens before; and that Celia Johnson, the Edwina-lookalike actress in the lead role, had appeared in Coward and Mountbatten's *In Which We Serve* as the wife of the Mountbatten character.

'I have just seen "Brief Encounter" in our private cinema, and cannot refrain from writing to tell you how deeply it moved me', wrote Dickie to Noël.[54] The two men had drifted apart somewhat in recent years, but something about *Brief Encounter* had affected Dickie on an intimate level. It is almost the only instance among all his papers in which he can be seen to respond emotionally to any piece of art.[55]

So great had been the drama inside Delhi that it would have been possible to forget that the Punjab had not yet calmed. Richard Symonds drove up the Grand Trunk Road in late September, and observed fresh Muslim corpses by the side of the road. At a railway station, he saw a band of 1000 Sikhs, armed with spears and kirpans, awaiting the arrival of the Pakistan Express train, with its consignment of Muslim refugees. When he arrived at the huge Kurukshetra refugee camp, it was to a scene of total disaster: cut off by monsoon rains and flooding, the camp had little food, no clothing, no blankets, no lighting, no medical supplies, and twice the number of people that it could accommodate in its tents.[56]

On 21 September, the Mountbattens took Nehru, Patel and a few others on a round trip in Dickie's plane to view the Punjab migrations. Near Ferozepur, they found the first caravan – and followed it for over fifty miles against the stream of refugees without finding its source.[57] The refugees moved slowly, in bullock carts or on foot, carrying children, the elderly and the infirm on their backs. Vultures followed the convoys, waiting for deaths which came frequently. Exhausted families would sometimes be forced to abandon their invalid relatives by the roadside rather than carry them further.[58] Suffering pushed the communities further apart. Punjabi Hindu women entering Delhi openly rejoiced at the sight of streets filled with Muslim corpses. According to Nirad Chaudhuri, 'the group of corpses which drew forth the strongest expression of delight from the ladies was that of a mother lying dead with her dead baby clasped in her arms.'[59]

That night, the party returned to Government House, where the Sunday film was *A Matter of Life and Death*, and the Sunday dinner was austere. The severe rations in Government House became severer still under Edwina's watchful eye. When Lord Listowel, the former Secretary of State for India and now Secretary of State for

Burma, came to visit, the Mountbattens threw a full ceremonial banquet with all the state pomp – and served a first course of cabbage-water, followed by a main course of one slice of Spam with a potato, and finished off with a solitary biscuit and a small piece of cheese.[60] 'The ADCs are mad with rage at me', Edwina wrote with satisfaction, 'as they think food can be spirited out of the skies'.[61]

Even after Delhi was subdued the situation outside Government House remained dire. The camps had not been prepared: there was no water, no food, no sanitation, no security. Anees Kidwai, the widow of a murdered government official and sister-in-law of Communications Minister Rafi Ahmed Kidwai, went to work in the camp at the Purana Qila. She described a shambolic mass of tents among which 'naked children, unkempt women, girls without their heads covered and men overcome with anger wandered up and down endlessly'.[62] Still no one kept count of how many Muslim refugees there were. By the middle of September, around 60 per cent of the Muslims of Old Delhi and 90 per cent of the Muslims of New Delhi were thought to have left their homes. There were thousands clustered into each of the biggest camps, at the Purana Qila and Humayun's Tomb: perhaps 60,000 in each, perhaps 80,000, perhaps even 100,000. Thousands more had been killed – was it 20,000 now? 30,000? No one knew.[63] Someone had counted 137 mosques damaged, a few of which had been forcibly converted into Hindu temples, looted for their libraries, and hung with flags of the fundamentalist Hindu Mahasabha. Gandhi mourned, and condemned the desecration as 'a blot on Hinduism and Sikhism'.[64]

To the north and east, Pakistan fared ill. Like India, it suffered riots; trains full of dead bodies turned up in its stations; rich Hindu merchants streamed out of its cities, despite efforts by the Pakistani government to persuade them to stay.[65] Grim conditions prevailed at West Pakistan's refugee camps. Richard Symonds remembered gaunt women with half-starved babies throwing themselves at his feet, their ration in some camps just two ounces of flour a day – enough to make one single chapati.[66] Unlike India, Pakistan had to deal with these problems on an empty treasury. The Punjab, its only profitable region, had collapsed. As a result of the migrations, Pakistan had lost

4 million people who had been settled, established and productive, and gained 5 million destitute refugees.[67] British India had not been poor, but the dominions had not yet agreed on the details by which its assets would be divided between them. In the meantime, India held on to the lot, while Pakistan struggled to cope. Even at the most basic level, the logistics of setting up the new government had proven impossible. When Ghulam Mohammed, the Finance Minister, had turned up in his Karachi office on 15 August for his first day's work, he had found it bare except for one table. Everything else had been sent on a train from Delhi, and looted en route.[68]

Jinnah was livid at what he saw as a deliberate sabotaging of Pakistan. In early September, Ismay had visited him in Karachi and, according to Alan Campbell-Johnson, found the Quaid-e-Azam seething on the brink of 'precipitate action'.[69] He wrote irate letters to Attlee, demanding the help of the Commonwealth; but Attlee had no intention of wading into a fight between two dominions.[70] Jinnah appealed to all the other Commonwealth governments directly, and Ismay began to suspect his aim was to push India out of the Commonwealth altogether.[71] At the beginning of October, Jinnah sent another long letter to Attlee. By then, the strain was making him ill. Jinnah's writing was full of spelling mistakes and repetition. 'I regret to say that every effort is being made to put difficulties in our way by our enemies in order to paralyse or cripple our State and bring about its collapse', he began. 'It is amazing that the top-most Hindu leaders repeatedly say that Pakistan will have to submit to the Union of India. Pakistan will never surrender'.[72] At the bottom, the usually sharp 'M.A. Jinnah' was signed with a tremulous hand.

Under the circumstances, Jinnah saw that he would have to cultivate international allies. On 7 September, he had told a cabinet meeting that communism could 'not flourish in the soil of Islam', and that Pakistan's interests would best be served by friendship with 'the two great democratic countries, namely, the U.K. and the U.S.A., rather than with Russia'.[73] Jinnah sought to present his new nation as a crucial strategic ally: a buffer zone between Communist Russia and dubious India, and a vantage point between China and the Middle East. For most of the nineteenth century, Britain and Russia had played the 'Great Game' for primacy in Central Asia. Now a new Great Game was beginning, and elements in the United States government were already beginning to realize that Pakistan – though they had opposed its creation – presented a more amenable prospect than India. From Jinnah's point of view, this had one great advantage: money. The Pakistani Finance Minister had already brought up the question of possible financial aid with the American Embassy in Karachi. Pakistan now asked the United States for a massive $2 billion loan, for the purposes of development and defence. In December, to the great disappointment of the Pakistani government, the Americans would offer a more realistic $10 million. But the Cold War was only just beginning; Pakistan's argument that it should be supported for being anti-Russian would be taken more seriously by the late 1950s, with happy results for its treasury.[74]

In the meantime, Jinnah was forced to go begging. He sent a letter to the Nizam of Hyderabad on 15 October, reminding him of the 'special claim' Pakistan had on his state, and that 'the resources of the Dominion of India are very vast whereas Pakistan is starting from scratch'. He concluded: 'Please do not think that I am trying to get more money. God is great, and we shall go through this dire calamity which has overtaken us.'[75] Three months later, he would ask the Nizam directly for a large loan.[76]

The status of Hyderabad troubled India, too. To Patel's embarrassment, Nehru put Mountbatten rather than him in charge of negotiation. Patel's relationship with Nehru, never great, was rapidly souring. Patel made it clear that he thought Nehru was too soft on Muslims. Nehru made it clear that he disliked Patel's Hindu-chauvinist tone. With almost half of his cabinet tending towards the establishment of India as a Hindu nation, Nehru had to fight an increasingly hard battle against the swell of fundamentalist feeling.[77] 'As long as I am at the helm of affairs India will not become a Hindu state,' Nehru announced in a public speech, with a deliberate dig at the orthodox members of his government. 'The very idea of a theocratic state is not only medieval but also stupid.'[78] Lord Addison visited Delhi and Karachi in October, and reported back to Attlee his fears about Patel. If Nehru's government fell, he warned, Patel would probably take over and install 'an iron-handed system', openly hostile to Pakistan.[79]

While the bigger problem of Hyderabad fermented, the Indian and Pakistani governments had their opening skirmish over another princely state. Junagadh was a small state wedged firmly amid Indian territory in Kathiawar. The Nawab of Junagadh was a Muslim, ruling over a population that was over four-fifths Hindu. Accession to Pakistan, while tricky, was not impossible: Junagadh had a port on the Arabian Sea, within reach of Karachi.[80] The Nawab wavered, before on 16 September his Muslim League government acceded to Pakistan.

Coming so soon after the great insurrection in Delhi had been quelled, the petty affair of Junagadh provoked a far more serious reaction than it warranted. Patel wanted to send troops in immediately. Nehru was more circumspect. Mountbatten suggested to Nehru and Liaquat that both India and Pakistan should abide by the results of a plebiscite, a procedure he hoped they would follow for any state. Nehru nodded dejectedly, but Liaquat's eyes lit up. Mountbatten noted that 'There is no doubt that the same thought was in each of their minds – "Kashmir!"'[81] Shortly afterwards, the Nawab packed up his beloved dogs – of which there were 800, each with its own keeper – and absconded to Pakistan, leaving his government and his subjects in some confusion.[82] At the beginning of November, India sent troops in at the invitation of the Junagadh administration, to the fury of Pakistan. The promised plebiscite, held in February 1948, would count only 91 votes for Pakistan, against 190,779 for India.[83]

Lord Addison's assessment of the situation between India and Pakistan made uncomfortable reading for those back in London. Jinnah was in such a weak position financially, militarily and administratively 'that he would be quite unable to take any action against India even if he wanted.' Rather, Addison believed, the Quaid-e-Azam was anxious to maintain, and possibly even increase, British involvement in Pakistan. 'I think it cannot be doubted that the danger to the British connection, and to the eventual success of our policy for the establishment of a progressive Indian democracy, comes much more from India than from Pakistan,' he concluded.[84] As far as the government in London was concerned, Mountbatten might well be on the wrong side.

*

By October, there were thought to be around 400,000 Hindu and Sikh refugees from the Punjab in Delhi. Thousands could not even fit into the tent city that Nehru had set up outside the capital, a sad and grimy echo of the gorgeous campsite that had been pitched there for his wedding, thirty-one years before. Delhi's own population had been devastated: 330,000 Muslims had left, representing around one third of the city's population.[85] Many refugees were obliged to sleep rough on Delhi streets, and courtyards, doorways and gutters were filled with their huddled bodies. The death toll continued to rise, not only from the epidemics of cholera, typhus and smallpox that issued forth from the unsanitary camps, but also from traffic accidents. Dozens of refugees who had collapsed, worn out, to sleep on the streets were run over each night.

'At times I could not believe my eyes or ears,' remembered Edwina a year later. 'All I can tell you is that the people I was privileged to work with did a superhuman job and I would like to say that they were of all religions, of all nationalities, and of all beliefs. I worked with Hindus, Muslims, Christians, Sikhs, Parsees, with people from India, Pakistan, Canada, China and America.'[86] She and Amrit Kaur continued to coordinate the relief effort, ensuring that vaccines were flown in from Bombay, Madras and Calcutta, and organizing campaigns to inoculate the migrants before they reached Delhi. Edwina also kept Betty Hutheesing on call to visit hospitals, clinics and camps. 'It was amazing to see her in those terrible places,' remembered Betty, 'neither patronizing, nor oversympathetic, but just talking naturally to the inmates. This is the hardest thing of all to do when people are destitute, hopeless or dying.'[87]

Edwina coped well, but the stress was exacting a terrible toll on Jawahar. 'Ever since I assumed charge of my office, I have done nothing but tried to keep people from killing each other or visited refugee camps and hospitals,' he said. 'All the plans which I had drawn up for making India a prosperous and progressive country have had to be relegated to the background.'[88] Speaking at the end of September, he did not yet know that arguably the greatest challenge of all was just about to begin.

CHAPTER 17

KASHMIR

KASHMIR IS OFTEN CALLED THE LOVELIEST OF THE SUBCONTINENT'S landscapes. Iced Himalayan peaks soar up from lush green valleys, dark forests sweep around the shores of glassy lakes. Before 1947, Muslims, Hindus, Buddhists and Sikhs had worked side by side in walnut groves and cherry orchards, saffron fields and lotus gardens. In ancient legends, Kashmir was supposed to have been an inland sea, from which a wicked demon emerged to terrorize the earth. The demon was finally quelled by the goddess Parvati, who dropped a mountain on him – one of those which now forms the backdrop to the regional capital, Srinagar. But, if a spirit of rage lived on beneath the mountain, the events of 1947 would awaken it.

Kashmir had come into existence as a princely state on 16 March 1846. The British had acquired the territory following the First Sikh War, but lacked the resources or the inclination to administer it. Instead they sold it under the Treaty of Amritsar to Gulab Singh, the Raja of Jammu, for 750,000 rupees. It is sometimes said that this sale was the root cause of the Kashmir conflict; either because Gulab Singh was a Dogra Hindu and most of the people were Muslims or because he was, in the words of the Viceroy, Lord Hardinge, 'the greatest rascal in Asia'.[1] But Kashmir had hosted a religiously mixed population for centuries before the beginning of Dogra rule and, for 101 years following the Treaty of Amritsar, it remained comparatively peaceable. Successive maharajas had ruled despotically, and had discriminated to various degrees against Muslims, but the region did not see any major incidents of unrest except once. In 1931, there had been Muslim riots against the regime of Gulab Singh's great-grandson, Maharaja Hari Singh; these were soon quashed, and did not inspire any widespread rebellion.[2] Though around three-quarters Muslim, the population was neither homogeneous nor especially orthodox. Buddhists formed the majority in remote Ladakh, perched high among the slopes of the Himalayas; while most of the population of lower-lying Jammu was Hindu. The stripped-down, casteless Bhakti form of Hinduism found favour with many. Mystical traditions such as Islamic Sufism had extensive roots in the vale.[3] When Jinnah had sent a Muslim League envoy to Kashmir in 1943 to assess its potential, the conclusion had been disheartening. 'No important religious leader has ever made Kashmir ... his home or even an ordinary centre of Islamic activities', wrote the envoy. 'It will require considerable effort, spread over a long period of time, to reform them and convert them into true Muslims.'[4]

All Kashmir's diverse and agreeable ways of life had continued in relative stability until soon after the partition of the subcontinent. Unlike the partition holocausts, whose effect was localized in time and space, the Kashmir crisis continues to pose one of the most serious threats to international stability that the world has ever seen. Within the space of three months, one of the most enchanting places on earth was transformed into the eastern front of a slow-burning but devastating war, between Islam and kaffirs (non-Muslims) on either side of the Arabian lands, and between Islam and Islam in the centre. The western front was to erupt just weeks later, in Palestine; the central battleground, in Iraq, was already on the boil.

It is impossible to tell the story of what happened in Kashmir in 1947 without upsetting at least one or, more likely, all of the factions that remain involved. The following year, the Indian and Pakistani governments presented their cases to the United Nations: their irreconcilable accounts of what had happened each lasted six hours.[5] Even at the time, international observers repeatedly complained that facts were hard to come by, and harder yet to prove. Sixty years of furious debate has fogged the view yet further.

It had always been assumed by the British, by the Muslim League, and indeed largely by Congress apart from Nehru himself, that Kashmir would eventually go to Pakistan.[6] Kashmir was the 'K' in Pakistan. Its population was predominantly Muslim. Its lines of trade and communication ran into Pakistan. Around one quarter of Kashmir's total revenue came from timber, which was floated down the Jhelum and Chenab Rivers and collected in towns in Pakistan. Other major exports were fruit and vegetables, also exported through Rawalpindi; and woollens, including the prized cashmere, pashmina and shahtoosh wools, which were sold through the West Punjab and the North-West Frontier Province.[7] There were only three roads running in and out of Kashmir. Two of them went into Pakistan, and one into India – but it was the Maharaja's private route, a crumbling track described optimistically on the Ordnance Survey maps as 'jeepable', and snowbound for five months of each year.[8]

Nehru held out hope that Kashmir would come into India. On 27 September, he had written to Patel that he thought Pakistan would infiltrate Kashmir soon, with a view to a full annexation just before the snows of winter made the region impossible to defend; and that therefore its accession to India should be assured at the earliest possible minute.[9] 'Kashmir affects me in a peculiar way', Nehru would write to Edwina Mountbatten a few months later; 'it is a kind of mild intoxication – like music sometimes or the company of a beloved person'.[10] His family's descent from Kashmir is the first thing he describes on the first page of his 1936 autobiography. During the struggle for independence, he would often recuperate after his prison sentences with a vacation in the Kashmiri mountains. For a person who had never quite fitted in – too British for India, too Indian for Britain – he had a powerful sense of belonging in Kashmir. 'I have a sense of coming back to my own', he wrote to his daughter, Indira, in 1940; 'it is curious how race memories persist, or perhaps it is all imagination'.[11] His love for the state was about more than its beauty and harmony, though these were powerful pulls. The implication of some historians that India claimed Kashmir because Nehru liked going there for his holidays is a little unfair. Nehru had long been a passionate supporter of the Congress-aligned

National Conference in Kashmir, an overwhelmingly Muslim political party led by his friend Sheikh Abdullah that constituted the effective opposition to the Maharaja. To him, the state was a powerful symbol of his belief that India could not become a Hindustan, that Congress was a party for all faiths, and that Muslims were no less Indian than Hindus. In the context of a subcontinent that had descended into all-out holy wars, it is easy to see why such principles might have become an obsession with the secular Nehru. Unfortunately, the same principles allowed him to be manipulated by Vallabhbhai Patel, who was by now talking along openly Islamophobic lines and eyeing an aggressively anti-Pakistan foreign policy. While Nehru thought in terms of high ideals, Patel was concerned with enlarging Hindu India at the expense of Pakistan.

The decision of the Maharaja, Sir Hari Singh, not to accede to Pakistan by 15 August had been based on what was generally seen as a whimsical notion of remaining independent. Both the British and Pakistani governments assumed that the Maharaja would soon enough come to his senses and throw his lot in with Pakistan. But the Maharaja was showing little sign of coming to his senses, and every sign of losing his grip. He was under pressure from his wife and her brother, who served as his Household Minister – both of whom were strongly in favour of joining India. Torn, he consulted his astrologer, who held out for independence in picturesque terms, telling him that the stars showed the flag of Gulab Singh flying from Lahore to Ladakh.[12] The Maharaja consequently dismissed his moderate Prime Minister, who had apparently recommended accession to Pakistan, and the British officers who had remained in his armed and police forces.[13] He restocked his ranks from among his own Dogra people. Noting a change in the wind, Muslim units swiftly began to desert the Kashmir Army.

During September and October 1947, the Maharaja's Dogra-led troops carried out a campaign of sustained harassment, arson, physical violence, and genocide against Muslim Kashmiris in at least two areas – Poonch, right on the border with Pakistan, and pockets of southern Jammu.[14] Just as in the Punjab, precise numbers were impossible to assess. According to some sources, more or less the entire Muslim population of Jammu, amounting to around half a million people, was displaced, with around 200,000 of those disappearing completely, 'having presumably been butchered, or died from epidemics or exposure', noted Ian Stephens, the editor of the Calcutta *Statesman*.[15] The Maharaja meant to create a buffer zone of uninhabited land, approximately three miles wide, between Kashmir and Pakistan.[16] Muslims were pushed into Pakistan, or killed. Hindus were sent the other way, deeper into Kashmir. India would deny that any holocaust had taken place, perhaps because it had secretly been providing arms to the Dogra side: the figures are open to question, but the fact that Muslim civilians were persecuted by the Maharaja's troops is not.[17] C.B. Duke, the British Deputy High Commissioner in Lahore, went to assess the situation in the third week of October. He saw around twenty burnt-out villages along the Chenab River inside the Kashmir border, and noted that many of them contained the ashes of a mosque – 'it was the Muslims who were suffering,' he concluded.[18] The Maharaja had ordered ethnic cleansing under the guise of a defensive strategy.

Thousands of refugees, mostly Muslims from Jammu, began to pour into Pakistan's Sialkot district, bringing with them sickening tales of atrocities. As it happened, Sialkot was on the frontier of Pathan tribal territory. In driving out the Muslims on his borders, the Maharaja had driven them straight into the arms of the most fearsome Islamic fighting force on earth. 'This is a dangerous game for the Maharaja to play,' noted Duke, 'and is likely to lead to large-scale disturbances in Kashmir and incursion by neighbouring Muslim tribesmen.'[19] He was right. The Pathans, who had for months been hearing tales of Sikh and Hindu outrages against their Muslim brothers and sisters in the Punjab, were already gearing up for what they did best: making war.[20] Thousands of Pathan tribesmen were raised by former railway guard Khurshid Anwar, described by a British diplomat as 'a complete adventurer', who had made a fortune during the war, though no one was clear as to how.[21] The tribesmen, mostly Afridis and Mahsuds from the North-West Frontier, tied a bright strip of cloth around their rifles, a sign of their oaths not to return home until they had avenged the deaths of Muslims in the Punjab.[22] In tribal groups, the warriors swept down from the mountains and massed on the Kashmir border.

British observers were convinced that the government of the North-West Frontier Province was doing its best to hold Anwar's tribesmen back, though without much success. Kashmir, warned Duke, 'has always been regarded by the lean and hungry tribesmen of the North West Frontier as a land flowing with milk and honey, and if to the temptation of loot is added the merit of assisting oppressed Muslims the attractions will be well nigh irresistible'.[23] Meanwhile, Pakistani officials on the borders stopped the supply of petrol, sugar and other goods to Kashmir. India would allege that the officials were acting with the knowledge and consent of the Pakistani government, a charge Pakistan hotly denied. Either way, according to the British High Commissioner to Pakistan, the responsibility on the ground lay with Rawalpindi's District Commissioner, one Abdul Haq, who 'appears to be conducting a private war of his own against Kashmir' along with his brother, a civil servant in the Ministry of Defence.[24]

By 20 October, a more public war seemed inevitable. The Maharaja's troops crossed the border into Pakistan, and attacked four large villages with mortars, grenades and automatic fire. A British officer on the scene estimated the casualties at 1750, excluding those who had been taken to hospital.[25] The following night, around 2000 of the massed tribesmen left Pakistan from the Hazara district of the North-West Frontier Province, and marched on Kashmir via the Jhelum Valley. Despite extensive research by the Indian government, the United Nations and independent researchers, no conclusive evidence has ever been found to confirm Indian suspicions that Jinnah was directing this invasion.[26]

The tribesmen headed for Srinagar, sacking towns and villages on the way, and recruiting local Muslim troops which had deserted from the Kashmir Army. They were held at Baramula by the Maharaja's army on 25 October. The result was a massacre, during which the town was reduced to ashes by Mahsud tribesmen. In their frenzy, the Mahsuds failed to distinguish between Kashmiri Muslims and Kashmiri kaffirs. Among the dead was a Muslim youth, nailed to a cross in the town square.[27] Khurshid Anwar suggested that the tribesmen stop looting, and consequently lost control of them. The tribal council spent two days debating whether to have him killed and replaced. This gave the Maharaja, trembling in Srinagar, time to consider his next move.[28]

India's top civil servant, V.P. Menon, was dispatched to Srinagar to speak to the Maharaja and his Prime Minister. According to the British High Commissioner, Menon 'so alarmed them that they were convinced that accession to India offered the only hope of salvation'.[29] The two of them packed up and bolted for Jammu in the small hours of 27 October in a fleet of American limousines, leaving no administration in the capital.[30] Public order collapsed. In Delhi, pressure to send troops grew, led by the hawkish Vallabhbhai Patel. Mountbatten insisted that troops could not be sent in unless Kashmir formally acceded to India first. It was a curious condition to demand. Had the Maharaja, as head of an independent state, asked India to help defend against an invasion, his action would have been legal. Had India responded to such a call, its action would have been legal, too.[31] Many in Pakistan smelled a rat.

Nehru cabled to Attlee in London: 'I should like to make it clear that the question of aiding Kashmir in this emergency is not designed in any way to influence the state to accede to India.'[32] The integrity of Nehru's sentiments was undermined when, the very next day, the Maharaja wrote to Mountbatten agreeing to do just that.[33] There is some muddiness in the evidence as to whether Indian troops were sent in before the instrument of accession was signed or delivered, and even as to whether it was signed or delivered at all.[34] The original seems to have disappeared from the Indian archives. But the question of when exactly the Maharaja signed the instrument is a red herring. He had already deserted his capital by the time he even requested the instrument, and had lost control of his state. Under such circumstances, it is doubtful that he was still the Maharaja in any meaningful sense, and whether he had the authority to accede to either dominion.[35] But Nehru's mind was filled with visions of losing his ancestral state to a plague of murderous tribesmen. Their faith did not matter to him; their brutality did, and the thought of yet more destruction, rape and slaughter impelled him to act rashly. The British High Commissioner in Pakistan telegraphed urgently to London that India should not accept Kashmir's accession without a plebiscite, but it was too late.[36] Nehru and

Mountbatten accepted the accession, and prepared to fly Indian troops to Kashmir.

The fact of the Maharaja's personal involvement in genocide was not known in Delhi at this point, but this cannot entirely excuse Nehru's action.[37] Nehru had spent much of his adult life excoriating the British for defending 'princely rights'. The Maharaja's antecedents had purchased their territory from a regime that Nehru had long held illegitimate. He had ruled autocratically over a population, much of which was hostile to his authority. Nehru would have pointed out that his friend Sheikh Abdullah had also requested that Indian troops be sent. This is true, but held little weight with the Pakistani government, which believed Abdullah to be a Congress stooge. Moreover, Abdullah's opinion had no impact on India's legal case for Kashmir, which rested solely on the flimsy fact of the Maharaja's acquiescence.

Sam Manekshaw, India's Director of Military Operations, remembered the meeting that took place in Delhi at this time. Nehru, as usual, was attempting to contextualize the Kashmir situation, talking about it in relation to Russia, the United States, the United Nations and so on. Eventually, Patel exploded: 'Jawaharlal, do you want Kashmir, or do you want to give it away?'

'Of course I want Kashmir,' replied Nehru.

Before he could add anything else, Patel turned to Manekshaw, and said: 'You have your orders.' It was Patel who went off to All-India Radio and ordered a command requisitioning private aircraft, and Patel who organized the fly-in of Indian troops to Kashmir the next day. Only later did Mountbatten realize that the Home Minister must have had the whole operation planned in advance.[38]

That evening, Ian Stephens dined with the Mountbattens, and 'was startled by their one-sided verdicts on affairs', he wrote. 'They seemed to have become wholly pro-Hindu.'[39] This statement was not fair. Neither Mountbatten nor Nehru saw the situation in terms of Hindu versus Muslim, but both were profoundly opposed to religious extremism in any form, and both suspected the worst of Jinnah. Mountbatten told Stephens that Jinnah was waiting in Abbottabad, ready to drive triumphantly into Srinagar, 'where he had hoped to have his breakfast – quite in the fashion of the Kaiser at the beginning of World War No. 1', according to the Indian High Commissioner to Pakistan.[40] It has since been shown that Jinnah spent all of late October in Karachi and Lahore.[41]

On 27 October, India flew numbers of its 1st Sikh battalion into Srinagar, and these quickly secured the Vale of Kashmir. 'If we had vacillated and delayed even by a day, Srinagar might have been a smoking ruin', Nehru wrote to his sister Nan, though a British pilot reporting on the situation in Srinagar that day described it as 'complete calm' when the Indian forces arrived.[42] Jinnah took the greatest exception to his arch-rival Nehru's actions. Incensed, he ordered Pakistan's troops in to defend Kashmir against India, but was persuaded to cancel his order when Auchinleck threatened to withdraw all British officers from the Pakistan Army.[43]

The same day, Edwina Mountbatten arrived in Lahore for a tour of refugee camps in West Punjab. Crossing the Indus, she paused for five minutes to watch the river fishermen as the sun set. It was, according to her fellow relief worker Richard Symonds, 'the only time she knocked off on our three day tour'.[44] The rest of the time she spent visiting camps, talking to refugees, and planning further extractions of supplies from the government.

The following evening, her party was in Rawalpindi when she was called upon by General Gracey, acting Commander-in-Chief of the Pakistan Army. Gracey warned Edwina that war between Pakistan and India might break out at any point. He confessed that he would probably be required to arrest her, but chivalrously offered to take her to dinner first. She accepted. The following day, she continued to Sialkot, to see camps where Hindu Kashmiri refugees waited with increasing anxiety to be evacuated to India. They recounted stories of Muslim atrocities, and a local Sikh official told her that he had seen Pakistani troops in civilian dress crossing into Kashmir.[45] That afternoon, Edwina flew back to Delhi, taking with her a frightening and one-sided view of the situation to impart to Dickie and Jawahar.

Edwina's story, based on hearsay, of Pakistani troops being sent into Kashmir would have confirmed all Jawahar's worst suspicions. Now Dickie began to worry about the influence his wife and Jawahar had over each other. The Mountbattens were overheard having a row about it: 'He's very emotional, very emotional about

Kashmir,' Dickie had warned her.[46] The Kashmir situation was profoundly worsened by the deep and personal loathing between Nehru and Jinnah. Both men suspected the worst possible motives in each other. Nehru became convinced that Jinnah had organized and directed the Pathan tribesmen to invade Kashmir. According to British officials on the scene, Jinnah was innocent – though they conceded that the Pakistani government had passively supported the invasion by keeping local supply routes open.[47] But the fact was that Jinnah could not have stopped the tribesmen, even had he wanted to. To send Pakistan's army to fight the Pathans would have provoked a civil war, and that might have excited the interest of the Afghans and potentially even the Russians. Nor did he have the resources. Most of the weapons and stocks owed to the Pakistan Army were still in India.[48] The correct course of action would have been for Jinnah to warn Nehru of the tribesmen's approach and explain frankly why they could not be stopped; because he did not do this, Nehru assumed there was a conspiracy.

Similarly, Nehru failed to inform Jinnah that the Maharaja had asked for help and that he was sending troops. As a result, Jinnah became convinced that Nehru had meant all along for Kashmir to be dragged into India by force.[49] Yet as late as 28 October, Nehru wrote in a private letter to Nan: 'For my part, I do not mind if Kashmir becomes more or less independent, but it would have been a cruel blow if it had become just an exploited part of Pakistan.'[50]

Mountbatten attempted to resolve this situation by arranging a meeting between himself, Nehru, Patel, Liaquat and Jinnah in Delhi. Edwina told a reporter over whiskies and ginger that, 'You can solve any problem if you work as pals,' and her husband agreed.[51] But friendly sentiment was in short supply. Jinnah refused to come to Delhi; Patel refused to leave. Instead, it was agreed that Mountbatten and Nehru would go to Lahore – a concession which Mountbatten only managed to get the Indian cabinet to allow by not telling his ministers that Jinnah had forced it on to him.[52] The talks were fixed for 1 November.

It was not to be. On the afternoon of 31 October, the Pakistani government issued a lengthy and provocative press release, accusing the Maharaja and Sheikh Abdullah of 'conspiring' with the Indians, while refusing its own overtures of 'friendly co-operation'. Moreover, it alleged, the Indian government had deliberately used the tribesmen's incursion to justify 'the pre-planned scheme for the accession of Kashmir by India troops with the object of holding down the people of Kashmir who have been driven to rebellion by this well-calculated and carefully planned oppression.'[53] Lord Ismay arrived at the British High Commission in Delhi at midnight to inform the High Commissioner, Sir Terence Shone, that Nehru would not be going to Lahore after all. Shone reported to the Commonwealth Relations Office that Mountbatten 'has no doubt that this decision is right since [the] Indian Cabinet feel so strongly on this matter that if Nehru were to insist on going in the face of this gross defamation he would undoubtedly be thrown out.'[54]

At a more reasonable hour of that morning, Mountbatten telephoned Jinnah and told him that Nehru was unwell.[55] Mountbatten turned up in Lahore alone, with no power to negotiate a settlement. Consequently, the talks were of little use, and the main result of them seems to have been that the rankling dislike of the Governors-General for each other increased. Both left the meeting with a new distrust of the other's motives: Mountbatten believing that Jinnah was directing the raiders, and Jinnah believing that Mountbatten was directing the Indian Army.[56]

Just three days later, the *Pakistan Times* reported that Mountbatten – whom it described in an epithet both politically and factually incorrect as 'conqueror of the Japs' – was commanding operations for India in Kashmir. Any Pakistani officers familiar with Mountbatten's record as an operational commander might well have started planning their victory party, but the implication was that Mountbatten represented Britain, and therefore that Britain was siding with India. 'The military colossus of the Government of India and the best British Generals and Commanders are, therefore, co-operating to crush a tiny half-organised ill-equipped and General-less force of [*sic*] the people of Kashmir have mustered', it said.[57] Sir Laurence Grafftey-Smith and Duke, the two most senior British diplomats in Pakistan, both worried that Mountbatten's position and attitude were stirring up 'anti-British feeling'.[58]

In all the calamities of Pakistan's young life, the hand of Dickie could be detected: the mysterious delay in the publication of the Radcliffe award; the failure to arrest known Sikh troublemakers just before partition; and now the accession of Kashmir to India. The Pakistani Minister of Finance offered Grafftey-Smith his acid congratulations on Britain's 'latest victory over Pakistan'. More and more Pakistanis were beginning to believe that the British government 'are led by the nose by Lord Mountbatten, who is himself led by the nose by Mr. Nehru, who in his turn, is frightened of Mr. Patel, Pakistan's greatest individual enemy.' He may as well have added, as plenty of commentators later would, an extra link in the chain: Lady Mountbatten, occupying an undefined position between her husband and the Prime Minister. 'We have so long been the "Aunt Sally" of politics in India that our reappearance in that role is hardly surprising', wrote Grafftey-Smith resignedly. 'But it is regrettable.'[59]

In Kashmir, fighting had spread to Uri at the mouth of the valley, and into the south-west.[60] On 5 November, 120 trucks mysteriously arrived in the city of Jammu. Local Muslims were rounded up and told that they would be taken to the Pakistan border, then released across it. Five thousand civilian men, women and children complied and got into the trucks. Instead of driving to the border, the trucks turned the other way, and took the Muslims further into the heart of Jammu. The convoy halted, the guards got out, and then, with machine guns and blades, massacred their charges. A few hundred escaped by hiding in fields or canals. The rest were killed.[61]

The physical temperature was steadily dropping. By December, the valley and surrounding hills would be icebound. Supplies to the Indian Army were already falling short. The Indian Army's Sikh troops were becoming restive, and it was rumoured that they had demanded a Sikh state, to include Amritsar, Simla and the East Punjab. The Maharaja of Patiala was said to be encouraging the scheme.[62] Against this Sikh objective was the similarly aggressive ambition of the Pathan tribesmen. Sydney Smith, a reporter for the *Daily Express* who had managed to get himself kidnapped by Pathans near Baramula, confirmed on his release that tribal leaders chanted prayers every night for the success of their jihad against the

Sikhs. 'Every tribal leader agrees on the war aims', wrote Smith. 'They are: To wipe out Sir Hari Singh's minority rule in Kashmir; to march on and exterminate the chief Sikh State, Patiala; to capture Amritsar and try – one day – to reach New Delhi.'[63]

Kashmir was becoming another chapter in the centuries-long story of conflict between Sikhs and Pathans for control of the North-West Frontier. As a result, Nehru was being pushed into an ever more mil-itant position by his cabinet's fears that a soft response to Muslim incursions in Kashmir would trigger more communal riots across India. Mountbatten, though he did advise military operations, became increasingly desperate to rein Nehru in. At a defence com-mittee meeting on 4 November, Mountbatten advised strongly against sending India's Sikh troops into Muslim areas of Mirpur and Poonch, even for 'liberation purposes'. He pointed out that, in such areas, it would be impossible to distinguish between hostile persons and friends, and that it was likely that the army would make mistakes and aggravate the situation. Instead, the Indian government should find a way of stopping the fighting through communication with the Pakistani government.[64]

But Mountbatten would not be around to supervise the Indian Army at this crucial point, for he had already accepted an invitation to fly back to Britain with Edwina for his nephew's royal wedding. He had originally hoped to have Nehru come with them, though that was untenable now; Patel, on the other hand, had been conspicu-ously encouraging of the Governor General's little break away from India.[65] Edwina was appalled that they might leave India in a state of acute crisis. She hated the thought of being dragged away from her relief work and, as she confided to Alan Campbell-Johnson, was 'concerned about the construction that might be put on their departure to London'. She suggested cancelling the trip, but Campbell-Johnson talked her out of it on the grounds that to do so would be to acknowledge that there was a problem.[66]

For some weeks, Edwina had been feeling that Dickie did not live up to the obsessive pace she set. She had been in Amritsar for a con-ference with the refugee commissioner and the military when news came through that her elder daughter, Patricia, had given birth to a baby boy. 'I gathered that I was a Grandmama and that you were both flourishing and that Daddy was at the Chief's House playing roulette!' she wrote to her. 'Very 1947!! Women work and men play!'[67] The joke was not light-hearted. Edwina was now working an average of eighteen hours a day. Dickie still seemed to be able to fit in riding, exercise, genealogy and regular massages. Tension between the two of them ran high, and the fights grew more serious. On 10 November, they got back on their plane for the two-day journey to London, Edwina still full of misgivings.

With the Mountbattens out of the way, Nehru's first action was to take his long-threatened trip to Kashmir. On 12 November, he addressed a meeting at Srinagar: 'I pledge before you on behalf of myself and the people of India that we – India and Kashmir – shall ever remain together.'[68] He wrote at length to Attlee of hospitals, convents and libraries ransacked. 'I saw large numbers of Muslim women with their ears torn, because their earrings had been pulled out,' he stated, implying that the raiders were responsible. 'The population of Kashmir Valley, which is chiefly Muslim, complain bitterly of this outrageous behaviour and begged us to continue to protect them.'[69]

The Mountbattens arrived back in London that same day, and embarked upon a flurry of social and political events. In private Edwina was unable to disguise how furious she was with her husband, and they had a series of rows. She insisted on seeing her former lover, Malcolm Sargent, on one of the two nights they would have had together at Broadlands.[70] Mountbatten went to see Churchill, and had a fight with him, too. Churchill patted him on the back, gave him a glass of port and a cigar, and then told him categorically that his sending British soldiers 'to crush and oppress the Muslims in Kashmir' was an act of gross betrayal. He described Nehru and Patel as 'enemies of Britain', and the Muslims as Britain's allies; and accused Mountbatten of planning and organizing 'the first victory of Hindustan' (he refused to call it India) 'against Pakistan'. Churchill told Mountbatten that he should leave India, 'and not involve the King and my country in further backing traitors'.[71]

The King and Queen hosted pre-wedding parties, which the Mountbattens attended. 'The most lovely sight I have ever seen', wrote Noël Coward, enchanted by the sight of Buckingham Palace full of glittering celebrities in full evening dress and decorations. 'Everyone looking shiny and happy; something indestructible.'[72] The following day saw an afternoon party at St James's Palace so that guests could view the thousands of wedding presents. Members of the public had already been permitted to admire them, at a shilling a peek; everything from a 175-piece porcelain dinner service from the Chiang Kai-sheks, to a gold tiara from Haile Selassie, to dozens of pairs of nylon stockings sent in by ordinary people. Mountbatten had brought the present that excited the most comment – a fringed piece of khadi spun by Gandhi on his own spinning wheel. 'Such an indelicate gift,' thundered Queen Mary, apparently under the impression that the Mahatma had sent Princess Elizabeth his loincloth.[73]

That evening, Dickie attended his nephew's stag night at the Dorchester Hotel. The twelve men present drank sherry, champagne, port and beer, and afterwards cheerfully assaulted some photographers, ripping their cameras off them and throwing flashbulbs so that they exploded with loud bangs against the wall.[74] The next morning, 20 November, 2000 people – and one Pekingese dog, hidden in Lady Munnings's muff – packed into Westminster Abbey.[75] The crowned heads of Europe sat in the sacrarium, with Dickie and Edwina in pride of place. They had arrived looking handsome, the full Mountbatten wattage disguising the frosty state of their private relationship. Churchill walked in, 'his beaming smile almost as broad as his waistline', according to Leo Amery; 'rather looking as if the whole thing were his own show and he the genial parent or godparent of the Bride ... The contrast between him and Attlee, trying to look as if he wasn't there, very striking.'[76]

The bride, in ivory silk and 10,000 pearls, walked down the aisle to join her tall, blond and apparently not too hungover groom at the altar. A full traditional ceremony followed, during which the future Queen promised to obey her husband. He had been created Duke of Edinburgh the day before, so that his wife need not suffer the name Mrs Philip Mountbatten.[77] It had been reported that the Edinburghs were thinking of joining Uncle Dickie in India for their honeymoon, though in view of the situation there by November 1947 it is probably fortunate that this came to nothing.[78] Instead, they had a week

at Broadlands, beleaguered by a phalanx of royal watchers, who followed them into the local town, lurked in the shrubbery, and even
queued outside the church after services to have a go at sitting in the
seats warmed by the royal couple.[79]

The Mountbattens flew back to India on 24 November. Much had
happened during their vacation. Liaquat Ali Khan stated that
Pakistan wanted to refer the Kashmir issue to the United Nations.
Jawaharlal Nehru charged high Pakistani officials with inciting the
tribesmen in Kashmir. A force of Afghans from Khost crossed the
border into Kashmir, reportedly armed with Russian equipment.[80]
The President of the Congress Party, J.B. Kripalani, resigned in fear
of an imminent war between India and Pakistan.

Mountbatten was horrified. Without his steadying hand, the
Indian Army had moved into militant action; it did not stretch the
imagination to work out that this might have been precisely the
reason Patel was so keen for him to go away. Just before he had left
for London, he had reluctantly authorized Indian columns to move
to Mirpur and Poonch, for the sole purpose of relieving the gar-
risons already there. 'During my absence in London this object
changed', he wrote to Nehru. 'It then evidently became the purpose
of the Government of India to attempt to impose their military will
on the Poonch and Mirpur areas.' He protested that the inhabitants
were mostly Muslim, and reminded Nehru that it would be
'morally unjustifiable' to use force to coerce them into India.[81]

Immediately after stepping off the plane, Edwina, whose fears
about leaving India had been proven right, went off to see Gandhi,
and then Amrit Kaur. But there was no doubt about who she
wanted to see most: it was Jawahar. More or less every day she saw
or spoke to him now. The Government House diaries reveal the two
of them meeting for dinner on 2 December, at his home on 3
December, at hers on 4 December, and so on throughout the winter.
Soon, she was happy enough to be kind to Dickie again. 'Thanks
for being so sweet and understanding during these days in
England', she wrote, though she had the note sent round to his
room by a servant rather than taking it to him herself.[82] On her
forty-sixth birthday, she took the afternoon off for a visit to the Taj
Mahal, the world's greatest monument to love in sparkling white

marble and lapidary, built by the heartbroken Shah Jahan in memory of his wife, Mumtaz.[83]

At the end of November, Dickie flew his mistress, Yola Letellier, out to Delhi. Edwina invited Malcolm Sargent, and ignored him. 'I fear I've hardly set eyes on them', wrote Edwina of their guests.[84] Her friendships with Jawahar and Gandhi cast her London friends in the shade. During her friends' visits, she kept up the regular trips to Jawahar's house in York Road. For both Edwina and Jawahar, it was the ideal relationship. Only in each other's company could the two of them relax and lose themselves in endless conversations.[85] Their talks were almost always about ideas rather than gossip, but were never dry or sterile. Ideas were what made them passionate. In their romantic lives, Jawahar and Edwina alike had always sought intimacy without suffocation. With each other, they found it.

According to Nehru's secretary, M.O. Mathai, Nehru paid a brief visit to Lucknow in the winter of that year. Sarojini Naidu was then the Governor of the United Provinces, and a rumour spread that Nehru was in Lucknow to propose to his old girlfriend, Sarojini's daughter Padmaja Naidu. Padmaja was ecstatic, and prepared herself to accept. When Jawahar turned up, he was with Edwina. Padmaja locked herself in a room and refused to meet the Governor General's wife.[86] Later, when Padmaja came to stay with him, Jawahar would find one of his framed photographs of Edwina smashed on the floor.[87]

On Kashmir, Nehru's attitude was hardening, and he appeared to be losing interest in holding a plebiscite.[88] On 6 December, he went again to the state and met the Maharaja's son – 'a very bright boy', he told Indira.[89] Mountbatten had desperately attempted to stop him from going.[90] Edwina's friends Richard Symonds and Horace Alexander, both relief workers, had paid a lengthy visit to Kashmir and afterwards sent Nehru a report. Symonds had described the conditions in Poonch, where the inhabitants had revolted against the Maharaja of Kashmir back in September or October, apparently before the Pathan raiders invaded. Nehru was furious, for the existence of a prior revolt would strengthen Pakistan's argument that the raiders had responded to a cry for help from oppressed Kashmiri Muslims. 'I don't care a damn what happens to Poonch,' he shouted.

'They can go to Pakistan or Hell for all I care.' Symonds and Alexander passed on suggestions made to them by Liaquat – that all non-Kashmiri troops should be removed from Kashmir, and replaced by a temporary United Nations government, pending a plebiscite. This made matters worse. 'These people do not deserve to be listened to. They have behaved disgustingly and *I will not have*' – as he banged on the table three times with his fist – 'a single Pakistani soldier in Kashmir.'[91]

Mountbatten, too, was beginning to think about calling in the international arbitrator. When Liaquat and Nehru met on 8 December, they argued for five hours straight before a pained Mountbatten interrupted them and begged them to telegraph the United Nations Security Council and get a team sent over immediately.[92] Nehru was reluctant to accept United Nations involvement. Just a week before, the UN had voted to partition Palestine between Arabs and Jews. Trouble had flared immediately in Damascus, Jenin, Tel Aviv, Acre and Nablus. Nehru did not see that the UN's roles of peacekeeping or supervising a plebiscite were relevant until there was a peace to keep; in the meantime, a reference to the UN would involve admitting that the situation was one of war between India and Pakistan.[93] His attitude came in for much criticism. In a moment of irritation, the British High Commissioner in Karachi would write that 'We seem to be faced with a choice between what may be loosely described as natural justice and the appeasement of one man who, since he is himself a Kashmiri pundit, is blinded to realities by emotions passionately involved.' For this, he earned a swift reprimand from Attlee.[94]

On 12 December, India and Pakistan finally announced an agreement on the partition of their assets. Pakistan was to get 750 million rupees of British India's sterling assets and cash balances (slightly less than one-fifth of the total), one-third of its military stocks, and 17.5 per cent of its liabilities. It was good news for the ailing dominion and its ailing leader. Just two weeks before, it had been reported that Jinnah had been bedridden secretly for a month. No details of his illness were disclosed.[95] 'I understand that he is now living on the edge of a nervous breakdown,' reported the British High Commissioner to Pakistan.[96] Nehru's friend Sri Prakasa, the Indian High Commissioner to Pakistan, sent him a long report on the situation in Karachi. While Jinnah was 'not quite a broken man as he was reported to be, he is not himself now and he has become extraordinarily sensitive', Prakasa noted. The sensitivity was not surprising, bearing in mind that Prakasa had heard of three separate attempts to assassinate Jinnah, all of which had been kept from the press. Some said the plotters were Sikhs. Others said they were Punjabi Muslims, angry at what they perceived as Jinnah's abandonment of them in the Indian Punjab. Either way, the last attempt had been 'particularly nasty'. The would-be assassins had broken into Jinnah's compound, killing one guard and seriously injuring another. Prakasa described Jinnah as increasingly isolated – not just by his illness, but also by his attitude. He took no advice, except from one person. 'I am almost inclined to think that his sister, Miss Fatima, is his evil genius.'[97]

The British High Commissioner, Sir Laurence Grafftey-Smith, went to see Jinnah shortly after this, and found that, though 'wispily frail in body', the 'fire of his fanatical ardour is certainly in no way diminished'. Jinnah harangued him with regard to his bugbear, 'which has now acquired the strength of an obsession' – that the person most responsible for the disaster of partition was Dickie Mountbatten.[98]

Mountbatten, meanwhile, permitted himself a brief escape from the vicissitudes of Delhi life. On 12 December, he flew with Edwina and Yola to Jaipur, one of India's most beautiful cities, a pink sandstone metropolis set in the heart of princely Rajputana. They stayed with the Maharaja, whose silver jubilee they were to celebrate. He had succeeded to the throne at the age of eleven, since which time he had ruled over three million people. His glamorous Maharani had been *Tatler* magazine's cover girl just five months before, was said to be very Western-minded, and played tennis with the Queen when she was in London.[99] Dickie and Edwina stayed at the Rambagh Palace, a huge and spectacular estate. They watched a lot of polo, and attended a lot of banquets; Edwina was taken to visit schools, and Dickie to shoot ducks. At his jubilee durbar the Maharaja walked barefoot across the palace grounds, wearing garlands of flowers and

a white plume held in place by a sumptuously jewelled turban orna-
ment. The Mountbattens followed: Dickie in full dress uniform,
Edwina in lamé with a coronet of laurel leaves and five strands of
pearls.[100] Afterwards, the Maharaja gave a very nice speech about
Dickie, crediting him with waging all sorts of battles in Burma.[101]

From Jaipur, the Mountbattens flew on to Bombay; he to visit soldiers, she to visit refugee camps and women's organizations. They
returned to Delhi on 18 December to find that, once again, problems
had blown up in their absence. Patel had ordered a freeze on 550
million rupees (£40 million) of Pakistan's sterling assets, on the
grounds that it would be used to arm invaders of 'Indian territory' in
Kashmir. Jinnah and Liaquat were furious. The Pakistani treasury
had only 20 million rupees left in it, and they were facing a serious
financial crisis.[102] Mountbatten presided over another hopeless meeting in New Delhi on 21 and 22 December, at which Liaquat and
Nehru reached a complete deadlock. After sustained lobbying,
Mountbatten persuaded Nehru to refer the Kashmir problem to the
United Nations – a concession which he considered a great achievement, for 'Nehru has been as temperamental and difficult over the
Kashmir issue as he [had] ever known him'.[103] To Mountbatten's
horror, Nehru had begun to talk of sending Indian troops into
Pakistan to take out the 'nerve centres' from which raiders were
being sent. The friendship between Dickie and Jawahar, recently so
cordial, was rapidly souring. Jawahar's relationship with Edwina
remained strong, but even she could not always lift his despair. 'I am
afraid I have had no peace whatever for an age', he wrote, 'and I
think rather longingly sometimes of the quiet days I had in prison.'[104]

On 25 December, Jinnah celebrated Christmas with a Pakistani
Christian community.[105] In Delhi, Mountbatten spent it writing
Nehru an extremely long and agonized letter about Kashmir. 'I
have never and will never from my experience of war subscribe to
the view that the operations which are now starting to take place
are anything but of the most dangerous and risky character,' he
declared. Correctly, he pointed out that the modern weapons and
great resources of India counted for nothing in the face of guerrilla
warfare. 'The raiders with the local population on their side can
take on our forces at their will. This process is bound to wear down

our army and our resources.' He deplored the possibility of sending Indian troops into Pakistan in the frankest terms: 'Each time I have heard you say it I have been more and more appalled.' He predicted that it would lead to war between India and Pakistan, and observed that the idea that such a war 'could be confined to the sub-Continent, or finished off quickly in favour of India without further complication, is to my mind a fatal illusion.' He reiterated the need to call in the United Nations, but the most striking message to emerge from the letter was the simplest. Several times, he repeated and underlined the phrase 'stop the fighting'.[106]

Nehru replied the next day. 'We have not started the fighting,' he protested. 'I am convinced that the whole of this business has been very carefully planned on an extensive scale.' After Kashmir, he wrote, the next objective would be Patiala; then the East Punjab; then Delhi itself. 'On to Delhi is the cry all over West Punjab.'[107]

The Mountbattens had been due to set off on another trip to Gwalior. By the time Dickie received Nehru's letter, and panicked, he considered the hour too late to cancel, though he believed that there was an immediate danger of war between India and Pakistan. He had been furious when Attlee threatened to have him superseded as Viceroy. Now it was he who sent a message to Attlee begging him to come out personally and take the crisis out of his hands.[108] Attlee refused to do so.[109] Mountbatten also asked Nehru to contact Attlee with a full report on Kashmir – though Nehru, again struck down with a cold at an inopportune moment, was confined to his bed and could not. Attlee sent him a sternly worded message telling him not to move forces into Pakistan, even if he thought such an action would constitute self-defence. 'I am gravely disturbed by your assumption that India would be within her rights in international law', he wrote. Moreover, Indian hopes for a quick and sharp campaign were 'very optimistic . . . all military history goes to shew how difficult it is to deal with the tribes of the N.W. Frontier'.[110]

While these debates were going on, India began to drop half-ton bombs on Pathan tribes along the 500-mile front of Kashmir's south-west. Within India, the government's standing was precarious. There was a strike by half a million textile and industrial workers on 29 December, and a riot led by communist students against Congress in

Bombay two days later. Finally, on the very last day of 1947, Nehru gave in to Mountbatten's persuasion and instructed the Indian ambassador in Washington to submit an appeal to the UN Security Council.[111] In under five months, the two nations of India and Pakistan had embroiled themselves in an irresolvable war.

CHAPTER 18

MAYBE NOT TODAY,
MAYBE NOT TOMORROW

AFTER NEHRU HAD SHOUTED AT HIM OVER POONCH AT THE
beginning of December, Edwina's friend Richard Symonds had been
struck down with typhoid. Gandhi had taken him in at Birla House
to convalesce, and G.D. Birla himself had slipped him brandy behind
the Mahatma's back. Symonds had been visited by Patel, with gentle
words; Gandhi, 'more charming & amusing than I have ever known
him'; and Nehru himself, contrite after his outburst, 'twirling &
sniffing at one deep red rose, like Ferdinand the Bull'. Gandhi had
invited some Christian women to decorate Symonds's room for
Christmas, which they did with great enthusiasm. Unfortunately, all
the baubles, streamers and tinsel were tied to the ceiling fan and,
when the Pakistani High Commissioner turned up to talk about
Kashmir, he had become so involved in his grievances that he accidentally switched it on.[1]

The High Commissioner's ceiling fan disaster was an apt
metaphor for the political situation as a whole. So worked up had
the politicians on both sides become about the details of who had
acceded when, and which soldiers had been sent in where, that they
had accidentally set off one of the most serious ongoing security
crises in history. Mountbatten's state of open desperation by the end
of 1947 demonstrated that he, at least, had begun to realize the full
magnitude of what had been unleashed. His insistence on taking the

Kashmir issue to the United Nations had been based on two sincere beliefs: first, that conflict between India and Pakistan would escalate; and second, that the better option was to cool the governments down and persuade them to talk. He was right on the first point. When the UN Security Council met in January, it observed that the danger of an imminent attack by India on Pakistan from the East Punjab was 'clearly acute'.[2] Meanwhile, the British High Commissioner in Karachi observed that any invasion by India would 'uncork a Jehad' in retaliation.[3]

On the second point, though, the decision to involve the United Nations was problematic. The Indian government was not prepared to talk, except about how much blame should be put on Pakistan for aiding the tribesmen.[4] But, if the Security Council adopted a resolution blaming the Pakistani government, India might order a full invasion of Pakistan. The best chance of peace, it considered, was to persuade Pakistan to call off the tribesmen; but Pakistan would not do so unless the safety of Muslims in Kashmir could be guaranteed.[5] The UN would have to send in a neutral peacekeeping force – and the only troops who had knowledge of the language and the terrain were British.[6] The British government reacted to the suggestion that it might put its soldiers back into the subcontinent with abject horror.[7]

Rather than calming the two dominions down, the chance to air their grievances at enormous length on the international stage would rile them up.[8] Attlee telegraphed his most important ambassadors on 10 January to emphasize that under no circumstances should they allow Pakistan to think they were siding with India, because 'In view of Palestine situation this would carry the risk of aligning the whole of Islam against us.'[9]

Attlee's fears were prescient. Israel was due to become an independent state on 14 May, prompting an immediate response characterized by the Pakistani newspaper *Light*. Under the headline 'America's challenge to Islam', the *Light* contrasted Washington's refusal to recognize Pakistani Kashmir with its keenness to recognize the state of Israel. The article described the United States' backing for Israel against the Arabs as 'the first link in the chain of planned acts of hostility' against Islam, and regretted that its policies were pitting Islam against its natural ally, democracy.[10]

In fact, Britain effectively did side with Pakistan. The British delegation at the UN was scrupulous in its insistence that India and Pakistan both had valid claims to the territory, and heavy in its implication that the Muslim majority in Kashmir gave Pakistan the edge.[11] But in India, as well as in Pakistan, the retreat of the British left a new world superpower to take the blame. According to Mountbatten, by the end of January, Nehru was describing the UN as 'an American racket'.[12]

Kashmir was threatening to become a major focus for the Cold War. On 13 January, the British Ambassador in Moscow reported that the Russians suspected that Britain had made a secret military agreement with Pakistan. The Soviet press claimed openly that Britain was 'inciting Pakistan to seize Kashmir'.[13] It was an easy accusation to make, for the armies of India and Pakistan were still to a significant extent commanded by British officers. Dickie Mountbatten was not the only serviceman whose position had become awkward, and the absurdity of the situation soon threatened mutinies. Stafford Cripps alerted Attlee to a private letter from the Royal Indian Air Force's Air Marshal T.W. Elmhirst, who stated frankly that he would resign if sent to fight the Pakistanis in Kashmir. 'I am not prepared to command the *King's* Indian Air Force to battle against the *King's* Pakistan Air Force commanded by a friend of mine,' he wrote. 'It's quite time H.M.G. took a firm line.'[14] London had issued a stern warning that no British officers were to serve in Kashmir, but many of the men in question felt strong personal ties to their fellow soldiers and loyalty to the dominion they served. It was impossible to stop them working from the sidelines. Richard Symonds, who served on the United Nations commission in Kashmir after he recovered from his illness, described a farcical situation. The British Commanders-in-Chief of the Indian and Pakistani forces would ring each other up as if they were arranging a tea-party: 'If you bomb this,' they would say, 'we shall shell that.'[15]

The last four months of 1947 had witnessed a spectacular revival in the popularity of Mohandas Gandhi in political circles. With his image boosted by the success of his fast in Calcutta and ministrations in Delhi, he had resumed his role as a guru to many of the leading lights of the Indian government. Despite this renewed demand for his spiritual leadership, the Mahatma himself remained disconsolate. 'I must achieve something or die in the attempt', he wrote.[16] Stories of communal outrages distressed him; the presence of armed police and the military in Delhi horrified him. 'Votaries of non-violence today have had to put their trust in the weapons of violence', he observed. 'What a severe test it is going to be for us.'[17] But both Nehru and Patel made daily pilgrimages to his sparse, airy chamber in the opulent Birla House.

To the distress of Gandhi, Nehru and Patel – never the best of friends – were developing a deep antipathy towards each other, splitting and stalling the government. Patel viewed Nehru's scrupulously unjudgemental treatment of India's remaining Muslims as indulgent and dangerous to national security. He also resented Nehru's attempts to root out the Hindu nationalists of the Rashtriya Swayamsevak Sangh (RSS), describing them as 'patriots who love their country'.[18] Many observers thought that, once the freedom struggle was over, Congress should have split.[19] A strong right wing under Patel, and a strong left wing under Nehru, might have produced a balanced two-party system. But Congress stayed together, united more by sentimentality than by a common political goal. When Patel chose Hindu nationalist Purshottam Das Tandon for Congress President, a man who openly supported an aggressive policy towards Pakistan and opposed industrialization, many of Nehru's usual supporters walked out of the party in protest. Nehru was isolated, and Patel had placed himself at the centre of the party, with the interests of the landowning and industrial elite behind him.[20] On 6 January, Nehru told Gandhi that he had reached an impasse. Either Patel had to go, or he would.

One week later, to the surprise of even his closest intimates, Gandhi embarked upon his final fast. Before, he had always discussed the intention to fast at great length; the period of warning and discussion had been an essential part of the tactic. This time, both Nehru and Patel had seen him in the morning before the fast began, and Gandhi had said not a word. The only member of the government he told was Amrit Kaur. Amrit confided to a member of the British High Commission's staff that she thought it would really be the fast unto death at last. The aged Mahatma could not hope to live for more than five or six days without sustenance. Ostensibly, Gandhi was fasting to stop Hindus attacking Muslims in Delhi. 'Other sources suggest that the fast is due to the bad state of relations between Nehru and Patel which they say have been worse during the last week than ever before,' noted the British High Commissioner. 'Gandhi hopes that his fast will rally mass public opinion to Nehru's more liberal views.'[21]

Gandhi slept on a cot in Birla House while the public filed past to observe him.[22] The Mountbattens were in Bikaner for another princely visit, though the Maharaja cancelled the state banquet out of respect for Gandhi's fast. When they returned to Delhi, Edwina took Dickie with her to visit Gandhi for the first time. Previously, the Mahatma had always come to see him. 'It takes a fast to bring you to me!' exclaimed Gandhi with a twinkle in his eye.[23] Though his sense of humour remained, Gandhi seemed so weak that, as she left, Edwina wept. Jawahar also came to visit Gandhi that day; he, too, could not hold back tears. When he heard a crowd of refugees outside Birla House chanting, 'Let Gandhi die!' Jawahar's sorrow turned to fury. 'How dare you say these words!' he shouted, running at the protesters. 'Come and kill me first!' The cowards scattered.[24]

Patel had been unmovable on the question of unfreezing the 550 million rupees that India still owed to Pakistan, and Nehru was unwilling to challenge his cabinet on the issue. Mountbatten claimed that he had told Gandhi the situation, at which point Gandhi offered to fast. 'And they were terribly upset that he'd agreed to this – terribly upset that he'd done it with me and not with them,' Mountbatten remembered. 'And he got them absolutely by the short hairs; they had to give up.'[25] This latter-day reminiscence of Mountbatten's is contradicted by his own report of 3 February 1948, in which he admits that he, too, had only been told about Gandhi's fast at the last minute, that the reason for it 'will, I think, forever remain a mystery', and that Gandhi had come up with the scheme 'without consulting me'.[26] Still, it is true that, during one of Nehru's visits, Gandhi asked him to pay Pakistan its due. Without hesitation, Nehru ordered it to be done. The cabinet, though reluctant, could not disobey a direct request from the ailing

Mahatma, whose political influence at last matched his moral influence.[27]

As it had in Calcutta, Gandhi's fast brought results from the people at large as well as the government. Representatives from across Delhi sent assurances that Muslim life, property and religion in Delhi would be respected. Nehru brought the messages to the Mahatma's cot and, on 18 January, Gandhi gave up his fast. Together with the Muslim minister Abul Kalam Azad, Nehru took turns to feed the old man fruit juice.

Quickly Gandhi recovered his strength, but not his optimism. 'India will virtually become a prison if the present conditions continue,' he said on breaking his fast. 'It may be better that you allow me to continue my fast and if God wills it He will call me.'[28] Two days later, he was addressing his daily prayer meeting in the grounds of Birla House when a bomb exploded only yards away. Both Jawahar and Edwina rushed to the scene, but found Gandhi unhurt and unflustered, declaring that he had merely thought the army must have been at work nearby.[29] Edwina congratulated him on his cool response, but Gandhi was modest. 'If somebody fired at me point blank and I faced his bullet with a smile, repeating the name of Rama in my heart,' Gandhi told her, 'I should be deserving of congratulations.'[30]

The bomb-thrower was a young Hindu refugee from West Punjab, caught in the act of lighting the fuse; he also had a live grenade on him. The police suspected that he was not acting alone. Rumours were rife about an extreme Hindu nationalist group from Bombay who saw Gandhi as the betrayer of Hinduism, and who had been inflamed by his efforts to save Muslim lives. Yet Gandhi refused any extra security at prayer meetings – except for demanding that every Hindu or Sikh brought a Muslim friend.[31]

On 23 January, the Mountbattens left for a tour of Bhopal, Nagpur and Madras. The atmosphere remained tense, and in Amritsar a wild protest trampled the national flag into the dirt. Three days after the incident, on 29 January, Nehru spoke in Amritsar district, his voice shaking with passionate anger as he denounced the action as traitorous, and communal organizations such as the RSS as unfit for India's greatness. A non-Muslim member of his audience was arrested for carrying two hand grenades.[32]

On the morning of 30 January, Margaret Bourke-White went to interview Gandhi, and found him deeply depressed. 'I can no longer live in darkness and madness,' he murmured. 'I cannot continue.' Later, he was visited by Betty Hutheesing, Indira Gandhi and Padmaja Naidu, bringing with them Indira's four-year-old son, Rajiv. While the adults talked and joked, Rajiv played with some jasmine flowers that had been brought for Gandhi. He wrapped them around the old man's feet, but was stopped with a gentle hand. 'You must not do that,' said the Mahatma. 'One only puts flowers around dead people's feet.'[33]

That afternoon, Gandhi shared a meal of goat's milk, vegetables and oranges with Vallabhbhai and Maniben Patel. He got up and, supported by his grand-nieces Abha and Manu, walked down the colonnade that ran from outside his ground-floor quarters to the large and beautiful back garden of Birla House. He was about ten minutes late for the prayer meeting that day, and a crowd of around five hundred had gathered. As he walked through the bowing attendees towards his platform at the centre of the garden, a young man stepped out and pressed his palms together, with the traditional Hindi greeting, 'Namaste.' Manu caught his hand to move him out of Gandhi's way, but he pushed her over. The man looked Gandhi in the eyes, pulled out a Beretta pistol, and fired three shots point-blank into the Mahatma's chest. 'He Ram' – 'Oh Rama' – Gandhi was heard to say as he sank to the ground.

Immediately, there was chaos. As Gandhi was cradled by his devotees and carried back to the house, the assassin was seized and pummelled by thirty-two-year-old diplomatic officer Herbert Reiner of Springdale, Connecticut.[34] A doctor was found within minutes, but he was no use. Mohandas Karamchand Gandhi was dead.

Crimson blood spread across Gandhi's white shawl, and the news spread through Delhi nearly as fast. Betty Hutheesing had gone on to a friend's house, and asked her Muslim driver to take her home. The driver began to tremble and could hardly start the car. 'My God, I hope it wasn't a Muslim,' he said.[35] It was not. The murderer was Nathuram Godse, a Bombay Brahmin and member of the fundamentalist Hindu Mahasabha, an organization linked to the same RSS that Patel had recently endorsed so glowingly. He and his co-conspirator, Narayan Apte, had bonded over a shared hatred of Muslims, and love of detective novels: Apte preferred Agatha Christie, while Godse's favourite was Erle Stanley Gardner.[36] Godse was unpenitent for the murder of Gandhi, and asked that no mercy be shown to him. After a trial a few months later, he would be hanged.

Nehru's niece, Nayantara Pandit, had been having tea with Indira Gandhi when they heard the news. They too rushed to Birla House. Shortly after they arrived, someone whispered, 'Jawaharlal,' and Indira's father walked in. He had heard that Mohandas had been shot, but did not realize until he saw the body that his guru was dead. He knelt by Gandhi's side, tears running down his face as he clutched the Mahatma's lifeless hand. 'I had never seen him so grief-stricken before', Nayantara wrote to her mother, Nan Pandit, 'like a lost child.'[37] She was moved to note that her uncle, to whom it fell to lead the world's mourning, had to sublimate his personal grief to the needs of his nation. 'When Mamu [Uncle] rose to his feet he had regained complete self-control,' she noted. 'Those who could bear to look at his face during those days saw a strained white mask through which only the eyes revealed stark anguish.'[38] Nayantara's aunt, Betty, remembered going into the quiet room and noticing Jawahar standing in the corner. 'His face was drawn and tortured as it had not been even when our father died', she wrote. 'I was quite con-trolled, or stunned, until then, but the agony which showed so clearly on Bhai's face made me break down.'[39]

Devadas Gandhi arrived to press his father's still-warm arm, and stayed with the body through the night. Dickie Mountbatten was there as soon as possible, but without Edwina, who had stayed in Madras and was trying desperately to organize her flight back. A tin can had been placed on the lawn to mark the spot where the Mahatma had been killed. People were clustered around it, scraping up bits of the bloodstained soil to carry off in their handkerchiefs for posterity.[40] Inside Gandhi's chamber, the silence was broken only by the smashing of glass. The crowds massing outside pressed forwards so powerfully that they broke the windows of Birla House.[41]

Nehru went outside and climbed up the gates to address the people. Three times during his speech he broke down in tears. When he climbed down, he was visibly shaking.[42] His words were not recorded but, soon afterwards, he went on All-India Radio to give another such speech to the nation. 'The light has gone out from our lives and there is darkness everywhere,' he began, his voice quavering. 'And I do not know what to tell you and how to say it.' But he did know how to say it: and he said it beautifully. 'The light has gone out, I said, and yet I was wrong. For the light that shone in this country was no ordinary light. The light that has illumined this country for these many, many years will illumine this country for many more years, and a thousand years later that light will still be seen in this country, and the world will see it, and it will give solace to innumerable hearts. For that light represented something more than the immediate present; it represented the living, eternal truths reminding us of the right path, drawing us from error, taking this ancient country to freedom.'[43]

The next morning, Gandhi's body was washed in a Hindu rite, garlanded with khadi and scattered with rose petals. In an inappropriately militaristic gesture, it was placed on an army weapons-carrier, drawn by 200 men of the services in a procession of 5100 troops, surrounded by armoured cars. The cortège took almost five hours to pass through the streets of New Delhi, packed with hundreds of thousands of people clad in the pure white of mourning, up towards Old Delhi and Raj Ghat, on the west bank of the Jumna River. Betty Hutheesing, Indira Gandhi and Padmaja Naidu walked behind the carriage. Though it was January, halfway through the nine-mile walk they were sodden with sweat, and Indira had begun to sway. Some soldiers in a jeep took pity on them and drove them the rest of the way.[44] Overhead, three aeroplanes showered petals on to the procession. One million people were estimated to be waiting at the ghat by late afternoon, including Dickie Mountbatten, in full uniform. Edwina, exhausted and grief-stricken after a sleepless night organizing a plane to take her back to Delhi, was sitting next to Jawaharlal Nehru on the dry earth. Unrecognized in the crowd was Gandhi's eldest son, Harilal, who had never reconciled with his father and was now suffering from tuberculosis. Harilal was drunk. A few months later he, too, would be dead.

Gandhi's body was laid on a pyre of sandalwood, and Nehru, in a unique departure from his own strict codes against any form of religious observance, went forward to kiss his guru's feet. The pyre was lit by another of Gandhi's sons, Ramdas, to a cry from the crowds and a rush forward. The danger of the flames was immediately obvious. Nehru, who had been staring into space in quiet desolation, jumped up and shoved his way through to the front of the crowd, shouting at people to sit down, and pushing them down if they did not comply. Dickie and Edwina Mountbatten sat immediately, forcing the ranks behind them to follow suit. The crowd dropped to the ground, and a further tragedy was averted.[45] (The fact that the Mountbattens had deigned to sit on dry earth amid a crowd of Indians raised a few eyebrows in London. A report from the *Daily Telegraph* with a picture of the Mountbattens sitting cross-legged beside Patel and Baldev Singh was torn out by Winston Churchill. He underlined the description of the Governor General and his wife 'squatting on the ground'.)[46] Prayers were chanted, hymns sung, and the entirety of Gandhi's beloved Bhagavad Gita read aloud as the sun slowly set. The flames burned until morning.

'Gandhi has been assassinated', wrote Noël Coward in his diary that day. 'In my humble opinion, a bloody good thing but far too late.'[47] This churlish remark indicated just how far the Mountbattens had come from their London set. Millions felt Gandhi's loss, but few so personally as Edwina Mountbatten. Yet it did not trigger a reconciliation with her husband. Instead, Edwina sat down and poured her heart out in a letter to Jawahar.[48] She had been getting closer to him for several months. Now she turned to him for comfort, and he to her.[49] There was little that any of the Mountbattens' friends could do to repair Dickie's and Edwina's marriage, though some of them were involved in it rather too closely. The new year had been followed by another series of scorching rows, prompting Peter Murphy – still living with the Mountbattens in Delhi – to write Edwina a letter begging her to give her husband another chance. 'It distresses me so that you ever imagine that you are not a very great deep love in his life,' he said. 'What it seems you *don't* know is the unfailing affection and loyalty that he feels for you and that he has spoken of so freely to me.'[50] It may have been true, but it did nothing to help. At one point

Dickie, Edwina and Yola had such a bitter and ugly 'three-cornered row' that Yola almost left India.[51] Mountbatten later confided to his Private Secretary, John Barratt, that Edwina had been 'difficult' in India, and put it down to the menopause that she was undergoing at the time. 'He made several oblique references to her relationship with Nehru,' remembered Barratt.[52]

Meanwhile, that relationship became closer. In public, Jawahar and Edwina were formal; in private, they were inseparable.[53] Letters became fervent. 'What did you tell me and what did I say to you . . .?' mused Jawahar to Edwina in a letter written after one of their many late-night meetings. 'The more one talks, the more there is to say and there is so much that it is difficult to put into words.'[54] Edwina's support was warm, but never controlling. 'In those days of tension, and later when she came to stay with my brother after he became Prime Minister of the Republic of India, she was one of the few people left who could break his sombre moods,' remembered Jawahar's sister, Betty. 'When she was there, Bhai's laughter would ring through the house as it used to when we were young.'[55] Dickie showed no sign of feeling excluded by the relationship. He pasted into his own private photograph album a selection of pictures from early February, when he and Edwina went to the Kumbh Mela at Allahabad with Jawahar. They rode in an ornate howdah atop a giant elephant to the confluence of the Ganges and the Jumna. Thousands lined the riverbanks and waved flags. One snapshot of Dickie, Edwina, Jawahar and Pamela was captioned simply, in Dickie's handwriting, 'Family visit to Allahabad'.[56]

From the sorrow and tragedy of Gandhi's death, some hope emerged. Mountbatten took the opportunity to tell Patel and Nehru that Gandhi's last great wish had been to see the two of them brought together. Weeping, the two men embraced.[57] Furthermore, though the long-anticipated final sacrifice had not been made by his own hand, it had, nonetheless, achieved a little of what he had spent much of his life pleading for. After a small spate of attacks on Hindu Mahasabha members in Bombay, India calmed, and the harassment of the Muslim population of Delhi ceased.[58] Refugees were rehoused in the Punjab. Stalls and shops reopened in Connaught Place. Unwittingly, with his act of hatred, Nathuram Godse had brought

Hindus and Muslims together. 'What is all the snivelling about?' Sarojini Naidu asked Gandhi's mourners defiantly. 'Would you rather he had died of decrepit old age or indigestion? This was the only death great enough for him.'[59]

On 2 February, the Indian government outlawed all communal organizations and private armies, specifically the Hindu Mahasabha, the RSS, the Sikh Akali Dal, and the Muslim League National Guard. The threat of further assassinations remained, and all eyes turned to the safety of Nehru. Nehru's friend Krishna Menon, now High Commissioner to London, sent Mountbatten a letter asking him to intervene personally to protect the Prime Minister. 'I am worried about Jawaharlal', he wrote. 'Is it not possible for something drastic to be done to prevent him taking unnecessary risks. He won't listen to anyone else.'[60] Mountbatten went further than Menon intended. He and Edwina attempted to persuade Nehru to move in with them. 'We offered him a self-contained flat with a separate entrance and said we would take in thirty other Government servants in one of the wings so that the accommodation vacated by them could be given to refugees,' Mountbatten wrote, 'but I was unable to persuade Panditji to move into the safety of Government House.'[61] Nehru was, however, persuaded to have his own house surrounded by armed guards. His niece, Rita Pandit, was staying with him at the time and wrote to her mother of his irritation: 'He hates all these regulations but abides by them – yesterday he said he felt freer in jail than he does now, & I can see why.'[62] He endured it all with composure. 'Jawaharlal is as magnificent as ever, and bearing up in spite of his overwhelming sorrow and responsibility; and so is Amrit', wrote Edwina Mountbatten to Agatha Harrison. 'I love them both.'[63]

In Pakistan, things were not going well for Jinnah. The prospect of open war with India continued to loom on West Pakistan's southern border. Now, on its northern border, the government of Afghanistan was furious with him, believing he had armed the tribesmen on their frontier.[64] In the face of a resurgent Islamic nationalism inside his own state, he continued to insist that 'Pakistan is not going to be a theocratic State to be ruled by priests with a divine mission. We have many non-Muslims – Hindus, Christians and Parsees – but they are all Pakistanis. They will enjoy the same rights and privileges as any other citizens and will play their rightful part in the affairs of Pakistan.'[65] Jinnah's strategy to achieve Pakistan by exploiting the extremes of identity politics had been extraordinarily successful. Unfortunately, his plan to run Pakistan as a progressive liberal democracy with a moderate Islamic flavour had been markedly less well worked out. Moreover, many of Jinnah's religious supporters had had a very different idea of what Pakistan might be. The maulvis, maulanas and pirs, whom he had spent two decades stirring up, would not return meekly to their boxes.

For all his strength and bluster, in private Jinnah was falling apart. He had suffered from tuberculosis for a decade, and his deterioration was obvious to the very few who were allowed to meet him. Margaret Bourke-White was one of them, sent to take a new portrait for the cover of *Life*. When she arrived at his house, she was fobbed off with a discreet code: 'The Quaid-e-Azam has a bad cold.'

Bourke-White knew Fatima Jinnah fairly well, and was able to sweet-talk her way into another appointment – on the condition that she would not take any close-up pictures. 'And when I saw his face, I knew why,' she remembered. 'The change was terrifying. There seemed to be a spiritual numbness concealing something close to panic underneath. As I went ahead with my pictures, his sister slipped up before each photograph and tried gently to uncurl his desperately clenched hands.'[66]

Jinnah's old loathing of Nehru had spilled over into an even greater loathing of Mountbatten.[67] He was convinced that India's Governor General was working to turn the Commonwealth against him, and he was not wrong. On 8 February, Mountbatten wrote Attlee an extraordinary letter – which, constitutionally, he was not supposed to write at all, for communication with Attlee was supposed to go through Nehru. In it, he implied that British policy was now anti-India and pro-Pakistan, criticized the attitude of the British at the UN, and admitted that 'I am being attacked on all sides for having given advice which is proving to be so disastrous' in involving the UN at all. The Indian government, he said, believed that Britain and the United

States were backing Pakistan as part of their goal of maintaining Muslim solidarity in the Middle East. 'It appears to me that Russia may well win India to her side by sponsoring her case,' he warned. 'I must point out that if this does come to pass the only result will be that India is thrown into the arms of Russia; and Russia will appear throughout this country as the saviour of India against the machination of the United States and the United Kingdom.'[68]

The letter was an open threat, and Attlee took it as such, sending back a stinging rebuke two days later. He pointed out that a Security Council resolution exactly in line with India's request would have led to war. 'Is it impossible for you to get these sorts of ideas into the heads of the Indian Government?' he asked. 'I realise of course that the difficulties are aggravated by Nehru's own emotional attitude to Kashmir.' He added that the threat of Russian influence 'does not make our flesh creep at all'.[69]

The rebuke prompted a lengthy response, in which Mountbatten complained about 'British support for American power politics'. He added, in hurt tones, that he did not believe that Nehru's government would survive if 'it were tamely to accept an award by the Security Council in favour of Pakistan; and it is for this reason that I drew your attention in my previous telegram to the grave consequences that such an award might entail.'[70] Someone at the British end highlighted this paragraph.

'Mountbatten finds his present constitutional position of friendly adviser irksome at times,' noted Campbell-Johnson. 'He can no longer step in between London and Delhi, and his only link now is with the King, who strictly separates his various sovereignties.'[71]

In the last week of February, alarming rumours began to reach Mountbatten's ears. The Pakistani government was preparing a genocide case, naming him as responsible for the Punjab massacres. Mountbatten fired off another urgent telegram to Attlee. Attlee's enquiries revealed the worrying fact that there was indeed reason to believe Pakistan's suggestion that Sir Cyril Radcliffe had altered the boundary award at the last moment, though it was not known whether this was done at the behest of Mountbatten. If the matter was to be pursued further, they would have to talk to Radcliffe – but this 'does not seem very desirable', noted the Commonwealth

Relations Secretary, Philip Noel-Baker. Noel-Baker sent a strictly personal message to the Pakistani government, carefully worded so as to avoid denying anything that might well be true: 'it would be most unwise and highly improper to introduce these allegations', the draft read; 'unwise, because we should certainly contest them; and improper because they would affect the honour and reputation of the King's Representative in India, who has no means of defending himself in public.' The bluff worked. Pakistan agreed that it would make no reference to a dubious change in the boundary award.[72] Britain was saved from a deeply embarrassing investigation, and Mountbatten from potential ruin.

With the drama in Kashmir, the problem of Hyderabad had almost been forgotten. Mountbatten had finally managed to conclude a standstill agreement with the state at the very end of November, though the Hyderabad delegation had objected to every possible detail, kicking up fusses over substituting the word 'shall' for the word 'will' in one clause, and over the use of a comma as opposed to their preferred semi-colon in another.[73] A few days later, a Hindu protester threw a hand-grenade at the Nizam's car. The Nizam was fortunate to escape without injury.

By the spring, the Governor General and the Nizam had lost patience with each other. Mountbatten wrote to the Nizam's former advocate, Walter Monckton, that the Nizam had 'been behaving queerly since your departure'. Almost simultaneously, the Nizam wrote to Monckton to the effect that Mountbatten wanted to force him to join India, but that 'he had better not interfere with this matter since political situation may aggravate if he does so'.[74] Consequently, Mountbatten washed his hands of Hyderabad. Patel took over and, by March, the Indian government had begun to use its geographical encirclement of Hyderabad to start an economic blockade.[75] Monckton got into a heated argument over these sanctions with Patel at the beginning of March, and for a moment it looked as if another war might break out. But, during lunch the next day, Patel suffered a massive heart attack, which would incapacitate him for several months. Once again, and with much reluctance, Mountbatten had to step in.

Mountbatten sent a last warning letter to the Nizam at the end of April, but refused to go to Hyderabad himself. Instead, he sent his press attaché. Campbell-Johnson flew to Hyderabad on 15 May, and was taken to meet the Nizam. The eccentric Nizam was renowned for being the world's worst-dressed billionaire, and that day was clad in a threadbare dressing-gown. They spoke in a dark, cluttered Victorian reception room, under the arresting gaze of a portrait of King George V. The Nizam expounded his view of Islam, complained about Palestine, and declared troublingly that 'Constitutional monarchy may be all very well in Europe and the west; it has no meaning in the East.'[76]

The Mountbattens, meanwhile, travelled the length and breadth of India, trying to fit into a few months the trips to every state that had taken most viceroys the fullness of their five-year terms. They inspected guards and hospitals in Cawnpore, visited the Buddhist temple at Sarnath, went by motor-boat to have tea at Ramnagar Fort, explored the caves at Bhubaneshwar, presented colours to the infantry in Trivandrum, cruised the backwaters in Travancore, ascended the hills at Ooty, laid foundation stones in Bundi, and opened engineering colleges in Anand. Edwina often toured without her husband, visiting Untouchable centres and leper clinics.

The furthest of these trips took the Mountbattens to Rangoon in newly independent Burma. There was a grand party at the President's house, at which the Mountbattens were presented to a wide array of Burmese notables including Aung San Suu Kyi, the one-year-old daughter of their late friend, Aung San.[77] The following day, Mountbatten returned the magnificent thirty-feet-high Hlutdaw Throne to the nation. The mood was happy, but tensions between Aung San's Anti-Fascist People's Freedom League and communist factions ran close to the surface. 'There are the symptoms here of complete political disintegration,' noted Alan Campbell-Johnson ominously.[78] All over the world, hostility was building. A communist coup in Czechoslovakia at the end of February had sparked fears in Washington that Finland, Italy, Austria and France might be next to fall into the Russian embrace. By the beginning of March, there was at least some reassurance from India. Nehru informed the US State Department that it would be 'unthinkable' for India to side with

Russia in another world war.[79] West Bengal outlawed the Communist Party and arrested 400 activists at the end of March, provoking an estrangement between Nehru and his American communist friend Paul Robeson, as well as a strike of 15,000 Bombay mill workers.

But the sticking point was still Kashmir. Some feared that Mountbatten's close friendship with Nehru might be holding him back from telling the Prime Minister just how hopeless the situation was. 'Panditji is capable of hearing profoundly unpleasant things,' the Governor of West Bengal, Chakravarty Rajagopalachari, hinted to Mountbatten during a tea-party in Calcutta.[80] He would hear them soon enough, whether or not Mountbatten was prepared to tell him. Soon afterwards Sir Hari Singh, now effectively an ex-Maharaja and a wretched figure, arrived at Government House to stay with the Mountbattens.[81] While he was there, news came through of the final UN Security Council resolution on Kashmir, requiring India to withdraw as well as Pakistan. It was a huge disappointment for Nehru, more so because it had the backing of the British government.[82] Pakistan was disappointed, too, because under the new resolution it was required to call off the tribesmen before India withdrew. 'Oh dear', wrote Horace Alexander to Edwina, 'I sometimes think our greatest crime against India was to turn all her best sons into lawyers.'[83] Even Edwina had to admit that 'Panditji, with all his understanding, statesmanship and fair-mindedness, is not always so easy to discuss Kashmir with'.[84] Jawahar arranged to visit Kashmir in May to celebrate a victory over the Pakistani tribesmen. He wanted to take Edwina, but not Dickie, with him. This plan was hastily dropped in the first week of May, with good reason. The appearance of the Governor General's wife in war-torn Kashmir on the arm of the Indian Prime Minister would have been distasteful both to the Pakistani and to the British governments.[85] Jawahar went alone for the celebrations, and Edwina visited Kashmir with Amrit Kaur two weeks later.[86] Edwina was shocked by the poor provision for welfare in Srinagar, but was impressed to see women running reconstruction and relief efforts. 'It is always true that good comes out of evil', she wrote to Sheikh Abdullah afterwards, 'and there is no doubt that this crisis has brought out women to play their full part in their country's affairs in a way which would otherwise have taken years of evolution to achieve.' Immediately on the evening of her return to Delhi, she went to see Nehru and convinced him to send more government help through her United Council for Relief and Welfare.[87]

Mountbatten's term as Governor General was undefined, though he had signed up as Viceroy on the basis of an end-date of June 1948. He preferred April, though Patel, according to Campbell-Johnson, had tried to persuade him to stay on for five years; Nehru, too, had asked him for another year. The date remained June 1948. Finding a successor would prove troublesome, for the role was effectively a retirement from party politics. Edwina suggested Patel; and, for obvious reasons, Nehru was 'immensely taken' with the idea of his greatest adversary in Congress being put out to pasture. But, when Mountbatten offered him the job, Patel simply 'roared with laughter'.[88] Nehru's second choice was Rajagopalachari, but the Governor of West Bengal was a wise man, and did not want the job at all. Nehru had first offered it to him on 30 March, and he asked for a few days to think it over. A begging letter from Nehru arrived a week later. 'I do hope you will not disappoint us', he wrote. 'We want you here to help us in many ways. The burden on some of us is more than we can carry.' With the greatest disinclination, Rajagopalachari accepted, and was named Mountbatten's successor on 3 May.[89]

Three days after the announcement, Nehru wrote Rajagopalachari a sad letter. 'Our politics have lost all real character or moral basis and we function as pure opportunists,' he confessed, alluding to events since the death of Gandhi. 'I have little doubt that we are rapidly deteriorating and becoming reactionary in our outlook and activities.' He concluded: 'I feel that it will be good for me as well as for India if I was out of the picture for a while.'[90]

Rajagopalachari sent back a telegram immediately, admitting he had been deeply moved by Nehru's words. 'I feel you should be Governor-General instead of me and let Sardar [Patel] be Prime Minister', he wrote. 'Much preferable to my appointment. You are big enough to understand the spirit in which I suggest this.'[91] But Nehru was not ready to retire into a ceremonial role, and even less so to hand over the prime ministership to Patel. Depressed though he was at the destruction of his vision for a free India, he was still driven to mend it. Edwina could sense his tension and his exhaustion. She persuaded him to take a few days up in the hills with her, as they had the year before: 'getting you to Mashobra to talk naturally and informally had become an obsession', she wrote to Jawahar afterwards.[92]

The next day, Jawahar drove with Dickie, Edwina and their daughter, Pamela, up to the retreat at Mashobra in a red open-topped car. The drive into the mountains from Delhi took many hours, suddenly switching into a vertiginous ascent when the flat expanse of the Punjab rucks up into the green hills at the base of the Himalayas. Hot, dusty roads give way to cool hillside tracks, and then to thickly wooded slopes, lightly veiled in the mist that lingers before the monsoon rains. As usual, Jawahar's mood lightened in direct proportion to the altitude.

Dickie liked Jawahar; and, though it was a very high risk in political terms, his wife's affair presented a relatively low risk in personal terms. As he must have known, Edwina could not leave him for the Prime Minister of India. Better to allow Edwina to carry on with Jawahar, than to risk her going off with someone else in circumstances he might not be able to control. 'Please keep this to yourselves but she and Jawarhalal [sic] are so sweet together', he wrote to his elder daughter, Patricia. 'They really dote on each other in the nicest way and Pammy and I are doing everything we can to be tactful and help. Mummy has been incredibly sweet lately and we've been such a happy family.'[93] And so Edwina and Jawahar walked together among the wild strawberry bushes during the days, and drove with Pamela along winding roads to the brightly lit town of Simla in the evenings. Dickie stayed behind at the house to devote himself with his trademark zealous jollity to his family tree. He had devised a system, based on that used in cattle-breeding, for working out exactly how any two people on it were related by comparing their alphanumeric codes.[94] It is hard to imagine what he can have been doing with it, several thousand miles away from the Battenberg archives, in a lodge surrounded by pine forests outside a rickety old Himalayan town. Perhaps his obsession was about reinforcing a sense of stability and family continuity, but it also gave his wife the space and privacy she had always wanted.

She made the most of it. Edwina and Jawahar met early every morning in the garden. They drove together along the Tibet Road, stopping for picnics in the woods. They stayed up late and alone after Dickie and Pamela had retired to bed. When Jawahar came to see Edwina in her room, he somehow upset an inkstand. 'They were both too busy mopping it up to be abashed', wrote Edwina's official biographer, leaving the mystery of why they should have been abashed to the imagination of the reader.[95] 'Mr Nehru was obviously a very lonely man,' remembered Patricia Mountbatten years later, 'and my mother was somebody who had not been able to communicate or make easy relationships with anybody, even with her own husband. I think the fact that these two had this similar lack in their lives, which the other person fulfilled, gave them a very strong relationship to each other.'[96] The Mountbattens' other daughter, Pamela, agreed: 'I've often been asked whether I think Nehru and my mother were in love. The answer undoubtedly is yes, they were.'[97]

Dickie was not entirely the noble martyr. He attended plays at Simla's Gaiety Theatre, and fell for an 'exceptionally lovely Anglo-Indian girl' in one of the leading roles. He flirted with her at dinner; afterwards she asked for his autograph, and held his hand for just a little too long. 'Isn't it maddening I just can't do anything about it', Dickie wrote to Patricia. 'She was just my cup of tea. Pammy was amused but luckily I don't think Mummy noticed anything.'[98] Edwina's attention was indeed elsewhere. Even a decade later, Jawahar would reminisce to her about his sudden realization at Mashobra 'that there was a deeper attachment between us, that some uncontrollable force, of which I was only dimly aware, drew us to each other'.[99] Their relationship had worked because it allowed both Jawahar and Edwina their own private space; but suddenly being together around the clock did not seem so undesirable after all. The intensity of their feelings both exhilarated and frightened them. They made a pact that their work would always have to come first.

'I had four very quiet and restful days in Mashobra', Jawahar wrote to Indira. 'I did no work at all, although I took many papers. I was not in the mood to work.'[100] On the day he left, Edwina saw him off at half-past six in the morning. 'I hated seeing you drive away this morning', she wrote afterwards; 'you have left me with a strange sense of peace and happiness. Perhaps I have brought you the same?'[101] Dickie showed films at the Governor General's Lodge – *This Time for Keeps*, and *The Unfinished Dance*. Edwina, distracted and petulant with Dickie, awaited her reply from Jawahar. It had been sent as soon as he returned to Delhi. 'Life is a dreary business', he wrote, 'and when a bright patch comes it rather takes one's breath away'.[102] The Mountbattens returned to Delhi on 25 May, and were taken that evening to see the Indian National Theatre's production of *A Bill of Divorcement*.

As the mercury in the thermometers climbed again, the capital became hot and dusty. 'But I love Delhi even like this and India and Indians', wrote Edwina, 'and my heart aches at the thought of leaving them so soon.'[103] In the swift jumble of events that characterized their last weeks in India, a few final dramatic scenes were played out. Negotiations with Hyderabad broke off for good on 17 June, ending with a telephone message from Monckton to Mountbatten with a single word: 'Lost'.[104] India indicated that it might intensify its blockade of the state, but there was no time to fix it. Four days later, the Mountbattens were to leave.

Unable to leave behind him a settlement with Hyderabad or peace in Kashmir, Mountbatten bequeathed to Nehru, Patel, V.P. Menon and Rajagopalachari a memorandum on the future of India. Admitting upfront that 'it would be gross conceit if I were to try and continue to influence the Government of India after my departure', he then launched into nineteen pages of gross conceit. He covered everything: the progress of nationalization, being nice to the Civil Service, the establishment of an honours system, compulsory holidays for the Prime Minister and Deputy Prime Minister, aircraft factories in Bangalore, training procedures for the Royal Indian Navy, the installation of air conditioning in all government offices. He was particularly concerned that India should become an oil-rich state. 'Clearly the first requirement is to find the oil,' he noted. 'To me it seems quite incredible that there should be oil to the north and west of India and oil to the east of India, but no oil has been found in India apart from Assam.' Geological surveys had previously drawn the conclusion that, incredible though it may have seemed, there really was none. No matter. Mountbatten recommended that they be redone. He further suggested that ambassadors and governors be chosen on the basis of their wives. 'If there are two candidates available, one for a Governorship and one for an Ambassador's post,' he explained, 'and one has a wife really competent to help with the welfare services of her husband's province, then I suggest that the one with the wife should always be sent to the Governorship, and the one without to the Ambassadorial post. But of course where possible men appointed to posts of this standing should have wives, and, as I have said above, their qualities are very nearly as important as their husbands!'[105]

Very nearly; perhaps even more so, in some respects, to judge from the great volume of letters pouring into Government House praising Edwina for her work with the victims of partition. Among them was one from Jawahar, asking whether she might stay to continue that work. It was an astonishing suggestion. Edwina could not have left her husband to live in India and carry on a close relationship with the Prime Minister without triggering the greatest scandal since the abdication of her friend Edward VIII. It might have been greater still. No one would have started a war over the King marrying Wallis Simpson, but Edwina's relationship with Jawahar had potentially devastating political implications. Mountbatten's viceroyalty was widely thought to have favoured India over Pakistan, to the extent of meddling with international boundaries; the suggestion that he had dabbled in Kashmir had added fuel to the fire. If it emerged now that his wife was romantically involved with Jawaharlal Nehru, with whom she had been extensively photographed since March 1947, it would have opened every decision Mountbatten had made to scrutiny. Few would have believed the line later perfected by official biographers that Jawahar's and Edwina's affair had not begun until May 1948. There was far too much evidence of an intimate long-term friendship. The scandal would have provided a firm base for any allegations of pro-Nehru bias that anyone wanted to sling around, and as such could have prompted a cascade of disasters: at the very least an investigation into the

Radcliffe award and the naming of Mountbatten in the genocide case that the Pakistani government had been advised to tone down; quite feasibly more civil unrest; perhaps even another full-scale war between Pakistan and India. The security of three nations – Britain, India and Pakistan – rested on this one love affair being kept quiet. On a personal level, too, Jawahar could not have remained in office in the face of such a story; though, in view of his frequent admissions of dissatisfaction and an inclination to leave office that year, perhaps it was this aspect of the idea that appealed to him.

Edwina replied that they had both agreed that they had to face reality and remember their pact to put duty before desire. It was not possible for them to be together. 'How wise and right you are', Jawahar wrote back, 'but wisdom brings little satisfaction. A feeling of acute malaise is creeping over me, and horror seizes me when I look at a picture in my mind of your shaking thousands of hands on the night of the 20th and saying your final goodbye.' But, he concluded: 'Dickie and you cannot bypass your fate, just as I cannot bypass mine.'[106]

Inevitably, the Mountbattens' last days became a parade of social events: presenting medals to staff, inspecting troops, holding luncheon parties, broadcasting to the nation. A photographer from the *Illustrated Weekly of India* turned up at Government House to take a series of pictures of the Mountbattens at home: the largest of which was one of Edwina settled in a brocade-upholstered armchair, engrossed in a copy of Nehru's bestselling historical memoir, *The Discovery of India*.[107] Edwina itemized the twenty-two Indian charitable societies of which she was president, most of which dealt with refugees, trafficked women and children, and the poor. She offered the vice-presidency of the United Council for Relief and Welfare, the organization she had started in response to the partition crisis, to Jawahar. 'If there were no other adequate reason for associating myself with the Council,' he replied, accepting it, 'the fact that it might enable me to work with you in a common task would be reason enough.'[108]

Jawahar held a farewell reception for the Mountbattens on 19 June. The following afternoon, all three drove from the Delhi Gate to the Red Fort, through crowds estimated at a quarter of a million which had assembled for a spontaneous street party. Their Rolls

Royces filled up with blossoms; spectators heaped garlands on to them as they progressed along Chandni Chowk. Dickie saluted as he ascended a dais draped with a Mughal-style velvet canopy. Edwina pressed her palms together, bowed her head, and addressed the crowd in Hindi with the traditional greeting: 'Namaste.' So enthused were the spectators that they rushed forward, breaking down the police barriers. According to the *Indian News Chronicle*, 'it was the dynamic personality of Pandit Nehru that restored order' – the 'dynamic personality' being a standard journalistic euphemism for Jawahar landing a punch on a troublemaker.[109]

That night, the outgoing Governor General and his wife held their final reception, complete with jugglers, conjurors and a band. Dickie and Edwina themselves served refreshments.[110] A banquet was given at Government House, with Dickie sitting between Amrit Kaur and Indira Gandhi, and Edwina opposite, next to Jawahar. Photographs from the evening show Jawahar's eyes downcast, his expression insuppressibly sad. After dinner, he gave a speech in honour of Edwina. It was virtually an open declaration of love.

> The gods or some good fairy gave you beauty and high intelligence, and grace and charm and vitality – great gifts – and she who possesses them is a great lady wherever she goes. But unto those who have, even more shall be given: and they gave you something that was even rarer than those gifts – the human touch, the love of humanity, the urge to serve those who suffer and who are in distress. And this amazing mixture of qualities results in a radiant personality and in the healer's touch.
>
> Wherever you have gone you have brought solace, and you have brought hope and encouragement. Is it surprising, therefore, that the people of India should love you and look up to you as one of themselves and should grieve that you are going? Hundreds of thousands have seen you personally in various camps and other places and in hospitals, and hundreds of thousands will be sorrowful at the news that you have gone.[111]

At these words, Edwina burst into tears. Jawahar, too, was inconsolable, and was too upset to listen to Edwina's eventual speech of thanks. The time came for an exchange of presents: Mountbatten gave the Indian government a set of gold plates, and it gave him a silver tray, engraved all over with the signatures of cabinet ministers and provincial governors. In the centre, it read: 'with affection and good wishes and as a token of friendship, Jawaharlal Nehru.' Nehru had tried to secure for Mountbatten something he would have prized even more: he had written to the King just after their return from Mashobra, suggesting Mountbatten be upgraded from an earldom even higher up the ranks of the nobility. The King's secretary replied that 'adequate recognition' of the Mountbattens' service had already been given.[112]

In private, they gave each other more personal gifts. Edwina gave Jawahar an eighteenth-century gold box, an emerald ring and a silver St Christopher medallion that her mother had given to her father. The last bemused him slightly: 'Am I supposed to wear it round my neck?' he wrote, tongue in cheek. 'Heaven forbid.'[113] He gave her an ancient coin, a box of mangoes and a copy of his auto-biography. Dickie sent Jawahar an engraved silver box with the latter's name hopelessly mixed up on it. He would never master the spelling, nor for that matter the pronunciation, of the name Jawaharlal, usually rendering it Jawrhalal or Jahawarlal.[114] Jawahar wrote to Edwina she must not tell her husband of his mistake, noting that he rather liked it – the inscription reminded him so much of Dickie.

Early in the morning of 21 June, the Mountbattens drove to Palam airfield in an open carriage drawn by six horses through a parade of cheering Indians. Outside Government House, one of the horses jibbed and refused to move. 'Even the horses won't let you go!' shouted a voice from the crowd. The front pair had to be removed, and the carriage went on to Palam with four.[115] A large military assembly greeted the former viceregal family. The band played Rabindranath Tagore's anthem, 'Jana Gana Mana' ('Thou art the ruler of the minds of all people'), and 'God Save the King'. Edwina accepted two garlands of jasmine from the crowd. Dickie's face was tight with emotion; reporters noted that Jawahar, too, was 'visibly moved'. Edwina hugged Rajagopalachari as Jawahar shook hands with Dickie and kissed Pamela on the cheek. As Dickie moved on to shake hands with his successor, Jawahar bowed his head to Edwina, and clasped, then kissed, her hand. The hour had come. Whatever she was feeling inside, Edwina had to get on the plane with her husband. At half past eight precisely, the York's propellers began to spin, and it took off for the last time from the tarmac at Delhi.[116]

The new Governor General, Chakravarty Rajagopalachari, was a sharply observant man. 'Lord Mountbatten has wound up Indo-British history in a manner which has secured for Britain a re-conquest', he wrote to Attlee, before concluding enigmatically: 'It is only those who have seen with their eyes how our Prime Minister and the people of India have bid adieu to the late Governor-General and his noble wife that can realise the full meaning of what I have said.'[117]

PART IV

AFTERWARDS

CHAPTER 19

A KISS GOODBYE

THAT WAS IT, THEN: THE LARGEST EMPIRE THE WORLD HAD ever hosted was gone. At its peak soon after the First World War, the British Empire had claimed an area of well over 14 million square miles – more than six times the size of the Roman Empire – and 500 million people. Of those, 400 million had been Indian. The day after the Mountbattens left India, King George VI issued a proclamation formally dropping the title 'Emperor of India'. The new Governor General, Chakravarty Rajagopalachari, wrote to Mountbatten, quoting a piece from the *Manchester Guardian* that said he 'ended the long British rule of India not with a whimper but with an unmistakable bang'. Rajagopalachari added: 'Now we here all know that it was not a bang but with a kiss you left us.'[1]

Dickie and Edwina emerged from their plane back at Northolt looking exhausted, lined and rumpled. Edwina arrived back in Britain not, she felt, to a much-needed rest, but to a life of emptiness. 'Idleness to Edwina was things not happening, and uneventfulness to her was sheer hell,' one of her friends remembered. 'You could see the pain on her face – adding to all those lines.'[2]

'Life is lonely and empty and unreal', Edwina wrote to Jawahar. Her husband dragged her to garden parties at Buckingham Palace – 'a waste of time', she thought, 'but Dickie insists.'[3] The pain of her absence was felt in India, too. Jawahar wrote to Edwina that he could still sense her 'fragrance on the air', and that he read and re-read her letters. 'I lose myself in dreamland, which is very unbecoming in a PM,' he confessed. 'But then I am only incidentally a PM.'[4] To Dickie, too, he admitted a sense of loss. 'It is extraordinary how the Mountbattens seemed to fill Delhi and without them there is a kind of vacuum', he wrote. He had written 'seem', and added the 'ed' later.[5]

When Rajagopalachari had described the Mountbattens leaving India with a kiss rather than a bang, he had been writing literally. All over the world, newspapers printed a picture of him hugging Edwina as she left Delhi. He sent a cutting of it from the *Madras Mail* to Dickie. 'The Madras folk must have frowned at this unorthodox posture,' he noted with some amusement.[6] Some British folk frowned, too: 'Throughout the British world many an appetite for breakfast must have been ruined,' opined the weekly *Truth*, describing the hug as a sign of 'a lack of respect towards European women'.[7] Dickie wrote in disgust about this 'vile article', noting angrily that 'this is what one has to expect from the worst reactionary paper in England'.[8]

Not everyone was delighted to have the Mountbattens back. On 25 June, Attlee sounded out Churchill about whether he and his wife would be likely to accept invitations to a dinner for the Mountbattens. Churchill returned a snub.[9] At a garden party of Anthony Eden's, Mountbatten walked over to Churchill with arms outstretched. Churchill scowled, and transfixed him with a sausagey finger. 'Dickie, stand there!' he snapped. 'What you did to us in India was like whipping your riding crop across my face!' According to Mountbatten, the Conservative leader would not speak to him again for seven years, though from their letters Churchill's reaction seems to have been less operatic.[10] At the party, Churchill had asked a thorny question about the speed of arms transfers from India to Pakistan, but he accepted Mountbatten's answer and wrote a warm letter afterwards.[11]

Both Mountbattens were called upon to speak at the East India Association at the Imperial Institute about their time in India. 'Dickie . . . told the story straightforwardly from his point of view, though naturally skating over Kashmir and Hyderabad,' observed

Leo Amery. 'Then Edwina, looking very handsome and evidently speaking most effectively, though unfortunately I could catch very little of what she said.'[12] She began with a friendly crack at her husband: 'I will confess he has always been my number one pin-up boy.' But she finished on a tribute to Nehru: 'My husband has referred to India's magnificent Prime Minister, Jawaharlal Nehru, and I would like to say what an inspiration he has been to all of us who have tried to help him in the past difficult months. He has been an inspiration to the doctors and nurses, to the welfare workers, and to the refugees themselves. I shall always remember the help and courage and the wise counsel he gave to me and to my colleagues at all times.'[13] The contrast between the pin-up boy and the magnificent inspiration defined her relationships with the two men. With Dickie, she was in an affectionate, sexless companionship; with Jawahar, she had found something more profound and more passionate.

The importance of the relationship to both Mountbattens is obvious from the correspondence between Jawahar and Dickie. On 3 July Jawahar, noting the seriousness of the situations in Kashmir and Hyderabad, warned Dickie that his proposed visit to Britain in September or October 'might not come off'.[14] Dickie responded with several feverish pages of cajoling, trying every tack from, 'You will find the experience of getting out of India and looking at your country from the outside world an exhilarating experience', to 'You will require a measure of rest, or at all events a change in your very busy routine', to reminding him of his 'valuable contacts in London', to joking that 'Unless you can come away for a reasonable while, there must be something wrong with your organisation!'[15]

On receipt of Nehru's letter, Mountbatten had fired off a suggestion to Attlee that they might meet with Cripps, Noel-Baker and Krishna Menon to discuss the situation. In a lapse of fair-mindedness, he omitted any Pakistani or even pro-Pakistan names from this list.[16] Afterwards, he reported happily to Nehru that the letter sent to Liaquat had been 'just about the strongest that has ever been sent'.[17] He also noted that he was 'doing what I can to keep Winston from making any statements about India, though this is not an easy one.'[18] But the problems were not so readily fixed and, by 1 August, Nehru admitted to Mountbatten that India was 'in open, though formally undeclared, war with Pakistan in Kashmir'.[19] 'How I wish I could still be with you in Delhi,' replied Mountbatten.[20] At the end of a long letter to Jawahar, detailing all the things he had done to resolve the situation, Dickie noted that: 'We all expect you over in October, and the sooner you can come in October, the more we can see of you, and no-one, neither the King, the Prime Minister, nor your late Governor-General, and certainly not his wife, would hear of your not coming, whatever the circumstances.'[21]

The circumstances changed quickly for, on 11 September 1948, Mohammad Ali Jinnah finally succumbed to his illness. He had been on his way to Karachi. Fatima remembered him speaking in delirium: 'Kashmir . . . Give them . . . the right . . . to decide . . . Constitution . . . I will complete it . . . soon . . . Refugees . . . give them . . . all assistance . . . Pakistan.'[22] According to his doctor, Jinnah saw Liaquat and told him that Pakistan was 'the biggest blunder of my life'. Further yet, he declared: 'If now I get an opportunity I will go to Delhi and tell Jawaharlal to forget about the follies of the past and become friends again.'[23] It is impossible to prove whether Jinnah actually said these words or not; either way, he was to have no further opportunity for a rapprochement. He was taken from the airport to the Governor General's house in an ambulance, which broke down after four miles on a main road in the middle of a refugee settlement with traffic honking by. The heat sizzled, flies buzzing around the Quaid-e-Azam's ashen face as Fatima attempted to fan them away. It was an hour before another ambulance could be found. Jinnah was taken back to Government House, where Fatima watched him sleep for about two hours. 'Oh, Jin,' she remembered thinking, 'if they could pump out all my blood, and put it in you, so that you may live.' He woke one final time and whispered to her 'Fati, khuda hafiz. . . . la ilaha il Allah . . . Mohammad . . . rasul . . . Allah.'[24] His head slumped to the right. He had died with the confession of faith just past his lips.

Two days after Jinnah's death, India swooped on Hyderabad, the only contentious princely state other than Kashmir that still remained outside India or Pakistan. The Nizam appealed to the UN, but soon dropped his resistance. 'There is still the most wide-spread misunderstanding over here about the action taken in Hyderabad,'

Mountbatten reported back to Rajagopalachari a week later, 'since even quite intelligent people seem to regard it as an act of military aggression and conquest.'[25]

'So your wish is being fulfilled,' Rajagopalachari teased Mountbatten on 5 October, 'and Jawaharlalji is put into the plane & despatched to Broadlands!'[26] Nehru was officially received at Heathrow, but his first action after that was to go to the Mountbattens' small flat: 'it is a change from Govt House', he wrote to Indira.[27] For Edwina, his midnight visit was 'too lovely'.[28] The very next day, she drove him to Broadlands. Dickie tactfully ensured that he would be absent for much of the time at Dartmouth and at a 'very boring' Rotary Club dinner. 'Edwina will be awaiting you', he wrote to Jawahar.[29] The two of them, alone at last in the privacy of her estate, were able to talk, laugh and cry together, to embrace, and to press each other's hands on walks by the river.[30] Even after Dickie turned up, the weekend was a great success, so much so that Jawahar changed his plans so that he might return the following weekend as well.[31] The Mountbattens had always been comfortable with ménages-à-trois, and Jawahar was fitted in with their family life without difficulty – though he startled the servants by standing on his head when they brought him his grapefruit and cereal. 'Funny fellow,' boomed Dickie. 'That explains why he sees the world upside down!'[32] The days were filled with dinner parties, games on the lawn, riding in the grounds, card games and gossip.[33] 'The Mountbatten family derived a lot of amusement from a letter Dickie received from a gentleman in Calcutta', wrote Jawahar to Indira, 'suggesting that in the interest of Indo-British friendship, Pamela should marry me!'[34]

Even in London, Nehru spent much of his time in the company of Mountbatten, and more yet in that of his wife. There was a reception for the Commonwealth Prime Ministers in the underwriters' room at Lloyd's of London, at which the Mountbattens were greeted with a huge round of applause by the assembled guests. Photographs of the event in the *Tatler* showed a now familiar scene: Edwina pressed closely to Jawahar's side and laughing with him, while Dickie hovered in the background.[35] He viewed this theoretical rival for his wife's heart with a sort of proud affection. 'He has literally taken, not only everyone that matters in England, but all the Commonwealth Representatives, by storm', Dickie wrote to Rajagopalachari. 'The King sat down and wrote me one of his rare letters after he had left saying that he wished me to know what a deep impression Jawaharlal had made on him and how much he liked him.'[36] Mountbatten had taken great care to make sure this came about, writing a letter to the King to introduce his 'great friend Nehru' and enclosing a full briefing on how the latter's invasion of Hyderabad had liberated the grateful Nizam from the thrall of fanatics. 'Don't forget that whereas Jinnah lost no chance of insulting the Crown – Nehru has gone out of his way to be courteous about it,' he ended, precisely inverting the truth.[37] The subject of all this effort had mixed feelings. 'I am told I made a hit, from Buckingham Palace downwards', Jawahar wrote to Indira. 'I basked in all this praise and adulation. But at the same time I felt rather uncomfortable and somewhat out of place and counterfeit.'[38]

Despite his lifelong insistence that Indian freedom demanded a total rejection of all ties to Britain, Jawahar was soon to agree to keep India in the Commonwealth. This controversial decision was widely described as the 'Great Betrayal' within India, and as 'The most extraordinary *volte-face* my brother made' by Nehru's own sister, Betty Hutheesing. It was during talks with the Commonwealth Prime Ministers, she wrote, that Nehru became convinced that India should remain within the Britannic orbit. True, the Commonwealth provided links of trade and foreign policy; but 'to this must be added the pull of his strong friendship with the Mountbattens', Betty noted.[39] Once again, it seemed the Mountbattens had saved India for Britain.

The Mountbattens had spun out the end of their personal empire. Their interventions over Kashmir, Hyderabad and the Commonwealth were welcomed, and even solicited, by the Indian government. But they were still only in their forties, and could hardly spend the rest of their lives acting as India's occasional agents in Britain. Shortly after Nehru's departure from London, they returned to Malta, and Dickie to the command of a cruiser squadron. Having been the first gentleman among 400 million in India, he was now only thirteenth in precedence on a tiny island. Officers who had served under him a few years before at South East Asia Command, and in India, now stood senior to him. Moreover, there was no longer a war on; and peace deprived both Dickie and Edwina of their primary function, which had been to make war and to clean up after it, respectively.

Edwina had no more interest in pursuing a life of tedious naval wifedom than ever. Instead, she threw herself back into the only work available. Over the next few years, tours for her charities would take her around England and the Channel Islands, to Germany, Austria and Trieste on the continent, and around Africa. But, most often of all, they would take her to the east: to Hong Kong, Singapore, Malaya and Ceylon, always by way of Delhi.[40]

Edwina and Jawahar wrote every day at first. Inevitably, this tailed off to once a week and finally once a fortnight, but the letters remained intimate until the end. Jawahar sent Edwina presents from wherever he was in the world: sugar from the United States (when it was rationed in Britain), cigarettes from Egypt, pressed ferns from Sikkim, a book of photographs of erotic sculptures from the Temple of the Sun in Orissa. 'I must say they took my breath away for an instant', he wrote. 'There was no sense of shame or of hiding anything.' Edwina replied that she had found the sculptures fascinating. 'I am not interested in sex as sex', she wrote. 'There must be so much more to it, beauty of spirit and form and in its conception. But I think you and I are in the minority! Yet another treasured bond.'[41]

Whenever possible, they spent time with each other. Edwina went to India every year, a fact that did not escape criticism. In 1953, Nehru was forced to defend Lady Mountbatten in the Indian parliament when Communist Party members accused her of trying to manoeuvre him into committing India to a defence pact with the Middle East. A dramatic scene ensued, with Nehru shouting, 'That's a lie!' and banging his fist on the table, while the Communists shouted, 'No lie!' back at him. The incident was struck from the official record, but made it into British newspapers.[42]

'It seems to me that the time has come when it should be pointed out to Edwina by one of Her Majesty's Ministers that these visits of hers to the Indian capital do not further the general interests of the

Commonwealth', wrote the Queen's Private Secretary to Churchill's Private Secretary.[43] If a minister ever did get up the courage to point this out to Edwina, it did not stop her. Once, at a reception for Commonwealth leaders in London, Jawahar upset the other delegates by spending all evening deep in conversation with Edwina and then conspicuously leaving with her.[44] On another occasion, when Jawahar and Edwina were staying together at Nainital in the Himalayan foothills, the Governor's son was sent to summon the guests for dinner. Unwittingly, he opened the door of the Prime Minister's suite, and was confronted by the sight of Jawahar and Edwina in an embrace. He tactfully retreated, and nothing was ever said about the incident.[45] These were the days of discretion in political life.

Though such stories were never made fully public, hints of them leaked out. An anti-Nehru party in Delhi began using the slogan, 'Break open Rama's heart, you will find Sita written on it; break open Nehru's heart, you will find Lady Mountbatten written on it.'[46] Neither ever bothered refuting the rumours. 'I have come to the conclusion that it is best to ignore them as any argument about them feeds them or at any rate draws people's attention to them', Jawahar wrote to Dickie. Dickie himself had been fending off remarkably widespread speculation that he was planning a coup to install himself as King Louis of Britain, and somehow simultaneously lead a communist revolution. 'Edwina has told me about the various rumours and stories about you,' Jawahar added. 'I was a little surprised as well as amused to learn of them.' He advised him, too, to make no comment and let them go away.[47] Whenever he was in Britain for a conference or diplomatic visit, he would stay with Edwina at Broadlands. During these sojourns, Dickie would remove himself to their London address.

Several times in the 1950s Edwina threatened divorce. Each time, Dickie responded with tolerant dignity which melted her heart and brought her back. 'I've never attempted to stop you or hold you and I never shall', he wrote; 'I'm not that selfish.'[48] The Mountbattens achieved a sort of harmony and mutual affection. It was to her husband Edwina entrusted her love letters from Jawahar in 1952. Following a haemorrhage, she had to undergo dangerous surgery.

She presented Dickie with a sealed letter before the doctor gave her the anaesthetic, telling him where they were. 'You will realize that they are a mixture of typical Jawaha [*sic*] letters, full of interest and facts and really historic documents', she had written. 'Some of them have no "personal" remarks at all. Others are love letters in a sense, though you yourself will realize the strange relationship – most of it spiritual – which exists between us. J. has obviously meant a very great deal in my life in these last years and I think I in his. Our meetings have been rare and always fleeting but I think I understand him, and perhaps he me, as well as any human beings *can* ever understand each other.'[49]

It was an odd sort of confession, and not an apology. Edwina pulled through the operation, but Dickie opened the letter. 'I'm glad you realize that I know and have always understood the very special relationship between Jawaha and you – made the easier by my fondness and admiration for him and by the remarkably lucky fact that among my many defects God did not add jealousy in any shape or form', he wrote to her. 'That is why I've always made your visits to each other easy and been faintly hurt when at times . . . you didn't take me into your confidence right away.'[50] Dickie remained, as he had always been, utterly besotted with Edwina. If he had to compromise on, or even facilitate, her relationships with others in order to keep her, that was better than losing her entirely.

In Delhi, Nehru moved into a grander house, Teen Murti Bhavan (Three Statues House), the former villa of the British Commander-in-Chief. He felt lost in it, though Indira and Padmaja Naidu stayed with him and helped make it his own.[51] He went on long and arduous tours of India, to the consternation of his family and friends.[52] On a tour of Maharashtra, Jawahar travelled over 200 miles every day; Padmaja went with him, and rested while he made speeches and attended meetings. He had particularly looked forward to seeing the old fort at Ahmednagar, in which he had been imprisoned for almost three years. He arrived to find his nostalgia thwarted. There was a plaque on the wall of a room in which he had not stayed, commemorating his internment in it. He pointed out this error, and was met with indignation. 'I was told that they had done this on the best authority!' he wrote to Indira. 'Indeed they were reluctant to accept my evidence!'[53] In the garden, he was confronted by a pomegranate tree with another plaque claiming falsely that the tree had been planted by him.

Yet he persisted in his tours. Nehru was at his happiest whenever he was in the centre of a crowd of ordinary people. The bigger the crowd, the happier he was; if it became unruly and broke through police cordons, he enjoyed it all the more. If it threatened danger, he would create a distraction by leaping into the fight. Nehru's security men were required less often to protect him from the crowd, than to protect it from him. His bodyguard G.K. Handoo 'had to wrestle with him on many occasions to stop him from jumping into the crowd', remembered his security chief. 'Held fast by Handoo's arms, Pandit Nehru would glare at him, but soon he would break into a smile and enquire if anyone had been injured.'[54]

Dickie's and Jawahar's correspondence continued, always following the same pattern. Nehru occasionally brought up his frustration over Kashmir; Mountbatten tried to persuade him to start training up younger politicians to replace the ageing veterans of the freedom fight who still dominated Congress. The latter issue had bothered Mountbatten since before independence. At the end of July 1947, he had told Nehru that his candidates for the Indian cabinet were too old and he should include some new blood, 'otherwise I fear Congress really will be finished within a year.'[55] Five years later, he was still pushing the same line, warning Nehru that he 'might slip on a banana-peel one day' and no successor would have been primed.[56]

But what Dickie and Jawahar wrote about, more than anything else, was Edwina. They sent each other proud news of her achievements, and updates on her activities, overwork and health. 'Edwina has been overworking as usual', wrote Dickie to Jawahar, 'and has had a cold but won't give in. She needs a rest but will never take one as we both know.'[57] Jawahar noted: 'The only way, apparently, for her to get some rest is to come to India. So I hope she will do so this winter.'[58]

She came almost every winter, often for several weeks. Dickie once went with her, in 1956. Every other time, he left them to each other, writing to Jawahar that he was 'delighted' that Edwina was visiting him on her way to Singapore, and adding: 'Don't let her go visiting, inspecting, speechifying, and doing her usual round of activities. She has overworked a great deal and really needs a rest.'[59] On one occasion, Edwina was due to visit Jawahar in Delhi but collapsed shortly before in Malta, and almost had to call the trip off on doctors' orders. She concealed the extent of her illness, but Dickie gave her a bland letter to take to Jawahar about politics, and inside hid a five-page update on her condition. Edwina had been desperate to go, for Jawahar had promised her a visit to the Ajanta Caves, a series of 2000-year-old Buddhist retreats carved out of a mountainside in the Deccan. The caves are filled with jewel-like frescoes, revealing ancient Buddhist India to have been a place of extraordinary richness, imagination and sensuality. 'How beautiful are the painted Bodhisattvas and the women of Ajanta!' Jawahar had written after first seeing them in the 1930s. 'One looks at those lovely and graceful figures almost with pain. They have a dreamlike quality, far removed from the vulgarity and cheapness of the life we see.'[60] Edwina only agreed to postpone her trip after Jawahar had sent her a telegram promising not to go to the caves without her. They finally went together in 1957, Edwina describing it as 'an enormous thrill'.[61]

The two men in Edwina's life were open with each other about their feelings. Dickie always emphasized that he would rather that Edwina 'should really get fit again and take things easy for as long as she likes' rather than hurrying back to him. Jawahar wrote forlornly to Dickie of 'a certain emptiness' that struck him whenever Edwina left.[62]

Mountbatten had written very properly to the King in April 1949 that, now he had returned to active service in the Navy, it would no longer be possible for him to advise Nehru: 'there is obviously no question of my taking part in any discussions', he wrote. 'I am sure you will agree that this is right.'[63] He was unable to stick to this rule. Both Mountbattens often met with government and opposition politicians on Nehru's behalf, to 'put the position of India'.[64]

Edwina's politics caused increasing friction with the British government. She was criticized in the media and in the Admiralty for allowing the communist Yugoslav leader, Tito, to entertain her in 1952. The oft-married Tito had invited her to lunch at his villa, and she had been charmed by his 'fine physique, good looks and vital personality'.[65] The Admiralty warned the Mountbattens that they were close to the line, prompting Dickie to write an aggrieved letter to Churchill. 'You know how strongly I feel that no serving officer should involve himself in politics in any way', he wrote.[66] Yet the archives reveal that he continued actively to advise Nehru throughout the 1950s and even into the 1960s, after he became Chief of Defence Staff for the British government. On matters of foreign policy – Goa, Kashmir, China – the two wrote often.[67] As a serving officer in the British Navy, it was injudicious of Mountbatten to advise the Prime Minister of another dominion; to set about selling him arms, on the other hand, was downright reckless. When Nehru stayed with the Mountbattens in 1955, Dickie suggested that he might buy the Gnat, an aircraft manufactured by Follands, and that he could transfer production of it to India. A factory was set up in Bangalore, with parts supplied from England. Gnats would be used extensively in the 1965 war with Pakistan.[68]

On 20 November 1949, Princess Elizabeth had flown to Malta to join her husband at the Mountbattens' villa. It was the beginning of a decade of close association between the Mountbattens and the Edinburghs, as the royal couple were then known. 'I always feel most bogus in this kind of circle', Edwina wrote to Jawahar. Then again, Dickie flourished in it.[69]

When King George VI died in 1952, Elizabeth became Queen. Quick off the mark as ever, Dickie held a dinner party at Broadlands only days after his cousin's death. He called for champagne, to celebrate the fact that the 'House of Mountbatten' now reigned. Prince Ernest Augustus of Hanover was among the guests; he reported the anecdote to the late King's mother, Queen Mary, and it precipitated an explosive reaction. Winston Churchill had returned to office as Prime Minister the previous year. His Private Secretary was summoned, and sent back to his master with explicit instructions to reverse this *coup d'état*.[70] The secretary remembered that Philip argued not for the name Mountbatten, but for Edinburgh, after his dukedom.[71] Neither option appealed to Queen Mary, Queen Elizabeth the Queen Mother, the royal household, nor the cabinet.

The last of these august bodies came down hard in favour of a rever-
sion to the unadorned Windsor.

Faced with such trenchant opposition, the twenty-five-year-old
Queen Elizabeth II issued a royal proclamation on 4 April declaring
that she and her descendants would indeed continue to bear the
name of Windsor. Quotes attributed to Philip on receipt of this news
range from the petulant ('I am the only man in the country not
allowed to give his name to his children'), to the anguished ('I'm
nothing but a bloody amoeba'), to the bitterly angry ('All they
wanted was my sperm. I'm nothing but a fucking sperm factory to
them').[72] Each boils down to the same point. 'What the devil does
that damned fool Edinburgh think that the family name has got to
do with him,' Queen Mary remarked shortly afterwards, proving
him right.[73]

Elizabeth's coronation the following year brought Nehru back to
London. He stayed at Claridge's, where Nehru's aide, eager to ensure
that the trip went smoothly, took the liberty of sending the prime
ministerial pyjamas to the hotel laundry service. When Nehru found
out, he rebuked the aide. 'Do you know that the laundry service in
this hotel costs more than the price of the clothes?' he scolded. He
proceeded to wash his own clothes in the hotel sink, and even to iron
his achkan neatly afterwards.[74] It was one among many economies
which, when compared to the spendthrift young Jawahar of his
Cambridge days, indicate that Gandhi's influence was not without its
benefits. Nehru travelled on commercial flights rather than private
jets, and took buses rather than chauffeur-driven cars.[75] He was
intolerant of any fuss or ceremony. On 1 June, he had been invited to
a pre-coronation party at Buckingham Palace. A long list of protocol
instructions arrived, detailing when to arrive, what to wear, how to
shake hands, how to back away from the Queen after shaking
hands, and so on. 'I am not going to do any of this,' remarked
Jawahar. 'Let those who want to shake hands with the Queen do so.
I can't do it.'[76]

He took Indira to the party but, as usual, ended up with Edwina.
Things went off badly. The pair of them got into a fight with Oliver
Lyttelton, the Colonial Secretary, over the Mau Mau rebellion in
Kenya. Lyttelton commented on the rebellion's 'terrible savagery', to

which Edwina rejoined: 'On both sides.' Jawahar added curtly that the British would achieve nothing by shooting Africans. Lyttelton was outraged at both of them. 'I am thinking of sending Edwina the photographs of some of the atrocities so she cannot repeat her disgraceful remarks', he wrote to Churchill.[77] Churchill promised to take it up with the Queen, and shortly afterwards tried to block Edwina from accompanying her husband on an official visit to Turkey. Dickie reassured him that Edwina denied making the Mau Mau remarks, and that in any case she had already accepted the Turkish invitation. Reluctantly, Churchill allowed her to go, and in fact it would be Dickie who would get into trouble with him on the trip, for inviting a controversial journalist aboard the HMS *Surprise*.[78]

When Nehru emerged from Buckingham Palace with Indira in tow, he saw Churchill waiting for his car, and went to greet him. Afterwards, Churchill said to Indira, 'I didn't expect it. This man whom I have jailed so many times has conquered hate. He acts without a trace of rancour.'[79] Indira noticed that there were tears in Churchill's eyes as he spoke.

The defrosting of relations between Churchill and Nehru which occurred at the coronation seems to have precipitated a change in the former's attitude to India. 'If I had been returned in 1945 I would have introduced a constituent assembly for India,' Churchill told Rab Butler and Lord Salisbury over lunch at Chequers shortly afterwards. 'Of course, they might have got rid of us anyway, but I'd have liked to try.' He regretted that the British had not befriended the Indians, and had instead dealt with them only in political terms.[80]

Churchill even invited Nehru's sister, Nan Pandit, then Indian High Commissioner to Britain, to visit him at Chartwell while he recovered from a stroke. He was not supposed to drink alcohol or walk in the garden to show her his prized carp, and within minutes had done both. When he noticed his security guards following discreetly down the garden, remembered Nan, 'he flared into a temper that was so like my father, the similarity could not be ignored and I had difficulty in restraining a smile.' The pair of them sat on a bench, and Churchill put his hand on Nan's arm.

'We killed your husband, didn't we?' he said. Ranjit Pandit, a gentle, unassuming Sanskrit scholar, had been imprisoned with Jawahar and most of the rest of the family following Quit India. A sentence in a British jail had made his asthma and pleurisy worse, and he died in 1944, shortly after his release. Nan was so taken aback at Churchill's words that she did not know what to say.

'Every man only lives to his appointed hour,' she replied eventually.[81]

Britain's wrongs against the Nehru family were not so readily forgiven by Nan's cook, Budhilal. Some years after her meeting with Churchill, Nan was hosting an ambassadorial dinner for his successor, Anthony Eden. Budhilal, who had been at the ale, staged a strike in the kitchen, declaring that he would never cook for the prime minister of a nation that had imprisoned Nan, and wielding a soup ladle in an emphatic manner. Taken aback, Nan returned to her guests in the drawing room, and whispered her plight to Edwina Mountbatten. Having organized refugee camps for hundreds of thousands, Edwina had little trouble getting the dinner party together. Over dessert, she revealed the truth to Nan's guests, who found it rather funny. 'My mother, slowly emerging from a state of shock, was even able to manage a wan smile,' added Nan's daughter.[82]

After forty years of effort, Mountbatten finally stepped into his father's shoes and became First Sea Lord in 1955. The following year came the Suez crisis, that last and most foolhardy flourish of British imperial delusion. 'Thank goodness Philip isn't here,' remarked the Queen, on being told that the Egyptian dictator Gamal Abdel Nasser had nationalized the Suez Canal.[83] Dickie Mountbatten was around, and he opposed Britain's invasion wholeheartedly, as did his wife and Jawaharlal Nehru. Mountbatten was told by the Ministry of Defence that he had no right to give political advice. Immediately, he offered his resignation to Eden; it was refused.[84]

There were other ways to make his views heard. In his unique position of confidant to the monarch, Mountbatten was heard to whisper in her ear that, 'I think they are being absolutely lunatic.'[85] Acting on Mountbatten's word, Elizabeth exercised her constitutional right to advise Eden not to invade. He exercised his constitutional right to ignore her. Britain invaded; the United States cut off its credit; and Eden was forced into a humiliating withdrawal. He resigned the following year. Mountbatten was promoted to Chief of the Defence Staff.

It is said that Dickie became a particularly close confidant of the Queen during the 1950s.[86] He always carried four pictures with him: Edwina as a young woman in white fur and pearls, one each of Patricia and Pamela, and one of Elizabeth, smiling, relaxed and unusually sexy in a white gown and long gloves. It was signed 'Lilibet', the nickname by which her intimate circle have always known her.[87]

In April 1958, Nehru announced that he wanted to resign and return to private life, telling a press conference shortly afterwards that he felt 'rather stale and flat'.[88] For once, the roles were reversed, and Edwina told him to take a rest. He took a month's holiday, trekking in the Kullu Valley, high in the Himalayas. 'Tell me whether I should continue to write to you or *not*?' wrote Edwina tentatively. 'I shall well understand if you say "not a note for the next months".'

Jawahar wrote back passionately. 'How do you think I would fare if months passed without a letter from you?' he asked. 'Have you realized what your letters mean to me?'[89] Two months later, in July, the *Economic Weekly* published an anonymous article under the headline 'After Nehru', predicting that on his departure Congress would fragment into petty interests of caste, religion and region. Remembering the Chanakya article of 1937, some wondered whether Nehru had written another anonymous diatribe against himself.[90] Only the sustained pleading of his colleagues persuaded Nehru to stay in office after his vacation – in opposition to the views of his closest friends. 'I understand only too well J.L [Jawahar Lal]'s desire to quit his office', wrote Amrit Kaur to Edwina, 'and I only wish he had lived up to what his inner voice told him.'[91]

Mountbatten believed that Nehru wanted to 'die with his boots on', but there is no reason to doubt the sincerity of his wish to retire.[92] Amrit Kaur wrote to Edwina the following year: 'I never see JL. I feel sorry for him because he *is* a lonely person.'[93] He talked to Indira's friend Marie Seton at length about his desperation to visit a tea shop or a bookstore without being mobbed. 'The trouble with power is that one doesn't know if one is still a human being or not,' he told her. 'I want to remain human.'[94]

His depression worsened as India's relations with China deteriorated. Nehru had always believed in pan-Asian identity. In 1958, China invaded Tibet, sending refugees scattering across the border into India – including the Dalai Lama himself, who set up court at Dharamsala in the Himalayas. 'It is going to be heavy weather all round', wrote Nehru to Indira.[95] It was she who persuaded her father to offer asylum to the Dalai Lama, which he did – to the intense annoyance of the Chinese government. By the middle of 1959, many were predicting that China would invade India next. 'Look at the terrain, and tell me how the Chinese can invade,' Mountbatten told American troops in South Carolina on 12 October 1959. 'I'd hate to plan that campaign.'[96] Nine days later, Chinese troops entered Indian territory in Ladakh, high in the mountains of Kashmir.[97] That troubled state would henceforth be disputed between three nations.

The first society event of 1960 was the wedding of Pamela Mountbatten to the interior designer David Hicks. Noël Coward, among the guests, remembered it as being 'hilarious and most enjoyable'. Hampshire was hit by a blizzard, and all the lights at Broadlands fused during the reception. Afterwards, when a coach left for the station, it broke down before it got out of the drive. The guests inside, including Walter Monckton's wife, Biddy, and Coward himself, had to get out into the snow in their morning suits and silk gowns, and push.[98]

The following day, 17 January 1960, the *Sunday Express* reported that the name of Mountbatten was to be restored to the royal house. Three weeks later, the Queen announced that 'while I and my children shall continue to be styled and known as the House of Windsor, my descendants other than descendants enjoying the style, title or attribute of Royal Highness and the titular dignity of Prince or Princess and female descendants who marry and their descendants shall bear the name of Mountbatten-Windsor.'[99]

Edwina did not stay around to enjoy her husband's triumph. On the day after her daughter's wedding, she left for Delhi. There she met Jawahar again: seventy now, to her fifty-eight, but still looking remarkably young. The same could not be said for her. Edwina's face was lined, but her delight at seeing Jawahar illuminated it. The effect was clear to everyone.[100] On 26 January, the pair of them attended the Indian Republic Day parade, and a reception afterwards in the Mughal Gardens. Memories of the magical night of 15 August 1947, when so many of the same people had celebrated in the same garden, hung in the air. Edwina and Jawahar chatted with the guest of honour, the Russian President, Marshal Voroshilov. Marie Seton was struck by Edwina's radiance. 'She moved easily about, unconcerned, talking to people with unselfconscious vivacity', she wrote; 'as she talked she shed the charm of her independent spirit.' Observing Edwina and Jawahar together, she noted, 'Some people believed that she exerted a great influence on Jawaharlal, but at least one of his friends was of the opinion that it was she who hung on every word he said.'[101] In fact, their admiration was mutual, and undiminished by the passing years.

The days were filled with charity work, and the evenings with quiet dinners at Jawahar's house. One afternoon, Jawahar hosted a display of folk dancing from all over India. Seton was present again, and was able to see the happiness of Jawahar and Edwina firsthand. Every group of dancers wanted to be photographed with Jawahar, and Seton delighted in watching him 'caper around with group after group', now wearing a tribal cloak, now a skull-cap, now a garland of flowers. Seton sat down with Edwina on the grass to watch a troupe of war dancers from Nagaland, spinning and dipping fiercely, clad in little more than feathers.

Edwina turned to Marie and remarked, 'Don't they have beautiful bottoms?'

'Very beautiful,' Marie replied.[102]

Soon afterwards, Edwina left Delhi for Malaya, and hopped from there to Singapore, Brunei, and finally Borneo, arriving on 18 February. She was driven to the house of Robert Noel Turner, Chief Secretary of North Borneo, and his wife Evelyn. After only a brief rest, she went on to the St John Ambulance headquarters. That night, Turner was impressed with her vivacity at their dinner party.[103]

The next morning, the heavy mountain mists briefly cleared, and

Evelyn Turner woke Edwina at seven to show her the spectacular view. Edwina emerged on to the balcony in a silk dressing-gown to look up at the heights of Mount Kinabalu. 'It's venerated by the Dusuns who live on the lower slopes,' Turner told her. 'They believe it is the resting place of the souls of the dead.'[104] The mists rose again only minutes later and obscured the mountain once more.

When Edwina returned to the house that evening, she complained of tiredness. The Turners' secretary suggesting calling a doctor, but Edwina would not have it. She got herself up again and went to the St John dinner that evening. When she arrived back at the house, she almost collapsed; but, righting herself, she dismissed it as only a headache and went to bed, refusing even an aspirin. The next day, Edwina grudgingly submitted to a medical examination. The doctor thought she had influenza, or early stage malaria; but she would not be put off her programme, and continued on to two hospital visits and a coffee party before finally allowing Mrs Turner to send her to bed with an egg flip. She insisted on attending a St John parade and an official reception that evening. Guests noticed that she looked pale and drawn despite her efforts to smile, and that she left after only twenty minutes.

At 7.30 the next morning, the Turners' secretary knocked on Edwina's door. There was no reply. She opened it to see the Countess Mountbatten of Burma lying on the bed. Her body was already cold. She had suffered heart failure a few hours before. Still one of the world's richest women, she had had no splendid possessions with her: only a pile of old letters on the bedside table. She must have been reading them when she died, for a few, having fluttered from her hands, were strewn across her bed. They were all from Jawaharlal Nehru.[105]

In Delhi, Marie Seton was waiting to hear the historian Arnold Toynbee lecture at Sapru House, when she saw Jawahar arrive. 'I noticed that his face was expressionless and self-contained, and that he took no notice of anyone.' When the audience sat down in the hall, the chairman rose to announce that Edwina Mountbatten had died that morning. A gasp ran through the hall, and everyone rose to their feet for a spontaneous memorial silence. Seton and her friends were deeply concerned for Nehru. 'Despite the self-control he demonstrated at the Toynbee lecture, I think it [Edwina's] was the death which left him most bereft of companionship', she wrote; 'she was the friend who had stimulated and encouraged him most.'[106] Just as after the death of Gandhi, Nehru's public face would be a mask, hiding his private grief.

Back in Britain, Mountbatten received over 6000 letters and telegrams of condolence, which were delivered almost hourly to Broadlands by the Post Office. Dickie's valet found him in the drawing room, crumpling one between his trembling fingers and weeping.[107] Three months later, Noël Coward met him for lunch, and noted that he had 'aged a good deal since Edwina's death'.[108] Dickie could not sleep properly for the next three years.[109]

Edwina had a horror of being interred in the claustrophobic family vault at Romsey Abbey, and had asked her husband to bury her 'in a sack at sea'.[110] HMS *Wakeful* was offered by the Admiralty, and sailed from Portsmouth. The coffin was discharged into the waves from beneath a Union Jack. Mountbatten, in tears, kissed a wreath of flowers before throwing it into the sea.[111] The *Wakeful* was escorted by an Indian frigate, the *Trishul*. Jawaharlal Nehru had sent it all the way to the English Channel, just to cast a wreath of marigolds into the waves after Edwina's coffin.

CHAPTER 20

ECHOES

AFTER EDWINA'S DEATH, JAWAHAR HAD NOT PERMITTED HIMSELF public grief; but the age he had defied for so many years began to catch up with him. His face puffed, and developed liver spots. He began to resemble his father in the latter's last years. He went to London, fell ill, and had to be examined by the Queen's physician and a kidney specialist. Marie Seton saw him a few months later, and believed him to be 'dying by inches', crushed under the burden of responsibility he felt for the collapse of relations with China, and deprived of the close friends who had supported him.[1] Politically, he had become erratic. Nan Pandit wrote to Dickie Mountbatten, asking him to tell her brother to delegate more: 'The only person who could control him was darling Edwina,' Dickie replied.[2] The question of his successor began to bother a wider circle of people. 'The Prime Minister is like the great banyan tree,' said S.K. Patil, the Minister for Food. 'Thousands shelter beneath it but nothing grows.'[3] The remark irritated Nehru, perhaps because it was true.

Another trip was planned, this time to the United States. Relations between India and the United States had long been frosty, owing to American support for Pakistan on one side, and Indian support for China on the other.[4] However, when John F. Kennedy became President, heaping praise on Nehru's 'soaring idealism', there was some hope of a thaw.[5] A visit by Nehru was planned for November 1961.

On 6 November, Nehru arrived in New York with Indira. The Kennedys took them aboard Air Force One for the flight to Washington. The President read the papers, while the First Lady immersed herself in the writings of André Malraux. Nehru read the *National Geographic* and the *New York Daily News*. Indira flicked through a copy of *Vogue*.[6]

The formal talks began the next day. Kennedy brought up a range of topics which usually interested Nehru very much – Berlin, Vietnam, nuclear testing, Indo-Pakistani relations – and yet the Indian premier seemed out of sorts, and could not be induced to grunt out more than a sentence or two in reply.[7] The meeting finally ended at 12.30, and Kennedy, crestfallen, went for a walk on the back lawn with the American Ambassador to India, J.K. Galbraith. 'He thought he had done badly,' Galbraith remembered; 'I fail to see how he could have done better.'[8]

That evening Nehru dined with Kennedy. During the dinner, Nehru eased up considerably – not least, noted Galbraith, because he 'had sat between Mrs. Kennedy and her sister and with the light of love in his eyes'.[9] The rest of the trip went without a hitch.

There was not long to wait for the sequel. On 13 March 1962, Jackie Kennedy descended from an Air India jet at New Delhi, accompanied by her sister, Lee Radziwill. Jawahar himself stood waiting for them at the bottom of the ramp. The next evening, she went to a party at Teen Murti Bhavan. In the light of a half-moon, traditional dancers and musicians performed on a stage. From among a sea of beautiful and elaborate saris, Jackie emerged in a simple, floor-sweeping dress of lambent turquoise. 'I am having a signal lack of success in soft-pedaling emphasis on clothes,' admitted Galbraith.[10] She sat with Jawahar under a canopy made of flower petals to watch the show. Both she and her sister were charmed, Lee describing him as 'the most fascinating, gentle and sensual man I ever met'.[11]

Two days later was the Hindu spring festival, Holi, and Galbraith took Jackie to Teen Murti Bhavan to say goodbye to Jawahar. Motilal Nehru had begun a family tradition of standing outside his house at Holi, wearing a dhoti and kurta in spotless white, and waiting for the huge crowds which trampled up the driveway to embrace him and cover him in red and purple festive powders. 'By the time they finished he was a chromatic mess and he loved it,' remembered Betty.[12] Jawahar continued this tradition as Prime Minister. When Jackie arrived, she found him outside the house, wearing a white sherwani, laughing as thousands of people turned up to pelt him with paint, powder and water. 'Oh, I must do that, too!' she exclaimed.[13]

The First Lady had made a tremendous impression in India. Soon afterwards, Galbraith called on Nehru. 'I noticed, incidentally, that in his upstairs sitting room where he has pictures of the really important people in his life – Gandhi, Motilal Nehru (his father), Tagore and Edwina Mountbatten – there is now a significant addition, to wit: Mrs. Jacqueline B. Kennedy. It is the picture of J.B.K. and the Prime Minister walking arm in arm in the White House garden.'[14]

Open war with China that year invigorated him briefly. 'Nehru looked younger and more vigorous than at any time in recent months,' noted Galbraith, 'and told me that the tension of the crisis agreed with him.'[15] Mountbatten visited in 1963, and they talked extensively about Kashmir, though more extensively still about Edwina. 'This is almost the first time he has been prepared to talk freely about her,' Mountbatten wrote in his diary, 'and we both exchanged sentimental memories of the time we were all together in India.'[16] It was a warm remembrance, but Nehru was declining.

The British High Commissioner in Delhi reported back to London on 3 January 1964 that the succession was 'sewn up' for Indira Gandhi, 'the one thing in which the Prime Minister was now really interested'.[17] Overall, the signs were that Nehru had not groomed Indira for the succession. He had supported her when she turned down government jobs, though he had not stood in her way when she took them. But, as his friends and colleagues melted away, she remained a constant companion, and his clarity of democratic vision seemed to blur. There was by no means universal support for her in government circles. When Mountbatten visited India shortly after the British High Commissioner had made his report, he and the President, Sarvepalli Radhakrishnan, agreed that Indira should not be given the external affairs portfolio that her father was apparently thinking of granting her.[18]

Jawahar had a minor stroke in January at the annual Congress session in Bhubaneshwar. Dickie visited again, and found his old friend 'shockingly weak and uncomprehending'.[19] He urged him not to keep working flat-out. 'That is what Edwina did, to the great distress of all who loved her whom she left behind', he wrote.[20] On 27 May, Jawahar rose at dawn and suffered a second stroke and a heart attack. He lost consciousness and, a few hours later, he died.

Two enormous blocks of ice were placed either side of Jawahar's body, which lay in state at Teen Murti Bhavan in temperatures of 110 degrees, surrounded by garlands of lilies, roses, bougainvillea and, of course, Indian marigolds.[21] The crowds were so thick that cars could not pass, and Nehru's sisters were obliged to struggle through on foot.[22] His friends came to look upon his sad-looking but peaceful countenance, and pay their respects. The first Englishman to arrive was Dickie Mountbatten, who flew in with the British Prime Minister, Sir Alec Douglas-Home. There were the women who had loved Nehru, too: Mridula Sarabhai, a scion of one of India's leading industrial families, in a white khadi salwar kameez, self-possessed and meditative; Padmaja Naidu, wandering about sadly as if lost, looking suddenly aged. 'Padmaja had never married,' noted Marie Seton, 'perhaps ever hoping to be asked by the man she so much loved.'[23]

Soon, Nehru's house was filled with uninvited guests – Hindu pandits, Buddhist lamas, Muslim maulvis and Christian priests – who sat by his body and recited prayers. Nehru's will had stated, 'I wish to declare with an earnestness that I do not want any religious ceremonies performed for me after my death. I do not believe in any such ceremonies and to submit to them, even as a matter of form, would be hypocrisy.'[24] His daughter and his government had seen fit to disregard this unambiguous wish. The crowds at his funeral were said to exceed even those who had turned out for Gandhi's, most clad in the traditional white of Indian mourning. Hundreds of thousands – some reports said millions – stood in a mile-long crescent around the ridge. There was an atmosphere of quiet reflection, rather than grief, that impressed all the foreign observers.[25]

Jawahar's younger grandson, Sanjay Gandhi, lit the pyre. 'The face most contorted by emotion was not an Indian face,' remembered Marie Seton, 'but that of the once blithe Louis Mountbatten. He appeared to sag at the sight of the alabaster head of Jawaharlal ... Theirs had been a harmony of difference, cemented by their mutual admiration for the Mahatma, on the one hand, and the very human Edwina, on the other.'[26] Dickie's admiration for the Mahatma might have been retrospective, but it was beyond doubt that he and Jawahar had been brought together by their love of the same woman.

The scent of sandalwood and camphor oil drifted into the afternoon heat as the priests Jawahar had disdained all his life chanted mantras around his body.[27] Perhaps inspired by the recurring dream of his childhood, Nehru had requested that most of his ashes be scattered from an aeroplane, 'so that they might mingle with the dust and soil of India and become an indistinguishable part of India'.

'Now that Nehru is gone we shall no longer have the enormously valuable access to the India Government's inner councils which Lord Mountbatten's personal friendship with him gave us at crucial moments,' complained the British High Commission in Delhi.[28] Mountbatten himself had other things to worry about. Douglas-Home's Conservative government lost an election, and a Labour administration under Harold Wilson came in. Mountbatten soon clashed with Denis Healey, his new boss at the Ministry of Defence. Mountbatten wanted to abandon the separate Chiefs of Staff and integrate the three services into one department; Healey suspected that Mountbatten really wanted more control for himself. 'I doubt if anyone else in my time could have met the requirements of a Chief of Defence Staff as Mountbatten conceived the post', wrote Healey; 'few other officers shared his confidence in his own qualifications for such a job.'[29]

Mountbatten attracted the disapproval of his colleagues by attempting to have himself made a Field Marshal and an Air Marshal, in addition to an Admiral, prompting an official to write icily to the Prime Minister that 'only members of the Royal Family have held five-star rank in all three Services'.[30] During this period Sir

Gerald Templer, Chief of the General Staff, allegedly remarked to Mountbatten's face that, 'Dickie, you're so bloody crooked that if you swallowed a nail, you'd shit a corkscrew!'[31]

Sidelined, Mountbatten occupied his time with reorganizational fantasies and technological flights of fancy. His great ally was his Chief Scientific Adviser, Sir Solly Zuckerman, a scientist distinguished originally in the field of monkey and ape behavioural science. Zuckerman had been involved in government work since before the Second World War, when someone at the Ministry of War, concerned with the effects of bomb blasts on the human body, apparently said: 'What about calling in that monkey fellow?'[32] Many exploded chimps later, it was conclusively established that the effect was detrimental.[33] But Zuckerman had caught the eye of Dickie Mountbatten, who had appointed him to his staff at Combined Operations. By the 1960s, the two men formed what was known in Whitehall as the 'Zuckbatten Axis', bent on spreading technological innovation throughout the services.[34]

Mountbatten's interest in science occasionally crossed the line into science fiction, and he was keen for the Ministry of Defence to spend its time investigating the paranormal. He was excited when a giant carcass was found on the west coast of Tasmania, with no recognizable head, eyes or appendages. He sent news clippings to Zuckerman, wondering whether it might be a sea-monster, and badgered him to take the matter up with the Zoological Society. Zuckerman replied that, 'It has been determined that it is "a lump of whale meat".' Having been defeated over his sea-monster, Mountbatten looked to the skies. 'I have long been fascinated by Flying Saucers', he wrote to Zuckerman a few months later, enclosing an imaginative magazine article on the subject. 'Should Flying Saucers not be investigated further?' Zuckerman wrote a kindly reply, explaining that it was not possible to establish conditions under which flying saucers might be impartially observed. 'It is the same problem as with ghosts,' he noted, perhaps hoping to forestall his friend's next initiative.[35]

When the time came for Dickie's reappointment to be considered, Healey interviewed the top forty people in the Ministry of Defence. Only one supported Mountbatten's reappointment, and that was an old friend of his – Sir Kenneth Strong, the Director General of Intelligence. 'When I told Dickie of my decision not to reappoint him, he slapped his thigh and roared with delight,' Healey remembered; 'but his eyes told a different story.'[36]

In retirement, there would be little for Dickie to do – though this never stopped him from doing it. He ran the Nehru Memorial Trust, raising £100,000 by 1966 to fund Indian scholars at British universities.[37] He organized the Nehru Memorial Lecture, and ensured a decent attendance: Prince Charles was induced to leave a day's shooting on his twentieth birthday to show up.[38] Harold Wilson considered sending him to Rhodesia to sort out Ian Smith after that country's white minority declaration of independence in 1965; Mountbatten leapt at the chance, and the Queen was in favour, but her courtiers quashed the idea.[39] He was made responsible for a government report on prison reform. He made documentaries, taking a hand in the BBC's notorious *Royal Family*, held by many commentators to have been the beginning of widespread public disrespect for the monarchy; in the programme the Queen bought an ice lolly, and Prince Philip was seen to barbecue a sausage.[40] There was also a twelve-part series on himself to be fussed over, presenting his reputation as a great British hero. He was unwilling to share his script with the government, which worried about the political effect in Pakistan of his self-aggrandizing attitude.[41] It was easy to see what they meant. At the end of the series, Dickie's summing up was characteristic: 'All I want to know is: was I right, were they wrong?' he asked. 'Will they eventually come round and see it? Or are they so dumb that it will have to be their children or grandchildren who will perhaps see this series of films in fifty years' time and see that I was fairly reasonable and the people who thought I was wrong were the ones who were unreasonable.'[42]

Most of all, though, Mountbatten wrote letters. The phrase 'letters in green ink' has long been used in the media to denote an eccentric strain of correspondence from members of the public. Mountbatten's letters were typed in emerald green, on pale mint-green paper, embossed with a forest-green crest, and signed dandyishly with his decisive, upslanting script, 'Mountbatten of Burma', in sea green ink. Dozens of these letters are to be found in the British and Indian national archives. 'What in God's name has happened in the Ministry of Defence?' he wrote to Solly Zuckerman, before launching into a diatribe against nuclear weapons.[43] 'I have been so worried about the situation in the sub-continent', he wrote to General Cariappa of the Indian Army, and confessed that he had been 'doing everything I can behind the scenes to try and explain India's case'.[44] The letters include multiple invitations, such as that extended to Harold Wilson in May 1966 for a private dinner with Mountbatten. Wilson's secretary noted at the top that 'The Prime Minister does *not* wish to take this up.'[45]

After Nehru's death, there had been no more great figures of independence to step into his shoes. The man who succeeded him, Lal Bahadur Shastri, had been chosen as the least objectionable candidate. The possibility of Nehru's daughter, Indira Gandhi, becoming Prime Minister had been dismissed as fanciful. But Shastri made her his Secretary of State for Information and Broadcasting and, when he died suddenly in January 1966, her name came up again. In a restrained and clever campaign which would be echoed forty years later by her daughter-in-law, Sonia Gandhi, Indira played a subtle game of flirtation with the media and the party. This only served to endear her to an electorate which preferred its politicians to play hard to get. Finally, after a great deal of prevaricating, Indira shyly conceded that she would accept the prime ministership if the Congress President wished her to do so. 'I am wholeheartedly overjoyed at this wonderful turn of events', wrote Dickie Mountbatten. 'How delighted your dear father would have been and Edwina also.'[46]

President Lyndon B. Johnson was similarly smitten when she visited the United States in March. 'What a nice girl, and how beautiful,' he said to the Indian Ambassador, describing the forty-eight-year-old woman who had just become Prime Minister of the world's largest democracy. He declared an interest in bolstering her support. 'You tell me what to do. Send her food? Attack her? I'll do whatever you say.' Indira herself, fielding a diplomatic enquiry about how Johnson should address her, showed her true character. 'He can call me Madam Prime Minister, he can call me Prime Minister, he can call me Mr Prime Minister if he wants,' she snapped. 'You can tell him that my colleagues call me "Sir".'[47]

Unlike Jawahar, Indira found the processes of democratic government irritating and cumbersome. Soon she started to act without
recourse to it. 'My position among the people is uncontested,' she
declared.[48] When she attacked the princes for their privy purses,
Mountbatten was shocked and upset. 'I do hope Indu will do nothing that could in any way dishonour her father's word', he wrote to
Nan Pandit, 'and I have written to her to this effect in as friendly a
way as possible.'[49]

But Mountbatten's main worries were closer to home. In London,
the spirit of revolution was also in the air. When the Labour Party
had been elected to power, the first person that Harold Wilson
invited to lunch at 10 Downing Street had been Cecil King, a large,
terse, ambitious newspaper magnate who controlled 40 per cent of
the national circulation.[50] King had supported Labour throughout
the election, but by the summer of 1965 he had lost all faith in
Wilson.[51] King and Hugh Cudlipp, an old friend and chairman of the
Mirror, decided that if Wilson would not change or go, he should be
ousted by force. But who could lead the coup and replace Wilson at
the head of a new, post-democratic administration? The answer had
come to them by 12 August 1967, when King reported: 'Cudlipp had
some talk a few weeks ago with Mountbatten at some dinner. Hugh
asked him if it had been suggested to him that our present style of
government might be in for a change. He said it had. Hugh then
asked if it had been suggested that he might have some part to play
in such a new regime? Mountbatten said it had been suggested, but
that he was far too old.'[52]

The idea floated around for some months before Cudlipp finally
set up a meeting between Mountbatten and King, on 8 May 1968, in
Mountbatten's flat on Kinnerton Street. Solly Zuckerman also
attended.[53] King launched into a list of Wilson's failings. If the government continued as it was, he said, the towns would be awash
with blood, and there would be machine guns on street corners.
Instead, he proposed a velvet revolution, but raised the question of
who could head the replacement government of 'national unity':
someone competent and non-partisan, who could command the confidence of the public.[54] Was Mountbatten interested?

Mountbatten was, according to Zuckerman 'for a moment

beguiled'.[55] He turned to Zuckerman and asked him what he thought. Zuckerman got up and went to the door. 'This is rank treachery,' he said. 'I am a public servant and will have nothing to do with it. Nor should you, Dickie.'[56] Mountbatten tried to restrain him for a few moments, but he walked out. Afterwards, according to King's diary, Mountbatten told him that morale in the services was low, and the Queen was 'desperately worried' over the situation.[57] Cudlipp later admitted that Mountbatten told him he had raised the question of a coup with the Queen that month.[58]

Private Eye magazine would later allege that Mountbatten had gone much further with this plan than this tale allowed, and even that he had begun to compile a list of military friends who might support him. The magazine claimed that it was Zuckerman who talked him out of it.[59] Rumours in the highest circles at Buckingham Palace suggest the *Eye* had the right idea, but the wrong saviour. It was not Solly Zuckerman who talked Mountbatten out of staging a coup and making himself President of Britain. It was the Queen herself.[60]

On 25 June 1970, Earl Mountbatten of Burma celebrated his seventieth birthday. He threw a weekend party at Broadlands, stocked with British and European royalty and other dignitaries. When the last of the guests left on the Monday morning, Mountbatten patted his valet on the shoulder. 'Charles, that was the best birthday party of my life,' he said. 'Only one person was missing. I wish she had been alive to see it.'[61] A decade after Edwina's death, he was still mourning.

By the 1970s, Mountbatten had outlived most of those whom he felt were his equals or superiors in class, style and outlook. Edwina had died in 1960; Alanbrooke in 1963; Nehru in 1964; Churchill and Ismay in 1965; Peter Murphy in 1966; the Duke of Windsor would go in 1972. He ate his meals alone in front of the television, watching *Panorama*, *World in Action*, and *Horizon*. He still enjoyed the company of women, but would not remarry: a man of his genealogical consciousness would not wish to jeopardize the position of his existing family, especially when – most unusually – he had secured a special remainder so that his title might pass to his daughter, Patricia. He was also obliged to spend some time fending off rumours about guardsmen when, in 1975, his name was whispered in connection with an exposé in the *Daily Mirror* about gay orgies at the Life Guards' barracks in London. 'I might have been accused of many things in my life but hardly of the act of homosexuality', he wrote indignantly in his diary.[62] He was accused of it again after a maid walked in while a photographer was attempting to remove the Admiral's trousers, for reasons apparently connected with portraiture.[63] He had continued his relationship with Yola Letellier.[64] But any thoughts Mountbatten had about marrying other women were crowded out by the memory of Edwina. 'If I lived for another hundred years,' he told his valet, 'I would not meet another woman to compare with Her Ladyship.'[65]

With all his fancies of leading the nation returning to the dust whence they had come, Dickie was left functionless again. He took up any number of charitable presidencies and patronages. No Boy Scout troupe went unaddressed, no dinner-dance unattended, no regional administrative office unopened. The Queen took pity on him and made him Governor of the Isle of Wight, his childhood home. The former Viceroy of mighty India, who had wielded the power of life or, often, death over 400 million people, was entitled in this new role to attend council luncheons. With his great friend, Barbara Cartland, he collaborated on a romance novel, *Love at the Helm*. The hero is a dashing naval officer, Captain Conrad 'Tiger' Horn, with a penchant for neatly kept uniforms.[66]

Indira Gandhi won a massive victory in the 1971 elections. That year, East Pakistan rebelled against West Pakistan. Indira sent troops to aid the rebels, and following an horrific civil war, East Pakistan seceded from Jinnah's dream to become Bangladesh.

In June 1975, Nan Pandit was in London for a wedding. She was queuing for breakfast at the Indian Students' Hostel when she heard that, following accusations of electoral malpractice, an 'emergency' had been declared in India. Indira had suspended all human rights: property could not be owned, professions could not be pursued, and there was no freedom of movement, association, or speech. Total censorship had been imposed, especially on quotations about freedom from the writings of Gandhi, Nehru and Tagore. 'It was reminiscent of the midnight knock of forty years ago in Hitler's Germany,' Nan remembered.[67]

The emergency was a time of terror. Bulldozers cleared deprived areas, whose inhabitants were given as little as forty-five minutes' notice to vacate them, in order to make way for property developers under the slogan 'Make Delhi Beautiful'.[68] Indira's son, Sanjay, ran a programme to tackle overpopulation. His sterilization campaign put so much pressure on provincial officials to show results that stories became common of men being kidnapped and forcibly castrated, and the same men being operated upon two or even three times to make up the figures. Indira had her favourite slogan – 'Indira is India, and India is Indira' – displayed in colossal letters around the arcades of Connaught Circus.[69]

Mountbatten was horrified. 'I cannot tell you how infinitely saddened I am at what is being done to the memory of your great brother, Jawaharlal', he wrote to Nan. 'It is a tragedy, of course, that his own daughter, Indu, and that unfortunate young son of hers, Sanjay, should have behaved in such a way during the Emergency, to make it possible for the name of Nehru to be besmirched.'[70] Indira cancelled the emergency on 18 January 1977 and called an election, in the belief that she would win it. She did not, and a rickety coalition of Hindu nationalists, Sikhs, farmers and the extreme right took over. Indira was shocked and hurt, more so yet when the new government imprisoned her. For all her 'Indira is India' rhetoric, she had badly misjudged the popular temperature.[71]

Dickie had agreed with Nan that he would not see Indira publicly on her visit to London after her release in 1978, but would invite her to see him privately.[72] Had he not wished to draw attention to the meeting, he could have picked a less conspicuous middleman. On 13 November, Barbara Cartland – in trademark searing pink and feathers, and with a white Pekingese dog under her arm – arrived at Claridge's to whisk off Mrs Gandhi in her Rolls Royce Silver Cloud. They drove to Dickie's flat and stayed for half an hour, for what can only have been an uncomfortable chat. 'We managed to keep off the Emergency', Dickie reported to Nan, 'and to talk in a friendly way about the old days with her father and you and the family generally.'[73] Reporters congregated to observe the surreal scene. Did Indira read Miss Cartland's books, they wondered – with an eye to the Indian setting of her 249th novel, *Flowers for the God of Love*, published that week? 'Of course she does,' snapped Miss Cartland.[74] And what on earth did the three of them talk about, the crumbling semi-royal playboy, the disgraced Indian dictator, and the romance novelist? 'We discussed inflation,' replied Miss Cartland, then slammed shut the door of her car, and drove Indira back to the hotel.[75]

Dickie's main focus became that of his own dynastic succession, through the proxy of the Prince of Wales. Mountbatten had been behind the decisions to send Prince Charles to Gordonstoun, Cambridge and the Navy; he had encouraged him to play polo; he had provided the younger man with a weekend place away from his parents at Broadlands, to which girlfriends could be invited; he had even tried, and failed, to persuade Philip and Elizabeth to have their son's ears pinned back before he went to school, which might have spared him a great deal of bullying from classmates and, later, the media.[76] In the summer of 1979, he was orchestrating a putative relationship between Charles and a pretty young aristocrat called the Hon. Amanda Knatchbull. Miss Knatchbull happened to be Mountbatten's granddaughter, and the opportunity to strengthen the concentration of his own blood in the royal veins was too delicious for the ageing schemer to pass up. He attempted to organize a trip to India, taking Charles and Amanda with him, but the potential for press intrusion put an end to that. Instead, he wrote to Nan that he might come alone, for he wanted to visit 'the Ajunta [sic] Caves which I have never actually seen myself'.[77] The opposition of Amanda's parents to Mountbatten's matchmaking, and the apparent lack of attraction between the couple, doomed the relationship.

In the summer of 1979, Mountbatten set off for his usual August holiday at Cliffoney in Eire. He had been warned about the threat of terrorism from the Irish Republican Army, then active on both sides of the border. 'The IRA are not looking for an old man like me,' he told his valet.[78] On the morning of 27 August, Mountbatten was up early and bustling around Classiebawn Castle, a Victorian gothic house in Sligo that had been inherited many years before by Edwina. Meanwhile, down at the nearby harbour of Mullaghmore, one or more Provisional IRA operatives levered up the green-painted planks in the centre aft of the Mountbatten family's fishing boat, the *Shadow V*. They packed twenty-five kilogrammes of ammonium nitrate and nitroglycerine, mixed to form a gelignite explosive, into the hull, and attached a remote detonator before withdrawing to the hillside by the quay.

Mountbatten was to spend the day aboard the *Shadow V* with his daughter Patricia and her husband, Lord Brabourne, along with their teenaged twin sons, Nicholas and Timothy Knatchbull. Lord Brabourne's mother, Doreen, and a local lad called Paul Maxwell, completed the party. Shortly before lunchtime they motored into Donegal Bay. As they got into open water Lord Brabourne turned to his father-in-law and said, 'You are having fun today, aren't you?'[79] At that moment, the terrorists pressed their button, and a massive explosion blasted the *Shadow V* into woodchips. Paul Maxwell, Nick Knatchbull and Earl Mountbatten of Burma were killed instantly; the others seriously injured – in the dowager Lady Brabourne's case, fatally. Patricia remembered thinking about how her father had been sunk on the *Kelly* thirty-eight years before, and how he had told her he covered his nose and mouth to prevent himself from drowning. She was very nearly killed as well and was to spend weeks on a life-support machine. 'My father had always been particular that the boat should be fully painted,' she remembered years later. 'I've still got some in my eyes, which is rather nice. I like having a souvenir of the boat.'[80] Mountbatten was found floating face down in the water. He had told friends he wished to die at sea.[81]

In the summer of 1907, a Cambridge undergraduate called Jawaharlal Nehru had visited Dublin. He had been thrilled by the reaction of the dissident political group Sinn Fein, when they were excluded from a nationalist meeting at Mansion House. They simply held a rally outside it, attracting far more spectators than were inside – including Jawahar himself. 'Their policy is not to beg for favours but to wrest them', he had written to his father, Motilal. 'They do not want to fight England by arms but "to ignore her, boycott her and quietly assume the administration of Irish affairs".'[82] Had Jawaharlal Nehru been alive in 1979, he would have been horrified by the actions of the Provisional IRA in the name of the same cause. And it would not have passed him by that the target was inappropriate. Mountbatten was no colonial oppressor or Unionist stooge. He died because he was posh.

Mountbatten had spent many happy hours planning his own funeral. 'How very macabre,' remarked his son-in-law, Lord Brabourne. 'Doesn't it upset you?' 'The only thing that upsets me is that I won't be there,' Mountbatten had replied.[83] Everything for this last great show went off just as the old man would have wanted, from the six scarlet cushions he had ordered to bear his crowns and crests, to the perfectly chosen hymns – 'He Who Would Valiant Be' and 'For Those in Peril on the Sea'.[84] One unplanned detail was a wreath that read 'From H.G.S. to H.G.F.', signifying 'from honorary grandson to honorary grandfather'.[85] 'Life will never be the same now that he has gone', wrote the honorary grandson, Charles, Prince of Wales, in his diary.[86] Ashley Hicks, Mountbatten's real grandson, summed it up the best. 'For Grandpapa, in a way it was the most tremendous of all ends,' he said. 'It stopped him from going gaga; it stopped him from fading into obscurity and it stopped people from being sorry for him. It was the most marvellously dramatic end.'[87]

Today, the India created by the Mountbattens, Nehru, Gandhi and Jinnah is on the way up. Mercedes-Benz and BMW cars hurtle around Connaught Circus alongside rickshaws and the occasional wandering cow; glass-panelled corporate headquarters tower over the internet cafés and sportswear shops that now fill the colonnades that were ransacked by a civil war only sixty years ago. The Punjab is rich again, both in India and in Pakistan. New cities have sprung up on both sides of its border to proclaim the proud, modernist ambitions of those nations. The Indian Punjab has Chandigarh, an elegant sprawl designed, at Nehru's request, by Le Corbusier. The Pakistani Punjab has Islamabad, now the nation's capital. India's great cities boom with industry, from the films and finance of Bombay to the infotech and biotech of Bangalore. Pakistan's great cities have not enjoyed the same prosperity. Despite the patronage it has received from the United States, the burgeoning of radical Islam in parts of Pakistan and its political volatility has made it a less appetising prospect for foreign investors.

Neither Nehru nor Jinnah has bequeathed exactly the legacy he would have wanted to his nation. Nehru's vision encompassed an inclusive democracy, a planned economy, and substantial investment in education. Some of these have fallen by the wayside, and he would have been horrified to observe the religious violence, disregard for the environment, and callousness towards the poor that have beleaguered India since his death. Others have succeeded remarkably, notably in the culture of science and technology, the availability of education, and the principle of secular democracy. But Nehru had seventeen years at the head of India to make his mark. Jinnah had just one at the head of Pakistan. After his death, there was little by the way of strong leadership beyond Liaquat Ali Khan, who was assassinated in 1951 in Rawalpindi. Into the vacuum rushed an assortment of religious fundamentalists and military dictators, and the political history of Pakistan in the sixty years following independence has been one of constant struggle, with democracy pitted against corruption, extremism, the military, and foreign interests. India has suffered no shortage of corruption or extremism either, but, with one brief exception during Indira Gandhi's prime ministership in the 1970s, democracy has held.

Serious problems face each part of the former British Indian Empire. Like India, Pakistan is a beautiful and fascinating country, with a massive pool of native English speakers, and incredible potential for tourism, commerce and industry. But if it is to catch up with India's economic pace it will need greater stability and a rebuilding of Jinnah's progressive ideals. Bangladesh, the nation that was designed to be unworkable, has seen some economic growth, but is constrained by its climate and geography. Every year, the monsoon rains swell the tributaries of the Ganges, Brahmaputra and Meghna rivers, and a huge part of Bangladesh floods. Droughts and cyclones add to the nation's woes, while its population continues to rise. Meanwhile, India's impressive development statistics mask a society split by some of the most shocking divisions of wealth visible anywhere in the world. Efforts to alleviate poverty and eradicate caste have progressed, but at a painfully slow pace. In many parts of the country, India's new rich enjoy their fabulous wealth behind the iron gates and armed guards of private towns, from which the poor are physically excluded. India suffers simultaneously from the strictures of poverty and the diseases of affluence. It contains 50 per cent of the world's hungry, and more than half of all children under five are malnourished.[88] Simultaneously, India's enormous middle class – estimated at around 300 million people – is experiencing an obesity epidemic.

The structures of British rule are visible everywhere but, in a sub-continent that has seen dozens of empires come and go, such relics do not seem out of place. In Delhi's Imperial Hotel, where Jinnah was nearly murdered by Khaksars, the British raj is now a selling point. Bollywood stars pop in to enjoy 'memsahib's tea' on the lawn, and spend 50,000 rupees on a handbag in the Chanel boutique. Outside, shoeless, half-starved children wait at the traffic lights to beg ten-rupee notes from rickshaw passengers. From each of these notes, in one of the least appropriate tributes imaginable, smiles the face of Mohandas K. Gandhi.

The Viceroy's House, later Government House, is now Rashtrapati Bhavan, the home of the President of the Republic of India. Nehru eventually succeeded in getting rid of the British crown and won republican status in 1950; the first president was Rajendra Prasad, and since then incumbents have included Muslims, a Sikh and a Dalit (the modern name for Untouchables). Birla House, Gandhi's last residence, and Teen Murti House, Nehru's home, are tourist attractions. Frozen behind glass panels, Mohan's and Jawahar's spectacles, notepads, clothes, shoes and books are dis-played like holy relics, gazed upon by crowds of schoolchildren. There is still a picture of Edwina Mountbatten in Jawaharlal Nehru's study.

Up in the hills at Simla, the Viceregal Lodge is now the Indian Institute of Advanced Studies. Perhaps more than anywhere else in India, Simla provides a snapshot of how the legacy of the raj has been incorporated into independent Indian life. Half-timbered shops sell Scottish knitwear alongside glittering sari fabric; restaurants serve pizzas alongside bhajis. Schoolchildren wear neat uniforms indistinguishable from those of British public schools, and many of the old baronial mansions have become hotels. The locals still tell tales of British ghosts. A group of Victorians in bonnets and breeches is said to appear on the benches on Mall Road; an English gentleman haunts tunnel 103 of the narrow-gauge railway; a beautiful *angrez churail*, an English vampiress with backwards feet and hands, entices Indian men to their doom if they walk at night near the thick deodar trees at the Boileauganj junction.[89] But these imperial nightmares are fading, replaced by the sense that the once-despised British raj is now just another part of history, and that the present is all about pushing forward. 'Gandhi lived in a different world', a marketing executive from Delhi told a newspaper. 'If he were alive now, he'd probably say there was nothing wrong with materialism but you had to get the balance right.'[90] He would not; but even the Mahatma cannot be allowed to stand in the way of an economic boom.

India today is not Gandhi's India, though there remains an enormous affection for him. There are elements of Gandhi's India in the nation's spirituality; elements of Nehru's India in its education, culture and technology; elements of Jinnah's India in the parts that remain outside; and even elements of the Mountbattens' India in the continuing membership of the Commonwealth held by India, Pakistan and Bangladesh. Though the echoes of 1947 still resonate around Kashmir, and Jinnah's Pakistans have taken a very different route from the one he might have wanted, the vast and diverse nation of India has its sights fixed firmly on the future.

NOTES

(See Abbreviations in Notes, pp. 427–8)

PROLOGUE: A TRYST WITH DESTINY

1 The clocks had been set two hours forward that summer rather than the usual one.
2 Clemenceau cited in Muggeridge, *The Thirties*, p. 76.
3 Mildred A. Talbot to Walter S. Rogers, 27 August 1947. MP: MB1/K148 (I).
4 JN to DM, 22 June 1947. *SWJN* (2), vol 3, p 179.
5 *Manchester Guardian*, 15 August 1947, p. 5. It is not clear from reports what form the effigy took.
6 Midnight had changed him, too: DM had been Viscount Mountbatten of Burma until he was granted an earldom at that hour.
7 DM cited in Collins & Lapierre, *Mountbatten and the Partition of India*, p. 78; see also Collins & Lapierre, *Freedom at Midnight*, p. 311.
8 EA, report on present position in India, 24 August 1947. TNA: DO 121/69.
9 JN to Krishna Nehru, 23 May 1931. Nehru, *Nehru's Letters to His Sister*, pp. 25–6.
10 See Chaudhuri, *Thy Hand Great Anarch!*, p. 817.

I. EMPIRE

1. IN THEIR GRATITUDE OUR BEST REWARD

1 Wolpert, *A New History of India*, pp. 128–30; Gilmartin, *Empire and Islam*, p. 13.
2 Shireen Moosvi (ed.), *Episodes in the Life of Akbar: Contemporary Records and Reminiscences* (National Book Trust of India, New Delhi, 1994), pp. 39, 60–4; Bamber Gascoigne, *The Great Moghuls* (1971; Jonathan Cape, London, 1985), pp. 86, 95–7.
3 This assessment of England in the 1570s has been drawn from: John Guy, *Tudor England* (Oxford University Press, Oxford, 1988), pp. 30–52; G.R. Elton, *England Under the Tudors* (Methuen & Co., London, 1955), pp. 229–51; J.B. Black, *The Reign of Elizabeth, 1558–1603* (1936; second edition, Clarendon Press, Oxford, 1959), pp. 251–67. Modern life expectancy statistics are from the World Health Organization's *World Health Report*, 2005.
4 Philip Stubbs cited in J.B. Black, *The Reign of Elizabeth*, p. 267.
5 Ralph Fitch, undated letter, c. 28 September 1585. J. Courtenay Locke, (ed.), *The First Englishmen in India: Letters and Narratives of Sundry Elizabethans Written by Themselves* (George Routledge & Sons, London, 1930), p. 103. An 'ounce' is a snow leopard, and a 'buffle' a buffalo.

6 William Dalrymple, *White Mughals* (HarperCollins, London, 2002) is an enjoyable account of this phenomenon.

7 Adam Smith, *The Wealth of Nations* (1776; Pickering & Chatto, London, 1995), vol I, p. 115.

8 Thomas Babington Macaulay, 10 July 1833; in *The Complete Works of Lord Macaulay: Speeches, Poems & Miscellaneous Writings* (Longmans, Green & Co., London, 1898), vol 1 (vol 11 of complete set), p. 559.

9 Judd, *The Lion and the Tiger*, p. 47. It is sadly not true that General Sir Charles Napier sent a single word Latin telegram – 'Peccavi', or 'I have sinned' – on capturing Sindh. The quote was attributed to him in a cartoon in *Punch*. Furthermore, it is probably untrue that Lord Dalhousie sent 'Vovi' ('I vowed') on taking Oudh, nor that the captors of Lucknow in 1857 sent 'Nunc fortunatus sum' ('I am in luck now').

10 Mike Dash, *Thug: The True Story of India's Murderous Cult* (Granta Books, London, 2005) is a very readable investigation into thuggee.

11 Abul Kalam Azad, in Sen, *1857*, p. x. Azad overstates the case by suggesting that the British deliberately concealed a motive of conquest behind a trading company. Even MKG admitted that the East India Company was not set up to conquer: 'They had not the slightest intention at the time of establishing a kingdom', he wrote (*Hind Swaraj*, p. 23). But he is certainly justified in arguing that the unofficial capacity of the East India Company allowed it to behave in ways the Crown could not; and it is true that the great Mughals would not have tolerated a similar incursion by an army.

12 Gandhi, *Hind Swaraj*, p. 23.

13 It is politically correct in India to refer to the revolt of 1857 as the 'First War of Independence'. But this is misleading, for it had no connection to the later independence movement; moreover, there was no second war of independence. Its traditional British name, the 'Indian Mutiny', may be offensive to some, but retains an authentic flavour of the attitudes of the time.

14 David, *The Indian Mutiny*, pp. 52–5.

15 Karl Marx, 'Investigation of Tortures in India', 28 August 1857. Marx & Engels, *The First Indian War of Independence*, pp. 59–63. Progressive Indians as well as the British favoured the end of suttee, and a notable campaign against it was led by Ram Mohan Roy and Dwarakanath Tagore. Many Indians were also supportive of the Company's policies on education and social welfare. Sen, *1857*, p. 5; Abul Kalam Azad, in Sen, *1857*, pp. xiv–xv; also Nehru, *The Discovery of India*, pp. 293–4.

16 David, *The Indian Mutiny*, pp. 80–4, 90–1; Ward, *Our Bones are Scattered*, pp. 106–7.

17 Sen, *1857*, pp. 67–8.

18 Some Gurkhas mutinied at Jutogh, near Simla, causing panic among the Europeans. But the town itself was left alone by the rioters. Pubby, *Shimla Then and Now*, pp. 30–3.

19 Karl Marx, 'The Future Results of the British Rule in India', 22 July 1853. Marx & Engels, *The First Indian War of Independence*, p. 26.

20 Sen, *1857*, pp. 114, 150; Abul Kalam Azad, in ibid, p. xvi; Ward, *Our Bones are Scattered*, pp. 442, 455, 510; Wolpert, *A New History of India*, p. 235.

21 David, *The Indian Mutiny*, pp. 305–6; Sen, *1857*, p. 110. Bahadur Shah II was eventually transported to Burma and kept in obscurity until he died.

22 Hutheesing, *We Nehrus*, p. 16.

23 Patrick French has rightly pointed out that the term 'the raj' was popularised by

DM. 'Raj' means 'rule' – it is possible to have 'Mughal raj', 'Congress raj', 'swaraj' (self-rule) and so on. In Britain and the West, 'the raj' is understood to refer specifically to the British raj, and it has been used in that sense throughout this book. In India, the term 'Angrez sarkar' was usually employed. French, *Liberty or Death*, p. 442.

24 Cited in Tendulkar, *Mahatma*, vol 1, p. 2.

25 There is an account of their tour in Liversidge, *The Mountbattens*, pp. 34–7.

26 Nehru, *An Autobiography*, p. 417.

27 See Prithwis Chandra Ray, *Indian Famines: Their Causes and Remedies* (Cherry Press, Calcutta, 1901), table opposite p. 10.

2. MOHAN AND JAWAHAR

1 Gandhi, *An Autobiography*, pp. 34–40; Fischer, *Life of Mahatma Gandhi*, pp. 28–9, 33; Tendulkar, *Mahatma*, vol 1, p. 31.

2 Kasturbai's surname is sometimes given as Nanakji or Kapadia.

3 Gandhi, *Daughter of Midnight*, pp. 16–18.

4 MKG cited in ibid, p. 212.

5 The Raj became less keen on Congress when Hume tried to broaden its base and recruited Muslims, peasant proprietors and townspeople over the next two years. *ODNB*, vol 28, pp. 735–7; Hamid, *Disastrous Twilight*, p. 3.

6 Gandhi, *An Autobiography*, pp. 42–4. This analysis is indebted to Koestler, *The Lotus and the Robot*, pp. 145–9.

7 Gandhi, *An Autobiography*, pp. 52–4; Fischer, *Life of Mahatma Gandhi*, p. 35; Tendulkar, *Mahatma*, vol 1, p. 33.

8 Gandhi, *An Autobiography*, p. 56.

9 Tendulkar, *Mahatma*, vol 1, pp. 32–3.

10 Fischer, *Life of Mahatma Gandhi*, p. 37.

11 Symonds, *In the Margins of Independence*, p. 88; Gandhi, *An Autobiography*, p. 87.

12 Fischer, *Life of Mahatma Gandhi*, pp. 39–40.

13 Tendulkar, *Mahatma*, vol 1, p. 36.

14 St Augustine had put forward the same principle in Christianity. MKG would later amend his motto to 'Truth is God'.

15 Gandhi, *An Autobiography*, pp. 113–7; Tendulkar, *Mahatma*, vol 1, pp. 44–5.

16 Tendulkar, *Mahatma*, vol 1, p. 43.

17 Fischer, *Life of Mahatma Gandhi*, p. 67; Erikson, *Gandhi's Truth*, p. 179; Tendulkar, *Mahatma*, vol 1, p. 60.

18 Morton, *The Women in Gandhi's Life*, p. 59.

19 Gandhi, *Daughter of Midnight*, pp. 75–87; Morton, *The Women in Gandhi's Life*, pp. 75–6.

20 Fischer, *Life of Mahatma Gandhi*, pp. 69–71.

21 MKG in 1932, cited in Fischer, ibid, p. 331.

22 Tendulkar, *Mahatma*, vol 1, p. 103.

23 MKG to Kasturba Gandhi, n.d. (9 November 1908). Cited in Gandhi, *Daughter of Midnight*, p. 158. The letter was written in Gujarati and there is a different translation in *CWMG*, vol 9, p. 106.

24 Tendulkar, *Mahatma*, vol 1, p. 216.

25 Akbar, *Nehru*, pp. 28–9.

26 Pandit, *The Scope of Happiness*, pp. 51–2.

27 Nehru, *An Autobiography*, p. 7. Several biographers have pointed out the Freudian implications of this story.

28 Fischer, *Life of Mahatma Gandhi*, p. 461.

29 Hutheesing, *We Nehrus*, pp. 22–3.

30 Nehru, *An Autobiography*, pp. 7–8.

31 According to Sarup (later Vijaya Lakshmi Pandit), she only became close to her brother after her entry into politics in the 1930s. Ultimately, they became the closest of allies and friends. Brittain, *Envoy Extraordinary*, pp. 35–6.

32 Nehru, *An Autobiography*, pp. 15–16.

33 Ibid, p. 19.

34 Sahgal, *Prison and Chocolate Cake*, p. 129.

35 Akbar, *Nehru*, p. 5.

36 Brown, *Nehru*, p. 38; Brittain, *Envoy Extraordinary*, p. 36.

37 Nehru, *An Autobiography*, pp. 19–21.

38 Ibid, p. 20.

39 JN to Motilal Nehru, 14 May 1909. *SWJN* (1), vol 1, p. 68.

40 The legal position did not stop others – including MKG's son Devadas – from marrying outside their castes. But the law would remain unchanged until JN himself initiated the Hindu Marriages Validity Act of 1949. Ali, *Private Face of a Public Person*, p. 10.

41 JN to Motilal Nehru, cited in Kalhan, *Kamala Nehru*, p. 6.

42 JN to Motilal Nehru, ibid, p. 7.

43 Brown, *Nehru*, p. 38.

44 Nehru, *An Autobiography*, p. 25.

45 Adams & Whitehead, *The Dynasty*, p. 18.

46 Ibid, pp. 30–1.

47 Nehru, *An Autobiography*, p. 26.

48 Ibid, p. 33.

49 Ibid, p. 28. JN cites Dickinson, and the original quote is to be found in E.M. Forster, *Goldsworthy Lowes Dickinson* (1934; Edward Arnold, London, 1973), p. 117. See also Syed Mahmud, 'In and out of prison', in Zakaria (ed.), *A Study of Nehru*, p. 158.

50 Asaf Ali cited in Bakshi, *Kamala Nehru*, p. 169.

51 Hutheesing, *We Nehrus*, p. 8.

52 Bakshi, *Kamala Nehru*, pp. 6–7.

53 Hutheesing, *We Nehrus*, p. 12.

54 Nehru, *An Autobiography*, p. 37.

55 Ibid, p. 38.

56 Sahgal, 'The Making of Mrs. Gandhi', p. 197.

57 MKG, 6 February 1916. CWMG, vol 13, pp. 213–14.

58 Erikson, *Gandhi's Truth*, pp. 284–6; Nehru, *An Autobiography*, p. 533.

59 Nehru, *An Autobiography*, p. 72.

60 MKG in *Young India*, 23 February 1921. Reprinted in Gandhi, *Hind Swaraj*, p. xiii.

61 Gandhi, *Hind Swaraj*, pp. 42, 44, 46.

62 Fischer, *Life of Mahatma Gandhi*, p. 107.

63 Ibid, p. 230; Gandhi, *Daughter of Midnight*, pp. 211–12.

64 Harilal Gandhi to MKG, 31 March 1915, cited in Kumar, *Brahmacharya*, p. 81. See also Gandhi, *Daughter of Midnight*, p. 174.

65 John H. Morrow, Jr, *The Great War: An Imperial History* (Routledge, London & New York, 2004), pp. 312–4.

66 Nehru, *The Discovery of India*, p. 336.

67 Vijaya Lakshmi Pandit cited in Brittain, *Envoy Extraordinary*, p. 45.

3. CIVIS BRITANNICUS SUM

1 King Carlos I and his brother, Crown Prince Luis Felipe, were both shot by a gang. Luis Felipe took a few hours longer to die, and therefore could have been said to reign briefly.

2 The family owned estates in Germany, and had a large portion of their liquid assets in Russia. During the First World War, inflation devalued the German estates, which were eventually sold for knock-down prices. The Russian assets disappeared during the Revolution. Hough, *Edwina*, p. 68.

3 Lambton, *The Mountbattens*, p. 45.

4 DM cited in Terraine, *The Life and Times of Lord Mountbatten*, p. 25; Hough, *Louis & Victoria*, p. 265; see also Hough, *Edwina*, p. 59; Liversidge, *The Mountbattens*, p. 99; Ziegler, *Mountbatten*, p. 34.

5 Asquith cited in Martin Gilbert, *Winston S. Churchill*, vol III (Heinemann, London, 1971), p. 147.

6 WSC wrote: 'The Prime Minister thought & I agree with him that a letter from you to me indicating that you felt that in some respects yr usefulness was impaired & that patriotic considerations wh at this juncture must be supreme in yr mind wd be the best form of giving effect to yr decision. To this letter I wd on behalf of the Govt write an answer. This correspondence cd then be made public and wd explain itself.' Cited in ibid, pp. 148–9.

7 WSC's letter to Prince Louis is cited in ibid, p. 149. His enthusiasm for Fisher's candidacy is recorded in the same volume, pp. 144–5.

8 The King made Prince Louis a Privy Counsellor to cheer him up, thereby putting him in a position of even greater access to state secrets than he had had as First Sea Lord. King George V's diary, 29 October 1914. Cited in Harold Nicolson, *King George V: His Life and Reign* (1952: Constable, London, 1979), p. 251.

9 Hough, *Edwina*, p. 60. Ziegler thought this story 'almost too picturesque to be credible', but admitted that it would have been 'a characteristic gesture'. Ziegler, *Mountbatten*, p. 36.

10 DM to G.S. Hugh-Jones, cited in Ziegler, *Mountbatten*, p. 36.

11 King George V cited in Aronson, *Crowns in Conflict*, p. 154.

12 Prince Louis of Battenberg cited in Hoey, *Mountbatten*, p. 63.

13 'impossible': Prince Louis of Battenberg cited in Hough, *Louis & Victoria*, p. 320. Despite his English identity, Prince Louis always spoke with a strong German accent. See Martin Gilbert, *Winston S. Churchill*, vol II (Heinemann, London, 1967), p. 553.

14 This account is summarized from the vivid reconstruction in Greg King & Penny Wilson, *The Fate of the Romanovs* (John Wiley & Sons, Hoboken, NJ, 2003), pp. 306–13, 316–31.

15 Anon, *Mountbatten: Eighty Years in Pictures*, p. 31. DM would regularly hold forth on how the gallant King George had tried to offer his Russian cousins asylum in Britain in their hour of peril, but had been prevented from doing so by Lloyd George on grounds that it might be politically damaging. As it would emerge many years later, precisely the opposite had been the case. It was the King who had fobbed Downing Street off, having received a pile of angry letters from his subjects protesting against any offer of succour to his controversial cousins – leaving the imperial family to be butchered in a cellar. There is a detailed account in Rose, *King George V*, pp. 210–18.

16 Report by P.J. Harrison, Royal Naval College, Dartmouth, Spring 1915. In Anon, *Mountbatten*, p. 47.

17 *Daily Telegraph*, 28 August 1979, p. 12.

18 There is also a fictional Order of the White Elephant, situated in Burma rather than Thailand, which should not be confused with the real one. William McGonagall (*c*.1825–1902), often described with some understatement as Scotland's worst poet, was created 'Sir William Topaz McGonagall, Knight of the Order of the White Elephant, Burmah' in 1894. Although McGonagall affected this style and title for the rest of his life, the letter announcing his elevation to the Order had in fact been a hoax by some Edinburgh university students. Colin Walker, *McGonagall: A Selection* (1993; Birlinn, Edinburgh, 1998), pp. 13, 20–3.

19 Roberts, *Eminent Churchillians*, p. 60.

20 Hough, *Edwina*, p. 61; Ziegler, *Mountbatten*, pp. 46–7.

21 John Alfred Wyllie, *India at the Parting of the Ways: Monarchy, Diarchy, or Anarchy?* (Lincoln Williams Ltd, London, 1934), p. 129.

22 CWMG, vol 15, p. 436.

23 Collett, *The Butcher of Amritsar*, pp. 202–3.

24 Cited in Read & Fisher, *The Proudest Day*, p. 4.

25 Ibid, p. 5.

26 Collett, *The Butcher of Amritsar*, p. 256. There were no white men among Dyer's troops.

27 Read & Fisher, *The Proudest Day*, p. 8; Collett, *The Butcher of Amritsar*, pp. 261–3. The Congress committee of investigation put the death toll at 1200 and those injured at 3600, though this may have been too high. Hutheesing, *We Nehrus*, p. 42, footnote.

28 Tagore cited in Kripalani, *Tagore, Gandhi and Nehru*, p. 19.

29 Hutheesing, *We Nehrus*, p. 43.

30 French, *Liberty or Death*, p. 58.

31 Reginald Dyer cited in Fischer, *Life of Mahatma Gandhi*, p. 204.

32 Collett, *The Butcher of Amritsar*, p. 380.

33 Metcalf, *Ideologies of the Raj*, p. 228; Collett, *The Butcher of Amritsar*, p. 292.

34 CWMG, vol 15, pp. 243–5.

35 MKG cited in French, *Liberty or Death*, p. 20.

36 S.R. Singh, 'Gandhi and the Jallianwala Bagh Tragedy: A Turning Point in the Indian Nationalist Movement', V.N. Datta & S. Settar, eds., *Jallianwala Bagh Massacre* (Pragati Publications, Delhi, 2000), pp. 196–9.

37 See the dedication in Chaudhuri, *Autobiography*, and his clarification in 'My hundredth year', *The Granta Book of India*, ed. Ian Jack (Granta Books, London, 2005), p. 284. The story of St Paul challenging the Romans can be found in Acts 16.

38 Nehru, *An Autobiography*, pp. 43–4.

39 MKG to Lord Hardinge, 1 August 1920. CWMG, vol 18, pp. 104–6.

40 Hutheesing, *We Nehrus*, p. 44.

41 Edward, *Letters from a Prince*, 17 March 1920, pp. 317–18.

42 Ibid, 18 March 1920, p. 318.

43 Mountbatten, *Diaries 1920–22*, 30 May 1920, p. 69.

44 Edward, *Letters from a Prince*, 26 March 1920, p. 323.

45 Ibid, 24 August 1920, p. 467. See also Anon, *Mountbatten*, pp. 64–5.

46 King George V to Prince Edward, Prince of Wales. Cited in Rose, *King George V*, p. 306.

47 Mountbatten, *Diaries 1920–22*, 17 April 1920, pp. 30–1; 30 May 1920, pp. 68–9; 11 June 1920, p. 78; Edward, *Letters from a Prince*, 11 June 1920, pp. 399–400; Ziegler, *Mountbatten*, pp. 55–6. Sadly, Digger fell ill after escaping in

Trinidad. Despite, or perhaps owing to, the Prince's efforts to revive it with brandy, the creature perished.

48 Edward, *Letters from a Prince*, p. 348.
49 Ibid, 28 August 1920, p. 470.

4. DREAMING OF THE EAST

1 Edward, *Letters from a Prince*, p. 424.
2 Windsor, *A King's Story*, p. 178.
3 Clair Price, 'Gandhi and British India', *New York Times*, 10 July 1921, section III, p. 12.
4 MKG cited in the *Statesman* (weekly edition), 9 November 1921, p. 13.
5 Ibid, 23 November 1921, p. 11.
6 MP: MB1/A16. See also Mountbatten, *Diaries 1920–22*, 10 November 1921, p. 178.
7 Alfred Duff Cooper, *Old Men Forget: The Autobiography of Duff Cooper* (Rupert Hart-Davis, London, 1953), 4 November 1920, p. 103.
8 Windsor, *A King's Story*, p. 165.
9 Cited in *Times of India*, 1 November 1921, p. 6; *Statesman* (weekly edition), 9 November 1921, p. 3.
10 Windsor, *A King's Story*, p. 167.
11 *Times of India*, 19 November 1921, p. 8.
12 Ibid, p. 9.
13 MKG cited in ibid, 21 November 1921, p. 11.
14 *Statesman* (weekly edition), 23 November 1921, p. 4; *Times of India*, 21 November 1921, p. 11.
15 Reuter correspondent, *Illustrated London News*, 17 December 1921, p. 829.
16 *Times of India*, 1 December 1921, p. 9.
17 Mountbatten, *Diaries 1920–22*, 1 December 1921, p. 203.
18 MP: MB1/A16. Handle with care.
19 *Illustrated London News*, 7 January 1922, pp. 10–11.
20 Ibid, p. 3.
21 Windsor, *A King's Story*, pp. 169–70.
22 Ibid, p. 170.
23 Mountbatten, *Diaries 1920–22*, 9 December 1921, p. 211.
24 Dance card in MP: MB1/A16.
25 EA to Dennis Holman, n.d., MP: MB1/R231.
26 Hough, *Edwina*, p. 42.
27 Ibid, p. 44. Janet Morgan dismisses the story of EA being bullied on the grounds that girls are generally 'more sympathetic' than boys and would not be likely to go in for anti-Semitic teasing. Morgan, *Edwina Mountbatten*, pp. 71–2.
28 Hough, *Edwina*, pp. 44–5.
29 MP: MB2/K3; Morgan, *Edwina Mountbatten*, pp. 76–9.
30 EA to Dennis Holman, n.d., MP: MB1/R231.
31 Morgan, *Edwina Mountbatten*, p. 92.
32 Dennis Holman, 'Lady Mountbatten's Story', part 1. *Woman*, 22 September 1951; Hough, *Edwina*, pp. 66–7.
33 Press cutting in MP: MB2/K5.
34 DM to EA, 15 January 1922. Cited in Ziegler, *Mountbatten*, p. 68.
35 Nehru, *An Autobiography*, pp. 49, 52.
36 Pandit, *The Scope of Happiness*, pp. 79–80.

37 Nehru, *An Autobiography*, p. 42

38 Ibid, pp. 79–80; *Statesman* (weekly edition), 14 December 1921, p. 14.

39 See Nayantara Sahgal's comment in Nehru, *Before Freedom*, p. 35.

40 Hutheesing, *We Nehrus*, p. 51.

41 The Viceroy, Lord Reading, wrote to King George V, 'Allahabad is undoubtedly the place which is blackest in the record, and where the hartal most completely succeeded. The reasons in the main were that leaders of the non-cooperation movement had been arrested a day or two before, and particularly one Moti Lal Nehru, who was a most successful member of the Bar and had lived in rather princely style. He gave up his practice and became a follower of Gandhi. Undoubtedly he exercised a powerful influence over Allahabad, and his arrest just before the Prince's arrival led to the demonstrations of complete absence of the Indians from the streets.' 23 February 1922. Cited in Chopra et al., *Secret Papers from the British Royal Archives*, p. 225.

42 *Daily Express*, 13 December 1921.

43 *Times of India*, 13 December 1921, p. 9.

44 Windsor, *A King's Story*, p. 170.

45 *Times of India*, 13 December 1921, p. 9.

46 Hutheesing, *We Nehrus*, p. 52.

47 *Times of India*, 16 December 1921, p. 10.

48 Hutheesing, *We Nehrus*, p. 51.

49 Ibid, p. 59.

50 *News of the World*, 18 December 1921; *Daily Express*, 27 December 1921.

51 *Times of India*, 27 December 1921, pp. 11–12; *Statesman* (weekly edition), 28 December 1921, p. 3; *Indian Mirror* (Calcutta), 29 December 1921; *Morning Post*, 27 December 1921; *Daily Express*, 27 December 1921.

52 *Statesman* (weekly edition), 28 December 1921, p. 17; Dance card in MP: MB1/A16.

53 Cited in the *Statesman* (weekly edition), 4 January 1922, p. 15.

54 Mountbatten, *Diaries 1920–22*, 13 January 1922, p. 237.

55 *Statesman* (weekly edition), 19 January 1922, p. 10.

56 Mountbatten, *Diaries 1920–22*, 13 January 1922, p. 237.

57 *Statesman* (weekly edition), 19 January 1922, p. 11.

58 Mountbatten, *Diaries 1920–22*, 15 January 1922, p. 239.

59 Allen & Dwivedi, *Lives of the Indian Princes*, pp. 104–5.

60 The *Illustrated London News* published a profile of MKG and a large illustration, describing him as 'The de Valera of India', after Eamon de Valera, the Irish leader then negotiating for the establishment of the Irish Free State. *Illustrated London News*, 21 December 1921, pp. 876–7.

61 Fischer, *Life of Mahatma Gandhi*, p. 219; Wolpert, *A New History of India*, p. 307; Menon, *The Transfer of Power in India*, p. 29; Dalton, *Mahatma Gandhi*, p. 48.

62 MKG in *Young India*, 16 February 1922. See also Fischer, *Life of Mahatma Gandhi*, p. 219.

63 MKG had set these six conditions for swaraj out in a previous article: *Young India*, 23 February 1921. Reprinted in his *Hind Swaraj*, p. xii.

64 Sir Conrad Corfield, 'The Princely India I Knew', version 1, unpublished manuscript, p. 25. Corfield Papers, CSAS.

65 Sir George Lloyd cited in Brecher, *Nehru*, p. 79; Sir Conrad Corfield, 'The Princely India I Knew', p. 25.

66 MKG in *Young India*, 16 February 1922. See also Fischer, *Life of Mahatma Gandhi*, p. 220; CWMG, vol 22, pp. 415–21.

67 Nehru, *An Autobiography*, p. 84.
68 Ibid, pp. 374, 377, 379, 380.
69 Hough, *Edwina*, p. 71.
70 Holman, 'Lady Mountbatten's story', part 1.
71 Mountbatten, *Diaries 1920–22*, 14 February 1922, p. 255.
72 Mountbatten, *Diaries 1920–22*, 16 February 1922, p. 256.
73 Lady Reading cited in Anon, *Mountbatten: Eighty Years in Pictures*, p. 76; Ziegler, *Mountbatten*, p. 69.
74 DM to Victoria, Dowager Marchioness of Milford Haven, 26 February 1922. Cited in Ziegler, *Mountbatten*, p. 69.
75 *Statesman* (weekly edition), 23 March 1922, p. 5.

5. PRIVATE LIVES

1   According to the *Daily Telegraph*. The *Star* proclaimed it the wedding of the century, but in retrospect this looks like overkill. Ziegler, *Mountbatten*, p. 70.
2   'Mountbatten', *Secret History*, Channel 4 Television.
3   Anon, *Mountbatten*, pp. 86–93.
4   The DM-friendly version of the story first appeared in a biography of Prince Louis of Battenberg and his wife, sanctioned by DM (Hough, *Louis & Victoria*, p. 348). It was repeated with even more dramatic emphasis in a biography of the Queen, with Princess Andrew telephoning her brother DM in desperation and DM rushing to the rescue via the King and Lord Curzon (Nicholas Davies, *Elizabeth: Behind Palace Doors*, Mainstream, London, 2000, p. 56). This is completely untrue. It is well-documented that the scheme to rescue the Greek royal family was conceived and directed entirely by the Foreign Office, through Commander Gerald Talbot. The King afterwards expressed his approval by appointing Talbot a Knight Commander of the Royal Victorian Order, but that was the extent of his involvement. Historian Kenneth Rose put the evidence to DM in 1977, at which point DM 'generously admitted that he had been misled by his "rather defective memory" of events half a century earlier'. Rose, *King George V*, p. 348.
5   Dennis Holman, 'Lady Mountbatten's Story', part 1.
6   Ibid, part 2, *Woman*, 29 September 1951.
7   Hoey, *Mountbatten*, pp. 80–1; Ziegler, *Mountbatten*, p. 107.
8   Morgan, *Edwina Mountbatten*, p. 184; DM cited p. 191.
9   According to Lady Pamela Hicks, 'Mountbatten', *Secret History*, Channel 4 Television.
10 EA to Dennis Holman, n.d. MP: MB1/R231. Philip spent most of his time with DM's elder brother George, the Marquess of Milford Haven, and his wife, Nada.
11 Hough, *Edwina*, pp. 90–1.
12 Cited in Ziegler, *Mountbatten*, p. 111; Morgan, *Edwina Mountbatten*, p. 191.
13 Ziegler, *Mountbatten*, p. 111; *San Francisco Chronicle*, 3 October 1926, feature section, p. 3.
14 Lady Pamela Hicks in 'Mountbatten', *Secret History*, Channel 4 Television.
15 DM to EA, 12 January 1927. Cited in Ziegler, *Mountbatten*, p. 112; see also Morgan, *Edwina Mountbatten*, pp. 198–9.
16 EA to DM, 3 September 1928. Cited in Ziegler, *Mountbatten*, p. 113.
17 See, for example, Mrs [May] Meyrick, *Secrets of the 43* (John Long, London, 1933), p. 160.
18 Ziegler, *Mountbatten*, p. 111; Chisholm & Davie, *Beaverbrook*, p. 265.

19 Morgan, *Edwina Mountbatten*, p. 219.

20 Lady Pamela Hicks in 'Mountbatten', *Secret History*, Channel 4 Television.

21 Lady Brabourne cited in Hoey, *Mountbatten*, p. 85.

22 'Mountbatten', *Secret History*, Channel 4 Television.

23 EA to DM, 2 September 1933. Cited in Ziegler, *Mountbatten*, p. 113.

24 Ibid, p. 115.

25 Coward, *Future Indefinite*, p. 304.

26 Ibid, p. 304.

27 Ibid, p. 305. The word 'gay' was in use to denote 'homosexual' by this point, though not very widely. Coward may have enjoyed the mischievous double-entendre.

28 Anon, *Mountbatten*, p. 104.

29 Noël Coward to DM, 21 June 1934. MP: MB1/A48.

30 Ziegler, *Mountbatten*, p. 82. Both DM's official biographer, Philip Ziegler, and his harshest critic, Andrew Roberts, have concluded that the rumours of homosexuality were untrue. See Ziegler, *Mountbatten*, pp. 52–3; Roberts, *Eminent Churchillians*, p. 58.

31 Smith, *Fifty Years with Mountbatten*, pp. 46–8.

32 Hough, *Edwina*, p. 110.

33 Dennis Holman, 'Lady Mountbatten's Story', part 2.

34 Hailey cited in Menon, *The Transfer of Power in India*, p. 32.

35 Motilal Nehru cited in Hutheesing, *We Nehrus*, p. 49.

36 Fischer, *Life of Mahatma Gandhi*, p. 229; Gandhi, *Daughter of Midnight*, p. 234.

37 MKG to Manilal Gandhi, 3 April 1926. Cited in Gandhi, *Daughter of Midnight*, p. 240.

38 Fischer, *Life of Mahatma Gandhi*, pp. 362–3.

39 Koestler, *The Lotus and the Robot*, p. 149.

40 Nehru, *An Autobiography*, p. 513.

41 Ibid, p. 512.

42 Ibid, p. 515.

43 Ibid, p. 191.

44 Morton, *The Women in Gandhi's Life*, p. 172.

45 Indira Gandhi cited in Kalhan, *Kamala Nehru*, p. 73.

46 Ibid, p. 56.

47 Kamala Nehru cited in ibid, p. 34.

48 Nehru, *The Discovery of India*, p. 23.

49 JN cited in Hutheesing, *We Nehrus*, p. 70.

50 Kalhan, *Kamala Nehru*, p. 33.

51 Kamala Nehru to Syed Mahmud, 4 May 1927. Cited in Ali, *Private Face of a Public Person*, p. 22.

52 Kamala Nehru to Syed Mahmud, cited in ibid, p. 23.

53 Syed Mahmud, 'In and out of prison', in Zakaria (ed.), *A Study of Nehru*, p. 161.

54 Hutheesing, *We Nehrus*, p. 73.

55 Kendall, *India and the British*, p. 425.

56 Hutheesing, *We Nehrus*, p. 77.

57 Menon, *The Transfer of Power in India*, p. 34.

58 Hutheesing, *We Nehrus*, p. 78.

59 Nehru, *An Autobiography*, pp. 177–8.

60 Ibid, pp. 179–80.

61 Hutheesing, *We Nehrus*, p. 79; JN cited in Akbar, *Nehru*, p. 215.

62 Irwin cited in Menon, *The Transfer of Power in India*, p. 38.

6. WE WANT NO CAESARS

1 Erikson, *Gandhi's Truth*, p. 443. The salt tax provided £25 million out of an annual revenue of £800 million.
2 Nehru, *An Autobiography*, p. 85.
3 Dalton, *Mahatma Gandhi*, pp. 99–100.
4 Khilnani, *The Idea of India*, p. 67. Most of the imperial revenue from India was brought in by the manipulation of currency and the balance of payments.
5 Hutheesing, *We Nehrus*, p. 85.
6 Wolpert, *A New History of India*, p. 315 makes a comparison with Moses.
7 MKG cited in Kendall, *India and the British*, p. 328.
8 MKG cited in Erikson, *Gandhi's Truth*, p. 445.
9 Miller, *I Found No Peace*, p. 135.
10 Nehru, *An Autobiography*, p. 293. The Aga Khan had been a long-term correspondent of MacDonald's. A sample letter was written by the Aga Khan to MacDonald from the Hotel Ritz in Paris on 19 June 1915: 'We want English statesmen when the war's conclusion is in sight to forget the evil councils [*sic*] of suspicious narrow "white" Imperialists and also of a narrow service interest & to grant us at once & graciously the modest claims we are fully sure we can accept without any risk of our making a "mess" of it.' TNA: PRO 30/69/1218.
11 Muggeridge, *The Thirties*, p. 72.
12 MacDonald's diary, 18 December 1930 and 13 January 1931. Cited in Marquand, *Ramsay MacDonald*, p. 581.
13 WSC, 23 February 1931, cited in Martin Gilbert, *Winston S. Churchill*, vol V, 1922–1939 (Heinemann, London, 1976), p. 390.
14 Lord Irwin cited in Hutheesing, *We Nehrus*, p. 97.
15 Hutheesing, *We Nehrus*, p. 100; Adams & Whitehead, *The Dynasty*, p. 90.
16 Willingdon to King George V, 28 September 1931. Chopra et al., *Secret Papers from the British Royal Archives*, p. 296.
17 Lester, *Entertaining Gandhi*, p. 34. Perhaps the newspapers had been inspired by the true story of the Maharaja of Jaipur bringing two colossal silver urns of Ganges water for his visit in 1902 – apparently, he put little trust in the sanctity of London tap water. *The Times*, 22 May 1902, p. 4.
18 As to whom: MKG's biographer says it was Chaplin's idea, while Chaplin's autobiography implies the opposite. Fischer, *Life of Mahatma Gandhi*, p. 307; Chaplin, *My Autobiography*, p. 368. Lester attributes it to 'Mr. Charlie Chaplin's friend'. Lester, *Entertaining Gandhi*, p. 71.
19 Chaplin, *My Autobiography*, p. 367.
20 Lester, *Entertaining Gandhi*, pp. 79–80.
21 Willingdon to King George V, 15 November 1931. Cited in Chopra et al., *Secret Papers from the British Royal Archives*, p. 298.
22 Sir Charles Wigram to Lord Willingdon, 2 December 1931. Cited in Rose, *King George V*, p. 353.
23 King George V and MKG cited in ibid, p. 353. See also Lord Templewood in 'Gandhi' by Francis Watson & Maurice Brown, radio programme, episode 3 ('Gandhi in England'), 18 November 1956. CSAS: Benthall Papers, Box 2, file 2.
24 Windsor, *A King's Story*, p. 245.
25 Nehru, *An Autobiography*, p. 293.
26 Muggeridge, *The Thirties*, p. 75. See also *The Times*, 29 December 1931, p. 8.
27 The second to last Viceroy, Lord Wavell, later wrote: 'I wonder if we shall ever have any chance of a solution till the three intransigent, obstinate, uncompromising

principals are out of the way: Gandhi (just on 75), Jinnah (68), Winston (nearing 70).' Wavell, *The Viceroy's Journal*, 11 July 1944, p. 79.

28 Cited in French, *Liberty or Death*, p. 170.

29 Lord Randolph Churchill cited in WSC's speech at the Round Table Conference, Cannon St, City of London, 12 December 1930. Churchill, *India*, p. 40. WSC cited his father's words again in the House of Commons on 12 December 1946.

30 CRA cited in Williams, *A Prime Minister Remembers*, p. 205.

31 Jinnah, *My Brother*, p. 33.

32 Bourke-White, *Portrait of Myself*, p. 281.

33 George E. Jones, in the *New York Times*. Cited in Fischer, *Life of Mahatma Gandhi*, p. 425. See also Jones, *Tumult in India*, p. 124.

34 MAJ to Durga Das in 1920, cited in Ahmed, *Jinnah, Pakistan and Islamic Identity*, p. 62.

35 Iqbal and MAJ cited in ibid, pp. 76–7.

36 Fischer, *Life of Mahatma Gandhi*, p. 426; Bourke-White, *Portrait of Myself*, p. 281; Ahmed, *Jinnah, Pakistan and Islamic Identity*, pp. 23, 201 has a selection of quotes about MAJ's supposed penchant for ham sandwiches. There is no credible evidence for this.

37 Ahmed, *Jinnah, Pakistan and Islamic Identity*, p. 87.

38 Ibid, pp. 88, 178.

39 Before her marriage, Ruttie wrote to Padmaja as 'my dear lotus-maiden' – Padmaja means 'born from the lotus' in Sanskrit – in letters full of girlish endearments. 'Your letter gave me exquisite pleasure,' she wrote in 1916. 'My conflicting emotions make me suffer more than anything. I suppose they do you too!' A week later, she assured Padmaja that 'your sweet emotions shall be my own secret.' She also wrote her poems: 'Love came to me once in flowerlike sweetness, & I breathed it's [sic] fragrance till it sickened & satiated.' Ruttie Petit to Padmaja Naidu, 18 May 1916, 4 July 1916, 12 July 1916, 27 January 1917. NML: Papers of Padmaja Naidu, correspondence with Ruttie Jinnah.

40 Ahmed, *Jinnah, Pakistan and Islamic Identity*, p. 15.

41 Cited in French, *Liberty or Death*, p. 88.

42 MAJ cited in Fischer, *Life of Mahatma Gandhi*, p. 427.

43 JN and MAJ cited in 'In memory of Jinnah', *Economist*, 17 September 1949, p. 618.

44 See also Grigg, *Myths About the Approach to Indian Independence*, pp. 7–8. MAJ and Motilal Nehru enjoyed a cordial friendship, and MAJ continued to believe in a united India until the late 1930s.

45 MKG in 1920, cited in Fischer, *Mahatma Gandhi*, p. 362.

46 Nehru, *An Autobiography*, p. 370.

47 Pandit, *The Scope of Happiness*, p. 41.

48 Nehru, *An Autobiography*, p. 370.

49 Ambedkar, *Gandhi and Gandhism*, p. 25.

50 Ibid, p. 83; Dutt, *Gandhi, Nehru and the Challenge*, p. 20. Dutt points out that large numbers of Untouchables were converting to Buddhism or Sikhism at this point.

51 Willingdon to King George V, 18 May 1933. Chopra et al., *Secret Papers from the British Royal Archives*, p. 311.

52 Ambedkar, *Gandhi and Gandhism*, pp. 72–3.

53 Ambedkar went on to greatness: he would one day write free India's constitution, and ensured that the Gandhians on his committee were overruled. He married a Brahmin woman and eventually converted to Buddhism.

54 Rajendra Prasad, *Devastated Bihar* (Bihar Central Relief Committee, Patna, 1934), p. 6.
55 Fischer, *Life of Mahatma Gandhi*, p. 350; C.F. Andrews, *The Indian Earthquake* (George Allen & Unwin, London, 1935), pp. 68–72.
56 Nehru, *An Autobiography*, p. 490; see also Brecher, *Nehru*, pp. 199–200.
57 Tagore cited in C.F. Andrews, *The Indian Earthquake* (George Allen & Unwin, London, 1935), p. 73; Fischer, *Life of Mahatma Gandhi*, pp. 350–1.
58 Gandhi, *Daughter of Midnight*, p. 261; Fischer, *Life of Mahatma Gandhi*, p. 231; Koestler, *The Lotus and the Robot*, p. 144.
59 Morton, *The Women in Gandhi's Life*, pp. 214–18.
60 Nehru, *An Autobiography*, pp. 566–7.
61 Kamala Nehru cited in ibid, p. 567.
62 JN, *Prison Diary*, 1 February 1935. *SWJN* (1), vol 6, p. 312.
63 Kalhan, *Kamala Nehru*, pp. 56–7.
64 JN to Vijaya Lakshmi Pandit, 10 September 1935, in Nehru, *Before Freedom*, p. 160.
65 JN to Vijaya Lakshmi Pandit, in ibid, p. 173.
66 Gandhi, *Letters to a Friend*, p. 14.
67 Nehru, *The Discovery of India*, p. 23.
68 Ibid, pp. 31–2.
69 Adams & Whitehead, *The Dynasty*, p. 94; Frank, *Indira* p. 74.
70 Hutheesing, *We Nehrus*, pp. 86–7.
71 Adams & Whitehead, *The Dynasty*, pp. 97–8; Frank, *Indira*, pp. 63–4, 93–5.
72 Sahgal, 'The Making of Mrs. Gandhi', *South Asian Review*, vol. 8, no 3 (April 1975), p. 196.
73 Gandhi with an 'i' means 'grocer', and is commonly found in Gujarati Hindus of the Modh Bania caste, such as MKG. The Parsi surname has a different root and is usually spelt Gandhy or Ghandy. Feroze's sister, Tehmina Kershasp Gandhy, continued to use the original spelling. Ali, *Private Face of a Public Person*, p. 35, note 11.
74 *People*, 29 May 1932, p. 10.
75 Morgan, *Edwina Mountbatten*, p. 225.
76 Hough, *Edwina*, p. 125.
77 Norman Birkett cited in Hough, *Edwina*, p. 126.
78 Ibid, p. 127. Robeson did have a serious affair with a white English actress called Yolande Jackson.
79 Holman, 'Lady Mountbatten's Story', part 2; Hough, *Edwina*, pp. 120–1.
80 Collins & Lapierre, *Mountbatten and the Partition of India*, p. 7.
81 Unnamed source cited in Hough, *Edwina*, p. 122.
82 DM cited in Morgan, *Edwina Mountbatten*, p. 299.
83 Edward, *Letters from a Prince*, 18 April 1920, p. 346. See also his letters of 20 October 1919, p. 263; and 11 April 1920, p. 340.
84 Anon, *Mountbatten*, p. 122.
85 Noël Coward to DM, 19 November 1936. MP: MB1/A48.
86 Hough, *Edwina*, p. 133.
87 Smith, *Fifty Years with Mountbatten*, pp. 53–4.
88 Prince Albert, Duke of York, cited in James Brough, *Margaret: The Tragic Princess* (W. H. Allen, London, 1978), p. 64.
89 Pandit, *The Scope of Happiness*, p. 150.
90 Hough, *Edwina*, p. 133.
91 DM to King George VI, 11 December 1936. Cited in Ziegler, *Mountbatten*, p. 95.
92 MAJ cited in Jalal, *The Sole Spokesman*, p. 22.

93 Moon, *Divide and Quit*, pp. 13–15.
94 Margaret Bondfield, British Minister of Labour from 1929–31, was the first.
95 Pandit, *The Scope of Happiness*, p. 156.
96 See Gilmartin, *Empire and Islam*, pp. 52–62.
97 Wolpert, *A New History of India*, pp. 317–8; Ahmed, *Jinnah, Pakistan and Islamic Identity*, p. 58.
98 MAJ cited in Jalal, *The Sole Spokesman*, p. 45.
99 JN to Krishna Hutheesing, 27 October 1933. Nehru, *Nehru's Letters to His Sister*, p. 34.
100 Hutheesing, *We Nehrus*, p. 83. See also Vijaya Lakshmi Pandit, 'The Family Bond', in Zakaria (ed.), *A Study of Nehru*, p. 126.
101 Nehru, *Autobiography*, p. 204.
102 *SWJN* (1), vol 8, pp. 520–3.
103 Getz, *Subhas Chandra Bose*, pp. 50–1.

7. POWER WITHOUT RESPONSIBILITY

1 Fischer, *Life of Mahatma Gandhi*, p. 428.
2 Nehru, *The Discovery of India*, p. 403.
3 Kendall, *India and the British*, p. 329.
4 MKG cited in *The Times*, 4 July 1940, p. 3; CWMG, vol 72, p. 230. See also CWMG, vol 72, p. 188.
5 MKG cited in Fischer, *Life of Mahatma Gandhi*, p. 374.
6 MKG, 9 September 1938, CWMG, vol 74, p. 309.
7 CWMG, vol 72, p. 70; see also p. 100.
8 MKG, 22 June 1940. CWMG vol 78, p. 344. He expressed hope that the Germans would exercise 'discrimination' in how much they honoured Hitler.
9 MKG cited in Fischer, *Life of Mahatma Gandhi*, p. 376. The more generally accepted figure for Jewish deaths in the Holocaust is six million.
10 High Commissioner for South Africa to the Dominions Office, 26 May 1942. CP: CHAR 20/75.
11 JN cited in Gordon, *Brothers Against the Raj*, p. 477. See also Chaudhuri, *Thy Hand Great Anarch!*, p. 702.
12 Linlithgow cited in Jalal, *The Sole Spokesman*, p. 48.
13 Moon, *Divide and Quit*, p. 25; see also French, *Liberty or Death*, p. 133.
14 MAJ cited in Menon, *The Transfer of Power*, p. 71; MKG cited in Ahmed, *Jinnah, Pakistan and Islamic Identity*, p. 81.
15 WSC cited in Thorne, *Allies of a Kind*, p. 62.
16 Moon, *Divide and Quit*, p. 21; French, *Liberty or Death*, p. 124. See also Jalal, *The Sole Spokesman*, especially pp. 58–60.
17 Tara Singh cited in Hamid, *Disastrous Twilight*, p. 7.
18 Brown, *Nehru*, pp. 144, 147.
19 Ibid, p. 154.
20 DM to Prince Louis of Hesse, 10 May 1937. Cited in Ziegler, *Mountbatten*, p. 102.
21 Smith, *Fifty Years with Mountbatten*, p. 58.
22 Ziegler, *Mountbatten*, p. 126.
23 Read & Fisher, *The Proudest Day*, p. 413; Ziegler, *Mountbatten*, p. 127.
24 Ziegler, *Mountbatten*, pp. 128–9.
25 DM cited in Murphy, *Last Viceroy*, p. 98; see also Roberts, *Eminent Churchillians*, p. 61; Read & Fisher, *The Proudest Day*, pp. 413–4; Ziegler, *Mountbatten*, pp. 130–1.

26 Ziegler, *Mountbatten*, p. 138.
27 Healey, *The Time of My Life*, p. 259.
28 Ziegler, *Mountbatten*, p. 143.
29 DM to Patricia Mountbatten, 10 June 1941. Cited in Ziegler, *Mountbatten*, p. 144.
30 Heald, *The Duke*, p. 66. DM tactfully remembered Philip's exclamation as being 'Your face is absolutely brown and your eyes are bright red.' Terraine, *The Life and Times of Lord Mountbatten*, p. 79.
31 Coward, *Diaries*, 27 May 1941, p. 6.
32 Ibid, 3 July 1941, p. 7.
33 Ibid, 22 July 1941, p. 9.
34 Noël Coward to DM, 17 September 1941. MP: MB1/A48.
35 Lady Pamela Hicks, 'Mountbatten', *Secret History*.
36 Coward, *Diaries*, 22 December 1941, pp. 14–15.
37 Lord Attenborough, in 'Mountbatten', *Secret History*, Channel 4 Television.
38 Ronald Neame in 'The Carlton Film Collection: A Profile of *In Which We Serve*'.
39 Coward, *Diaries*, 27 October 1942, p. 19.
40 Noël Coward to DM, 2 November 1942. MP: MB1/A48.
41 Coward, *Diaries*, 9 November 1942, p. 19; see also 31 December 1943, p. 20.
42 Hough, *Edwina*, p. 144.
43 Myrtle Tuckwell cited in ibid, p. 152.
44 Roberts, *Eminent Churchillians*, p. 59.
45 Channon, *Chips*, 25 February 1942, p. 323.
46 Hough, *Edwina*, p. 160.
47 Anon, *Mountbatten*, p. 136; Terraine, *The Life and Times of Lord Mountbatten*, p. 83; see also Roberts, *Eminent Churchillians*, p. 63.
48 Ziegler, *Mountbatten*, pp. 168–9. There are signs that WSC nearly pushed his pet even further. Admiral Cunningham found the First Sea Lord, Sir Dudley Pound, having conniptions after WSC had threatened to retire him and replace him with DM. 'Naturally I told him to glue himself to his chair,' Cunningham said. General Ismay thought WSC was probably joking. He may have been, but it was becoming harder and harder to tell. Ibid, p. 175.
49 Read & Fisher, *The Proudest Day*, p. 415; Ziegler, *Mountbatten*, p. 187.
50 Eisenhower and Ismay cited in Ziegler, *Mountbatten*, pp. 180–1.
51 Ibid, pp. 187–9. Lieutenant–General William Anderson, personal assistant to one of the two Canadian Generals in charge of the Dieppe troops, remembered: 'The British were fighting all over the world. The Canadian army had done bugger-all. We were still just training and training. The pressure was on that we had to get into action!' Anderson cited in Whitaker & Whitaker, *Dieppe*, p. 97.
52 Whitaker & Whitaker, *Dieppe*, pp. 134–5.
53 Villa, *Unauthorized Action*, pp. 13, 30.
54 DM speaking to BBC Television, 1972. Cited in ibid, p. 41.
55 See accounts of Captain Denis Whitaker, Corporal John Williamson, Major Jim Green, Lieutenant Dan Doheny, Private Ron Beal and others, Whitaker & Whitaker, *Dieppe*, pp. 242–71; Villa, *Unauthorized Action*, pp. 14–15, 24.
56 Whitaker & Whitaker, *Dieppe*, p. xii.
57 Ziegler, *Mountbatten*, pp. 162–4.
58 Whitaker & Whitaker, *Dieppe*, pp. 15–16.
59 Ibid, p. 201.
60 Ibid, p. 7.
61 In the event, the Germans had another warning, too. Part of a flotilla carrying

commando raiders ran into a German naval convoy at 3.45a.m., an hour and a half before the frontal assault began – meaning the coastal ports were all alerted to the Allied fleet's presence in good time. Ibid, p. 235. See also TNA: DEFE 2/546, Appendix IV. Cited in ibid, p. 154.

62 Admiral Baillie-Grohman, on reading the post-action report, commented on 14 September 1942 that it should have been titled 'Lessons Learned By Captain Hughes-Hallett', and noted that almost everything in there could have been learned by reading Admiralty background pamphlets on Combined Operations. Villa, *Unauthorized Action*, p. 200.

63 Wolpert, *A New History of India*, p. 335.

64 Chiefs of Staff Committee, 1 April 1942. Cited in Thorne, *Allies of a Kind*, pp. 233–4.

65 CRA cited in ibid, p. 235.

66 Sherwood, *Roosevelt & Hopkins*, p. 511; Fischer, *Life of Mahatma Gandhi*, p. 389; Thorne, *Allies of a Kind*, p. 243. Roosevelt told his son Elliott during the Casablanca conference in January 1943 that what he favoured was that 'India should be made a commonwealth at once. After a certain number of years – five, perhaps, or ten – she should be able to choose whether she wants to remain in the Empire or have complete independence.' Elliott Roosevelt, *As He Saw It* (Duell, Sloan and Pearce, New York, 1946), pp. 74–5.

67 Wolpert, *A New History of India*, p. 336. Other senior figures in Congress, including Chakravarty Rajagopalachari, urged acceptance of the Cripps plan. Kux, *Estranged Democracies*, p. 14; Hamid, *Disastrous Twilight*, p. 7.

68 Moon, *Divide and Quit*, pp. 26–7.

69 Thorne, *Allies of a Kind*, p. 234.

70 Robert Skidelsky, *John Maynard Keynes: Fighting for Britain, 1937–1946* (Macmillan, London, 2000), pp. 341–2, 379–84.

71 Cabinet Committee, 20 December 1944 and 16 January 1945, cited in Thorne, *Allies of a Kind*, p. 642.

72 Fischer, *Life of Mahatma Gandhi*, p. 394.

8. A NEW THEATRE

1 Cited in Nehru, *The Discovery of India*, p. 454.

2 Linlithgow to WSC, 31 August 1942. CP: CHAR 20/79B, ff 103–4.

3 Nehru, *The Discovery of India*, pp. 460–4. JN himself guessed the death toll at 10,000. See also French, *Liberty or Death*, pp. 158–9.

4 Recollection of Vijaya Lakshmi Pandit, in Symonds, *In the Margins of Independence*, p. 14.

5 Ahmed, *Jinnah, Pakistan and Islamic Identity*, p. 82.

6 Ibid, p. 112.

7 Linlithgow to Leopold Amery, 31 August 1942. CP: CHAR 20/79B, ff 105–6.

8 Nehru, *The Discovery of India*, pp. 427–8.

9 MKG to Linlithgow, 31 December 1942. TNA: CAB 123/170.

10 Linlithgow cited in Fischer, *Life of Mahatma Gandhi*, p. 395.

11 MKG to Linlithgow, 29 January 1943. TNA: CAB 123/170.

12 Linlithgow to MKG, 5 February 1943. TNA: CAB 123/170.

13 MKG to Linlithgow, 7 February 1943. TNA: CAB 123/170.

14 Linlithgow to Leopold Amery, 8 February 1943. TNA: PREM 4/49/3, f 664; see also TNA: CAB 123/170.

15 Linlithgow to Leopold Amery, 6 January 1943. TNA: PREM 4/49/3.

16 Linlithgow to Leopold Amery, 12 February 1943. TNA: PREM 4/49/3, f 618.

17 WSC to Linlithgow, 11 February 1943. TNA: PREM 4/49/3, f 532.

18 Linlithgow to WSC, 15 February 1943. TNA: PREM 4/49/3, f 531.

19 Leopold Amery to Anthony Eden, 19 February 1943. TNA: PREM 4/49/3, ff 496–7.

20 Linlithgow to William Phillips, 19 February 1943. TNA: PREM 4/49/3, ff 498–9. See also Phillips, *Ventures in Diplomacy*, pp. 231–3.

21 Smuts to WSC, 25 February 1943. TNA: PREM 4/49/3, f 518.

22 WSC to Smuts, 26 February 1943. TNA: PREM 4/49/3.

23 WSC to Linlithgow, 27 February 1943. TNA: PREM 4/49/3, f 525.

24 Linlithgow to WSC, 27 February 1943. TNA: PREM 4/49/3, ff 522–3.

25 WSC to Smuts, 26 February 1943. TNA: PREM 4/49/3, f 516.

26 Nayyar, *Kasturba*, p. 65.

27 Ibid, p. 53.

28 Ibid, p. 67; Fischer, *Life of Mahatma Gandhi*, p. 422.

29 Morton, *The Women in Gandhi's Life*, p. 275; Fischer, *Life of Mahatma Gandhi*, p. 422.

30 Nayyar, *Kasturba*, pp. 70–1.

31 Morton, *The Women in Gandhi's Life*, pp. 277–8.

32 Major Desmond Morton cited in Roberts, *Eminent Churchillians*, p. 63.

33 Brooke cited in Ziegler, *Mountbatten*, pp. 197–8.

34 John Grigg, 'The Pride and the Glory', *Observer*, 2 September 1979; Ziegler, *Mountbatten*, pp. 198, 207–8. Captain Thomas Hussey, who chaired a Mulberry investigation committee, credited DM with the eventual solution of sinking ships to create a breakwater.

35 Ziegler, *Mountbatten*, p. 208.

36 DM cited in Anon, *Mountbatten*, p. 143; Dennis Holman, 'Lady Mountbatten's Story', part 3. *Woman*, 6 October 1951.

37 Ziegler, *Mountbatten*, p. 150. On one occasion at the White House, Roosevelt and DM had stayed up until 1.30 a.m., so absorbed had they been in their conversation.

38 Montgomery cited in Roberts, *Eminent Churchillians*, p. 71.

39 Brooke cited in Read & Fisher, *The Proudest Day*, p. 416.

40 Cunningham cited in Ziegler, *Mountbatten*, p. 222; Read & Fisher, *The Proudest Day*, p. 415.

41 DM to EA, August 1943. Cited in Ziegler, *Mountbatten*, p. 224. He was permitted the stripe, but not the full honours: opposition from the Chiefs of Staff, and from the Admiralty in particular, kept his ranks acting and unconfirmed.

42 DM to EA, 21 August 1943. Cited in ibid, p. 224–5; see also Morgan, *Edwina Mountbatten*, p. 323.

43 Ziegler, *Mountbatten*, p. 242.

44 Bradford, *King George VI*, pp. 483–4.

45 DM's diary, 11 September 1944, cited in Ziegler, *Mountbatten*, p. 251.

46 Anonymous member of DM's staff, cited in Hough, *Edwina*, p. 220.

47 Cannadine, *The Pleasures of the Past*, p. 62.

48 Ziegler, *Mountbatten*, pp. 260–7.

49 It is not clear whether Bose and the German woman in question, Emilie Schenkl, were married. They had a daughter, Anita, in 1942. Gordon, *Brothers Against the Raj*, pp. 446–7.

50 Getz, *Subhas Chandra Bose*, pp. 72–3.

51 Chaudhuri, *Thy Hand Great Anarch!*, pp. 783–4.

52 Browning cited in Ziegler, *Mountbatten*, p. 270.

53 Stilwell's diary, January–August 1944, cited in Thorne, *Allies of a Kind*, pp. 337, 453; Ziegler, *Mountbatten*, p. 247.

54 Anon, *Mountbatten*, pp. 152, 155.

55 Fischer, *Life of Mahatma Gandhi*, p. 474.

56 N.G. Goray to DM, 10 March 1978. MP: MB1/K148A.

57 Holman, 'Lady Mountbatten's Story', part 3.

58 EA to Bryan Hunter, 16 October 1951. MP: MB1/R231

59 DM to EA, 7 May 1945. Cited in Ziegler, *Mountbatten*, p. 306.

60 Lady Pamela Hicks in 'Mountbatten', *Secret History*, Channel 4 television.

61 DM to EA, 22 August 1944, cited in Ziegler, *Mountbatten*, p. 305.

62 EA to DM, 30 August 1944, cited in ibid. p. 306.

63 Driberg, *Ruling Passions*, p. 223.

64 DM in SEAC diary, May 1945; WSC minute, 20 May 1945, both cited in Thorne, *Allies of a Kind*, p. 611.

65 Driberg, *Ruling Passions*, p. 215.

66 EA cited in Masson, *Edwina*, p. 146.

67 Reminiscences of Major Grafton. MP: MB1/R679.

68 Paul Crook cited in Hough, *Edwina*, p. 176.

69 Cited in Hoey, *Mountbatten*, p. 76.

70 Driberg, *Ruling Passions*, p. 218.

71 Ibid, pp. 225–6.

72 DM's SEAC diary, 15 June 1945, cited in Thorne, *Allies of a Kind*, pp. 590–1.

73 Driberg, *Ruling Passions*, p. 216; Ziegler, *Mountbatten*, p. 321. DM became convinced in later life that it had been a mistake on his own part to hand Burma over to Aung San too quickly.

74 DM cited in Roberts, *Eminent Churchillians*, p. 76.

75 Driberg, *Ruling Passions*, p. 226.

9. NOW OR NEVER

1 Told to the author by Nayantara Sahgal, 8 April 2006. See also Healey, *The Time of My Life*, p. 259.

2 Cited in *The Times*, 20 September 1945, p. 4.

3 Keynes in Robert Skidelsky, *John Maynard Keynes: Fighting for Britain, 1937–1946* (Macmillan, London, 2000), p. 403. For expenditure on empire (£2 billion from 1942–44), see French, *Liberty or Death*, pp. 196–7.

4 CRA to King George VI, 8 March 1947. RA: PS/GVI/C 337/07.

5 WSC cited in M.S. Venkataramani, *Bengal Famine of 1943: The American Response*. (Vikas Publishing House, Delhi, 1973), p. 8.

6 Ibid, p. 4.

7 Famine Inquiry Commission, *Report on Bengal* (1944), p. 10; Sen, *Poverty and Famines*, pp. 65, 75–8.

8 Famine Inquiry Commission, *Report on Bengal* (1944), pp. 1–2.

9 K.S. Fitch, *A Medical History of the Bengal Famine, 1943–44* (Government of India Press, Calcutta, 1947), pp. 6–28.

10 Pandit, *The Scope of Happiness*, pp. 203–4.

11 Famine Inquiry Commission, *Report on Bengal* (1944), p. 104.

12 Among the guilty men were the Muslim League politicians Huseyn Shaheed Suhrawardy and Khwaja Nazimuddin, the latter then Premier of Bengal. Their involvement did little damage to their careers and both would serve as Prime Ministers of Pakistan in the 1950s.

13 Wavell, *Viceroy's Journal*, 5 July 1944, p. 78.

14 The India Secretary, Leo Amery, wrote to WSC: '. . . once it becomes known that no supplies are coming from outside the machinery of the Governments [sic] of India will be quite uncapable [sic] of preventing food going underground everywhere and famine conditions spreading with disastrous rapidity all over India. The result may well be fatal for the whole prosecution of the war, and that not only from the point of view of India as a base for further operations. I don't think you have any idea of how deeply public feeling in this country has already been stirred against the Government over the Bengal Famine, or what damage it has done to us in American eyes. It is the worst blow we have had to our name as an Empire in our lifetime. We simply cannot afford a repetition of it and on an even larger scale. Nothing after that would avail to keep India in the Empire.' Leo Amery to WSC, 17 February 1944. LAP: AMEL 2/2/4, file 1/4.

15 Hamid, *Disastrous Twilight*, pp. 23–6; Report on the Royal Indian Navy Mutiny, AP: MS Attlee dep. 32, ff 285–9.

16 Moon, *Divide and Quit*, pp. 62, 80.

17 Hutheesing, *We Nehrus*, p. 182.

18 *Malaya Tribune*, 19 March 1946.

19 F.V. Duckworth, Report on Visit of Pandit Jawaharlal Nehru to Malaya, 18–26 March 1946. TNA: CO 717/149/8.

20 Hutheesing, *We Nehrus*, p. 182; Hough, *Edwina*, p. 180; Ziegler, *Mountbatten*, p. 327; Seton, *Panditji*, p. 120.

21 L.F. Pendred, Director of Intelligence for SACSEA, report on Nehru's visit to Malaya. TNA: CO 717/149/8.

22 Ibid.

23 Campbell-Johnson, *Mission with Mountbatten*, p. 30.

24 Private collection of the Mountbatten Family.

25 Kux, *The United States and Pakistan*, pp. 6, 8. Clare Boothe Luce, the wife of *Time*'s publisher Henry Luce, was a close friend of JN's.

26 Ahmed, *Jinnah, Pakistan and Islamic Identity*, p. 114; Chaudhuri, *Thy Hand Great Anarch!*, p. 824.

27 See Khilnani, *The Idea of India*, pp. 161–3; Moon, *Divide and Quit*, pp. 50–1. In February 1947, Harold Macmillan visited MAJ in Karachi, and asked him why he had accepted the plan. MAJ replied that he had only done so under pressure and that it had been a great personal risk. 'But after all, you cannot argue for ever. We argued for weeks and months. Whether there can be a united India is a matter of argument or opinion. Finally I agreed to test it in practice.' MAJ cited in report of Harold Macmillan, 17 February 1947. CP: CHUR 2/43A. In 1997, the former MP Woodrow Wyatt, who had been on the Cabinet Mission, claimed that he had persuaded MAJ to accept the plan as 'the first step on the road' to Pakistan. Woodrow Wyatt, 'Even His Fasts Were a Fraud', *Spectator*, 9 August 1997, p. 15.

28 Sir Francis Fearon Turnbull, *Diary*, 19 May 1946. CP: MISC 51.

29 Lord Wavell cited in French, *Liberty or Death*, p. 245.

30 Sir Francis Fearon Turnbull, *Diary*, 24 May 1946. CP: MISC 51.

31 Eugénie Wavell to EA, 24 July 1946. MP: MB1/Q128.

32 Moon, *Divide and Quit*, pp. 52–5.

33 MAJ cited in Bourke-White, *Portrait of Myself*, p. 283. See also Jalal, *The Sole Spokesman*, p. 216.

34 Chaudhuri, *Thy Hand Great Anarch!*, p. 811.

35 Stephens, *Pakistan*, p. 105; Judd, *The Lion and the Tiger*, p. 177; Hutheesing, *We Nehrus*, pp. 186–7; French, *Liberty or Death*, p. 252.

36 Bourke-White, *Portrait of Myself*, p. 283.

37 Hutheesing, *We Nehrus*, p. 187.

38 Fischer, *Life of Mahatma Gandhi*, p. 476; Hutheesing, *We Nehrus*, p. 189.

39 MKG cited in Fischer, *Life of Mahatma Gandhi*, pp. 469–70.

40 Koestler, *The Lotus and the Robot*, pp. 149–50. MKG had previously caused controversy by receiving daily massages from young women and bathing with them. He claimed to keep his eyes closed during the latter. Kumar, *Brahmacharya*, p. 6.

41 Mehta, *Mahatma Gandhi and his Apostles*, pp. 201, 203. MKG's relationship with Manu Gandhi was protracted and intense, with a tone that it is difficult for those less spiritually perfect than MKG to hear as anything but romantic. It has been discussed at length in Kumar, *Brahmacharya*, pp. 315–62.

42 Bose, *My Days with Gandhi*, pp. 95–104.

43 Ibid, p. 169.

44 MKG cited in Erikson, *Gandhi's Truth*, p. 404.

45 WSC cited in Gilbert, *Never Despair*, p. 233.

46 Monckton to WSC, 18 May 1946. CP: CHUR 2/42A ff 59–60.

47 WSC to Clementine Churchill, 1 February 1945, cited in Gilbert, *Road to Victory*, p. 1166.

48 MAJ did, however, lobby WSC against proposals put forward by Liberal leader Sir Tej Bahadur Sapru for a united India, on the grounds that it would disappoint Muslims 'with most disastrous consequences, especially in regard to the war effort'. MAJ to WSC, repeated in WSC to Franklin D. Roosevelt, 4 March 1942. CP: CHAR 20/71A.

49 The Treason Act 1351, which is still in force, says among other things that treason occurs 'if a man do levy war against our lord the King in his realm, or be adherent to the King's enemies in his realm, giving to them aid and comfort in the realm, or elsewhere, and thereof be probably attainted of open deed by the people of their condition'.

50 During this period, WSC was also corresponding with the Untouchable leader, B.R. Ambedkar – apparently looking to throw in the Conservative Party's lot with any indigenous Indian organization that could help stall plans for independence. There is an extensive selection of this correspondence in CP: CHUR 2/42, and CHUR 2/42B. WSC received Ambedkar at Chartwell at the end of October 1946. CP: CHUR 2/42B/266. MAJ followed WSC's lead: in November and December 1946, headlines in *Dawn* announced that 'Qaed-e-Asam and Muslim League Have Always Befriended the Downtrodden' and articles proclaimed proudly that 'The Muslim League stands for the rights of all weak [i.e. oppressed] communities! In reaching an agreement with the Government or any other power, we will make every sacrifice necessary to obtain. . . every right for the Muslims, the Adivasis and the Untouchables!' See Pandey, *Remembering Partition*, p. 28.

51 WSC to MAJ, 3 August 1946. CP: CHUR 2/42B, ff 252–3.

52 The Muslim League's Liaquat Ali Khan, and the Sikh leader Baldev Singh, also came to London.

53 King George VI to CRA, 8 December 1946. Cited in Bradford, *George VI*, pp. 521–2.

54 Sir Eric Miéville to DM, 11 April 1947. *ToP*, vol X, p. 198.

55 CP: CHUR 2/42B/350.

56 QP: IOR Pos 10762. Also CP: CHUR 2/42B/374. MAJ also corresponded with Sir John Simon, who informed him that Lords Salisbury, Cranborne, Altrincham, Croft, Cherwell and Rankeillour would be interested in his cause. QP, as above.

57 M. Eleanor Herrington, 'American Reaction to Recent Political Events in India', *Asiatic Review*, vol xliv, no 158 (April 1948), pp. 178–9.

58 JN had met Robeson in London in 1938, six years after the latter's supposed affair with EA. Marie Seton, *Paul Robeson* (Dennis Dobson, London, 1958), p. 115. JN's sister Nan Pandit was also close friends with the Robesons. Pandit, *The Scope of Happiness*, pp. 254–5.

59 Sahgal, *Prison and Chocolate Cake*, p. 131.

60 Johnson to Roosevelt and Hull, 11 April 1942, cited in Kux, *Estranged Democracies*, p. 17.

61 Pandit, *The Scope of Happiness*, p. 227.

62 Cited in Kux, *Estranged Democracies*, p. 37; see also pp. 47–8.

63 CRA to Bevin, 25 March 1946. TNA: FO 800/470, f 30.

64 Kux, *Estranged Democracies*, p. 52.

65 French, *Liberty or Death*, p. 254.

66 Leopold Amery, *Diaries*, 21 November 1946. LAP: AMEL 7/40.

67 MAJ to CRA and WSC 6 July 1946. QP: IOR Pos 10762.

68 CRA cited in Williams, *A Prime Minister Remembers*, p. 208.

69 Ibid, p. 209. Rumours of a viceroyalty had occasionally attached themselves to DM before – Sir Mirza Ismail, at one time Prime Minister to the Nizam of Hyderabad, claimed to have suggested it to him in the early- to mid-1940s, and CRA had been considering him since January. Sir Mirza Ismail to Walter Monckton, 10 March 1947. WMP: 29, ff 88–9; French, *Liberty or Death*, p. 276.

70 CRA cited in Wheeler-Bennett, *Friends, Enemies and Sovereigns*, p. 149.

71 Marion Crawford, *The Little Princesses* (Cassell & Co, London, 1950), pp. 59–60.

72 Channon, *Chips*, 21 January 1941, p. 287.

73 DM to Sir Miles Lampson, cited in Pimlott, *The Queen*, p. 96.

74 King George VI to DM, 10 August 1944. Cited in Bradford, *George VI*, p. 557; Ziegler, *Mountbatten*, p. 308.

75 Pimlott, *The Queen*, pp. 97–100.

76 Philip to DM, cited in Bradford, *George VI*, p. 557; Ziegler, *Mountbatten*, p. 308.

77 CRA cited in Williams, *A Prime Minister Remembers*, p. 209.

78 DM tells an extremely colourful version of this story in Collins & Lapierre, *Mountbatten and the Partition of India*, pp. 10–11.

79 CRA cited in Williams, *A Prime Minister Remembers*, p. 210.

80 He had originally been offered a mere barony – actually a step down in precedence from being the son of a marquess, which he already was. Moreover, the fact that it was junior to the viscountcies offered to A.V. Alexander and Bernard Montgomery was received as an open snub. He was upgraded to a viscount on protesting. Ziegler, *Mountbatten*, p. 310.

81 Anonymous friend cited in Hough, *Edwina*, p. 183. A letter from DM to Jo Hollis, written on 16 December 1946, confirms this view: DM asks that his demotion be given the least possible publicity, and writes of the Chiefs of Staff that 'I hope they will be gracious enough to allow me to retain the actual parchments on which the Commissions are written as souvenirs.' TNA: CAB 127/25.

82 DM told Larry Collins and Dominique Lapierre in the 1970s that he had 'always had a very curious, subconscious desire to be Viceroy'. DM cited in Collins & Lapierre, *Mountbatten and the Partition of India*, p. 7. Henry Hodson added more points to the list of DM's objections, including the canard that DM was granted plenipotentiary powers by CRA, but these are unsupported by the documentary evidence. Hodson, *The Great Divide*, p. 201.

83 DM to CRA, 20 December 1946. MP: MB1/E5.

84 DM to CRA, 3 January 1947. MP: MB1/D246.

85 DM to CRA, 7 January 1947. MP: MB1/D246. DM had mentioned in passing the issue of 'a definite and specified date' on 3 January, but the letter of 7 January contained his first open demand. See also MP: MB1/E5.

86 CRA to Lascelles, 18 February 1947. TNA: PREM 8/558.

87 CRA cited in Williams, *A Prime Minister Remembers*, p. 208.

88 CRA to DM, 9 January 1947. MP: MB1/E5.

89 DM to CRA, 12 January 1947. MP: MB1/E5.

90 CRA to DM, 16 January 1947. MP: MB1/E5.

91 DM to Sir Stafford Cripps, 26 January 1947. MP: MB1/E5.

92 Report of Sir Frederick Burrows, in Wavell to Secretary of State for India, 16 February 1947. MP: MB1/D246.

93 Wavell to India Office, 17 February 1947. MP: MB1/D246.

94 CRA to Sir Alan Lascelles, 18 February 1947. TNA: PREM 8/558.

95 CRA to Sir Alan Lascelles, 22 February 1947. TNA: PREM 8/558.

96 CRA to DM, March 1947 [no day dated]. MP: MB1/D254; Ziegler, *Mountbatten*, pp. 358–9.

97 MP: MB1/E37, MB1/E38.

98 Admiral Sir Reginald Plunkett-Ernle-Erle-Drax to DM, 22 February 1947. MP: MB1/E37.

99 DM to Admiral Sir Reginald Plunkett-Ernle-Erle-Drax, 1 March 1947. MP: MB1/E37.

100 At the beginning of March 1947 JN had been sent an unsigned and undated official memorandum from India to London, saying that these files were being removed or destroyed. JN wrote to Wavell on 6 March. 'I do not know how far this information is correct. I hope it is not so because these records must contain information of great historical value and they should not be destroyed or transferred to other hands. May I beg of you to inquire into this matter and to stop any such vandalism of valuable material?' JN to Wavell, 6 March 1947. *SWJN* (2), vol 2, p. 275. Wavell replied on 15 March that the records in question possessed no historical interest. Anything else was being transferred to the UK High Commission in India. JN replied to him that he would like eminent historians to be put in charge of such an effort, and wondered why the UK High Commission should have any right to them. Wavell left soon after and never replied. See *SWJN* (2), vol 2, pp. 276, 282–6; *ToP*, vol X, p. 8.

101 Brendan Bracken cited in Roberts, *Eminent Churchillians*, pp. 80–1.

102 DM's valet, Charles Smith, alleged that JN had recommended DM for the post of Viceroy (Smith, *Fifty Years with Mountbatten*, p. 80), and Stanley Wolpert claimed that JN's friend Krishna Menon 'tirelessly urged' CRA to appoint DM (Wolpert, *Shameful Flight*, p. 129). Neither AP nor TNA offers any evidence to back this up.

103 Statement dated 22 February 1947. *SWJN* (2), vol 2, p. 44.

104 JN to Menon, 27 February 1947. *SWJN* (2), vol 2, p. 55.

105 Ibid, pp. 57–8. JN seemed to warm to Ismay: on 5 August 1947, he wrote to DM about the personal staff that the latter would retain as Governor General. He mentioned specifically that 'I am glad that Lord Ismay will be staying on.' JN to DM, 5 August 1947. *SWJN* (2), vol 3, p. 39. Krishna Menon had indeed met DM already, through EA. EA and Krishna had been friends even before the war, when the former was a borough councillor for St Pancras and an editor at Penguin Books. Hough, *Edwina*, p. 178.

106 Roberts, *Eminent Churchillians*, p. 69.

107 DM's own claim that he had been given 'plenipotentiary powers' by CRA is neither documented officially, nor borne out by subsequent events. However, previous Viceroys had not even been able to see MKG without authorization from London, and even the limited powers he had may be regarded as having allowed him more agency than his predecessors.

108 Pimlott, *The Queen*, pp. 100–1.

109 Philip cited in ibid; p. 89; Basil Boothroyd, *Philip: An Informal Biography* (Longman, London, 1971), p. 54.

110 Coward, *Diaries*, 18 March 1947, p. 83.

111 DM to Lieutenant-Commander Peter Howes, cited in Smith, *Fifty Years with Mountbatten*, p. 77. See also Ziegler, *Mountbatten*, p. 359.

II. THE END

10. OPERATION MADHOUSE

1 Woodrow Wyatt cited in Hough, *Edwina*, p. 185.

2 DM cited in ibid, p. 186.

3 EA cited in Morgan, *Edwina Mountbatten*, p. 382. EA also wrote in her diary that she would rather be doing relief work in Europe with Marjorie Brecknock. Ibid, pp. 383–4.

4 Collins & Lapierre, *Freedom at Midnight*, pp. 76–7.

5 Murphy, *Last Viceroy*, p. 243.

6 Collins & Lapierre, *Freedom at Midnight*, pp. 87–8; Ziegler, *Mountbatten*, p. 353. The novelist Salman Rushdie listed DM's attributes as being 'his inexorable ticktock, his soldier's knife that could cut subcontinents in three, and his wife who ate chicken breasts secretly behind a locked lavatory door.' Salman Rushdie, *Midnight's Children* (Jonathan Cape, London, 1981), p. 65. Collins & Lapierre claim EA had two terriers, but most other sources and photographs suggest that EA took only one to India.

7 Collins & Lapierre, *Freedom at Midnight*, pp. 86–7; see also DM cited in Collins & Lapierre, *Mountbatten and the Partition of India*, p. 18. Wavell, *Viceroy's Journal*, 22 March 1947, p. 432 gives a less dramatic account of this meeting.

8 Close, *Attlee, Wavell, Mountbatten*, p. 10, agrees.

9 Wavell, *Viceroy's Journal*, 2 December 1946, p. 389. During the Cabinet Mission the previous year, Lord Pethick-Lawrence had suggested the same scheme to CRA as the only serious option if open rebellion against British rule broke out. AP: MS Attlee dep. 37, ff 49–50. There is one piece of supposedly contemporary evidence to support the 'Madhouse' name: Shahid Hamid's diary from 26 June 1947 notes, 'Orders have been issued that India Command Joint Operation instructions No. 2 "Madhouse" is to be destroyed.' Hamid, *Disastrous Twilight*, p. 193. Attention has been drawn to the unreliability of Hamid's memoir elsewhere in this book.

10 CRA cited in Williams, *A Prime Minister Remembers*, p. 209.

11 Corfield, *The Princely India I Knew*, pp. 152–3.

12 CRA to King George VI, 15 March 1947. RA: PS/GVI/C 337/08.

13 Pethick-Lawrence to DM, 12 April 1947. *ToP*, vol X, p. 219.

14 Campbell-Johnson, *Mission with Mountbatten*, 22 March 1947, pp. 39–40.

15 British Pathé News Archive, film 2150.10. See also Hamid, *Disastrous Twilight*, p. 149.

16 DM cited in Collins & Lapierre, *Mountbatten and the Partition of India*, pp. 24–5; see also Roberts, *Eminent Churchillians*, p. 81.

17 DM cited in *The Times*, 25 March 1947, p. 4; see also Mountbatten, *Time Only to Look Forward*, p. 3.

18 Holman, 'Lady Mountbatten's Story', part 5; Campbell-Johnson, *Mission with Mountbatten*, 24 March 1947, p. 42.

19 Moon, *Divide and Quit*, pp. 77–9, 288. The official death toll for March was 2049, but Moon called this a significant underestimate. See also T.W. Rees, *Report of the Punjab Boundary Force*, AAS: Mss Eur F274/70.

20 W. Christie, Chief Commissioner Delhi, to A. E. Porter, Secretary to the Home Department, Government of India. 24 March 1947. NAI: Home Dept, Political Branch, F. No. 5/7/47 – Poll. (I).

21 *The Times*, 25 March 1947, p. 3.

22 W. Christie to A. E. Porter, 25 March 1947. NAI: Home Dept, Political Branch, F. No. 5/7/47 – Poll. (I).

23 *The Times*, 29 March 1947, p. 3.

24 Campbell-Johnson, *Mission with Mountbatten*, p. 41. DM wrote to both of them on the night of his arrival in India.

25 Ibid; 25 March 1947, pp. 43–4; ToP, vol X, pp. 10–11.

26 ToP, vol X, p. 17.

27 Campbell-Johnson, *Mission with Mountbatten*, 25 March 1947, p. 45; ToP, vol X, p. 91.

28 According to a famous story about Patel, in 1909 he had been in court when he was passed a telegram saying that his wife had died. Without changing his expression, he skimmed it, put it in his pocket, and continued with the case. French, *Liberty or Death*, pp. 51, 279.

29 All these quotes are from DM's notes on the meeting, 24 March 1947. SWJN (2), vol 2, p. 73; ToP, vol X, pp. 11–13.

30 *The Times*, 28 March 1947, p. 4.

31 EA to the East India Association, 13 October 1948, in *Asiatic Review*, vol xlv, no 161 (January 1949), p. 440.

32 Ibid.

33 Vijaya Lakshmi Pandit cited in Masson, *Edwina*, p. 244.

34 Hamid, *Disastrous Twilight*, p. 153. DM's official biographer, Philip Ziegler, wrote that EA's 'close relationship with Nehru did not start until the Mountbattens were on the verge of leaving India'. Ziegler, *Mountbatten*, p. 365.

35 These photographs may be seen in SWJN (2) vol 2; opposite pp. 81 and 513; *Illustrated Weekly of India*, 13 April 1947, p. 17; see also Wolpert, *Nehru*, p. 384; Hamid, *Disastrous Twilight*, p. 152.

36 EA to JN, March 1957; JN to EA, 12 March 1957, both cited in Morgan, *Edwina Mountbatten*, pp. 473–4.

37 Viceroy's Personal Report no. 1, 31 March 1947 (second draft). MP: MB1/D83. A very similar draft was finally sent on 2 April. ToP, vol X, pp. 90–4.

38 Stephens, *Pakistan*, p. 125.

39 Viceroy's notes, 31 March 1947. ToP, vol X, pp. 54–5; MP: MB1/D4.

40 Hamid, *Disastrous Twilight*, p. 156.

41 Linlithgow to Leopold Amery, 15 February 1943. TNA: PREM 4/49/3, ff 612–3; Wavell to Leopold Amery, 12 July 1944. TNA: PREM 4/49/3, f 451.

42 Unnamed Congressman cited in Wolpert, *A New History of India*, p. 348; see also Jones, *Tumult in India*, p. 79.

43 ToP, vol X, p. 69.

44 Ibid, pp. 70–1.

45 Campbell-Johnson, *Mission with Mountbatten*, p. 61; *ToP*, vol X, pp. 197–8.

46 DM, 'Reflections on Mr Jinnah 29 years later', MP: MB1/K137A.

47 See Ahmed, *Jinnah, Pakistan and Islamic Identity*, p. 127.

48 DM, 'Reflections on Mr Jinnah 29 years later'.

49 'psychopathic case': Viceroy's staff meeting, 11 April 1947. *ToP*, vol X, p. 190; and Viceroy's Personal Report no 3, in ibid, p. 300. All cited in Roberts, *Eminent Churchillians*, p. 82. DM was not the only person to describe MAJ in such terms. Sir Terence Shone, the British High Commissioner in India, wrote on 16 April 1947 that 'Jinnah appeared to be quite unbending in his insistence on Pakistan which, indeed, savoured of the psychopathic.' *ToP*, vol X, p. 279. American journalist George E. Jones was among those who described his 'repressed intensity [which] borders on the psychotic.' Jones, *Tumult in India*, p. 114.

50 'demagogue', 'reprehensible': Viceroy's Personal Report no. 4, 24 April 1947, *ToP*, vol X, p. 408; 'hysterical': Viceroy's Personal Report no. 17, 16 August 1947, *ToP*, vol XII, p. 761; 'Trotskyist': Viceroy's Personal Report no 11, 4 July 1947, *ToP*, vol XI, p. 896.

51 Viceroy's Interview no 35, 5–6 April 1946. *ToP*, vol X, p. 138.

52 Viceroy's Personal Report no 3, *ToP*, vol X, p. 299; Campbell-Johnson, *Mission with Mountbatten*, p. 58.

53 EA to Isobel Cripps, 20–27 April 1947. MP: MB1/Q19.

54 Fatimah Jinnah cited in Viceroy's Personal Report No. 5, 1 May 1947, *ToP*, vol X, p. 540.

55 MKG himself passed the reports of roasting alive to DM. MKG to DM, 7 April 1947. *ToP*, vol X, p. 146.

56 *The Times*, 7 April 1947, p. 3.

57 Ibid, 2 April 1947, p. 3.

58 Viceroy's Personal Interview no 41, 8 April 1947. *ToP*, vol X, p. 158.

59 *ToP*, vol X, pp 297–8; Campbell-Johnson, *Mission with Mountbatten*, p. 61.

60 *ToP*, vol X, pp. 212–3.

61 *ToP*, vol X, p. 405.

62 *ToP*, vol X, pp. 183–5; 320–4.

63 Viceroy's Personal Report no. 4, 24 April 1947, ibid, p. 405.

64 *ToP*, vol X, p. 398; Das, *End of the British-Indian Empire*, vol 1, p. 38.

65 EA to Isobel Cripps, 20–27 April 1947. MP: MB1/Q19.

66 *ToP*, vol X, p. 398. DM told an embellished version of this story in Collins & Lapierre, *Mountbatten and the Partition of India*, pp. 37–8.

67 Ismay cited in Campbell-Johnson, *Mission with Mountbatten*, p. 117.

68 *The Times*, 29 March 1947, p. 3.

69 *Illustrated Weekly of India*, 4 May 1947, Late News Supplement, p. 8; *The Times*, 29 April 1947, p. 4. The figure was given as 60,000 in the official 'Notes on Her Excellency's Tour of the N.W.F.P. and Punjab'; and later changed in that document to 150,000. MP: MB1/Q79. DM himself estimated 100,000, and described them as 'militant Pathans advancing on Government House'. MP: MB2/N14.

70 Collins & Lapierre, *Freedom at Midnight*, p. 146. Shahid Hamid claimed that the demonstration was organized by Caroe and had been friendly from the start, but this is contradicted by news reports of the day. Hamid, *Disastrous Twilight*, p. 168. See also *ToP*, vol X, p. 535.

71 *The Times*, 29 April 1947, p. 4.

72 Hodson, *The Great Divide*, p. 286.

11. A BARREL OF GUNPOWDER

1   *The Times*, 30 April, p. 30; *Illustrated Weekly of India*, 11 May 1947, p. 14; MP: MB1/Q79; *ToP*, vol X, p. 536.

2   Corfield, *The Princely India I Knew*, p. 151, 154.

3   Burrows cited in Viceroy's Personal Report no 5, 1 May 1947. *ToP*, vol X, p. 539.

4   CP: CHUR 2/43B, f 151.

5   MAJ cited in *The Times*, 2 May 1947, p. 4; *ToP*, vol X, p. 543.

6   Campbell-Johnson, *Mission with Mountbatten*, p. 59.

7   Viceroy's Interview no 41, 8 April 1947. *ToP*, vol X, p. 160.

8   EA to Isobel Cripps, 20–27 April 1947. MP: MB1/Q19.

9   *Illustrated Weekly of India*, 11 May 1947, p. 15.

10 EA cited in Morgan, *Edwina Mountbatten*, p. 398.

11 Viceroy's Personal Report No. 5, 1 May 1947, *ToP*, vol X, p. 537.

12 Report on visits of observation to refugee camps and hospitals. MP: MB1/Q79.

13 MP: MB1/Q79.

14 *Statesman* (daily edition), Calcutta, 2 May 1947, p. 5; Campbell-Johnson, *Mission with Mountbatten*, p. 82.

15 Seton, *Panditji*, p. 133.

16 EA to Lieutenant Colonel K.C. Packman, 1 May 1947. MP: MB1/Q78; *ToP*, vol X, p. 839.

17 MP: MB1/Q80.

18 Campbell-Johnson, *Mission with Mountbatten*, 24 March 1947, p. 43.

19 Lady Pamela Hicks, recorded by Mr B. R. Nanda, 14 October 1971, p. 5, NML: Oral History Project; MP: MB1/K202.

20 EA to Dowager Marchioness of Reading, 17 April 1947. MP: MB1/Q61.

21 Viceroy's Personal Report No. 3, 17 April 1947, *ToP*, vol X, p. 303.

22 Hough, *Edwina*, p. 187. The suggestion sometimes made that DM persuaded Congress to concede Pakistan to MAJ is misleading – both Congress and the British government had realized that they would have to concede to some extent following the Muslim League's strong showing in the elections of 1945–6. See Gopal, *Jawaharlal Nehru*, vol 1, p. 342.

23 Viceroy's Personal Report No. 5, 1 May 1947. *ToP*, vol X, p. 540.

24 *Hindustan Times* cited in Campbell-Johnson, *Mission with Mountbatten*, p. 84.

25 MP: MB1/D4.

26 MKG to Doon Campbell, 5 May 1947. Cited in Bose, *My Days with Gandhi*, p. 187.

27 Agatha Harrison to EA, 29 April 1947. MP: MB1/Q26. Harrison's emphasis.

28 DM speaking in 'Gandhi' by Francis Watson & Maurice Brown, radio programme, episode 4 ('The Last Phase'), 16 December 1956, Benthall Papers, CSAS, Box 2, file 2; Viceroy's Personal Report No, 6, 8 May 1947, *ToP*, vol X, p. 681.

29 *The Times*, 5 May 1947, p. 4.

30 Pubby, *Shimla Then and Now*, p. 63; Nigel Woodyatt, *Under Ten Viceroys* (Herbert Jenkins Ltd, London, 1922), pp. 51–2.

31 MKG cited in Pubby, *Shimla Then and Now*, p. 89.

32 Minutes of Viceroy's Fourth Staff Meeting, 28 March 1947. *ToP*, vol X, pp. 37–8.

33 *ToP*, vol X, p. 228.

34 Ibid, p. 335; for details of the Simla Conference, see Hodson, *The Great Divide*, pp. 120–9.

35 *ToP*, vol X, p. 373. 'I asked Nehru to come as my guest, as I thought he was nearing a breakdown from overwork,' DM explained to London. Viceroy's Personal Report No 7, 15 May 1947. *ToP*, vol X, p. 836.

36 JN to Indira Gandhi, 1 July 1945. Gandhi & Nehru, *Two Alone, Two Together*, p. 511. JN had been imprisoned for almost three years, his longest single internment.

37 EA cited in Morgan, *Edwina Mountbatten*, p. 399.

38 Kitchener made himself even less popular in India than he was in Britain. On the road between Simla and Mashobra, there is a long tunnel at the village of Sanjauli. Locals still tell the story about how one day Kitchener fell off his horse when riding through the tunnel, and was dragged by his stirrup. The villagers came out of their houses to watch this spectacle, but not one among them was moved to help the commander-in-chief.

39 Campbell-Johnson, *Mission with Mountbatten*, p. 88.

40 Lady Pamela Hicks, recorded by Mr B.R. Nanda, 14 October 1971, pp. 20–1.

41 DM to Sir Frederick Burrows, 9 May 1947. AAS: IOR Neg 15539, file 17; *Illustrated Weekly of India*, 11 May 1947, Late News Supplement, p. 8.

42 V.P. Menon, 8 May 1947. *SWJN* (2), vol 2, p. 116.

43 *Illustrated Weekly of India*, 11 May 1947, Late News Supplement, p. 1.

44 JN to DM, 11 May 1947. *SWJN* (2), vol 2, pp. 130–1; *ToP*, vol X, pp. 756–7. See also Gopal, *Jawaharlal Nehru*, p. 349.

45 DM referred to it as such from 12 April. See *ToP*, vol X, p. 207.

46 'A Note on the Draft Proposals', *SWJN* (2), vol 2, p. 134.

47 Ibid, p. 133.

48 DM cited in Collins & Lapierre, *Mountbatten and the Partition of India*, p. 57.

49 DM cited in Campbell-Johnson, *Mission with Mountbatten*, p. 89.

50 Minutes of the 13th miscellaneous meeting of the Viceroy, Simla, 11 May 1947. *SWJN* (2), vol 2, p. 140.

51 Close, *Attlee, Wavell, Mountbatten*, pp. 21–2; French, *Liberty or Death*, p. 301.

52 Ziegler, *Mountbatten*, p. 394.

53 Viceroy's Personal Report No, 7, 15 May 1947, *ToP*, vol X, p. 836.

54 Draft telegram from CRA to DM, 13 May 1947, in ibid, p. 806.

55 Leslie Rowan to CRA, 14 May 1947, in ibid, p. 818. See also Roberts, *Eminent Churchillians*, p. 129.

56 Ziegler, *Mountbatten*, pp. 383–4.

57 Morgan, *Edwina Mountbatten*, p. 400.

58 Azad, *India Wins Freedom*, pp. 183–4. In this extract Azad is referring to how JN was persuaded to accept partition, which he did, effectively, during the preparation of the plan in Simla.

59 Announcement cited in *The Times*, 16 May 1947, p. 6.

60 News bulletin, 22 May 1947. British Pathé News Archive, film 1185.11.

61 '. . . the Viceroy when in London reported that already at that date certain prominent Congress leaders, speaking as individuals and not on behalf of their party, had indicated in private conversation their belief that India would accept Dominion status within the Commonwealth as an ad interim measure if there could be a very early transfer of power; and that if this were effected at an early date there was good prospect that the portion of British India under Congress control would ultimately abstain from secession from the Commonwealth.' CRA to Sir Michael Adeane, 12 June 1947. RA: PS/GVI/C 280/272.

62 WSC to CRA, 21 May 1947. CP: CHUR 2/43A, f 121.

63 CRA to DM, March 1947 [no day dated]. MP: MB1/D254.

64 Campbell-Johnson, *Mission with Mountbatten*, p. 31.

65 Leo Amery to WSC, 4 June 1947. LAP: AMEL 2/2/4, file 2/4.

66 Montague Browne, *Long Sunset*, p. 114; Harold Evans, *Downing Street Diary: The Macmillan Years 1957–1963* (Hodder & Stoughton, London, 1981), pp. 24–5.

67 DM cited in Ziegler, *Mountbatten*, p. 384 and Collins & Lapierre, *Mountbatten and the Partition of India*, p. 61; WSC to CRA, 22 May 1947, CP: CHUR 2/43A, ff 116–7. DM contradicted his version of events himself in conversation with Narendra Singh Sarila. Singh Sarila, *The Shadow of the Great Game*, p. 295.

68 Leo Amery, *Diaries*, 27 May 1947. LAP: AMEL 7/41.

69 Wolpert, *Jinnah*, p. 326; Campbell-Johnson, *Mission with Mountbatten*, p. 97.

70 JN, interview to the United Press of America, Mussoorie, 24 May 1947. SWJN (2), vol 2, p. 171. See also Sir Claude Auchinleck, 'The military implication of Pakistan', 24 April 1947, cited in Hamid, *Disastrous Twilight*, p. 334.

71 Comments by MAJ, 21 May 1947. QP: IOR Pos 10762.

72 *Times of India*, 1 July 1947, p. 7.

73 EA sent her 'a little old box' of mother of pearl from London. EA to Fatima Jinnah, 31 May 1947. QP: IOR Pos 10762, reel 3. She sent similar boxes to Amrit Kaur and Sarojini Naidu. Morgan, *Edwina Mountbatten*, p. 403; MP: MB1/Q40.

12. LIGHTNING SPEED IS MUCH TOO SLOW

1   EA to Dorothy, Lady Bird, 2 June 1947. MP: MB1/Q8.

2   MKG, 1 June 1947, cited in Nanda, *In Search of Gandhi*, p. 154.

3   Campbell-Johnson, *Mission with Mountbatten*, p. 102 and plate opposite p. 97; Wolpert, *Jinnah*, p. 327.

4   Viceroy's Personal Report No. 8, 5 June 1947. ToP, vol X, p. 160.

5   Collins & Lapierre, *Mountbatten and the Partition of India*, pp. 45–6; ToP, vol XI, p. 161.

6   ToP, vol XI, p. 53.

7   Brown, *Nehru*, pp. 172–3.

8   French, *Liberty or Death*, p. 304. JN and MAJ cited in *The Times*, 4 June 1947, p. 3.

9   Mountbatten, *Time Only to Look Forward*, p. 11.

10 Leo Amery, *Diaries*, 3 June 1947. LAP: AMEL 7/41. WSC replied to the announcement in support of dominion status and paid tribute to CRA and DM.

11 Harold Nicolson, *Diaries and Letters*, ed. Nigel Nicolson (Collins, London, 1966–68) 3 June 1947, vol 3, p. 100.

12 DM cited in Collins & Lapierre, *Mountbatten and the Partition of India*, p. 49.

13 EA cited in Hough, *Edwina*, p. 186.

14 DM to the East India Association, 29 June 1948. *Asiatic Review*, vol xliv, no 160 (October 1948), p. 348.

15 Even after the announcement of 15 August, JN believed for some time that dominion status would be an interim stage, and did not grasp that the British were actually intending to leave. Gopal, *Jawaharlal Nehru*, vol 1, p. 356.

16 Govind Ballabh Pant, ToP, vol X, p. 590. Abul Kalam Azad agreed: see Azad, *India Wins Freedom*, p. 199.

17 ToP, vol X, p. 357.

18 See Sir Eric Miéville, 29 March 1947. ToP, vol X, p. 47; Ismay, Viceroy's staff meeting, 11 April 1947. ToP, vol X, p. 192; Auchinleck in Hamid, *Disastrous Twilight*, p. 182.

19 Top-secret minute, n.d. (late April 1947). ToP, vol X, p. 440.

20 Campbell-Johnson, *Mission with Mountbatten*, p. 69.

21 Morgan, *Edwina Mountbatten*, p. 409.

22 If this was among DM's intentions, it worked. In her official report on the vice-royalty, EA noted that the transfer of power had happened ten and a half months ahead of schedule, and wrote: 'I feel I shall be forgiven if I place on record my wifely pride at the developments of the past few months.' EA, report on present position in India, 24 August 1947. TNA: DO 121/69. In the words of DM's official biographer, Philip Ziegler: 'I think it was one of the main motive forces that drove him on his career, was feeling that even though he was not able to satisfy his wife, by God he could impose himself on the rest of the world, but he did have a feeling of inadequacy as far as she was concerned.' 'Mountbatten', *Secret History*, Channel 4 Television.

23 See Campbell-Johnson, *Mission with Mountbatten*, p. 109; Lord Ismay cited in ibid, p. 81.

24 Listowel to DM (draft, approved), n.d. (27 June 1947). TNA: PREM 8/550.

25 MAJ cited in Ahmed, *Jinnah, Pakistan and Islamic Identity*, p. 87; the implication that MAJ was considering resigning is intriguing, but would soon be rescinded.

26 Campbell-Johnson, *Mission with Mountbatten*, pp. 115–6; Wolpert, *Jinnah*, pp. 329–30; Andreas Augustin, *The Imperial New Delhi* (The Most Famous Hotels in the World, 2005), pp. 83–5; Ahmed, *Jinnah, Pakistan and Islamic Identity*, p. 10; *The Times*, 10 June 1947, p. 4.

27 Dennis Holman, 'Lady Mountbatten's Story', part 4. *Woman*, 13 October 1951.

28 Singh, *Heir Apparent*, p. 47; Ziegler, *Mountbatten*, p. 414.

29 DM to the East India Association, 29 June 1948. *Asiatic Review*, vol xliv, no 160 (October 1948), p. 353.

30 JN, 'A Note on Kashmir', *ToP*, vol XI, p. 448; *SWJN* (2), vol 3, p. 229. See also Hamid, *Disastrous Twilight*, pp. 187–8, 191; Corfield, *The Princely India I Knew*, p. 172; Commonwealth Relations Office memorandum on developments in Kashmir up to 31 October 1947. TNA: DO 133/68.

31 Krishna Menon to DM, 14 June 1947. MP: MB1/E104. See also Hamid, *Disastrous Twilight*, p. 274; *SWJN* (2), vol 3, pp. 273–93.

32 Anonymous letter to Anand Bhavan, received 27 June 1947. NML: AICC papers, file G-11/1946, ff 81–93.

33 Viceroy's Personal Report No 14, 25 July 1947. *ToP*, vol XII, p. 334.

34 Campbell-Johnson, *Mission with Mountbatten*, p. 124; Heward, *The Great and the Good*, p. 38.

35 *Times of India*, 3 July 1947, p. 1; *Manchester Guardian*, 5 July 1947, p. 6.

36 'I want the Muslims of the Frontier to understand that they are Muslims first and Pathans afterwards and that the province will meet a disastrous fate if it does not join the Pakistan Constituent Assembly,' MAJ said on 28 June at Delhi. He described the NWFP as economically 'deficient' and geographically a 'nonentity'. MAJ cited in *Illustrated Weekly of India*, 29 June 1947 (Late News Supplement), p. 1.

37 *Times of India*, 4 July 1947, p. 3.

38 Ibid, 22 July 1947, p. 1.

39 *Liberator*, 27 July 1947, Delhi; and Giani Kartar Singh, both cited in Pandey, *Remembering Partition*, pp. 33–4.

40 JN to DM, 22 June 1947. *SWJN* (2), vol 3, p. 179.

41 MAJ cited in Viceroy's Personal Report No. 10, 27 June 1947. *ToP*, vol XI, p. 680.

42 WSC to CRA, 1 July 1947. CP: CHUR 2/43B, f 168.

43 CRA to WSC, 4 July 1947; WSC to CRA, 14 July 1947, both in CP: CHUR 2/43B, ff 199–200, 188–9.

44 TNA: PREM 8/549, ff 26–30.

45 A further clue had come when DM presented his draft proposals for the transfer of power to MAJ on 18 May. At that stage, there had been an A version and a B version: in A, there was to be one common constitutional Governor General for the two dominions; in draft B, there was to be a separate Governor General for each dominion. MAJ underlined the word 'separate' in his copy. It was the only word on the page he highlighted. QP: IOR Pos 10762.

46 EA to Lady Brabourne, cited in Morgan, *Edwina Mountbatten*, p. 408.

47 Viceroy's Personal Report No. 11, 4 July 1947. *ToP*, vol XI, pp. 899–900.

48 TNA: PREM 8/549, ff 26–30.

49 Judd, *The Lion and the Tiger*, pp. 184–5.

50 John Grigg, 'The Pride and the Glory', *Observer*, 2 September 1979.

51 French, *Liberty or Death*, p. 316.

52 Bakhtiar cited in Ahmed, *Jinnah, Pakistan and Islamic Identity*, pp. 132–3.

53 Ibid, pp. 146–7; Syed Sharifuddin Pirzada in Merchant, *The Jinnah Anthology*, p. 70.

54 Ian Stephens, a newspaper editor who observed the situation first-hand, wrote elliptically in 1963 that 'some Leaguers had come to suspect that Lord Mountbatten, in his proposed dual role, would subconsciously or otherwise load the dice against Pakistan, because of the friendships he and his wife had formed with leading Hindus. But Mr. Jinnah seemed to be above such suspicions.' Stephens, *Pakistan*, p. 175.

55 DM to CRA, 3 July 1947. TNA: PREM 8/549, f 3. See also Ziegler, *Mountbatten*, p. 398.

56 India Office memorandum, 7 July 1947. PREM 8/549, ff 38–40.

57 TNA: PREM 8/549, ff 26–30.

58 CP: CHUR 2/43B, ff 196–7; TNA: PREM 8/559, ff 18–19. See also Campbell-Johnson, *Mission with Mountbatten*, p. 132.

59 MAJ to WSC and CRA via Lord Ismay, 9 July 1947. CP: CHUR 2/43B/171–3.

60 DM to CRA, 9 July 1947. TNA: PREM 8/549, f 5.

61 EA to Dowager Marchioness of Reading, 27 July 1947. MP: MB1/Q61. 'Morally, logically as well as personally feel it's wrong', EA wrote privately; cited in Morgan, *Edwina Mountbatten*, p. 409.

62 *Times of India*, 14 July 1947, p. 1.

63 DM to CRA, 25 July 1947. MP: MB1/E5.

64 EA to Dowager Marchioness of Reading, 27 July 1947. MP: MB1/Q61.

13. A FULL BASKET OF APPLES

1 The old Viceroy's House in which DM had proposed had been given to Delhi University in 1933. Visitors may still observe a small plaque in the registrar's office commemorating the Mountbattens' engagement.

2 EA to Dowager Marchioness of Reading, 27 July 1947. MP: MB1/Q61.; EA to the East India Association, 13 October 1948. *Asiatic Review*, vol xlv, no 161 (January 1949), p. 446; MKG to EA, 18 July 1947. MP: MB2/N41.

3 Morgan, *Edwina Mountbatten*, p. 408.

4 Frances, Mrs Ambrose Diehl to EA, 27 July 1947. MP: MB1/Q20.

5 MAJ cited in Hamid, *Disastrous Twilight*, p. 206. This tends to contradict Alan Campbell-Johnson's assertion that MAJ once said: 'The only man I have ever been

impressed with in all my life was Lord Mountbatten. When I met him for the first time I felt he had "nur",' which Campbell-Johnson translates as 'divine radiance'. Campbell-Johnson, *Mission with Mountbatten*, p. 230. Like Hamid, Campbell-Johnson is an erratic source, but on this occasion Hamid's story is more convincing.

6 EA cited in Morgan, *Edwina Mountbatten*, p. 408.

7 *Times of India*, 19 July 1947, p. 6; 22 July 1947, p. 8.

8 Morgan, *Edwina Mountbatten*, p. 406; Masson, *Edwina*, p. 178.

9 EA to Dowager Marchioness of Reading, 27 July 1947. MP: MB1/Q61.

10 The assassination was later traced to his political opponent, U Saw.

11 Liaquat Ali Khan cited in Viceroy's Personal Report No 14, 25 July 1947. *ToP*, vol XII, p. 339.

12 Campbell-Johnson, *Mission with Mountbatten*, p. 138.

13 Viceroy's Personal Report no 13, 18 July 1947. *ToP*, vol XII, p. 231.

14 Viceroy's Personal Report no 14, 25 July 1947. *ToP*, vol XII, p. 339.

15 Carthill, *The Lost Dominion*, pp. 27–8.

16 See Sen, *The Argumentative Indian*, especially essays 1 and 6.

17 Carthill, *The Lost Dominion*, p. 27.

18 Lord Curzon to Queen Victoria, 12 September 1900. Cited in Chopra et al, *Secret Papers from the British Royal Archives*, p. 89. See also Gilmour, *Curzon*, pp. 184–5.

19 See Patrick French, *Younghusband: The Last Great Imperial Adventurer* (HarperCollins, London, 1994), p. 158.

20 Mountbatten, *Diaries 1920–22*, 25 November 1921, p. 196.

21 Hamid, *Disastrous Twilight*, p. 61.

22 Campbell-Johnson, *Mission with Mountbatten*, p. 192. Henry Hodson gives this figure as 20 lakh rupees (£150,000): Hodson, *The Great Divide*, p. 428.

23 Andreas Augustin, *The Imperial New Delhi*, p. 50.

24 'A Prince's Ransom', *Guardian*, 28 May 2001; 'A Paperweight Worth 400 Crores and Much More', *Hindu*, 24 August 2001.

25 Allen & Dwivedi, *Lives of the Indian Princes*, pp. 329–30; George Birdwood, *The Industrial Arts of India* (Chapman & Hall, London, 1880), vol 2, p. 118; Akshaya Mukul, 'National Treasure Up for Sale in Dubai', *Times of India*, 3 January 2006.

26 Miller, *I Found No Peace*, p. 152.

27 Malik Habib Ahmed Khan cited in ibid, p. 153.

28 Cited in French, *Liberty or Death*, p. 246.

29 Robin Jeffrey, 'Introduction', in Jeffrey, *People, Princes and Paramount Power*, p. 16.

30 Ziegler maintains that DM personally favoured the tactic of organizing princely states into blocs that might form separate nations – something like 'Plan Balkan' – as had Napoleon in Germany. But there was no time to institute such a complex plan and, in any case, Congress would have been furious. Ziegler, *Mountbatten*, pp. 405–6.

31 JN, 10 June 1947, cited in *ToP*, vol XI, p. 233.

32 Viceroy's Personal Report No 10, 27 June 1947, ibid, p. 687. See also Brown, *Nehru*, p. 174. Patel had been an outspoken critic of the princely states since the late 1920s, when he had described them as 'disorderly and pitiable', with 'no limits to their slavery'. On the other hand, he had already demonstrated an ability to make concessions to the privileged classes in order to keep the process running smoothly. Two months before, Indian citizenship policy had been established, with a clause stating that no titles should be conferred by the Union and no

citizen should accept titles from a foreign state. At Patel's suggestion, the ruling was not made retrospective. 'After all,' he had joked, 'some people have spent so much money in obtaining titles – let them keep them.' Patel cited in Krishna, *Sardar*, p. 296; *The Times*, 1 May 1947, p. 4.

33 CRA to DM, March 1947 [no day dated]. MP: MB1/D254.

34 Viceroy's Personal Report No 14, 25 July 1947. *ToP*, vol XII, p. 338.

35 Ziegler, *Mountbatten*, p. 411.

36 Patel cited in Krishna, *Sardar*, pp. 322, 319, 323.

37 Walter Monckton, for the Nizam of Hyderabad, described DM's methods as 'an exact replica of those in which Hitler indulged'; another agent told Sir Conrad Corfield that 'he now knew what Dolfuss felt like when he was sent for to see Hitler: he had not expected to be spoken to like that by a British officer: after a moment's pause he withdrew the word "British".' Both cited in Bradford, *George VI*, pp. 524–5.

38 Roberts, *Eminent Churchillians*, p. 102; Allen & Dwivedi, *Lives of the Indian Princes*, p. 317.

39 See, for example: James, *Raj*, pp. 624–9; Roberts, *Eminent Churchillians*, pp. 102–3; Cannadine, *Ornamentalism*, pp. 156–8. In fact, the Butler Committee, which looked into the question of princely rights and British responsibilities alongside the Simon Commission in the 1920s, produced an inconclusive and extremely complex set of findings, clear only in its statement that the states should not be transferred into a relationship with an independent Indian government without their permission. Hodson, *The Great Divide*, pp. 27–9. DM would doubtless have argued that they were not.

40 Hodson, *The Great Divide*, p. 22.

41 Pethick-Lawrence to DM, 18 April 1947. *ToP*, vol X, p. 327.

42 DM cited in Ziegler, *Mountbatten*, p. 408.

43 Nizam of Hyderabad to WSC, 19 June 1947; WSC to Nizam of Hyderabad, 24 June 1947; both WMP: 29, ff 201, 209.

44 Viceroy's Personal Report No 15, 1 August 1947. *ToP* vol XII, p. 454.

45 Patel cited in Krishna, *Sardar*, pp. 339–40.

46 Viceroy's Personal Report no 17, 16 August 1947, *ToP*, vol XII, p. 767; Allen & Dwivedi, *Lives of the Indian Princes*, p. 320; Ziegler, *Mountbatten*, p. 411; Hodson, *The Great Divide*, p. 380 (footnote).

47 Campbell-Johnson, *Mission with Mountbatten*, p. 54; *ToP*, vol X, p. 116.

48 *Times of India*, 7 July 1947, p. 7.

49 Allen & Dwivedi, *Lives of the Indian Princes*, p. 63.

50 Viceroy's Personal Report No 14, 25 July 1947. *ToP*, vol XII, p. 336.

51 Viceroy's Personal Report No 15, 1 August 1947. *ToP*, vol XII, p. 453.

52 Monckton to Sir Mirza Ismail, 21 February 1947. WMP: 29, ff 58–60.

53 Monckton, record of interview with MAJ, 4 June 1947. WMP: 29, f 192.

54 MAJ to Nizam of Hyderabad, 21 July 1947. WMP: 29, f 353.

55 Viceroy's Personal Report No 14, 25 July 1947. *ToP*, vol XII p. 337.

56 Monckton, note for the consideration of MAJ, 28 July 1947. WMP: 29, ff 417–9.

57 Memorandum from Monckton, 6 August 1947. WMP: 30, ff 23–5.

58 Monckton: note of interview with Ismay, 10 August 1947. WMP: 30, f 46; note of interview with HE the Viceroy, WMP: 30, f 51.

59 Campbell-Johnson, *Mission with Mountbatten*, pp. 140–2. DM's comment was remembered by the Maharawal of Dungarpur as 'I can see clearly through this crystal that the best course for your Ruler to adopt is to accede to India.' Maharawal of Dungarpur cited in Allen & Dwivedi, *Lives of the Indian Princes*,

p. 318. Narendra Singh Sarila, who was also present, remembered the Dewan in question being that of Bhavnagar, not Kutch. Singh Sarila, *The Shadow of the Great Game*, pp. 316–7.

60 Allen & Dwivedi, *Lives of the Indian Princes*, p. 319; Sydney Smith, 'Fate of India's Princes', *Sunday Express*, 3 August 1947, p. 4.

61 Ali Yavar Jung, 26 July 1947. WMP: 29, ff 390–2. Patel had also given DM a solid assurance that the government of India would raise no objection if Kashmir did what was widely supposed to be inevitable, and acceded to Pakistan. DM to the East India Association, 29 June 1948, *Asiatic Review*, vol xliv, no 160 (October 1948), p. 353.

62 Campbell-Johnson, *Mission with Mountbatten*, p. 143.

63 JN to DM, 27 July 1947. *SWJN* (2), vol 3, p. 264.

64 Viceroy's Personal Report No 15, 1 August 1947. *ToP*, vol XII, p. 450.

65 Hamid, *Disastrous Twilight*, p. 212. DM took the credit for persuading MKG to go in place of JN. DM to Henry V. Hodson, 3 October 1978. MP: MB1/K137A. See also Singh, *Heir Apparent*, pp. 50–1.

66 Campbell-Johnson, *Mission with Mountbatten*, p. 144.

67 William L. Richter, 'Traditional Rulers in Post-traditional Societies: The Princes of India and Pakistan', in Jeffrey, *People, Princes and Paramount Power*, p. 335.

14. A RAINBOW IN THE SKY

1 *Imperial Review*, August 1947, p. 19.

2 Thomas Babington Macaulay, *Minute on Indian Education*, 1835.

3 Metcalf, *Ideologies of the Raj*, p. 233. This argument is still used even today. See, for example, Neillands, *A Fighting Retreat*, pp. 41–2.

4 Sardar Dalip Singh cited in *Times of India*, 28 July 1947, p. 1.

5 DM cited in Collins & Lapierre, *Mountbatten and the Partition of India*, p. 30.

6 Campbell-Johnson, *Mission with Mountbatten*, p. 139.

7 French, *Liberty or Death*, p. 340.

8 Ismay to Lady Ismay, 5 August 1947. Cited in Ziegler, *Mountbatten*, p. 365.

9 JN to DM, 6 August 1947. *SWJN* (2), vol 3, p. 40; see also p. 43.

10 See Sen, *The Argumentative Indian*, essay 3; especially p. 55.

11 Jones, *Tumult in India*, pp. 92–3.

12 'The number of signatories is considerably higher,' Prasad noted, 'because it is not unusual for one postcard to bear more than one signature and there are packets which contain thousands of signatures.' Rajendra Prasad to JN, 7 August 1947. Prasad, *Correspondence*, vol 7, p. 91. See also JN to Rajendra Prasad, 7 August 1947. *SWJN* (2), vol 3, pp. 189–92. JN dismissed the cow protection campaign as being sponsored by Seth Dalmia, an enormously rich financier whose wartime ardour for Hitler had given way to a passion for Hindu nationalism and, it later emerged, tax evasion. 'Fadeout', *Time*, 10 October 1955.

13 Christopher Beaumont, in AAS: Mss Eur Photo Eur 358.

14 Roberts, *Eminent Churchillians*, p. 91.

15 Hamid, *Disastrous Twilight*, p. 170.

16 Shireen Moosvi (ed.), *Episodes in the Life of Akbar: Contemporary Records and Reminiscences* (National Book Trust of India, New Delhi, 1994), pp. xi–xii.

17 Akbar, *Nehru*, p. 438.

18 French, *Liberty or Death*, pp. 220–1, 372–3. French points out that, when the Indian Army was sent to Kashmir a few weeks later, it went by airlift rather than

by the Gurdaspur road anyway. However, against that must be laid the fact that Gurdaspur was still very dangerous riot-torn territory by the end of October 1947; moreover, the Indian government had to react extremely fast, and sending troops via Gurdaspur would have taken days. In October 1947, shortly before the conflict began, India began to improve the road between Pathankot and Jammu, which was opened in July 1948. JN described this road as 'the chief life-line for our troops and for supplies'. JN to Maharaja of Kashmir, 27 October 1947. *SWJN* (2), vol 4, p. 278.

19 French, *Liberty or Death*, p. 328.
20 Abell cited in Ziegler, *Mountbatten*, pp. 419–20.
21 Ziegler, *Mountbatten Revisited*, pp. 16–17; Kanwar Sain, *Reminiscences of an Engineer* (Young Asia Publications, New Delhi, 1978), pp. 120–4.
22 Christopher Beaumont, in AAS: Mss Eur Photo Eur 358; 'Mountbatten', *Secret History*; Ziegler, *Mountbatten Revisited*, p. 16; Ahmed, *Jinnah, Pakistan and Islamic Identity*, p. 137; Heward, *The Great and the Good*, pp. 49–50; Ziegler, *Mountbatten*, pp. 420–1; Lamb, *Birth of a Tragedy*, pp. 35–8; see also Hamid, *Disastrous Twilight*, pp. 222–3, 235.
23 DM to Ismay, 2 April 1948, cited in Ziegler, *Mountbatten Revisited*, p. 17.
24 Ibid, p. 17.
25 28 March 1947. *ToP*, vol X, p. 36.
26 *ToP*, vol X, pp. 242–55; 'rural slum', see also p. 509.
27 MAJ cited in *ToP*, vol X, p. 452. The Bengali Muslim League leader H.S. Suhrawardy proposed that Calcutta remain as a 'free city' under joint Indo-Pakistani control for six months; Vallabhbhai Patel's reply was 'Not even for six hours!' Hodson, *The Great Divide*, pp. 276–7.
28 Patel to DM, 13 August 1947. MP: MB1/D85.
29 Viceroy's Personal Report no 17, 16 August 1947. *ToP*, vol XII, p. 761.
30 Heward, *The Great and the Good*, p. 41.
31 The definition of a state under international law at this point was generally taken from the Montevideo Convention of 26 December 1933, in which it was defined as having a permanent population, a defined territory, a government, and a capacity to enter into relations with other states.
32 Campbell-Johnson, *Mission with Mountbatten*, p. 152.
33 Heward, *The Great and the Good*, p. 41.
34 Viceroy's Personal Report no 17, 16 August 1947. *ToP*, vol XII, p. 760.
35 *Manchester Guardian*, 14 August 1947, p. 5; *Times of India*, 14 August 1947, p. 1; Fischer, *Life of Mahatma Gandhi*, p. 511.
36 Viceroy's Personal Report no 16, 8 August 1947. *ToP*, vol XII, p. 594.
37 *Times of India*, 9 August 1947, p. 6.
38 Ibid, 8 August 1947, p. 1.
39 Azad, *India Wins Freedom*, p. 183. Jalal, *The Sole Spokesman*, is entirely about the theory; see especially pp. 241–93 on MAJ and DM.
40 MAJ, 11 August 1947. Cited in Merchant, *The Jinnah Anthology*, p. 11.
41 *Manchester Guardian*, 13 August 1947, p. 5.
42 Viceroy's Personal Report no 17, 16 August 1947. *ToP*, vol XII, p. 770.
43 Mildred A. Talbot to Walter S. Rogers, 27 August 1947. MP: MB1/K148 (I).
44 DM, 'Reflections on Mr Jinnah 29 years later', MP: MB1/K137A. See also DM to Henry V. Hodson, 7 April 1976, in which he wrote that 'The only period of genuine warm-hearted friendship occurred when I came to Karachi to stay with Jinnah for the transfer of power – but I can hardly put this in as an isolated & only example of my relations with Jinnah.' MP: MB1/K137A.

45 Gerry O'Neill cited in Ahmed, *Jinnah, Pakistan and Islamic Identity*, p. 23.
46 According to Sri Prakasa, India's High Commissioner in Pakistan. NAI: Home Dept, Political Branch, F. No. 57/25/47 - Poll. (I).
47 Ahmed, *Jinnah, Pakistan and Islamic Identity*, p. 186.
48 Singh Sarila, *The Shadow of the Great Game*, p. 94.
49 Campbell-Johnson, *Mission with Mountbatten*, p. 156.
50 DM to Pakistan Constituent Assembly, 14 August 1947. Mountbatten, *Time Only to Look Forward*, p. 58.
51 *Times of India*, 15 August 1947, p. 5.
52 Mildred A. Talbot to Walter S. Rogers, 27 August 1947. MP: MB1/K148 (I).
53 *Manchester Guardian*, 15 August 1947, p. 5.
54 DM, 'Reflections on Mr Jinnah 29 years later'.
55 DM cited in Wolpert, *Jinnah*, p. 342.
56 DM, 'Reflections on Mr Jinnah 29 years later'.
57 Viceroy's Personal Report no 17, 16 August 1947. *ToP*, vol XII, p. 771.
58 Campbell-Johnson, *Mission with Mountbatten*, p. 156.
59 CRA to DM, 14 August 1947; DM to CRA, 15 August 1947. TNA: PREM 8/571.
60 DM to EA, 18 August 1947. Cited in Ziegler, *Mountbatten*, p. 427.
61 'Delhi Bedecked for Independence Day', *Times of India*, 14 August 1947, p. 1.
62 JN to Vijaya Lakshmi Pandit, 10 August 1947. VLP: correspondence with JN.
63 Phillips Talbot to Walter S. Rogers, 19 August 1947. CSAS: Talbot Papers; MP: MB1/K148 (I).
64 Mildred A. Talbot to Walter S. Rogers, 27 August 1947. MP: MB1/K148 (I).
65 Cited in Mountbatten, *Time Only to Look Forward*, p. 63.
66 Campbell-Johnson, *Mission with Mountbatten*, p. 160.
67 Lady Pamela Hicks, recorded by Mr B.R. Nanda, 14 October 1971, p. 8.
68 Indira Gandhi cited in Hough, *Edwina*, p. 192.
69 Lady Pamela Hicks, recorded by Mr B.R. Nanda, 14 October 1971, pp. 8–9. See also Phillips Talbot to Walter S. Rogers, 19 August 1947; CSAS: Talbot Papers; also MP: MB1/K148 (I); Campbell-Johnson, *Mission with Mountbatten*, p. 160.
70 Viceroy's Personal Report no 17, 16 August 1947. *ToP*, vol XII, p. 772.
71 Hutheesing, *We Nehrus*, p. 202; Phillips Talbot to Walter S. Rogers, 19 August 1947, MP: MB1/K148 (I); Campbell-Johnson, *Mission with Mountbatten*, p. 161.
72 Viceroy's Personal Report no 17, 16 August 1947. *ToP*, vol XII, p. 773.
73 Campbell-Johnson, *Mission with Mountbatten*, p. 168.

III. THE BEGINNING

15. PARADISE ON EARTH

1 *Times of India*, 21 August 1947, p. 3.
2 DM to Patricia, Lady Brabourne, 14 August 1947. Cited in Ziegler, *Mountbatten*, p. 427. DM's emphasis.
3 '"Rejoicings": Happy Augury for the Future', *Times of India*, 18 August 1947, p. 6.
4 Sir Cyril Radcliffe to Mark Tennant, 13 August 1947. Cited in Heward, *The Great and the Good*, p. 42.
5 Schofield, *Kashmir*, p. 130.

6 Nishtar cited in *Times of India*, 18 August 1947, p. 1.

7 Hutheesing, *We Nehrus*, p. 205.

8 Campbell-Johnson, *Mission with Mountbatten*, p. 167.

9 Cited in Hutheesing, *We Nehrus*, p. 196.

10 Moon, *Divide and Quit*, pp. 115–6.

11 Ibid, pp. 93–4; Gopal, *Nehru*, vol ii, p. 13.

12 Campbell-Johnson, *Mission with Mountbatten*, p. 169.

13 Viceroy's Personal Report No. 17, 16 August 1947 (postscript, 17 August). MP: MB1/D85.

14 Phillips Talbot to Walter S. Rogers, 19 August 1947. MP: MB1/K148 (I).

15 *Times of India*, 18 August 1947, p. 1. See also *Manchester Guardian*, 19 August 1947, p. 6.

16 *Manchester Guardian*, 19 August 1947, p. 6; United Mills photograph album, MP: MB2/M6.

17 EA cited in Masson, *Edwina*, p. 202; Campbell-Johnson, *Mission with Mountbatten*, pp. 169–70.

18 *Manchester Guardian*, 20 August 1947, p. 5.

19 T.W. Rees, *Report of the Punjab Boundary Force*, AAS: Mss Eur F274/70.

20 Stephens, *Pakistan*, p. 183.

21 T.W. Rees, *Report of the Punjab Boundary Force*, AAS: Mss Eur F274/70.

22 *Manchester Guardian*, 21 August 1947, p. 4; 25 August 1947, p. 5.

23 Pandey, *Remembering Partition*, p. 122.

24 Report of Lord Ismay, 5 October 1947, TNA: DO 121/69.

25 Roberts, *Eminent Churchillians*, p. 112.

26 29 March 1947. *ToP*, vol X, pp. 44–5.

27 French, *Liberty or Death*, p. 332.

28 Population figures are from the 1941 census, as cited in Korbel, *Danger in Kashmir*, p. 50. More accurately, the figures in 1941 were 16,217,000 Muslims, 7,551,000 Hindus, and 3,757,800 Sikhs.

29 *Manchester Guardian*, 2 August 1947, p. 4; and 14 August 1947, p. 4; also Moon, *Divide and Quit*, pp. 83–4. Kartar Singh had apparently told the Raja of Faridkot in June that he was prepared to negotiate with MAJ for inclusion in Pakistan, but Tara Singh and Baldev Singh were implacably opposed. *ToP*, vol XI, p. 38.

30 See also Hamid, *Disastrous Twilight*, p. 164.

31 Roberts, *Eminent Churchilllians*, p. 115.

32 Campbell-Johnson, *Mission with Mountbatten*, pp. 149, 152; JN to Krishna Menon, 11 July 1948, MP: MB1/F39.

33 JN to Krishna Menon, 11 July 1948. MP: MB1/F39.

34 Viceroy's Report No 13, 18 July 1947. MP: MB1/D84.

35 Roberts, *Eminent Churchillians*, p. 132.

36 At a cabinet meeting on 23 May, CRA and his cabinet offered their moral support to DM's policy of using 'all the force required', but not more resources. *ToP*, vol X, p. 967.

37 DM Roberts, cited in *Eminent Churchillians*, p. 118.

38 JN cited in Neillands, *A Fighting Retreat*, p. 77.

39 Ziegler, *Mountbatten*, p. 435.

40 'The Strategic Value of India to the British Empire', 5 July 1946 in Hamid, *Disastrous Twilight*, pp. 310–1. There are extensive papers to back up the need for a faster release rate from the forces in AP: MS Attlee dep 47, November 1947.

41 JN in *SWJN* (2), vol 3, p. 300.

42 Ian Stephens: lecture on 'Pakistan', CSAS, 24 February 1969 (MP: MB1/K202);
    Moon, *Divide and Quit*, p. 280.
43 Rajagopalachari cited in Ziegler, *Mountbatten Revisited*, p. 22.
44 Figure as stated by Emmanuel Shinwell in the House of Commons, 3 February
    1948; 446 HC Deb 5s, cols 1629–30. Of the seven, two were murdered, and
    one was killed in a flying accident and was not even serving at the time. See
    also Ian Stephens: lecture on 'Pakistan', CSAS, 24 February 1969 (MP: MGI/
    K202).
45 'Edie Rutherford' is a pseudonym: the woman in question kept a diary for the
    Mass-Observation Archive, which changes all observers' names. Cited in Simon
    Garfield, *Our Hidden Lives: The Remarkable Diaries of Post-War Britain* (2004;
    Ebury Press, London, 2005), p. 438.
46 WSC to MAJ, n.d. [unsent, late August/September 1946]. CP: CHUR
    2/42B/231–2.
47 DM cited in Terraine, *The Life and Times of Lord Mountbatten*, p. 148.
48 EA to Kaysie Norton, 25 August 1947. MP: MB1/Q40.
49 Cited in Gopal, *Nehru*, vol ii, p. 14.
50 H.V.R. Iengar, 'P.M. at work', in Zakaria (ed.), *A Study of Nehru*, pp. 177–8.
51 Shudraka, *Mrcchakatika*, pp. 34, 59, 174. See also G.V. Devasthali, *Introduction
    to the Study of Mrcchakatika* (Poona Oriental Book House, Poona, 1951).
52 Maniben Patel to EA, 25 August 1947. MP: MB1/Q115.
53 Campbell-Johnson, *Mission with Mountbatten*, p. 176; Masson, *Edwina*,
    pp. 202–4.
54 EA to the East India Association, 13 October 1948. *Asiatic Review*, vol xlv, no
    161 (January 1949), p. 444.
55 See Pandey, *Remembering Partition*, pp. 68–9, 72–3. Pandey disputes the accu-
    racy of claims about the tattooing and branding of raped women, suggesting
    that it might be part of a patriarchal fantasy of female debasement. It is impossi-
    ble now, as it was at the time, to establish the truth. While Pandey is right to point
    out that some accounts rely on rumour and hearsay, it is not realistic to expect the
    victims of such crimes to produce neatly verifiable historical records. The victims
    would mostly have been illiterate women, either socially ostracized by their own
    communities or forcibly married into new communities.
56 Rameshwari Nehru cited in Pandey, *Remembering Partition*, p. 88. The Thoa
    Khalsa incident took place in March 1947, though similar events were observed
    in August.
57 *Manchester Guardian*, 29 August 1947, p. 5. See also Moon, *Divide and Quit*,
    p. 261.
58 JN to DM, *SWJN* (2), vol 4, p. 44.
59 *SWJN* (2), vol 4, p. 25, footnote.
60 JN to DM, 27 August 1947. *SWJN* (2), vol 4, p. 26.
61 Indira Gandhi cited in Hough, *Edwina*, p. 193.
62 *Manchester Guardian*, 25 August 1947, p. 5.
63 Moon, *Divide and Quit*, pp. 134–5.
64 *Manchester Guardian*, 30 August 1947, p. 5.
65 T.W. Rees, *Report of the Punjab Boundary Force*, AAS: Mss Eur F274/70.
66 Campbell-Johnson, *Mission with Mountbatten*, pp. 172, 174, 176; *Times of
    India*, 30 August 1947, p. 1.
67 'Gandhi' by Francis Watson & Maurice Brown, radio programme, episode 4
    ('The Last Phase'), 16 December 1956, in Benthall Papers, CSAS, Box 2, file 2;
    Fischer, *Life of Mahatma Gandhi*, pp. 511–2.

16. THE BATTLE FOR DELHI

1 The figure of 200,000 was estimated by Penderel Moon – but, though DM and others have quoted it as if it applied to the whole of India, Moon was in fact only calculating for the Punjab. However, he later considered that it might have been an overestimate.

2 See Pandey, *Remembering Partition*, pp. 88–91.

3 NAI: Home Dept, Political Branch, F. No, 27/2/1947 – Poll. (I).

4 T.W. Rees, *Report of the Punjab Boundary Force*, AAS: Mss Eur F274/70.

5 Mudie cited in Roberts, *Eminent Churchillians*, p. 127.

6 Dalton, *Mahatma Gandhi*, pp. 155–9; Fischer, *Life of Mahatma Gandhi*, pp. 512–3.

7 DM cited in Ziegler, *Mountbatten*, p. 436. This letter is reproduced in facsimile in Pyarelal, *Mahatma Gandhi*, vol 2, plate 2 between pp. 496–7.

8 Ziegler, *Mountbatten*, pp. 431–2.

9 Pandey, *Remembering Partition*, p. 123.

10 Morgan, *Edwina Mountbatten*, p. 415.

11 Sir Terence Shone to Lord Addison, 11 September 1947. TNA: PREM 8/584.

12 Report of Tek Singh, Superintendent of Police, Delhi, 10 October 1947. NAI: Home Department, Political Branch, F. No. 5/26/47 – Poll. (I).

13 Pandey, *Remembering Partition*, p. 129.

14 Campbell-Johnson, *Mission with Mountbatten*, p. 180.

15 DM cited in ibid, p. 181.

16 Ibid, p. 182.

17 Ziegler, *Mountbatten*, p. 433.

18 MKG was not a member of the United Council, but he discussed initiatives for it with EA and other members of its executive committee. MP: MB1/Q117.

19 Ibid.

20 Campbell-Johnson, *Mission with Mountbatten*, pp. 182–4.

21 Chaudhuri, *Thy Hand Great Anarch!*, pp. 838–42; Pandey, *Remembering Partition*, p. 123; Campbell-Johnson, *Mission with Mountbatten*, p. 206.

22 Chaudhuri, *Thy Hand Great Anarch!*, pp. 844–5.

23 *Times of India*, 8 September 1947, p. 8.

24 Sir Laurence Grafftey-Smith to Secretary of State for Commonwealth Relations, 10 September 1947. TNA: PREM 8/584; *The Times*, 9 September 1947, p. 4..

25 Sir Terence Shone to Secretary of State for Commonwealth Relations, 12 September 1947. TNA: PREM 8/584.

26 Pandey, *Remembering Partition*, p. 129; see also *Daily Mirror*, 9 September 1947.

27 Report of Lord Ismay, 5 October 1947, TNA: DO 121/69.

28 Patel cited in Sir Terence Shone to Secretary of State for Commonwealth Relations, 11 September 1947. TNA: PREM 8/584. See also *Times of India*, 9 September 1947, p. 1.

29 MAJ to CRA, 18 September 1947. TNA: PREM 8/584.

30 Sir Terence Shone to Secretary of State for Commonwealth Relations, 12 September 1947. TNA: PREM 8/584.

31 Sir Terence Shone to Secretary of State for Commonwealth Relations, 11 September 1947. TNA: PREM 8/584.

32 Sir Laurence Grafftey-Smith to Secretary of State for Commonwealth Relations, 10 September 1947. TNA: PREM 8/584.

33 Sir Laurence Grafftey-Smith to Secretary of State for Commonwealth Relations, 18 September 1947. TNA: PREM 8/584.

34 Chaudhuri, *Thy Hand Great Anarch!*, pp. 848–9.

35 JN cited in *Times of India*, 10 September 1947, p. 1.

36 JN to Rajendra Prasad, 19 September 1947, cited in Gopal, *Nehru*, vol ii, p. 16.

37 According to Shahid Ahmad Dehlavi, cited in Pandey, *Remembering Partition*, p. 142.

38 Pandey, *Remembering Partition*, pp. 140–1.

39 *Times of India*, 11 September 1947, p. 1.

40 JN cited in Moraes, *Jawaharlal Nehru*, p. 363.

41 Campbell-Johnson, *Mission with Mountbatten*, p. 189.

42 Sahgal, *From Fear Set Free*, p. 28; *Times of India*, 9 September 1947, p. 1; Brecher, *Nehru*, p. 365.

43 JN cited in Adams & Whitehead, *The Dynasty*, p. 131.

44 Symonds, *In the Margins of Independence*, pp. 33–4.

45 DM to King George VI, cited in Ziegler, *Mountbatten*, p. 433; see also DM's interview with JN, 8 September 1947, AAS: IOR Neg 15561/195A f 41.

46 EA cited in Morgan, *Edwina Mountbatten*, p. 427.

47 Vijaya Lakshmi Pandit cited in Brittain, *Envoy Extraordinary*, p. 135; see also Fischer, *Life of Mahatma Gandhi*, pp. 514–5.

48 Mohammed Yunus, cited in French, *Liberty or Death*, p. 387.

49 Richard Symonds, speaking on AAS: Mss Eur R207/5, side B.

50 Hutheesing, *We Nehrus*, pp. 208–10.

51 Morgan, *Edwina Mountbatten*, p. 427.

52 Nayantara Sahgal in conversation with the author, 8 May 2006.

53 Noël Coward to DM, 3 July 1945. MP: MB1/A48. 'I hope you have by now enjoyed THIS HAPPY BREED and BLITHE SPIRIT films; the new one, BRIEF ENCOUNTER, is practically finished and looks jolly nice. I often think of those gay cinematic evenings in the King's P.' MP: MB1/A48.

54 DM to Noël Coward, 21 October 1947. MP: MB1/A48.

55 'He read few books,' remembered DM's close friend Solly Zuckerman, 'but could be relied upon to master his briefs, reading slowly, sometimes with his lips moving as if he were reading aloud.' Solly Zuckerman, 'Working with a Man of Destiny', *Observer*, 2 September 1979.

56 Symonds, *In the Margins of Independence*, pp. 39–40.

57 Campbell-Johnson, *Mission with Mountbatten*, pp. 200–1; Morgan, *Edwina Mountbatten*, pp. 416–7.

58 Fischer, *Life of Mahatma Gandhi*, p. 516.

59 Chaudhuri, *Thy Hand Great Anarch!*, pp. 851–2.

60 Campbell-Johnson, *Mission with Mountbatten*, p. 186.

61 EA cited in Morgan, *Edwina Mountbatten*, p. 415.

62 Begum Anees Kidwai cited in Pandey, *Remembering Partition*, p. 131.

63 Ibid, pp. 123–4, 131.

64 MKG cited in Fischer, *Life of Mahatma Gandhi*, p. 520. See also JN to Vallabhbhai Patel, 22 October 1947, *SWJN* (2), vol 4, pp. 173–4. Hindu temples in Sind were vandalized at around the same time. Prakasa, *Pakistan*, p. 38.

65 V. Viswanathan, Deputy High Commissioner for India in Pakistan (Karachi), to S. Dutt, Secretary to the Government of India, Ministry of External Affairs and Commonwealth Relations, 30 October 1947. NAI: Home Dept, Political Branch, F. No. 57/25/47 – Poll. (I).

66 Symonds, *In the Margins of Independence*, pp. 49, 54.

67 Sir Arthur Waugh, 'India and Pakistan: The Economic Effects of Partition', *Asiatic Review*, vol xliv, no 158 (April 1948), p. 119.

68 Symonds, *In the Margins of Independence*, p. 116.
69 Campbell-Johnson, *Mission with Mountbatten*, p. 190.
70 MAJ to CRA, 18 September 1947; Arthur Henderson to CRA, 19 September 1947; both TNA: PREM 8/584.
71 Sir Terence Shone to Secretary of State for Commonwealth Relations, 22 September 1947. TNA: PREM 8/584.
72 MAJ to CRA, 1 October 1947. TNA: PREM 8/568.
73 Cited in Kux, *The United States and Pakistan*, p. 20.
74 Ibid, pp. 20–1.
75 MAJ to Nizam of Hyderabad, 15 October 1947. WMP: 30, f 317.
76 Memorandum, WMP: 31, ff 88–9.
77 Krishna, *Sardar*, pp. 402–3; Pandey, *Nehru*, p. 297; Gopal, *Nehru*, vol ii, pp. 14–15; Akbar, *Nehru*, pp. 454–5.
78 JN, 30 September 1947. *SWJN* (2), vol 4, p. 108.
79 Memorandum of Lord Addison to the Cabinet Commonwealth Affairs Committee, 3 November 1947. TNA: PREM 8/585.
80 Campbell-Johnson, *Mission with Mountbatten*, pp. 191–3.
81 DM cited in Ziegler, *Mountbatten*, p. 444.
82 Allen & Dwivedi, *Lives of the Indian Princes*, p. 328.
83 *The Times*, 25 February 1948, p. 3.
84 Memorandum of Lord Addison to the Cabinet Commonwealth Affairs Committee, 3 November 1947. TNA: PREM 8/585. See also Wavell, *Viceroy's Journal*, 20 November 1947, p. 437.
85 Pandey, *Remembering Partition*, p. 122.
86 EA to the East India Association, 13 October 1948. *Asiatic Review*, vol xlv, no 161 (January 1949), pp. 442–3.
87 Hutheesing, *We Nehrus*, pp. 206–7
88 JN, 30 September 1947. *SWJN* (2), vol 4, p. 107.

17. KASHMIR

1 Lord Hardinge cited in Schofield, *Kashmir in the Crossfire*, p. 54.
2 Ibid, pp. 100–3.
3 Jha, *Kashmir, 1947*, pp. 16–17.
4 Anonymous report to MAJ, 20 August 1943. Cited in ibid, p. 17.
5 Symonds, *In the Margins of Independence*, p. 73.
6 Commonwealth Relations Office memorandum on developments in Kashmir up to 31 October 1947. TNA: DO 133/68.
7 'The background of the Kashmir problem', 1948. TNA: DO 142/540.
8 Malgonkar, *The Men who Killed Gandhi*, p. 6.
9 JN to Vallabhbhai Patel, 27 September 1947. *SWJN* (2), vol 4, pp. 263–5.
10 JN to EA, 27 June 1948. Cited in Ziegler, *Mountbatten*, p. 445.
11 JN to Indira Gandhi, 29 May 1940, in Nehru & Gandhi, *Two Alone, Two Together*, p. 64.
12 Schofield, *Kashmir in the Crossfire*, p. 117; Jha, *Kashmir, 1947*, pp. 39, 40 (footnote).
13 Singh, *Heir Apparent*, p. 55.
14 There are eyewitness accounts in Symonds, *In the Margins of Independence*, pp. 67–8.
15 Stephens, *Pakistan*, p. 200; see also Lamb, *Birth of a Tragedy*, pp. 68, 129.
16 Extract from report of C.B. Duke, 23 October 1947. TNA: DO 133/68; Sir

Laurence Grafftey-Smith to Commonwealth Relations Office, n.d. (early November 1947?). TNA: DO 133/68.

17 Korbel, *Danger in Kashmir*, p. 65; French, *Liberty or Death*, p. 374. The Indian representative put it to the UN Security Council in 1948 that the Pakistani government sent agents and religious leaders to incite the Muslim population of Kashmir into rebellion. Based on the fact that the Maharaja and his antecedents had a long history of oppressing their Muslim subjects, and on the eyewitness reports of an overwhelming number of impartial observers, it is hard to swallow India's argument whole on this particular point.

18 Extract from report of C.B. Duke, 23 October 1947. TNA: DO 133/68; Commonwealth Relations Office memorandum on the Kashmir dispute, May 1948. TNA: DO 142/540.

19 Extract from report of C.B. Duke, 23 October 1947. TNA: DO 133/68.

20 Frank Messervy, 'Kashmir', *Asiatic Review*, vol xlv, no 161 (January 1949), p. 469.

21 C.B. Duke to Sir Laurence Grafftey-Smith, 4 December 1947. TNA: DO 133/69; Note by C.B. Duke, 8 December 1947. TNA: DO 133/69. See also Schofield, *Kashmir in the Crossfire*, p. 142.

22 Sir Laurence Grafftey-Smith to Commonwealth Relations Office, n.d. (early November 1947?). TNA: DO 133/68; Sydney Smith in the *Daily Express*, 10 November 1947, p. 1.

23 Extract from report of C.B. Duke, 23 October 1947. TNA: DO 133/68.

24 Sir Laurence Grafftey-Smith to Philip Noel-Baker, 22 October 1947. TNA: DO 133/68.

25 Sir Laurence Grafftey-Smith to Commonwealth Relations Office, n.d. (early November 1947?). TNA: DO 133/68.

26 Schofield, *Kashmir in the Crossfire*, p. 143; Khan, *Raiders in Kashmir*, p. 17; Commonwealth Relations Office memorandum on the Kashmir dispute, May 1948. TNA: DO 142/540; Korbel, *Danger in Kashmir*, p. 95.

27 Malgonkar, *The Men Who Killed Gandhi*, p. 9. The behaviour of the Mahsuds was deplored by tribal leaders, and they were withdrawn in disgrace. 'The Mahsuds were being allowed back again on their word of honour – for what it may be worth – that looting and murdering (at least of Europeans and Muslims) is forbidden.' Sir Laurence Grafftey-Smith to Philip Noel-Baker, 28 November 1947. TNA: DO 133/69. The figure for casualties at Baramula is often given as 11,000 or even 13,000 out of a population of 14,000; Major-General Akbar Khan of the Pakistan Army disputed these estimates, and Alastair Lamb has estimated casualties at being more like 500. The truth is impossible to ascertain. Khan, *Raiders in Kashmir*, p. 29; Lamb, *Birth of a Tragedy*, p. 115.

28 Note by C.B. Duke, 8 December 1947. TNA: DO 133/69.

29 Sir Laurence Grafftey-Smith to Commonwealth Relations Office, n.d. (early November 1947?). TNA: DO 133/68.

30 *Daily Express*, 28 October 1947, p. 1. The drive is memorably described in Singh, *Heir Apparent*, pp. 58–9.

31 Korbel, *Danger in Kashmir*, pp. 79–80; Ziegler, *Mountbatten*, p. 446; Schofield, *Kashmir in the Crossfire*, pp. 144–5.

32 JN to CRA, 25 October 1947. TNA: DO 142/496.

33 Messervy, 'Kashmir', p. 469.

34 See Schofield, *Kashmir in the Crossfire*, pp. 148–50.

35 Commonwealth Relations Office memorandum on the Kashmir dispute, May 1948. TNA: DO 142/540.

36 Sir Laurence Grafftey-Smith to Philip Noel-Baker, 27 October 1947. TNA: DO 133/68.

37 Stephens, *Pakistan*, p. 200. Stephens, a very well-connected source, says that government circles in Delhi became aware of it only by November.

38 Field-Marshal Manekshaw cited in French, *Liberty or Death*, p. 375; Adams & Whitehead, *The Dynasty*, p. 134.

39 Stephens, *Pakistan*, p. 203; see also Stephens, *Horned Moon*, p. 109.

40 Sri Prakasa to JN, 11 November 1947. NAI: Home Dept, Political Branch, F. No. 57/25/47 – Poll. (I).

41 Stephens, *Pakistan*, p. 203.

42 JN to Vijaya Lakshmi Pandit, 28 October 1947. VLP: correspondence with JN; Report of E. Isaacs, 6 November 1947. TNA: DO 133/68.

43 Commonwealth Relations Office memorandum on the Kashmir dispute, May 1948. TNA: DO 142/540.

44 Symonds, *In the Margins of Independence*, p. 58.

45 Ibid, pp. 59–60.

46 DM cited in Ahmed, *Jinnah, Pakistan and Islamic Identity*, p. 145.

47 Sir George Cunningham, Governor of the North-West Frontier Province, claimed on 28 October that there would have been 30,000–40,000, rather than 2000, Pathans in Kashmir by then if he had given them any encouragement, and emphasized that only by impressing on the leaders that the orders of MAJ and Liaquat were that they should hold fire was this much larger incursion prevented. C.B. Duke to Sir Laurence Grafftey-Smith, 28/29 October 1947. TNA: DO 133/68; see also Commonwealth Relations Office memorandum on the Kashmir dispute, May 1948. TNA: DO 142/540; see also Schofield, *Kashmir in the Crossfire*, p. 134.

48 Foreign Office to Ambassadors, 2 January 1948. TNA: DO 35/3162.

49 Commonwealth Relations Office memorandum on developments in Kashmir up to 31 October 1947. TNA: DO 133/68.

50 JN to Vijaya Lakshmi Pandit, 28 October 1947. VLP: correspondence with JN.

51 EA cited in *News Review*, 25 December 1947, p. 9.

52 Ismay to Noel-Baker, 31 October 1947. TNA: DO 133/68; see also Stephens, *Pakistan*, p. 206.

53 Cited in Shone to CRO, 1 November 1947 (1.15 a.m.). TNA: DO 133/68.

54 Shone to CRO, 1 November 1947 (1.15 a.m.). TNA: DO 133/68.

55 Liaquat Ali Khan to CRA, 4 November 1947. TNA: DO 142/496.

56 Ibid; Sir Terence Shone to Commonwealth Relations Office, 4 November 1947; DM's report, cited in Sir Terence Shone to Commonwealth Relations Office, 6 November 1947; both TNA: DO 133/68

57 Extract from *Pakistan Times*, 4 November 1947. Cited in C.B. Duke to Sir Laurence Grafftey-Smith, 5 November 1947. TNA: DO 133/68.

58 C.B. Duke to Sir Laurence Grafftey-Smith, 5 November 1947. TNA: DO 133/68.

59 Sir Laurence Grafftey-Smith to Sir Archibald Carter, 6 November 1947. TNA: DO 133/68.

60 Foreign Office to Ambassadors, 2 January 1948. TNA: DO 35/3162.

61 Symonds, *In the Margins of Independence*, p. 68.

62 Report of E. Isaacs, 6 November 1947. TNA: DO 133/68.

63 Sydney Smith in the *Daily Express*, 10 November 1947, p. 1.

64 Minutes, 4 November 1947, cited in DM to JN, 25 December 1947. TNA: DO 142/543.

65 DM to Lord Listowel, 8 August 1947. *ToP*, vol XII, p. 590; *SWJN* (2), vol 4, p. 27; see also AAS: IOR Neg 15561/195A, f 29; French, *Liberty or Death*, pp. 376–7.

66 Campbell-Johnson, *Mission with Mountbatten*, p. 234.

67 EA to Lady Brabourne, 1 November 1947. Cited in Morgan, *Edwina Mountbatten*, p. 418. It is not clear from the context whether 'Daddy' refers to DM or to Lord Brabourne, though usually in her letters to her daughters EA refers to DM as 'Daddy'. According to Philip Ziegler, DM was speaking to Walter Monckton about Hyderabad when he found out about the baby. Ziegler, *Mountbatten*, p. 452.

68 JN cited in anonymous article, 'The States of India and Pakistan: Advances Towards Responsible Government', *Asiatic Review*, vol xliv. no 157 (January 1948), p. 77; also in Memorandum of the Commonwealth Relations Office, TNA: DO 142/540.

69 JN to CRA, 23 November 1947. TNA: DO 142/496.

70 Morgan, *Edwina Mountbatten*, pp. 419–20.

71 DM, record of Governor General's interview with opposition leaders, 19 November 1947. AAS: IOR Neg 15561/195B, ff 94–7. See also Ziegler, *Mountbatten*, p. 461.

72 Coward, *Diaries*, 18 November 1947, p. 96.

73 Pimlott, *The Queen*, p. 133; Sarah Bradford, *Elizabeth: A Biography of Her Majesty the Queen* (Penguin, London, 2002), p. 125.

74 *Daily Express*, 20 November 1947, p. 1.

75 Pimlott, *The Queen*, p. 140.

76 Leo Amery, *Diaries*, 20 November 1947. LAP: AMEL 7/41.

77 MP: MB1/Y17.

78 *The Queen*, vol 195 no 9582, 23 July 1947, p. 8.

79 Pimlott, *The Queen*, p. 144.

80 Sir Laurence Grafftey-Smith to Philip Noel-Baker, 28 November 1947. TNA: DO 133/69.

81 DM to JN, 25 December 1947. TNA: DO 142/543.

82 EA to DM, cited in Morgan, *Edwina Mountbatten*, p. 419.

83 Masson, *Edwina*, pp. 210–1.

84 EA cited in Morgan, *Edwina Mountbatten*, p. 421.

85 Moraes, *Jawaharlal Nehru*, p. 328.

86 Mathai, *Reminiscences of the Nehru Age*, p. 204.

87 Morgan, *Edwina Mountbatten*, p. 435. The two women later became good friends.

88 Commonwealth Relations Office memorandum on the Kashmir dispute, May 1948. TNA: DO 142/540.

89 JN to Indira Gandhi, 6 December 1947. Gandhi & Nehru, *Two Alone, Two Together*, p. 549.

90 Sir Terence Shone to Commonwealth Relations Office, 5 December 1947. TNA: DO 133/69.

91 JN cited in Symonds, *In the Margins of Independence*, p. 85; also Richard Symonds, speaking on AAS: Mss Eur R207/5, side B; see also Lamb, *Birth of a Tragedy*, p. 65.

92 DM to JN, 25 December 1947. TNA: DO 142/543. See also Campbell-Johnson, *Mission with Mountbatten*, pp. 251–2.

93 Ziegler, *Mountbatten*, p. 449; Akbar, *Nehru*, p. 447.

94 Sir Laurence Grafftey-Smith to Commonwealth Relations Office, 18 March 1948. TNA: PREM 8/813.

95 *Daily Express*, 27 November 1947, p. 1.

96 Sir Laurence Grafftey-Smith to Commonwealth Relations Office, 1 December 1947. TNA: DO 133/69.

97 Sri Prakasato JN, 11 November 1947. NAI: Home Department, Political Branch, F. No. 57/25/47 – poll. (I).

98 Sir Laurence Grafftey-Smith to Philip Noel-Baker, 9 December 1947. TNA: DO 133/69.

99 The *Tatler and Bystander*, 23 July 1947, p. 97.

100 Ibid, 31 December 1947, pp. 422–3.

101 Maharaja Sawai Man Singh Bahadur of Jaipur cited in Mountbatten, *Time Only to Look Forward*, p. 75.

102 Sir Terence Shone to the Commonwealth Relations Office, 24 December 1947. TNA: DO 142/543; Foreign Office to Ambassadors, 2 January 1948. TNA: DO 35/3162.

103 Sir Terence Shone to Commonwealth Relations Office, 24 December 1947. TNA: DO 142/490.

104 JN to Agatha Harrison, 12 December 1947. *SWJN* (2), vol 4, p. 653.

105 Ahmed, *Jinnah, Pakistan and Islamic Identity*, p. 178.

106 DM to JN, 25 December 1947. TNA: DO 142/543.

107 JN to DM, 26 December 1947. TNA: DO 142/543. The Commonwealth Relations Office telegraphed JN's allegations to Grafftey-Smith in Pakistan, who agreed that Patiala was under threat, the Sikhs being the secondary target of the tribesmen, after loot. If they were encouraged in this direction by local authorities in Pakistan, though, it was more a matter of self-defence than strategy, for 'if the Pathans here have nothing better to do they will impartially loot the West Punjab'. Sir Laurence Grafftey-Smith to Commonwealth Relations Office, 3 January 1948. TNA: DO 142/490.

108 Sir Terence Shone to Commonwealth Relations Office, 28 December 1947, TNA: DO 142/543.

109 Commonwealth Relations Office to Sir Terence Shone, 29 December 1947. TNA: DO 142/490.

110 CRA to JN, 29 December 1947. TNA: DO 142/490. CRA had based his opinion on a letter written by Philip Noel-Baker, who had said that the Indian government 'appear to think that they can bring their present campaign to victory, and stifle resistance in Kashmir, if they cut off supplies and reinforcements to their opponents by occupying the Pakistan territory which now serves as their opponents' base. I do not know who can have given them such advice, but I believe it to be a dangerous military miscalculation. Many of those who are in the field against them are Poonchis or other Kashmiries [*sic*]; I know them to be excellent soldiers; I think it most unlikely that the Indian Army could successfully maintain enough troops in Kashmir to counter their guerrilla tactics, and to bring them to submission.' Philip Noel-Baker to Sir Terence Shone, 27 December 1947. TNA: DO 142/490.

111 Foreign Office to Ambassadors, 2 January 1948. TNA: DO 35/3162.

18. MAYBE NOT TODAY, MAYBE NOT TOMORROW

1 Richard Symonds to EA, 1 January 1948. MP: MB1/Q68; also Symonds, *In the Margins of Independence*, p. 88.

2 Commonwealth Relations Office memorandum on the Kashmir dispute, May 1948. TNA: DO 142/540.

3 Sir Laurence Grafftey-Smith to Commonwealth Relations Office, 7 January 1948. TNA: DO 142/542.

4 'The number of genuine tribesmen from the North West Frontier which have come into the area to assist these local insurgents appears . . . to be very small. It

should be remembered that the Poonch area produced 60,000 troops for the last war, most of whom are now home. These are formidable fighters.' Foreign Office to Ambassadors, 9 January 1948. TNA: DO 35/3162.

5 Commonwealth Relations Office memorandum on the Kashmir dispute, May 1948. TNA: DO 142/540.

6 Foreign Office to UN Delegation in New York, 12 January 1948. TNA: DO 142/490.

7 UK High Commissioner India to Commonwealth Relations Office, 5 January 1948. TNA: DO 142/542, Commonwealth Relations Office memorandum on the Kashmir dispute, May 1948. TNA: DO 142/540.

8 Brown, *Nehru*, pp. 178–9.

9 CRA to Philip Noel-Baker and embassies, 10 January 1948. TNA: DO 142/490.

10 The *Light* (Lahore), 16 May 1948, p. 3.

11 Akbar, *Nehru*, p. 448.

12 DM cited in Ziegler, *Mountbatten*, p. 450.

13 Sir M. Peterson to Foreign Office, 13 January 1948. TNA: DO 35/3162.

14 Cited in letter from J.G.P. Spicer to L.N. Helsby, 1 November 1948, TNA: CAB 127/143.

15 Symonds, *In the Margins of Independence*, p. 97.

16 MKG, fragment of a letter, 7 January 1948. *CWMG*, vol 90, p. 376.

17 MKG, fragment of a letter, 9 January 1948. *CWMG*, vol 90, p. 388.

18 Vallabhbhai Patel cited in French, *Liberty or Death*, pp. 359–60. See also *SWJN* (2), vol 5, pp. 21, 30; Akbar, *Nehru*, p. 454.

19 A top-secret telegram from the British High Commissioner to the Commonwealth Relations Office mentioned this possibility. Sir Terence Shone to Archibald Carter, n.d. (January 1948), TNA: DO 133/93.

20 Khilnani, *The Idea of India*, p. 75; Seton, *Panditji*, pp. 158–9.

21 UK High Commissioner (India) to Commonwealth Relations Office, 13 January 1948. TNA: DO 35/3162.

22 Bourke-White, *Portrait of Myself*, p. 292.

23 MKG cited in Governor General's Personal Report no. 8, 3 February 1948. AAS: Mss Eur D714/86.

24 Akbar, *Nehru*, p. 429.

25 DM cited in Collins & Lapierre, *Mountbatten and the Partition of India*, p. 36.

26 Governor General's Personal Report no. 8, 3 February 1948. AAS: Mss Eur D714/86. See also DM's record of the meeting, AAS: IOR Neg 15561/195C, ff 96–8.

27 Hutheesing, *We Nehrus*, p. 218; Brown, *Nehru*, pp. 179–80; *SWJN* (2), vol 5, pp. 6–7.

28 MKG, 18 January 1948. *CWMG*, vol 90, p. 444.

29 Campbell-Johnson, *Mission with Mountbatten*, p. 272.

30 MKG cited in Malgonkar, *The Men Who Killed Gandhi*, p. 153.

31 Report of ACB Symon to Philip Noel-Baker, 4 February 1948. TNA: PREM 8/741.

32 See speech in SWJN (2), vol 5, p. 32; also *Pioneer* (Lucknow), 29 January 1948, p. 1.

33 Hutheesing, *We Nehrus*, p. 222; Frank, *Indira*, p. 218.

34 Report of A.C.B. Symon to Philip Noel-Baker, 4 February 1948. TNA: PREM 8/741.

35 Hutheesing, *We Nehrus*, p. 224. Similar sentiments were expressed during a memorable scene in Salman Rushdie's *Midnight's Children*, in which Amina and Ahmed Sinai are at the cinema when news of MKG's assassination comes through. Amina's

relief when the assassin is revealed to have a Hindu name is obvious. 'By being Godse he has saved our lives!' Rushdie, *Midnight's Children*, p. 142.

36 Malgonkar, *The Men Who Killed Gandhi*, pp. 20–1, 85.
37 Nayantara Pandit to Vijaya Lakshmi Pandit, 18 February 1948. Private collection of Nayantara Sahgal.
38 Sahgal, *Prison and Chocolate Cake*, p. 219; also Moraes, *Jawaharlal Nehru*, p. 348.
39 Hutheesing, *We Nehrus*, p. 225.
40 Bourke-White, *Portrait of Myself*, p. 298.
41 Hutheesing, *We Nehrus*, p. 226.
42 According to journalist Pran Chopra, cited in Adams & Whitehead, *The Dynasty*, p. 137; see also Report of A.C.B. Symon to Philip Noel-Baker, 4 February 1948. TNA: PREM 8/741.
43 *SWJN* (2), vol 5, p. 35.
44 Hutheesing, *We Nehrus*, pp. 227–8.
45 Report of A.C.B. Symon, to Philip Noel-Baker, 4 February 1948. TNA: PREM 8/741.
46 CP: CHUR 2/44.
47 Coward, *Diaries*, 30 January 1948, p. 103.
48 Morgan, *Edwina Mountbatten*, p. 427.
49 Gopal, *Nehru*, vol ii, p. 26.
50 Peter Murphy to EA, cited in Morgan, *Edwina Mountbatten*, p. 423.
51 Ibid, p. 423.
52 Barratt with Ritchie, *With the Greatest Respect*, p. 47.
53 Hough, *Edwina*, p. 182.
54 JN to EA, cited in Morgan, *Edwina Mountbatten*, p. 429.
55 Hutheesing, *We Nehrus*, p. 198.
56 MP: MB2/N14.
57 Brown, *Nehru*, pp. 180–1; DM to Krishna Menon, 7 February 1948. MP:MB1/F37.
58 Pandey, *Remembering Partition*, p. 145; Dalton, *Mahatma Gandhi*, p. 167.
59 Sarojini Naidu cited in John Grigg, 'The Power and the Glory', *Observer*, 2 September 1979.
60 Krishna Menon to DM, 3 February 1948 (dated 1947 in error). MP: MB1/F37.
61 DM to Krishna Menon, 7 February 1948. MP:MB1/F37.
62 Rita Pandit to Vijaya Lakshmi Pandit, 17 February 1948. VLP: correspondence with Rita Dar.
63 EA to Agatha Harrison, 20 February 1948. Seton, *Panditji*, plate xix, between pp. 140–1.
64 Sir G. Squire to Foreign Office, 11 January 1948. TNA: DO 142/490.
65 MAJ cited in Ahmed, *Jinnah, Pakistan and Islamic Identity*, p. 178.
66 Bourke-White, *Portrait of Myself*, p. 291.
67 Campbell-Johnson, *Mission with Mountbatten*, p. 255.
68 DM to CRA, 8 February 1948. TNA: DO 142/496.
69 CRA to DM, 10 February 1948. TNA: DO 142/496.
70 DM to CRA, 11 February 1948. TNA: DO 142/496.
71 Campbell-Johnson, *Mission with Mountbatten*, p. 287.
72 DM to CRA, 24 February 1948; Philip Noel-Baker to CRA, 25 February 1948 and 26 February 1948; Philip Noel-Baker to Sir Terence Shone, 3 March 1948; all TNA: PREM 8/821; see also TNA: DO 142/496.
73 Campbell-Johnson, *Mission with Mountbatten*, p. 245; DM to Walter Monckton, 29 November 1947. WMP: 30, f 652.

74 Nizam of Hyderabad to Walter Monckton, 16 January 1948. WMP: 31, f 76.

75 Campbell-Johnson, *Mission with Mountbatten*, p. 313.

76 Nizam of Hyderabad cited in ibid, p. 329.

77 Campbell-Johnson, *Mission with Mountbatten*, pp. 300–1.

78 Ibid, p. 304.

79 Kux, *Estranged Democracies*, p. 68.

80 Rajagopalachari cited in Campbell-Johnson, *Mission with Mountbatten*, p. 297.

81 Ibid, p. 317.

82 UK High Commissioner in India to Commonwealth Relations Office, 18 April 1948. TNA: DO 142/496.

83 Horace Alexander to EA, 22 April 1948. MP: MB1/Q6.

84 EA to Horace Alexander, 19 May 1948. MP: MB1/Q6.

85 DM, report of an interview with JN, 3 May 1948. AAS: IOR Neg 15561/195F, f 23.

86 *SWJN* (2), vol 5, p. 271.

87 EA to Sheikh Abdullah, 30 May 1948. MP: MB1/Q101.

88 DM, report of interviews with JN and Vallabhbhai Patel, 20 April 1948. AAS: IOR Neg 15561/195A, f 45.

89 JN to Chakravarty Rajagopalachari, 30 March 1948; Chakravarty Rajagopalachari to JN, 2 April 1948; JN to Chakravarty Rajagopalachari, 11 April 1948; Chakravarty Rajagopalachari to JN, 15 April 1948. NML: Papers of Chakravarty Rajagopalachari, Inst. V, correspondence with JN.

90 JN to Chakravarty Rajagopalachari, 6 May 1948; all NML: Papers of Chakravarty Rajagopalachari, Inst. V, correspondence with JN.

91 Chakravarty Rajagopalachari to JN, 12 May 1948. NML: Papers of Chakravarty Rajagopalachari, Inst. V, correspondence with JN.

92 EA to JN, cited in Morgan, *Edwina Mountbatten*, pp. 427–8.

93 DM to Lady Brabourne, 12 June 1948. Cited in Ziegler, *Mountbatten*, p. 473.

94 Roberts, *Eminent Churchillians*, pp. 125–6.

95 Morgan, *Edwina Mountbatten*, p. 428.

96 Countess Mountbatten of Burma cited in Adams & Whitehead, *The Dynasty*, p. 148.

97 Lady Pamela Hicks in 'Mountbatten', *Secret History*, Channel 4 Television. Lady Pamela made a point of stating that she did not believe the relationship to be physical.

98 DM to Lady Brabourne, 22 May 1948, cited in Ziegler, *Mountbatten*, p. 460.

99 JN to EA, 12 March 1957, Cited in ibid, p. 473.

100 JN to Indira Gandhi, 19 May 1948. Nehru and Gandhi, *Two Alone, Two Together*, p. 553.

101 EA to JN, cited in Morgan, *Edwina Mountbatten*, p. 428.

102 JN to EA, cited in ibid, p. 429.

103 EA cited in ibid, p. 429.

104 Campbell-Johnson, *Mission with Mountbatten*, p. 349.

105 DM: farewell memorandum, in DM to Vallabhbhai Patel, 19 June 1948. MP: MB1/D150. Notably, India already had a female ambassador, Vijaya Lakshmi Pandit, who happened to be a widow. DM made no recommendations as to ambassadors' husbands.

106 JN to EA, cited in Morgan, *Edwina Mountbatten*, p. 430.

107 *Illustrated Weekly of India*, 20 June 1948, pp. 9–11.

108 JN to EA, 18 June 1948. MP: MB1/R447.

109 *Indian News Chronicle*, 21 June 1948, p. 1; *Statesman*, 21 June 1948, p. 1.

110 Holman, 'Lady Mountbatten's story', part 5.

111 JN cited in Holman, *Lady Louis*, p. 12.

112 JN to King George VI, 21 May 1948. RA: PS/GVI/C 280/292; Sir Alan Lascelles to JN, 17 June 1948. RA: PS/GVI/C 280/294; JN to Sir Alan Lascelles, 23 July 1948. RA: PS/GVI/C 280/296; Sir Alan Lascelles to JN, 29 July 1948. RA: PS/GVI/C 280/303.

113 JN to EA, cited in Morgan, *Edwina Mountbatten*, p. 432.

114 JN himself disliked his name, and had almost thought of changing it a decade before after 'a BBC announcer got hopelessly muddled over it and went on ha-haing'. JN to Krishna Menon, 25 March 1937, cited in Akbar, *Nehru*, p. 307. In contrast, DM seems to have had no trouble spelling Vallabhbhai Patel or Chakravarty Rajagopalachari's names.

115 MP: MB2/N14.

116 *Times of India*, 22 June 1948, pp. 1, 3.

117 Chakravarty Rajagopalachari to CRA, 23 June 1948. TNA: PREM 8/808.

IV. AFTERWARDS

19. A KISS GOODBYE

1 Chakravarty Rajagopalachari to DM, 23 June 1948. MP: MB1/F42.

2 Anonymous friend cited in Hough, *Edwina*, p. 199.

3 EA to JN, cited in Morgan, *Edwina Mountbatten*, p. 434.

4 JN to EA, cited in ibid, p. 435.

5 JN to DM, 3 July 1948. MP: MB1/F39.

6 Chakravarty Rajagopalachari to DM, 1 July 1948. MP: MB1/F42.

7 *Truth*, 2 July 1948, p. 2. See also Chakravarty Rajagopalachari to DM, 8 July 1948. MP: MB1/F42.

8 DM to Chakravarty Rajagopalachari, 16 July 1948. MP: MB1/F42.

9 CP: CHUR 2/153B, ff 286–7.

10 Wolpert, *Nehru*, p. 401.

11 DM to WSC, 23 July 1947. CP: CHUR 2/153B, f 281. WSC to DM, 4 August 1947. CP: CHUR 2/153B, f 282.

12 Leo Amery, *Diary*, 29 June 1948. LAP: AMEL 7/42.

13 EA to the East India Association, 29 June 1948. *Asiatic Review*, vol xliv, no 160 (October 1948), pp. 354–5.

14 JN to DM, 3 July 1948. MP: MB1/F39.

15 DM to JN, 15 July 1947. MP: MB1/F39.

16 DM to CRA, 6 July 1948. MP: MB1/E5.

17 DM to JN, 15 July 1947. MP: MB1/F39.

18 DM to JN, 28 July 1948. MP: MB1/F39.

19 JN to DM, 1 August 1948. MP: MB1/F39.

20 DM to JN, 15 August 1948. MP: MB1/F39; see also DM to JN, 10 September 1948. MP: MB1/F39.

21 DM to JN, 28 July 1948. MP: MB1/F39.

22 Jinnah, *My Brother*, p. 35.

23 MAJ cited in Akbar, *Nehru*, p. 433. See also Singh Sarila, *The Shadow of the Great Game*, p. 94.

24 Jinnah, *My Brother*, pp. 37–8. MAJ had said: 'Fati, may God protect you . . . There is no God but Allah . . . Mohammed is the messenger of Allah.'

25 DM to Chakravarty Rajagopalachari, 25 September 1948. MP: MB1/F42.
26 Chakravarty Rajagopalachari to DM, 5 October 1948: MP: MB1/F42.
27 JN to Indira Gandhi, 6 October 1948. Nehru & Gandhi, *Two Alone, Two Together*, p. 559.
28 EA cited in Morgan, *Edwina Mountbatten*, p. 437.
29 DM to JN, 25 September 1948. MP: MB1/F39.
30 Morgan, *Edwina Mountbatten*, p. 437.
31 DM to Chakravarty Rajagopalachari,16 October 1948. MP: MB1/F42.
32 Smith, *Fifty Years with Mountbatten*, pp. 87–8.
33 Hough, *Edwina*, p. 199.
34 JN to Indira Gandhi, 28 October 1948. Nehru & Gandhi, *Two Alone, Two Together*, p. 561.
35 The *Tatler & Bystander*, 27 October 1948, pp. 97–101.
36 DM to Chakravarty Rajagopalachari,16 October 1948. MP: MB1/F42.
37 DM to King George VI, 10 October 1948. RA: GVI/PRIV/01/24/174.
38 JN to Indira Gandhi, 28 October 1948. Nehru & Gandhi, *Two Alone, Two Together*, p. 561.
39 Hutheesing, *We Nehrus*, pp. 237–8.
40 EA to Dennis Holman, n.d. MP: MB1/R231.
41 JN to EA and EA to JN, cited in Morgan, *Edwina Mountbatten*, pp. 447–8.
42 *Daily Herald*, 27 February 1953, p. 1; *The Times*, 27 February 1953, p. 7.
43 Sir Alan Lascelles to J.R. Colville, 27 February 1953. TNA: PREM 11/340.
44 Akbar, *Nehru*, p. 569.
45 The witness was Russi Mody, later chief executive of Tata Steel; his father was Sir Homi Mody, Governor of Uttar Pradesh (formerly the United Provinces). The incident took place between 1949 and 1952. Ibid, pp. 390–1.
46 Cited in Mathai, *My Days with Nehru*, p. 154; see also Morgan, *Edwina Mountbatten*, p. 469.
47 JN to DM, 25 March 1952. MP: MB1/G28. See also Ziegler, *Mountbatten*, pp. 501–2.
48 DM cited in Morgan, *Edwina Mountbatten*, p. 475.
49 EA to DM, cited in ibid, p. 476.
50 DM to EA, cited in ibid, p. 476.
51 Rajkumari Amrit Kaur to EA, 6 August 1949. MP: MB1/R127.
52 Sahgal, *From Fear Set Free*, p. 141.
53 JN to Indira Gandhi, 2 May 1953. Nehru & Gandhi, *Two Alone, Two Together*, p. 583.
54 Mullik, *My Years with Nehru*, p. 51.
55 Viceroy's Personal Report No 15, 1 August 1947, *TOP*, vol XII, p. 452.
56 DM to JN, 18 February 1952. MP: MB1/G28.
57 DM to JN, 18 October 1953. MP: MB1/H167.
58 JN to DM, 16 November 1953. MP: MB1/H167.
59 DM to JN, 11 February 1954. MP: MB1/H167.
60 JN to Indira Nehru, 4 January 1937. Nehru & Gandhi, *Freedom's Daughter*, p. 307. During 1937, JN was romantically involved with Padmaja Naidu, whom he often compared to an 'Ajanta Princess'. Akbar, *Nehru*, pp. 393, 568.
61 EA to A. Wahid, 5 February 1957. MP: MB1/R573.
62 DM to JN, 25 January 1953. MP: MB1/H167; JN to DM, 20 March 1949. MP: MB1/F39.
63 DM to King George VI, 12 April 1949. RA: GVI/PRIV/01/24/178.
64 DM to JN, 18 April 1951. MP: MB1/G28.

65 EA cited in Morgan, *Edwina Mountbatten*, p. 454.
66 DM to WSC, 18 September 1952. TNA: PREM 11/340.
67 Seton, *Panditji*, p. 315.
68 Mullik, *My Years with Nehru*, pp. 125–31.
69 EA to JN, cited in Morgan, *Edwina Mountbatten*, p. 440.
70 Pimlott, *The Queen*, p. 184; Heald, *The Duke*, p. 102. The problem had been pointed out even before the wedding. Cyril Hankinson, editor of Debrett, wrote in *Queen* magazine that 'it may be decided to continue the Windsor Dynasty by a similar process [of proclamation as in 1917]. If this is not done, however, Princess Elizabeth's children will be of the House of Mountbatten.' *Queen*, vol 195, no 9582, 23 July 1947, p. 15.
71 Pimlott, *The Queen*, p. 183. Pimlott argues that Edinburgh was unacceptable because it was a title, rather than a family name, and that a conversion to the House of Mountbatten would have followed the precedent set by Prince Albert. In fact, the royal name acquired when Queen Victoria married Prince Albert – that of Saxe-Coburg Gotha – was a title. Albert's surname was either Wettin or Wipper, according to the College of Heralds. The House of Edinburgh would, therefore, have followed precedent; it would have been as patriotic as Windsor, and no more artificial; it would also have avoided any undesirable association with DM or the Battenberg family. It is hard to imagine what the objection to this could have been, apart from a simple dislike of Philip in the royal household.
72 Philip cited in Pimlott, *The Queen*, p. 185; Bradford, *Elizabeth*, p. 172; Lady Colin Campbell, *The Royal Marriages: Private Lives of the Queen and Her Children* (Smith Gryphon, London, 1993), p. 85.
73 Queen Mary cited in Pimlott, *The Queen*, p. 185.
74 Seshan, *With Three Prime Ministers*, p. 28.
75 See ibid, passim.
76 JN cited in Seshan, *With Three Prime Ministers*, p. 28.
77 Oliver Lyttelton cited in 'Mountbatten's Wife Enraged Churchill', *Daily Telegraph*, 3 January 2004. EA was herself outraged at Lyttelton's statement: see Morgan, *Edwina Mountbatten*, pp. 468–9.
78 TNA: FO 371/107577.
79 WSC cited in Seshan, *With Three Prime Ministers*, pp. 28–9; Henry Hodson attributes a similar story about WSC to Rab Butler rather than Indira Gandhi. Hodson, *The Great Divide*, p. 401.
80 WSC, 8 August 1953, cited in Moran, *Winston Churchill*, pp. 449–50.
81 Pandit, *The Scope of Happiness*, pp. 337–9. The conversation is reported more mildly in Pandit's book; this account was told to the author by Pandit's daughter, Nayantara Sahgal, 8 April 2006.
82 Sahgal, *From Fear Set Free*, p. 171; also Pandit, *The Scope of Happiness*, p. 347.
83 Queen Elizabeth II cited in Parker, *Prince Philip*, p. 220.
84 Healey, *The Time of My Life*, p. 171.
85 DM cited in Pimlott, *The Queen*, p. 254.
86 Ibid, pp. 470–1.
87 Private collection of the Mountbatten family, Broadlands.
88 JN cited in Seton, *Panditji*, p. 270.
89 EA and JN cited in Morgan, *Edwina Mountbatten*, p. 474.
90 Ramachandra Guha, 'A Mask That was Pierced', *Hindu*, 24 April 2005. Guha and Sunil Khilnani both guessed that the author was more likely to be Penderel Moon.
91 Amrit Kaur to EA, 21 July 1958. MP: MB1/R127.

92 DM cited in Seton, *Panditji*, p. 270.
93 Amrit Kaur to EA, 12 May 1959. MP: MB1/R127. Emphasis is Amrit Kaur's.
94 JN cited in Seton, *Panditji*, p. 253.
95 JN to Indira Gandhi, 23 April 1959. Nehru & Gandhi, *Two Alone, Two Together*, p. 625.
96 DM cited in Chaudhuri, *Thy Hand Great Anarch!*, pp. 822–3.
97 Mullik, *My Years with Nehru*, p. 168.
98 Coward, *Diaries*, 16 January 1960, p. 427.
99 *London Gazette*, 8 February 1960. It is clear that the Queen wanted to change her surname as a gift to Philip. TNA: LCO 2/8115, ff 8–11.
100 Hough, *Edwina*, p. 3.
101 Seton, *Panditji*, p. 281.
102 Ibid, pp. 282–3, and see plates between pp. 268–9.
103 Hough, *Edwina*, p. 7.
104 Robert Noel Turner cited in ibid, p. 8.
105 Morgan, *Edwina Mountbatten*, p. 480.
106 Seton, *Panditji*, p. 284.
107 Smith, *Fifty Years with Mountbatten*, p. 125.
108 Coward, *Diaries*, 15 May 1960, p. 439.
109 According to William Evans, in 'Mountbatten', *Secret History*.
110 Morgan, *Edwina Mountbatten*, p. 481.
111 'Mountbatten', *Secret History*.

20. ECHOES

1 Seton cited in Paul Gore-Booth to Sir Saville Garner, 16 April 1963. TNA: DO 196/210.
2 DM to Vijaya Lakshmi Pandit, 20 June 1962. Cited in Ziegler, *Mountbatten*, p. 602.
3 S.K. Patil cited in Galbraith, *Ambassador's Journal*, p. 175.
4 Mullik, *My Years with Nehru*, p. 107; Robert Schulman, *John Sherman Cooper: The Global Kentuckian* (University Press of Kentucky, Lexington, KY, 1976), p. 70.
5 Kux, *The United States and Pakistan*, p. 115.
6 Galbraith, *Ambassador's Journal*, p. 247, footnote.
7 According to B.K. Nehru, cited in Kux, *Estranged Democracies*, p. 193; see also pp. 194–5. See also Galbraith, *Ambassador's Journal*, p. 248.
8 Galbraith, *Ambassador's Journal*, p. 248.
9 Ibid, p. 249.
10 Ibid, p. 320.
11 Lee Radziwill, *Happy Times* (Assouline, New York, 2000), p. 110.
12 Hutheesing, *We Nehrus*, p. 28.
13 Jacqueline Kennedy cited in ibid, p. 28.
14 Galbraith, *Ambassador's Journal*, p. 353.
15 Ibid, 9 December 1962, p. 517.
16 Mountbatten, *From Shore to Shore*, p. 82.
17 Report from P.H. Gore-Booth to Sir Saville Garner, 3 January 1964. TNA: DO 196/311.
18 P.H. Gore-Booth, report of DM's account of a meeting with JN, 3 January 1964. TNA: DO 196/311.
19 Ibid.
20 DM cited in Brown, *Nehru*, p. 335.
21 Brittain, *Envoy Extraordinary*, pp. 160–1.

22 Pandit, *The Scope of Happiness*, p. 378.

23 Seton, *Panditji*, p. 472.

24 JN, will and testament, *SWJN* (2), vol 26, p. 612.

25 R.H. Belcher, report on the funeral of JN. TNA: PREM 11/4864.

26 Seton, *Panditji*, p. 474.

27 Brittain, *Envoy Extraordinary*, pp. 163–4.

28 Report by Acting British High Commissioner in India, R.H. Belcher, to Secretary of State for Commonwealth Development, 17 June 1964. PREM 11/4864; CRO ref: 2SEA 50/5/1.

29 Healey, *The Time of My Life*, pp. 261–2.

30 Patrick Nairne to Derek Mitchell, 26 March 1965. TNA: PREM 13/159. See also Solly Zuckerman to Michael Berry, 7 February 1964. MP: MB1/Z2; 'Peterborough', *Daily Telegraph*, 30 January 1964.

31 Healey, *The Time of My Life*, p. 257; Montague Browne, *Long Sunset*, p. 315.

32 John Beavan, 'The Man of Influence', *Daily Mirror*, 29 October 1964, p. 9.

33 TNA: HO 191/167, 195/6/65, 195/8/124, and several more.

34 Sampson, *Anatomy of Britain Today*, p. 364.

35 Solly Zuckerman to DM, 30 March 1962; DM to Solly Zuckerman, 14 June 1962; Solly Zuckerman to DM, 15 June 1962, all MP: MB1/Z2. DM's articles were 'Identity of Carcass Still a Scientific Mystery', *Nassau Daily Tribune*, 15 March 1962; 'Is Monster Unknown Extinct Sea Animal?', *Daily Gleaner*, 12 March 1962; *Envoy*, March/April 1960.

36 Healey, *The Time of My Life*, p. 258.

37 MP: MB1/K202.

38 *Yorkshire Post*, 15 November 1968.

39 Pimlott, *The Queen*, pp. 349–50.

40 Ibid, p. 387.

41 Sir Morrice James to Burke Trend, 9 August 1968. TNA: FCO 37/133.

42 DM cited in Roberts, *Eminent Churchillians*, p. 134.

43 DM to Solly Zuckerman, 21 February 1969. MP: MB1/Z1.

44 DM to General Cariappa, 5 December 1965. MP: MB1/K147.

45 DM to Harold Wilson, 24 May 1966. TNA: PREM 13/1072.

46 DM to Indira Gandhi, 19 January 1966. MP: MB1/K147.

47 Lyndon B. Johnson and Indira Gandhi cited in Adams & Whitehead, *The Dynasty*, p. 206.

48 Indira Gandhi cited in Sahgal, 'The Making of Mrs. Gandhi', p. 192.

49 DM to Vijaya Lakshmi Pandit, 25 August 1967. MP: MB1/K147.

50 King, *The Cecil King Diary 1965–1970*, p. 12; Sampson, *Anatomy of Britain Today*, p. 140.

51 King, *The Cecil King Diary 1965–1970*, p. 14.

52 Ibid, 12 August 1967, pp. 138–9.

53 Zuckerman, *Monkeys, Men and Missiles*, p. 463.

54 Healey, *The Time of My Life*, p. 337; Ziegler, *Mountbatten*, pp. 659–61.

55 Solly Zuckerman, 'Working with a Man of destiny', *Observer*, 2 September 1979.

56 Solly Zuckerman cited in Hugh Cudlipp, *Walking on the Water* (The Bodley Head, London, 1976), p. 326.

57 Cecil King's *Diary*, cited in 'Mountbatten and the Coup that Wasn't Quite', *The Times*, 3 April 1981, p. 4.

58 'Queen Told of "Coup" Threat', *Sunday Telegraph*, 16 August 1981, p. 3.

59 *Private Eye*, no 362, 31 Oct 1975, p. 5. There is a copy of this in MP: MB1/K162A.

60 Private information. See also King, *The Cecil King Diary 1965–1970*, 22 May 1969, p. 259; and Zuckerman, 'Working with a Man of Destiny'. There is a conspicuous hole in the otherwise regular correspondence file with Solly Zuckerman among DM's papers, between 29 January and 18 October 1968.

61 Smith, *Fifty Years with Mountbatten*, p. 157.

62 DM cited in Ziegler, *Mountbatten*, p. 53.

63 'Mountbatten', *Secret History*, Channel 4 Television.

64 Hoey, *Mountbatten*, p. 86; Smith, *Fifty Years with Mountbatten*, p. 96.

65 DM cited in Smith, *Fifty Years with Mountbatten*, p. 152.

66 Barbara Cartland, *I Reach for the Stars: An Autobiography* (Robson Books, London, 1994), p. 123.

67 Pandit, *The Scope of Happiness*, p. 2.

68 Frank, *Indira*, p. 402.

69 Adams & Whitehead, *The Dynasty*, pp. 261–5; Frank, *Indira*, pp. 404–7.

70 DM to Vijaya Lakshmi Pandit, 29 August 1977. VLP: correspondence with DM. See also Indira Gandhi to Barbara Cartland, 20 September 1981. Cited in Cartland, *I Reach for the Stars*, 1994, pp. 73–4.

71 Pandit, *The Scope of Happiness*, p. 27.

72 DM to Vijaya Lakshmi Pandit, 13 November 1978. VLP: correspondence with DM.

73 DM to Vijaya Lakshmi Pandit, 21 November 1978. VLP: correspondence with DM.

74 Barbara Cartland cited in the *Evening Standard*, 13 November 1978.

75 Barbara Cartland cited in the *Daily Telegraph*, 14 November 1978, p. 19. Six years later, Indira Gandhi would meet her death by assassination. She was shot with semi-automatic pistols by her Sikh bodyguards, in revenge for ordering the army into the Golden Temple at Amritsar. Her son Sanjay had been killed in a plane crash after flying loops over Delhi in 1980. Her other son, Rajiv Gandhi, became the third Nehru Prime Minister, winning a landslide in 1984 despite having little political experience. Following a disappointing tenure and lacklustre result at the 1989 elections, he resigned, though his personal popularity remained high. In 1991, he was on the verge of a return to power – but assassination awaited him too, strapped under the kurti of a Tamil suicide bomber. Rajiv's widow, Sonia Gandhi, an Italian he had met while studying at Cambridge, led a return to power by Congress in 2004. To the surprise of commentators, she became President of Congress rather than Prime Minister. Her son, Rahul, is often talked of as a future Prime Minister; her daughter, Priyanka Gandhi Vadra, has been active in Congress campaigns. Meanwhile Sanjay's widow, Maneka Gandhi, forced out of Congress by Indira, defected to the Hindu nationalist Bharatiya Janata Party and became a member of the Lok Sabha. Maneka's son, Varun Gandhi, has followed her into the BJP. It is not out of the question that the future of Indian democracy could see a billion people being offered an electoral choice between cousins.

76 Bradford, *Elizabeth*, p. 321; Smith, *Fifty Years with Mountbatten*, pp. 140–1; Pimlott, *The Queen*, pp. 358–9.

77 DM to Vijaya Lakshmi Pandit, 27 February 1979. VLP: correspondence with DM.

78 DM cited in Smith, *Fifty Years with Mountbatten*, p. 11.

79 Hoey, *Mountbatten*, p. 21.

80 Patricia Mountbatten speaking on *Woman's Hour*, Radio 4, 10 August 2005. See also Hoey, *Mountbatten*, p. 29.

81 Pimlott, *The Queen*, p. 470; Roberts, *Eminent Churchillians*, p. 136.

82 JN to Motilal Nehru, 7 November 1907. *SWJN* (1), vol 1, p. 37. See also Nehru, *An Autobiography*, p. 25.

83 Hoey, *Mountbatten*, p. 39.

84 Smith, *Fifty Years with Mountbatten*, p. 12; TNA: MEPO 10/31.
85 Barry, *Royal Service*, p. 95.
86 Charles cited in Pimlott, *The Queen*, p. 471.
87 Ashley Hicks cited in Hoey, *Mountbatten*, p. 32.
88 Statistics from United Nations World Food Programme.
89 These tales were collected by Minakshi Chaudhry in her entertaining *Ghost Stories of Shimla Hills* (Rupa & Co, New Delhi, 2005).
90 Cited in Amrit Dhillon, 'India's New Rich Go On Spending Spree', *Sunday Times*, 3 April 2005.

BIBLIOGRAPHY

There are two great problems facing any historian of the end of the British Empire in India and Pakistan: the sheer quantity of evidence, and the extreme nature of bias in most of it. The most popular work on the transfer of power has been *Freedom at Midnight* by Larry Collins and Dominique Lapierre. That book, largely and unquestioningly based on the rose-tinted reminiscences of Lord Mountbatten in the 1970s, is highly entertaining, but so imaginative that it is best read as a novelization of events. Meanwhile, the memoirs written by those closest to the action – including Maulana A.K. Azad's *India Wins Freedom*, Alan Campbell-Johnson's *Mission with Mountbatten* and Shahid Hamid's *Disastrous Twilight* – were all written with the benefit of considerable hindsight, and with overwhelming political motives.

This bibliography includes works that have been cited more than two or three times, or that have been used for general background. Further works have been cited in the Notes.

ABBREVIATIONS IN NOTES

AAS   Asian & African Studies, formerly the Oriental & India Office Collection, British Library, London.

AP   Attlee Papers, Modern Manuscripts, Bodleian Library, Oxford.

CP   Churchill Papers, Churchill Archive, Churchill College, Cambridge.

CRA   Clement Richard Attlee.

CSAS   Centre of South Asia Studies, University of Cambridge.

CWMG   *Collected Works of Mahatma Gandhi* (Government of India, New Delhi, 1958–94).

DM   Louis 'Dickie' Mountbatten.
EA   Edwina Ashley (later Edwina Mountbatten).
JN   Jawaharlal Nehru.
LAP   Amery Papers, Churchill Archive, Churchill College, Cambridge.
MAJ   Mohammad Ali Jinnah.
MKG   Mohandas Karamchand Gandhi.
MP   Mountbatten Papers, Hartley Library, Southampton University.
            Copies of the official parts of the papers are also available at
            Asian & African Studies, British Library, London; and at the
            National Archives, Kew, London.
NAI   National Archives of India, New Delhi.
NML   Nehru Memorial Library, New Delhi.
ODNB   *Oxford Dictionary of National Biography* (Oxford University
            Press, Oxford, 2004).
QP   Quaid-e-Azam Papers (Papers of Mohammad Ali Jinnah), Asian
            & African Studies, British Library, London. The original papers
            are held in the National Archives of Pakistan, Islamabad.
RA   Royal Archives, Windsor. Used with the permission of Her
            Majesty Queen Elizabeth II.
SWJN   *Selected Works of Jawaharlal Nehru*, edited by Sarvepalli
            Gopal. First series (1): (Jawaharlal Nehru Memorial Fund,
            New Delhi, 1972–82); Second series (2): (Jawaharlal Nehru
            Memorial Fund, New Delhi, 1984–).
TNA   The National Archives (formerly the Public Record Office),
            Kew, London.
ToP   *The Transfer of Power 1942–47*, 12 vols, edited by Nicholas
            Mansergh et al (HMSO, London, 1970–83)
VLP   Papers of Vijaya Lakshmi Pandit, Nehru Memorial Library,
            New Delhi.
WMP   Walter Monckton Papers, Modern Manuscripts, Bodleian
            Library, Oxford.
WSC   Winston Spencer Churchill.

OTHER SOURCES

Adams, Jad, and Phillip Whitehead. *The Dynasty: The Nehru-Gandhi
    Story* (Penguin Books & BBC Books, London, 1997)
Ahmed, Akbar S. 'The Hero in History: Myth, Media and Realities',
    History Today, vol 46, no 3, March 1996.
— *Jinnah, Pakistan and Islamic Identity: The Search for Saladin*
    (Routledge, London & New York, 1997)
Akbar, M.J. *Nehru: The Making of India* (Roli Books, New Delhi,
    2002)

Ali, Aruna Asaf, in association with G.N.S. Raghavan. *Private Face of a Public Person: A Study of Jawaharlal Nehru* (Radiant Publishers for Nehru Memorial Museum & Library, New Delhi, 1989)

Allen, Charles. *God's Terrorists: The Wahhabi Cult and the Hidden Roots of Modern Jihad* (Little, Brown, London, 2006)

— and Sharada Dwivedi. *Lives of the Indian Princes* (Century Publishing, London, 1984)

Ambedkar, B.R. *Gandhi and Gandhism* (Bheem Patrika Publications, Jullundur, 1970)

Anon. *Mountbatten: Eighty Years in Pictures* (Macmillan, London, 1979)

Aronson, Theo. *Crowns in Conflict: The Triumph and the Tragedy of European Monarchy, 1910–1918* (John Murray, London, 1986)

Azad, Abul Kalam. *India Wins Freedom: An Autobiographical Narrative* (Orient Longmans, Calcutta, 1959)

Bakshi, S.R., ed. *Kamala Nehru*. Indian Freedom-fighters; Struggle for Independence, vol. 76 (Om Publications, Faridabad, 1998)

Barratt, John, with Jean Ritchie. *With the Greatest Respect: The Private Lives of Earl Mountbatten of Burma and Prince & Princess Michael of Kent* (Sidgwick & Jackson, London, 1991)

Barry, Stephen P. *Royal Service: My Twelve Years as Valet to Prince Charles* (Macmillan Publishing Co, New York, 1983)

Bose, Nirmal Kumar. *My Days with Gandhi* (1953; Sangam Books, London, 1987)

Bourke-White, Margaret. *Portrait of Myself* (Collins, London, 1964)

Bradford, Sarah. *George VI* (1989; Penguin Books, London, 2002)

Brecher, Michael. *Nehru: A Political Biography* (Oxford University Press, London, 1959)

Brittain, Vera. *Envoy Extraordinary: A Study of Vijaya Lakshmi Pandit and Her Contribution to Modern India* (George Allen & Unwin, London, 1965)

Brown, Judith M. *Gandhi: Prisoner of Hope* (Yale University Press, New Haven & London, 1989)

— *Nehru: A Political Life* (Yale University Press, New Haven and London, 2003)

Burke, S.M. and Salim Al-Din Quraishi. *Quaid-i-Azam Mohammad Ali Jinnah: His Personality and His Politics* (1997; Oxford University Press, Karachi, 2003)

Campbell, Beatrix. *Diana, Princess of Wales: How Sexual Politics Shook the Monarchy* (The Women's Press, London, 1998)

Campbell-Johnson, Alan. *Mission with Mountbatten* (Robert Hale Ltd, London, 1951)

Cannadine, David. *The Pleasures of the Past* (Collins, London, 1989)

— *Ornamentalism: How the British Saw Their Empire* (Allen Lane: The Penguin Press, London, 2001)

Carrington, C.E. *An Exposition of Empire* (Cambridge University Press, Cambridge, 1947)

Carthill, A.L. *The Lost Dominion* (William Blackwood & Sons, Edinburgh & London, 1927)

Cartland, Barbara, inspired and helped by Admiral of the Fleet the Earl Mountbatten of Burma. *Love at the Helm* (Weidenfeld & Nicolson, London, 1980)

Channon, Sir Henry. *Chips: The Diaries of Sir Henry Channon.* Ed. Robert Rhodes James (1967; Phoenix, London, 1999)

Chaplin, Charles. *My Autobiography* (The Bodley Head, London, 1964)

Chaudhuri, Nirad C. *The Autobiography of an Unknown Indian* (Macmillan & Co, London, 1951)

— *Thy Hand Great Anarch! India 1921–1952* (Chatto & Windus, London, 1987)

Chisholm, Ann, and Michael Davie. *Beaverbrook: A Life* (Hutchinson, London, 1992)

Chopra, P.N., with Prabha Chopra and Padmsha Das. *Secret Papers from the British Royal Archives* (Kornak Publishers PVT Ltd, Delhi, 1998)

Churchill, Winston S. *India: Speeches and an Introduction* (Thornton Butterworth Ltd, London, 1931)

Close, H.M. *Attlee, Wavell, Mountbatten, and the Transfer of Power* (National Book Foundation, Islamabad, 1997)

Collett, Nigel. *The Butcher of Amritsar: General Reginald Dyer* (Hambledon & London, London & New York, 2005)

Collins, Larry, and Dominique Lapierre. *Freedom at Midnight* (1975; HarperCollins, London 1997)

— *Mountbatten and the Partition of India: vol. 1, March 22–August 15, 1947* (Garlandfold, London & Vikas Publishing House, New Delhi, 1982)

Connell, Brian. *Manifest Destiny: A Study in Five Profiles of the Rise and Influence of the Mountbatten Family* (Cassell & Co., London, 1953)

Corfield, Conrad. *The Princely India I Knew: From Reading to Mountbatten* (Indo-British Historical Society, Madras, 1975)

Coward, Noël. *Future Indefinite* (William Heinemann Ltd, London, 1954)

— *The Noël Coward Diaries.* Ed. Graham Payn and Sheridan Morley (Weidenfeld & Nicolson, London, 1982)

Dalton, Dennis. *Mahatma Gandhi: Nonviolent Power in Action* (Columbia University Press, New York, 1993)

Das, Manmath Nath. *End of the British-Indian Empire: Politics of 'Divide and Quit'. Select Documents, March-August 1947.* 2 vols (Vidyapuri, Cuttack, India, 1983)

David, Saul. *The Indian Mutiny: 1857* (Viking, London, 2002)

Deacon, Richard. *The Greatest Treason: The Bizarre Story of Hollis, Liddell and Mountbatten* (Century, London, 1989)

Dimbleby, Jonathan. *The Prince of Wales: A Biography* (Little, Brown and Company, London, 1994)

Driberg, Tom. *Ruling Passions* (Jonathan Cape, London, 1977)

Dutt, Vishnu. *Gandhi, Nehru and the Challenge* (Abhinav Publications, New Delhi, 1979)

Edward, HRH The Prince, Prince of Wales. *Letters from a Prince: Edward, Prince of Wales, to Mrs Freda Dudley Ward, March 1918–January 1921*. Edited by Rupert Godfrey (1998; Warner Books, London, 1999) *see also*: Windsor, Duke of.

Eilers, Marlene A. *Queen Victoria's Descendants* (Rosvall Royal Books, Falköping, Sweden, 1997)

Einstein, Albert. *Out of My Later Years* (Thames & Hudson, London, 1950)

Erikson, Erik H. *Gandhi's Truth: On the Origins of Militant Nonviolence* (Faber & Faber Ltd, London, 1970)

Evans, William. *My Mountbatten Years: In The Service of Lord Louis* (Headline, London, 1989)

Faligot, Roger. *Nous avons tué Mountbatten: l'IRA parle* (Editions Jean Picollec, Paris, 1981)

Ferguson, Niall. *Empire: How Britain Made the Modern World* (Allen Lane, London, 2003)

Fischer, Louis. *The Life of Mahatma Gandhi* (Jonathan Cape, London, 1951)

Fisher, Frederick B. *That Strange Little Brown Man Gandhi* (Ray Long & Richard R. Smith Inc, New York, 1932)

Frank, Katherine. *Indira: The Life of Indira Nehru Gandhi* (HarperCollins, London, 2001)

French, Patrick. *Liberty or Death: India's Journey to Independence and Division* (1997; Flamingo, London, 1998)

Galbraith, John Kenneth. *Ambassador's Journal: A Personal Account of the Kennedy Years* (Hamish Hamilton, London, 1969)

Gandhi, Arun. *Daughter of Midnight: The Child Bride of Gandhi* (Blake Publishing Ltd, London, 1998)

Gandhi, Indira. *Letters to a Friend 1950–1984*. Selected, with commentary, from correspondence with Dorothy Norman (Weidenfeld & Nicolson, London, 1985)

Gandhi, Indira and Jawaharlal Nehru. *Freedom's Daughter: Letters Between Indira Gandhi and Jawaharlal Nehru, 1922–39*, edited by Sonia Gandhi (Hodder & Stoughton, London, 1989)

— *Two Alone, Two Together: Letters Between Indira Gandhi and Jawaharlal Nehru, 1940–1964*, edited by Sonia Gandhi (Hodder & Stoughton, London, 1992)

Gandhi, Mohandas Karamchand. *Hind Swaraj* (1908; S. Ganesan & Co, Madras, 1921)

— *An Autobiography: Or, the Story of My Experiments with the Truth* translated by Mahadev Desai (1929; Penguin Classics, London, 2001)

Getz, Marshall J. *Subhas Chandra Bose: A Biography* (McFarland & Company, Jefferson, NC, 2002)

Gilbert, Martin. *Road to Victory: Winston S. Churchill, 1941–1945* (Heinemann, London, 1986)

— *'Never Despair': Winston S. Churchill, 1945–1965* (1988; Minerva, London, 1990)

Gilmartin, David. *Empire and Islam: Punjab and the Making of Pakistan* (University of California Press, Berkeley & London, 1988)

Gilmour, David. *Curzon* (1994; Papermac, London, 1995)

Gopal, Sarvepalli. *Jawaharlal Nehru: A Biography* (Jonathan Cape, London, 1975–84) 3 vols.

Gordon, Leonard A. *Brothers Against the Raj: A Biography of Indian Nationalists Sarat and Subhas Chandra Bose* (Columbia University Press, New York, 1990)

Grenier, Richard. *The Gandhi Nobody Knows* (Thomas Nelson, Inc, Nashville, TN, 1983)

Grigg, John. *Myths About the Approach to Indian Independence* (University of Texas at Austin, Austin, TX, 1995)

Hamid, Shahid. *Disastrous Twilight: A Personal Record of the Partition of India* (Leo Cooper/Secker & Warburg, London, 1986)

Hasan, Mushirul, with Priya Kapoor. *The Nehrus: Personal Histories* (Mercury Books, London, 2006)

Hatch, Alden. *The Mountbattens* (W. H. Allen, London, 1966)

Heald, Tim. *The Duke: A Portrait of Prince Philip* (Hodder & Stoughton, London, 1991)

Healey, Denis. *The Time of My Life* (1989; Penguin Books, London, 1990)

Heward, Edward. *The Great and the Good: A Life of Lord Radcliffe* (Barry Rose Publishers, Chichester, 1994)

Hodson, H.V. *The Great Divide: Britain – India – Pakistan* (1969; new edition, Oxford University Press, Karachi, 1985)

Hoey, Brian. *Mountbatten: The Private Story* (Sidgwick & Jackson, London, 1994)

Holman, Dennis. *Lady Louis: Life of the Countess Mountbatten of Burma* (Odhams Press, London, 1952)

Hough, Richard. *Louis and Victoria: The First Mountbattens* (Hutchinson, London, 1974)

— *Edwina: Countess Mountbatten of Burma* (Weidenfeld & Nicolson, London, 1983)

Hutheesing, Krishna, with Alden Hatch. *We Nehrus* (Holt, Rinehart & Wilson, New York, 1967)

Jalal, Ayesha. *The Sole Spokesman: Jinnah, the Muslim League, and the Demand for Pakistan* (Cambridge University Press, Cambridge, 1985)

James, Lawrence. *Raj: The Making and Unmaking of British India* (Little, Brown, London, 1997)

Jayawardena, Kumari and Malathi de Alwis, eds. *Embodied Violence: Communalising Women's Sexuality in South Asia* (Kali for Women, New Delhi, 1996)

Jeffrey, Robin, ed. *People, Princes and Paramount Power: Society and Politics in the Indian Princely States* (Oxford University Press, Delhi, 1978)

Jenkins, Roy. 'Jawaharlal Nehru', *Portraits and Miniatures: Selected Writings* (1993; Papermac, London, 1994)

Jha, Prem Shankar. *Kashmir, 1947: Rival Versions of History* (Oxford University Press, Delhi, 1996)

Jinnah, Fatima. *My Brother* (Quaid-e-Azam Academy, Karachi, 1987)

Jones, George E. *Tumult in India* (Dodd, Mead & Company, New York, 1948)

Judd, Denis. *The Lion and the Tiger: The Rise and Fall of the British Raj, 1600–1947* (Oxford University Press, Oxford, 2004)

Juneja, M.M. *The Mahatma and the Millionaire: A Study in Gandhi-Birla Relations* (Modern Publishers, Hisar, 1993)

Kalhan, Promilla. *Kamala Nehru: An Intimate Biography* (Vikas Publishing House PVT Ltd, Delhi, 1973)

Kendall, Patricia. *India and the British: A Quest for Truth* (Charles Scribner's Sons, London, 1931)

Khan, Akbar. *Raiders in Kashmir* (Pak Publishers, Karachi, 1970)

Khilnani, Sunil. *The Idea of India* (1997; Penguin Books, London, 2003)

King, Cecil. *Strictly Personal: Some Memoirs of Cecil H. King* (Weidenfeld & Nicolson, London, 1969)

— *The Cecil King Diary 1965–1970* (Jonathan Cape, London, 1972)

Koestler, Arthur. *The Lotus and the Robot.* With a new preface by the author (1960; Hutchinson & Co, London, 1966)

Korbel, Josef. *Danger in Kashmir* (Princeton University Press, Princeton, NJ, 1954)

Kripalani, K. R. *Tagore, Gandhi and Nehru* (Hind Kitabs Ltd, Bombay, 1947)

Krishna, B. *Sardar Vallabhbhai Patel: India's Iron Man* (HarperCollins, New Delhi, 1996)

Kumar, Girja. *Brahmacharya: Gandhi and His Women Associates* (Vitasta, New Delhi, 2006)

Kux, Dennis. *Estranged Democracies: India and the United States, 1941–1991* (1993; Sage Publications, New Delhi, 1994)

— *The United States and Pakistan, 1947–2000: Disenchanted Allies* (Woodrow Wilson Center Press, Washington DC; Johns Hopkins University Press, Baltimore & London, 2001)

Lal, Chaman. *Laugh with Gandhi* (Jhandewalan, New Delhi, 1969)

Lamb, Alastair. *Birth of a Tragedy: Kashmir 1947* (1994; Oxford University Press, Karachi, 2001)

Lambton, Antony. *The Mountbattens: The Battenbergs and Young Mountbatten* (Constable, London, 1989)

Lester, Muriel. *Entertaining Gandhi* (Ivor Nicholson & Watson, London, 1932)

Liversidge, Douglas. *The Mountbattens: From Battenberg to Windsor* (Arthur Barker Ltd, London, 1978)

Malgonkar, Manohar. *The Men Who Killed Gandhi* (1978; Macmillan, London, 1979)

Marquand, David. *Ramsay MacDonald* (1977; Richard Cohen Books, London, 1997)

Marx, Karl, and Friedrich Engels. *The First Indian War of Independence 1857–1859* (1959; Progress Publishers, Moscow, 1988)

Marx, Roland. *Mort d'un amiral: l'I.R.A. contre Mountbatten* (Calmann-Lévy, Paris, 1985)

Masson, Madeleine. *Edwina: The Biography of the Countess Mountbatten of Burma* (Robert Hale Ltd, London, 1958)

Mathai, M.O. *Reminiscences of the Nehru Age* (Vikas Publishing House, New Delhi, 1978)

— *My Days with Nehru* (Vikas Publishing House, New Delhi, 1979)

Mehta, Ved. *Mahatma Gandhi and His Apostles* (Andre Deutsch, London, 1977)

Menon, V.P. *The Transfer of Power in India* (1957; Sangam Books, New Delhi, 1981)

Merchant, Liaquat H., ed. *The Jinnah Anthology* (Oxford University Press, Karachi & Oxford, 1999)

Metcalf, Thomas R. *Ideologies of the Raj.* New Cambridge History of India series, vol III.4 (Cambridge University Press, Cambridge, 1994)

Meyer-Stabley, Bertrand. *Edwina Mountbatten: scandaleuse, libre, vice-reine des Indes* (Bartillat, Paris, 2005)

Miller, Webb. *I Found No Peace: The Journal of a Foreign Correspondent* (Penguin Books, Harmondsworth & New York, 1940)

Mira Behn (Madeleine Slade). *The Spirit's Pilgrimage* (Longmans, London, 1960)

— (as Mirabahen). *New and Old Gleanings* (Navajihan Publishing House, Ahmedabad, 1964)

Montague Browne, Anthony. *Long Sunset: Memoirs of Winston Churchill's Last Private Secretary* (1995; Indigo, London, 1996)

Montgomery, John. *The Twenties: An Informal Social History* (George Allen & Unwin, London, 1957)

Moon, Penderel. *Divide and Quit* (1961; Chatto & Windus, London, 1964)

Moraes, Frank. *Jawaharlal Nehru: A Biography* (Macmillan, New York, 1956)

Moran, Charles McMoran Wilson, Lord. *Winston Churchill: The Struggle for Survival, 1940–1965* (Constable, London, 1966)

Morgan, Janet. *Edwina Mountbatten: A Life of Her Own* (Harper-Collins, London, 1991)

Morley, Sheridan. *Noël Coward: A Talent to Amuse* (1969: Penguin Books, London, 1974)

Morton, Eleanor (pseudoyum: ie Elizabeth Stern). *The Women in Gandhi's Life* (Dodd, Mead & Co, New York, 1953)

Mountbatten, Lord Louis. *The Diaries of Lord Louis Mountbatten 1920–1922: Tours with the Prince of Wales*. Edited by Philip Ziegler (Collins, London, 1987)

Mountbatten of Burma, The Earl. *Time Only to Look Forward* (Nicholas Kaye, London, 1949)

— *From Shore to Shore: The Tour Diaries of Earl Mountbatten of Burma, 1953–1979*. Edited by Philip Ziegler (Collins, London, 1989)

Muggeridge, Malcolm. *The Thirties* (Hamish Hamilton, London, 1940)

Mullik, B.N. *My Years with Nehru, 1948–1964* (Allied Publishers, Bombay, 1972)

Murphy, Ray. *Last Viceroy: The Life and Times of Rear-Admiral the Earl Mountbatten of Burma* (Jarrolds, London, 1948)

Nanda, B.R. *In Search of Gandhi: Essays and Reflections* (Oxford University Press, New Delhi, 2002)

Nayyar, Sushila. *Kasturba, Wife of Gandhi*. Introduction by the late Mohandas Karamchand Gandhi (Pendle Hill, Wallingford, PN, 1948)

Nehru, Jawaharlal. *An Autobiography* (1936; new edition, The Bodley Head, London, 1958)

— *The Discovery of India* (1946; Meridian Books, London, 1951)

— *A Bunch of Old Letters: Written Mostly to Jawaharlal Nehru, and Some Written by Him* (Asia Publishing House, Bombay, 1958)

— *Nehru's Letters to His Sister* [ie Krishna Hutheesing]. Edited with an introduction by Krishna Nehru Hutheesing (Faber & Faber, London, 1963)

— *Before Freedom: Nehru's Letters to his Sister* [ie Vijaya Lakshmi Pandit]. Edited by Nayantara Sahgal (HarperCollins, New Delhi, 2000) *see also*: Gandhi, Indira and Jawaharlal Nehru.

Neillands, Robin. *A Fighting Retreat: The British Empire 1947–97* (Hodder & Stoughton, London, 1996)

Pandey, B.N. *Nehru* (Macmillan, London, 1976)

— ed. *The Indian Nationalist Movement, 1885–1947: Select Documents* (Macmillan, London, 1979)

Pandey, Gyanendra. *Remembering Partition: Violence, Nationalism and History in India* (Cambridge University Press, Cambridge, 2001)

Pandiri, Ananda M., compiler. *A Comprehensive, Annotated Biography on Mahatma Gandhi* (Greenwood Press, Westport, Connecticut and London, 1995)

Pandit, Vijaya Lakshmi. *The Scope of Happiness: A Personal Memoir* (1979; HarperCollins, New Delhi, 2000)

Parikh, Nilam. *Gandhiji's Lost Jewel: Harilal Gandhi* (National Gandhi Museum, New Delhi, 2001)

Parker, John. *Prince Philip: A Critical Biography* (Sidgwick & Jackson, London, 1990)

Phillips, William. *Ventures in Diplomacy* (John Murray, London, 1955)

Pimlott, Ben. *The Queen: Elizabeth II and the Monarchy* (1996; HarperCollins, London, 2002)

Prakasa, Sri. *Pakistan: Birth and Early Days* (Meenakshi Prakashan, Meerut, 1965)

Prasad, Rajendra. *Correspondence and Select Documents*, edited by Valmiki Choudhary. (Allied Publishers, New Delhi, 1984–88), 11 volumes.

Pubby, Vipin. *Shimla Now and Then* (1988; 2nd edition, Indus Publishing, New Delhi, 1996)

Pyarelal [ie Pyarelal Nayyar]. *Mahatma Gandhi: The Last Phase* (Navajivan Publishing House, Ahmedabad, 1956–58) 2 vols.

Read, Anthony, and David Fisher. *The Proudest Day: India's Long Road to Independence* (W.W. Norton & Company, New York & London, 1998)

Roberts, Andrew. *Eminent Churchillians* (Weidenfeld & Nicolson, London, 1994)

Rolland, Romain. *Mahatma Gandhi: The Man Who Became One with the Universal Being*, translated by Catherine D. Groth (Swarthmore Press, London, 1924)

Rose, Kenneth. *King George V* (1983; Phoenix Press, London, 2000)

Sahgal, Nayantara. *Prison and Chocolate Cake* (Victor Gollancz, London, 1954)

— *From Fear Set Free* (Victor Gollancz, London, 1962)

— 'The making of Mrs. Gandhi', *South Asian Review*, vol 8, no 3 (April 1975).

Sampson, Anthony. *Anatomy of Britain Today* (1965; Book Club Associates, London, 1969)

Schofield, Victoria. *Kashmir in the Crossfire* (I.B. Tauris, London & New York, 1996)

Sen, Amartya. *Poverty and Famines: An Essay on Entitlement and Deprivation* (1981; English Language Book Society/Oxford University Press, 1987)

— *The Argumentative Indian: Writings on Indian Culture, History and Identity* (2005; Penguin Books, London, 2006)

Sen, Surendra Nath. *1857*. With a Foreword by Maulana Abul Kalam Azad (Government of India Publications Division, Delhi, 1957)

Seshan, N. K. *With Three Prime Ministers: Nehru, Indira and Rajiv* (Wiley Eastern Ltd, New Delhi, 1993)

Seton, Marie. *Panditji: A Portrait of Jawaharlal Nehru* (Dennis Dobson, London, 1967)

Sherwood, Robert E. *Roosevelt and Hopkins: An Intimate History* (Harper & Brothers, New York, 1948)

Shudraka. *Mrcchakatika*. Translated as 'The Mrichchakati, or the Toy-Cart', in Horace Hayman Wilson, *Select Specimens of the Theatre of the Hindus, Translated from the Original Sanskrit* (Parbury, Allen, & Co, London, 1835), vol 1.

Shukla, Chandrashanker, ed. *Gandhiji As We Know Him: By Seventeen Contributors*. With a Foreword by Sarojini Naidu (Vora & Co, Bombay, n.d.)

Singh, Karan. *Heir Apparent: An Autobiography* (Oxford University Press, Delhi, 1982)

Singh Sarila, Narendra. *The Shadow of the Great Game: The Untold Story of India's Partition* (HarperCollins, New Delhi, 2005)

Smith, Charles. *Fifty Years with Mountbatten: A Personal Memoir By His Valet and Butler* (Sidgwick & Jackson, London, 1980)

Stephens, Ian. *Horned Moon* (Chatto & Windus, London, 1953)

— *Pakistan* (Ernest Benn, London, 1963)

Stoddard, Lothrop. *The New World of Islam* (Chapman & Hall, London, 1921)

Symonds, Richard. *In the Margins of Independence: A Relief Worker in India and Pakistan 1942–1949* (Oxford University Press, Karachi, 2001)

Tendulkar, D.G. *Mahatma: Life of Mohandas Karamchand Gandhi* (D.G. Tendulkar & Vithalbhai K. Jhaveri, Bombay, 1951–54). 8 vols.

Terraine, John. *The Life and Times of Lord Mountbatten: An Illustrated Biography Based on the Television History by John Terraine* (Hutchinson & Co, London, 1968)

Thorne, Christopher. *Allies of a Kind: The United States, Britain and the War against Japan, 1941–1945* (Hamish Hamilton, London, 1978)

Various. *The Edwina Mountbatten Papers* (Marr-Manning Trust, London, 1973—)

Villa, Brian Loring. *Unauthorized Action: Mountbatten and the Dieppe Raid* (1989; new edition, Oxford University Press, Oxford, 1994)

Ward, Andrew. *Our Bones are Scattered: The Cawnpore Massacres and the Indian Mutiny of 1857* (1996; John Murray, London, 2004)

Wavell, Archibald, Earl. *The Viceroy's Journal,* edited by Penderel Moon (Oxford University Press, London, 1973)

Wheeler-Bennett, John. *Friends, Enemies and Sovereigns* (Macmillan, London, 1976)

Whitaker, Denis, and Shelagh Whitaker. *Dieppe: Tragedy to Triumph* (McGraw-Hill Ryerson, Toronto & Montreal, 1992)

Williams, Francis. *A Prime Minister Remembers* (William Heinemann Ltd, London, 1961)

Windsor, The Prince Edward, Duke of. *A King's Story* (1951; Prion Books, London, 1998) *see also*: Edward, HRH The Prince.

Wolpert, Stanley. *A New History of India.* Seventh edition (1977; Oxford University Press, New York & Oxford, 2004)

— *Jinnah of Pakistan* (Oxford University Press, New York & Oxford, 1984)

— *Nehru: A Tryst with Destiny* (Oxford University Press, New York & Oxford, 1996)

— *Shameful Flight: The Last Years of the British Empire in India* (Oxford University Press, New York, 2006)

Zakaria, Rafiq, ed. *A Study of Nehru* (1959; revised edition, Times of India Publications, New Delhi, 1960)

Ziegler, Philip. *Mountbatten: The Official Biography* (Collins, London, 1985)

— *Mountbatten Revisited* (University of Texas, Austin, TX, 1995)

Zuckerman, Solly. *Monkeys, Men and Missiles: An Autobiography 1946–88* (Collins, London, 1988)

FILMOGRAPHY

Brief Encounter (dir. David Lean, 1945)
Caesar and Cleopatra (dir. Gabriel Pascal, 1945)
Gandhi (dir. Richard Attenborough, 1982)
In Which We Serve (dir. David Lean and Noël Coward, 1942)
Jinnah (dir. Jamil Dehlavi, 1998)
My Favorite Brunette (dir. Elliott Nugent, 1947)
British Pathé News Archive
'Mountbatten', *Secret History*, Channel 4 Television, 1995

A NOTE ON NAMES

Indian names and titles can be confusing for foreigners. For instance, Mohandas Karamchand Gandhi can be referred to as Mohan, Mohandas, Mohan Das, Mohandasbhai, Gandhi, Gandhiji, Mahatma, or Bapu, and many further combinations are possible.

Jawaharlal Nehru was often called 'Pandit Nehru' as a mark of his caste as a Kashmiri Pandit Brahmin; he attempted to prohibit the use of this title, but without success. Gandhi encouraged people to call him Bapu, meaning 'father', and was also widely known as 'Mahatma', a religious title meaning 'great soul'. Mohammad Ali Jinnah, the first Governor General of Pakistan, is often called the Quaid-e-Azam, or 'great leader'.

Hindu and Sikh princes were usually known as Raja (king) or Maharaja (great king); Muslim princes as Nawab. There are many exceptions: the Nizam of Hyderabad, Gaekwar of Baroda and Jam Sahib of Nawanagar were among those who enjoyed unique titles. The princes' chief ministers were usually known as Dewan.

The suffix –ji, which implies affectionate respect, is affixed liberally to names or titles – so Jawaharlal Nehru could be called Jawaharlalji, Nehruji or Panditji. The suffix –bhai, meaning 'brother', can similarly be added. Some names incorporate it, such as that of Vallabhbhai Patel; Jinnah's surname was originally Jinnahbhai. The feminine version is –ben or –bai. Some Hindu women, such as Kasturba Gandhi, adopt the suffix –bai to their first name on marriage, and –ba when they become the matriarch of the household.

British names are equally confusing. Louis Francis Albert Victor Nicholas Mountbatten was known to his family and friends as

Dickie. To everyone else he was His Serene Highness Prince Louis of Battenberg (1900–14), Lord Louis Mountbatten (1914–46), Viscount Mountbatten of Burma (1946–7), and eventually Earl Mountbatten of Burma (1947 onwards). The second of those titles was correctly shortened to Lord Louis, and the third and fourth to Lord Mountbatten. Mountbatten's personal staff persisted in addressing him as Lord Louis until the day he died.

A woman who marries a prince or the son of a peer takes her husband's title and first name, meaning that Mountbatten's wife Edwina was generally referred to as Lady Louis. (She was never 'Lady Edwina'; that would have denoted the daughter of a duke, marquess or earl. Edwina was only the daughter of a baron, Lord Mount Temple, and was therefore known before her marriage as the Hon. Edwina Ashley.) After 1946, Edwina would correctly have been addressed as Lady Mountbatten.

For the sake of consistency, all the people in this book have been referred to by their last name or first name, depending loosely on whether they are being viewed in a public or private context. Titles have been used occasionally for variety. Mohammad Ali Jinnah's first name has not been used, for his close friends and even his sister never called him Mohammad. They referred to him as Jinnah or, occasionally, Jin. Sikhs, all of whom bear the surname Singh if they are male and Kaur if they are female, and Muslims who bear the common surname Khan, have usually been referred to by their first names.

GLOSSARY

achkan	a long-sleeved coat, worn by men over trousers
Angrez	English
ashram	a village-style religious community and retreat
bagh	a garden or park
Bania	Gandhi's sub-caste, within the Vaishya caste: traders. Hard-bargaining salesmen may be described as 'banias' in a mildly derogatory sense
Bapu	Father; often used by his acolytes to refer to Gandhi
bhai	brother
brahmacharya	chastity. A person who practises brahmacharya is a brahmachari
Brahmin	the first caste: priests and academics
chaprasi	a bearer
communal	used as an adjective in India to describe a prejudice based on one's own 'community' identity, which may be defined by religion or caste. Muslim-Sikh rioting may be called 'communal rioting'; a protest by Untouchables against caste-Hindus may similarly be described as 'communal politics'. The British use of the word, to mean 'shared', is not common in the subcontinent
coolie	a porter or manual labourer; used in a derogatory sense by Europeans to describe any Indian
crore	ten million, or 100 lakhs. Written in India as 1,00,00,000
Dalit	'The oppressed', 'broken', or 'crushed'; modern term for Untouchables
darshan	the viewing of a sacred object
Dewan	a prime minister in an Indian princely state
dupatta	a long scarf worn by women
gaddi	throne (literally, cushion)
goonda	gangster, hooligan

gurdwara	a Sikh temple
Harijan	'child of God'; Gandhi's term for Untouchables
hartal	a day of prayer and fasting, functioning as a general strike
Jai Hind	'Victory to India': a slogan of Subhas Chandra Bose's Indian National Army, later adopted by more mainstream Indian politicians.
jatha	a band of fighting Sikhs
kaffir	Islamic term for a non-Muslim
karma	destiny; the credit built up in one life that determines one's station in the next incarnation
khadi	homespun cloth
ki jai	'victory to': shouted by Indian crowds as English-speaking crowds might shout 'three cheers for X!' or 'long live X!'
kirpan	a blade, which can be anything between a small ceremonial knife and a sword, carried by all Sikhs
Kshatriya	the second caste: warriors and rulers
kurta	a long shirt worn over trousers. The women's version is the kurti
lakh	one hundred thousand. Written in India as 1,00,000
lassi	a drink made from yoghurt and water, sold on most street corners
lathi	a bamboo cane with a metal tip, used by Indian policemen to control crowds
loya jirga	inter-tribal council, made up of the representatives of several tribes. Each tribe has its own jirga (council)
maidan	a grass-covered open space, parade ground or green; sometimes a race-course or battlefield
mamu	uncle
masjid	a mosque
memsahib	contraction of 'madam sahib', applied to European women
purna swaraj	complete self-rule
raj	rule, as in government; usually used in Britain to refer to the British administration of India between 1858–1947
sahib	equivalent to 'sir'; used to respected figures, and sometimes used to denote any European
satyagraha	'truth-force'; Gandhi's term for passive resistance or militant non-violence. A person who practises satyagraha is a satyagrahi
sepoy	Indian soldier serving in the British army
sherwani	a long coat worn over trousers in northern India and central Asia, associated often with Islamic dress

Sudra	the fourth caste: farmers and manual labourers
suttee, sati	Hindu female sacrifice; specifically, the burning of a widow on the funeral pyre of her husband
swadeshi	'home-made': Gandhi's campaign to persuade Indian consumers to buy Indian rather than British goods
swaraj	self-rule
thuggee	Hindu cult devoted to the goddess Kali, implicated in murders and robbery during the nineteenth century
Untouchable	a Hindu person born outside the four castes, considered unclean by orthodox Hindu society; also known at various stages as the Depressed Classes, Scheduled Castes, Harijans, and Dalits
Vaishya	the third caste: merchants
zindabad	'long live', as in 'Pakistan zindabad' – 'long live Pakistan'

PLACES

Some place names changed after the transfer of power to make their spelling more Indian, though a non-Indian English speaker may be more likely to pronounce them correctly by referring to the old spellings (Poona is now spelled Pune, but still pronounced 'Poona'). Many more were changed in the late 1990s and 2000s as part of a controversial Hindu nationalist movement. For instance, Bombay, named after the Portuguese Bom Bahia (Good Bay), has been renamed Mumbai after an obscure local Hindu goddess, Mumba Devi. The campaign has lately begun to propose renaming cities which presently have Muslim names with Hindu names: Allahabad would become Prayag, and Ahmedabad would become Karnavati. Because this story is set mainly in the 1940s, the names current then have been used throughout.

Bangalore	Bengaluru
Baroda	Vadodara
Benares	Varanasi
Bombay	Mumbai
Calcutta	Kolkata
Cawnpore	Kanpur
Dacca	Dhaka (Bangladesh)
Jullundur	Jalandhar

Jumna River	Yamuna River
Madras	Chennai
Mysore	Mysuru
Ooty (Ootacamund)	Udhagamangalam
Oudh	Awadh
Poona	Pune
Simla	Shimla
Trivandrum	Thiruvananthapuram
United Provinces	Uttar Pradesh

INDEX